ART AND AUTONOMY
A CRITICAL READER

EDITED BY
SVEN LÜTTICKEN

AFTERALL BOOKS

First published in 2022 by Afterall Books
in association with Verlag der Buchhandlung
Walther und Franz König, Köln

This publication was initiated by the Autonomy
Project, an initiative of the Dutch Art Institute,
Enschede/Arnhem; Grizedale Art Centre,
Cumbria; Liverpool School of Art and Liverpool
John Moores University; Lectoraat Kunst en
Publieke Ruimte (Gerrit Rietveld Academie,
Amsterdam; Sandberg Instituut, Amsterdam;
Universiteit van Amsterdam); Onomatopee,
Eindhoven; Onderzoekschool Kunstgeschiedenis/
Platform Moderne Kunst, Netherlands;
Kunstwissenschaft, Stiftung Universität
Hildesheim; Van Abbemuseum, Eindhoven

**Art and Autonomy
Project Advisory Board**
John Byrne, Jeroen Boomgaard,
Charles Esche and Noortje de Leij

Editor
Sven Lütticken

Managing Editor
Louis Hartnoll

Associate Editors
David Morris and Caroline Woodley

Research Assistants
Lara García Díaz, Florian Göttke
and Kim Kannler

AWP Research Interns
Bo Choy and Ella Sweeney

Copy Editor
Deirdre O'Dwyer

Design
Andrew Brash and Louis Hartnoll

Typefaces for interior
A2/SW/HK + A2-Type

Printed and bound by
die Keure, Bruges

This Critical Reader is printed on
FSC-certified papers

Distribution
Verlag der Buchhandlung Walther und Franz König
(Europe: verlag@buchhandlung-walther-koenig.de);
Cornerhouse Publications Ltd. – HOME (UK &
Ireland: publications@cornerhouse.org);
D.A.P. / Distributed Art Publishers, Inc. (outside
Europe: orders@dapinc.com)

Afterall
Central Saint Martins
Granary Building
1 Granary Square
London N1C 4AA, UK
www.afterall.org

Afterall is a Research Centre of University
of the Arts London

Director
Mark Lewis

Associate Directors
Charles Esche and Chloe Ting

Project Coordinator
Camille Crichlow

ISBN 978-3-96098-933-2 (Verlag der
Buchhandlung Walther und Franz König, Köln)
ISBN 978-1-84638-168-3 (Afterall Books)

The publishers have made every effort to contact the
copyright holders of the material included in this
book. However, if there are omissions, please let us
know (contact@afterall.org) and future editions will
be amended

A version of the introduction to this reader previously
appeared as 'Neither Autocracy nor Autonomism:
Notes on Autonomy and the Aesthetic', *e-flux journal*,
no.69, January 2016

Portions of Part Two of this reader were drafted by
John Byrne

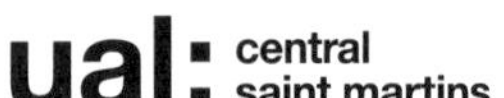

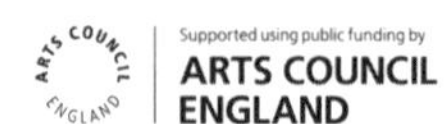

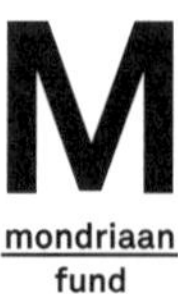

Contents

A User's Manual

This reader, structured in six thematic parts, follows a rough chronological outline, but with historical overlaps and returns. Reading this entire volume from beginning to end is one way to navigate its pages, but no doubt many readers will chart their own course. Although the focus throughout is on visual art, many texts deal with 'general aesthetics'. Each part is subdivided into sections that contain extracts from historical or contemporary texts alongside some complete essays, combining frequently discussed and often overlooked passages that are important in the present context. Any rare edits made to these texts are light and focus on stylistic consistency.

In contrast to the standard model for readers or anthologies, we print only a few key texts in their entirety (or close to it). The editorial comments provide some context for the fragments, integrating them into a textile that never presumes to forge the constituents into a seamless whole. The full source texts aren't seamless unities either; all texts are tissues of quotations, to quote Roland Barthes. Our selection and contextualisation offer, we hope, points of entry. The writings from which we have extracted fragments are well worth reading and rereading in their entirety, and it is easier to do this now than ever before. Having access to a public or university library is ideal, but the (legal and less than legal) online availability of sources makes it possible for most to follow up on tangents opened up by snippets in this book. We thus intend this reader to function as a tool that combines some of the properties of hypertext with those of obdurate physical presence.

As Walter Benjamin put it: 'There is no document of culture which is not at the same time a document of barbarism.'[1] A critical re-reading of the (Western) discourse on autonomy will, to some extent, replicate its exclusions; for the longest time, only some (mostly men, mostly white) were in a position to become authors. This leaves its imprint on the first parts of publication even as some sections function as an immanent autocritique – with Part Six discussing forms of theory and practice beyond Eurocentric confines. It is our belief that such a dialectical montage can produce more insight than any attempted abstract negation of a past deemed abhorrent. This reader proposes to tarry with history in its complexities and contradictions, its compromised critiques and unfinished revolutions, its structural violence and its grace notes.

---

[1]   Walter Benjamin, 'Eduard Fuchs, Collector and Historian', in *Selected Writings, vol.3, 1935-1938* (ed. Howard Eiland and Michael W. Jennings), Cambridge, MA: The Belknap Press of Harvard University Press, 2002, p.267; and Walter Benjamin, 'On the Concept of History', in *Selected Writings, vol.4, 1938-1940* (ed. Howard Eiland and Michael W. Jennings), Cambridge, MA: The Belknap Press of Harvard University Press, 2003, p.392.

INTRODUCTION:
AUTONOMY AND ART

Why autonomy? Why autonomy now? Why art and autonomy? Should Afterall not devote its Critical Readers to subjects of more immediately apparent cultural and social relevance – such as art and cognitive capitalism, art and the Anthropocene, or art and the decolonial? Though the term may lack immediate appeal (unless used in its Italian version, *autonomia*), questions pertaining to autonomy could hardly be more relevant and pressing in today's art world and academia. In 2009, when researchers affiliated with a number of different art institutions, art schools and universities in the Netherlands, the United Kingdom and Germany got together to form the Autonomy Project, this move was motivated in part by upheavals in the European cultural landscape.[1] These were upheavals not just in funding, but also in the entire ideology of art: art was increasingly seen as merely another economic sector that had to be immediately productive. What used to be regarded as a somewhat autonomous realm, art, was now part of the 'creative industries'.

In academia, too, old forms of autonomy were dwindling. In Holland, for instance, scholars in the humanities were increasingly forced to vie for research fun-ding specifically earmarked for research into/in collaboration with the creative industries, or research in the area of digital humanities or 'ehumanities'. And while staff's autonomy in determining the content of their research and of their teaching was declining, students were increasingly under pressure to collect credit points and prep themselves for a difficult job market while juggling two or three jobs to afford their studies in the first place. However, the founders of the Autonomy Project did not consider nostalgia for lost freedoms (in other words, for lost privileges) to be a viable option. The right-wing Dutch government that came into power in 2010 attacked art as a 'leftist hobby' that needed to be weaned off subsidies, inspired some to write rosy-tinted hymns to a lost age 'when art was still autonomous'. By contrast, the Autonomy Project aimed at investigating and problematising both historical and contemporary conceptions of autonomy while remaining convinced of the term's use-value.

Responding to the crisis in higher education in the UK, Sarah Amsler has noted:

> No stylised ideal of autonomy has ever been actualised within English universities. [...] It is often forgotten that this independence was itself a contingent effect of power; an elite and 'gentlemanly' understanding between elements of a ruling class whose exclusive education corresponded neatly to exclusive privileges of economic and political power. But this misremembering is also a way of drawing on the promise that at least some of these elite privileges – free access to university on merit, intellectual autonomy from the logics of state and market, and the right to a broadly liberal education – would be democratised through university expansion.[2]

In this sense, then, memories of autonomy – however partial and compromised such historical forms of autonomy may have been – could be more than just nostalgic self-indulgence in a dismal present: 'the idea that universities are socially protected spaces for autonomous inquiry and critique has grounded a belief amongst many scholars that teaching, research and the governance of the university should be relatively autonomous from the logics of both state and economy'.[3]

Autonomy has a habit of returning as a problem when the smooth operation of a given social or cultural system becomes untenable. In the summer of 1967, two prominent West German intellectuals debated each other on television: Theodor W. Adorno, the doyen of critical theory, and Arnold Gehlen, a conservative sociologist.[4]

The topic under discussion was the relation between freedom and institutions; between the constraints imposed by institutional structures and the growing desire for autonomy as manifested in the Dutch Provo movement – an anarchist and countercultural youth movement that in many ways prefigured May '68. Film footage of clashes between the Provos and Amsterdam police introduced the broadcast.[5] Gehlen, the conservative, praised institutions for their civilising role and for enabling human *Zusammenleben* (living together, or cohabitation). The university, for instance, creates a social context that facilitates research and critical thought. The elephant in the room was Gehlen's Nazi past; whereas Adorno had to flee the country, Gehlen was a member of the party and profited from the Nazi's purge of academia. For the likes of Gehlen in that period, institutions were crucial instruments of *Zucht*, a kind of spiritual and mental discipline that made them susceptible to *Führung* by anointed leaders such as Adolf Hitler.[6]

Although Adorno and Gehlen got on surprisingly well for much of the 1960s, sharing a *kulturkritische* scepticism vis-à-vis post-War consumer society, Adorno was all too aware of the reactionary implications of his colleague's 'institutionalism'.[7] Confronting his esteemed opponent, Adorno argued that even though institutions are not purely external but rather shaped by our mind and our social *habitus,* they can become ossified social structures that are imposed by coercion and, as such, experienced as alien, reified or objectified – *vergegenständlicht.*[8] It is true that institutions enable free acts in the first place, but they also undermine them. Look at the contemporary university, Adorno added, and specifically at the humanities: academics and students are doing anything but what they really want to do. Nobody forces them at gunpoint, but this does not mean they have real freedom – the freedom of subjects to determine their own destiny, to *self-legislate*. For Adorno, any freedom worth the name has to entail such self-legislation, or *autonomy* – a term which he actually substituted for 'freedom' at one point during the discussion.

If anything, doing what you feel should be done is even more impossible in today's corporate academia, and the Provo protests are not without contemporary overtones. They also hint at an aesthetic dimension that Adorno and Gehlen did not explicitly address. To a significant extent, the Provo movement derived its impetus from the provocative happenings that Robert Jasper Grootveld had started staging in the centre of Amsterdam, in turn based loosely on American artistic happenings and Fluxus events. Furthermore, Constant's utopia of New Babylon and its vision of the unalienated life of *homo ludens* came to be a crucial point of reference for Provo: the ex-Situationist artist's vision of a future society of life-as-play (made possible by automation) inspired the Provos to turn life into a series of happenings.[9] The revolt was an attempt at realising an aesthetic or a cultural revolution that would change not merely the political institutions but also the fabric of lived relations and the whole world of the senses.

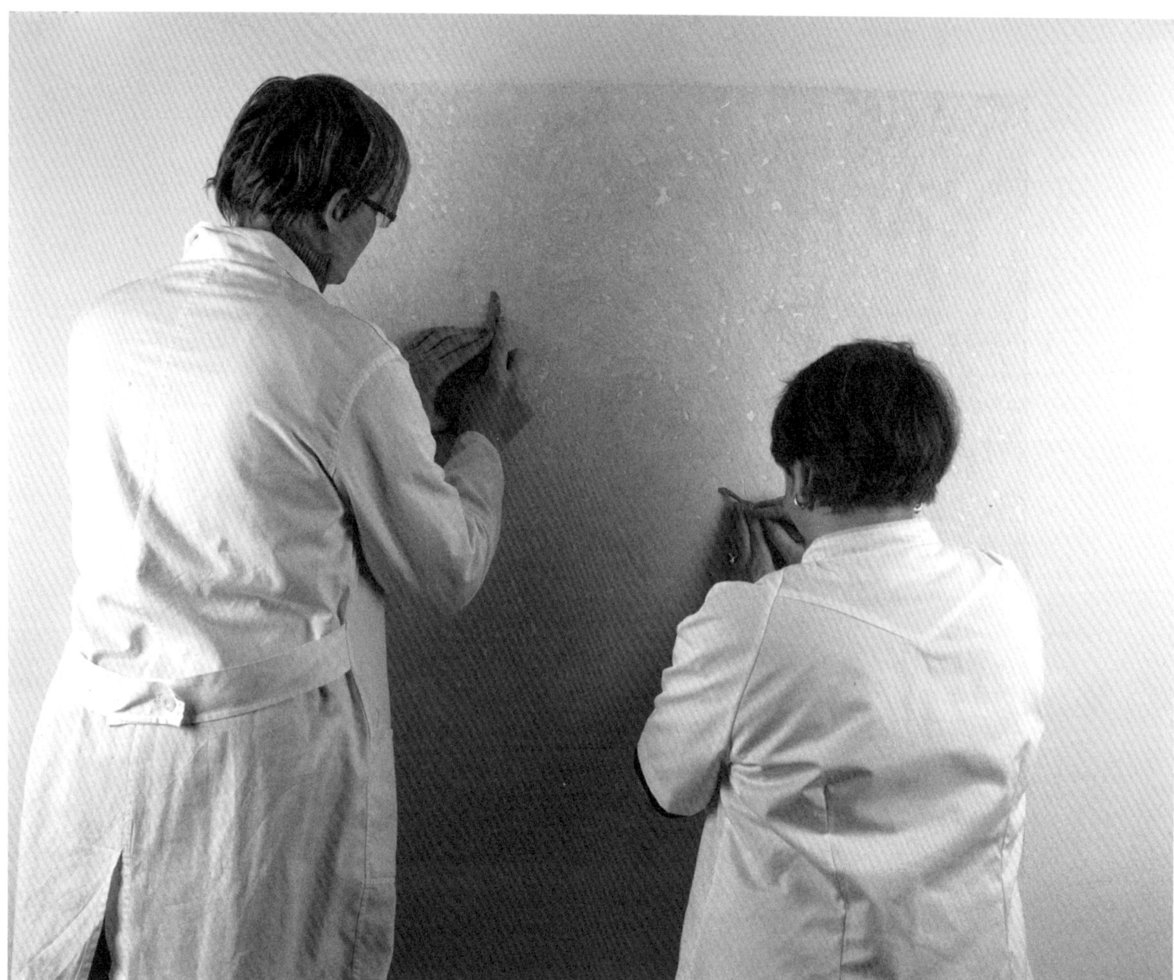

Hito Steyerl,
Adorno's Grey (detail), 2012,
single-channel HD video projection,
four angled screens, wall plot and
photographs
Courtesy the artist, Andrew Kreps
Gallery, New York and Esther
Schipper, Berlin

See pp.419-20 of this reader for
Hito Steyerl, 'Duty-Free Art'

Art and the Aesthetic

Autonomy is an Enlightenment value par excellence: the Enlightenment subject is supposed to be self-determined and critical. Of course, this subject can also be deconstructed as a patriarchal and colonial construction: after all, this ideal theoretical subject is supposedly incarnated as the male bourgeois property owner. It is only he who has the right to autonomy – bad luck for workers, women, Jews and people of colour! The concept of autonomy can be regarded as uncannily complicit with the bourgeois ideology of self-determining individualism, which in turn amounts to taking possession and staking out claims against those relegated to heteronomy. We should not stop there, however. Enlightenment conceptions of the autonomous subject or of imperious reason never went unchallenged.

When Alexander Gottlieb Baumgarten introduced aesthetics as a field of philosophical inquiry in 1750, he did so, in Terry Eagleton's phrasing, as a 'discourse of the body'.[10] With somatic and sensuous experience, what is heteronomous to the subject's status as pure cogito is complicated and compromised. To the extent that aesthetics claimed autonomy or its area of expertise, this amounted to a problematisation of the autonomy of the Enlightenment subject. After all, aesthetic experience and practice revolved around impure mixtures and intricate dialectical entanglements of freedom and determination, mind and body, subject and object. If the aesthetic held out a highly ideological promise of fulfilment within alienating modern society, an impossible promise of reconciliation, it also proffered a 'vision of human energies as radical ends in themselves which is the implacable enemy of all dominative or instrumentalist thought'.[11]

Fundamentally, the aesthetic constitutes a practico-theoretical engagement with what Eagleton has called the 'residually common world' of the senses.[12] Being an inquiry into embodied and sensate experience, aesthetics was far from limited to art. However, by the time G.W.F. Hegel lectured on aesthetics in the 1810s and 1820s, he focused on art and its historical development. Artworks came to function as paradigmatic aesthetic objects – objects of aesthetic experience and theory – because in artworks nature appears transformed by spirit; they are subjectified objects, in which matter appears transformed not by mechanical science but by a far more subtle and hermetic logic. The resulting cult of art, a major feature of German Romanticism, had contradictory effects. On the one hand, the Romantic poets and theorists wanted to 'romanticise' the whole world and turn the whole of life into lived art; this trope of the reconciliation of art and life, or the transformation of life through art, would begin in the late eighteenth century, pass via various avant-gardes and run right to the present. On the other hand, the cult of art produced 'an isolated enclave within which the dominant social order can find an idealised refuge from its actual values of competitiveness, exploitation and material possessiveness'.[13] The transformation of life was limited to the 'life of art'.

As an immanent critique of autonomy, aesthetics amounted to an autocritique of Enlightenment thought – an incomplete and complicit critique.[14] In contrast to some contemporary academics, the originators of aesthetic thought were not interested in theorising 'the autonomy of the aesthetic' in substantive terms. To the extent that there is an autonomy of the aesthetic, it must appear situational, in specific articulations of autonomy in sensate, embodied social forms. And this autonomy of the aesthetic takes the paradoxical form of the questioning and problematisation of claims for autonomy – including that of art. The aesthetic seeks to counteract the reduction of autonomy from a persistent problem to an ideological given. The comfortable assumption that art is structurally autonomous ultimately leads to aesthetic attrition, as in much late-modernist painting.

Maintaining philosophical aesthetics as a jealously guarded branch of philosophy would be counterproductive and anachronistic. The aesthetic prefigures and indeed inaugurates the shift from philosophy to 'theory', which Boris Groys has characterised with his characteristic flair for provocative simplification:

> Philosophy taught us to distrust religion and art, to trust our own reason instead. The man of the Enlightenment despised art, believing only in himself, in the evidences of his own reason. However, modern and contemporary critical theory is nothing other than a critique of reason, rationality and traditional logic.[15]

Groys's key progenitors of modern critical theory are Karl Marx, Friedrich Nietzsche and Sigmund Freud; in different ways, these thinkers all moved from idealist system building à la Hegel to modes of thinking grounded not in an abstract, notional subject, but in social, somatic or psychological reality.

In *Capital* (1867) Marx developed an in-depth analysis of *wage labour* and what he terms *commodity fetishism* – that is, the illusion that the value of commodities is autonomous rather than dependent on human labour.[16] With its account of the disjunction between sensuous appearance and underlying productive logic, the chapter on the commodity fetish is Marx's negative aesthetics. As the product of disavowed wage labour, the commodity constitutes an alienated world of false appearances that needs to be shattered by transformative and revolutionary praxis. In fact, wage labour and the commodity's seemingly autonomous 'whims' can be regarded as the reified counterparts to *praxis*. Defined in the 'Theses on Feuerbach' (1845) as ' human sensuous activity', Marx's concept of praxis is a post-idealist politicisation of the aesthetic as a transformative engagement with the material and sensuous world.[17]

Insofar as aesthetic experience has a specific autonomy, as Jacques Rancière has argued, this consists of a refusal of the autocracy of reason.[18] It is always ready to morph into more purposive rationality, becoming complicit with what Marx called the 'automatic subject' of value as constituted by the circulation of capital.[19] If the aesthetic problematises the relationship of autonomy and heteronomy, then this means that a form of praxis can be termed aesthetic insofar as it *lets autonomy appear sensibly as a problem*, in a world where subjectivities and objectifications are profoundly entangled, and where different agencies coexist and collide. While it may be true that the aesthetic and the political never quite coincide, aesthetic practice forever enacts and reenacts an asymptotic rapprochement between 'autonomous art' and social or political activism, pointing towards a synthesis that remains (partly) potential. Contra Rancière, this cannot be used as grounds for discrediting 'critical', 'political' or 'social' art practices – or aesthetic practices within the context of or in relation to art. Lack of measurable agency delegitimises them no more than their occasional direct successes in achieving specific political or social goals (which to some proves that 'this is not art but social activism'). One way or another, 'the autonomy of art' remains highly relative and structurally compromised.

Today, what were formerly known as art and culture are frequently recategorised as 'the creative industries'.[20] Under such neoliberal demands, both art and academia are rendered more immediately productive – now that they are no longer seen as relatively autonomous supplements of the 'real economy'. Both art and science need to be economically 'valorised' more directly than in the past, and both are ideologised as engines for the new knowledge-based creative economy of deindustrialised countries. Funding is allocated accordingly. As neoliberal programmes are imposed and become normalised, social fields are in their corollary process of decomposition. Everywhere, the relativity of 'relative autonomy' is becoming more pronounced. What if a 'field' is now a kind of scattered archipelago – an institutional, para- and extra-institutional Balkans of conflicting ideologies and practices? Perhaps the ultimate and most solid illusion today is not that of the quasi-autonomous life of any particular commodity fetish, nor that of the automaton-like autonomy of capital, but that of a techno-economic system that is constantly spawning new products and tools that demand an instant reschooling of the subject, a subject that has to keep up with developments to shore up its own much more precarious illusion of subjective autonomy.

We are all post-Fordist auto-productivists whose *autos* is less self-determination than self-design and self-control. The autonomous subject has become its own anxious autocrat, perpetually self-managing and self-optimizing while forever being illuminated by the dark light to data surveillance. As self-management takes the form of perpetual decision-making, it can revive a sense of individual subjective mastery. As the American art historian and theorist Jonathan Crary writes: 'The illusion of choice and autonomy is one of the foundations of this global regime of self-regulation.'[21] Always busy surviving and self-optimising, this self has no time to revolt, for to do so would be a waste of time and a career killer.[22]

From the Artwork to Art-Work

Modernist aestheticians such as Adorno focussed on the work of art as a privileged site in which the 'unsolved antagonisms of reality' are reconfigured time and again as 'immanent problems of form'.[23] Adorno acknowledged that the autonomisation of art was itself a consequence of the division of labour in capitalist society.[24] Nonetheless, for him the *faits sociaux* (social facts) enabling modernist art are in the end just that: heteronomous enabling conditions to which art cannot be reduced. A medium such as film was part of the culture industry and thus needed sociological perspectives; one chapter of Adorno and Hanns Eisler's book on film music is titled 'Sociological Aspects'.[25] By contrast, for Adorno *genuine* art is itself a higher form of sociology; it is critical theory in the form of aesthetic objects. If art had a 'double nature', as both autonomous and *fait social,* even its social dimension was ultimately articulated best mimetically, on the level of the autonomous artwork.[26]

Implicitly and explicitly, modernists such as Adorno could rely on Max Weber's account of modern society as predicated on the progressive functional differentiation and autonomisation of social spheres.[27] In a 1980 attack on postmodernism by Adorno's former pupil Jürgen Habermas, this Weberian model is deployed to defend modernism in art and the 'project of modernity' in general:

> [Weber] characterised cultural modernity as the separation of the substantive reason expressed in religion and metaphysics into three autonomous spheres. They are: science, morality and art. These came to be differentiated because the unified world-views of religion and metaphysics fell apart. Since the eighteenth century, the problems inherited from these older world-views could be arranged so as to fall under specific aspects of validity: truth, normative rightness, authenticity and beauty. They could then be handled as questions of knowledge, or of justice and morality, or of taste. Scientific discourse, theories of morality, jurisprudence and the production and criticism of art could in turn be institutionalised.[28]

Adorno had been well aware of the complicitness of these 'autonomous' spheres in maintaining a questionable social and economic order, yet he did not consider art's autonomy to be merely illusory. As a social fact in its own right, it enabled certain practices that were impossible outside the sphere of art. As a consequence, he considered avant-garde attempts to 'overcome' art or academia to be dangerous; while wary of Gehlen's institutionalism, he came to be at least as concerned by radical anti-institutionalism. 'Actionism is regressive': *Aktionismus* was Adorno's disparaging code word for young radicals such as Rudi Dutschke, who in turn regarded Adorno as a modernist mandarin who fiddled Arnold Schoenberg while Vietnam burned.[29]

In the 1950s, the term *action* had been promoted in the context of *action painting* by Harold Rosenberg, with the canvas allegedly becoming an 'arena in which to act' – for Jackson Pollock, Willem de Kooning and company.[30] Rosenberg's theory of the artistic act was an individualised Cold War transposition of the Marxist philosophy of praxis he had espoused in the context of Trotskyism during the 1930s. Praxis became a sequence of acts, of mock-heroic and existential actions. Praxis – as a 'human sensuous activity' as aesthetic as it is political – becomes an individual act that can be hung over a couch. Towards the end of the 1950s, Allan Kaprow and other neo-avant-gardists argued that it was now crucial to leave the painting and stage actions (or happenings, or events) more directly and theatrically, without a painting as intermediary.[31] *Aktion* was thus a term that discursively enacted the 'blurring of art and life' advocated by the neo-avant-garde. In line with the Situationist International (SI), who had advocated 'new forms of action in art and politics', the notion was applied both to more strictly artistic and to countercultural cum political actions.[32]

The post-Situationist group Subversive Aktion, which included Dutschke and former SI member Dieter Kunzelmann – and which used an entrist strategy to infiltrate the German Socialist Students' Union (SDS) – fell into the latter camp.[33] Artists or 'un-artists' from Kaprow and George Maciunas to Jean-Jacques Lebel and the Situationists advocated generalised and at times highly politicised forms of aesthetic praxis in which the external world is no longer purely external and confronted by a disembodied subject, but is instead made up of truly 'human sensuous activity'.

The revolutionary year of 1968 saw institutions such as the Museum of Modern Art in New York or the Stedelijk Museum in Amsterdam being contested by activist groups such the Art Workers' Coalition or Aksie BBK.[34] Many of the artists who would become known as practitioners of institutional critique participated in such groups and protests – aiming not for 'the abolition of art' but certainly for a radical overhaul of its infrastructure. Once the revolutionary impetus of the late 1960s had waned, institutional critique tended to take the form of individual critical gestures within institutions, which hosted them with more or less equanimity. These practices were marked by a covertly Adornian rejection of the transgressive gestures of the neo-avant-garde and aimed to make artistic practice critically reflexive rather than abandoning it in favour of generalised cultural-political *Aktionen*. Artists such as Marcel Broodthaers, Hans Haacke and Martha Rosler rejected both the modernist object and the avant-garde event or performance; both the modernist conviction 'that an object, by its distinction from all others, can serve as a mirror for an equally singular and independent subject' and the avant-garde belief in radically transgressive gestures that in fact leave the system intact and await their own institutional recuperation.[35]

In line with this tendency, Andrea Fraser has registered her doubts concerning 'formulations reach for a kind of pure autonomy, a kind of pure freedom, and in which avant-garde practices are sometimes identified with radical political practices, such as anarchist traditions and Autonomia'.[36] Resembling Adorno in this respect, institutional critique does not wish to smash institutions but to intervene in their dialectic of enablement and constraints, their processes of subjectivation and subjection. Avant-garde transgression is replaced by critical praxis inside the system. Fraser has argued that 'artistic autonomy' has four dimensions: aesthetic (the artwork as following its own intrinsic logic, free from instrumentalisation); economic (the bourgeois, modern art market); social (the art world as a relatively autonomous field with its own protocols and criteria); and political (which she identifies with freedom of speech and conscience).[37] While Fraser here uses a narrow definition of the aesthetic, identified with one aspect of 'artistic autonomy', her distinctions are nonetheless useful when discussing 'institutionalised' modern art.

If various avant-gardes and neo-avant-gardes sought to destroy or at least escape from the field of art, institutional critique à la Haacke or Fraser is an immanent critical practice within this field. However, when both selves and institutional structures are subject to permanent redesign, the old opposition between transgressive and immanent practices loses much of its relevance. If the term *autonomy* has any meaning in art, it is not as a label for a historical series of *artworks* that somehow have the property of 'being autonomous'. With institutional critique, artistic autonomy came to be redefined in terms of *art-work*, or artistic labour that aspires to become immanent critical practice. If institutional critique was highly critical of the artwork as object, it did not necessarily side with the object's familiar neo-avant-garde alternatives: transgressive *actions* that seek to escape institutional art altogether.

Institutional critique created a certain taboo in the art world of the 1970s and 1980s: 'autonomy' became identified with the very limited autonomy of the modernist work of art à la Clement Greenberg, revealed to be highly heteronomous and dependent on disavowed economic, political and ideological factors. Institutional critique sounded out the limits and the potential for autonomy within existing art-world structures, while largely refraining from using the term. This 'autonomy that dared not speak its name' contrasts to forms of social and political action in the shape of the Italian Autonomia movement and its cognates in other countries. A number of Italian activists and theorists shifted from a focus on workers' autonomy (*autonomia operaio*) to more general conception of an autonomy of movements and structures no longer necessarily containable within old-school conceptions of class struggle.[38] This also had an impact elsewhere; in Germany, for instance, the remains of actionism and related strands of left-wing activism and theorising morphed and crossbred in various ways, with former SDS member Karl Heinz Roth and others looking to Italian Operaismo and the beginnings of autonomia for alternative models. In 1975, Roth and others from the post-1968 Spont movement founded the periodical *Autonomie,* which was subtitled *Materialien gegen die Fabrikgesellschaft* (Materials Against Factory Society).

The real international success of post-Operaist and Autonomist thinkers such as Antonio Negri and Maurizio Lazzarato came later, from the 1990s on, when they started to have a significant impact on art discourse with their account of the transition from Fordism to post-Fordism, the rise of 'immaterial labour' and the *fabbrica diffusa* (*social factory*). This reception of Autonomia would ultimately come to blend with impulses from institutional critique in the work of theorists such as Gerald Raunig.[39] We do indeed live in a *Fabrikgesellschaft*, and the museum is a (part of the) factory. Artistic practice has become *project based*, and the focus has shifted from the artwork as object to artistic labour. This reflects the fundamental transformation in capitalism articulated by the post-Operaists and autonomists: art in the social factory.

By the time Andrea Fraser and Helmut Draxler organised the project *Services: The Conditions and Relations of Service Provision in Contemporary Project Oriented Artistic Practice*, in 1993–94, in which they analysed the service industries as a possible model for artistic project work, there was more room for nuance and differentiation.[40] It is precisely because 'immaterial' labour in its various forms is at the forefront of both commodification and precarisation that it has become something of a privileged site for contemporary art. Art becomes aesthetic practice by engaging with the contradictions of art-work and the regime it is part of. In this respect, as of the 1960s and 1970s, institutional critique had been at the forefront of articulating the transformations of not just art but the wider economy. And in fact, such practice was not limited to art. During the late 1980s, the feminist performance collective V-Girls, of which Fraser was a member, performed mock academic panels that reflected their own uncertain status in (relation to) academia and enacted their own subjected subjectivities in grotesquely distorted ways. Fraser (or Fraser's persona) would occasionally end some demonstration of her theoretical skills with a desperately peppy: 'I would like to conclude by saying that I am available for immediate employment.'

Institutional critique confronted the 'social fact' of modern art head-on, and certainly with the intention of having *some* impact – transforming parts of the field one intervention at a time. We should also acknowledge that the proliferation of alternative spaces and collective forms of working in the 1970s can be seen as a manifestation of institutional critique, as another outcome of the contestations of the late 1960s. Nonetheless, the stated affinity of artists such as Buren, Haacke or Fraser with Pierre Bourdieu's sociology of art and his analysis of the 'artistic field' and its institutions has also resulted in a sociologising fetishisation of said field.[41]

The practice of art was, of course, never truly autonomous in the sense of being free from external constraints and impulses. As Kerstin Stakemeier has emphasised, art being 'meticulously isolated as a field', and given relative autonomy, was precisely how the subsumption of art under capitalism operated *under modernism*.[42] Now this subsumption had become much more radical and extreme. If, as Fredric Jameson noted recently, 'the generic universal of art itself has disintegrated', then one consequence of this is the ever more complete inscription of art into the mainstream of capitalist accumulation and extraction.[43] In art as in academia, what used to be a carefully maintained reserve – for instance, a research facility in which processes that could be subject to *later* capitalisation had to be given some room to unfold – is now unhesitatingly mined much more directly. From a seeming alternative to capitalism, art has become capitalism's vanguard. What can autonomy mean and *be* under such circumstances?

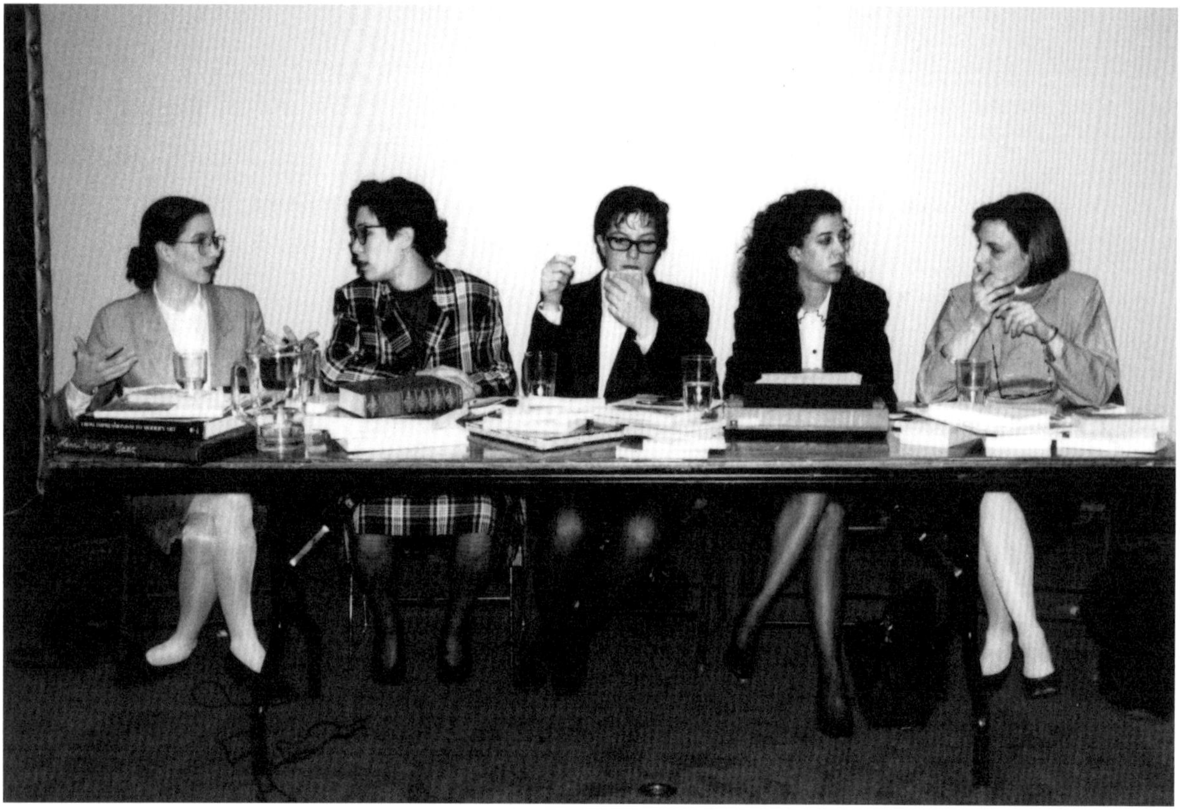

Performance view, The V-Girls, *The Question of Manet's 'Olympia': Posed and Skirted*, Institute of Contemporary Arts, London, May 1990. From left: Andrea Fraser, Jessica Chalmers, Marianne Weems, Erin Cramer and Martha Baer

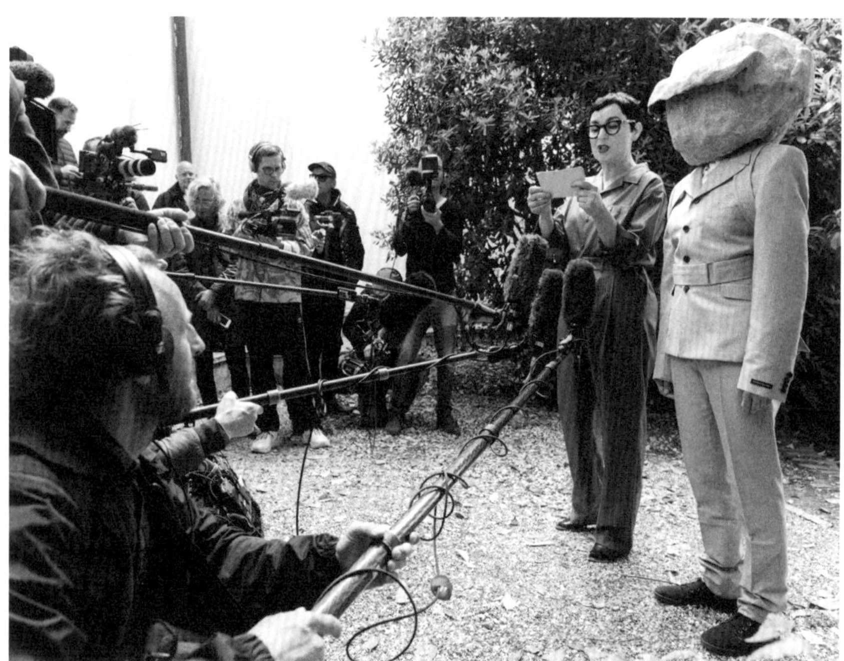

Helene Duldung (centre) leading opening press conference at presentation by Natascha Süder Happelmann (pseudonym of Natascha Sadr Haghighian), German Pavilion, 58th Venice Biennale, 2019
Photo: Jasper Kettner
Courtesy Natascha Sadr Haghighian and Galerie für Zeitgenössische Kunst, Leipzig

See pp.262–63 of this reader for more images and pp.348–50 for Natascha Sadr Haghighian, 'Dear Artfukts, Look at My Curve'

Are We the Robots of the Social Factory?

Already in the 1970s, corporate sponsorship and the influence of trustees had become a focus of Hans Haacke's work. The seemingly autonomous logic of capital transformed the art field from the inside. Today, the logic of capital has, in turn, largely merged with that of technoscience: if we pay up, we can get real-time algorithmic advice on which artists to buy and which to dump. Helmut Draxler has eloquently critiqued the avant-garde logic of transgression, of abandoning one's field, of becoming another – a better, more political – subject.[44] But what if institutions themselves become transgressive, what if subjects are already constantly being reshaped? When Rudi Dutschke coined the phrase 'the long march through institutions', he was thinking of a process in which revolutionaries undermine one institution after another from within.[45] As the revolutionary impetus of the late 1960s petered out, institutional critique at times replaced avant-garde transgression by an equally problematic fetishisation of immanent practice within institutions.

The neo-avant-garde had a point when it opposed the reduction of the aesthetic to institutional art. Actionism's refusal to accept institutional and disciplinary limits, to respect functional differentiation, is highly relevant at the present historical juncture – which is, after all, marked by an erosion of relative autonomy in art as in academia and elsewhere. However, it is no longer a matter of choosing between *anti-institutional aesthetic practice* (1960s neo-avant-garde tendencies) and *embedded critical practice within institutions* (1970s institutional critique). As aesthetic practice and theoretical practice navigate institutional as well as extra-institutional contexts and interstices, the complementary nature of both approaches is made clear. Existing institutions such as museums or universities should be engaged with and used to the extent that this is possible and productive, but they should not constitute the horizon.

In May 1968, the Situationist-dominated Council for Maintaining the Occupations at the Sorbonne put out a poster decreeing the 'End of the University'.[46] In the early twenty-first century, universities and museums alike are occupied by rather different forces. In dealing with such institutions, it may be wise to consider them already gone, already plundered and ruined. But these ruins are not the crumbling-yet-still-solid edifices seen in Old Master paintings. Ruination now takes the form of constant liquefaction. Workplaces literally disappear, with unworkable 'flexi-work stations' at Dutch universities having the effect (and no doubt the unstated intention) of severing ties of solidarity between and among staff members and students. A situation marked by the liquefaction of institutions and the erosion of the relative autonomy of fields presents huge problems, but also possibilities. As the Vidya Ashram collective has put it:

> Now the global order is reinventing itself. In the information age, there is not going to be a privileged set of knowledge producers who will be allowed an autonomous space, a safe haven to explore and invent. Knowledge will be harnessed from the whole cultural field and subjected to regimes of cognitive measurement, knowledge management and information enclosures.[47]

A few years ago, in the context of the promotion of digital humanities, a number of Amsterdam-based institutions poured significant funding into the new Center for Humanities and Technology (CHAT), to enable researchers to use IBM's Watson system for cognitive computing, network analytics, visualisation, text and social analytics, and search and data representation.[48] With underfunded academics bending their research agenda to come up with something – anything – that could get them a bit of cash, this might have seemed opportune; but although CHAT had an inaugural budget of 65 million euros, that money was earmarked to promote a very particular research agenda. The 'call for proposals' gave researchers a full *three weeks* to develop a proposal. Since the project also represented something of a power grab by linguists and historians, art historians were offered some suggestions patently irrelevant in relation to contemporary artistic practice: 'Can we detect meaningful relationships between artworks when we do not understand the semantic labels (due to language differences), or with insufficient clues (untitled works)? Can we search for artworks on the basis of pattern recognition of e.g. colour, composition, texture, rhythm?'[49] Dreaming of a cut of that 65 million euro pot, some art historians started brainstorming: Should we rather focus on discourse analysis, and have Watson parse thousands of texts on the basis of keywords? Which keywords? *Autonomy* perhaps? In the end, no proposal was made by this group.

In many respects, the Autonomy Project was the polar opposite of CHAT: institutionally embedded but informal and springing from genuine research interests, low-tech and interested in aesthetic practice as an alternative mode of organising. This is not to deny, of course, that quantitative research and cognitive computing present worthwhile avenues for research. A humanist defence of the isolated researcher against the evil machine would be regressive and unhelpful; clearly the point cannot be a resuscitation of some deliriously autocratic Enlightenment subject. Autonomy needs to be defined in terms of assemblages that include technological tools as well as institutions. What was disquieting about the Amsterdam CHAT project was how this proprietary version of cognitive computing was naturalised and never questioned. To open up serious debates about these and other matters would require conceiving of the university, as Sarah Amsler puts it, 'as a site of struggle, or education as a reason for it', but this is something that few academics are willing to do.[50] Staff and students find it difficult to organise and undertake collective action – if they see the need for it at all. Many have been depoliticised by the perpetual need to perform, and to compete. Amsler sees such development as symptomatic of a 'deep neoliberalism' that

> moves beyond daily erosions of autonomy to become a hollowing out of the relationships, ideas and subjectivities that help maintain critical spaces from neoliberal rationality and a temporal contracting of the distance between these spaces. If we can identify how and why these processes become possible, we might also get a better grip on how critical spaces can be reclaimed or created.[51]

Again, the question as to labour arises, with greater urgency than before. Why *should* we work (and spend public money) on making IBM's Watson smarter when the working conditions imposed on us are so grotesque? Like electronics industry workers at Foxconn or Pegatron, most academics may be easily replaceable by the next eager candidate available for immediate employment. Self-design and self-surveillance do their job – until they don't.

In line with the Italian Autonomia of the 1970s, later movements, from alter-globalism to Occupy Wall Street, have insisted on autonomy not as a property of the subject, but as 'collective adventure' produced by transversal connections and groupings.[52] The success of autonomist theory and activism in the art world can be seen as a continuation and intensification of the aesthetic critique of the Enlightenment concept of the autonomous subject and of its even more abstracted double, the autonomous will. But can there be an 'autonomous' rather than 'managerial' university? And to what extent can or must this have its own independent and permanent infrastructure? Can existing institutions become such autonomous organisations, or do they need to be supplemented with shadowy para-institutions? In Fred Moten and Stefano Harney's words, the only viable option with American universities – but perhaps also universities elsewhere – may be to 'undercommon' them:

> [I]t cannot be denied that the university is a place of refuge, and it cannot be accepted that the university is a place of enlightenment. In the face of these conditions one can only sneak into the university and steal what one can. To abuse its hospitality, to spite its mission, to join its refugee colony, its gypsy encampment, to be in but not of – this is the path of the subversive intellectual in the modern university.[53]

On the other hand, in the case of smaller institutions, the transformation and 'liquefaction' can take on the form of an activist praxis by, for instance, the director and curatorial team. A case in point is the Van Abbemuseum in Eindhoven, where Charles Esche and Galit Eilat organised *Picasso in Palestine* (2011), initiated by Khaled Hourani of the International Academy of Art Palestine. The museum's apparatus was used to send Picasso's *Buste de Femme* (1943) to Palestine, where most institutional niceties that are taken for granted elsewhere are absent; indeed, Israel has blocked and sabotaged the formation and maintenance of institutions, including that of a Palestinian state, for decades. *Picasso in Palestine* emphasised and exacerbated the painting's status as art – as a painting by Picasso that allows for certain kinds of aesthetic experience. Precisely because bringing this artwork to Palestine as object – as producer or enabler of such an experience – was so grotesquely difficult, the painting there acquired different meanings and functions – an unexpected use-value that enriched rather than cancelled out the work's aesthetic qualities. In the process, the work mapped the inequalities and asymmetries in today's 'globalisation', which is the continuation of imperialism and colonialism with different means – including those of international law.

Picasso in Palestine dealt with a highly specific situation, and did so by foregrounding the various forms of curatorial, critical, artistic, legal, police and manual labour involved – all revolving around a precious and precarious object.[54] Rather than addressing Israel's stranglehold on Palestine from an external vantage point, the project foregrounded the contradictions of working in a 'global' economy marked by asymmetries and inequalities between different forms of migration (workers and commodities, Western and subaltern subjects). *Picasso in Palestine* took as its point of departure a quintessential modernist artwork and showed its entanglement in activities that ensure its transportation, its protection, its legal status and so on. The *art-work* in the sense of labour – noun becomes verb. Many contemporary practices seek to revert or at least counteract the concealment of labour, but 'the labour that went into the work of art' can be manifold and contradictory, and it may include the labour of guards or cleaners needed for maintenance of the system.

In the midst of institutional turmoil, new forms of cooperation and new alliances can emerge not only within liquid institutions and ex-fields, but also between them. When the same 'ironclad logic' of financialised capital – as enabled by technoscience as financial capital – is imposed on all different fields and occupations, then is there not potentially a common ground? In art as in academia, those who opt out or are left out may no longer consider themselves to be part of the same 'field' as some of their (former) peers. Does this not also create new possibilities for networks of solidarity within but also *between* (ex-)fields? Networks emerge in which collaboration between artists, lecturers, students, activists and illegal immigrants may start to make more sense than the usual field-immanent activities of pursuing gallery exhibitions or grants for mega research projects. This means, for instance, that artists and others seeking out collaboration with those excluded from the Empire of global capitalism are encountering the 'margins' of contemporary labour.[55] As the integration of semi-autonomous fields and workers into neoliberal capitalism is being pushed forward, divisions between legal and illegal, first-class and second-class citizens, workers and nonworkers are proliferating.

What has happened in the last decades is the progressive subjugation of art and academia to an economistic logic that allows for no alterity, no other criteria. In the same process, the institution becomes networked and diffused, spreading out even as it intensifies its grasp on subjectivation and introduces ever greater numbers of cultural and intellectual workers into precarity.[56] Meanwhile, the 'reinvention of the global order' has by now spawned an international of nationalist and neofascist movements, from the US and Brazil to various European countries, Russia and Turkey. Triumphant after the collapse of the USSR in 1989–91, neoliberalism posited an entrepreneurial self that was as regressive as it was aggressive in its sovereign disregard for others and society. Today, this neoliberal subject has spawned an army of autonomous little assholes on social media. While complaining about 'cancel culture' and attacking feminists or racial and sexual minorities, they leave a trial of data that can be used to target them by the likes of Steve Bannon and Cambridge Analytica. Autonomous self-assertion turns out to be a symptom suitable for pattern recognition.

As global capitalism meets its economic as well as its ecological limits, hymns to economic growth have been replaced by the naked upward redistribution of wealth. Art has become a crucial asset for the diversified portfolio of the 0.1 per cent; and this at a time when migrants and minorities are exposed to systemic violence, excluding them from the market and from society as a racialised surplus. It is no fluke that some of the wealthier protagonists and enablers of neofascist policies are also collectors of contemporary art; there is only a seeming contradiction between the supposed 'cosmopolitanism' of contemporary art and white nationalism or the far-right. Much as populists like to attack 'the cultural elite', the success of contemporary art and the rise of neofascism are two different sides of the same polyhedron. The revelation, for instance, that Warren B. Kanders, as vice-chairman of the Whitney Museum of American Art, owned a company producing teargas used against immigrants on the US-Mexico border was not surprising. But of course, it took protracted activism by artists to finally force him out (of the Whitney, that is).

With the intensifying contradictions and conflicts generating a sense of precarity and vulnerability, the impetus to stay on the 'right side' of economic and social divisions is often strong and overpowering: to wrest self-entrepreneurial autonomy from precarity, to become a fighting machine, to kiss ass and punch down. Artists become alt-right trolls and are embraced by once respectable galleries eager to cash in on hateful memes executed with post-internet sheen. However, if art's and academia's inscription in the automatic logic of (finance) capital entails a loss of a specific type of disciplinary autonomy, this generates possibilities as well as dismal symptoms – that seem to have intensified during the COVID-19 pandemic. In this reader we focus on artistic and theoretical practices that thrive on the loss of modern(ist) areas of exclusive competence to try to forge alliances and foster solidarity under increasingly difficult circumstances.

Operaismo at times glorified workers' autonomy in ways that seemed reductive and cartoonish. Autonomist feminists and feminist autonomists have long insisted that autonomy needs to be understood not in terms of a delusional autarky, but as the ability to choose one's dependencies.[57] At their best, today's autonomists strive for an autonomy of chosen dependencies; an autonomy that practices entanglement, that dances with heteronomy, that starts from an acknowledgement of the need for collaboration, co-individuation and co-creation. Meaningful aesthetico-political praxis will often be slow or intermittent. In the *fabbrica diffusa* of contemporary capitalism, autonomy can only occur as the assembly and assemblage of disparate workers and nonworkers. Everything conspires against this occurring. It is time to conspire back.

Notes

1   The institutions were the Dutch Art Institute, Enschede/Arnhem; Grizedale Art Centre, Cumbria; Liverpool School of Art and Liverpool John Moores University; Lectoraat Kunst en Publieke Ruimte (Gerrit Rietveld Academie, Amsterdam; Sandberg Instituut, Amsterdam; Universiteit van Amsterdam); Onomatopee, Eindhoven; Onderzoekschool Kunstgeschiedenis/ Platform Moderne Kunst, Netherlands; Kunstwissenschaft, Stiftung Universität Hildesheim; Van Abbemuseum, Eindhoven.

2   Sarah Amsler, 'Beyond All Reason: Spaces of Hope in the Struggle for England's Universities', *Representations*, vol.116, no.1, Fall 2011, p.68.

3   *Ibid.*

4   Presented by Alexander von Cube, 'Die Freiheit und die Institution' (Freedom and the Institution) was broadcast on Westdeutscher Rundfunk (WDR) television on 3 June 1967. Documentation has been posted online with a 1965 date, and a number of recent German academic publications have erroneously repeated it. The reference at the broadcast's start to the dissolution of the Provo movement (which happened on 13 May 1967) should make it clear that 1965 cannot be correct. The confusion may be due to the famous 1965 radio debate between Adorno and Gehlen, 'Ist die Soziologie eine Wissenschaft vom Menschen?' (Is Sociology a Science of Man?), which shares similarities with the televised discussion.

5   The footage is from Louis van Gasteren's film *Omdat mijn fiets daar stond* (*Because My Bike Was Standing There*, 1966), which documents police violence against Provos and others after the opening of an exhibition that documented and criticised police actions during the wedding of Princess Beatrix and Claus von Amsberg.

6   On Gehlen's career, his partial post-War rehabilitation and his dialogue with Adorno in the 1960s, see Monika Boll, *Nachtpogramm. Intellektuelle Gründungsdebatten in der frühen Bundesrepublik*, Münster: LIT, 2004, pp.137-38, 190-97, 238-42.

7   On the other hand, as Max Horkheimer noted in 1950, the Nazis had instrumentalised the anti-institutional reaction against all reified and ossified structures; even while seeming to celebrate institutions of the state, of the army, and of the party, society had in fact become a permanently *actionistic* state of exception, wherein institutional safeguards against tyranny did not exist. Adorno and Horkheimer's position was thus a dialectical one – not anti-institutional per se, but aware of the need to keep or make institutions humane and flexible. See *ibid.*, p.150. This shared outlook notwithstanding, Horkheimer's stance grew far more conservative than Adorno's.

8   Adorno here references G.W.F. Hegel's notion of *objective spirit*, Émile Durkheim's concept of *faits sociaux* (social facts) and Thorstein Veblen's understanding of institutions in terms of *habits of thought*.

9   Constant and New Babylon were feted in *Provo*, no.4, October 1965.

10   Terry Eagleton, *The Ideology of the Aesthetic*, Oxford: Blackwell, 1990, p.13. See also Part One of this reader, pp.32-33.

11   *Ibid.*, p.9.

12   *Ibid.*, p.2.

13   *Ibid.*

14   On the complicity of various strands of modern aesthetic theory and practice with modern Western racism, see Part Six of this reader, pp.357-415.

15   Boris Groys, 'Under the Gaze of Theory', *e-flux journal*, no.35, May 2012, available at http://www.e-flux.com/journal/under-the-gaze-of-theory/ (last accessed on 31 May 2016).

16   On praxis and labour see, for instance, Josefine Wikström, 'Practice Comes Before Labour: An Attempt to Read Performance through Marx's Notion of Practice', *Performance Research: A Journal of the Performing Arts*, vol. 17, no. 6., 2016, pp.22-27.

17   Karl Marx, 'Theses on Feuerbach' (trans. W. Lough), in *Collected Works of Marx and Engels, vol.5, 1845-1847*, London: Lawrence & Wishart, 1976, p.6.

18   See Jacques Rancière, 'The Aesthetic Revolution and Its Outcomes: Emplotments of Autonomy and Heteronomy', in Part One of this reader, pp.81-94.

19   Karl Marx, *Capital: A Critique of Political Economy, Volume I* (trans. Ben Fowkes), London: Penguin, 1990, p.255. This is discussed by Kerstin Stakemeier in 'Art as Capital – Art as Service – Art as Industry: Timing Art in Capitalism', in Beatrice von Bismarck et al. (ed.), *Timing: On the Temporal Dimension of Exhibiting*, Berlin: Sternberg Press, 2014, pp.15-38.

20   For instance, in a country such as the Netherlands the state actively pushes research on (and in the service of) the creative industries, syphoning resources into areas like design and new media.

21   Jonathan Crary, *24/7: Late Capitalism and the Ends of Sleep*, London and New York: Verso, 2013, p.46.

22   See Byung-Chul Han, *Psychopolitik. Neoliberalismus und die neuen Machttechniken*, Frankfurt am

Main: Fischer, 2014.

23   Theodor W. Adorno, *Aesthetic Theory* (1970; trans. Robert Hullot-Kentor, ed. Gretel Adorno and Rolf Tiedemann), London: Althone Press, 1997, p.6.

24   Theodor W. Adorno and Hanns Eisler, *Composing for the Films*, London: Althone Press, 1994, pp.45-61; reprinted in Part Five of this reader, pp.310-21.

25   *Ibid.*

26   Adorno famously defines art's double character as both autonomous and *fait social* in *Aesthetic Theory*, *op. cit.*, p.5.

27   See Max Weber, *Gesammelte Aufsätze zur Religionssoziologie*, vol.1 (1920), Tübingen: Mohr, 1988, pp.536-73.

28   Jürgen Habermas, 'Modernity: An Incomplete Project,' in Hal Foster (ed.), *The Anti-Aesthetic: Essays on Postmodern Culture*, Seattle: Bay Press, 1983, p.9.

29   T.W. Adorno, 'Marginalia to Theory and Praxis' (1968), in *Critical Models: Interventions and Catchwords* (trans. Henry W. Pickford), New York: Columbia University Press, 2005, pp.259-78, especially 273. In his attack on 'actionism', Adorno here uses the impoverished and undialectical notion of praxis (as antithetically opposed to 'theory') that he had accused his opponents of employing.

30   Rosenberg launched the term 'action painting' in 'The American Action Painters', *ARTnews*, December 1952, pp.22-23, 48-50. The article was widely assumed to be based on Pollock's practice, although it does not include mention a single artist's name (and Rosenberg was much closer to de Kooning). See also Sven Lütticken, *History in Motion: Time in the Age of the Moving Image*, Berlin: Sternberg Press, 2013, pp.223-32.

31   Allan Kaprow, 'The Legacy of Jackson Pollock', *ARTnews*, October 1958, pp.24-26, 55-57.

32   The reference here is to Guy Debord's 1963 text 'The Situationists and the New Forms of Action in Art and Politics'. A translation from the French by Ken Knabb is available at http://www.cddc. vt.edu/sionline/si/newforms.html (last accessed on 19 September 2020).

33   On the Subversive Aktion and its links to the Situationist International, see Aribert Reimann, *Dieter Kunzelmann: Avantgardist, Protestler, Radikaler*, Göttingen: Vandenhoeck & Ruprecht, 2009, pp.49-122.

34   See also Part Three of this reader, pp.167-215.

35   Brian Holmes, 'Artistic Autonomy and the Communication Society', *Third Text*, vol.18, no.6, 2004, p.548; reprinted in Part Four of this reader, pp.340-41.

36   Andrea Fraser, 'Autonomy and Its Contradictions', 2015 revised version of an essay originally published in *Open!*, no.23, 2012; reprinted in Part Three of this reader, pp.203-10.

37   *Ibid.*

38   On Operaismo and Autonomia, see Parts Four and Five of this reader, pp.217-57 and 289-352.

39   Gerald Raunig, 'Instituent Practices: Fleeing, Instituting, Transforming', in *Art and Contemporary Critical Practice: Reinventing Institutional Critique*, G. Raunig and Gene Ray (ed.), London: MayFlyBooks, 2009, pp.3-11.

40   *Services: Conditions and Relations of Contemporary Project Oriented Artistic Practice* was exhibited first at the Kunstraum der Universität Lüneburg, from 29 January-February 20, 1994, and subsequently toured other art spaces.

41   See, for instance, Haacke and Fraser's obituaries of Bourdieu in *October*, no. 101, Summer 2002, pp.4-11.

42   Kerstin Stakemeier, 'Art as Capital - Art as Service - Art as Industry: Timing Art in Capitalism', in Beatrice von Bismarck et al. (ed.), *Timing: On the Temporal Dimension of Exhibiting*, Berlin: Sternberg Press, 2014, p.21.

43   Fredric Jameson, 'The Aesthetics of Singularity', *New Left Review*, no.92, March/April 2015, p.107.

44   Helmut Draxler, 'The Politics of Relational Form', lecture delivered at 'Art and its Frames: Continuity and Change', symposium at the Kunstraum der Leuphana Universität Lüneburg, 14 June 2014.

45   'Langer Marsch durch die Institutionen' is a well-known phrase in Germany. On Dutschke's original use, see Manfred Kittel, *Langer Marsch durch die Institutionen? Politik und Kultur in Frankfurt nach 1968*, Munich: Oldenbourg, 2011, p.6.

46   See René Viénet, *Enragés and Situationists in the Occupations Movement* (1968; trans. Loren Goldner and Paul Sieveking), New York: Autonomedia, 1992, chapter 8, available at http://www. cddc.vt.edu/sionline/si/enrages08.html (last accessed on 17 September 2020).

47   Vidya Ashram, 'The Global Autonomous University', in Edu-Factory Collective (ed.), *Towards a Global Autonomous University*, New York: Autonomedia, 2009, p.166.

48   See Sally Wyat (KNAW) and David Millen (IBM) (ed.), *Meaning and Perspective in the Digital Humanities: A White Paper for the Establishment of a Center for Humanities and Technologies (CHAT)*, Amsterdam: Royal Netherlands Academy of Arts and Sciences, 2014, available at https://www.knaw. nl/shared/resources/actueel/publicaties/pdf/meaning-and-perspectives-in-the-digital-humanities-white-paper-chat (last accessed on 17 September 2020).

49   *Ibid.*, p.53.

50   S. Amsler, 'Beyond All Reason', *op. cit.*, p.80.

51   *Ibid.*, p.68.

52   B. Holmes, 'Artistic Autonomy and the Communication Society', *op. cit.*

53   Stefano Harney and Fred Moten, *The Undercommons: Fugitive Planning & Black Study*, London, New York and Port Watson: Minor Compositions, 2013, p.26.

54   See Michael Baers, 'No Good Time for an Exhibition: Reflections on the Picasson in Palenstine Project', parts 1 and 2, *e-flux journal*, no.33-34, March-April 2012, available at https://www.e-flux.com/journal/33/68274/no-good-time-for-an-exhibition-reflections-on-the-picasso-in-palestine-project-part-i/ and https://www.e-flux.com/journal/34/68343/no-good-time-for-an-exhibition-reflections-on-the-picasso-in-palestine-project-part-ii/ (last accessed on 17 September 2020).

55   See Parts Two and Six of this reader, pp.101-65 and 355-413.

56   On the transformation of the institution from site into network, see André Rottmann, 'Networks, Techniques, Institutions: Art History in Open Circuits', *Texte zur Kunst*, no.81, 2011, pp.142-44. On the 'integration into precarity', see Hito Steyerl, 'The Institution of Critique', in G. Raunig and G. Ray (ed.), *Art and Contemporary Critical Practice*, *op. cit.*, pp.13-19.

57   The slogan 'Autonomie ist selbstbestimmte Abhängigkeit' (autonomy is self-determined dependency) was the title of the 1995 Autonomie-Kongress in Berlin. See Part Five of this reader, p.237 and the documentation provided in *Autonomie-Kongreß der undogmatischen linken Bewegungen: Standpunkte - Provokationen - Thesen*, Münster: Unrast Verlag, no date, pp.20-35. The latter was recently cited in Bini Adamczak, *Beziehungsweise Revolution. 1917, 1968 und kommende*, Frankfurt: Suhrkamp, 2017, p.99. The variation 'self-determination is the right to choose your dependencies' is attributed to Vivian Ziherl by Jonas Staal in 'To Make a World, Part II: The Art of Creating a State', in *e-flux journal* no. 60, December 2014, https://www.e-flux.com/journal/60/61062/to-make-a-world-part-ii-the-art-of-creating-a-state/ (last accessed on 17 September 2020).

PART ONE:
ART AND LIFE

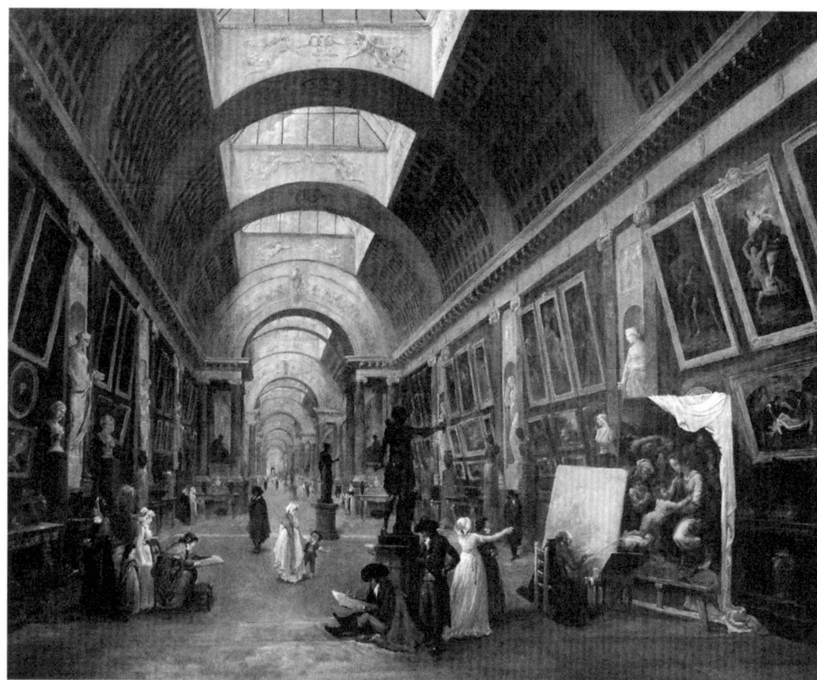

Hubert Robert, *Project for the Grande Galerie of the Louvre*, 1796, oil on canvas, 115 × 145cm

Opposite page: Hubert Robert, *Imaginary View of the Grand Gallery in Ruins*, 1796, oil on canvas, 33 × 40cm

Around 1800, art became radically unmoored. In the wake of the French Revolution of 1789, royal and church property was nationalised and monasteries disbanded; museums opened to house the 'homeless' artworks. After years of preparation, the museum at the Louvre opened its doors in 1793, and the Musée des Monuments Français in 1795. Napoleon's campaigns meant that works from large parts of Europe were now within the grasp of the French state. In 1796, the theorist Quatremère de Quincy published letters in which he bemoans the decontextualisation of Italian artworks, considered in danger of losing specificity and aesthetic value once transported to the Louvre.[1] That same year, the painter Hubert Robert, who was deeply involved in the Louvre's transformation, exhibited a painting that showed his proposal for a renovated Grande Galerie, with custom-designed skylights turning the grand corridor into a perfect space for the study of art – a new kind of art-historical viewing device.[2]

Among the admiring visitors of the Musée du Louvre were the brothers August Wilhelm and Friedrich Schlegel, key figures of German Romanticism who also had close contacts with Sulpiz and Melchior Boisserée, collectors of many late medieval artworks in the German territories occupied by Napoleon. This gave a boost to the rediscovery of the art of the Middle Ages, which the Romantics glorified as embedded in daily life, not locked away in alienating museums – even while these very museums were crucial in enabling the romantic 'religion of art' in the first place. And this *Kunstreligion* was not limited to visual art. Poets and composers developed a heightened sense of calling, which made traditional notions of literary patronage as problematic as working for an art market that privileged less ambitious work.

While the arts were still divided between different disciplines, these disciplines were increasingly seen as different manifestations of one transcendental essence: Art. As Raymond Williams puts it in his *Keywords* (1976/83) compendium:

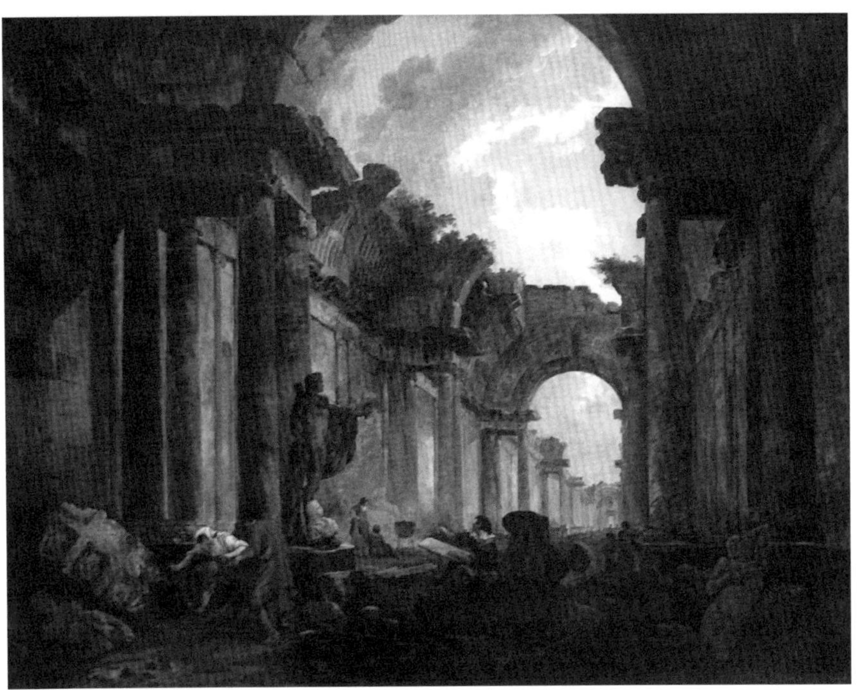

Art has been used in English from thirteenth century, the immediate forerunner of *art*, Old French, ultimately traceable from *artem*, Latin – skill. It was widely applied, without predominant specialisation, until last period of the seventeenth century, in matters as various as mathematics, medicine and angling. In the medieval university curriculum the **arts** ('the seven arts' and later 'the LIBERAL (q.v.) arts') were grammar, logic, rhetoric, arithmetic, geometry, music and astronomy, and **artist,** from the sixteenth century, was first used in this context, though with almost contemporary developments to describe any skilled person (as which it is in effect identical with **artisan** until last period of the sixteenth century) or a practitioner of one of the **arts** in another grouping, those presided over by the seven muses: history, poetry, comedy, tragedy, music, dancing, astronomy. Then, from last period of the seventeenth century, there was an increasingly common specialised application to a group of skills not hitherto formally represented: painting, drawing, engraving and sculpture. The now dominant use of **art** and **artist** to refer to these skills was not fully established until last period of the nineteenth century, but it was within this grouping that in the last period of the eighteenth century, and with special reference to the exclusion of engravers from the new Royal Academy, a now *general distinction between* **artist** and **artisan** – the latter being specialised to 'skilled manual worker' without 'intellectual' or 'imaginative' or 'creative' purposes – was strengthened and popularised. This development of **artisan,** and the middle period of the nineteenth century definition of *scientist*, allowed the specialisation of **artist** and the distinction not now of the *liberal* but of the **fine arts.**

The emergence of an abstract, capitalised **Art,** with its own internal but general principles, is difficult to localise. There are several plausible eighteenth century uses, but it was in the nineteenth century that the concept became general. It is historically related, in this sense, to the development of CULTURE and AESTHETICS (qq.v.). [William] Wordsworth wrote to the painter [Benjamin Robert] Haydon in 1815: 'High is our calling, friend, Creative Art.' The now normal association with *creative* and *imaginative*, as a matter of classification, dates effectively from last period of the eighteenth century and the first period of the nineteenth century. The significant adjective **artistic** dates effectively from the middle period of the nineteenth century. **Artistic temperament** and **artistic sensibility** date from the same period. So too does **artiste,** a further distinguishing specialisation to describe performers such as actors or singers, thus keeping **artist** for painter, sculptor and eventually (from the middle period of the nineteenth century) writer and composer.[3]

Such evolutions in jargon may register cultural and social shifts with some delay. The 'autonomisation' of art did not happen overnight. In the early sixteenth century, both the Italian Renaissance and the Northern Reformation did much to foster a sense that visual art has some merit in its own right, not just as a representation of Eternal Truths or as propaganda for temporal powers.[4] Between the sixteenth and eighteenth centuries, and more rapidly and substantially in the latter, the development of the art market and of academies, art theory and exhibitions all contributed to this growing relative autonomy.[5] Nonetheless, the 'aesthetic turn' inaugurated by philosophers and philosophising poets from the mid-eighteenth to the early-nineteenth century changed the terms of the debate radically. These writers theorised Art at its most general and fundamental, though at some point they usually also differentiated between the different arts. In this reader, we deal with Art mostly through visual art – but, as Part Four in particular will stress, visual art has itself become rather 'general', encompassing ever more media and intermedial forms

When aesthetics emerged as a branch of philosophy in the eighteenth century, it was not as a philosophy of Art or of the arts, but as a philosophy of the senses. Modern philosophy tried to found itself on reason alone, on the subject as pure cogito; in the process, it cut itself off from the world. Aesthetics was philosophy's attempt to reconnect reason and sense, subject and object. Art became central to this project because in art, matter already seemed to be informed by reason; whatever its medium, the work of art is a sensuous object that appears to be truly sensible, yet we cannot fully grasp its essential workings. Constructed according to an obscure logic, the artwork is a bridge between philosophy and the world, but also a constant challenge to philosophy's claim to dominion. The artwork is endlessly talked about, debated; thus, as Terry Eagleton has put it, it constitutes a 'residually common world'.[6] But what is the nature of this aesthetic world?

In his book *The Ideology of the Aesthetic* (1990), Eagleton casts an unsparing eye on aesthetics as an ideology that purports to resolve the contradictions of modern bourgeois society. The artwork becomes a site of reconciliation, an embodiment of the mind that momentarily appears to take away the alienation of wage labour – but which, in this account, ultimately reinforces dominant class interests. However, Eagleton also stresses that this aesthetic ideology has its progressive potential, and can in fact be read as, or turned into, a powerful critique of 'bourgeois possessive individual and appetitive egoism' – in other words, of a kind of imperialist autonomy of the self-serving privileged bourgeois.

The emergence of the aesthetic as a theoretical category is closely bound up with the material process by which cultural production, at an early stage of bourgeois society, becomes 'autonomous' – autonomous, that is, of the various social functions which it has traditionally served. Once artefacts become commodities in the market place, they exist for nothing and nobody in particular, and can consequentially be rationalised, ideologically speaking, as existing entirely and gloriously for themselves. It is this notion of autonomy or self-referentiality which the new discourse of aesthetics is centrally concerned to elaborate; and it is clear enough, from a radical political viewpoint, just how disabling any such idea of aesthetic autonomy must be. It is not only, as radical thought has familiarly insisted, that art is thereby conveniently sequestered from all other social practices, to become an isolated enclave within which the dominant social order can find an idealised refuge from its own values of competitiveness, exploitation and material possessiveness. It is also, rather more subtly, that the idea of autonomy – of a mode of being which is entirely self-regulating and self-determining – provides the middle class with just the ideological model of subjectivity it requires for its material operations. Yet this concept of autonomy is radically double-edged: if on the one hand it provides a central constituent of bourgeois ideology, it also marks an emphasis on the self-determining nature of human powers and capacities which becomes, in the work of Karl Marx and others, the anthropological foundation of a revolutionary opposition to bourgeois society. The aesthetic is at once, as I try to show, the very secret prototype of human subjectivity in early capitalist society, and a vision of human energies as radical ends in themselves which is the implacable enemy of all instrumentalist thought. It signifies a creative turn to the sensuous body, as well as an inscribing of that body with a subtly oppressive law; it represents on the one hand a liberatory concern with concrete particularity, and on the other hand a specious form of universalism.[7]

Of all the tensions or contradictions in which the aesthetic is wrapped up, that between Art and Life has been debated with particular fervour. Aesthetics was never just a philosophy of art: fundamentally, it aimed to serve up visions of a full life amidst alienating structures and strictures. And while this could have a conservative and conciliatory function, some practitioners actually attempted to create, or at least prefigure, such an aesthetic life in the here and now.

Aestheticise the World

The mediating and conciliatory function of the aesthetic is very clear from Immanuel Kant's *Critique of the Power of Judgment* (1790).[8] In this treatise, Kant places particular emphasis on the need for pure aesthetic judgements to be 'disinterested'; that is to say, our appreciation of the beautiful cannot depend on whether we derive some primary sensuous gratification from it. If aesthetics tried to give embodied sensuous experience its due, Kant sublimated and formalised this experience almost beyond recognition – paving a way for formalist approaches to art. The judgment of taste claims autonomy, and to allow one's judgment to be shaped by the verdicts of others 'would be heteronomy'.[9] Tradition and consensus, then, can be downright harmful; aesthetic judgement has the power to explode them, or at least to challenge them. But who has the capacity to make such autonomous judgements? In attempting to demonstrate the aesthetic and disinterested nature of the judgement of taste, Kant does not hesitate to cast an indigenous American chief in the role of an all too interested 'primitive', thus establishing a hierarchy between Enlightened European philosophers and those who are unable to suspend their desires in favour of aesthetic judgement.[10]

IMMANUEL KANT, *CRITIQUE OF THE POWER OF JUDGMENT*

Reprinted from *Critique of the Power of Judgment*, Cambridge: Cambridge University Press, 2000, pp.89-91. Emphasis in the original. First published in 1790. Translated from the German by Paul Guyer and Eric Matthews. Translators' notes have been removed.

§ 1. The judgement of taste is aesthetic.
In order to decide whether or not something is beautiful, we do not relate the representation by means of understanding to the object for cognition, but rather relate it by means of the imagination (perhaps combined with the understanding) to the subject and its feeling of pleasure or displeasure. The judgment of taste is therefore not a cognitive judgment, hence not a logical one, but is rather aesthetic, by which is understood one whose determining ground **cannot** be **other than subjective**. Any relation of representations, however, even that of sensations, can be objective (in which case it signifies what is real in an empirical representation); but not the relation to the feeling of pleasure and displeasure, by means of which nothing at all in the object is designated, but in which the subject feels itself as it is affected by the representation.

To grasp a regular, purposive structure with one's faculty of cognition (whether the manner of representation be distinct or confused) is something entirely different from being conscious of this representation with the sensation of satisfaction. Here the representation is related entirely to the subject, indeed to its feeling of life, under the name of the feeling of pleasure or displeasure, which grounds an entirely special faculty for discriminating and judging that contributes nothing to cognition but only holds the given representation in the subject up to the entire faculty of representation, of which the mind becomes conscious in the feeling of its state. Given representations in a judgment can be empirical (hence aesthetic); however, the judgment that is made by means of them is logical if in the judgment they are related to the object. Conversely, however, even if the given representations were to be rational but related in a judgment solely to the subject (its feeling), then they are to that extent always aesthetic.

§ 2. The satisfaction that determines the judgment of taste is without any interest.

The satisfaction that we combine with the representation of the existence of an object is called interest. Hence such a satisfaction always has at the same time a relation to the faculty of desire, either as its determining ground or else as necessarily interconnected with its determining ground. But if the question is whether something is beautiful, one does not want to know whether there is anything that is or that could be at stake, for us or for someone else, in the existence of the thing, but rather how we judge it in mere contemplation (intuition or reflection). If someone asks me whether I find the palace that I see before me beautiful, I may well say that I don't like that sort of thing, which is made merely to be gaped at, or, like the Iroquois sachem, that nothing in Paris pleased him better than the cook-shops; in true **Rousseauesque** style I might even vilify the vanity of the great who waste the sweat of the people on such superfluous things; finally I could even easily convince myself that if I were to find myself on an uninhabited island, without any hope of ever coming upon human beings again, and could conjure up such a magnificent structure through my mere wish, I would not even take the trouble of doing so if I already had a hut that was comfortable enough for me. All of this might be conceded to me and approved; but that is not what is at issue here. One only wants to know whether the mere representation of the object is accompanied with satisfaction in me, however indifferent I might be with regard to the existence of the object of this representation. It is readily seen that to say that it is **beautiful** and to prove that I have taste what matters is what I make of this representation in myself, not how I depend on the existence of the object. Everyone must admit that a judgment about beauty in which there is mixed the least interest is very partial and not a pure judgment of taste. One must not be in the least biased in favour of the existence of the thing, but must be entirely indifferent in this respect in order to play the judge in matters of taste.

For Kant, the aesthetic became crucial in that it seemed to suggest a bridge between two realms. On one side there is the realm of 'pure reason', which concerns our experience of the outside world and the ways such experience follows fixed laws that we cannot consciously control. Our experience of the sensuous world both entangles us in and separates us from it – we can never be sure that the way in which our senses and the mind structure sense data reflects the 'real' order of things. The realm of 'practical reason', on the other side, deals with moral judgements that are supposedly exercised freely and autonomously. Kant's philosophy thus separates the subject of reason from the world and splits the subject itself. Ultimately, it is only the subject of 'practical reason' that has any freedom, though this is undermined by the fact that Kant's moral will is a curiously abstract voice of moral reason that ultimately occupies the place of the subject rather than being one of its faculties.[11] Such reason seems to be eerily autonomous from the subject, paving the way for the technocratic and 'purposive reason' of industrial capitalism. It is precisely here that the aesthetic experience – aesthetic judgement – at least appears to offer autonomy to a unified, actual human subject:

> That nature has the property of containing an occasion for us to perceive the inner purposiveness in the relationship of our mental powers in the judging of certain of its products, and indeed as something that has to be explained as necessarily and universally valid on the basis of a supersensible ground, cannot be an end of nature, or rather be judged by us as such a thing: because otherwise the judgment that would thereby be determined would be grounded in heteronomy and would not, as befits a judgment of taste, be free and grounded in autonomy.[12]

Das Ding an sich, 'the thing-in-itself', may be inaccessible, but aesthetic judgement suggests that beautiful objects function as if the world and reason are actually in harmony, with the subject being in control.

The *Critique of the Power of Judgement* (with its accounts of both aesthetic and teleological judgement) went far in overcoming – or glossing over – the chasms Kant had created. A younger set of thinkers would try to reintegrate and transcend his split and abstracted subject. These authors lived and worked in a Germany that was a patchwork of small absolutist states that to a greater or lesser extent supported the arts and sciences, but that usually did not allow any political dissent. The duchy Sachsen-Weimar-Eisenach, in particular, prided itself on patronage of the arts and humanities; the capital city of Weimar is still associated in the German imaginary with the so-called *Weimarer Klassik* (Weimar Classicism) and its main protagonists, the poets Johann Wolfgang von Goethe and Friedrich Schiller. In 1789 – the year of the French Revolution – Schiller was appointed professor at the University of Jena, the most prominent centre of higher education in the duchy, and to mark the occasion he gave a lecture espousing an Enlightenment view of 'universal history': 'What Is, and to What End Do We Study Universal History?'

The previous year Schiller had published a historical work on the Netherlands' fight for independence in the sixteenth and seventeenth centuries. Like many German intellectuals and artists, Schiller was also electrified by the outbreak of the French Revolution – only to grow wary of its excesses. The gradual Napoleonic invasion of 1801–07 created an upsurge in German nationalism and Romantic glorification of the past. In a country lacking self-determination, in which the French celebration of Reason appeared as a part-alluring, part-frightening foreign cult, the aesthetic became ever more important as a synthesis and reconciliation of freedom and necessity, of the mind and the world of the senses, of subject and object.

In *Letters on the Aesthetic Education of Mankind* (1795), Schiller attempts to show that aesthetic activity can reconcile not just reason and the senses, but also do away with social conflict and the dulling 'mechanical' nature of modern life. With his notion of the 'play instinct', Schiller tries to better Kant. He argues that 'man' is split between the 'sensuous instinct' and the 'formal instinct': the first anchors us in the world and gives us over to time, and it would also get us completely lost among a myriad of impressions and desires; the second gives laws (for judgments of knowledge and for moral action), which purport to be timeless and exist independent of experience. The play instinct is the synthesis of the two. Far from being a matter of disinterested aesthetic judgment, it allows us to actively shape the world, to engage with sensuous stuff in time and to form our environment in accordance with our desires. This conception of play as aesthetic activity goes beyond 'autonomous' art and would have significant repercussions in later art and theory.

FRIEDRICH SCHILLER, *LETTERS ON THE AESTHETIC EDUCATION OF MANKIND*

Translation reprinted from *Literary and Philosophical Essays: French, German and Italian*, Harvard Classics, vol.32, New York: Collier, 1909-14, pp.221-322, available at http://www. bartleby.com/32/ (last accessed on 17 September 2020). Reproduced with minor amendments.

Letter XI

[...] Now, although an infinite being, a divinity could not *become* (or be subject to time), still a tendency ought to be named divine which has for its infinite end the most characteristic attribute of the divinity; the absolute manifestation of power – the reality of all the possible – and the absolute unity of the manifestation (the necessity of all reality). It cannot be disputed that man bears within himself, in his personality, a predisposition for divinity. The way to divinity – if the word 'way' can be applied to what never leads to its end – is open to him in every *direction*.

Considered in itself and independently of all sensuous matter, his personality is nothing but the pure virtuality of a possible infinite manifestation, and so long as there is neither intuition nor feeling, it is nothing more than a form, an empty power. Considered in itself, and independently of all spontaneous activity of the mind, sensuousness can only make a material man; without it, it is a pure form; but it cannot in any way establish a union between matter and it. So long as he only feels, wishes and acts under the influence of desire, he is nothing more than the world, if by this word we point out only the formless contents of time. Without doubt, it is only his sensuousness that makes his strength pass into efficacious acts, but it is his personality alone that makes this activity his own. Thus, that he may not only be a world, he must give form to matter, and in order not to be a mere form, he must give reality to the virtuality that he bears in him. He gives matter to form by creating time, and by opposing the immutable to change, the diversity of the world to the eternal unity of the Ego. He gives a form to matter by again suppressing time, by maintaining permanence in change, and by placing the diversity of the world under the unity of the Ego.

Now from this source issue for man two opposite exigencies, the two fundamental laws of sensuous-rational nature. The first has for its object absolute *reality*; it must make a world of what is only form, manifest all that in it is only a force. The second law has for its object absolute *formality*; it must destroy in him all that is only world, and carry out harmony in all changes. In other terms, he must manifest all that is internal, and give form to all that is external. Considered in its most lofty accomplishment, this twofold labour brings us back to the idea of humanity which was my starting point.

Letter XII

[...] If the sensuous instinct only produces *accidents*, the formal instinct gives laws, laws for every judgment when it is a question of knowledge, laws for every will when it is a question of action. Whether, therefore, we recognise an object or conceive an objective value to a state of the subject, whether we act in virtue of knowledge or make of the objective the determining principle of our state; in both cases we withdraw this state from the jurisdiction of time, and we attribute to it reality for all men and for all time, that is, universality and necessity. Feeling can only say: 'That is true *for this subject* and *at this moment*', and there may come another moment, another subject, which withdraws the affirmation from the actual feeling. But when once thought pronounces and says: '*That is*', it decides for ever and ever, and the validity of its decision is guaranteed by the personality itself, which defies all change. Inclination can only say: 'That is good *for your individuality* and *present necessity*'; but the changing current of affairs will sweep them away, and what you ardently desire today will form the object of your aversion tomorrow. But when the moral feeling says: 'That ought to be', it decides for ever. If you confess the truth because it is the truth, and if you practice justice because it is justice, you have made of a particular case the law of all possible cases, and treated one moment of your life as eternity.

Accordingly, when the formal impulse holds sway and the pure object acts in us, the being attains its highest expansion, all barriers disappear, and from the unity of magnitude in which man was enclosed by a narrow sensuousness, he rises to the *unity of idea*, which embraces and keeps subject the entire sphere of phaenomena. During this operation we are no longer in time, but time is in us with its infinite succession. We are no longer individuals but a species; the judgment of all spirits is expressed by our own, and the choice of all hearts is represented by our own act. [...]

Letter XIV

[...] The sensuous instinct wishes to be determined, it wishes to receive an object; the formal instinct wishes to determine itself, it wishes to produce an object. Therefore the instinct of play will endeavour to receive as it would itself have produced, and to produce as it aspires to receive.

The sensuous impulsion excludes from its subject all autonomy and freedom; the formal impulsion excludes all dependence and passivity. But the exclusion of freedom is physical necessity; the exclusion of passivity is moral necessity. Thus the two impulsions subdue the mind: the former to the laws of nature, the latter to the laws of reason. It results from this that the instinct of play, which unites the double action of the two other instincts, will content the mind at once morally and physically. Hence, as it suppresses all that is contingent, it will also suppress all coercion, and will set man free physically and morally. When we welcome with effusion someone who deserves our contempt, we feel painfully that *nature is constrained*. When we have a hostile feeling against a person who commands our esteem, we feel painfully the *constraint of reason*. But if this person inspires us with interest, and also wins our esteem, the constraint of feeling vanishes together with the constraint of reason, and we begin to love him, that is to say, to play, to take recreation, at once with our inclination and our esteem.

Moreover, as the sensuous impulsion controls us physically, and the formal impulsion morally, the former makes our formal constitution contingent, and the latter makes our material constitution contingent, that is to say, there is contingence in the agreement of our happiness with our perfection, and reciprocally. The instinct of play, in which both act in concert, will render both our formal and our material constitution contingent; accordingly, our perfection and our happiness in like manner. And on the other hand, exactly because it makes *both of them* contingent, and because the contingent disappears with necessity, it will suppress this contingence in both, and will thus give form to matter and reality to form. In proportion that it will lessen the dynamic influence of feeling and passion, it will place them in harmony with rational ideas, and by taking from the laws of reason their moral constraint, it will reconcile them with the interest of the senses.

Letter XV

[...] Beauty is neither extended to the whole field of all living things nor merely enclosed in this field. A marble block, though it is and remains lifeless, can nevertheless become a living form by the architect and sculptor; a man, though he lives and has a form, is far from being a living form on that account. For this to be the case, it is necessary that his form should be life, and that his life should be a form. As long as we only think of his form, it is lifeless, a mere abstraction; as long as we only feel his life, it is without form, a mere impression. It is only when his form lives in our feeling, and his life in our understanding, he is the living form, and this will everywhere be the case where we judge him to be beautiful.

But the genesis of beauty is by no means declared because we know how to point out the component parts, which in their combination produce beauty. For to this end it would be necessary to comprehend that *combination itself,* which continues to defy our exploration, as well as all mutual operation between the finite and the infinite. The reason, on transcendental grounds, makes the following demand: There shall be a communion between the formal impulse and the material impulse – that is, there shall be a play instinct – because it is only the unity of reality with the form, of the accidental with the necessary, of the passive state with freedom, that the conception of humanity is completed. Reason is obliged to make this demand, because her nature impels her to completeness and to the removal of all bounds; while every exclusive activity of one or the other impulse leaves human nature incomplete and places a limit in it. Accordingly, as soon as reason issues the mandate 'a humanity shall exist', it proclaims at the same time the law 'there shall be a beauty'. Experience can answer us if there is a beauty, and we shall know it as soon as she has taught us if a humanity can exist. But neither reason nor experience can tell us how beauty can be, and how a humanity is possible.

We know that man is neither exclusively matter nor exclusively spirit. Accordingly, beauty, as the consummation of humanity, can neither be exclusively mere life, as has been asserted by sharp-sighted observers who kept too close to the testimony of experience, and to which the taste of the time would gladly degrade it; nor can beauty be merely form, as has been judged by speculative sophists, who departed too far from experience, and by philosophic artists, who were led too much by the necessity of art in explaining beauty; it is rather the common object of both impulses, that is, of the play instinct. The use of language completely justifies this name, as it is wont to qualify with the wordplay what is neither subjectively nor objectively accidental, and yet does not impose necessity either externally or internally. As the mind in the intuition of the beautiful finds itself in a happy medium between law and necessity, it is, because it divides itself between both, emancipated from the pressure of both. The formal impulse and the material impulse are equally earnest in their demands, because one relates in its cognition to things in their reality and the other to their necessity; because in action the first is directed to the preservation of life, the second to the preservation of dignity, and therefore both to truth and perfection. But life becomes more indifferent when dignity is mixed up with it, and duty on longer coerces when inclination attracts. In like manner the mind takes in the reality of things, material truth, more freely and tranquilly as soon as it encounters formal truth, the law of necessity; nor does the mind find itself strung by abstraction as soon as immediate intuition can accompany it. In one word, when the mind comes into communion with ideas, all reality loses its serious value because it becomes *small*; and as it comes in contact with feeling, necessity parts also with its serious value because it is *easy*.

But perhaps the objection has for some time occurred to you: Is not the beautiful degraded by this, that it is made a mere play? And is it not reduced to the level of frivolous objects which have for ages passed under that name? Does it not contradict the conception of the reason and the dignity of beauty, which is nevertheless regarded as an instrument of culture, to confine it to the work of being a mere play? And does it not contradict the empirical conception of play, which can coexist with the exclusion of all taste, to confine it merely to beauty?

But what is meant by a *mere play*, when we know that in all conditions of humanity that very thing is play, and *only* that is play which makes man complete and develops simultaneously his twofold nature? What you style *limitation*, according to your representation of the matter, according to my views, which I have justified by proofs, I name *enlargement*. Consequently, I should have said exactly the reverse: man is serious *only* with the agreeable, with the good and with the perfect, but he *plays* with beauty. In saying this we must not indeed think of the plays that are in vogue in real life, and which commonly refer only to his material state. But in real life we should also seek in vain for the beauty of which we are here speaking. The actually present beauty is worthy of the really, of the actually, present play impulse; but by the ideal of beauty, which is set up by the reason, an ideal of the play instinct is also presented, which man ought to have before his eyes in all his plays.

Therefore, no error will ever be incurred if we seek the ideal of beauty on the same road on which we satisfy our play impulse. We can immediately understand why the ideal form of a Venus, of a Juno and of an Apollo is to be sought not at Rome but in Greece, if we contrast the Greek population, delighting in the bloodless athletic contests of boxing, racing and intellectual rivalry at Olympia, with the Roman people, gloating over the agony of a gladiator. Now the reason pronounces that the beautiful must not only be life and form, but a living form, that is, beauty, inasmuch as it dictates to man the twofold law of absolute formality and absolute reality. Reason also utters the decision that man shall only *play* with beauty, and he *shall only play* with *beauty*.

For, to speak out once for all, man only plays when in the full meaning of the word he is a man, and *he is only completely a man when he plays*. This proposition, which at this moment perhaps appears paradoxical, will receive a great and deep meaning if we have advanced far enough to apply it to the twofold seriousness of duty and of destiny. I promise you that the whole edifice of aesthetic art and the still more difficult art of life will be supported by this principle. But this proposition is only unexpected in science; long ago it lived and worked in art and in the feeling of the Greeks, her most accomplished masters; only they removed to Olympus what ought to have been preserved on earth. Influenced by the truth of this principle, they effaced from the brow of their gods the earnestness and labour which furrow the cheeks of mortals, and also the hollow lust that smoothes the empty face. They set free the ever serene from the chains of every purpose, of every duty, of every care, and they made *indolence* and *indifference* the envied condition of the godlike race; merely human appellations for the freest and highest mind. As well the material pressure of natural laws as the spiritual pressure of moral laws lost itself in its higher idea of necessity, which embraced at the same time both worlds, and out of the union of these two necessities issued true freedom. Inspired by this spirit, the Greeks also effaced from the features of their ideal, together with desire or inclination, all traces of volition, or, better still, they made both unrecognisable, because they knew how to wed them both in the closest alliance. It is neither charm nor is it dignity which speaks from the glorious face of the Juno Ludovisi; it is neither of these, for it is both at once. While the female god challenges our veneration, the godlike woman at the same times kindles our love. But while in ecstasy we give ourselves up to the heavenly beauty, the heavenly self-repose awes us back. The whole form rests and dwells in itself – a fully complete creation in itself – and as if she were out of space, without advance or resistance; it shows no force contending with force, no opening through which time could break in. Irresistibly carried away and attracted by her womanly charm, kept off at a distance by her godly dignity, we also find ourselves at length in the state of the greatest repose, and the result is a wonderful impression, for which the understanding has no idea and language no name. [...]

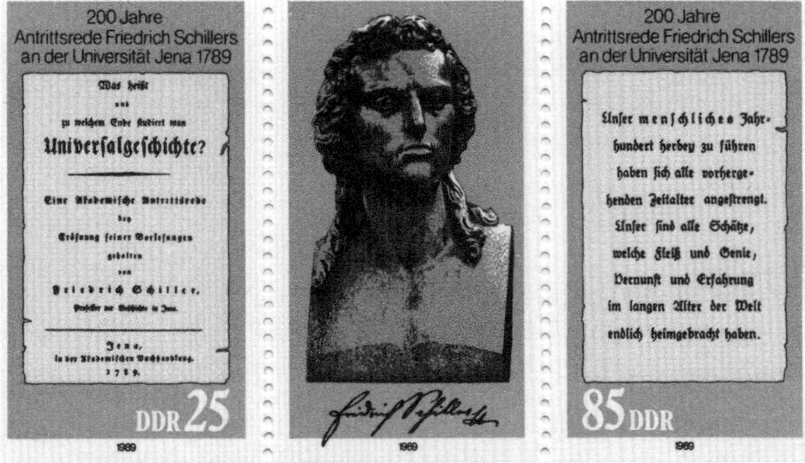

Commemorative stamps issued in 1989
by the German Democratic Republic for the
bicentenary of Friedrich Schiller's lecture
'What Is, and to What End Do We Study,
Universal History?'

[...] Duty and stern necessity must change their forbidding tone, only excused by resistance, and do homage to nature by a nobler trust in her. Taste leads our knowledge from the mysteries of science into the open expanse of common sense, and changes a narrow scholasticism into the common property of the human race. Here the highest genius must leave its particular elevation, and make itself familiar to the comprehension even of a child. Strength must let the Graces bind it, and the arbitrary lion must yield to the reins of love. For this purpose taste throws a veil over physical necessity, offending a free mind by its coarse nudity, and dissimulating our degrading parentage with matter by a delightful illusion of freedom. Mercenary art itself rises from the dust; and the bondage of the bodily, in its magic touch, falls off from the inanimate and animate. In the aesthetic state the most slavish tool is a free citizen, having the same rights as the noblest; and the intellect which shapes the mass to its intent must consult it concerning its destination. Consequently, in the realm of aesthetic appearance, the idea of equality is realised, which the political zealot would gladly see carried out socially. It has often been said that perfect politeness is only found near a throne. If thus restricted in the material, man has, as elsewhere appears, to find compensation in the ideal world.

Does such a state of beauty in appearance exist, and where? It must be in every finely harmonised soul; but as a fact, only in select circles, like the pure ideal of the church and state - in circles where manners are not formed by the empty imitations of the foreign, but by the very beauty of nature; where man passes through all sorts of complications in all simplicity and innocence, neither forced to trench on another's freedom to preserve his own, nor to show grace at the cost of dignity.

In his discussion of the Juno Ludovisi in Letter XV, Schiller notes how the work completely blends the formal and the sensuous, the moral and the material; it is a sensory thing exhibiting an obscure yet compelling logic. But aesthetic speculations and practices were never limited to specific objects. In fact, prefiguring the avant-garde trope of 'the merging of art and life', Schiller criticises the Greeks by stating that 'they removed to Olympus what ought to have been preserved on earth'. Here we have the profoundly ambiguous proto-programme of an aesthetic revolution: not an abstract imposition of Reason on more or less willing subjects (as in the French Revolution), but a transformation of life from the inside out. However, as Schiller's last letter suggests, this could easily remain a privileged project limited to 'select circles': this suggests that for the time being an elite will have to substitute for a more generalised 'state of beauty'. The modern art world would institutionalise this substitution.

Schiller's project is profoundly Romantic in its attempt to merge life and art, even though the Weimar poet in many respects differed from the *Frühromantiker* (early Romantics) around the Schlegel brothers, whose base was in near Jena. While Schiller remained in thrall to Ancient Greece, Friedrich Schlegel and Novalis looked towards post-antique, 'modern' art and literature - the art of the Romance languages and the literary romances of the Middle Ages, especially the German Middle Ages. Indeed, Romanticism would increasingly stage a cult of the Germanic Middle Ages as the paradigmatic period in which art, religion and 'the people' were still one, before the onset of modern rationalism and the division of labour.

Like Schiller, the Romantics paradoxically pushed the cult of art as a field endowed with a high mission to the point where aesthetic autonomy turns against art. The painter Caspar David Friedrich, who received important impulses from the Schlegel circle, dreamt of having his *Cross in the Mountains* (also known as the *Tetschen Altar*, c.1807) function as an altarpiece in the chapel of the castle at Tetschen, rather than as an 'autonomous' artistic commodity in a private collection.[13] His attitude reflects a situation in which the basic infrastructure of the art world as we know it had already been established: exhibitions, museums, galleries and art criticism. The Romantics dreamed of a flight from this emerging institutional sphere, aiming to reintegrated alienated art into more organic forms of life. Their peculiar mixture of the reactionary and the revolutionary is particularly evident in some of Novalis's philosophical fragments, the first of which were published in 1798. Giving a more religious slant to Schiller's attempt to reform society through the aesthetic, Novalis exults poetry and its mission to 'romanticise' the world:

> In the beginning poet and priest were one – and only later ages have separated them. But the true poet has always remained a priest, just as the true priest has always remained a poet – and ought not the future bring the old state of affairs back again? [...]
>
> The world must be made Romantic. In that way one can find the original meaning again. To make Romantic is nothing but a qualitative raising to a higher power. In this operation the lower self will become one with a better self. Just as we ourselves are such a qualitative exponential series. This operation is as yet quite unknown. By endowing the commonplace with a higher meaning, the ordinary with mysterious respect, the known with the dignity of the unknown, the finite with the appearance of the infinite, I am making it Romantic. The operation for the higher, unknown, mystical, infinite is the converse – this undergoes a logarithmic change through this connection – it takes on an ordinary form of expression. Romantic philosophy. *Lingua romana*. Raising and lowering by turns.[14]

Such dense and suggestive fragments are a quintessentially Romantic form: the Romantics used the fragment as an aesthetic-theoretical device that allowed for speculation not bound by systemic order. In that sense, the fragment was perfectly suited for 'potentialising' mundane reality, for seeing the extraordinary in the common. The fragment was as poetical as it was philosophical, and one might argue that it comes closest to embodying the ideal posited by Friedrich Schlegel in another fragment – that of Romantic poetry as a 'progressive universal poetry' that can absorb almost anything, endlessly, in an open-ended montage.

> Romantic poetry is a progressive, universal poetry. Its aim isn't merely to reunite all the separate species of poetry and put poetry in touch with philosophy and rhetoric. It tries to and should mix and fuse poetry and prose, inspiration and criticism, the poetry of art and the poetry of nature; and make poetry lively and sociable, and life and society poetical; poeticise wit and fill and saturate the forms of art with every kind of good, solid matter for instruction, and animate them with the pulsations of humour. It embraces everything that is purely poetic, from the greatest systems of art, containing within themselves still further systems, to the sigh, the kiss that the poetising child breathes forth in artless song. It can so lose itself in what it describes that one might believe it exists only to characterise

poetical individuals of all sorts; and yet there still is no form so fit for expressing the entire spirit of an author: so that many artists who started out to write only a novel ended up by providing us with a portrait of themselves. It alone can become, like the epic, a mirror of the whole circumambient world, an image of the age. And it can also - more than any other form - hover at the midpoint between the portrayed and the portrayer, free of all real and ideal self-interest, on the wings of poetic reflection, and can raise that reflection again and again to a higher power, can multiply it in an endless succession of mirrors. It is capable of the highest and most variegated refinement, not only from within outwards, but also from without inwards; capable in that it organises - for everything that seeks a wholeness in its effects - the parts along similar lines, so that it opens up a perspective upon an infinitely increasing classicism. Romantic poetry is in the arts what wit is in philosophy, and what society and sociability, friendship and love are in life. Other kinds of poetry are finished and are now capable of being fully analysed. The romantic kind of poetry is still in the state of becoming; that, in fact, is its real essence: that it should forever be becoming and never be perfected. It can be exhausted by no theory and only a divinatory criticism would dare try to characterise its ideal. It alone is infinite, just as it alone is free; and it recognises as its first commandment that the will of the poet can tolerate no law above itself. The romantic kind of poetry is the only one that is more than a kind, that is, as it were, poetry itself: for in a certain sense all poetry is or should be romantic.[15]

Early Romanticism was still marked by enthusiasm for the Enlightenment and the French Revolution, even while the Romantics wanted to complete this revolution by reinfusing it with art and poetry in order to create a 'mythology of reason' (to quote from a philosophical programme that has been variously ascribed to Friedrich Hölderlin, F.W.J. Schelling and the young Hegel).[16]

However, during the Napoleonic era the Romantics around Friedrich Schlegel increasingly turned to Catholicism and took to lambasting the alienating effects of reason and modernity in favour of a picture-perfect ideal of the Middle Ages as a time of lived piety manifesting itself in aesthetic forms. One can already see the kernel of this in the first Novalis fragment above. Schlegel became a proponent of a group of young painters dubbed the Nazarenes (his son-in-law, Philipp Veit, among them), who lived in an abandoned monastery in Rome as they tried to take art back to the 'glory days' of just before the Protestant Reformation; Albrecht Dürer and Raphael were their twin gods. Goethe, the dominant literary figure of the day, had nothing but scorn for such a project: 'This is the first time in the history of art that significant talents have shaped themselves backwards, by returning into the mother's womb in order to initiate a new artistic epoch.'[17]

Goethe and Schiller, the *Weimarer Klassiker*, took Greek antiquity as their benchmark, opposed the Romantics' wild imagination, and pitted Neoclassical form against Romantic 'formlessness'. However, the *Klassik* was not a monolithic bloc. As its two pillars, Goethe and Schiller could in some ways have hardly be more distinct. Goethe insisted that the work of art be largely autonomous from changing social mores and moral conceptions. This is a view he shared with the writer and critic Karl Philipp Moritz, with whom he became close during his Italian journey. In essays such as 'Versuch einer Vereinigung aller Künste und Wissenschaften unter den Begriff des in sich selbst Vollendeten' (Attempt to Unify All Arts and Sciences Under the Concept of Completion-in-Itself, 1785) and 'Über die bildende Nachahmung des

Schönen' (On the Formative Imitation of Beauty, 1788) Moritz theorised the artwork as a self-sufficient entity that serves no practical interests but is dedicated to the 'inner perfection' that is beauty. He contrasts the artwork with the useful artefact: the 'merely useful object' is not complete in itself but finds its purpose in being used by the subject.[18] Thus, the opposition between the 'autonomous' artwork (a term Moritz does not yet use) and utility is already embedded in early manifestations of aesthetic theory.[19]

In his 1835 treatise *The Romantic School*, the late-Romantic poet and critic Heinrich Heine critiqued the Goethean conception of art by contrasting it with Schiller's.

HEINRICH HEINE, *THE ROMANTIC SCHOOL*

Reprinted from *The Romantic School*, New York: Henry Holt, 1882, pp.55-58. Translated from the German by S.L. Fleishman.

Starting with this idea, the Goetheans viewed art as a separate, independent world, which they would rank so high that all the changing and changeable doings of mankind, their religions and systems of morality, should surge far below it.

I cannot unconditionally endorse this view; but the Goetheans were led so far astray by it as to proclaim art in and of itself as the highest good. Thus they were induced to hold themselves aloof from the claims of the world of reality, which, after all, is entitled to precedence. [...]

Schiller united himself to the world of reality much more decidedly than did Goethe; and he deserves praise for this. The living spirit of the times thrilled through Friedrich Schiller; it wrestled with him; it vanquished him; he followed it to battle; he bore its banner, and, lo! it was the same banner under which the conflict was being enthusiastically waged across the Rhine, and for which we are always ready to shed our heart's best blood. Schiller wrote for the grand ideas of the Revolution; he razed the bastilles of the intellect; he helped to erect the temple of freedom, that colossal temple which shelters all nations like a single congregation of brothers: in brief, he was a cosmopolitan.

He began his career with that hate of the past which we behold in *The Robbers*.[1] In this work he resembles a diminutive Titan who has run away from school, got tipsy with schnapps and throws stones at Jupiter's windows. He ended with that love for the future which already in his *Don Carlos*[2] blossoms forth like a field of flowers. Schiller is himself that Marquis Posa who is simultaneously prophet and soldier, and battles for that which he foretells. Under that Spanish cloak throbs the noblest heart that ever loved and suffered in Germany. [...]

While Schiller devotes himself to the history of the race, and becomes an enthusiast for the social progress of mankind, Goethe, on the other hand, applies himself to the study of the individual, to nature and to art. The physical sciences

---

[1] Editors' note: First performed in 1781.
[2] EN: First performed in 1787.

must of necessity have finally become a leading branch of study with Goethe, the pantheist, and in his poems, as well as in his scientific works, he gave us the result of his researches. His indifferentism was to a certain extent the result of his pantheistic views. [...] No, God does not manifest himself in all things equally, as Wolfgang Goethe believed, who, through such a belief became an indifferentist, and, instead of devoting himself to the highest interests of humanity, occupied himself with art, anatomy, theories of colour, botanical studies and observations of the clouds. No, God is manifest in some things to a greater degree than in others. He lives in motion, in action, in time. His holy breath is wafted through the pages of history, which is God's true book of record. Friedrich Schiller felt this, and became an historian, a 'prophet of the past', and wrote the *Revolt of the Netherlands*, the *Thirty Years' War*, the *Maid of Orleans*, and *William Tell*.[3]

Schiller, in other words, did not write the *Letters on the Aesthetic Education of Mankind* to glorify great and self-sufficient artistic monuments such as the Juno Ludovisi, but in order to place them in the context of an aesthetic play instinct that also has more mundane manifestations. Heine, who in his youth had been profoundly marked by the Schlegel group, had become a biting critic of their reactionary tendencies. In Schiller, he saw a more felicitous attempt to overcome the limits of art's relative autonomy, to make art beget action. Meanwhile, Goethe's work remained admirable but also dead in its splendid autonomy from life.

---

[3]   EN: *Revolt of the Netherlands* is dated 1788, *Thirty Years' War* is dated 1791, *Maid of Orleans* was first performed 1801 and *William Tell* is dated 1804.

'The Autonomy of Art': On the Emergence of a Concept

Art historians write retrospectively about 'the autonomy of art in the Italian Renaissance' or about sixteenth- and seventeenth-century 'meta-paintings' as indices of artistic autonomy; the artists in question played with their medium rather than glorifying kings or God.[20] And it is indeed perfectly possible to trace the signs of a relative autonomisation of art in the early modern age, even in the absence of the term. The concept of 'the autonomy of art' is itself the product of several centuries of accelerating historical change. When critics and journalists used the term *autonomy* in the press during the first decades of the nineteenth century, it was often in reference to the autonomy of certain regions or countries, or in reference to the Kantian moral will rather than the Kantian judgement of taste. It is only in the 1830s and 1840s that the phrase 'autonomy of art' can be found with any regularity. Heinrich Heine, who lived in Paris from 1831 until his death in 1856, was one of the pioneers. In 1837, in 'Letters on the French Stage', he noted:

> Victor Hugo is actually not as yet esteemed here in France at his full value. German critics and German impartiality mete out his merits with a better measure, and honour him with higher praise. This want of recognition is due not only to contemptibly petty criticism, but to political partisan feeling. The Carlists regard him as a renegade, who, while his lyre still rang with the lost chords of a song of consecration [*Salbungslied*] for Charles X, tuned it to a hymn on the Revolution of July. The Republicans mistrust his zeal for the popular cause, and spy out in every phrase a secret predilection for nobility and Catholicism. Even the Invisible Church of the St. Simonians, which is everywhere and nowhere, like the Christian Church before Constantine, disowns him; for these men regard art as a priesthood, and require that every work of the poet, the painter, the sculptor or musician shall in itself bear witness to its higher consecration and set forth its holy mission, which is the making happy and beautiful of the human race. The works of Victor Hugo indicate no such moral standard, and they sin against all the noble but erroneous laws of the new church. I call them erroneous, because, as you know, I am for the autonomy of art, which should be the handmaid of neither religion nor politics, for it is in itself its own aim, like the world itself. Here we encounter the same narrow-minded or one-sided reproaches which Goethe had to endure from the pious brethren, and, like him, so must Victor Hugo bear the unjust accusation that he has no enthusiasm for the ideal, that he is without moral basis, is a cold-hearted egoist and so forth. And add to this a false criticism, which declares that the best which there is to praise in him, his talent for sensuous or material form and creation [*sinnlichen Gestaltung*], is a fault, and adds that in these creations there is a want of deep poetry, *la poésie intime*; outline and colour are everything to him; he gives us only superficial [*äusserlich fassbare*] poetry; he is material; in short, they blame in him his most praiseworthy, peculiar talent, his sense for the plastic.[21]

Having experienced the censorship of the reactionary German states of the post-Napoleonic era, Heine was equally suspicious of progressive attempts to instrumentalise the arts. Though he collaborated on Karl Marx and Arnold Ruge's *Deutsch-Französische Jahrbücher* in 1844 and on the Marx-dominated periodical *Vorwärts* later that same year, his later pronouncement that 'the future belongs to the communists' had a ring of ambivalence.[22] Heine had always insisted that art should not be made the servant of any particular extraneous cause. In the second half of the 1830s, his rejection of all instrumentalisation appeared to bring him close to a Goethean conception of art as a self-sufficient world, as his justified concerns over political censorship and repression led him to pronounce the autonomy of art in the starkest terms. One example can be found in Heine's 1838 letter to Karl Gutzkow: 'The autonomy of art is what is at stake here, not the moral needs of a respectable married citizen of some corner of Germany. My motto remains: "Art is for the purpose of art, just as love is the purpose of love, and even life that of life itself."'[23]

Following Heine, in the 1840s the concept of the autonomy of art also started to feature in the historical and theoretical writings of the German poet and critic Robert Eduard Prutz. In his 1841 study about an obscure proto-Romantic group of German poets, *Der Göttinger Dichterbund. Zur Geschichte der Deutschen Literatur* (The Göttingen Society of Poets: A Contribution to the History of German Literature), Prutz gives us his understanding of the aim of poetry, which is to both integrate and transcend 'individual pathos, the living individual drive' into 'the general and universal of art'.[24] In particular, this had been the mission of German poetry since the Enlightenment, culminating in the works of Goethe and Schiller: to mediate between subject and object, between 'individual, living conviction and traditional, conventional dogma', and to annihilate these oppositions through a 'lively development of interiority'.[25] Reflecting his closeness to some of the radical Left Hegelians of the time (he was subject to police surveillance for his political views), Prutz's praise for Schiller concerns his refusal to let art be 'just art'. Like Heine, Prutz stresses that Schiller foregrounds the political promise of the aesthetic:

> Schiller thus moves beyond the boundaries of the merely subjective world, mere feeling, savouring and self-formation: he steps out in conquest into the world, wishing to subjugate his poetry to history. Schiller grows up and educates himself against the tumult of the French Revolution, which also resonates through Germany and here too stirs people to contemplation and reflection. There is an emerging awareness that the subject, in order to attain his full rights, his full existence, must also participate in history, in the state and in its political development. Yet initially this insight remains purely theoretical, freedom ('Man is free, though he be born in chains!') remains ideational, a postulate, a dogma that is demanded and taught, but not yet satisfied or realised. In this, Schiller finds himself at a disadvantage vis-à-vis Goethe: all is completion in Goethe, all is inception and promise in Schiller; Goethe the ripe fruit, Schiller the bud.[26]

In the end, 'the state and the subject' will have to be reconciled, and 'only political freedom will create poets for us once again'.[27] Later in the same volume he continues: 'For, with the sun of our freedom, the beautiful, heart-warming orb of the new poetry will rise, heralded by the rose-tinged dawn of Schiller's poetry.'[28] Poets such as Schiller thus anticipated a free society in which subjectivity can unfold without fear of reprisal. Prutz notes, however, that Schiller could develop such an anticipation of freedom beyond the confines of 'mere' art precisely because the Enlightenment had defended art's autonomy from conventional morality: the German Enlightenment thinker and critic Friedrich Nicolai 'very readily conceived the notion of a separation of poetry from morals, thus paving the way for the era of geniuses that he would so doggedly combat, and for art's complete autonomy'. [29]

Prutz took up this motif in his 1845 work, *Die Geschichte des deutschen Journalismus* (The History of German Journalism), which returns to the German Enlightenment, focussing on Gotthold Ephraim Lessing:

> After Klopstock came Lessing. His contribution to world history lies in being the first to have understood and expressed the autonomy of art. As a consequence, he became the true consciousness of his era, the driving force of this turning point, which experienced its full, unopposed breakthrough in his oeuvre.[30]

In this book, Prutz again stresses the need for freedom to be realised not just ideally, in literature, but in social and political reality. Schiller was the poet who made the transition 'from the idea of Art to the idea of Freedom'.[31] In the realm of philosophy, it had been Hegel who acted as a new Lessing, as 'the man of critique and of consciousness'.[32] Post-Schiller and post-Hegel, a new era was dawning, which would not necessarily be marked by the towering artistic achievement of a single artistic genius, by a new Goethe. The new era will not culminate in a book or in a philosophical system, but in 'a free creation of history'.[33] Art will indeed have become life, or rather active social *praxis* – to use the term that was introduced by the Hegelian August von Cieszkowski in 1838, and which would be picked up by Marx.[34]

Meanwhile, in France Heine's defence of the 'autonomy of art' against political disenfranchisement fed into Théophile Gautier's *l'art pour l'art* aestheticism. Heinean overtones can be discerned in Gautier's defence of Charles Baudelaire's *Les Fleurs du mal* (The Flowers of Evil, 1862):

> That type of critic who, not understanding the autonomy of art, asks the poet to teach, prove, moralise, in a word, to be useful, has been greatly perturbed by M. Baudelaire's book. The big word 'immoral' has been spilled on him, a word full of Jesuitism, ignorance and bad faith.[35]

And again, in 1868:

> With these ideas one can well understand that Baudelaire believed in the absolute self-government of Art [*l'autonomie absolue de l'art*], and that he would not admit that poetry should have any end outside itself, or any mission to fulfil other than that of exciting in the soul of the reader the sensation of supreme beauty – beauty in the absolute sense of the term. To this sensation he liked to add a certain effect of surprise, astonishment and rarity. As much as possible he banished from poetry a too realistic imitation of eloquence, passion and a too exact truth. As in statuary one does not mould forms directly after Nature, so he wished that, before entering the sphere of Art, each object should be subjected to a metamorphosis that would adapt it to this subtle medium, idealising it and abstracting it from trivial reality.
>
> Such principles are apt to astonish us, when we read certain of the poems of Baudelaire in which horror seems to be sought like pleasure; but that we should

not be deceived, this horror is always transfigured by character and effect, by a ray of Rembrandt, or a trait of Velázquez, who portrayed the race under sordid deformity. In stirring up in his cauldron all sorts of fantastically odd and enormous ingredients, Baudelaire can say, with the witches of *Macbeth*, 'Fair is foul, and foul is fair.' This sort of intentional ugliness is not, then, in contradiction to the supreme aim of Art; and the poems, such as the 'Sept Vieillards' and the 'Petits Vieilles', have snatched from the poetical Saint John who dreams in Patmos this phrase, which characterises so well the author of the *Flowers of Evil*: 'You have endowed the sky of Art with one knows not what macabre ray; you have created a new *frisson*.'

But it is, so to speak, only the shadow of the talent of Baudelaire, a shadow ardently fiery or coldly blue, which allows him to give the essential and luminous touch. There is a serenity in his nervous, febrile and tormenting talent. On the highest summits he is tranquil: *pacem summa tenent*.[36]

It is striking that a defence of the autonomy of art against political instrumentalisation (Heine) could on the one hand (Prutz) generate the demand of a realisation of the aesthetic in the form of emancipatory or revolutionary praxis, while on the other hand (Gautier) it led to a wilful self-limitation of what art is and can or should do. Art was to have no other mission than 'that of exciting in the soul of the reader the sensation of supreme beauty'. Autonomy is here understood as *autonomy from* any outside interference; it is no longer the *autonomy to* question the limits of art and to engage with the 'outside' as an essential element of aesthetic practice.

L'art pour l'art aestheticism was only one possible response to the vexed question of the relation between radical politics and radical art, between the artistic and the political avant-garde. It is significant that the notion of 'the autonomy of art' emerges at the moment when the 'art for art's sake' doctrine is formulated, but it is no less significant that some of Heine's and much of Prutz's work points in different directions, towards different assemblages of 'art' and 'autonomy' in which what is at stake is not so much self-legislation of the artistic field as modes of agency and experience that challenge the aestheticist or modernist purification and autonomisation of art.

The Two Avant-Gardes

A long and eventful history connects our present to, but also separates it from, the inaugural statements of aesthetic theory and the aesthetic regime. A 'plot' that plays out time and again throughout these centuries is that of the difficult relationship between the artist and the social and political vanguard. The result is a shaggy-dog story with endless rapprochements, joint actions and misunderstandings, schisms and exclusions.

In the bohemian cafés of the early and mid-nineteenth century, artists mingled freely with philosophers and various social reformers and (would-be) revolutionaries. Before Marxism, there were various stripes of romantic or utopian socialism; Heinrich Heine knew followers of Henri de Saint-Simon such as Père Enfantin and Olinde Rodrigues. The latter has been credited with writing the Saint-Simonian tract 'L'artiste, le savant et l'industriel' (The Artist, the Scientist and the Industrialist, 1825), which contains the first use of the term *avant-garde* (a military concept) in relation to art: 'It is we, artists, that will serve as your avant-garde.'[37] Which is to say: the artists will prophetically announce the coming society and make the people ready for a new order administered technocratically by scientists and industrialists.

Heine was not the only one who found this a less than enticing prospect, and relations between the artistic and political avant-garde remained contentious. However, early socialism frequently appeared in an aesthetic register. The writings of Charles Fourier were, in their own way, as aesthetic as poems or paintings; they too envisaged a reconciliation with the senses and a 'redistribution of the sensible', to use Jacques Rancière's terminology.[38] The young Marx sketched his own aesthetic utopia when he wrote that in communist society it would be 'possible for me to do one thing today and another tomorrow, to hunt in the morning, fish in the afternoon, rear cattle in the evening, criticise after dinner, just as I have a mind, without ever becoming hunter, fisherman, shepherd or critic'.[39]

In its rejection both of the abstract idealist subject and undialectical accounts of the object, Marx's notion of praxis reads as profoundly aesthetic:

> The chief defect of all previous materialism – that of Feuerbach included – is that things [*Gegenstand*], actuality, sensuousness, are conceived only in the form of the *object*, or of *contemplation*, but not as *human sensuous activity, practice*, not subjectively. Hence it happened that the *active* side, in contradistinction to materialism, was set forth by idealism – but only abstractly, since, of course, idealism does not know real, sensuous activity as such.[40]

Under capitalism and the condition of wage labour, however, we face the negation of true praxis – a negation that stints the subject's development. Capitalist wage labour is predicated on the division of labour; that is, rather than combining different occupations, the worker is forced to behave like a robotic monomaniac. In modernity, art becomes so important precisely because it is seen as a sphere in which aesthetic education can alleviate the symptoms of specialisation. Art is the fragment that refuses to be fragment, laying claim to a lost totality. Even so, it remains the product of the modern division of labour – produced by specialists in the superstructure of the capitalist economy.

The notion of intellectual production forming a 'superstructure' that functions as an ideological distortion of the economic 'base' was introduced by Marx and Friedrich Engels in *The German Ideology* (1845-46). This superstructure has a certain relative autonomy that is ultimately a sham, as it is based on a disavowal of the forces of production and the social relations – and the contradictions that are brewing between them:

> Division of labour only becomes truly such from the moment when a division of material and mental labour appears.[4] From this moment onwards consciousness *can* really flatter itself that it is something other than consciousness of existing practice, that it *really* represents something without representing something real; from now on consciousness is in a position to emancipate itself from the world and to proceed to the formation of 'pure' theory, theology, philosophy, morality, etc. But even if this theory, theology, philosophy, morality, etc. comes into contradiction with the existing relations, this can only occur because existing social relations have come into contradiction with existing productive forces; moreover, in a particular national sphere of relations this can also occur through the contradiction, arising not within the national orbit, but between this national consciousness and the practice of other nations,[5] i.e. between the national and the general consciousness of a nation (as is happening now in Germany).[41]

Later, in the 1859 preface of *A Contribution to the Critique of Political Economy*, Marx again stresses that the totality of productive relations (social relations between people as mediated or enabled by productive means) is the real basis, from which legal and political superstructures arise. However, this time he also specifically mentions art as part of the superstructure:

> The mode of production of material life conditions the general process of social, political and intellectual life. It is not the consciousness of men that determines their existence, but their social existence that determines their consciousness. [...] It is always necessary to distinguish between the material transformation of the economic conditions of production, which can be determined with the precision of natural science, and the legal, political, religious, artistic or philosophic – in short, ideological forms in which men become conscious of this conflict and fight it out.[42]

The latter remark should not be taken to mean that art, law or philosophy are fully reducible to their ideological function; as a lover of literature, Marx would never have assented to such an oversimplification.[43] His writings are suffused with literary allusions, but Marx never published any systematic examination of art or of the 'superstructure' in general, and some of his pronouncements were taken by later Marxists as justification for reductionist theories in which art could indeed only ever be an expression of bourgeois ideology or a direct expression of proletarian class consciousness.

Often Marxist in orientation, the 'social history of art' has sought to restore complexity to our understanding of art's and the artist's social and political existence. In

---

[4]   The first form of ideologists, *priests*, is coincident.

[5]   *Religions*. The Germans and *ideology* as such.

his 1973 study of Gustave Courbet, for instance, T.J. Clark analyses the artist not as someone who paints a political programme, but as a painterly master of the 'inarticulate response' who causes outrage precisely because he mixes up codes and presents the public with highly ambiguous tableaux.[44] In a striking passage, Clark describes how Courbet placed himself outside of accepted and acceptable classes by reviving the avant-garde's association with 'Bohemia' – the urban underclass that was idealised as a carefree playground for slumming young bourgeois in literary works such as Henri Murger's *Scènes de la vie de bohème* (Scenes of Bohemian Life, 1851).

———————

T.J. CLARK, *IMAGE OF THE PEOPLE: GUSTAVE COURBET AND THE 1848 REVOLUTION*

Reprinted from *Image of the People: Gustave Courbet and the 1848 Revolution*, London: Thames & Hudson, 1973, pp.33-34.

In the early days, for a few days after the 1830 revolution, Bohemia had been a comfortable part of the *avant-garde,* supported by doting fathers and therefore carefree, fashionable, unscrupulous (Gautier, Houssaye, Nerval, Roger de Beauvoir had been its leading lights). But that group had broken up and gone its separate ways, into various kinds of accommodation with the market and the official world of art. Bohemia, after that, was an unassimilated class, wretchedly poor, obdurately anti-bourgeois, living on in the absolute, outdated style of the 'Romantics', courting death by starvation.

[...] It was this Bohemia, this confused, indigent, shifting population, with its Romantic postures, that Jules Vallès tried to rescue from Murger and myth in his book *Les Réfractaires* [The Refractories], published in 1865. He tried to show the real Bohemia: a world of grinding poverty, of absolute refusal of bourgeois society, rather than the sowing of flippant wild oats. It was not an irrelevant book for Vallès the Socialist and revolutionary to write; for Bohemia in mid-nineteenth-century Paris was a real social class, a real locus of dissent. And if we want to locate it within the complex social structure of Paris, we should put it alongside not the students of the Latin quarter but the *classes dangereuses*. It was this dangerous element – this mob of unemployed, criminals and *déclassés* of every sort, the first victims, the first debris of industrialism – which made up one part of the rebel fighting forces in June 1848. The great social historian of the June Days, Rémi Gossez, closes his description of the class origins of the insurgents by saying that the last category of the rebels comprised 'social outcasts of all kinds: tramps, street-porters, organ-grinders, ragpickers, knife-grinders, tinkers, errand-boys and all those who lived by the thousand little occupations of the streets of Paris, and also that confused, drifting mass known as *la Bohème*'.[6]

[...] This was Daumier's Bohemia: the ragpickers and organ-grinders of Gossez's list come straight from his canvases. This was Courbet's Bohemia,

---

6   Rémi Gossez, 'Diversité des antagonismes sociaux vers le milieu du XIXe siècle', *Revue économique* no.3, 1956, p.451.

this was Journet's, this was Baudelaire's ('Perhaps the future belongs to the *déclassés?...*': letter to Ancelle, 5 March 1852).[7] It was a life-style *and* a social situation. [...] It meant a place between the *classes dangereuses* of proletarian Paris and the intelligentsia; between two classes which were themselves strange, intricate misfits in any class system, and remained unsure of whose side they were on. So that in June the intelligentsia stayed loyal – ferociously loyal – to the Government, and many of Baudelaire's friends fought with the Latin Quarter detachment: and the *classes dangereuses* closed ranks with the Garde Mobile, and slaughtered rebels with the best of them. Courbet hesitated and abstained on utopian grounds. Baudelaire fought for the rebels, with Bohemia. One wonders what Journet did and said in June.

The crazed Fourierist 'prophet' Jean Journet was painted by Courbet in 1850 as *L'Apôtre Jean Journet* (*The Apostle Jean Journet*). This monumental portrait was based on a popular print of the Wandering Jew that Courbet would again use for his own self-portrait in *La Rencontre* (*The Meeting,* or *Bonjour, Monsieur Courbet*) in 1854.[45] *L'Apôtre Jean Journet* was shown at the 1850–51 Paris Salon alongside *Un enterrement à Ornans* (*A Burial at Ornans,* 1849–50); like that scandalous piece, it is a work sui generis, not comfortably fitting into any established genre, and showing monumental subjects that appeared to challenge rigid class categories.

Courbet was a sympathiser and friend of the libertarian socialist Pierre-Joseph Proudhon, but the latter's understanding of Courbet's art was not particularly profound, and Courbet was not interested in illustrating political theses. His paintings were nonetheless an aesthetic-political affront to Louis Napoléon's Second Empire, forged in the 1851 coup d'état. In 1855, during the Exposition Universelle in Paris, Courbet staged his own counter-exhibition, a solo show in a building erected specially for the occasion, with a manifesto-like text extolling his artistic autonomy.

---

[7]   Charles Baudelaire, *Correspondance générale* (ed. Jacques Crépet I), vol.1, Paris: Conard, 1947, pp.151-52.

GUSTAVE COURBET, 'THE REALIST MANIFESTO'

Reprinted from Linda Nochlin (ed.), *Realism and Tradition in Art, 1848-1900: Sources and Documents*, Englewood Cliffs, NJ: Prentice-Hall, 1966, pp.33-34. Translation from the French by L. Nochlin.

The title of Realist was thrust upon me just as the title of Romantic was imposed upon the men of 1830. Titles have never given a true idea of things: if it were otherwise, the works would be unnecessary.

Without expanding on the greater or lesser accuracy of a name which nobody, I should hope, can really be expected to understand, I will limit myself to a few words of elucidation in order to cut short the misunderstandings.

I have studied, outside of any system and without prejudice, the art of the ancients and the art of the moderns. I no more wanted to imitate the one than to copy the other; nor, furthermore, was it my intention to attain the trivial goal of *art for art's sake*. No! I simply wanted to draw forth from a complete acquaintance with tradition the reasoned and independent consciousness of my own individuality.

To know in order to be able to create, that was my idea. To be in a position to translate the customs, the ideas, the appearance of my epoch, according to my own estimation; to be not only a painter, but a man as well; in short, to create living art - this is my goal.

Quillenbois, caricature of Gustave Courbet's *The Meeting*, 1854, *L'Illustration*, 21 July 1855

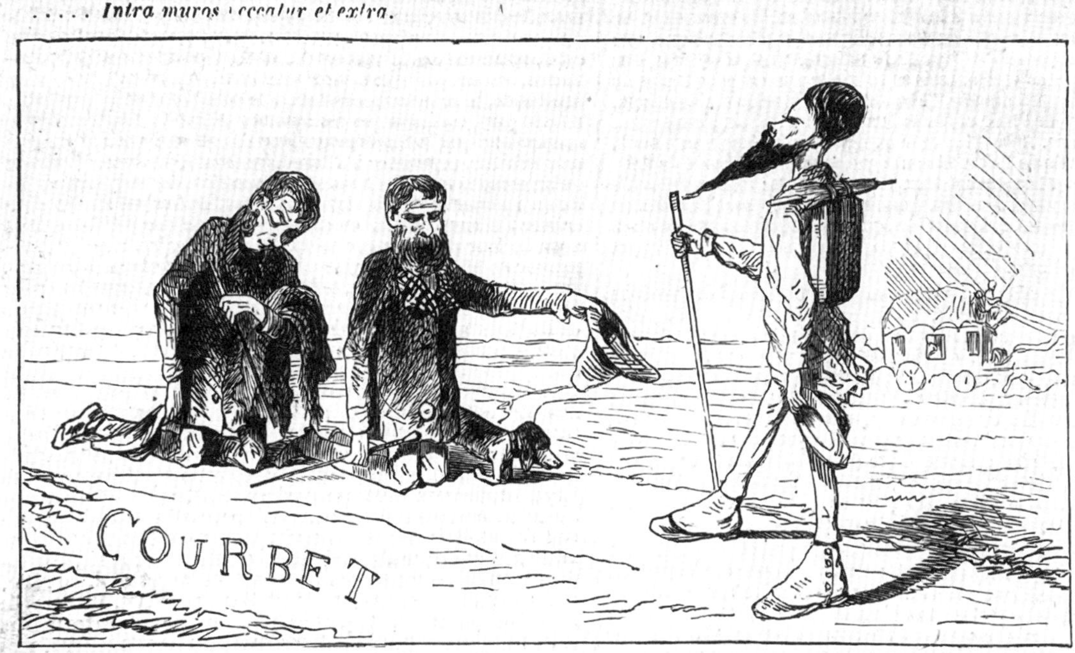

L'adoration de M. Courbet, imitation réaliste de l'adoration des Mages.

In 1871, after the Franco-Prussian War had put an end to Napoléon's Second Empire, Courbet was active in the Paris Commune. For this, he was heavily penalised after a massacre by government troops had violently 'restored order'. One of the Commune's acts had been the toppling of the Vendôme column as a symbol for Napoléonic oppression; Courbet was often seen as the instigator of this act, though this is highly debatable. In 1967, the Situationist International – an avant-garde movement that we will return to, and whose English section included a young T.J. Clark – glorified this as an exemplary act of artistic transgression:

> The project of art – for Blake, for Nietzsche – became the transvaluation of all values and the destruction of all that prevents it. Art became negation: in Goya, in Beethoven or in Gericault, one can see the change from celebrant to subversive within the space of a lifetime. But a change in the definition of art demanded a change in its forms and the nineteenth century was marked by an accelerating and desperate attempt at improvising new forms of artistic attack. Courbet began by touting his pictures round the countryside in a marquee and ended in the Commune by superintending the destruction of the Vendôme column (the century's most radical artistic art, which its author immediately disowned).[46]

In the later decades of the nineteenth century, the freedoms promised by anarchism seemed more inviting to artists than the party discipline of communism or social democracy. The 1880s and 1890s saw a thriving anarchist culture – one often associated with the wave of bombings that culminated in 1894, when the police clamped down. The anarchist concept of 'propaganda of the deed' meant that the populace had to be shaken from its stupor by extreme acts. In fact, it seems likely that the symbolist aesthete and art critic Félix Fénéon, who was the first advocate of Georges Seurat and of Neo-Impressionism, was also the 'author' of one such deed – exploding a bomb in a fancy Parisian restaurant, seriously injuring one customer.[47]

Aside from this rather disastrous side of anarchist politics, the movement was also not always immune from an instrumentalising view of art. Artists who were committed anarchists, such as Camille Pissarro and his son Lucien, contributed illustrations to anarchist publications but were uneasy with some of the demands made on them. On 7 December 1895, Jean Grave's journal *Les Temps Nouveaux* published a remarkable letter by 'L.P.' (Lucien Pissarro) responding to an article in a previous issue.

LUCIEN PISSARRO, LETTER TO *LES TEMPS NOUVEAUX*

Reprinted from Aline Dardel (ed.), *"Les Temps
Nouveaux", 1895-1914: Un hebdomanaire anarchiste
et la propagande par l'image*, Paris: Réunion des
Musées Nationaux, 1987, p.42. Translation from
the French by Sven Lütticken.

25 November 1895

Comrades,

We are searching for the truth, aren't we? So let me put forward thoughts that were brought to my mind after reading the article 'Art et Société' in the last issue of *Les Temps Nouveaux*. Like you, I believe there cannot be any integral development of the individual artist without libertarian communism. We agree on this point, but I think you are mistaken as far as your conception of artistic production goes.

The distinction you establish between 'Art for Art' and Art with a social aim doesn't exist. All production that really is a work of art is social (whether the author wants it or not), because the person who has produced it shares with his fellow men the most vivid and distinct emotions he experienced in front of the spectacle of nature.

Following the ideas you express, you seem to establish hierarchies between artworks based on their direct usefulness for propaganda. I don't think this is true. A certain work of art exclusively conceived with an eye to pure Beauty will make human intellectuality more pure than numerous others with didactic pretensions, because that work of pure beauty will have broadened the aesthetic conception of other individuals.

I also believe those ideas conflict with the theory of individual autonomy. Indeed, I would be morally uncomfortable in my conceptions if I believed it's better to produce in one tendency than in another. You do accept that absolute freedom for the artist in a future society, so why not accept it for all times? What's true remains true. One shouldn't paint any landscape, then? For I can't really see the anarchist landscape! That is, I see it clearly, but not in the choice of subject matter. Corot, Monet, Pissarro etc. ... have made some by interpreting the landscape in a new way, destroying in the process the aesthetic conventions popular at the time.

[Jean] Grave, in his beautiful latest book, says that the true scholar is not the one who studies to acquire honours and wealth, but the one who studies to know more with no other preoccupation in mind. It is very true, but is it less so for the artist? Mustn't his constant research tend towards Beauty?

For, being the product of his milieu, man's productions are influenced by it, but following that person's nature, in a more or less discernable way. An artist whose reactionary opinions are well known may nevertheless leave an oeuvre of bitter criticism against our contemporary society, and a traditionalist artist may make you regret the lack of harmony in today's society all the more through his works, which express a poetry of happy melancholy.

To produce for the masses, you say? Today's masses having been kept in an almost complete ignorance, there are too many big inequalities between men. Should those who had the chance to cultivate their intellectual abilities not use them, then? Or should they play them down in order to be understood by the greatest number? It is thus abnegation, devotion you are asking for. Is it not better to produce what is the truth for oneself, even if it means being understood by only ten people who will help others to understand, and so on? Is it not like that that progress is accomplished?

This misunderstanding between revolutionary writers and artists has been going on for a while; it has produced on the side of the artist, these 'ivory towers', 'intellectual aristocracy' and other rigmarole. Wouldn't an anarchist artist be allowed to try (however imperfectly!) to dissipate it? Yes, wouldn't you agree? This is also what communism is.

Yours,
L.P.

The October Revolution in 1917 changed the situation drastically. In the young Soviet Union, many artists and intellectuals – often with anarchist rather than Bolshevik sympathies – leapt at the chance to participate in an actual revolutionary transformation of society and sought to forge alliances between their aesthetic agendas and official policies. However, by the late 1920s Socialist Realism was established as the retrograde official doctrine, and under Joseph Stalin deviation from official dogma would be a dangerous game.

In the West, where discipline was much more difficult to enforce, the 1920s and early 1930s saw a revival of serious Marxist theorising, with authors such as Karl Korsch, Georg Lukács and Walter Benjamin attempting to rescue Marx both from social-democratic distortions and from nascent Stalinist dogma. This led to Korsch's expulsion from the German Communist Party. Nonetheless, as Nazism became stronger, theorists and artists such as Bertolt Brecht and John Heartfield were drawn ever closer into Moscow's orbit. In a 1935 letter to the council communist Paul Mattick, Heartfield's brother Wieland Herzfelde critiqued Mattick's rejection of Bolshevik Party dictatorship and Stalinist terror in words that are hard to take seriously, even though they were written in earnest: 'take a good look at pictures of Stalin. Does such a dandy seem intent on terror? Can't you see his slightly ironic smile with which he receives all the (admittedly not very tasteful) hero worship that comes his way?'[48]

In France, Surrealism entered into a long and complicated alliance with the Moscow-directed French Communist Party during the late 1920s and early 1930s. The journal *La Révolution surréaliste* was discontinued and replaced by *Le Surréalisme au service de la révolution*, and under communist auspices the Surrealists organised the 1931 anti-colonial exhibition 'L'exposition anti-impérialiste: La vérité sur les colonies' (Anti-Imperialist Exhibition: The Truth of the Colonies), in which a variety of appropriated Western and non-Western objects sought to drive home the point that it was Western colonialism that was barbaric, not the colonised cultures.

However, the problem for the Party was that André Breton and his allies (excepting defectors such as Louis Aragon, who became a loyal communist) did not want to surrender their autonomy. More specifically, they did not want to accept a narrow, limited definition of 'the revolution'. For them, the revolution would not just have to entail the replacement of capitalism with a different economic structure; it would also, and perhaps primarily, have to be a true aesthetic revolution, a liberation of men and women, and particularly a liberation of their psyches, of their repressed desires.

Like Korsch, Benjamin and Adorno, the Surrealists considered the 'superstructure' of art and theory to be of crucial importance in its own right.

For the artistic and theoretical avant-garde of these decades, it was not a matter of replacing bourgeois 'false consciousness' and affirmative culture with proletarian class consciousness and socialist realism. Rather, culture had to be exploded from the inside out – in the case of the Surrealists, tapping into the explosive potential of the unconscious. The Party was not amused. As Stalinism became ever more repressive, hopes were pinned on the exiled Leon Trotsky, who had been co-responsible for turning the Soviet Union into a top-down party dictatorship rather than a society run bottom-up by soviets (workers' councils). While anarchists and council communists were not about to let him forget this, for others Trotsky represented an alternative to Stalin, and the promise of a communist state that would not descend into totalitarianism.

In 1938, Breton and Trotsky met in Mexico and co-wrote the manifesto 'Towards a Free Revolutionary Art', which was published that autumn in *Partisan Review* – the New York–based Trotskyist journal that would publish Clement Greenberg's 'Avant-Garde and Kitsch' one year later. [49] The text was co-signed by Breton and the Mexican muralist Diego Rivera (without Trotsky). Arguing that even 'socialist' states should be anarchist when it comes to art, the manifesto calls for non-Stalinist alliance between artistic and political progressives that would briefly take shape in the short-lived International Federation of Independent Revolutionary Art.

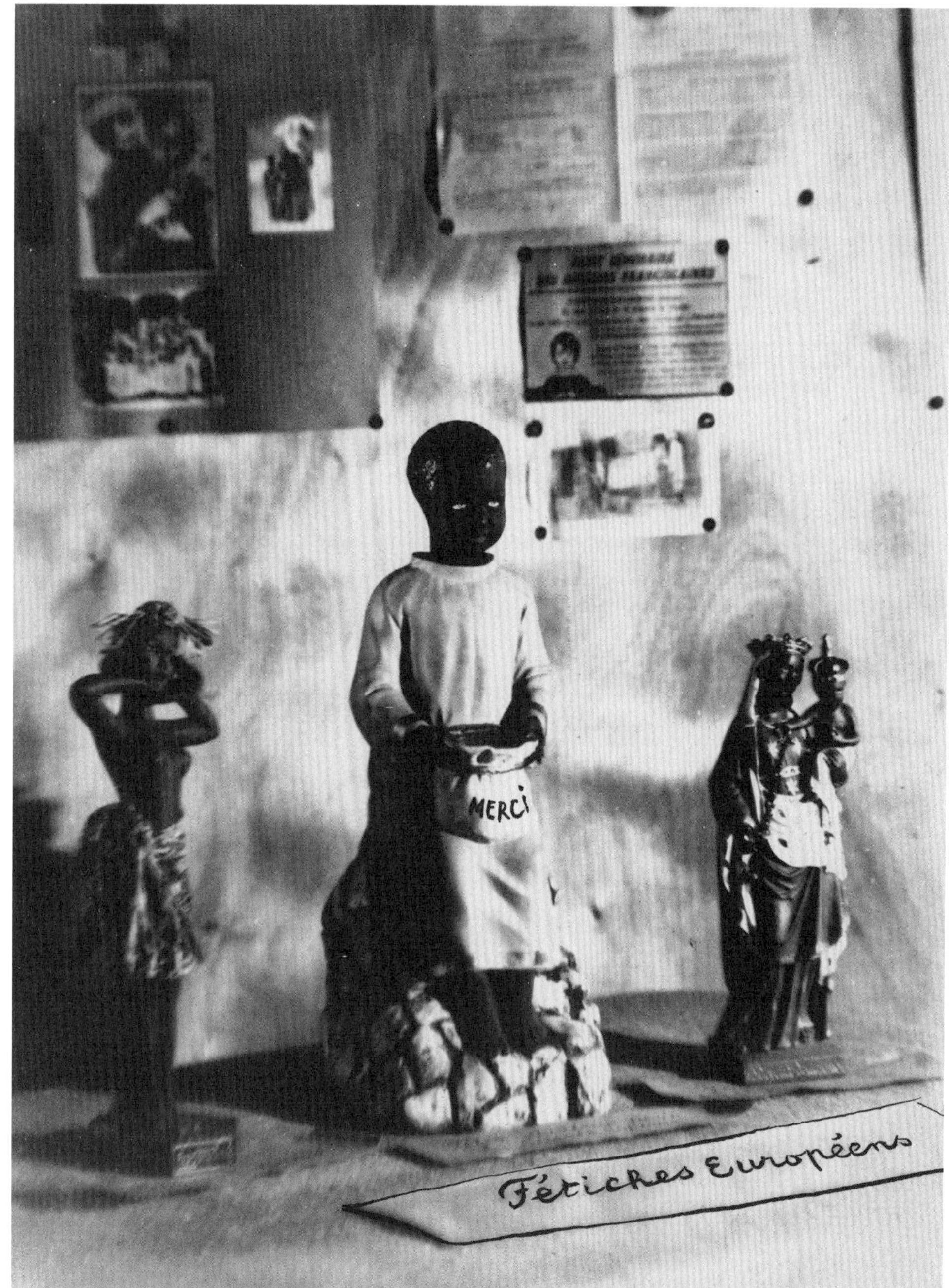

Installation views, 'The Truth
about the Colonies', September 1931–
February 1932, Palais des Soviets, Paris

Above: Display of 'European fetishes'
including Christian devotional figurines
such as the Madonna and Child and
chromolithographs used by colonial
missionaries

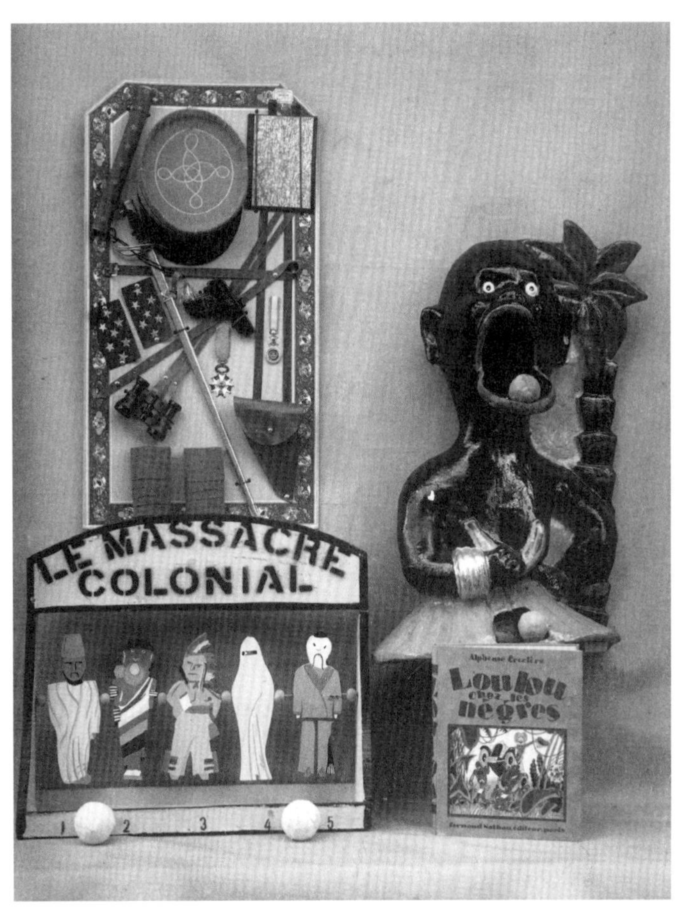

Display of colonial paraphernalia
including weaponry, tools, military
accoutrements, ceramic figure and
printed matter

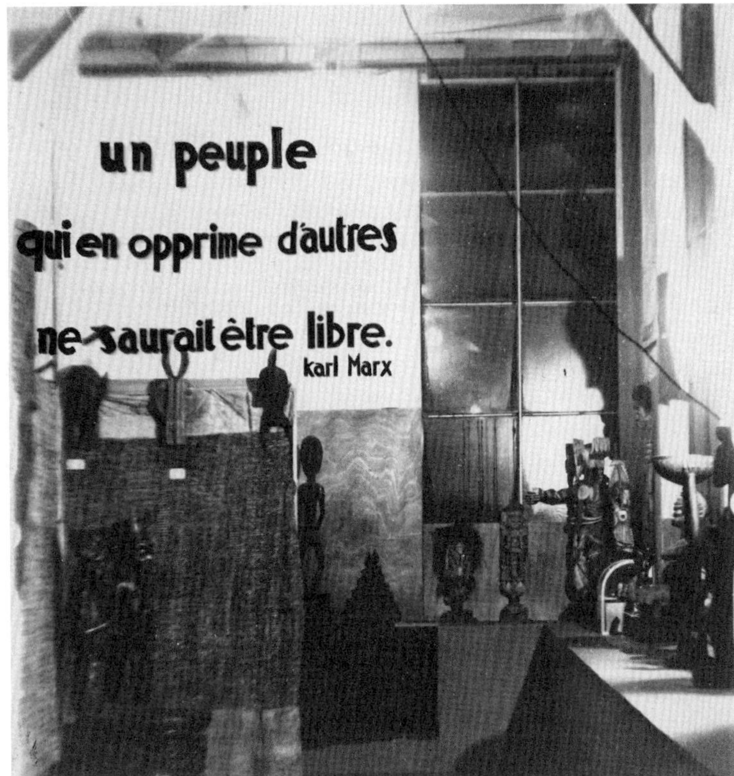

Display featuring a statement
attributed to Karl Marx (in fact from
an 1847 speech about Poland by
Friedrich Engels): 'A nation cannot
be free and at the same time continue
to oppress other nations.'

ANDRÉ BRETON AND DIEGO RIVERA [AND LEON TROTSKY], 'MANIFESTO: TOWARDS A FREE REVOLUTIONARY ART'

Reprinted from *Partisan Review*, vol.6, no.1,
Autumn 1938, pp.49-53. Translation by Dwight
MacDonald.

We can say without exaggeration that never has civilisation been menaced so seriously as today. The Vandals, with instruments which were barbarous and so comparatively ineffective, blotted out the culture of antiquity in one corner of Europe. But today we see world civilisation, united in its historic destiny, reeling under the blows of reactionary forces armed with the entire arsenal of modern technology. We are by no means thinking only of the world war that draws near. Even in times of 'peace', the position of art and science has become absolutely intolerable.

Insofar as it originates with an individual, insofar as it brings into play subjective talents to create something which brings about an objective enriching of culture, any philosophical, sociological, scientific or artistic discovery seems to be the fruit of a precious *chance*, that is to say, the manifestation, more or less spontaneous, of necessity. Such creations cannot be slighted, whether from the standpoint of general knowledge (which interprets the existing world) or of revolutionary knowledge (which, the better to change the world, requires an exact analysis of the laws which govern its movement). Specifically, we cannot remain indifferent to the intellectual conditions under which creative activity takes place, nor should we fail to pay all respect to those particular laws which govern intellectual creation.

In the contemporary world we must recognise the ever more widespread destruction of those conditions under which intellectual creation is possible. From this follows of necessity an increasingly manifest degradation not only of the work of art but also of the specifically 'artistic' personality. The regime of Hitler, now that it has rid Germany of all those artists whose work expressed the slightest sympathy for liberty, however superficial, has reduced those who still consent to take up pen or brush to the status of domestic servants of the regime, whose task it is to glorify it on order, according to the worst possible aesthetic conventions. If reports may be believed, it is the same in the Soviet Union where Thermidorean reaction is now reaching its climax.

It goes without saying that we do not identify ourselves with the currently fashionable catchword 'Neither fascism nor communism!' – a shibboleth which suits the temperament of the Philistine, conservative and frightened, clinging to the tattered remnants of the 'democratic' past. True art, which is not content to play variations on ready-made models but rather insists on expressing the inner needs of man and of mankind in its time – true art is unable *not* to be revolutionary, not to aspire to a complete and radical reconstruction of society. This it must do, were it only to deliver intellectual creation from the chains which bind it, and to allow all mankind to raise itself to those heights which only isolated geniuses have achieved in the past. We recognise that only the social revolution can sweep clean the path for a new culture. If, however, we reject all solidarity with the bureaucracy now in control of the Soviet Union, it is precisely because, in our eyes, it represents not communism but its most treacherous and dangerous enemy.

The totalitarian regime of the USSR, working through the so-called 'cultural' organisations it controls in other countries, has spread over the entire world a deep twilight hostile to every sort of spiritual value. A twilight of filth and blood in which, disguised as intellectuals and artists, those men steep themselves who have made of servility a career, of lying for pay a custom, and of the palliation of crime a source of pleasure. The official art of Stalinism mirrors with a blatancy unexampled in history their efforts to put a good face on their mercenary profession.

The repugnance which this shameful negation of principles of art inspires in the artistic world – a negation which even slave states have never dared to carry so far – should give rise to an active, uncompromising condemnation. The *opposition* of writers and artists is one of the forces which can usefully contribute to the discrediting and overthrow of regimes which are destroying, along with the right of the proletariat to aspire to a better world, every sentiment of nobility and even of human dignity.

The communist revolution is not afraid of art. It realises that the role of the artist in a decadent capitalist society is determined by the conflict between the individual and various social forms which are hostile to him. This fact alone, insofar as he is conscious of it, makes the artist the natural ally of revolution. The process of *sublimation*, which here comes into play, and which psychoanalysis has analysed, tries to restore the broken equilibrium between the integral 'ego' and the outside elements it rejects. This restoration works to the advantage of the 'ideal of self', which marshals against the unbearable present reality all those powers of the interior world, of the 'self', which are *common to all men* and which are constantly flowering and developing. The need for emancipation felt by the individual spirit has only to follow its natural course to be led to mingle its stream with this primeval necessity: the need for the emancipation of man.

The conception of the writer's function which the young Marx worked out is worth recalling. 'The writer,' he declared, 'naturally must make money in order to live and write, but he should not under any circumstances live and write in order to make money. ... The writer by no means looks on his work as a *means*. It is *an end in itself* and so little a means in the eyes of himself and of others that if necessary he sacrifices his existence to the existence of his work. ... *The first condition of freedom of the press is that it is not a business activity.*' It is more than ever fitting to use this statement against those who would regiment intellectual activity in the direction of ends foreign to itself, and prescribe, in the guise of so-called 'reasons of State', the themes of art. The free choice of these themes and the absence of all restrictions on the range of his exploitations – these are possessions which the artist has a right to claim as inalienable. In the realm of artistic creation, the imagination must escape from all constraint and must, under no pretext, allow itself to be placed under bonds. To those who urge us, whether for today or for tomorrow, to consent that art should submit to a discipline which we hold to be radically incompatible with its nature, we give a flat refusal and we repeat our deliberate intention of standing by the formula: *complete freedom for art.*

We recognise, of course, that the revolutionary State has the right to defend itself against the counterattack of the bourgeoisie, even when this drapes itself in the flag of science or art. But there is an abyss between these enforced and temporary measures of revolutionary self-defence and the pretension to lay commands on intellectual creation. If, for the better development of the forces of material production, the revolution must build a *socialist* regime with centralised control, to develop intellectual creation an *anarchist* regime of individual liberty should from the first be established. No authority, no dictation, not the least trace of orders from above! Only on a base of friendly cooperation, without constraint from outside, will it be possible for scholars and artists to carry out their tasks, which will be more far-reaching than ever before in history.

It should be clear by now that in defending freedom of thought we have no intention of justifying political indifference, and that it is far from our wish to revive a so-called 'pure' art which generally serves the extremely impure ends of reaction. No, our conception of the role of art is too high to refuse it an influence on the fate of society. We believe that the supreme task of art in our epoch is to take part actively and consciously in the preparation of the revolution. But the artist cannot serve the struggle for freedom unless he subjectively assimilates its social content, unless he feels in his very nerves its meaning and drama and freely seeks to give his own inner world incarnation in his art.

In the present period of the death agony of capitalism, democratic as well as fascist, the artist sees himself threatened with the loss of his right to live and continue working. He sees all avenues of communication choked with the debris of capitalist collapse. Only naturally, he turns to the Stalinist organisations which hold out the possibility of escaping from his isolation. But if he is to avoid complete demoralisation he cannot remain there, because of the impossibility of delivering his own message and the degrading servility which these organisations exact from him in exchange for certain material advantages. He must understand that his place is elsewhere, not among those who betray the cause of the revolution, and of mankind, but among those who with unshaken fidelity bear witness to the revolution, among those who, for this reason, are alone able to bring it to fruition, and along with it the ultimate free expression of all forms of human genius.

The aim of this appeal is to find a common ground on which may be reunited all revolutionary writers and artists, the better to serve the revolution by their art and to defend the liberty of that art itself against the usurpers of the revolution. We believe that aesthetic, philosophical and political tendencies of the most varied sort can find here a common ground. Marxists can march here together with anarchists, provided both parties uncompromisingly reject the reactionary police-patrol spirit represented by Joseph Stalin and by his henchman, [Juan] García Oliver.

We know very well that thousands on thousands of isolated thinkers and artists are today scattered throughout the world, their voices drowned out by the loud choruses of well-disciplined liars. Hundreds of small local magazines are trying to gather youthful forces about them, seeking new paths and not subsidies. Every progressive tendency in art is destroyed by fascism as 'degenerate'. Every free creation is called 'fascist' by the Stalinists. Independent revolutionary art must now gather its forces for the struggle against reactionary persecution. It must proclaim aloud the right to exist. Such a union of forces is the aim of the *International Federation of Independent Revolutionary Art* which we believe it is now necessary to form.

We by no means insist on every idea put forth in this manifesto, which we ourselves consider only a first step in the new direction. We urge every friend

and defender of art, who cannot but realise the necessity for this appeal, to make
himself heard at once. We address the same appeal to all those publications of
the left wing which are ready to participate in the creation of the International
Federation and to consider its task and its methods of action.

When a preliminary international contact has been established through
the press and by correspondence, we will proceed to the organisation of local
and national congresses on a modest scale. The final step will be the assembly of
a world congress which will officially mark the foundation of the International
Federation.

Our aims:

The independence of art – for the revolution;

The revolution – for the complete liberation of art!

The Breton-Trotksy manifesto was written in a desperate geopolitical situation. Trotsky
himself would soon be murdered by Stalin's thugs; and, of course, fascism and
National Socialism were on the rise, with Adolf Hitler's Third Reich being poised to
overrun Europe.

Benito Mussolini's fascism in particular attracted its share of international artistic admirers. It was not just Italian Futurists who put their art in the service of fascism, but also Dutch artists such as the symbolist Jan Toorop and a pioneer of abstract
art, Erich Wichman. Wichman, who travelled to Italy in 1923, espoused an abstract
notion of freedom and evinced no small degree of petulance in dedicating a series of
lithographs to Il Duce: 'Because I have always and exclusively done what seemed right
to me, in my country which for this made me suffer from hunger most atrocious, I
likewise here and now claim the right to do what I think is right; the right to dedicate
this work to you, Benito Mussolini.'[50]

That artists fell under the sway of fascism, even as fascist governments clamped
down on artistic freedom and basic human rights, should come as no surprise. Fascism
– and German National Socialism in particular – was the culmination of a reactionary
version of the aesthetic project. This project had been nationalised and racialised early
on.[51] The German Romantics pitted the art and culture of the German Volk against
French civilisation, and later the composer, conductor and theatre director Richard
Wagner would promote his *Gesamtkunstwerk* as an aesthetic mass for the German
Volksgemeinschaft, from which Jews were to be excluded. For Wagner, Jews were by
definition alien to German culture and by default corrupted art during the process of
their integration. The Nazis practiced Wagnerianism on a grand scale, though Hitler's
petty-bourgeois taste meant that modern artists who were ardent Nazis, such as Emil
Nolde, saw their work branded 'degenerate' by a regime they supported.

For avant-garde fascist sympathizers, Italy was more accommodating; it attracted and gave a platform to a poet of the stature of Ezra Pound. During the Second
World War, Pound produced a series of speeches for Italian radio in which he praised
Mussolini and attacked Franklin D. Roosevelt, Western capitalism and international
Jewry. He lambasted capitalism as a system built on the liquefaction and liquidation
of all that is solid; the resulting erosion of tradition, according to Pound, was causing
people to be shackled by debt. At a moment when industrial genocide was already well
underway, Pound dug into the grab-bag of anti-Semitic tropes to identify the evils of
this capitalist system with an international Jewish conspiracy. He ranted in his radio
speech of 15 March 1942:

The enemy is *Das Leihkapital.* Your Enemy is *Das Leihkapital,* international, wandering Loan Capital. Your enemy is not Germany, your enemy is money on loan. And it would be better for you to be infected with typhus, and dysentery, and Bright's disease, than to be infected with this blindness which prevents you from understanding HOW you are undermined, how you are ruined.

The big Jew is so bound up with this Leihkapital that no one is able to unscramble that omelette. It would be better for you to retire to Darbyshire and defy New Jerusalem, better for you to retire to Gloucester and find one spot that is England than to go on fighting for Jewry and ignoring the process.

It is an outrage that any clean lad from the country – I suppose there are STILL a few ENGLISH lads from the country – it is an outrage that any nice young man from the suburbs should be expected to die for Victor Sassoon, it is an outrage that any drunken footman's by-blow should be asked to die for Sassoon.

As to your Empire, it was not all of it won by clean fighting. But however you got it, you did for a time more or less justify keeping it, on the ground that you exported good government or better government than the natives would have had without England.[52]

Pound's fascism was shaped by an obsessive concern over enslavement to gold and debt. Falsely concretising complex systemic features in the figure of the usurious and corrupt Jew, Pound turned himself into a propagandist for ethnic cleansing. After the war, he was committed to a mental clinic. In 1948 he was awarded the Bollingen Prize for poetry in his native US following the publication of *The Pisan Cantos* (written in 1945) – a decision that sparked heated debate. Was it acceptable to honour a fascist apologist in the name of Poetry, seen as an autonomous art?

In the context of the budding Cold War, when Soviet Communism was the enemy, many answered in the affirmative. Though Pound had produced fascist propaganda, separating his ideological rants from his poetry made it possible to use the latter as a shining example of the kind of Great Art that could only flourish in the West, and certainly not behind the Iron Curtain. The Cold War thus had its cultural spin-off, with the CIA secretly backing the anti-communist Congress for Cultural Freedom, which attracted a fair deal of former New York Trotskyists who were in the process of becoming neoconservative 'hawks'.[53]

The ideological gridlock of those years was challenged by relatively marginal individuals and groups, such as the young Parisian bohemians of the Lettrist International – which later cofounded the Situationist International. A 1954 Lettrist text from the fourth issue of *Potlatch* sees the group (Michèle Bernstein, André-Frank Conord, Mohamed Dahou, Guy Debord, Jacques Fillon and Gil J. Wolman) attack the Western pacification of the workers' struggle through trade unionism and rearticulate the project of a transformation of society that would have to be as aesthetic as political and economic.

Jan Toorop, *Portrait of
Benito Mussolini*, 1927,
charcoal on wood, 46 × 38cm
Courtesy Photo Collection RKD –
Netherlands Institute for
Art History, The Hague

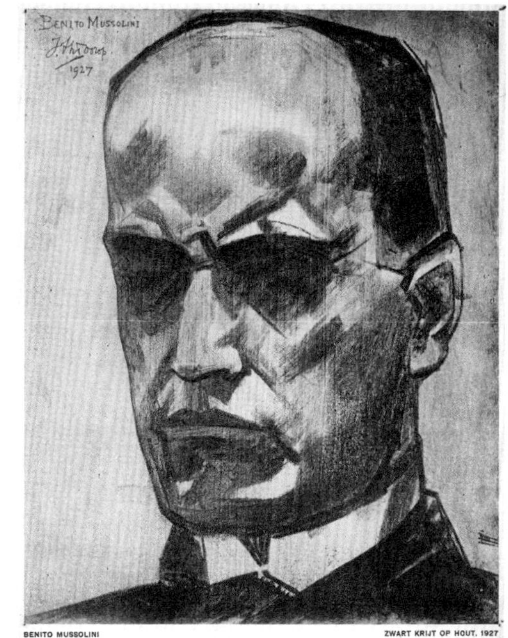

Erich Wichman, dedication to
Mussolini in the print portfolio
Idealisten II, 1923, lithograph on paper,
15.5 × 10.5cm
Courtesy and © Centraal Museum Utrecht

LETTRIST INTERNATIONAL, 'THE MINIMUM LIFE'

Reprinted from *Potlatch*, no.4, 13 July 1954, available at http://www.cddc.vt.edu/sionline/ presitu/potlatch4.html (last accessed on 18 September 2020). Translation by Gerardo Denis and Reuben Keehan.

One can never tire of saying that unionism's current concessions are condemned to failure; less by their division and their dependence on official organisations than by the poverty of their programmes.

One can never tire of telling the exploited workers their lives are at stake, lives that are irreplaceable and boundless in potential; that their most beautiful years are at stake, passing slowly but surely by, without any worthwhile enjoyment, without their ever having taken up arms.

We don't need to demand greater security or a raise in the 'minimum wage', but that the masses are no longer kept at a minimum life. We don't just need to demand bread, we need to demand fun.

In the 'Economic statute on light labour', defined last year by the Commission of Collective Conventions, a statute that is an unbearable injury to all that can still be expected from humans, the role of leisure – not to mention culture – was set at the level of serialised detective novels.

There's no other way out.

And what's more, with its detective novels, as with its Press and its trans-Atlantic Cinema, this regime extends its prisons in which nothing is left to gain – but where there is nothing to lose but our chains.

It is not the question of increase to salaries that should be posed, but that of the conditions forced on people in the West.

It is necessary to refuse to struggle inside the system to obtain concessions to details immediately called into question or regained elsewhere by capitalism. The problem of the survival or destruction of the system must be posed radically.

It is not necessary to talk of possible compromises, but of unacceptable realities: just ask the Algerian workers at the Regié Renault plant where their free time is, or their country, their dignity, their wives. Ask them what they have to hope for. The social struggle must not be bureaucratic, it must be passionate. To judge the disastrous effects of professional unionism, it is enough to analyse the spontaneous strike of August 1953; its basic resolution; its sabotage by scabs; its abandonment by the CGT [Confédération générale du travail; General Confederation of Labour], who had neither brought about the strike nor used it to extend itself victoriously. It is necessary, on the contrary, to become aware of a few facts that can make the debate passionate: for example, the fact that our friends exist all over the world, and that in their struggles, we see ourselves; the fact also that we do not expect any compensation outside of what we must invent and build ourselves.

This is a matter of courage.

The Situationist International, founded in 1957, was a volatile artistic-political mix, with the painters involved being suspect for producing works for the capitalist art market. In the early 1960s, the movement became less 'artistic' and more of a full-fledged 'revolutionary avant-garde' intent on toppling the 'society of the spectacle'. Still aesthetic, however, was the goal of a revolution of everyday life, of the realisation of a post-capitalist life of playful activity, of 'constructed situations', of lived poetry.

In June 1963, Guy Debord wrote 'The Situationists and the New Forms of Action in Art and Politics' to accompany the Situationists' anti-nuclear exhibition 'Destruction of the RSG-6', outlining the need for an 'interrelated' political-artistic approach:

THE SITUATIONIST MOVEMENT can be seen as an artistic avant-garde, as an experimental investigation of possible ways for freely constructing everyday life, and as a contribution to the theoretical and practical development of a new revolutionary contestation. From now on, any fundamental cultural creation, as well as any qualitative transformation of society, is contingent on the continued development of this sort of interrelated approach.

The same society of alienation, totalitarian control and passive spectacular consumption reigns everywhere, despite the diversity of its ideological and juridical disguises. The coherence of this society cannot be understood without an all-encompassing critique, illuminated by the inverse project of a liberated creativity, the project of everyone's control of all levels of their own history.

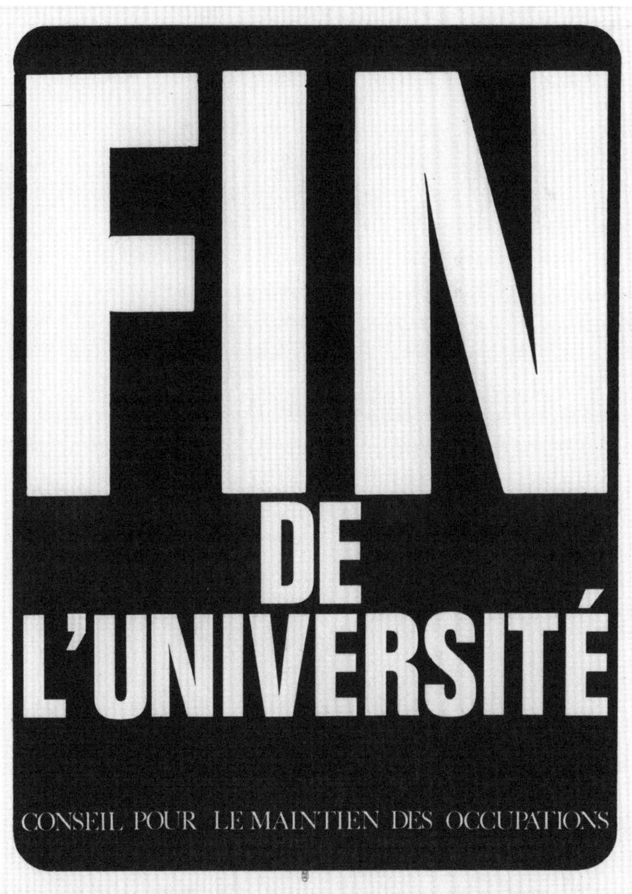

Poster by Conseil pour le
maintien des occupations,
May 1968

To revive and bring into the present this *inseparable*, mutually illuminating project and critique entails appropriating all the radicalism borne by the workers' movement, by modern poetry and art, and by the thought of the period of the supersession of philosophy, from Hegel to Nietzsche. To do this, it is first of all necessary to recognise, without holding on to any consoling illusions, the full extent of the defeat of the entire revolutionary project in the first third of this century and its official replacement, in every region of the world and in every domain of life, by delusive shams and petty reforms that camouflage and preserve the old order.[54]

Debord later noted that the Situationist programme had 'promised nothing more than an autonomy without rules or restrictions'.[55] The Situationists, then, embraced and exacerbated the value of autonomy, but in the sense of a lived and embodied collective practice that foreshadows later conceptions of Autonomia.[56]

In turn, the Situationists were indebted to the French group Socialisme ou Barbarie, to whom they were close for a part of the 1960s. Socialisme ou Barbarie's Cornelius Castoriadis emphasised the need for workers' autonomous self-management. A 1975 text by Castoriadis argues that any discussion of autonomy, even if beginning in individual terms, ultimately necessitates a switch to the social level:

> ... one cannot want autonomy without wanting it for everyone and that its realisation cannot be conceived of in its full scope except as a collective enterprise. If by this term we no longer mean the inalienable freedom of an abstract subject or the domination of a pure consciousness over an undifferentiated material, essentially 'the same' for all and forever, a primary obstacle that freedom would have to overcome ('passions', 'inertia', etc.); if the problem of autonomy is that the subject meets in itself a sense that is not its own and that it must transform this sense in using it; if autonomy is the relation in which others are always present as the otherness *and* as the self-ness of the subject, then autonomy can be conceived of, even in philosophical terms, only as a social problem and as a social relation.[57]

In the 1950s, Castoriadis corresponded with the Dutch council communist Anton Pannekoek, who had always defended bottom-up creation of workers' councils against the Leninist party model.[58] This held great appeal for the Situationists; while the SI had started out with a romantic revolt against labour as such, by the late 1960s the creation of workers' councils became their default option, as it seemed to be a viable tool for effecting the transition to a post-capitalist society that would ultimately do away with alienating labour altogether. The SI's moment appeared to have come in May '68, when Situationist-inspired slogans could be seen all over Paris. At the Sorbonne, the Situationists around Debord dominated the Occupation Committee of the People's Free Sorbonne University, as well as the more general Council for Maintaining the Occupations, which focussed not just on the Sorbonne but also on occupations at other universities and at factories, which were crucial to the 'councilist' agenda.

To make it absolutely clear that this was a different kind of revolution – not one in the service of Maoist or Stalinist ideology – the Sorbonne committee sent telegrams to Beijing and Moscow. The 17 May 1968 telegram to the Politburo of the Communist Party of the USSR rejected the whole of Bolshevism, including Trotsky, who in stamping out the 1921 Kronstadt rebellion had helped crush the councilist element:

SHAKE IN YOUR SHOES BUREAUCRATS STOP THE INTERNATIONAL POWER OF THE WORKERS COUNCILS WILL SOON WIPE YOU OUT STOP HUMANITY WON'T BE HAPPY TILL THE LAST BUREAUCRAT IS HUNG WITH THE GUTS OF THE LAST CAPITALIST STOP LONG LIVE THE STRUGGLE OF THE KRONSTADT SAILORS AND OF THE MAKHNOVSHCHINA AGAINST TROTSKY AND LENIN STOP LONG LIVE THE 1956 COUNCILIST INSURRECTION OF BUDAPEST STOP DOWN WITH THE STATE STOP LONG LIVE REVOLUTIONARY MARXISM STOP OCCUPATION COMMITTEE OF THE PEOPLE'S FREE SORBONNE[59]

The Situationists ended up gambling on the Revolution to realise a society that would be humane and, in a profound sense, aesthetic. In doing so, they abandoned the use of means that most people would consider to be properly aesthetic – that is, they abandoned the means of art in favour of avant-garde activism. In recent years, long after his Situationist involvement, T.J. Clark has launched what might be termed a neo-modernist defence of artists who responded to the 'horrors' of the twentieth century not with such activism but by withdrawing into a private aesthetic world:

> But artists are seldom brave, nor need they be; and out of their honest cowardice, or blithe self-absorption, or simple revulsion from the world around them can come, in times of catastrophe, the fullest recognition of what catastrophe is – how it enters and structures everyday life. And as for artists who did *not* retreat or regress during the period in question [1905-56] – who went on believing in some version of modernity's movement forward, toward rationality or transparency or full disenchantment – they were too often involved (the record is clear) in a contorted compromise with the tyrannies and duplicities just listed. Better a private dreamworld, it seems to me, than a glib facsimile of the common good. Better Chagall's Vitebsk than Rodchenko's White Sea Canal – better Miró than Léger, or Matisse than Piscator, or Kahlo than Rivera, or De Chirico than De Stijl.[60]

This is a polemical rejoinder to those art historians who construct a clear genealogy of 'progressive' art and downplay the complexity of artists' political entanglement and the compromising moments that ensue (one imagines that Clark had Benjamin H.D. Buchloh in mind as he was writing). It is true enough that Aleksandr Rodchenko's propaganda photographs of the work on Stalin's White Sea Canal, during which thousands of forced labourers died, would make Leni Riefenstahl blush, and Clark's point about measuring all art with some reductive political yardstick is well taken. However, he constructs strangely undialectical oppositions – no doubt in part because of the polemical intent. Why is De Stijl here equated with 'a glib facsimile of the common good'? Are we really faced with a binary choice between private dreams and potentially totalitarian commitment? Or, at least, were these the only options in the early twentieth century? What about Joan Miró's activities in the Surrealist group, which insisted that seemingly private dreamworlds can be socially transformative?

The Avant-Garde Will Be Institutionalised

With his focus on artists expressing 'the fullest recognition of what catastrophe is', T.J. Clark has come a long way from his 1960s participation in the Situationist International – with its aesthetico-political programme that aimed at combatting the catastrophe of the spectacle, of alienation and nuclear deterrence. During the upheavals of this period, Adorno worked on his *Aesthetic Theory*, which would be edited and published posthumously in 1970. This monumental work develops an art theory that is far removed from the avant-gardism of his old friend Walter Benjamin, who in the 1930s had issued rousing calls for the transformation of art in keeping with technological developments and the revolutionary transformation of society in the Soviet Union.

By contrast, the heroes of Adorno's modernist aesthetic are Arnold Schoenberg and Samuel Beckett rather than Sergei Eisenstein or Bertolt Brecht (let alone Breton or Debord).[61] In such art, social content is articulated indirectly, filtered and fractured through rigorous forms. 'Art's double character as both autonomous and *fait social* is incessantly reproduced on the level of its autonomy.'[62] In the context of the 1960s, with its politicisation of art, this was somewhat out of sync with the times. However, as the 1970s progressed and art continued to exist semi-autonomously as a special-interest commodity, one aspect of Adorno's critical modernism seemed to be exactly to the point: his disparagement of avant-garde attempts to 'overcome' art.

It comes as no surprise that Adorno is frequently invoked in Peter Bürger's *Theory of the Avant-Garde* (1974). In this influential book, Bürger argues that the project of the historical avant-garde, the negation of 'autonomous' bourgeois-modernist art, was itself negated by the post-War institutionalisation of avant-garde strategies. Bürger takes a long view of autonomy, using terms that are derived from sociology and the social history of art; what he is dealing with is the relative autonomy of even early modern bourgeois art as functionally differentiated from other social fields. It was this relative autonomy that various avant-gardes attacked in order to merge art into a transformative force that Bürger calls *Lebenspraxis* (life praxis).

However, Bürger – a literary scholar – does not seem to have been terribly familiar with the scope of neo-avant-garde practice in the 1960s (particularly movements such as the Situationist International, which can hardly be said to have commodified the historical avant-garde). His argument is mostly based on Neo-Dada assemblage and Pop art. At a moment when it was clear that the infrastructure of art had survived the late 1960s, and that art was becoming ever more integrated in what Adorno and Max Horkheimer called the culture industry, Bürger's account nonetheless manages to articulate a central problem for the 1970s and the future: how to deal not just with the survival of semi-autonomous institutional art, but with its transfiguration into something on a par with Prada bags and luxury yachts.

PETER BÜRGER, 'THE NEGATION OF THE AUTONOMY OF ART BY THE AVANT-GARDE'

Reprinted from Peter Bürger, *Theory of the Avant-Garde*, Minneapolis: University of Minnesota Press, 1984, pp.47-54. First published in 1974. Translated from the German by Michael Shaw.

In scholarly discussion up to now, the category 'autonomy' has suffered from the imprecision of the various subcategories thought of as constituting a unity in the concept of the autonomous work of art. Since the development of the individual subcategories is not synchronous, it may happen that sometimes courtly art seems already autonomous, while at other times only bourgeois art appears to have that characteristic. To make clear that the contradictions between the various interpretations result from the nature of the case, we will sketch a historical typology that is deliberately reduced to three elements (purpose or function, production, reception), because the point here is to have the nonsynchronism in the development of individual categories emerge with clarity.

A. Sacral Art (example: the art of the High Middle Ages) serves as cult object. It is wholly integrated into the social institution 'religion'. It is produced collectively, as a craft. The mode of reception also is institutionalised as collective.[8]

B. Courtly Art (example: the art at the court of Louis XIV) also has a precisely defined function. It is representational and serves the glory of the prince and the self-portrayal of courtly society. Courtly art is part of the life praxis of courtly society, just as sacral art is part of the life praxis of the faithful. Yet the detachment from the sacral tie is a first step in the emancipation of art. ('Emancipation' is being used here as a descriptive term, as referring to the process by which art constitutes itself as a distinct social subsystem.) The difference from sacral art becomes particularly apparent in the realm of production: the artist produces as an individual and develops a consciousness of the uniqueness of his activity. Reception, on the other hand, remains collective. But the content of the collective performance is no longer sacral, it is sociability.

C. Only to the extent that the bourgeoisie adopts concepts of value held by the aristocracy does bourgeois art have a representational function. When it is genuinely bourgeois, this art is the objectification of the self-understanding of the bourgeois class. Production and reception of the self-understanding as articulated in art are no longer tied to the praxis of life. Habermas calls this the satisfaction of residual needs, that is, of needs that have become submerged in the life praxis of bourgeois society. Not only production but reception also are now individual acts. The solitary absorption in the work is the adequate mode of appropriation of creations removed from the life praxis of the bourgeois, even though they still claim to interpret that praxis. In Aestheticism, finally, where bourgeois art reaches the stage of self-reflection, this claim is no longer made.

---

8   On this, see the recent essay by R. Warning, 'Ritus, Mythos und geistliches Spiel', in Wilhelm Furhmann, *Terror und Spiel. Probleme der Mytbenrezeption*, Munich: Wilhelm Fink, 1971, pp.211-39.

Apartness from the praxis of life, which had always been the condition that characterised the way art functioned in bourgeois society, now becomes its content. The typology we have sketched here can be represented in the accompanying tabulation (the vertical lines in boldface refer to a decisive change in the development, the broken ones to a less decisive one).

	Sacral Art	Courtly Art	Bourgeoise Art
Purpose or function	cult object	representational object	portrayal of bourgeoise self-understanding
Production	collective craft	individual	individual
Reception	collective (sacral)	collective (sociable)	individual

The tabulation allows one to notice that the development of the categories was not synchronous. Production by the individual that characterises art in bourgeois society has its origins as far back as courtly patronage. But courtly art still remains integral to the praxis of life, although as compared with the cult function, the representational function constitutes a step toward a mitigation of claims that art play a direct social role. The reception of courtly art also remains collective, although the content of the collective performance has changed. As regards reception, it is only with bourgeois art that a decisive change sets in: its reception is one by isolated individuals. The novel is that literary genre in which the new mode of reception finds the form appropriate to it.[9] The advent of bourgeois art is also the decisive turning point as regards use or function. Although in different ways, both sacral and courtly art are integral to the life praxis of the recipient. As cult and representational objects, works of art are put to a specific use. This requirement no longer applies to the same extent to bourgeois art. In bourgeois art, the portrayal of bourgeois self-understanding occurs in a sphere that lies outside the praxis of life. The citizen who, in everyday life has been reduced to a partial function (means-ends activity) can be discovered in art as 'human being'. Here, one can unfold the abundance of one's talents, though with the proviso that this sphere remain strictly separate from the praxis of life. Seen in this fashion, the separation of art from the praxis of life becomes the decisive characteristic of the autonomy of bourgeois art (a fact that the tabulation does not bring out adequately). To avoid misunderstandings, it must be emphasised once again that autonomy in this sense defines the status of art in bourgeois society but that no assertions concerning the contents of works are involved. Although art as an institution may be considered fully formed toward the end of the eighteenth century, the development of the contents of works is subject to a historical dynamics, whose terminal point is reached in Aestheticism, where art becomes the content of art.

---

[9]   Hegel already referred to the novel as 'the modern bourgeois epic' (G.W.F. Hegel, *Aesthetics: Lectures on Fine Art*, vol.2 (trans. T.M. Knox), Oxford: Oxford University Press, p.1092. Translation amended by SL.)

The European avant-garde movements can be defined as an attack on the status of art in bourgeois society. What is negated is not an earlier form of art (a style) but art as an institution that is unassociated with the life praxis of men. When the avant-gardistes demand that art become practical once again, they do not mean that the contents of works of art should be socially significant. The demand is not raised at the level of the contents of individual works. Rather, it directs itself to the way art functions in society, a process that does as much to determine the effect that works have as does the particular content.

The avant-gardistes view its dissociation from the praxis of life as the dominant characteristic of art in bourgeois society. One of the reasons this dissociation was possible is that Aestheticism had made the element that defines art as an institution the essential content of works. Institution and work contents had to coincide to make it logically possible for the avant-garde to call art into question. The avant-gardistes proposed the sublation of art – sublation in the Hegelian sense of the term: art was not to be simply destroyed, but transferred to the praxis of life where it would be preserved, albeit in a changed form. The avant-gardistes thus adopted an essential element of Aestheticism. Aestheticism had made the distance from the praxis of life the content of works. The praxis of life to which Aestheticism refers and which it negates is the means-ends rationality of the bourgeois everyday. Now, it is not the aim of the avant-gardistes to integrate art into this praxis. On the contrary, they assent to the aestheticists' rejection of the world and its means-ends rationality. What distinguishes them from the latter is the attempt to organise a new life praxis from a basis in art. In this respect also, Aestheticism turns out to have been the necessary precondition of the avant-gardiste intent. Only an art the contents of whose individual works is wholly distinct from the (bad) praxis of the existing society can be the centre that can be the starting point for the organisation of a new life praxis.

With the help of Herbert Marcuse's theoretical formulation concerning the twofold character of art in bourgeois society, the avant-gardiste intent can be understood with particular clarity. All those needs that cannot be satisfied in everyday life, because the principle of competition pervades all spheres, can find a home in art, because art is removed from the praxis of life. Values such as humanity, joy, truth, solidarity are extruded from life as it were, and preserved in art. In bourgeois society, art has a contradictory role: it projects the image of a better order and to that extent protests against the bad order that prevails. But by realising the image of a better order in fiction, which is semblance [*Schein*] only, it relieves the existing society of the pressure of those forces that make for change. They are assigned to confinement in an ideal sphere. Where art accomplishes this, it is 'affirmative' in Marcuse's sense of the term. If the twofold character of art in bourgeois society consists in the fact that the distance from the social production and reproduction process contains an element of freedom and an element of the noncommittal and an absence of any consequences, it can be seen that the avant-gardistes' attempt to reintegrate art into the life process is itself a profoundly contradictory endeavor. For the (relative) freedom of art vis-à-vis the praxis of life is at the same time the condition that must be fulfilled if there is to be a critical cognition of reality. An art no longer distinct from the praxis of life but wholly absorbed in it will lose the capacity to criticise it, along with its distance.

During the time of the historical avant-garde movements, the attempt to do away with the distance between art and life still had all the pathos of historical progressiveness on its side. But in the meantime, the culture industry has brought about the false elimination of the distance between art and life, and this also allows one to recognise the contradictoriness of the avant-gardiste undertaking.[10]

In what follows, we will outline how the intent to eliminate art as an institution found expression in the three areas that we used above to characterise autonomous art: purpose or function, production, reception. Instead of speaking of the avant-gardiste work, we will speak of avant-gardiste manifestation. A Dadaist manifestation does not have work character but is nonetheless an authentic manifestation of the artistic avant-garde. This is not to imply that the avant-gardistes produced no works whatever and replaced them by ephemeral events. We will see that whereas they did not destroy it, the avant-gardistes profoundly modified the category of the work of art.

Of the three areas, the intended purpose or function of the avant-gardiste manifestation is most difficult to define. In the aestheticist work of art, the disjointure of the work and the praxis of life characteristic of the status of art in bourgeois society has become the work's essential content. It is only as a consequence of this fact that the work of art becomes its own end in the full meaning of the term. In Aestheticism, the social functionlessness of art becomes manifest. The avant-gardiste artists counter such functionlessness not by an art that would have consequences within the existing society, but rather by the principle of the sublation of art in the praxis of life. But such a conception makes it impossible to define the intended purpose of art. For an art that has been reintegrated into the praxis of life, not even the absence of a social purpose can be indicated, as was still possible in Aestheticism. When art and the praxis of life are one, when the praxis is aesthetic and art is practical, art's purpose can no longer be discovered, because the existence of two distinct spheres (art and the praxis of life) that is constitutive of the concept of purpose or intended use has come to an end.

We have seen that the production of the autonomous work of art is the act of an individual. The artist produces as individual, individuality not being understood as the expression of something but as radically different. The concept of genius testifies to this. The quasitechnical consciousness of the makeability of works of art that Aestheticism attains seems only to contradict this. Valéry, for example, demystifies artistic genius by reducing it to psychological motivations on the one hand, and the availability to it of artistic means on the other. While pseudo-romantic doctrines of inspiration thus come to be seen as the self-deception of producers, the view of art for which the individual is the creative subject is let stand. Indeed, Valéry's theorem concerning the force of pride (*orgueil*) that sets off and propels the creative process renews once again the notion of the individual character of artistic production central to art in bourgeois society.[11]

---

[10]   On the problem of the false sublation of art in the praxis of life, see Jürgen Habermas, *Strukturwandel der Öffentlichkeit. Untersuchungen zu einer Kategorie der bürgerlichen Gesellschaft*, Neuwied and Berlin: Luchterhand, 1962, §18, p.176 ff. [Editors' Note: For the English-language translation, see J. Habermas, *The Structural Transformation of the Public Sphere: An Inquiry into a Category of Bourgeois Society* (trans. Thomas Burger with the assistance of Frederick Lawrence), Cambridge, MA: MIT Press, 1991, p.158 ff.]

[11]   See Peter Bürger, 'Funktion und Bedeutung des *orgueil* bei Paul Valéry', *Romanistisches Jahrbuch*, vol.16, 1965, pp.149-68.

In its most extreme manifestations, the avant-garde's reply to this is not the collective as the subject of production but the radical negation of the category of individual creation. When Duchamp signs mass-produced objects (a urinal, a bottle drier) and sends them to art exhibits, he negates the category of individual production. The signature, whose very purpose it is to mark what is individual in the work, that it owes its existence to this particular artist, is inscribed on an arbitrarily chosen mass product, because all claims to individual creativity are to be mocked. Duchamp's provocation not only unmasks the art market where the signature means more than the quality of the work; it radically questions the very principle of art in bourgeois society according to which the individual is considered the creator of the work of art. Duchamp's Ready-Mades are not works of art but manifestations. Not from the form-content totality of the individual object Duchamp signs can one infer the meaning, but only from the contrast between mass-produced object on the one hand, and signature and art exhibit on the other. It is obvious that this kind of provocation cannot be repeated indefinitely. The provocation depends on what it turns against: here, it is the idea that the individual is the subject of artistic creation. Once the signed bottle drier has been accepted as an object that deserves a place in a museum, the provocation no longer provokes; it turns into its opposite. If an artist today signs a stovepipe and exhibits it, that artist certainly does not denounce the art market but adapts to it. Such adaptation does not eradicate the idea of individual creativity, it affirms it, and the reason is the failure of the avant-gardiste intent to sublate art. Since now the protest of the historical avant-garde against art as institution is accepted as art, the gesture of protest of the neo-avant-garde becomes inauthentic. Having been shown to be irredeemable, the claim to be protest can no longer be maintained. This fact accounts for the arts-and-crafts impression that works of the avant-garde not infrequently convey.[12]

The avant-garde not only negates the category of individual production but also that of individual reception. The reactions of the public during a Dada manifestation where it has been mobilised by provocation, and which can range from shouting to fisticuffs, are certainly collective in nature. True, these remain reactions, responses to a preceding provocation. Producer and recipient remain clearly distinct, however active the public may become. Given the avant-gardiste intention to do away with art as a sphere that is separate from the praxis of life, it is logical to eliminate the antithesis between producer and recipient. It is no accident that both Tzara's instructions for the making of a Dadaist poem and Breton's for the writing of automatic texts have the character of recipes.[13] This represents not only a polemical attack on the individual creativity of the artist; the recipe is to be taken quite literally as suggesting a possible activity on the part of the recipient. The automatic texts also should be read as guides to individual production. But such production is not to be understood as artistic production, but as part of a liberating life praxis. This is what is meant by Breton's demand that poetry be practiced (*pratiquer la poésie*). Beyond the coincidence

---

[12]   Examples of neo-avant-gardiste paintings and sculptures to be found in the catalogue of the exhibition *Sammlung Cremer. Europäische Avantgarde 1950–1970* (ed. G. Adriani), Tübingen, 1973.

[13]   Tristan Tzara, 'Pour faire un Poeme dadaiste', in *Lampisteries précedées des sept manifestes dada*, publisher unknown, 1963, p.64; and André Breton, 'Manifeste du surréalisme' (1924), in *Manifestes du surréalisme*, Paris: Coli. Idees 23, 1963, p.42f.

of producer and recipient that this demand implies, there is the fact that these concepts lose their meaning: producers and recipients no longer exist. All that remains is the individual who uses poetry as an instrument for living one's life as best one can. There is also a danger here to which Surrealism at least partly succumbed, and that is solipsism, the retreat to the problems of the isolated subject. Breton himself saw this danger and envisaged different ways of dealing with it. One of them was the glorification of the spontaneity of the erotic relationship. Perhaps the strict group discipline was also an attempt to exorcise the danger of solipsism that surrealism harbours.[14]

In summary, we note that the historical avant-garde movements negate those determinations that are essential in autonomous art: the disjunction of art and the praxis of life, individual production and individual reception as distinct from the former. The avant-garde intends the abolition of autonomous art by which it means that art is to be integrated into the praxis of life. This has not occurred, and presumably cannot occur, in bourgeois society unless it be as a false sublation of autonomous art.[15] Pulp fiction and commodity aesthetics prove that such a false sublation exists. A literature whose primary aim it is to impose a particular kind of consumer behaviour on the reader is in fact practical, though not in the sense the avant-gardistes intended. Here, literature ceases to be an instrument of emancipation and becomes one of subjection.[16] Similar comments could be made about commodity aesthetics that treat form as mere enticement, designed to prompt purchasers to buy what they do not need. Here also, art becomes practical but it is an art that enthrals.[17] This brief allusion will show that the theory of the avant-garde can also serve to make us understand popular literature and commodity aesthetics as forms of a false sublation of art as institution. In late capitalist society, intentions of the historical avant-garde

---

[14]   On the Surrealists' conception of groups and the collective experiences they sought and partially realised, see Elisabeth Lenk, *Der springende Narziss. André Breton's poetischer Materialismus*, Munich: Rogner & Bernhard, 1971, pp.57ff, 73f.

[15]   One would have to investigate to what extent, after the October Revolution, the Russian avant-gardistes succeeded to a degree, because social conditions had changed, in realising their intent to reintegrate art in the praxis of life. Both B. Arvatov and S. Tretjakov turn the concept of art as developed in bourgeois society around and define art quite straightforwardly as socially useful activity: 'The pleasure of transforming the raw material into a particular, socially useful form, connected to the skill and the intensive search for the suitable form - those are the things the slogan "art for all" should mean.' Sergej Tretjakov, 'Die Kunst in der Revolution und die Revolution in der Kunst', in H. Boehncke (ed.), *Die Arbeit des Schriftstellers*, Reinbek bei Hamburg: Rowohlt, 1971, p.13. 'Basing himself on the technique which is common to all spheres of life, the artist is imbued with the idea of suitability. It is not by subjective taste that he will allow himself to be guided as he works on his material but by the objective tasks of production.' Boris Arvatov, 'Die Kunst im System der proletarischen Kultur', in *Kunst und Produktion*, p.15. [EN: For the English-language translation, see B. Arvatov, *Art and Production* (ed. John Roberts and Alexei Penzin, trans. Shushan Avagyan), London: Pluto Press, 2017, p.93ff.] With the theory of the avant-garde as a point of departure, and with concrete investigations as guide, one should also discuss the problem of the extent (and of the kinds of consequences for the artistic subjects) to which art as an institution occupies a place in the society of the socialist countries that differs from its place in bourgeois society.

[16]   See Christa Bürger, *Textanalyse als Ideologiekritik. Zur Rezeption zeitgenössischer Unterhaltungsliteratur*, Frankfurt: Athenaum, 1973.

[17]   See Wolfgang Fritz Haug, *Kritik der Warenästhetik*, Frankfurt a.M.: Suhrkamp, 1971. [EN: For the English-language translation, see W.F. Haug, *Critique of Commodity Aesthetics: Appearance, Sexuality and Advertising in Capitalist Society* (trans. Robert Bock), Cambridge: Polity Press, 1986.]

are being realised but the result has been a disvalue. Given the experience of
the false sublation of autonomy, one will need to ask whether a sublation of the
autonomy status can be desirable at all, whether the distance between art and
the praxis of life is not requisite for that free space within which alternatives to
what exists become conceivable.

Bürger's analysis proved both influential and controversial. His conclusion in this
chapter – that we should be grateful for art's autonomy and the 'distance between art
and the praxis of life' for offering us a 'free space' – is not terribly satisfying. Is this
not exactly the kind of pacifying function that art has all too often had, giving us an
imaginary free space, a free space for the imagination to play in and to leave the rest
alone? Furthermore, Bürger's notion of *Lebenspraxis* remains as abstract as many
of the avant-garde's own pronouncements on the need to 'overcome art' in order to
'merge art with life' and 'transform life aesthetically'. Here, the notion of life becomes
subject to 'imaginistic freezing', in Peter Osborne's words.[63] It evokes a wholeness and
a rejection of social divisions and specialisations that remains a vague promise – and
the neo-avant-garde is decried by Bürger for betraying this beautiful pipe dream.
However, with Hal Foster we might argue that 'the project of the avant-garde is no
more concluded in its neo moment than it is enacted in its historical moment':

> Bürger takes the romantic rhetoric of the avant-garde, of rupture and revolution,
> at its own word. In doing so he misses crucial dimensions of its practice. For
> example, he misses its *mimetic* dimension, whereby the avant-garde mimics the
> degraded world of capitalist modernity in order not to embrace it but to mock it
> (as in Cologne Dada). He also misses its *utopian* dimension, whereby the avant-
> garde proposes not what can be so much as what *cannot* be – again as a critique of
> what is (as in De Stijl).[64]

Foster advocates for practices by artists such as Michael Asher, Marcel Broodthaers
and Hans Haacke – artists who work critically within the institutions of art.[65] As
Foster puts it, 'the neo-avant-garde at its best addresses the institution with a creative
analysis at once specific and deconstructive (not a nihilistic attack at once abstract
and anarchistic, as so often with the historical avant-garde)'.[66] As for the institutionalisation of the avant-garde and the transformation of the art world into a sector of the
culture industry, Foster admits:

> A reconnection of art and life *has* occurred, but under the terms of the culture
> industry, not the avant-garde, some devices of which were long ago assimilated
> into the operations of spectacular culture (in part through the very repetitions
> of the neo-avant-garde). This much is due to the devil, but only this much. Rather
> than render the avant-garde null and void, these developments have produced
> new spaces of critical play and prompted new modes of institutional analysis.
> And the reworking of the avant-garde in terms of aesthetic forms, cultural-polit-
> ical strategies and social positionings has proved the most vital project in art and
> criticism over the last three decades at least.[67]

Reconsidering the Aesthetic Project

In the twenty-first-century art world, Peter Bürger–style defences of the autonomous 'free space' of art will have a hard time avoiding complicitness with the framing conditions of this space. In a deregulated and financialised Goldman Sachs economy, visual art has become a favourite blue-chip investment. Meanwhile, new forms of activism attack this pseudo-autonomous art world – in the name of a higher autonomy. From Occupy to Extinction Rebellion and decolonial activism in museums, we see groups and movements deploying aesthetic means in public spaces in the form of embodied assemblies and choreographed protests, while the institutions of art are being politicised from the inside by artistic-activist coalitions who take them to task for their dodgy trustees and sponsorship deals.

It is significant that the art theory of this century's first decades has been marked by a reconsideration of the aesthetic project as a whole, since its origins in the late eighteenth century, and of its structural logic and fundamental contradictions; this includes the contradiction between art and politics, which is the 'politicised' version of the dichotomy of 'art' and 'life', and, as such, immanent to the aesthetic itself. The crucial thinker here is Jacques Rancière, who in the 1960s was part of the Marxist circle around Louis Althusser. In his later work, Rancière attempts to go beyond the modernism/avant-garde or Adorno/Debord divide by delineating the 'aesthetic regime of art' that was inaugurated by the Romantics and idealists around 1800. The founders of the aesthetic regime conceived of the artwork in a radically different way than the preceding 'representational regime' had done. In the aesthetic regime, the artwork became an opaque *objet de pensée*, a mixture of logos and pathos. As such, it did indeed appear to bridge the gulf between the sensible and the sensuous without ever effecting a synthesis. Moreover, in so far as it was aesthetic, art could never be truly autonomous.

In his 2002 essay 'The Aesthetic Revolution and Its Outcomes', Rancière returns to Schiller and the Juno Ludovisi, who here becomes a precursor to the 'showrooms of the avant-garde', in an ambitious attempt to identify the structural antinomies of the aesthetic regime and to trace the 'emplotments' of autonomy and heteronomy.

JACQUES RANCIÈRE, 'THE AESTHETIC REVOLUTION AND ITS OUTCOMES: EMPLOTMENTS OF AUTONOMY AND HETERONOMY'

Reprinted from *New Left Review*, no.14, March–
April 2002, pp.133-51.

At the end of the fifteenth of his *Letters on the Aesthetic Education of Mankind* Schiller states a paradox and makes a promise. He declares that 'Man is only completely human when he plays', and assures us that this paradox is capable 'of bearing the whole edifice of the art of the beautiful and of the still more difficult art of living'. We could reformulate this thought as follows: there exists a specific sensory experience – the aesthetic – that holds the promise of both a new world of Art and a new life for individuals and the community. There are different ways of coming to terms with this statement and this promise. You can say that they virtually define the 'aesthetic illusion' as a device which merely serves to mask the reality that aesthetic judgement is structured by class domination. In my view that is not the most productive approach. You can say, conversely, that the statement and the promise were only too true, and that we have experienced the reality of that 'art of living' and of that 'play', as much in totalitarian attempts at making the community into a work of art as in the everyday aestheticised life of a liberal society and its commercial entertainment. Caricatural as it may appear, I believe this attitude is more pertinent. The point is that neither the statement nor the promise were ineffectual. At stake here is not the 'influence' of a thinker, but the efficacy of a plot – one that reframes the division of the forms of our experience.

This plot has taken shape in theoretical discourses and in practical attitudes, in modes of individual perception and in social institutions – museums, libraries, educational programmes; and in commercial inventions as well. My aim is to try to understand the principle of its efficacy, and of its various and antithetical mutations. How can the notion of 'aesthetics' as a specific experience lead at once to the idea of a pure world of art and of the self-suppression of art in life, to the tradition of avant-garde radicalism and to aestheticisation of common existence? In a sense, the whole problem lies in a very small preposition. Schiller says that aesthetic experience will bear the edifice of the art of the beautiful *and* of the art of living. The entire question of the 'politics of aesthetics' – in other words, of the aesthetic regime of art – turns on this short conjunction. The aesthetic experience is effective inasmuch as it is the experience of that *and*. It grounds the autonomy of art, to the extent that it connects it to the hope of 'changing life'. Matters would be easy if we could merely say – naïvely – that the beauties of art must be subtracted from any politicisation, or – knowingly – that the alleged autonomy of art disguises its dependence upon domination. Unfortunately this is not the case: Schiller says that the 'play drive' – *Spieltrieb* – will reconstruct both the edifice of art and the edifice of life.

Militant workers of the 1840s break out of the circle of domination by reading and writing not popular and militant, but 'high' literature. The bourgeois critics of the 1860s denounce Flaubert's posture of 'art for art's sake' as the embodiment of democracy. Mallarmé wants to separate the 'essential language' of poetry from common speech, yet claims that it is poetry which gives the community the 'seal' it lacks. Rodchenko takes his photographs of Soviet workers or gymnasts from an overhead angle which squashes their bodies and movements, to construct the surface of an egalitarian equivalence of art and life. Adorno says that art must be entirely self-contained, the better to make the blotch of the unconscious appear and denounce the lie of autonomised art. Lyotard contends that the task of the avant-garde is to isolate art from cultural demand so that it may testify all the more starkly to the heteronomy of thought. We could extend the list *ad infinitum*. All these positions reveal the same basic emplotment of an *and*, the same knot binding together autonomy and heteronomy.

Understanding the 'politics' proper to the aesthetic regime of art means understanding the way autonomy and heteronomy are originally linked in Schiller's formula.[18] This may be summed up in three points. Firstly, the autonomy staged by the aesthetic regime of art is not that of the work of art, but of a mode of experience. Secondly, the 'aesthetic experience' is one of heterogeneity, such that for the subject of that experience it is also the dismissal of a certain autonomy. Thirdly, the object of that experience is 'aesthetic', in so far as it is not – or at least not only – art. Such is the threefold relation that Schiller sets up in what we can call the 'original scene' of aesthetics.

Sensorium of the goddess

At the end of the fifteenth letter, he places himself and his readers in front of a specimen of 'free appearance', a Greek statue known as the Juno Ludovisi. The statue is 'self-contained', and 'dwells in itself', as befits the traits of the divinity: her 'idleness', her distance from any care or duty, from any purpose or volition. The goddess is such because she wears no trace of will or aim. Obviously, the qualities of the goddess are those of the statue as well. The statue thus comes paradoxically to figure what has not been made, what was never an object of will. In other words: it embodies the qualities of what is not a work of art. (We should note in passing that formulas of the type 'this is' or 'this is not' a work of art, 'this is' or 'this is not a pipe', have to be traced back to this originary scene, if we want to make of them more than hackneyed jokes.)

Correspondingly, the spectator who experiences the free play of the aesthetic in front of the 'free appearance' enjoys an autonomy of a very special kind. It is not the autonomy of free Reason, subduing the anarchy of sensation. It is the suspension of that kind of autonomy. It is an autonomy strictly related to a withdrawal of power. The 'free appearance' stands in front of us, unapproachable,

---

[18]   I distinguish between three regimes of art. In the ethical regime, works of art have no autonomy. They are viewed as images to be questioned for their truth and for their effect on the ethos of individuals and the community. Plato's *Republic* offers a perfect model of this regime. In the representational regime, works of art belong to the sphere of imitation, and so are no longer subject to the laws of truth or the common rules of utility. They are not so much copies of reality as ways of imposing a form on matter. As such, they are subject to a set of intrinsic norms: a hierarchy of genres, adequation of expression to subject matter, correspondence between the arts, etc. The aesthetic regime overthrows this normativity and the relationship between form and matter on which it is based. Works of art are now defined as such, by belonging to a specific sensorium that stands out as an exception from the normal regime of the sensible, which presents us with an immediate adequation of thought and sensible materiality. For further detail, see Jacques Rancière, *Le Partage du sensible. Esthétique et Politique*, Paris: La Fabrique Editions, 2000. [Editors' Note: For the English-language translation, see J. Rancière, *The Politics of Aesthetics: The Distribution of the Sensible* (trans. Gabriel Rockhill), London and New York: Continuum, 2011.]

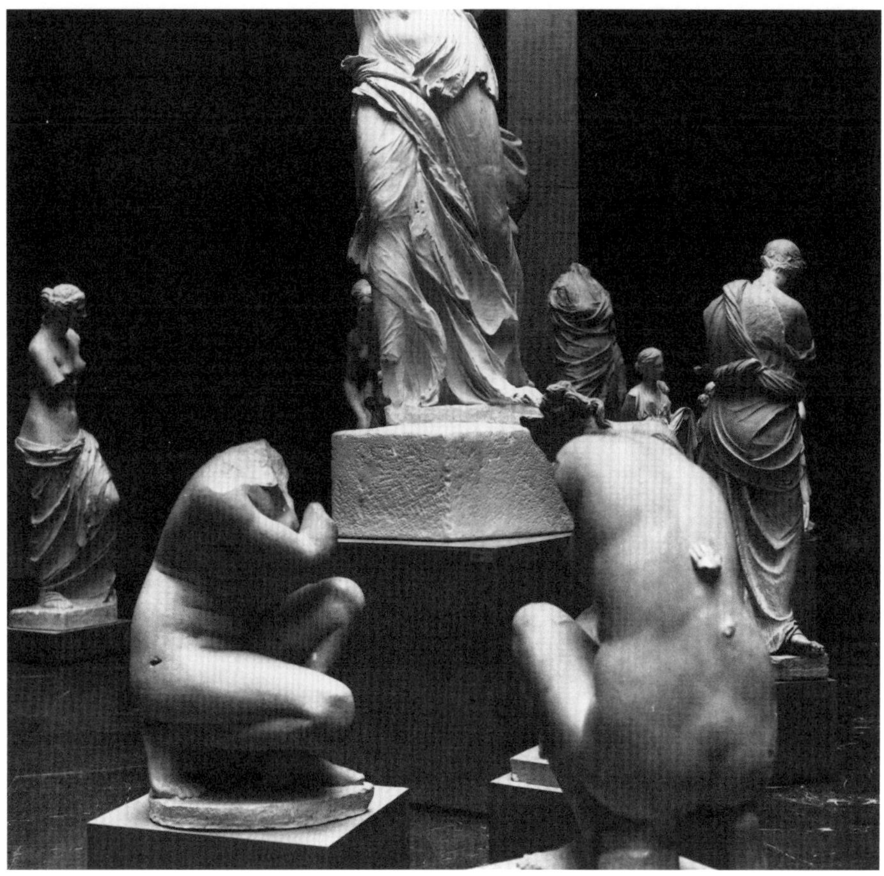

unavailable to our knowledge, our aims and desires. The subject is promised the possession of a new world by this figure that he cannot possess in any way. The goddess and the spectator, the free play and the free appearance, are caught up together in a specific sensorium, cancelling the oppositions of activity and passivity, will and resistance. The 'autonomy of art' and the 'promise of politics' are not counterposed. The autonomy is the autonomy of the experience, not of the work of art. To put it differently, the artwork participates in the sensorium of autonomy inasmuch as it is not a work of art.

Now this 'not being a work of art' immediately takes on a new meaning. The free appearance of the statue is the appearance of what has not been aimed at as art. This means that it is the appearance of a form of life in which art is not art. The 'self-containment' of the Greek statue turns out to be the 'self-sufficiency' of a collective life that does not rend itself into separate spheres of activities, of a community where art and life, art and politics, life and politics are not severed one from another. Such is supposed to have been the Greek people whose autonomy of life is expressed in the self-containment of the statue. The accuracy or otherwise of that vision of ancient Greece is not at issue here. What is at stake is the shift in the idea of autonomy, as it is linked to that of heteronomy. At first autonomy was tied to the 'unavailability' of the object of aesthetic experience.

Then it turns out to be the autonomy of a life in which art has no separate existence – in which its productions are in fact self-expressions of life. 'Free appearance', as the encounter of a heterogeneity, is no more. It ceases to be a suspension of the oppositions of form and matter, of activity and passivity, and becomes the product of a human mind which seeks to transform the surface of sensory appearances into a new sensorium that is the mirror of its own activity. The last letters of Schiller unfold this plot, as primitive man gradually learns to cast an aesthetic gaze on his arms and tools or on his own body, to separate the pleasure of appearance from the functionality of objects. Aesthetic play thus becomes a work of aestheticisation. The plot of a 'free play', suspending the power of active form over passive matter and promising a still unheard-of state of equality, becomes another plot, in which form subjugates matter, and the self-education of mankind is its emancipation from materiality, as it transforms the world into its own sensorium.

So the original scene of aesthetics reveals a contradiction that is not the opposition of art versus politics, high art versus popular culture, or art versus the aestheticisation of life. All these oppositions are particular features and interpretations of a more basic contradiction. In the aesthetic regime of art, art is art to the extent that it is something else than art. It is always 'aestheticised', meaning that it is always posed as a 'form of life'. The key formula of the aesthetic regime of art is that art is an autonomous form of life. This is a formula, however, that can be read in two different ways: autonomy can be stressed over life, or life over autonomy – and these lines of interpretation can be opposed, or they can intersect.

Such oppositions and intersections can be traced as the interplay between three major scenarios. Art can become life. Life can become art. Art and life can exchange their properties. These three scenarios yield three configurations of the aesthetic, emplotted in three versions of temporality. According to the logic of the *and*, each is also a variant of the politics of aesthetics, or what we should rather call its 'metapolitics' – that is, its way of producing its own politics, proposing to politics rearrangements of its space, reconfiguring art as a political issue or asserting itself as true politics.

Constituting the new collective world
The first scenario is that of 'art becoming life'. In this schema art is taken to be not only an expression of life but a form of its self-education. What this means is that, beyond its destruction of the representational regime, the aesthetic regime of art comes to terms with the ethical regime of images in a two-pronged relationship. It rejects its partitioning of times and spaces, sites and functions. But it ratifies its basic principle: matters of art are matters of education. As self-education art is the formation of a new sensorium – one which signifies, in actuality, a new ethos. Taken to an extreme, this means that the 'aesthetic self-education of humanity' will frame a new collective ethos. The politics of aesthetics proves to be the right way to achieve what was pursued in vain by the aesthetics of politics, with its polemical configuration of the common world. Aesthetics promises a non-polemical, consensual framing of the common world. Ultimately the alternative to politics turns out to be aestheticisation, viewed as the constitution of a new collective ethos. This scenario was first set out in the little draft associated with Hegel, Hölderlin and Schelling, known as the 'Oldest System-Programme

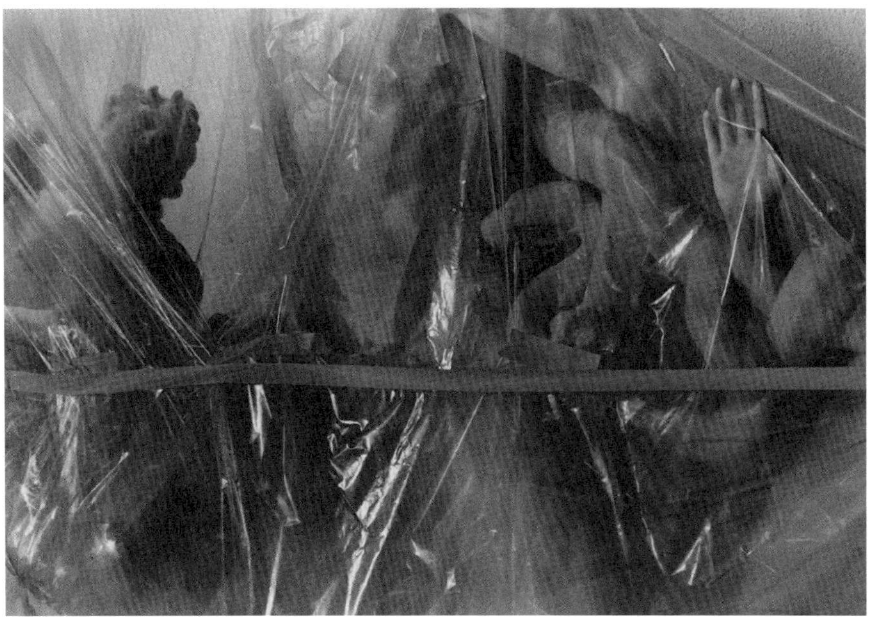

of German Idealism'. The scenario makes politics vanish in the sheer opposition between the dead mechanism of the State and the living power of the community, framed by the power of living thought. The vocation of poetry – the task of 'aesthetic education' – is to render ideas sensible by turning them into living images, creating an equivalent of ancient mythology, as the fabric of a common experience shared by the elite and by the common people. In their words: 'mythology must become philosophy to make common people reasonable and philosophy must become mythology to make philosophers sensible'.

This draft would not be just a forgotten dream of the 1790s. It laid the basis for a new idea of revolution. Even though Marx never read the draft, we can discern the same plot in his well-known texts of the 1840s. The coming Revolution will be at once the consummation and abolition of philosophy; no longer merely 'formal' and 'political', it will be a 'human' revolution. The human revolution is an offspring of the aesthetic paradigm. That is why there could be a juncture between the Marxist vanguard and the artistic avant-garde in the 1920s, as each side was attached to the same programme: the construction of new forms of life, in which the self-suppression of politics would match the self-suppression of art. Pushed to this extreme the originary logic of the 'aesthetic state' is reversed. Free appearance was an appearance that did not refer to any 'truth' lying behind or beneath it. But when it becomes the expression of a certain life, it refers again to a truth to which it bears witness. In the next step, this embodied truth is opposed to the lie of appearances. When the aesthetic revolution assumes the shape of a 'human' revolution cancelling the 'formal' one, the originary logic has been overturned. The autonomy of the idle divinity, its unavailability had once promised a new age of equality. Now the fulfilment of that promise is identified with the act of a subject who does away with all such appearances, which were only the dream of something he must now possess as reality.

But we should not for all that simply equate the scenario of art becoming life with the disasters of the 'aesthetic absolute', embodied in the totalitarian figure of the collectivity as a work of art. The same scenario can be traced in more sober attempts to make art the form of life. We may think, for instance, of the way the theory and practice of the Arts and Crafts movement tied a sense of eternal beauty, and a medieval dream of handicrafts and artisan guilds, to concern with the exploitation of the working class and the tenor of everyday life, and to issues of functionality. William Morris was among the first to claim that an armchair is beautiful if it provides a restful seat, rather than satisfying the pictorial fantasies of its owner. Or let us take Mallarmé, a poet often viewed as the incarnation of artistic purism. Those who cherish his phrase 'this mad gesture of writing' as a formula for the 'intransitivity' of the text often forget the end of his sentence, which assigns the poet the task of 'recreating everything, out of reminiscences, to show that we actually are at the place we have to be'. The allegedly 'pure' practice of writing is linked to the need to create forms that participate in a general reframing of the human abode, so that the productions of the poet are, in the same breath, compared both to ceremonies of collective life, like the fireworks of Bastille Day, and to private ornaments of the household.

It is no coincidence that in Kant's *Critique of [the Power of] Judgement* significant examples of aesthetic apprehension were taken from painted décors that were 'free beauty' insofar as they represented no subject, but simply contributed to the enjoyment of a place of sociability. We know how far the transformations of art and its visibility were linked to controversies over the ornament. Polemical programmes to reduce all ornamentation to function, in the style of Loos, or to extol its autonomous signifying power, in the manner of Riegl or Worringer, appealed to the same basic principle: art is first of all a matter of dwelling in a common world. That is why the same discussions about the ornament could support ideas both of abstract painting and of industrial design. The notion of 'art becoming life' does not simply foster demiurgic projects of a 'new life'. It also weaves a common temporality of art, which can be summed up in a simple formula: a new life needs a new art. 'Pure' art and 'committed' art, 'fine' art and 'applied' art, alike partake of this temporality. Of course, they understand and fulfil it in very different ways. In 1897, when Mallarmé wrote his *Un coup de dés*, he wanted the arrangement of lines and size of characters on the page to match the form of his idea – the fall of the dice. Some years later Peter Behrens designed the lamps and kettles, trademark and catalogues of the German General Electricity Company. What have they in common?

The answer, I believe, is a certain conception of design. The poet wants to replace the representational subject-matter of poetry with the design of a general form, to make the poem like a choreography or the unfolding of a fan. He calls these general forms 'types'. The engineer-designer wants to create objects whose form fits their use and advertisements which offer exact information about them, without commercial embellishment. He also calls these forms 'types'. He thinks of himself as an artist, inasmuch as he attempts to create a culture of everyday life that is in keeping with the progress of industrial production and artistic design, rather than with the routines of commerce and petty-bourgeois consumption. His types are symbols of common life. But so are Mallarmé's. They are part of the project of building, above the level of the monetary economy, a symbolic economy that would display a collective 'justice' or 'magnificence', a celebration of the human abode replacing the forlorn ceremonies of throne and religion. Far from each other as the symbolist poet and the functionalist engineer may seem, they share the idea that forms of art should be modes of collective education. Both industrial production and artistic creation are committed to doing something else than what they do – to create not only objects but a sensorium, a new partition of the perceptible.

Framing the life of art
Such is the first scenario. The second is the schema of 'life becoming art' or the 'life of art'. This scenario may be given the title of a book by the French art historian Elie Faure, *The Spirit of Forms* [1937]: the life of art as the development of a series of forms in which life becomes art. This is in fact the plot of the Museum, conceived not as a building and an institution but as a mode of rendering visible and intelligible the 'life of art'. We know that the birth of such museums around 1800 unleashed bitter disputes. Their opponents argued that the works of art should not be torn away from their setting, the physical and spiritual soil that gave birth to them. Now and then this polemic is renewed today: the museum denounced as a mausoleum dedicated to the contemplation of dead icons, separated from the life of art. Others hold that, on the contrary, museums have to be blank surfaces so that spectators can be confronted with the artwork itself, undistracted by the ongoing culturalisation and historicisation of art.

Both, in my view, are mistaken. There is no opposition between life and mausoleum, blank surface and historicised artefact. From the beginning the scenario of the art museum has been that of an aesthetic condition in which the Juno Ludovisi is not so much the work of a master sculptor as a 'living form', expressive both of the independence of 'free appearance' and of the vital spirit of a community. Our museums of fine arts don't display pure specimens of fine art. They display historicised art: Fra Angelico between Giotto and Masaccio, framing an idea of Florentine princely splendour and religious fervour; Rembrandt between Hals and Vermeer, featuring Dutch domestic and civic life, the rise of the bourgeoisie and so on. They exhibit a time-space of art as so many moments of the incarnation of thought.

To frame this plot was the first task of the discourse named 'aesthetics', and we know how Hegel, after Schelling, completed it. The principle of the framing is clear: the properties of the aesthetic experience are transferred to the work of art itself, cancelling their projection into a new life and invalidating the aesthetic revolution. The 'spirit of forms' becomes the inverted image of the aesthetic revolution. This reworking involves two main moves. First, the equivalence of activity and passivity, form and matter, that characterised the 'aesthetic experience' turns out to be the status of the artwork itself, now posited as an identity of consciousness and unconsciousness, will and un-will. Second, this identity of contraries at the same stroke lends works of art their historicity. The 'political' character of aesthetic experience is, as it were, reversed and encapsulated in the historicity of the statue. The statue is a living form. But the meaning of the link between art and life has shifted. The statue, in Hegel's view, is art not so much because it is the expression of a collective freedom, but rather because it figures the distance between that collective life and the way it can express itself. The Greek statue, according to him, is the work of an artist expressing an idea of which he is aware and unaware at the same time. He wants to embody the idea of divinity in a figure of stone. But what he can express is only the idea of the divinity that he can feel and that the stone can express. The autonomous form of the statue embodies divinity as the Greeks could at best conceive of it – that is, deprived of interiority. It does not matter whether we subscribe to this judgement or not. What matters is that, in this scenario, the limit of the artist, of his idea and of his people, is also the condition for the success of the work of art. Art is living so long as it expresses a thought unclear to itself in a matter that resists it. It lives inasmuch as it is something else than art, that is a belief and a way of life.

This plot of the spirit of forms results in an ambiguous historicity of art. On the one hand, it creates an autonomous life of art as an expression of history, open to new kinds of development. When Kandinsky claims for a new abstract expression an inner necessity, which revives the impulses and forms of primitive art, he holds fast to the spirit of forms and opposes its legacy to academicism. On the other hand, the plot of the life of art entails a verdict of death. The statue is autonomous in so far as the will that produces it is heteronomous. When art is no more than art, it vanishes. When the content of thought is transparent to itself and when no matter resists it, this success means the end of art. When the artist does what he wants, Hegel states, he reverts to merely affixing to paper or canvas a trademark.

The plot of the so-called 'end of art' is not simply a personal theorisation by Hegel. It clings to the plot of the life of art as 'the spirit of forms'. That spirit is the 'heterogeneous sensible', the identity of art and non-art. The plot has it that when art ceases to be non-art, it is no longer art either. Poetry is poetry, says Hegel, so long as prose is confused with poetry. When prose is only prose, there is no more heterogeneous sensible. The statements and furnishings of collective life are only the statements and furnishings of collective life. So the formula of art becoming life is invalidated: a new life does not need a new art. On the contrary, the specificity of the new life is that it does not need art. The whole history of art forms and of the politics of aesthetics in the aesthetic regime of art could be staged as the clash of these two formulae: a new life needs a new art; the new life does not need art.

Metamorphoses of the curiosity shop
In that perspective the key problem becomes how to reassess the 'heterogeneous sensible'. This concerns not only artists, but the very idea of a new life. The whole affair of the 'fetishism of the commodity' must, I think, be reconsidered from this point of view: Marx needs to prove that the commodity has a secret, that it ciphers a point of heterogeneity in the commerce of everyday life. Revolution is possible because the commodity, like the Juno Ludovisi, has a double nature – it is a work of art that escapes when we try to seize hold of it. The reason is that the plot of the 'end of art' determines a configuration of modernity as a new partition of the perceptible, with no point of heterogeneity. In this partition, rationalisation of the different spheres of activity becomes a response both to the old hierarchical orders and to the 'aesthetic revolution'. The whole motto of the politics of the aesthetic regime, then, can be spelled out as follows: let us save the 'heterogeneous sensible'.

There are two ways of saving it, each involving a specific politics, with its own link between autonomy and heteronomy. The first is the scenario of 'art and life exchanging their properties', proper to what can be called, in a broad sense, Romantic poetics. It is often thought that Romantic poetics involved a sacralisation of art and of the artist, but this is a one-sided view. The principle of 'Romanticism' is rather to be found in a multiplication of the temporalities of art that renders its boundaries permeable. Multiplying its lines of temporality means complicating and ultimately dismissing the straightforward scenarios of art becoming life or life becoming art, of the 'end' of art; and replacing them with scenarios of latency and re-actualisation. This is the burden of Schlegel's idea of 'progressive universal poetry'. It does not mean any straightforward march of progress. On the contrary, 'romanticising' the works of the past means taking them as metamorphic elements, sleeping and awakening, susceptible to different re-actualisations, according to new lines of temporality. The works of the past can be considered as forms for new contents or raw materials for new formations. They can be re-viewed, re-framed, re-read, re-made. It is thus that museums exorcised the rigid plot of the 'spirit of forms' leading to the 'end of arts', and helped to frame new visibilities of art, leading to new practices. Artistic ruptures became possible, too, because the museum offered a multiplication of the temporalities of art, allowing for instance Manet to become a painter of modern life by re-painting Velásquez and Titian.

Now this multi-temporality also means a permeability of the boundaries of art. Being a matter of art turns out to be a kind of metamorphic status. The works of the past may fall asleep and cease to be artworks, they may be awakened and take on a new life in various ways. They make thereby for a continuum of metamorphic forms. According to the same logic, common objects may cross the border and enter the realm of artistic combination. They can do so all the more easily in that the artistic and the historic are now linked together, such that each object can be withdrawn from its condition of common use and viewed as a poetic body wearing the traces of its history. In this way the argument of the 'end of art' can be overturned. In the year that Hegel died, Balzac published his novel *La Peau de chagrin* [The Wild Ass's Skin, 1831]. At the beginning of the novel, the hero Raphael enters the show-rooms of a large curiosity shop where old statues and paintings are mingled with old-fashioned furniture, gadgets and household goods. There, Balzac writes, 'this ocean of furnishings, inventions, works of art and relics made for him an endless poem'. The paraphernalia of the shop is also a medley of objects and ages, of artworks and accessories. Each of these objects is like a fossil, wearing on its body the history of an era or a civilisation. A little further on, Balzac remarks that the great poet of the new age is not a poet as we understand the term: it is not Byron but Cuvier, the naturalist who could reconstitute forests out of petrified traces and races of giants out of scattered bones.

In the show-rooms of Romanticism, the power of the Juno Ludovisi is transferred to any article of ordinary life which can become a poetic object, a fabric of hieroglyphs, ciphering a history. The old curiosity shop makes the museum of fine arts and the ethnographic museum equivalent. It dismisses the argument of prosaic use or commodification. If the end of art is to become a commodity, the end of a commodity is to become art. By becoming obsolete, unavailable for everyday consumption, any commodity or familiar article becomes available for art, as a body ciphering a history and an object of 'disinterested pleasure'. It is re-aestheticised in a new way. The 'heterogeneous sensible' is everywhere. The prose of everyday life becomes a huge, fantastic poem. Any object can cross the border and repopulate the realm of aesthetic experience.

We know what came out of this shop. Forty years later, the power of the Juno Ludovisi would be transferred to the vegetables, the sausages and the merchants of Les Halles by Zola and Claude Lantier, the Impressionist painter he invents, in *Le Ventre de Paris* [The Belly of Paris, 1873]. Then there will be, among many others, the collages of Dada or Surrealism, Pop Art and our current exhibitions of recycled commodities or video clips. The most outstanding metamorphosis of Balzac's repository is, of course, the window of the old-fashioned umbrella shop in the Passage de l'Opéra, in which Aragon recognises a dream of German mermaids. The mermaid of *Le Paysan de Paris* [Paris Peasant, 1926] is the Juno Ludovisi as well, the 'unavailable' goddess promising, through her unavailability, a new sensible world. Benjamin will recognise her in his own way: the arcade of outdated commodities holds the promise of the future. He will only add that the arcade has to be closed, made unavailable, in order that the promise may be kept.

There is thus a dialectic within Romantic poetics of the permeability of art and life. This poetics makes everything available to play the part of the heterogeneous, unavailable sensible. By making what is ordinary extraordinary, it makes what is extraordinary ordinary, too. From this contradiction, it makes a kind of politics - or metapolitics - of its own. That metapolitics is a hermeneutic of signs. 'Prosaic' objects become signs of history, which have to be deciphered. So the poet becomes not only a naturalist or an archaeologist, excavating the fossils and unpacking their poetic potential. He also becomes a kind of symptomatologist, delving into the dark underside or the unconscious of a society to decipher the messages engraved in the very flesh of ordinary things. The new poetics frames a new hermeneutics, taking upon itself the task of making society conscious of its own secrets, by leaving the noisy stage of political claims and doctrines and sinking to the depths of the social, to disclose the enigmas and fantasies hidden in the intimate realities of everyday life. It is in the wake of such a poetics that the commodity could be featured as a phantasmagoria: a thing that looks trivial at first sight, but on a closer look is revealed as a tissue of hieroglyphs and a puzzle of theological quibbles.

Infinite reduplication?

Marx's analysis of the commodity is part of the Romantic plot which denies the 'end of art' as the homogenisation of the sensible world. We could say that the Marxian commodity steps out of the Balzacian shop. That is why the fetishism of the commodity could allow Benjamin to account for the structure of Baudelaire's imagery through the topography of the Parisian arcades and the character of the *flâneur*. For Baudelaire loitered not so much in the arcades themselves as in the plot of the shop as a new sensorium, as a place of exchange between everyday life and the realm of art. The *explicans* and the *explicandum* are part of the same poetical plot. That is why they fit so well; too well, perhaps. Such is more widely the case for the discourse of *Kulturkritik* in its various figures - a discourse which purports to speak the truth about art, about the illusions of aesthetics and their social underpinnings, about the dependency of art upon common culture and commodification. But the very procedures through which it tries to disclose what art and aesthetics truly are were first framed on the aesthetic stage. They are figures of the same poem. The critique of culture can be seen as the epistemological face of Romantic poetics, the rationalisation of its way of exchanging the signs of art and the signs of life. *Kulturkritik* wants to cast on the productions of Romantic poetics the gaze of disenchanted reason. But that disenchantment itself is part of the Romantic re-enchantment that has widened *ad infinitum* the sensorium of art as the field of disused objects encrypting a culture, extending to infinity, too, the realm of fantasies to be deciphered and formatting the procedures of that decryption.

So Romantic poetics resists the entropy of the 'end of art' and its 'de-aestheticisation'. But its own procedures of re-aestheticisation are threatened by another kind of entropy. They are jeopardised by their own success. The danger in this case is not that everything becomes prosaic. It is that everything becomes artistic – that the process of exchange, of crossing the border reaches a point where the border becomes completely blurred, where nothing, however prosaic, escapes the domain of art. This is what happens when art exhibitions present us with mere reduplications of objects of consumption and commercial videos, labelling them as such, on the assumption that these artefacts offer a radical critique of commodification by the very fact that they are the exact reduplication of commodities. This indiscernibility turns out to be the indiscernibility of the critical discourse, doomed either to participate in the labelling or to denounce it *ad infinitum* in the assertion that the sensorium of art and the sensorium of everyday life are nothing more than the eternal reproduction of the 'spectacle' in which domination is both mirrored and denied.

This denunciation in turn soon becomes part of the play. An interesting case of this double discourse is the recent exhibition, first presented in the United States as 'Let's Entertain', then in France as 'Beyond the Spectacle'.[19] The Parisian exhibition played on three levels: first, the Pop anti-high-culture provocation; second, Guy Debord's critique of entertainment as spectacle, meaning the triumph of alienated life; third, the identification of 'entertainment' with the Debordian concept of 'play' as the antidote to 'appearance'. The encounter between free play and free appearance was reduced to a confrontation between a billiard table, a bar-football table and a merry-go-round, and the neo-classical busts of Jeff Koons and his wife.

Entropies of the avant-garde
Such outcomes prompt the second response to the dilemma of the de-aestheticisation of art – the alternative way of reasserting the power of the 'heterogeneous sensible'. This is the exact opposite of the first. It maintains that the dead-end of art lies in the romantic blurring of its borders. It argues the need for a separation of art from the forms of aestheticisation of common life. The claim may be made purely for the sake of art itself, but it may also be made for the sake of the emancipatory power of art. In either case, it is the same basic claim: the sensoria are to be separated. The first manifesto against kitsch, far prior to the existence of the word, can be found in Flaubert's *Madame Bovary* [1856]. The whole plot of the novel is, in fact, one of differentiation between the artist and his character, whose chief crime is to wish to bring art into her life. She who wants to aestheticise her life, who makes art a matter of life, deserves death – literarily speaking. The

---

19   EN: 'Let's Entertain: Life's Guilty Pleasures', Walker Art Center, Minneapolis, 12 February-30 April, 2000, curated by Phillip Vergne. The exhibition travelled to the Musée national d'art moderne, Centre Georges Pompidou under the title 'Sons et lumières' between 15 November-18 December 2000, and to other venues.

cruelty of the novelist will become the rigour of the philosopher when Adorno
lays the same charge against the equivalent of Madame Bovary – Stravinsky, the
musician who thinks that any kind of harmony or disharmony is available and
mixes classical chords and modern dissonances, jazz and primitive rhythms,
for the excitement of his bourgeois audience. There is an extraordinary pathos
in the tone of the passage in *Philosophy of New Music* [1958] where Adorno
states that some chords of nineteenth-century salon music are no longer audible,
unless, he adds, 'everything be trickery'. If those chords are still available, can
still be heard, the political promise of the aesthetic scene is proved a lie, and the
path to emancipation is lost.

Whether the quest is for art alone or for emancipation through art, the
stage is the same. On this stage, art must tear itself away from the territory of
aestheticised life and draw a new borderline, which cannot be crossed. This is a
position that we cannot simply assign to avant-garde insistence on the autonomy
of art. For this autonomy proves to be in fact a double heteronomy. If Madame
Bovary has to die, Flaubert has to disappear. First he has to make the sensorium
of literature akin to the sensorium of those things that do not feel: pebbles, shells
or grains of dust. To do this, he has to make his prose indistinguishable from that
of his characters, the prose of everyday life. In the same way the autonomy of
Schoenberg's music, as conceptualised by Adorno, is a double heteronomy: in
order to denounce the capitalist division of labour and the adornments of commodification, it has to take that division of labour yet further, to be still more
technical, more 'inhuman' than the products of capitalist mass production. But
this inhumanity, in turn, makes the blotch of what has been repressed appear
and disrupt the perfect technical arrangement of the work. The 'autonomy' of
the avant-garde work of art becomes the tension between two heteronomies,
between the bonds that tie Ulysses to his mast and the song of the sirens against
which he stops his ears.

We can also give to these two positions the names of a pair of Greek divinities, Apollo and Dionysus. Their opposition is not simply a construct of the
philosophy of the young Nietzsche. It is the dialectic of the 'spirit of forms' in
general. The aesthetic identification of consciousness and unconsciousness,
logos and *pathos*, can be interpreted in two ways. Either the spirit of forms is
the *logos* that weaves its way through its own opacity and the resistance of the
materials, in order to become the smile of the statue or the light of the canvas
– this is the Apollonian plot – or it is identified with a *pathos* that disrupts the
forms of *doxa*, and makes art the inscription of a power that is chaos, radical
alterity. Art inscribes on the surface of the work the immanence of *pathos* in the
logos, of the unthinkable in thought. This is the Dionysian plot. Both are plots
of heteronomy. Even the perfection of the Greek statue in Hegel's *Aesthetics* is
the form of an inadequacy. The same holds all the more for Schoenberg's perfect construction. In order that 'avant-garde' art stay faithful to the promise of
the aesthetic scene it has to stress more and more the power of heteronomy that
underpins its autonomy.

Defeat of the imagination?

This inner necessity leads to another kind of entropy, which makes the task of
autonomous avant-garde art akin to that of giving witness to sheer heteronomy.

This entropy is perfectly exemplified by the 'aesthetics of the sublime' of Jean-François Lyotard. At first sight this is a radicalisation of the dialectic of avant-garde art which twists into a reversal of its logic. The avant-garde must indefinitely draw the dividing-line that separates art from commodity culture, inscribe interminably the link of art to the 'heterogeneous sensible'. But it must do so in order to invalidate indefinitely the 'trickery' of the aesthetic promise itself, to denounce both the promises of revolutionary avant-gardism and the entropy of commodity aestheticisation. The avant-garde is endowed with the paradoxical duty of bearing witness to an immemorial dependency of human thought that makes any promise of emancipation a deception.

This demonstration takes the shape of a radical re-reading of Kant's *Critique of [the Power of] Judgement*, of a reframing of the aesthetic sensorium which stands as an implicit refutation of Schiller's vision, a kind of counter-originary scene. The whole 'duty' of modern art is deduced by Lyotard from the Kantian analysis of the sublime as a radical experience of disagreement, in which the synthetic power of imagination is defeated by the experience of an infinite, which sets up a gap between the sensible and the supersensible. In Lyotard's analysis this defines the space of modern art as the manifestation of the unrepresentable, of the 'loss of a steady relation between the sensible and the intelligible'. It is a paradoxical assertion: firstly, because the sublime in Kant's account does not define the space of art, but marks the transition from aesthetic to ethical experience; and secondly, because the experience of disharmony between Reason and Imagination tends towards the discovery of a higher harmony – the self-perception of the subject as a member of the supersensible world of Reason and Freedom.

Lyotard wants to oppose the Kantian gap of the sublime to Hegelian aestheticisation. But he has to borrow from Hegel his concept of the sublime, as the impossibility of an adequation between thought and its sensible presentation. He has to borrow from the plot of the 'spirit of forms' the principle of a counter-construction of the originary scene, to allow for a counter-reading of the plot of the 'life of forms'. Of course this confusion is not a casual misreading. It is a way of blocking the originary path from aesthetics to politics, of imposing at the same crossroad a one-way detour leading from aesthetics to ethics. In this fashion the opposition of the aesthetic regime of art to the representational regime can be ascribed to the sheer opposition of the art of the unrepresentable to the art of representation. 'Modern' works of art then have to become ethical witnesses to the unrepresentable. Strictly speaking, however, it is in the representational regime that you can find unrepresentable subject matters, meaning those for which form and matter cannot be fitted together in any way. The 'loss of a steady relation' between the sensible and the intelligible is not the loss of the power of relating, it is the multiplication of its forms. In the aesthetic regime of art nothing is 'unrepresentable'.

Much has been written to the effect that the Holocaust is unrepresentable, that it allows only for witness and not for art. But the claim is refuted by the work of the witnesses. For example, the paratactic writing of Primo Levi or Robert Antelme has been taken as the sheer mode of testimony befitting the experience of Nazi de-humanisation. But this paratactic style, made up of a concatenation of little perceptions and sensations, was one of the major features of the literary revolution of the nineteenth century. The short notations at the beginning of Antelme's book *L'Espèce humaine* [The Human Race, 1947], describing the latrines and setting the scene of the camp at Buchenwald, answer to the same pattern as the description of Emma Bovary's farmyard. Similarly, Claude Lanzmann's film *Shoah* [1985] has been seen as bearing witness to the unrepresentable. But what Lanzmann counterposes to the representational plot of the US television series *The Holocaust* [1978] is another cinematographic plot – the narrative of a present inquiry reconstructing an enigmatic or an erased past, which can be traced back to Orson Welles's Rosebud in *Citizen Kane* [1941]. The argument of the 'unrepresentable' does not fit the experience of artistic practice. Rather, it fulfils the desire that there be something unrepresentable, something unavailable, in order to inscribe in the practice of art the necessity of the ethical detour. The ethics of the unrepresentable might still be an inverted form of the aesthetic promise.

In sketching out these entropic scenarios of the politics of aesthetics, I may seem to propose a pessimistic view of things. That is not at all my purpose. Undeniably, a certain melancholy about the destiny of art and of its political commitments is expressed in many ways today, especially in my country, France. The air is thick with declarations about the end of art, the end of the image, the reign of communications and advertisements, the impossibility of art after Auschwitz, nostalgia for the lost paradise of incarnate presence, indictment of aesthetic utopias for spawning totalitarianism or commodification. My purpose has not been to join this mourning choir. On the contrary I think that we can distance ourselves from this current mood if we understand that the 'end of art' is not a mischievous destiny of 'modernity', but the reverse side of the life of art. To the extent that the aesthetic formula ties art to non-art from the start, it sets up that life between two vanishing points: art becoming mere life or art becoming mere art. I said that 'pushed to the extreme', each of these scenarios entailed its own entropy, its own end of art. But the life of art in the aesthetic regime of art consists precisely of a shuttling between these scenarios, playing an autonomy against a heteronomy and a heteronomy against an autonomy, playing one linkage between art and non-art against another such linkage.

Each of these scenarios involves a certain metapolitics: art refuting the hierarchical divisions of the perceptible and framing a common sensorium; or art replacing politics as a configuration of the sensible world; or art becoming a kind of social hermeneutics; or even art becoming, in its very isolation, the guardian of the promise of emancipation. Each of these positions may be held and has been held. This means that there is a certain undecidability in the 'politics of aesthetics'. There is a metapolitics of aesthetics which frames the possibilities of art. Aesthetic art promises a political accomplishment that it cannot satisfy, and thrives on that ambiguity. That is why those who want to isolate it from politics are somewhat beside the point. It is also why those who want it to fulfil its political promise are condemned to a certain melancholy.

In situating various modernist or avant-garde positions as options within the aesthetic regime, Rancière runs the risk of painting a panorama in which all options are equal, and cancel each other out. The 'regime' becomes more of a closed system than a historical formation in which, at different times, option A, B or Z may hold more potential than at others. And if those who want art to fulfil its political promise are 'condemned to a certain melancholy', then why would anybody ever do anything else than paint still-lives? In fact, Rancière at times suggests that 'political art' is not so much one option among others as it is a uniquely problematic one: whilst the true 'aesthetics of politics' lies in the 're-configuration of the common through political processes of subjectivation' and a genuine 'politics of aesthetics' resides in 'the practices and modes of visibility of art that re-configure the fabric of sensory experience', the 'political art' that Rancière critiques remains stuck in representation and mimesis.[68] This is an art that illustrates political points and does little else.

While Rancière here paints with a broad brush, and appears to discredit art that makes a concrete political intervention, it is true that there is no easy synthesis or identity between artistic and activist practice. Rather, there is a stubborn historical contradiction; we might say that this contradiction, this dialectic, helps to constitute the aesthetic itself. The aesthetic derives whatever autonomy it has from its active engagement with heteronomous entanglement. It is a realm of activity that actively courts impurity and antinomy – and herein lies part of its specificity. Aesthetic practice is always both less and more than either art or politics. 'Aesthetic art' is aesthetic to the extent that it questions and challenges its autonomy. As Adorno – who was no fan of 'activist' art – put it:

> The tendency to perceive art either in extra-aesthetic or preaesthetic fashion, which to this day is undiminished by an obviously failed education, is not only a barbaric residue or a danger of regressive consciousness. Something in art calls for this response. Art perceived strictly aesthetically is art aesthetically misperceived. Only when art's other is sensed as a primary layer in the experience of art does it become possible to sublimate this layer, to dissolve the thematic bonds, without the autonomy of the artwork becoming a matter of indifference. Art is autonomous and it is not; without what is heterogeneous to it, its autonomy eludes it.[69]

Those moments when art is defined in terms of either 'pure art' or a kind of activism completely ruled by political objectives constitute an aesthetic failure. In so far as the artwork is aesthetic, it is a conflict. It is not self-identical, secure in its autonomy. It is an assemblage – an assemblage of faultlines and rifts. Work with the constitutive contradictions of the aesthetic in fact characterises a lot of the more interesting contemporary activity.

In 2010, Gulf Labor – a coalition of artists, academics, curators and other cultural workers – began protesting against the labour conditions of construction workers on Saadiyat Island, beside Abu Dhabi in the United Arab Emirates, where yet another Guggenheim Museum is, at the time of this volume's publication, in development. If Napoleon brought art from all over Europe to his imperial capital, today's mega-museums are themselves mobile, sprouting branches everywhere. Even if these protests do not lead to any 'results' in the sense of a policy change at the Guggenheim, the project itself is a result. It actively engages in the dialectic of autonomies, of a relative artistic autonomy built on invisible exploitation and a precarious political autonomy of artists – not as disembodied subjects channelling some Kantian will, but as embodied, social subjects.

Some may be more entitled to speak and act than others: historically, only a small subset of well-educated white men were deemed capable of aesthetic creation and aesthetic judgement, and historical forms of inequity don't tend to disappear overnight. The 'emplotments' of art and autonomy were always gendered and racialised – something which Rancière rarely reflects upon. It is feminist, queer and decolonial theory that have challenged the implicit (and, at times, explicit) hierarchies of the aesthetic regime. In a text from the year 2000, Amelia Jones notes that 'Kant's model of aesthetic judgement relies explicitly on the capacity of the beautiful object to inspire pure taste and elevated pleasure in the viewer', while it also 'requires that this viewer maintain his integrity by claiming to be disinterested' – and that these objects have often been women, i.e. idealised white female nudes. For Jones, the 'aesthetic is precisely the conceptual structure that enabled the traffic in images/in women called the art market, which itself has traditionally supported the vast and intricate system of privilege that might be reduced to the dualistic circuit that opposes the artist [bound by identification to the viewer and, as we shall see, to 'God'] to the objects of exchange (women, paintings, slaves).'[70]

Is the whole concept of aesthetics, as developed in the eighteenth century, not a colonial construct imposing Eurocentric canons and conventions; should it be replaced by a 'decolonial aesthesis' that leaves Kant to rot (or roll) in his grave?[71] Such a proposition is a curious return of modernist 'tabula rasa' rhetoric in the age of memefied cultural theory. For better or worse, the historical record is more complex. While there is no lack of evidence for modern art and theory's implication in capitalist, colonialist or patriarchal structures, in this reader we want to focus precisely on those forms of aesthetic practice and theory that constitute more critical 'emplotments', however imperfect and incomplete. It would be a miracle if even the most radical aesthetic practices would manage to magic away their constitutive contradictions, to square the circle and arrive at some ultimate synthesis of the artistic and the political whilst remaining free from any kind of problematic entanglement. Who in their right mind would expect such practices to pull off this feat? At their best, then as now, they engage with their own constituent contradictions as so much material to work with, and work through.

Notes

1   Quatremère de Quincy, *Lettres à Miranda – Sur le déplacement des monuments de l'art de l'Italie* (1796), Paris: Macula, 1989.

2   On this painting and its counterpart (further discussed in this book's Coda), see *Hubert Robert 1733-1808. Un peintre visionnaire* (exh. cat.), Paris: Musée du Louvre and Somogy, 2016, pp.436-41.

3   Raymond Williams, *Keywords: A Vocabulary of Culture and Society* (1976), rev. ed., New York: Oxford University Press, 1983, p.41. Emphasis in original. Abbreviated terms in original appear here in full.

4   On the Renaissance, see Michael Müller (ed.), *Autonomie der Kunst. Zur Genese und Kritik einer bürgerlichen Kategorie*, Frankfurt: Suhrkamp Verlag, 1972. On reflexivity in sixteenth- and seventeenth-century Northern painting as an indicator of autonomisation, see also Victor I. Stoichita, *The Self-Aware Image: An Insight into Early Modern Meta-Painting* (trans. Anne-Marie Glasheen), Cambridge: Cambridge University Press, 1996.

5   On the emergence of the public exhibition in the eighteenth century, see Oskar Bätschmann, *The Artist in the Modern World: The Conflict Between Market and Self-Expression*, Cologne: DuMont, 1998. Se also Larry Shiner, *The Invention of Art: A Cultural History*, Chicago: University of Chicago Press, 2001.

6   Tery Eagleton, *The Ideology of the Aesthetic*, Oxford: Blackwell, 1990, p.2.

7   *Ibid.*, pp.8-9.

8   For a number of years, English-language editions of this text mistranslated Kant's title *Kritik der Urteilskraft* as *Critique of Judgement*, thereby ignoring that *Urteilskraft* is a compound word combining 'power of' (*kraft*) and 'judgement' (*Urteil*).

9   Immanuel Kant, *Critique of the Power of Judgement* (trans. Paul Guyer and Eric Matthews), Cambridge: Cambridge University Press, 2000, p.163. In the phrase 'Taste makes claim merely to autonomy', the word 'merely' (*bloß*) was added by Kant in the second, partially revised edition.

10   See Part Six of this reader, pp.355-413.

11   Peter Osborne, 'Theorem 4. Autonomy: Can It Be True of Art and Politics at the Same Time?', *The Postconceptual Condition: Critical Essays*, London: Verso, 2018, pp.61-72; selections from this essay are reprinted in Part Four of this reader, pp.221-23.

12   I. Kant, *Critique of the Power of Judgment*, op. cit., p.224.

13   Joseph Leo Koerner, *Caspar David Friedrich and the Subject of Landscape*, rev. ed., London: Reaktion, 2009, pp.56-82.

14   Novalis, *Philosophical Writings* (trans. and ed. Margaret Mahony Stoljar), Albany, NY: SUNY Press,1997, pp.36, 60.

15   Friedrich Schlegel, *Friedrich Schlegel's Lucinde and the Fragments* (trans. Peter Firchow), Minneapolis: University of Minnesota Press, 1971, pp.175-76, fragment 116.

16   This single-page manuscript appears to be in Hegel's handwriting. It surfaced in 1913 and was published in 1917 by Franz Rosenzweig under the title 'Das älteste Systemprogramm des deutschen Idealismus' (The Oldest Systematic Programme of German Idealism).

17   Johann Wolfgang von Goethe, letter to Sulpiz Boisserée, 14 Feb 1814; cited in James Garratt, 'Mendelssohn and the rise of musical historicism', in *The Cambridge Companion to Mendelssohn*, Cambridge: Cambridge University Press, 2004, p.58.

18   See Karl Philipp Moritz, 'Über den Begriff des in sich selbst Vollendeten', in *Karl Philipp Moritz Werke. Reisen, Schriften zur Kunst und Mythologie* (ed. Horst Günther), vol.2, Frankfurt: Insel, 1993, pp.543-48.

19   See Part Two of this reader, pp.101-65.

20   See the publications listed in footnote 4.

21   Heinrich Heine, 'Sixth Letter on The French Stage' (1831), in *The Works of Heinrich Heine* (trans. Charles Godfrey Leland), vol.4, *The Salon, or Letters on Art, Music, Popular Life and Politics*, London: William Heinemann, 1893, pp.205-06.

22   The statement about communists and the future is from the preface to the French-language edition of *Lutetia* (1855). An English-language translation can be found in Jost Hermand and Robert C. Holub (ed.), *The Romantic School and Other Essays* (trans. Gilbert Cannan and R.C. Holub), New York: Continuum, 1985, p.299.

23   Letter to Karl Gutzkow (trans. Gilbert Cannan), 23 August 1838, in *Heinrich Heine's Memoirs: From His Works, Letters, and Conversations* (ed. Gustav Karpeles), vol 2, London: William Heineman, 1910, p.73. Translation amended from the German by Sven Lütticken.

24   Robert Eduard Prutz, *Der Göttinger Dichterbund. Zur Geschichte der Deutschen Literatur*, Leipzig: Otto Wiegand, 1841, p.58. Translated from the German by Helen Ferguson.

25   *Ibid.*, p.70.

26   *Ibid.*, p.405.

27   *Ibid.*, pp.309-10.

28   *Ibid.*, p.406.

29   *Ibid.*, pp.138-39.

30   R.E. Prutz, *Geschichte des deutschen Journalismus*, Hannover: Rius, 1845, p.68. Translated from the German by Helen Ferguson. On Lessing, see Part Five of this reader, pp.292-93.

31   *Ibid.*, p.71.

32   *Ibid.*

33   *Ibid.*, p.72.

34   See August von Cieszkowski, *Prolegomena zur Historiosophie*, Berlin: Veit und Comp, 1838.

35   Théophile Gautier, 'Charles Baudelaire' (1862), *Baudelaire: Un demi-siècle de lectures des Fleurs du mal (1855-1905)* (ed. André Guyaux), Paris: Presses Sorbonne Université, 2007, p.353. Translated from the French by Catherine Petit and Paul Buck.

36   Théophile Gautier, *Charles Baudelaire: His Life* (1868; trans. Guy Thorne), New York: Brentano's, 1915, pp.25-27.

37   Olinde Rodrigues, cited in Matei Calinescu, *Five Faces of Modernity: Modernism, Avant-Garde, Decadence, Kitsch, Postmodernism*, Durham, NC: Duke University Press, 1987, p.102.

38   See Jacques Rancière, *The Politics of Aesthetics: The Distribution of the Sensible* (trans. Gabriel Rockhill), London and New York: Continuum, 2004.

39   Karl Marx and Friedrich Engels, 'The German Ideology', *Collected Works of Marx and Engels*, vol.5, 1845-47, London: Lawrence & Wishart, 1991, p.47.

40   K. Marx, 'Theses on Feuerbach' (1845), in *ibid.*, p.6. Although commentators often recognise the centrality of the theses and Marx's early engagement with Feuerbach for the development of historical materialism, the eleven notes contained therein are comprised of notes collected and posthumously published by Engels in 1888, five years after Marx's death.

41   K. Marx and F. Engels, 'The German Ideology', *op. cit.*, p.45. As with the 'Theses on Feuerbach', it was not until much after this early manuscript was written, in 1846, that it successfully made it to publication. While various editions had been published by that point, it was not until 1932, following the editorial efforts of David Ryazanov, Vladimir Viktorovich Adoratskii and the Marx-Engels Institute in Moscow, that the first complete edition of 'The German Ideology' was printed. Further, the history of this document's preparation is somewhat fraught. For instance, in 1931 the Marx-Engels Institute itself was subject to political intervention when Ryazanov, its director, was arrested for engaging in counterrevolutionary activities, and the Stalin-backed Adoratskii was placed at the helm. Questions have been raised regarding the different political and authorial influences on the early complete editions of the text. For extensive commentary on this history and a critical account of various influences on the text, see Terrell Carver and Daniel Blank, *A Political History of the Editions of Marx and Engels's 'German Ideology Manuscripts'*, New York: Palgrave Macmillan, 2014.

42   Karl Marx, *A Contribution to the Critique of Political Economy* (trans. S.W. Ryazanskaya), London: Lawrence & Wishart, 1981, pp.20-21.

43   On Marx's literary tastes, see S.S. Prawer, *Karl Marx and World Literature* (1976), London: Verso, 2011.

44   T.J. Clark, *Image of the People: Gustave Courbet and the 1848 Revolution*, London: Thames & Hudson, 1973, p.155.

45   *Ibid.*, p.32.

46   T.J. Clark, Christopher Gray, Donald Nicholson-Smith and Charles Radcliffe, 'The Revolution of Modern Art and the Modern Art of Revolution' (1967), available at http://www.cddc.vt.edu/sionline/si/modernart.html (last accessed on 19 September 2020).

47   Joan Ungersma Halperin, *Félix Fénéon: Aesthete and Anarchist in Fin-de-Siècle Paris*, New Haven, CT: Yale University Press, 1988, pp.267-95. If Ungersma Halperin makes a convincing case for Fénéon's 'authorship' on the basis of circumstantial evidence and, at times, of hearsay, a recent Parisian exhibition and catalogue ('Félix Fénéon: Anarchiste, critique d'art, éditeur, collectionneur', Musée d'Orsay, Musée du quai Branly - Jacques Chirac and Musée de l'Orangerie, 28 May-29 September 2019) sidestepped the question by focussing on Fénéon's virtuoso performance in court and subsequent acquittal.

48   Wieland Herzfelde, letter to Paul Mattick, 19 August 1935, cited in Gary Roth, *Marxism in a Lost Century: A Biography of Paul Mattick*, Chicago: Maymarket Books, 2015, p.157.

49   See Part Five of this reader, pp.289-352.

50   Erich Wichman, dedication of lithograph portfolio *Idealisten II* (1923). Translated from the Dutch by Sven Lütticken.

51   For an excellent recent study of French and German art history, see Éric Michaux, *Les invasions barbares. Une généaologie de l'histoire de l'art*, Paris: Gallimard, 2015.

52   Ezra Pound, 'England,' radio speech no.16, 15 March 1942, in Leonard W. Doob (ed.), *'Ezra Pound Speaking': Radio Speeches of World War II*, Westport, CT: Greenwood Press, 1978, pp.59-60.

53   See Frances Stonor Saunders, *The Cultural Cold War: The CIA and the World of Arts and Letters*, New York: The New Press, 2000; on Pound and the Bollingen Prize, see pp.249-51.

54   Guy Debord, 'The Situationists and New Forms of Action in Politics and Art', available at http://www.cddc.vt.edu/sionline/si/newforms.html (last accessed on 19 September 2020). Translated from the French by Kenn Knabb.

55   Guy Debord, 'In girum imus nocte et consumimur igi' (1978), available at http://www.bopsecrets.org/SI/debord.films/ingirum.htm (last accessed on 19 September 2020). Transled from the French by Kenn Knabb.

56   See Part Four of this reader, pp.217-57.

57   Cornelius Castoriadis, *The Imaginary Institution of Society* (trans. Kathleen Blamey), Cambridge: Polity Press, 2005, pp.107-08.

58   See Asad Haider and Salar Mohandes, 'Deviations, part 1: the Castoriadis-Pannekoek exchange', *Libcom.org*, 2013, available at https://libcom.org/library/deviations-part-1-castoriadis-pannekoek-exchange (last accessed on 19 September 2020).

59   Telegram from Occupation Committee of the People's Free Sorbonne University to the Politburo of the USSR, 17 May 1968 (trans. Kenn Knabb), available at http://www.cddc.vt.edu/sionline/si/telegrams.html (last accessed on 19 September 2020).

60   T.J. Clark, *Picasso and Truth*, Princeton, NJ: Princeton University Press, 2013, p.19.

61   Gretel Adorno and Rolf Tiedemann, 'Editors' Afterword', in Theodor W. Adorno, *Aesthetic Theory* (1970; trans. Robert Hullot-Kentor, ed. G. Adorno and R. Tiedemann), London: Althone Press, 1997, p.366. As the editors note, the following quote from Friedrich Schlegel's *Critical Fragments* was intended to also act as the book's motto: 'What is called the philosophy of art usually lacks one of two things: either the philosophy or the art.'

62   *Ibid.*, p.5.

63   Peter Osborne, 'Temporalization as Transcendental Aesthetics: Avant-Garde, Modern, Contemporary,' in *Nordic Journal of Aesthetics*, no.44-45 (2012-13), p.37.

64   Hal Foster, *The Return of the Real*, Cambridge, MA: MIT Press, 1996, pp.15-16.

65   See Part Three of this reader, pp.167-215.

66   *Ibid.*, p.20. Emphasis removed.

67   *Ibid.*, p.21. Note removed.

68   Jacques Rancière, *Dissensus: On Politics and Aesthetics*, trans. and ed. Steven Corcoran, London: Continuum, 2010, p.148.

69   T.W. Adorno, *Aesthetic Theory, op. cit.*, p.6.

70   Amelia Jones, '"Every Man Knows Where and How Beauty Gives Him Pleasure": Beauty Discourse and the Logic of Aesthetics', in *X-TRA*, vol. 2, no. 2 (Spring 2000), available at https://www.x-traonline.org/article/beauty-discourse-and-the-logic-of-aesthetics (last accessed on 19 September 2020).

71   See Walter Mignolo and Rolando Vazquez, 'Decolonial AestheSis: Colonial Wounds/Decolonial Healings', in *Social Text* online, 15 July 2013, available at https://socialtextjournal.org/periscope_article/decolonial-aesthesis-colonial-woundsdecolonial-healings/ (last accessed on 19 September 2020).

PART TWO:
USEFUL ART

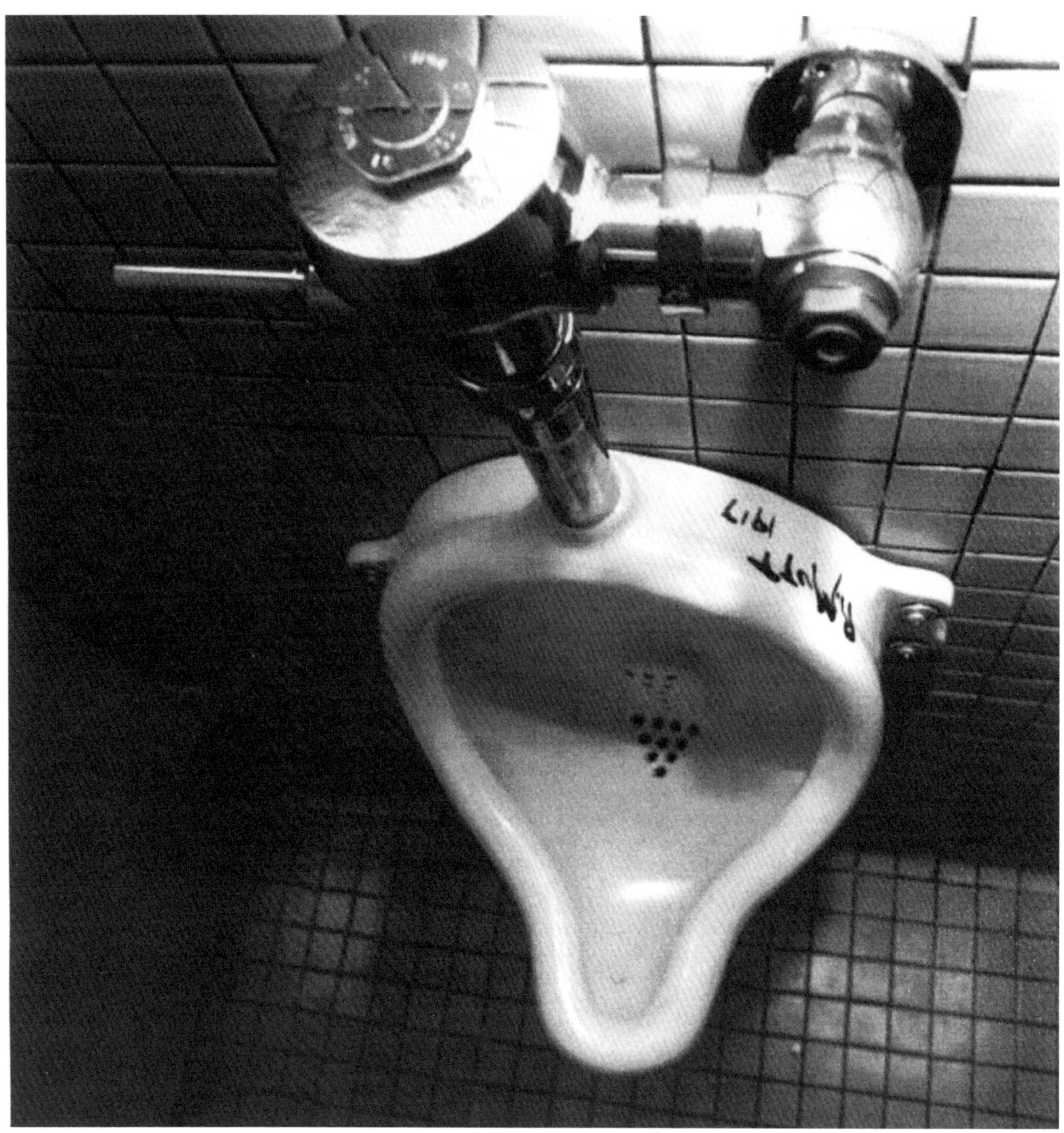

Urinal at Queens Museum of Art,
New York, as part of Arte Útil project,
begun 2013
Courtesy Studio Bruguera

If the avant-garde dreamed of a 'reconciliation of art and life', the latter term was made to stand in for everything excluded from the rarefied sphere of art – everything and the kitchen sink. In fact, a lowly object such as a kitchen sink would seem to stand for non-artistic and extra-aesthetic life par excellence. It is not by chance that his defence of *l'art pour l'art* in the preface to *Mademoiselle de Maupin* (1835), Théophile Gautier singled out an even lowlier item of plumbing:

> There is nothing truly beautiful but that which can never be of any use whatso-ever; everything useful is ugly, for it is the expression of some need, and man's needs are ignoble and disgusting like his own poor and infirm nature. The most useful place in a house is the water-closet.[1]

In his 2007 book *De la beauté des latrines* (On the Beauty of Latrines), the film theorist and filmmaker Noël Burch discusses this passage as a foundational modernist gesture.[2] In Burch's feminist and Marxist reading, Gautier's refusal of utility and ugliness (which become coterminous) is elitist in that it seeks to protect a sphere of rarefied and purified aesthetic experience, but it is also gendered, as it is women who are most identified with the domestic sphere, reproductive labour and bodily functions.

From Gautier to the present, the spectre of usefulness has haunted art and aesthetic theory – as has its twin ghost, the spectre of uselessness. Various proponents of aestheticism and modernism felt that if art was to be autonomous, it had to guard itself against a relapse into a heteronomy that was often identified with utility; on the other hand, critics of aestheticism and modernism attempted to combat the social uselessness of 'autonomous' art *and* its all too real uses as a manifestation of bourgeois ideology by making art directly 'productive'. In today's hyper-speculative art world, such critiques return with a vengeance.

Again focussing on plumbing, in the context of her Arte Útil project artist Tania Bruguera has stated that Marcel Duchamp's *Fountain* (1917) should be put back in the bathroom.[3] The artistic fetish should become functional and useful – this is what Bruguera's polemical proposal aims to drive home, and the rather ambiguous sexual connotations of Duchamp's tilted urinal, with its play on male and female anatomical features, seem of secondary importance in this context. In order to assess how such a contemporary stance on 'useful art' derives from and differs from its precedents, we once again need to create a genealogy of intersecting and sometimes conflicting historical strands.

Labour and Value(s)

It is hardly surprising that the most industrialised country of the mid-nineteenth century, Britain, would be at the forefront of that period's debates about aesthetic labour as a refuge from industrial alienation. The increasing industrialisation of all forms of production, from the mechanisation of farming techniques to the mass production of cloth for global export, brought a concomitant set of concerns over the future of craft, skill and quality. In this situation, the aesthetic came to be understood as a bridge between freedom and necessity, as a kind of experience that promised the synthesis of sensuous plenitude and political liberty, in a world that was yet to be. In the process, the artwork and the work of making art began to be imbued with a special sense of value – as offering a sanctuary for necessary and essentialist forms of useful labour within increasingly alienated forms of production.

These debates tended to look back at romanticised historical precedents – usually the Middle Ages – before the introduction of alienated and mechanical forms of labour; the work of aesthetic reformers such as John Ruskin and William Morris often had such medievalising traits. It was also in Britain that Karl Marx – financially supported by his friend Friedrich Engels, who managed a textile factory in Manchester – developed his mature work, the foremost of which is the first volume of *Capital: A Critique of Political Economy* (1867). Marx's analysis begins by distinguishing between a commodity's qualitative use-value and a quantitative, instrumentalised and alienating exchange-value. In turn, Marx's economic analysis would have profound effects on attempts to reform or revolutionise art in order to prevent it from being reduced to the status of high-end commodities for a wealthy elite.

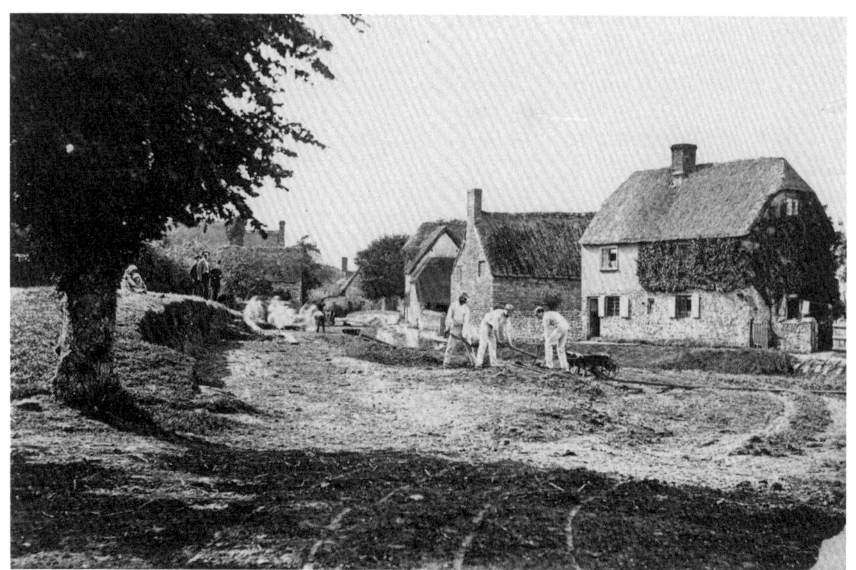

This page and opposite: Henry W. Taunt, Untitled (labourers working on the Ruskin Road, North Hinksey Oxfordshire), 1874
Courtesy Oxfordshire County Council – Oxfordshire History Centre

Following spread: Joseph Nash, *Amateur navvies at Oxford, Undergraduates making a road as suggested by Mr Ruskin*, 1874
illustration for *The Graphic*, 27 June 1984
Courtesy and © akg-images

Ruskin was highly visible as an author, lecturer and organiser. His publications and activities, which span the Victorian era, can give us some guidance for reading later debates in which the aesthetic, moral, ethical and political functions of art were discussed and pitted against the growing antinomies of use-value and exchange-value. During the early part of his career, Ruskin tended towards a reading of art that drew largely upon his unique descriptive powers (aligned with his own ability as a draughtsman) and provided a critical aid to an extended readership that also wished to develop its own enjoyment of painting, sculpture and architecture. This Ruskin is still known as a champion of J.M.W. Turner's work. However, his lectures on art from 1870 mark a decisive shift in his thinking; he began to insist on the embedded social role and function of art, and to distinguish good art from bad in terms of its ability to satisfy public and civic need through education and use.

What unites both of Ruskin's perspectives, and often obfuscates the fundamental differences between his 'early' and 'late' outlooks, is his suspicion of industry, technology and mass-produced culture. This rejection of industry and technology was widely shared in the period. In Germany, Richard Wagner invoked the German medieval past and lambasted the modern age and its nascent culture industry, even while using the latest technologies, such as electrical light, in the staging of his operas.[4] Wagner started out as a Romantic Socialist, fighting alongside Mikhail Bakunin on the barricades during the 1849 May Uprising in Dresden, but his romanticisation of the pre-industrial had reactionary (and anti-Semitic) traits that became ever more pronounced as time went by. Ruskin, meanwhile, called for moral and ethical progress while insisting upon more conservative forms of tradition and heritage (he described himself as being both a socialist and a Tory).

Ruskin's insistence in his 1870 lectures that no nation can be a good nation if it does not first provide for its poor, and that the strength of its School of Art depends upon this provision, follows from an equal insistence that art is to be practiced as a means to re-examine a world in which the harsh realities of industrialised labour have become manifest and manifold.

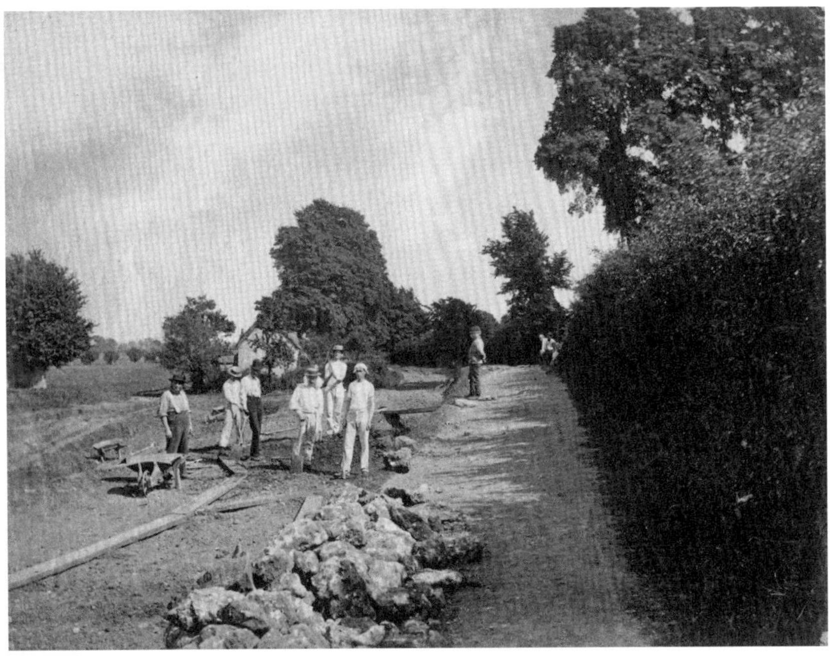

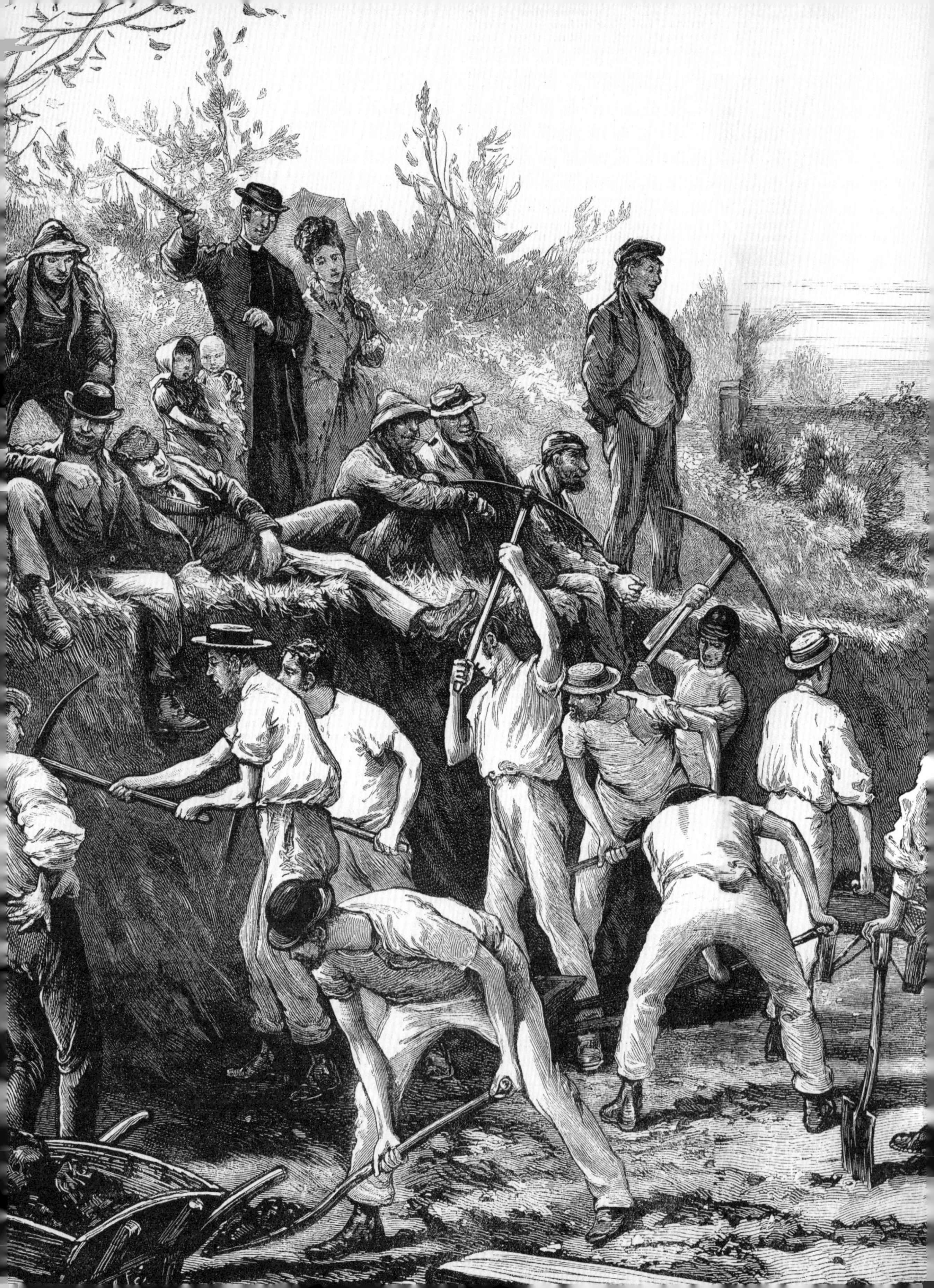

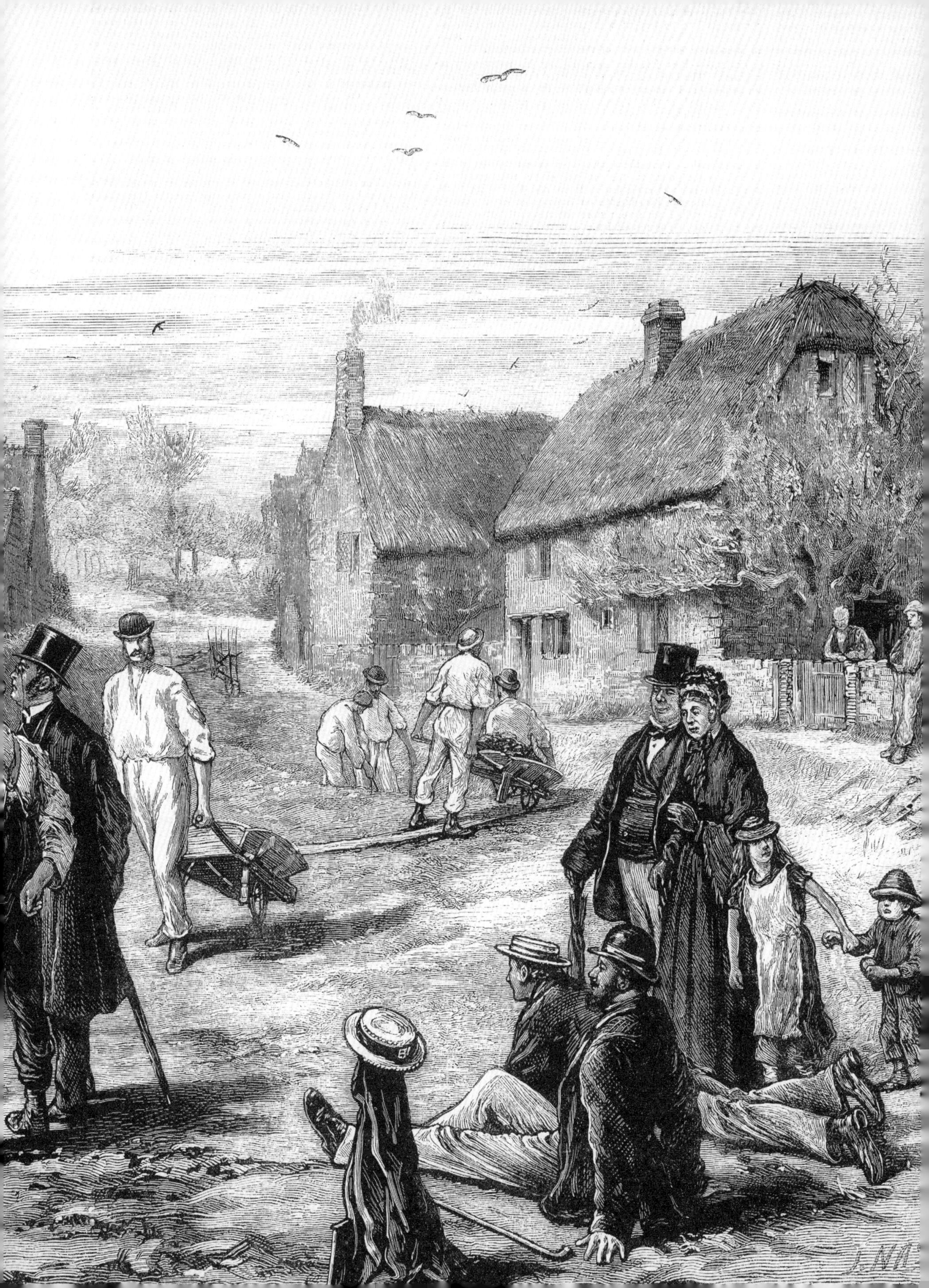

JOHN RUSKIN, 'LECTURE IV: THE RELATION OF ART TO USE'

Reprinted from '"Lectures on Art" (Inaugural
Course Delivered at Oxford in Hilary Term, 1870)',
The Works of John Ruskin, Library Edition (ed.
Edward Tyas Cook and Alexander Wedderburn),
vol.20, London: George Allen, 1905, pp.95-97,
100-10, 114-15.

97. Our subject of enquiry today, you will remember, is the mode in which fine art is founded upon, or may contribute to, the practical requirements of human life.

Its offices in this respect are mainly twofold: it gives Form to knowledge, and Grace to utility; that is to say, it makes permanently visible to us things which otherwise could neither be described by our science, nor retained by our memory; and it gives delightfulness and worth to the implements of daily use, and materials of dress, furniture and lodging. In the first of these offices it gives precision and charm to truth; in the second it gives precision and charm to service. For, the moment we make anything useful thoroughly, it is a law of nature that we shall be pleased with ourselves, and with the thing we have made; and become desirous therefore to adorn or complete it, in some dainty way, with finer art expressive of our pleasure.

And the point I wish chiefly to bring before you today is this close and healthy connection of the fine arts with material use; but I must first try briefly to put in clear light the function of art in giving Form to truth.

98. Much that I have hitherto tried to teach has been disputed on the ground that I have attached too much importance to art as representing natural facts, and too little to it as a source of pleasure. And I wish, in the close of these four prefatory lectures, strongly to assert to you, and, so far as I can in the time, convince you, that the entire vitality of art depends upon its being either full of truth, or full of use; and that, however pleasant, wonderful or impressive it may be in itself, it must yet be of inferior kind, and tend to deeper inferiority, unless it has clearly one of these main objects, either *to state a true thing*, or to *adorn a serviceable one.* It must never exist alone - never for itself; it exists rightly only when it is the means of knowledge, or the grace of agency for life.

99. Now, I pray you to observe - for though I have said this often before, I have never yet said it clearly enough - every good piece of art, to whichever of these ends it may be directed, involves first essentially the evidence of human skill and the formation of an actually beautiful thing by it.

Skill, and beauty, always then; and, beyond these, the formative arts have always one or other of the two objects which I have just defined to you - truth, or serviceableness; and without these aims neither the skill nor their beauty will avail; only by these can either legitimately reign. All the graphic arts begin in keeping the outline of shadow that we have loved, and they end in giving to it the aspect of life; and all the architectural arts begin in the shaping of the cup and the platter, and they end in a glorified roof.

Therefore, you see, in the graphic arts you have Skill, Beauty and Likeness; and in the architectural arts, Skill, Beauty and Use; and you *must* have the three. in each group, balanced and co-ordinate; and all the chief errors of art consist in losing or exaggerating one of these elements.

100. For instance, almost the whole system and hope of modern life are founded on the notion that you may substitute mechanism for skill, photograph for picture, cast iron for sculpture. That is your main nineteenth-century faith, or infidelity. You think you can get everything by grinding – music, literature and painting. You will find it grievously not so; you can get nothing but dust by mere grinding. Even to have the barley-meal out of it, you must have the barley first; and that comes by growth, not grinding. But essentially, we have lost our delight in Skill; in that majesty of it which I was trying to make clear to you in my last address, and which long ago I tried to express, under the head of ideas of power. The entire sense of that, we have lost, because we ourselves do not take pains enough to do right, and have no conception of what the right costs; so that all the joy and reverence we ought to feel in looking at a strong man's work have ceased in us. We keep them yet a little in looking at a honeycomb or a bird's nest; we understand that these differ, by divinity of skill, from a lump of wax or a cluster of sticks. But a picture, which is a much more wonderful thing than a honeycomb or a bird's nest, have we not known people, and sensible people too, who expected to be taught to produce that, in six lessons?

101. Well, you must have the skill, you must have the beauty, which is the highest moral element; and then, lastly, you must have the verity or utility, which is not the moral, but the vital element; and this desire for verity and use is the one aim of the three that always leads in great schools, and in the minds of great masters, without any exception. They will permit themselves in awkwardness, they will permit themselves in ugliness; but they will never permit themselves in uselessness or in unveracity. [...]

105. And now let us think of our own work, and ask how that may become, in its own poor measure, active in some verity of representation. We certainly cannot begin by drawing kings or queens; but we must try, even in our earliest work, if it is to prosper, to draw something that will convey true knowledge both to ourselves and others. And I think you will find greatest advantage in the endeavour to give more life and educational power to the simpler branches of natural science: for the great scientific men are all so eager in advance that they have no time to popularise their discoveries, and if we can glean after them a little, and make pictures of the things which science describes, we shall find the service a worthy one. Not only so, but we may even be helpful to science herself; for she has suffered by her proud severance from the arts; and having made too little effort to realise her discoveries to vulgar eyes, has herself lost true measure of what was chiefly precious in them.

106. Take Botany, for instance. Our scientific botanists are, I think, chiefly at present occupied in distinguishing species, which perfect methods of distinction will probably in the future show to be indistinct; in inventing descriptive names of which a more advanced science and more fastidious scholarship will show some to be unnecessary, and others inadmissible; and in microscopic investigations of structure. [...] In the meantime, our artists are so generally convinced of the truth of the Darwinian theory that they do not always think it necessary to show any difference between the foliage of an elm and an oak; and the gift books of Christmas have every page surrounded with laboriously engraved garlands of rose, shamrock, thistle and forget-me-not, without its being thought proper by the draughtsman, or desirable by the public, even in the case of those uncommon flowers, to observe the real shape of the petals of any one of them.

107. Now what we especially need at present for educational purposes is to know, not the anatomy of plants, but their biography – how and where they live and die, their tempers, benevolences, malignities, distresses and virtues. We want them drawn from their youth to their age, from bud to fruit. [...] And all this we ought to have drawn so accurately, that we might at once compare any given part of a plant with the same part of any other, drawn on the like conditions. Now, is not this a work which we may set about here in Oxford, with good hope and much pleasure? I think it is so important, that the first exercise in drawing I shall put before you will be an outline of a laurel leaf. [...]

108. Next, in Geology, which I will take leave to consider as an entirely separate science from the zoology of the past, which has lately usurped its name and interest. In geology itself we find the strength of many able men occupied in debating questions of which there are yet no data even for the clear statement; and in seizing advanced theoretical positions on the mere contingency of their being afterwards tenable; while, in the meantime, no simple person, taking a holiday in Cumberland, can get an intelligible section of Skiddaw, or a clear account of the origin of the Skiddaw slates; and while, though half the educated society of London travel every summer over the great plain of Switzerland, none know, or care to know, why that is a plain, and the Alps to the south of it are Alps; and whether or not the gravel of the one has anything to do with the rocks of the other. And though every palace in Europe owes part of its decoration to variegated marbles, and nearly every woman in Europe part of her decoration to pieces of jasper or chalcedony, I do not think any geologist could at this moment with authority tell us either how a piece of marble is stained, or what causes the streaks in a Scotch pebble.

109. Now, as soon as you have obtained the power of drawing, I do not say a mountain, but even a stone, accurately, every question of this kind will become to you at once attractive and definite; you will find that in the grain, the lustre, and the cleavage lines of the smallest fragment of rock, there are recorded forces of every order and magnitude, from those which raise a continent by one vol-canic effort, to those which at every instant are polishing the apparently com-plete crystal in its nest, and conducting the apparently motionless metal in its vein; and that only by the art of your own hand, and fidelity of sight which it develops, you can obtain true perception of these invincible and inimitable arts of the earth herself; while the comparatively slight effort necessary to obtain so much skill as may serviceably draw mountains in distant effect will be instantly rewarded by what is almost equivalent to a new sense of the conditions of their structure. [...]

113. Lastly, in Zoology. What the Greeks did for the horse, and what, as far as regards domestic and expressional character, Landseer has done for the dog and the deer, remains to be done by art for nearly all other animals of high organisation. [...] I have placed in your Educational series a wing by Albert Dürer, which goes as far as art yet has reached in delineation of plumage; while for the simple action of the pinion it is impossible to go beyond what has been done already by Titian and Tintoret; but you cannot so much as once look at the rufflings of the plumes of a pelican pluming itself after it has been in the water, or carefully draw the contours of the wing either of a vulture or a common swift, or paint the rose and vermilion on that of a flamingo, without receiving almost a new conception of the meaning of form and colour in creation. [...]

115. Now it is quite probable that some of you, who will not care to go through the labour necessary to draw flowers or animals, may yet have pleasure in attaining some moderately accurate skill of sketching architecture, and greater pleasure still in directing it usefully. Suppose, for instance, we were to take up the historical scenery in Carlyle's *Frederick* [*History of Friedrich II of Prussia, Called Frederick the Great,* 1858-65]. Too justly the historian accuses the genius of past art, in that, types of too many such elsewhere, the galleries of Berlin – 'are made up, like other galleries, of goat-footed Pan, Europa's Bull, Romulus's She-Wolf and the correggiosity of Correggio; and contain, for instance, no portrait of Friedrich the Great; no likenesses at all, or next to none at all, of the noble series of Human Realities, or any part of them, who have sprung, *not* from the idle brains of dreaming Dilettanti, but from the Head of God Almighty, to make this poor authentic Earth a little memorable for us, and to do a little work that may be eternal there'. So Carlyle tells us – too truly! We cannot now draw Friedrich for him, but we can draw some of the old castles and cities that were the cradles of German life – Hohenzollern, Hapsburg, Marburg and such others; we may keep some authentic likeness of these for the future. Suppose we were to take up that first volume of *Friedrich*, and put outlines to it: shall we begin by looking for Henry the Fowler's tomb – Carlyle himself asks if he has any – at Quedlinburg, and so downwards, rescuing what we can? That would certainly be making our work of some true use.

116. But I have told you enough, it seems to me, at least today, of this function of art in recording fact; let me now finally, and with all distinctness possible to me, state to you its main business of all; its service in the actual uses of daily life.

You are surprised, perhaps, to hear me call this its main business. That is indeed so, however. The giving brightness to picture is much, but the giving brightness to life more. And remember, were it as patterns only, you cannot, without the realities, have the pictures. *You cannot have a landscape by Turner, without a country for him to paint; you cannot have a portrait by Titian, without a man to be portrayed.* I need not prove that to you, I suppose, in these short terms; but in the outcome I can get no soul to believe that the beginning of art *is in getting our country clean, and our people beautiful.* I have been ten years trying to get this very plain certainty – I do not say believed – but even thought of, as anything but a monstrous proposition. To get your country clean, and your people lovely; I assure you that is a necessary work of art to begin with! There has indeed been art in countries where people lived in dirt to serve God, but never in countries where they lived in dirt to serve the devil. There has indeed been art where the people were not all lovely – where even their lips were thick – and their skins black, because the sun had looked upon them; but never in a country where the people were pale with miserable toil and deadly shade, and where the lips of youth, instead of being full with blood, were pinched by famine, or warped with poison. And now, therefore, note this well, the gist of all these long prefatory talks. I said that the two great moral instincts were those of Order and Kindness. Now, all the arts are founded on agriculture by the hand, and on the graces, and kindness of feeding, and dressing, and lodging your people. [...]

117. Now look at the working out of this broad principle in minor detail; observe how, from highest to lowest, health of art has first depended on reference to industrial use. There is first the need of cup and platter, especially of cup;

for you can put your meat on the Harpies',[1] or on any other, tables; but you must have your cup to drink from. And to hold it conveniently, you must put a handle to it; and to fill it when it is empty you must have a large pitcher of some sort; and to carry the pitcher you may most advisably have two handles. Modify the forms of these needful possessions according to the various requirements of drinking largely and drinking delicately; of pouring easily out, or of keeping for years the perfume in; of storing in cellars, or bearing from fountains; of sacrificial libation, of Panathenaic treasure of oil, and sepulchral treasure of ashes, and you have a resultant series of beautiful form and decoration, from the rude amphora of red earth up to Cellini's vases of gems and crystal, in which series, but especially in the more simple conditions of it, are developed the most beautiful lines and most perfect types of severe composition which have yet been attained by art.

118. But again, that you may fill your cup with pure water, you must go to the well or spring; you need a fence round the well; you need some tube or trough, or other means of confining the stream at the spring. For the conveyance of the current to any distance you must build either enclosed or open aqueduct; and in the hot square of the city where you set it free, you find it good for health and pleasantness to let it leap into a fountain. On these several needs you have a school of sculpture founded; in the decoration of the walls of wells in level countries, and of the sources of springs in mountainous ones, and chiefly of all, where the women of household or market meet at the city fountain. [...]

120. Well, the gist of this matter lies here then. Suppose we want a school of pottery again in England, all we poor artists are ready to do the best we can, to show you how pretty a line may be that is twisted first to one side, and then to the other; and how a plain household blue will make a pattern on white; and how ideal art may be got out of the spaniel's colours of black and tan. But I tell you beforehand, all that we can do will be utterly useless, unless you teach your peasant to say grace, not only before meat, but before drink; and having provided him with Greek cups and platters, provide him also with something that is not poisoned to put into them. [...]

124. Now, I have given you my message, containing, as I know, offence enough, and itself, it may seem to many, unnecessary enough. But just in proportion to its apparent non-necessity, and to its certain offence, was its real need, and my real duty to speak it. The study of the fine arts could not be rightly associated with the grave work of English Universities without due and clear protest against the misdirection of national energy, which for the present renders all good results of such study on a great scale, impossible. I can easily teach you, as any other moderately good draughtsman could, how to hold your pencils, and how to lay your colours; but it is little use my doing that, while the nation is spending millions of money in the destruction of all that pencil or colour has to represent, and in the promotion of false forms of art, which are only the costliest and the least enjoyable of follies. And therefore these are the things that I have first and last to tell you in this place; that the fine arts are not to be learned by Locomotion, but by making the homes we live in lovely, and by staying in them; that the fine arts are not to be learned by Competition, but by doing our quiet best in our own way; that the fine arts are not to be learned by Exhibition, but by doing what is right, and making what is honest, whether it be exhibited or not; and, for the sum

---

[1]   Virgil, *Aeneid*, book 3, 209.

of all, that men must paint and build neither for pride nor for money, but for love; for love of their art, for love of their neighbour, and whatever better love may be than these, founded on these. I know that I gave some pain, which I was most unwilling to give, in speaking of the possible abuses of religious art; but there can be no danger of any, so long as we remember that God inhabits cottages as well as churches, and ought to be well lodged there also. Begin with wooden floors; the tessellated ones will take care of themselves; begin with thatching roofs, and you shall end by splendidly vaulting them; begin by taking care that no old eyes fail over their Bibles, nor young ones over their needles, for want of rushlight, and then you may have whatever true good is to be got out of coloured glass or wax candles. And in thus putting the arts to universal use, you will find also their universal inspiration, their universal benediction. I told you there was no evidence of a *special* Divineness in any application of them; that they were always equally human and equally Divine; and in closing this inaugural series of lectures, into which I have endeavoured to compress the principles that are to be the foundations of your future work, it is my last duty to say some positive words as to the Divinity of all art, when it is truly fair, or truly serviceable.

For Ruskin, then, art 'must never exist alone – never for itself; it exists rightly only when it is the means of knowledge, or the grace of agency for life'. According to this line of thinking, 'knowledge' and 'utility' are interwoven. For instance, insofar as drawing contributes to our knowledge of the natural world, this constitutes another form of utility. However, terms such as *utility* and *usefulness* are notoriously slippery.

In the first volume of *Capital*, Marx offers an alternative to Ruskinian moralising. He distinguishes between a commodity's exchange-value, which is purely quantitative, and its use-value, which remains resistant to quantification while underpinning everything. Exchange-value is abstraction to use-value's concretion. The commodity thus has a twofold nature, and the relation between the two incommensurable types of value becomes a formidable theoretical challenge. It is by dissecting labour, which in turn is revealed to be twofold, that Marx begins to unpack the problem.[5]

KARL MARX, 'THE DUAL CHARACTER OF THE LABOUR EMBODIED IN COMMODITIES'

Reprinted from Karl Marx, *Capital: A Critique of Political Economy, Volume 1*, London: Penguin, 1990, pp.131–38. First published in 1867. Translated from the German by Ben Fowkes.

As use-vales, commodities differ above all in quality, while as exchange-values they can only differ in quantity, and therefore do not contain an atom of use-value.

If then we disregard the use-values of commodities, only one property remains, that of being products of labour. But even the product of labour has already been transformed in our hands. If we make abstraction from its use-value, we abstract also from the material constituents and forms which make it a use-value. It is no longer a table, a house, a piece of yarn or any other useful thing. All its sensuous characteristics are extinguished. Nor is it any longer the product of the labour of the joiner, the mason or the spinner, or of any other particular kind of productive labour. With the disappearance of the useful character of the products of labour, the useful character of the kinds of labour embodied in them also disappears; this in turn entails the disappearance of the different concrete forms of labour. They can no longer be distinguished, but are all together reduced to the same kind of labour, human labour in the abstract.

Let us now look at the residue of the products of labour. There is nothing left of them in each case but the same phantom-like objectivity; they are merely congealed quantities of homogenous human labour, i.e. of human labour-power expended without regard to the form of its expenditure. All these things now tell us is that human labour-power has been expended to produce them, human labour power is accumulated in them. As crystals of this social substance, which is common to them all, they are values – commodity values.

We have seen that when commodities are in the relation of exchange, their exchange-value manifests itself as something totally independent of their use-value. But if we abstract from their use-value, there remains their value, as it has just been defined. The common factor in the exchange relation, or in the exchange-value of the commodity, is therefore its value. The progress of the investigation will lead us back to exchange-value as the necessary mode of expression, or form of appearance, of value.

In this passage, Marx already begins to discuss the twofold nature of labour itself. On the one hand, we have work that creates use-value, as a necessary condition for the subsistence and reproduction of mankind, independent of the socially produced division of labour. On the other hand, there is 'abstract labour', or human labour power in general, which is subject to the division of labour and made measurable and compatible as a commodity in its own right. Workers sell their labour power, their generalised and abstract labour, for a certain amount of money.

Initially the commodity appeared to us as an object with a dual character, possessing both use-value and exchange-value. Later on it was seen that labour, too, has a dual character: insofar as it finds its expression in value, it no longer possesses the same characteristics as when it is the creator of use-values. I was first to point out and examine critically this twofold nature of the labour contained in commodities.[2] As this point is crucial to an understanding of political economy, it requires further elucidation.

Let us take two commodities, such as a coat and 10 yards of linen, and let the value of the first be twice the value of the second, so that, if 10 yards of linen = W, the coat = $2W$.

The coat is a use-value that satisfies a particular need. A specific kind of productive activity is required to bring it into existence. This activity is

---

2   Karl Marx, *A Contribution to the Critique of the Political Economy* (trans. S.W. Ryazanskaya), London: Lawrence and Wishart, 1971, pp.41-42.

determined by its aim, mode of operation, object, means and result. We use the abbreviated expression 'useful labour' for labour whose utility is represented by the use-value of its product, or by the fact that its product is a use-value. In this connection we consider only its useful effect.

As the coat and the linen are qualitatively different use-values, so also are the forms of labour through which their existence is mediated – tailoring and weaving. If the use-values were not qualitatively different, hence not the products of qualitatively different forms of useful labour, they would be absolutely incapable of confronting each other as commodities. Coats cannot be exchanged for coats, one use-value cannot be exchanged for another of the same kind.

The totality of heterogeneous use-values or physical commodities reflects a totality of similarly heterogeneous forms of useful labour, which differ in order, genus, species and variety: in short, a social division of labour. This division of labour is a necessary condition for commodity production, although the converse does not hold; commodity production is not a necessary condition for the social division of labour. Labour is socially divided in the primitive Indian community, although the products do not thereby become commodities. Or, to take an example nearer home, labour is systematically divided in every factory, but the workers do not bring about this division by exchanging their individual products. Only the products of mutually independent acts of labour, performed in isolation, can confront each other as commodities.

To sum up, then: the use-value of every commodity contains useful labour, i.e. productive activity of a definite kind, carried on with a definite aim. Use-values cannot confront each other as commodities unless the useful labour contained in them is qualitatively different in each case. In a society whose products generally assume the form of commodities, i.e. in a society of commodity producers, this qualitative difference between the useful forms of labour which are carried on independently and privately by individual producers develops into a complex system, a social division of labour.

It is moreover a matter of indifference whether the coat is worn by the tailor or by his costumer. In both cases it acts as a use-value. So, too, the relation between the coat and the labour that produced it is not in itself altered when tailoring becomes as a special trade, an independent branch of the social division of labour. Men made clothes for thousands of years, under the compulsion of the need for clothing, without a single man ever becoming a tailor. But the existence of coats, of linen, of every element of material wealth not provided in advance by nature, had always to be mediated through a specific productive activity appropriate to its purpose, a productive activity that assimilated particular natural materials to particular human requirements. Labour, then, as the creator of use-values, as useful labour, is a condition of human existence which is independent of all forms of society; it is an eternal natural necessity which mediates the metabolism between man and nature, and therefore human life itself.

Use-values like coats, linen, etc., in short, the physical bodies of commodities, are combinations of two elements, the material provided by nature, and labour. If we subtract the total amount of useful labour of different kinds which is contained in the coat, the linen, etc., a material substratum is always left. This substratum is furnished by nature without human intervention. When man engages in production, he can only proceed as nature does herself, i.e. he can only change the form of the materials.[3] Furthermore, even in this work of modification he is constantly helped by natural forces. Labour is therefore not the only source of material wealth, i.e. of the use-values it produces. As William Petty says, labour is the father of material wealth, the earth is its mother.[4]

Let us now pass from the commodity as an object of utility to the value of commodities.

We have assumed that the coat is worth twice as much as the linen. But this is merely quantitative difference, and does not concern us at the moment. We shall therefore simply bear in mind that if the value of a coat is twice that of 10 yards of linen, 20 yards of linen will have the same value as a coat. As values, the coat and the linen have the same substance, they are the objective expressions of homogeneous labour. But tailoring and weaving are qualitatively different forms of labour. There are, however, states of society in which the same man alternately makes clothes and weaves. In this case, these two different modes of labour are only modifications of the labour of the same individual and not yet fixed functions peculiar to different individuals, just as the coat our tailor makes today, and the pair of trousers he makes tomorrow, require him only to vary his own individual labour. Moreover, we can see at a glance that in our capitalist society a given portion of labour is supplied alternatively in the form of tailoring and in the form of weaving, in accordance with changes in the direction of the demand for labour. This change in the form of labour may well not take place without friction, but it must take place.

If we leave aside the determinate quality of productive activity, and therefore the useful character of the labour, what remains is its quality of being an expenditure of human labour-power. Tailoring and weaving, although they are qualitatively different productive activities, are both a productive expenditure of human brains, muscles, nerves, hands etc., and in this sense both human labour. They are merely two different forms of the expenditure of human labour-power. Of course, human labour-power must itself have attained a certain level of development before it can be expended in this or that form. But the value of a commodity represents human labour pure and simple, the expenditure of human labour in general. And just as, in civil society, a general or a banker plays a great part but man as such plays a very mean part,[5] so, here too, the same is true of human labour. It is the expenditure of simple labour-power, i.e. of the labour-power possessed in his bodily organism by every ordinary man, on the average,

---

[3] 'All the phenomena of the universe, whether produced by the hand of man or indeed by the universal laws of physics, are not to be conceived of as acts of creation but solely as a reordering of matter. Composition and separation are the only elements found by the human mind whenever it analyses the notion of reproduction; and so it is with the reproduction of value' (use-value, although Verri himself, in this polemic against the Physiocrats, is not quite certain of the kind of value he is referring to) 'and wealth, whether earth, air and water are turned into corn in the fields, or the secretions of an insect are turned into silk by the hand of man, or some small pieces of metal are arranged together to form a repeating watch'. Pietro Verri, *Meditazioni sulla economia politica*, first printed in 1771 in Custodi's edition of the Italian economists, *Parte moderna*, vol.15, pp.21-22.

[4] Translator's Note: *A Treatise of Taxes and Contributions*, published anonymously by William Petty, London, 1667, p.47.

[5] Cf. Hegel, *Philosophie des Rechts*, Berlin, 1840, p.250, para.190. TN: Hegel says here: 'In civil society as a whole, at the standpoint of needs, what we have before us is the composite idea which we call man. Thus this is the first time, and indeed the only time, to speak of man in this sense.' *Hegel's Philosophy of Right* (trans. T.M. Knox), Oxford: Oxford University Press, 1952, p.127.

without being developed in any special way. *Simple average labour*, it is true, varies in character in different countries and at different cultural epochs, but in a particular society it is given. More complex labour counts only as *intensified*, or rather *multiplied* simple labour, so that a smaller quantity of complex labour is considered equal to a larger quantity of simple labour. Experience shows that this reduction is constantly being made. A commodity may be the outcome of the most complicated labour, but through its *value* it is posited as equal to the product of simple labour, hence it represents only a specific quantity of simple labour.[6] The various proportions in which different kinds of labour are reduced to simple labour as their unit of measurement are established by a social process that goes on behind the backs of the producers; these proportions therefore appear to the producers to have been handed down by tradition. In the interests of simplification, we shall henceforth view every form of labour-power directly as simple labour-power; by this we shall simply be saving ourselves the trouble of making the reduction.

Just as, in viewing the coat and the linen as values, we abstract from their different use-values, so, in the case of the labour represented by those values, do we disregard the difference between its useful forms, tailoring and weaving. The use-values coat and linen are combinations of, on the one hand, productive activity with a definite purpose, and, on the other, cloth and yarn; the values coat and linen, however, are merely congealed quantities of homogeneous labour. In the same way, the labour contained in these values does not count by virtue of its productive relation to cloth and yarn, but only as being an expenditure of human labour-power. Tailoring and weaving are the formative elements in the use-values coat and linen, precisely because these two kinds of labour are of different qualities; but only in so far as abstraction is made from their particular qualities, only in so far both possess the same quality of being human labour, do tailoring and weaving form the substance of the values of the two articles mentioned.

Coats and linen, however, are not merely values in general, but values of definite magnitude, and, following our assumption, the coat is worth twice as much as the 10 yards of linen. Why is there this difference in value? Because the linen contains only half as much labour as the coat, so that labour-power had to be expended twice as long to produce the second as to produce the first.

While, therefore, with reference to use-value, the labour contained in a commodity counts only qualitatively, with reference to value it counts only quantitatively, once it has been reduced to human labour pure and simple. In the former case it was a matter of the 'how' and the 'what' of labour, in the latter of the 'how much', of the temporal duration of labour. Since the magnitude of the value of a commodity represents nothing but the quantity of labour embodied in it, it follows that all commodities, when taken in certain proportions, must be equal in value.

If the productivity of all the different sorts of useful labour required, let us say, for the production of a coat remains unchanged, the total value of the coats produced will increase along with their quantity. If one coat represents x days'

---

6   The reader should note that we are not speaking here of the wages or value the worker receives for (e.g.) a day's labour, but of the value of the commodity in which his day labour is objectified. At this stage of our presentation, the category of wages does not exist at all.

labour, two coats will represent $2x$ days' labour, and so on. But now assume that the duration of the labour necessary for the production of a coat is doubled or halved. In the first case, one coat is worth as much as two coats were before; in the second case two coats are only worth as much as one was before, although in both cases one coat performs the same service, and the useful labour contained in it remains of the same quality. One change has taken place, however: a change in the quantity of labour expended to produce the article.

In itself, an increase in the quantity of use-values constitutes an increase in material wealth. Two coats will clothe two men, one coat will only clothe one man, etc. Nevertheless, an increase in the amount of material wealth may correspond to a simultaneous fall in the magnitude of its value. This contradictory movement arises out of the twofold character of labour. By 'productivity' of course, we always mean the productivity of concrete useful labour; in reality this determines only the degree of effectiveness of productive activity directed towards a given purpose within a given period of time. Useful labour becomes, therefore, a more or less abundant source of products in direct proportion as its productivity rises or falls. As against this, however, variations in productivity have no impact whatever on the labour itself represented in value. As productivity is an attribute of labour in its concrete useful form, it naturally ceases to have any bearing on that labour as soon as we abstract from its concrete useful form. The same labour, therefore, performed for the same length of time, always yields the same amount of value, independently of any variations in productivity. But it provides different quantities of use-values during equal periods of time; more, if productivity rises; fewer, if it falls. For this reason, the same change in productivity which increases the fruitfulness of labour, and therefore the amount of use-values produced by it, also brings about a reduction in the value of this increased total amount, if it cuts down the total amount of labour-time necessary to produce the use-values. The converse also holds.

On the one hand, all labour is an expenditure of human labour-power, in the physiological sense, and it is in this quality of being equal, or abstract, human labour that it forms the value of commodities. On the other hand, all labour is an expenditure of human labour-power in a particular form and with a definite aim, and it is in this quality of being concrete useful labour that it produces use-values.[7]

---

[7]   In order to prove that 'labour alone is the ultimate and real standard by which the value of all commodities can at all times and places be estimated and compared', Adam Smith says this: 'Equal quantities of labour, at all times and places, must have the same value for the labourer. In this ordinary state of health, strength and activity; in the ordinary degree of his skill and dexterity, he must always lay down the same portion of his ease, his liberty, and his happiness.' A. Smith, *An Inquiry into the Nature and Causes of the Wealth of Nations*, ed. Edwin Cannan, Chicago: University of Chicago Press, 1977, p.54. (TN: Here, as elsewhere occasionally, Marx quotes an English author in German. This explains certain slight divergences from the original English text.) On the one hand, Adam Smith here (but not everywhere) confuses his determination of value by the quantity of labour expended in the production of commodities with the determination of the values of commodities by the value of labour, and therefore endeavours to prove that equal quantities of labour always have the same value. On the other hand, he has a suspicion that, in so far as labour manifests itself in the value of commodities, it only counts as an expenditure of labour-power; but then again he views this expenditure merely as the sacrifice of rest, freedom and happiness, not as also man's normal life-activity. Of course, he has the modern wage-labourer in mind. Adam Smith's anonymous predecessor [...] is much nearer the mark when he says: 'One man has employed himself a week in providing this necessary of life ... and he that gives him some other in exchange, cannot make a

As 'concrete useful labour', work creates use-values; however, when we are dealing with abstract labour in the form of labour power sold by the worker to the capitalist, this produces *value*. Here, Marx drops the use of qualifiers and talks of value *as such* as the product of abstract labour – of quantified labour-power – under specific relations of production. This is not a theory of supply and demand. Adopting and adapting David Ricardo's labour theory of value, for Marx value is determined by the 'socially necessary labour time' spent on producing something. This can be seen as a critique of the 'autonomisation' of exchange-value in what Marx dubbed commodity fetishism: the illusion that the value of commodities are determined by their interplay on the market. *In fact*, their value is determined by socially necessary labour time. The opposition between use-value and exchange-value is thus extended into a triad.

Rather than claiming to explain how one form of value is 'translated' into the other, Marx presents a dialectical constellation in which the three terms mutually problematise each other. Any 'functioning' commodity must have a use-value, or possibly several different use-values to different people, otherwise it would fail to ever find a buyer. However, we cannot quantify use-value in order to determine a commodity's exchange-value; there is fundamental contradiction between these concepts.[6] An important point in the present context is that use-value need not refer only to objects that have a clear 'practical' function – such as coats, cars or cornflakes. In fact, Marx states categorically that 'nothing can be a value without being an object of utility. If the thing is useless, so is the labour contained in it; the labour does not count as labour, and therefore creates no value'.[7] Use-value is historically and culturally specific. Marx's examples are typically linen, coats, watches and the like; his remarks on the early culture industry are intermittent and far from consistent. Yet, remarks such as the above speak to the commodification of knowledge in the 'teaching factory' while his observations on authors and singers, make it clear that he was aware of the beginnings of the culture industry:

Milton, who wrote *Paradise Lost*, was an unproductive worker. On the other hand, a writer who turns out work for his publisher in factory style is a productive worker. Milton produced *Paradise Lost* as a silkworm produces silk, as the activity of *his own* nature. He later sold his product for £5 and thus became a merchant. But the literary proletarian of Leipzig who produces books, such as compendia on political economy, at the behest of his publisher is pretty nearly a productive worker since his production is taken over by capital and only occurs in order to increase it. A singer who sings like a bird is an unproductive worker. If she sells her song for money, she is to that extent a wage-labourer or merchant. But if the same singer is engaged by an entrepreneur who makes her sing to make money, then she becomes a productive worker, since she *produces* capital directly.

better estimate of what is a proper equivalent, than by computing what cost him just as much labour and time: which in effect is no more than exchanging one man's labour in one thing for a time certain, for another man's labour in another thing for the same time.' Unknown, *Some Thoughts on the Interest of Money in General, and Particularly in the Publick Funds*, London, 1738, p.39. Note by Engels to the fourth German edition: The English language has the advantage of possessing two separate words for these two different aspects of labour. Labour which creates use-values and is qualitatively determined is called 'work', as opposed to 'labour'; labour which creates value and is only measured quantitatively is called 'labour', as opposed to 'work'. (TN: Unfortunately, English usage does not always correspond to Engels' distinction. We have tried to adopt it where possible.)

A schoolmaster who instructs others is not a productive worker. But a schoolmaster who works for wages in an institution along with others, using his own labour to increase the money of the entrepreneur who owns the knowledge-mongering institution, is a productive worker. But for the most part, work of this sort has scarcely reached the stage of being subsumed even formally under capital, and belongs essentially to a transitional stage.[8]

Marx's fundamental assertion that any commodity – no matter how 'immaterial' – must have a use-value applies to even to *l'art pour l'art*, but this did not prevent Ruskin from attacking art he considered to be pure aestheticism without any social use. In Letter 79 of *Fors Clavigera*, first published in 1877, Ruskin famously launched a scathing critique of a series of paintings by James McNeill Whistler, accusing the artist of seeking 'two hundred 200 guineas for flinging a pot of paint in the public's face'.[9] Whistler sued Ruskin for libel, and, after a long, public court hearing, Whistler scored a pyrrhic victory: he won the case but went bankrupt in the process, receiving an award of one farthing in damages. In fact, Ruskin's criticism of Whistler in Letter 79 forms only a very small part of a wide-ranging polemic in support of Working Men's Guilds, which Ruskin associated with the qualitative and ethical value of non-alienated labour, and with art's potential to play a role in the improvement of everyday social environments, education and civil society.

In this context, Ruskin also praises the work of the Pre-Raphaelite Edward Burne-Jones. What is interesting here is Ruskin's acknowledgement that the flaws, mistakes and problems embodied in Burne-Jones's work evidence a moral and ethical labour of art that runs counter to the precise and machine-driven accuracy of everyday mass-produced objects. Seen in this light, it is not the speed or expressiveness of Whistler's work that so provoked Ruskin, but the presentation of such work as a disembodied and decorative commodity:

> Lastly, the mannerisms and errors of these pictures, whatever may be their extent, are never affected or indolent. The work is natural to the painter, however strange to us; and it is wrought with utmost conscience of care, however far, to his own or our desire, the result may yet be incomplete. Scarcely so much can be said for any other pictures of the modern schools: their eccentricities are almost always in some degree forced; and their imperfections gratuitously, if not impertinently, indulged. For Mr. Whistler's own sake, no less than for the protection of the purchaser, Sir Coutts Lindsay ought not to have admitted works into the gallery in which the ill-educated conceit of the artist so nearly approached the aspect of wilful imposture. I have seen, and heard, much of Cockney impudence before now; but never expected to hear a coxcomb ask two hundred guineas for flinging a pot of paint in the public's face.[10]

The paintings in question were a series of impressionistic renditions of night-time fireworks. During his evidence at the libel trial in 1878, Whistler offered a defence of his rationale for making them, which encapsulated a move towards the conception of art as being culturally autonomous:

> By using the word 'nocturne' I wished to indicate artistic interest alone, divesting the picture of any outside anecdotal interest which might have been otherwise attached to it. A nocturne is an arrangement of line, form and colour first. The

picture is throughout a problem that I attempt to slve. I make use of any means, any incident or object in nature, that will bring about this symmetrical result.[11]

Although his ideas echo those of some proponents of *l'art pour l'art*, such as Gautier and Baudelaire, Whistler never foreclosed the possibility of a moral, ethical or political reading of an artwork. Instead, his arguments for an autonomous art were based around the proposition that the kind of immaterial and aesthetic values that art represented could only develop in isolation from the material necessities and conditions of everyday existence.

In the same year that Ruskin published Letter 79, William Morris delivered to the Trades' Guild of Learning in London his lecture 'The Lesser Arts' (1877), which outlines an impassioned argument for the social integration of art and design into the fabric of contemporary culture. Profoundly marked by Ruskin (and then, from 1883 on, by Marx), Morris feared that the existing divisions of labour in industrialised Britain and Europe were impoverishing the moral, ethical and political infrastructure of culture and society. For Morris, art – and, more importantly, the production of a new popular art – should play a necessary role in providing an alternative to the existing conditions of mass-produced 'squalor' and their associated class divisions.

Morris's belief was that a useful art would not merely be decoration for a blighted environment, but would offer a cultural common denominator through which a truly egalitarian society would emerge. In doing so, he began to articulate a relationship between art, use and political change that directly informed later avant-garde attempts to weld formal experimentation to revolutionary political agendas.

WILLIAM MORRIS, 'THE LESSER ARTS'

Reprinted from William Morris, *Hopes and Fears for Art & Signs of Change* (1882), Bristol: Thoemmes Press, 1994, pp.25-27.

Unless something or other is done to give all men some pleasure for the eyes and rest for the mind in the aspect of their own and their neighbours' houses, until the contrast is less disgraceful between the fields where beasts live and the streets where men live, I suppose that the practice of the arts must be mainly kept in the hands of a few highly cultivated men, who can go often to beautiful places, whose education enables them, in the contemplation of the past glories of the world, to shut out from their view the everyday squalors that the most of men move in. Sirs, I believe that art has such sympathy with cheerful freedom, open-heartedness and reality, so much she sickens under selfishness and luxury, that she will not live thus isolated and exclusive. I will go further than this and say that on such terms I do not wish her to live. I protest that it would be a shame to an honest artist to enjoy what he had huddled up to himself of such art, as it would be for a rich man to sit and eat dainty food amongst starving soldiers in a beleaguered fort.

I do not want art for a few, any more than education for a few, or freedom for a few.

No, rather than art should live this poor thin life among a few exceptional men, despising those beneath them for an ignorance for which they themselves are responsible, for a brutality that they will not struggle with - rather than this, I would that the world should indeed sweep away all art for a while, as I said before I thought it possible she might do; rather than the wheat should rot in the miser's granary, I would that the earth had it, that it might yet have a chance to quicken in the dark.

I have a sort of faith, though, that this clearing way of all art will not happen, that men will get wiser, as well as more learned; that many of the intricacies of life, on which we now pride ourselves more than enough, partly because they are new, partly because they have come with the gain of better things, will be cast aside as having played their part, and being useful no longer. I hope that we shall have leisure from war - war commercial, as well as war of the bullet and the bayonet; leisure from the knowledge that darkens counsel; leisure above all from the greed of money, and the craving for that overwhelming distinction that money now brings: I believe that as we have even now partly achieved LIBERTY, so we shall one day achieve EQUALITY, which, and which only, means FRATERNITY, and so have leisure from poverty and all its griping, sordid cares.

Then having leisure from all these things, amidst renewed simplicity of life we shall have leisure to think about our work, that faithful daily companion, which no man any longer will venture to call the Curse of labour: for surely then we shall be happy in it, each in his place, no man grudging at another; no one bidden to be any man's *servant*, every one scorning to be any man's *master*: men will then assuredly be happy in their work, and that happiness will assuredly bring forth decorative, noble, *popular* art.

Morris's attempt to create a revival of crafts can be seen as a form of aestheticism: a utilitarian aestheticism that attempts to aestheticise the whole of life. However, the concept of aestheticism is more commonly associated with those who, in the lineage of Gautier, created an elitist cult of *l'art pour l'art* that was resolutely opposed to Morris's socialism, or any attempt to effect a wider social transformation. The *locus classicus* of aestheticist doctrine is Oscar Wilde's preface to his novel *The Picture of Dorian Gray* (1891). Sixteen years prior, in 1875, a young Wilde had pushed wheelbarrows full of paving stones as part of Ruskin's project to have his students pave a road in Hinksey, near Oxford, in celebration of healthy and unalienated manual labour. In the *Dorian Gray* preface, the mature Wilde launches into a series of statements asserting that the role of the artist is to to 'reveal art and to conceal the artist' through the production of beautiful, useless objects. Dancing ironic pirouettes around the reader, Wilde queers the notion of autonomous art, transforming it into a masquerade in the face of Victorian morals.

OSCAR WILDE, PREFACE TO *THE PICTURE OF DORIAN GRAY*

Reprinted from Oscar Wilde, *The Picture of Dorian Gray*, London: Penguin Books, 1985, pp.3-4. First published in *The Fortnightly Review*, March 1891.

The artist is the creator of beautiful things.

To reveal art and conceal the artist is art's aim.

The critic is he who can translate into another manner or a new material his impression of beautiful things.

The highest, as the lowest, form of criticism is a mode of autobiography.

Those who find ugly meanings in beautiful things are corrupt without being charming. This is a fault.

Those who find beautiful meanings in beautiful things are the cultivated. For these there is hope.

They are the elect to whom beautiful things mean only Beauty.

There is no such thing as a moral or an immoral book. Books are well written, or badly written. That is all.

The nineteenth-century dislike of Realism is the rage of Caliban seeing his own face in a glass.

The nineteenth-century dislike of Romanticism is the rage of Caliban not seeing his own face in a glass.

The moral life of man forms part of the subject-matter of the artist, but the morality of art consists in the perfect use of an imperfect medium. No artist desires to prove anything. Even things that are true can be proved.

No artist has ethical sympathies. An ethical sympathy in an artist is an unpardonable mannerism of style.

No artist is ever morbid. The artist can express everything.

Thought and language are to the artist instruments of an art.

Vice and virtue are to the artist materials for an art.

From the point of view of form, the type of all the arts is the art of the musician. From the point of view of feeling, the actor's craft is the type.

All art is at once surface and symbol.

Those who go beneath the surface do so at their peril.

Those who read the symbol do so at their peril.

It is the spectator, and not life, that art really mirrors.

Diversity of opinion about a work of art shows that the work is new, complex and vital.

When critics disagree the artist is in accord with himself.

We can forgive a man for making a useful thing as long as he does not admire it. The only excuse for making a useless thing is that one admires it intensely.

All art is quite useless.

Productivism Against Mammonart

In the twentieth century, the growing disparagement of the artwork's subject matter and social functions culminated in various strands of formalism in art criticism and art history. The most important formalist critic of the early twentieth century is no doubt Roger Fry, who curated the groundbreaking exhibition 'Manet and the Post-Impressionists' at the Grafton Galleries in London in 1910. Not only did this show provide the first opportunity for an English audience to see a collection of modern French works together under one roof, it cemented a lineage of modern art that began with Édouard Manet and was consolidated in the work of Paul Cézanne; it also provided Fry and his ally and collaborator Clive Bell with an opportunity to interpret this art as being about a set of autonomous formal concerns. Bell's 1914 essay 'The Aesthetic Hypothesis' insists that a work of art should rely upon its use of line, form and colour alone to provide a harmonious visual impact, thereby guaranteeing an aesthetic experience in those who are sensitive enough to receive it.

Fry, however, was a more considered and less polemical writer than Bell. As curator of painting at the Metropolitan Museum of Art in New York (1905-10) and editor of Burlington Magazine (1909-19), he commanded a position that enabled him to establish formalist criticism as a credible and viable approach. Furthermore, like a number of post-Impressionist artists, Fry aimed to reintegrate an art of purified forms into daily life through decorative schemes; to this end, he founded the Omega Workshops in London, in 1913. Fry, the designers he worked with and many of their clients were members of the Bloomsbury Group - an informal set of artistic bohemians who famously 'loved in triangles', exploring open marriages and bisexual relationships. Fry's art, thus, was not pure formalism.[12] It was in this milieu that Virginia Woolf—who published a biography of Fry shortly before her death—wrote her classic feminist essay *A Room of One's Own* (1929), arguing that women need a room of their own both in literal terms (a space to write in) and in a metaphorical sense (creating room for themselves within literary culture and the canon).

Meanwhile, changes were afoot in the world at large. Fry's essay 'Art in a Socialism', from 1916, muses on the social role of the artist in the capitalist present and in a future socialist society. By positing true creativity as a gift that can never be subject to managerial or bureaucratic calculations, Fry identifies the artist as occupying a space which is necessarily outside the bureaucratic decision-making policies of cultural politics. Any socialist attempt to administer and regiment the arts inevitably runs the risk of producing instrumentalised and mediocre pseudo-art:

> We come now to the crucial problem itself, the genuine artist - the only really anti-social intransigent kind. I have assumed all along that we do want him to exist. However good socialists we may be, we all have, I believe, a hard core of anarchism within us which claims the gratifications of the individual spirit as one of the supreme goods of life, and many of us know that the artist is necessary for this. I sometimes think that Wagner was right in his theory (I suppose based on Schopenhauer's) that art is *par excellence* the spiritual food of those who are emancipated, while religion must always remain the chief spiritual gratification of the mass of mankind. In any case, much as I detest our capitalist civilisation, I would hardly change it for a socialism which was set on the elimination of the genuine artist.

Now the one clear advantage which our present capitalist state has in this respect is the toleration of social parasites. In America, where public opinion objects violently to the idle and harmless parasite, artists can hardly exist at all – in practice they are forced to lead their parasitic existence in Paris and London, where they can escape notice.

Let us admit that the chance of the gift for artistic creation falling to one of the comparatively restricted number of parasites is a small one, but it does occur, and the mere chance being open gives us the hope that the type may always just survive. [...]

We have now pared down our problem to its ultimate core: how to give a livelihood to the real artist; and admitting that our socialist state is willing to do this, how it can distinguish the real artist, since it would not wish, under the heading artists, to support in idleness or useless activity a vast body of shirkers. And here I am rather by way of asking for suggestions than laying down any prescriptions. [...]

One thing is certain: no bureaucratic or official or executive body must ever be allowed a determining voice in what kind of art is worthwhile. Without some such proviso, some statute more rigid and resistant than the Habeas Corpus Act, the case for art in our socialist state is hopeless.[13]

The following year, the October Revolution in Russia radically changed the political landscape in Europe. In the tumultuous period following the 1917 Revolution, various avant-garde artists and movements tried to show the compatibility of their formal revolutions with the social and political revolutionary process – even while many, such as Kazimir Malevich, were at loggerheads with fundamental Bolshevik tenets such as the cult of labour (against which Malevich offered a celebration of laziness).[14]

Malevich attempted to utilise his Suprematist forms for public works such as posters and monuments, which were meant to play an active role in the transformation of society – rather than being mere vessels for ideology. Over the course of the 1920s, such a position became increasingly untenable. Leon Trotsky intervened in the country's debates about artistic and social revolution with Литература и революция (Literature and Revolution, 1923–24), discussing avant-garde writers such as Vladimir Mayakovsky and Sergei Tretyakov. Trotsky argued against the nascent doctrine of Socialist Realism. Rather than producing propaganda in the guise of formally retrograde, idealising depictions of the working class in its current state, art should be allowed to develop, by its own means, into the truly revolutionary tool of a future, liberated proletariat. At the same time, the path towards this revolutionary art to come could not be willed into existence by any self-selecting group of avant-garde bohemians, whether they be poets or painters:

The original Futurism of Russia, as has already been said, was the revolt of Bohemia, that is, of the semi-pauperised left wing of the intelligentsia, against the closed-in and caste-like aesthetics of the bourgeois intelligentsia. Through the outer layer of this poetic revolt was felt the pressure of deep social forces, which Futurism itself did not quite understand. The struggle against the old vocabulary and syntax of poetry, regardless of all its Bohemian extravagances, was a progressive revolt against a vocabulary that was cramped and selected artificially with the view of being undisturbed by anything extraneous. [...] Without exaggerating the dimensions of this 'revolution' in language, we must realise that Futurism has pushed out of poetry many worn words and phrases, and has made

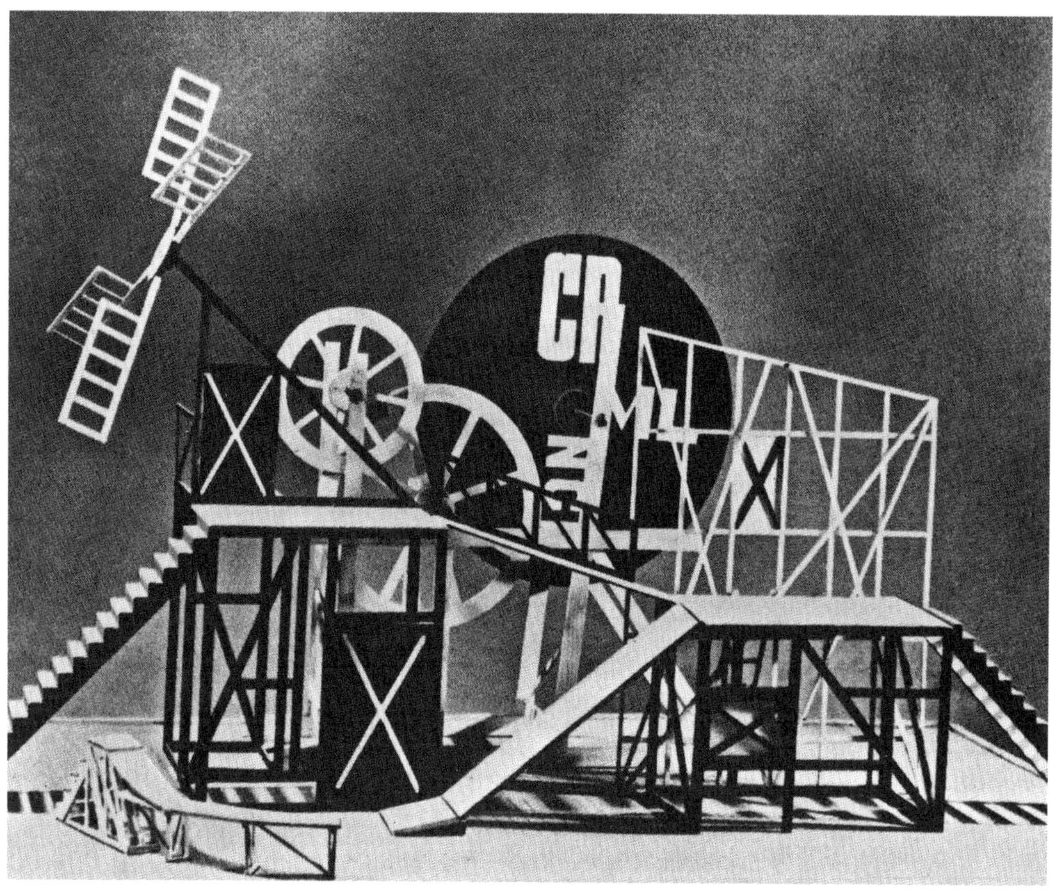

them full-blooded again and, in a few cases, has happily created new words and phrases which have entered, or are entering, into the vocabulary of poetry and which can enrich the living language. [...]

When one breaks a hand or a leg, the bones, the tendons, the muscles, the arteries, the nerves and the skin do not break and tear in one line, nor afterwards do they grow together and heal at the same time. So, in a revolutionary break in the life of society, there is no simultaneousness and no symmetry of processes either in the ideology of society, or in its economic structure. The ideologic premises which are needed for the revolution are formed before the revolution, and the most important ideologic deductions from the revolution appear only much later. It would be extremely flippant to establish by analogies and comparisons the identity of Futurism and Communism, and so form the deduction that Futurism is the art of the proletariat. Such pretensions must be rejected. But this does not signify a contemptuous attitude towards the work of the Futurists. In our opinion they are the necessary links in the forming of a new and great literature. But they will prove to be only a significant episode in its evolution.[15]

Opposite page: Liubov Popova, set design for *The Magnanimous Cuckold* by Fernand Crommelynk, directed by Vsevolod Meyerhold, Actors Theatre, Moscow, 1922

Liubov Popova, sketch of working clothes for actor no. 7 in *The Magnanimous Cuckold*, 1921, gouache, coloured paper, ink and pencil on paper, 32.8 × 23.1cm

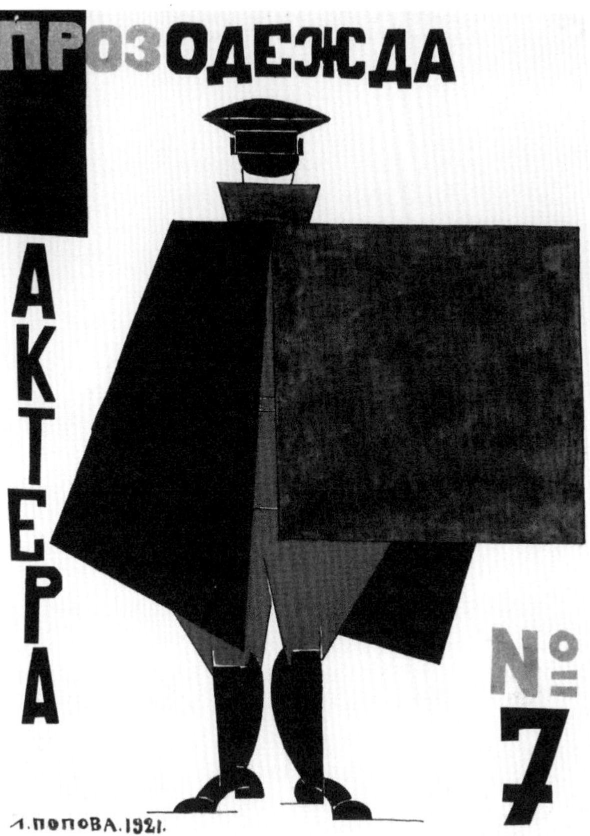

Thus art, in conjunction with the revolutionary transformation of society, will undergo a qualitative change that will render it unrecognisable by pre-revolutionary standards. Precisely because of this, Trotsky deemed it foolish to try to forge the culture of the future today. Hence his critique of the Proletkult (proletarian culture) movement:

> Such terms as 'proletarian literature' and 'proletarian culture' are dangerous, because they erroneously compress the culture of the future into the narrow limits of the present day. They falsify perspectives, they violate proportions, they distort standards, and they cultivate the arrogance of small circles, which is most dangerous.[16]

Proletkult was an avant-garde artists' organisation that played an important but precarious role in the early Soviet Union; the Bolsheviks, including Trotsky, eyed its autonomous stance with suspicion. Later, in exile, Trotsky would come to rely on avant-garde admirers who saw in him an alternative to Stalin. While *Literature and Revolution* is far from proposing a Stalinist purge of the arts, its attack on 'the arrogance of small circles' can be read as a harbinger of things to come.

Constructivism was affiliated with the Proletkult movement, especially when the more politically oriented Constructivists moved in a Productivist direction. As Productivists, the Constructivist artists were no longer content to produce 'constructions' which, while having an abstract and technical look, remained 'autonomous' artworks; they wanted to work with and in modern industry. Trying to enter and reform – or revolutionise – production, they attempted to create a truly socialist material culture in which objects would be 'comrades' (as Alexsandr Rodchenko put it) rather than capitalist commodities.

In Germany, the feminist Marxist critic Lu Märten lauded Proletkult for abandoning the artwork as commodity in favour of a transformed life. It was only by changing habits that a deadening daily life stifling women could be overcome.[17] For the Constructivists, the main way to contribute to such as project was through the designing of furniture, household items, packaging for consumer goods, clothing, wallpaper, advertising and propaganda – as well as set designs for theatre productions. Productivism thus has a rather consumerist side, especially during the 'liberal' New Economic Policy (NEP) period, and female Productivists such as Varvara Stepanova gave the move 'into production' a rather different inflection than that suggested by the industrial-minded rhetoric of certain male theorists and artists (including Rodchenko, her husband).[18]

Photomontage was also a crucial medium for Constructivism and Productivism. Perfect for advertising and agitprop, for book covers and posters, the technique was key for a 'Productivism of the image'. As Benjamin Buchloh puts it:

> The Productivist artists realised that in order to address a new audience not only did the techniques of production have to be changed, but the forms of distribution and institutions of dissemination and reception had to be transformed as well. The photomontage technique, as an artistic procedure that supposedly carries transformative potential *qua* procedure, as the Berlin Dadaists seem to have believed, therefore, in the work of Rodchenko and Lissitzky, becomes integrated as only *one* among several techniques – typography, advertising, propaganda – that attempted to redefine the representational systems of the new society.[19]

In the West, it was the former Berlin Dadaist John Heartfield who came closest to this Productivist understanding of photomontage, with the book covers he designed for his brother Wieland Herzfelde's publishing house Malik-Verlag and in his many montages distributed by the communist press mogul and Soviet agent Willi Münzenberg. Heartfield's 1928 cover for *Die goldne Kette*, the German translation of Upton Sinclair's 1925 book *Mammonart*, features a grid showing 'art treasures' from across the ages, with a George Grosz cartoon of a fat bourgeois smoking a cigar in front – the bourgeoisie owns history by owning the great art of the past.

Mammonart was written as an alternative survey of the history of art and its cultural evaluation. A popular American writer with close to one hundred books published in his name, Sinclair saw himself not as a 'muckraking' journalist but rather as an anti-capitalist, anti-authoritarian voice of reason. Not lacking in self-confidence, he predicted that *Mammonart* would be used as a school textbook on art in the Soviet Union. Although Sinclair's work is not part of the accepted canon of art criticism and theory, *Mammonart* is a compelling statement of a series of concerns around the complicity of artistic practice (especially the work and labour of allegedly autonomous artists) with the rich and the growing commodification of art as *the* luxury good of choice.

UPTON SINCLAIR, 'WHO OWNS THE ARTISTS'

Reprinted from Upton Sinclair, *Mammonart:*
An Essay in Economic Interpretation, Pasadena, CA:
self-published, 1925, pp.7–9.

Throughout this book the word artist is used, not in the narrow sense popular in America, as a man who paints pictures and illustrates magazines; but in its broad sense, as one who represents life imaginatively by any device, whether picture or statue or poem or song or symphony or opera or drama or novel. It is my intention to study these artists from a point of view so far as I know entirely new; to ask how they get their living, and what they do for it; to turn their pockets inside out, and see what is in them and where it came from; to put to them the question already put to priests and preachers, editors and journalists, college presidents and professors, school superintendents and teachers: WHO OWNS YOU, AND WHY?

The book will present an interpretation of the arts from the point of view of the class struggle. It will study artworks as instruments of propaganda and repression, employed by the ruling classes of the community; or as weapons of attack, employed by new classes rising into power. It will study the artists who are recognised and honoured by critical authority, and ask to what extent they have been servants of ruling class prestige and instruments of ruling class safety. It will consider also the rebel artists, who have failed to sever their masters, and ask what penalties they have paid for their rebellion.

The book purposes to investigate the whole process of art creation, and to place the art function in relation to the sanity, health and progress of mankind. It will attempt to set up new canons in the arts, overturning many of the standards now accepted. A large part of the world's art treasures will be taken out to the scrapheap, and a still larger part transferred from the literature shelves to the history shelves of the world's library.

Since childhood the writer has lived most of his life in the world's art. For thirty years he has been studying it consciously, and for twenty-five years he has been shaping in his mind the opinions here recorded; testing and revising them by the artworks which he has produced, and by the stream of other men's work which has flowed through his mind. His decisions are those of a working artist, one who has been willing to experiment and blunder for himself, but who has also made it his business to know and judge the world's best achievements.

The conclusion to which he has come is that mankind is today under the spell of utterly false conception of what art is and should be; of utterly vicious and perverted standards of beauty and dignity. We list six great art lies now prevailing in the world, which this book will discuss:

Lie Number One: the Art for Art's Sake lie; the notion that the end of art is in the artwork, and that the artist's sole task is perfection of form. It will be demonstrated that this lie is a defensive mechanism of artists run to seed, and that its prevalence means degeneracy, not merely in art, but in the society where such art appears.

Lie Number Two: the lie of Art Snobbery; the notion that art is something esoteric, for the few, outside the grasp of the masses. It will be demonstrated

that with few exceptions of a special nature, great art has always been popular
art, and great artist have swayed the people.

Lie Number Three: the lie of Art Tradition; the notion that new artists
must follow old models, and learn from the classics how to work. It will be demonstrated that vital artists make their own technique; and that present-day
technique is far and away superior to the technique of any art period preceding.

Lie Number Four: the lie of Art Dilettantism; the notion that the purpose
of art is entertainment and diversion, an escape from reality. It will be demonstrated that this lie is a production of mental inferiority, and that the true purpose of art is to alter reality.

Lie Number Five: the lie of the Art Pervert; the notion that art has nothing
do with moral questions. It will be demonstrated that all art deals with moral
questions; since there are no other questions.

Lie Number Six: the lie of Vested Interests; the notion that art excludes
propaganda and has nothing do with freedom and justice. Meeting that issue
without equivocation, we assert:

*All art is propaganda. It is universally and inescapably propaganda;
sometimes unconsciously, but often deliberately, propaganda.*

As commentary on the above, we add, that when artists or art critics make
the assertion that art excludes propaganda, what they are saying is that their
kind of propaganda is art, and other kinds of propaganda are not art. Orthodoxy
is my doxy, and heterodoxy is the other fellow's doxy.

Sinclair's debunking of commodified bourgeois art, whose apogee is easel painting, was the flipside to the Productivists' attempts to give art a new social function
by going 'from easel painting to machine' (to quote the title of Russian critic Nikolai
Tarabukin's book, *Ot mol'berta k mashine*). This was not limited to visual artists and
designers; authors such as Tretyakov gave a Productivist turn to literature by embrac-
ing the potential of the press. When curator Alfred H. Barr, Jr. visited the Soviet Union
to prepare for his landmark exhibition 'Cubism and Abstract Art', which opened in
1936 at the Museum of Modern Art in New York, he noted with some bemusement
that Tretyakov had become a journalist. In the West, literary Productivism was
theorised and defended by Walter Benjamin, who also embraced the revolutionary
potential of new media (film, photography) to transform audience reactions and, in
the end, to change society.[20] Benjamin's ally Bertolt Brecht can also be seen as a literary productivist, using radio and film as well as the stage; his 'epic theatre' sought to
activate audience members through the 'distantiation effect'.

The political commitment of some of these artists led them ever more deeply into
the clutches of Stalinism. After the Second World War, Brecht and Heartfield lived
and worked in the Soviet vassal state of East Germany (the German Democratic
Republic). During this period, art in the US and the West of Europe was dominated
by a seemingly depoliticised modernism, which could in fact be used as a cultural
weapon in the Cold War by being made to represent the 'Free West'. However, by the
second half of the 1960s the rediscovery of authors and artists such as Benjamin,
Brecht and Heartfield picked up speed. Neo-Productivist elements can be found in
a number of 1960s and 1970s art practices that considered art as an agent of social
change and disparaged the objecthood and commodity status of artworks.

For George Maciunas, the self-appointed chairman of Fluxus, the aim of advanced art practice during the 1960s was to reintegrate itself in the social fabric. In contrast to Andy Warhol's celebration of the remoteness and alienation offered by the circulation of the media image, Maciuna's task was to replace the production of expensive artworks for a small elite with a new and useful form of art practice that was capable of integrating itself into the current conditions of work and labour, which it would help reshape. In 1966, Maciunas designed a pamphlet titled *Communists Must Give Revolutionary Leadership in Culture* by Henry Flynt; to the bewilderment and irritation of some of Maciunas's associates, he regarded Fluxus as a revolutionary avant-garde in line with Constructivism and Productivism.

Fluxus festivals and events, and the many cheap 'Fluxkits' Maciunas assembled and filled with artistic jokes and games, were continuing the fight against precious art objects. From an 'elephant', the artwork had to become a 'butterfly', to quote Tarabukin again.[21] While Maciunas and Fluxus were practicing their art at a time when centralised forms of monopoly capitalism were reaching their peak (and also showing immanent signs of decline), his rhetoric was intentionally reminiscent of Trotsky's call for a new and useful role for both art and artist – giving an American spin to Soviet models by emphasising 'career opportunities' in a 1964 letter to artist Tomas Schmit:

> Fluxus objectives are social (not aesthetic). They are connected to the LEF group of 1929 in the Soviet Union (ideologically) and concerned with: gradual elimination of the fine arts (music, theatre, poetry, fiction, painting, sculpture etc. etc). This is motivated by the desire to stop the waste of material and human resources (like yourself) and direct it to socially constructive ends. Such as applied arts: industrial design, journalism, architecture, engineering, graphic-typographic arts, printing etc. They are almost closely related fields to fine arts and offer the best alternative profession to fine artists. All clear till now?
>
> Thus Fluxus is definitely against art object as non-functional commodity – to be sold and to make [a] livelihood for an artist. It could temporarily have pedagogical function of teaching people the needlessness of art, including the eventual needlessness of Fluxus itself.[22]

This rejection of the 'non-functional' artistic commodity was widespread. In 1961, the budding Dutch Nul group, which was affiliated with the Zero group in Germany and Nouveau Réalisme in France, announced an 'international exhibition of NOTHING' in 'the world's first gallery for the latest [or, the last] art'. The show, conveniently scheduled to open on 1 April, had an announcement that took the form of a 'Manifesto Against Nothing', written largely by Carl Laszlo, who was a co-signatory alongside international allies including Piero Manzoni and (future) Fluxus artist and gallerist Arthur Kopke.[23] The manifesto stated that 'a painting is worth as much as no painting' and that 'no art market [*Kunsthandel*] is as efficient as an art market'.[24] On the day of the announced opening, the gallery remained closed, and a second manifesto, designed like an obituary called 'THE END', was distributed.

NUL GROUP, 'THE END'

Reprinted from Wim Beeren (ed.), *Actie,
werkelijkheid en fictie in de kunst van de jaren
'60 in Nederland*, Rotterdam: Museum Boijmans
Van Beuningen, 1979, p.31. Translated from
the Dutch by Sven Lütticken.

Since the liberation [in 1945], Our People have succeeded in raising themselves
to the level of a Welfare State in which only the freedom to be poor and destitute
has lost its right to exist. All of this has happened without any great flowering in
the cultural sphere. While Dutch Art has fallen to a provincial level, the value
of the Guilder is soaring. Up to now it was sacrilege to question the slogan 'No
people can live without culture'. However, today we declare:

**The Dutch people have no need for art for their well-being. In fact, good
riddance to art!**
Your cleaning lady fights her boredom with modern music, your dentist collects
modern art, your accountant amuses himself with Tinguely's machines:
You can no longer use art to improve your status!
Therefore, a group of prominent artists had taken the initiative to:
1. Decide to stop making artistic products.
2. Promote the liquidation of all institutions that still [make a] profit from art.

Thus we've closed the avant-garde Kopke gallery in Copenhagen, breaking
off all commercial relations. In this country, we're starting with Galerie 207
(Willemsparkweg 207) in Amsterdam. Henceforth the undersigned will occupy
themselves exclusively with the dissolving of art circles and the closing of exhibition spaces, which can finally be given a more dignified purpose.

On behalf of Galerie 207 in Amsterdam: **Cornelius Rogge**
The provisional action committee:
**Armando (Amsterdam), Bazon Brock (Itzehoe), Henderikse (Düsseldorf),
Arthur Kopke (Copenhagen), Silvano Lora (Paris), Piero Manzoni (Milan),
Megert (Berne), Henk Peeters (Arnhem), Schoonhoven (Delft)**[25]

This April Fool's Day stunt had clearly been informed by practices such as Manzoni's
and Yves Klein's. (Klein had, after all, purified the white cube and turned it into a void
at the Iris Clert Gallery in Paris in 1958.) Here, however, this 'zero' aesthetic becomes
a form of proto-institutional critique. It is not so much that the art space needs to be
emptied out and turned into an 'immaterial zone of pictorial sensibility' *à la* Klein;
rather, it needs to be closed down and art as we know it overcome. Or has it, we might
ask, already been overcome? On the one hand, the authors declare that the affluent
society of the Cold War no longer needs culture, nor any specialised 'artistic products';
on the other, these products are said to be everywhere, as people use art as another way
to fight boredom. What, on this level, is the difference between Jean Tinguely and a
popular TV show? The end of art has already occurred because of contemporary art's
fatal success (in which 'provincial' Dutch art, however, hardly seems to partake). The
closing of the gallery as a specialist and elitist institution, then, is only consequential.

To close down galleries, to call for the discontinuation of art production, is a strike against what art has become in the name of what it could be. The late 1960s and early 1970s saw occasional short strikes, such as the Art Strike Against Racism, War and Oppression on 22 May 1970 in New York, which was the result of the Art Workers' Coalition calling on institutions to keep their doors closed on that day. Throughout the period, the gesture of artists closing down specific exhibitions or institutions became increasingly common. In 1974, Gustav Metzger proposed something grander: a three-year strike, effective from 1977 to 1980, that would supposedly be enough to bring down the entire art-industrial complex.

GUSTAV METZGER, 'ART STRIKE 1977-1980'

Reprinted from Christos M. Joachimides and
Norman Rosenthal (ed.), *Art into Society - Society
into Art* (exh. cat.), London: ICA, 1974, p.79.

Artists engaged in political struggle act in two key areas: the use of their art for direct social change; and actions to change the structures of the art world. It **needs** to be understood that this activity is necessarily of a reformist, rather than revolutionary, character. Indeed this political activity often serves to consolidate the existing order, in the West, as well as in the East.

The use of art for social change is bedevilled by the close integration of art and society. The state supports art, it needs art as a cosmetic cloak to its horrifying reality, and uses art to confuse, divert and entertain large numbers of people. Even when deployed against the interests of the state, art cannot cut loose the umbilical cord of the state. Art in the service of revolution is unsatisfactory and mistrusted because of the numerous links of art with the state and capitalism. Despite these problems, artists will go on using art to change society.

Throughout the century, artists have attacked the prevailing methods of production, distribution and consumption of art. These attacks on the organisation of the art world have gained momentum in recent years. This struggle, aimed at the destruction of existing commercial and public marketing and patronage systems, can be brought to a successful conclusion in the course of the present decade.

The refusal to labour is the chief weapon of workers fighting the system; artists can use the same weapon. To bring down the art system it is necessary to call for years without art, a period of three years – 1977 to 1980 – when artists will not produce work, sell work, permit work to go on exhibition, and refuse collaboration with any part of the publicity machinery of the art world. This total withdrawal of labour is the most extreme collective challenge that artists can make to the state.

The years without art will see the collapse of many private galleries. Museums and cultural institutions handling contemporary art will be severely hit, suffer loss of funds and will have to reduce their staff. National and local government institutions will be in serious trouble. Art magazines will fold. The international ramifications of the dealer/museum/publicity complex make for vulnerability; it is a system that is keyed to a continuous juggling of artists, finance, works and information - damage one part, and the effect is felt worldwide.

Three years is the minimum period required to cripple the system, while a longer period of time would create difficulties for artists. The very small number of artists who live from the practice of art are sufficiently wealthy to live on their capital for three years. The vast majority of people who produce art have to subsidise their work by other means; they will, in fact, be saving money and time. Most people who practice art never sell their work at a profit, do not get the chance to exhibit their work under proper conditions, and are unmentioned by the publicity organs. Some artists may find it difficult to restrain themselves from producing art. These artists will be invited to enter camps, where making of art works is forbidden, and where any work produced is destroyed at regular intervals.

In place of the practice of art, people can spend time on the numerous historical, aesthetic and social issues facing art. It will be necessary to construct more equitable forms for marketing, exhibiting and publicising art in the future. As the twentieth century has progressed, capitalism has smothered art - the deep surgery of the years without art will give it a new chance.

In order for Metzger's Art Strike to succeed, it would have to be adopted widely. Needless to say, this didn't happen, but such proposals have the value of articulating the constraints and contradictions of praxis within, yet against, the art world.[26] In 1979 - during the proposed period of Metzger's strike - Yugoslav artist Goran Đorđević sent a questionnaire to hundreds of artists, asking:

Would you agree to take part in an international strike of artists? As a protest against the art system's unbroken repression of the artist and the alienation from the results of his practice. It would be very important to demonstrate a possibility of coordinating activity independent from art institutions, and organise an International strike of artists. This strike should represent a boycott of art system in a period of several months. Duration, exact date of beginning and forms of boycott will be worked out on the completion of the list of enrolled artists and propositions. Please give notice of this to the artists you know. The deadline for applications/suggestions is 15/05/79.[27]

That same year, Belgian artist Guillaume Bijl imagined an 'Art Liquidation Project', which he ascribed to the government, rather than to himself. Bijl penned a fake manifesto in which the state - or some unnamed agency speaking 'in the name of the state' - announced that it would close down all museums, and subsequently all private galleries, since art had proven to be non-functional and unproductive. Art spaces would be converted to more 'useful' functions, such as driving schools, hospitals, training centres and tax offices.

GUILLAUME BIJL, 'PROJECT FOR ART LIQUIDATION'

Reprinted from *M HKA Ensembles*, available at
http://ensembles.mhka.be/events/guillaume-
bijl-44a5e8f8-ae50-48d8-9ecf-3f600d7cebf7/
assets/48368 (last accessed on 19 September 2020).
Translation from the Flemish by Sven Lütticken.

BY ORDER OF THE STATE
- Due to art's non-functional nature.
- Due to the lack of space that several ministries have had to contend with recently.
- Due to the economic marginality of the art market, which is rife with tax evasion?
- Due to the annually rising costs of the ministry of culture.
- Due to the mounting general crisis, for which a solution needs to be found urgently.
- Due to the degrading nature of the new tendencies in art.
- Due to the anarchist mentality of many contemporary artists.

WE ARE OBLIGED TO CLOSE ALL MUSEUMS and transform them, as quickly as possible, into spaces suited for more practical purposes;
ART GALLERIES ARE TO FOLLOW; with the same aim.

THEY WILL BE REPLACED BY A.O.:
- Tax audit offices (department of the Ministry of Finance).
- Hospital wards (department of the Ministry of Health).
- Retraining centres (department of the Ministry of Labour).
- Military training centres (department of the Ministry of Defence).
- Career guidance services (department of the Ministry of Education).
- Data banks (department of the Ministry of Justice).
- Driving Schools (department of the Ministry of Roads and Bridges).

This text became the basis for Bijl's practice, which involved the temporary transformation of art spaces into simulations of various types of offices and shops. Some of these were, in fact, devoted to the kind of conspicuous consumption that was characteristic of the Ronald Reagan/Margaret Thatcher/Helmut Kohl era; *Chaussures Icécé* (1980), for instance, mimicked a fancy shoe shop. Bijl also created fake art exhibitions with works by fake artists. In this manner, the original starting point of his practice – art being attacked for being unproductive – was flipped around. With his installations, Bijl did not in fact perpetuate the Productivist critique of 'useless' art; rather, he showed the integration of art into an economy that was increasingly dependent on luxury goods and 'cultural commodities'.

The Potlatch of Consumerism

The Productivists were not alone in attacking the uselessness of art. In 1941, Adorno felt compelled to defend culture against an attack that had been launched by the sociologist Thorstein Veblen. Veblen analysed art as – and more or less reduced art to – a form of 'conspicuous consumption' by the 'leisure class'. While Adorno found much to agree with in Veblen's work, he was concerned by the puritanical reflexes that made Veblen attack all culture as waste, and his longing back for a simpler culture in which good workmanship was the only art:

> The economic in Veblen remains implicitly defined as the 'profitable'. His talk of economics converges with that of the businessman who rejects an unnecessary expense as uneconomical. The concepts of the useful and the useless presupposed in such thinking are not subjected to analysis. Veblen demonstrates that society functions uneconomically in terms of its own criteria. This is both much and little; much, because he thus glaringly illuminates the unreason of reason, little, because he fails to grasp the interdependence of the useful and the useless. He leaves the question of the useless to heteronomous categories produced by the intellectual division of labour and makes himself a cultural efficiency expert whose vote can be vetoed by his aesthetic colleagues. He fails to see in the opposition of jurisdictions itself an expression of the fetishistic division of labour. While as economist he is all too sovereign in his treatment of culture, cutting it from the budget as waste, he is secretly resigned to its existence outside the budgetary sphere. He fails to see that its legitimacy or illegitimacy can be decided only through insight into society as a totality, not from the departmental perspective of the questioner. Thus a moment of buffoonery is inherent in his critique of culture.[28]

If Adorno thus cautioned against totalising conceptions of efficiency and productivity, the French philosopher and renegade Surrealist Georges Bataille waged a full-on war against what he regarded as the cult of production in both the Soviet Union and the capitalist West. His opening salvo was his 1933 essay 'La Notion de dépense' (The Notion of Expenditure), but the campaign would continue for the rest of his life.[29] Opposing the subjugation of life to the imperatives of production and Fordist efficiency, Bataille lauded premodern cultures precisely because they were not beholden to the notion of the subject as a putatively autonomous yet disciplined and productive member of society; not having been corrupted by the lure of an ultimately instrumentalist concept of autonomy, these societies prized sovereignty. In contrast to the modern subject, seemingly autonomous yet enslaved by work, the sovereign individual is not afraid to transcend the mundane world of use-value, to court excessive waste and the *petite mort* of sexual climax.

> The sovereignty I speak of has little to do with the sovereignty of States, as international law defines it. I speak in general of an aspect that is opposed to the servile and the subordinate. In the past, sovereignty belonged to those who, bearing the names of chieftain, pharaoh, king, king of kings, played a leading role in the formation of that being with which we identify ourselves, the human being of

today. But it also belonged to various divinities, of which the supreme god was one of the forms, as well as to the priests who served and incarnated them, and who were sometimes indistinguishable from the kings; it belonged, finally, to a whole feudal and priestly hierarchy that was different only in degree from those who occupied its pinnacle. But further, it belongs essentially to all *men* who possess and have never entirely lost the value that is attributed to gods and 'dignitaries'. [...]

What distinguishes sovereignty is the consumption of wealth, as against labour and servitude, which produce wealth without consuming it. The sovereign individual consumes and doesn't labour, whereas at the antipodes of sovereignty the slave and the man without means labour and reduce their consumption to the necessities, to the products without which they could neither subsist nor labour. [...]

The sovereign, if he is not imaginary, truly enjoys the products of this world – beyond his needs. His sovereignty resides in this. Let us say that the sovereign (or the sovereign life) begins when, with the necessities ensured, the possibility of life opens up without limit.

Conversely, we may call sovereign the enjoyment of possibilities that utility doesn't justify (utility being that whose end is productive activity). Life *beyond utility* is the domain of sovereignty.[30]

For Bataille, planning and constructing the future through work – whether under capitalism or in Stalinist communism – resulted in people's enslavement to a linear and teleological temporality. In one of his books he published a photograph of a voodoo ritual in which a participant is licking a severed ram's head.[31] In such rituals, historical time is annulled: 'What is sovereign in fact is to enjoy the present time without having anything else in view but this present time.'[32] The modern Western subject is always focussed on a future that is to be conquered (more production, more accumulation); the sovereign is not.

In modern societies, the remaining experiences of sovereignty include eroticism, art and the worker taking revenge on the cult of use and production by squandering his income on alcohol. Such experiences are poor descendants of the *potlatch*, a ritual among the indigenous peoples of North American of excessive mutual gifts that, in Bataille's interpretation, proved that some societies revolved not around utility and growth but around the ritualistic destruction of objects and use-value. Drawing on the anthropological work of Marcel Mauss, Bataille turned the potlatch into Exhibit A of his critique of modernity. In the 1950s, the future Situationists (then known as Internationale Lettriste) likewise felt the potlatch's lure, naming their newsletter after the ritual.

The budding Situationists, too, glorified the useless, the improductive – life as *fête* and *dérive*. Rather than critiquing specific forms of 'conspicuous consumption' as useless and noxious, the Situationists attacked all forms of capitalist consumption as substitutes for real experience and true enjoyment: as spectacle in which people consume their alienated labour in the form of images. For the Situationists, as for Bataille, the issue was not with true consumption as waste, as excess, as life, but with consumption in the service of production and exploitation. This was the capitalist pseudo-potlatch: those who can afford it (or not, as the case may be) pay for 'luxury' goods that are nothing but impoverished replacements (*Ersatz*). Art was part of the problem: it had been made economically and socially useful by being institutionalised and commodified, becoming bourgeois and capitalist through and through. In their own version of the 'art strike', the Situationists demanded that artists stop making identifiable and commodifiable artworks (such as paintings) in order to work towards an unalienated life to come, to fight for an unrestricted autonomy. As Debord would later put it, looking back at the elaboration of the Situationist project and programme:

> Thus was mapped out a programme calculated to undermine the credibility of the entire organisation of social life. Classes and specialisations, work and entertainment, commodities and urbanism, ideology and the state – we showed that it all needed to be scrapped.[33]

Art was one of the 'specialisations' that needed to be scrapped – a pseudo-autonomous field to be abandoned. Painters in the SI, such as Asger Jorn, were understandably reluctant to give up their practice. In *Value and Economy* (1962), written after he left the SI (whilst continuing to finance them from his picture sales), Jorn attempted to argue that art, while entangled in commodification, is ultimately about the production of aesthetic 'countervalues' or qualities:

> The artwork in its highest form is *valuable quality*: the form that always distributes its content without even being exhausted. It fills itself up in the most wonderful way. Art is the spiritual creation which preserves its quality simultaneously with spreading its value. This singularity has provided material for innumerable explanations about the metaphysical and religious essence of art, whilst at the same time the rationalists have simply denied that there is anything called art. The reason for this special character of art, which Marx was the first to acknowledge but the last to understand, is, however, quite a simple condition. Art never supplies values. Art gives nothing. It takes all. Art is the strength needed to influence a body and liberate the values confined in that body. Art is thus a destroyer of human quality and integrity, and it is this destruction of one's own absolute integrity that one experiences as beauty. The secret of art consists of the simple fact that it is more blessed to give than to take, but also that this blessedness is dependent on a *voluntary* giving, so that what is given is felt as a *surplus*, a wealth, and not a duty. This is the simple materialistic explanation of the value of the artwork and for all the other things called spiritual values. Art is opium for the people. It undoes, subverts, liberates.
>
> In relation to the practical values, art is thus a countervalue, the value of productive pleasure. *Art is the call for a discharge of energy* without a precise goal, except the one that the received can discover.[34]

Starting in the late 1960s, the French sociologist and philosopher Jean Baudrillard synthesised elements from Bataille and the Situationists, among others, into a critique of the Marxist understanding of production. As a member of the Utopie group in the late 1960s and 1970s, Baudrillard was involved in the critical reception of post-War urbanism and consumer culture by this group of architects and theorists. In two essays that were originally published in *Utopie* in 1972–73, Baudrillard launched an attack on Marx's notion of use-value and his insistence on the bodily and qualitative nature of work or labour.

We have seen that Marx, while keeping use-value and exchange-value analytically separate, nonetheless stated that exchange-value presupposes use-value of whatever kind; this can also be 'immaterial' use (for novels, paintings and so on). Turning Marx on his head, Baudrillard argues for the primacy of exchange-value: 'Exchange-value makes the use-value of products appear as its anthropological horizon. The exchange-value of labour power makes use-value visible as the originality and concrete finality of the act of labour, as its "generic" alibi. The logic of signifiers produces "evidence" of the "reality" of the signified and of the referent.'[35]

Baudrillard's 1972 book *Towards a Critique of the Political Economy of the Sign* argued that in modern commodity/media culture exchange-value is transmuted into *sign value*. 'Functionalist design', such as a Bauhaus chair, produces 'functionality' as sign value. In other words, while we may think that use-value has to come first, what we posit as use-value is a second-degree abstraction. Our notions of 'utility' *are the product of capitalism*; they are informed and shaped by exchange-value even when we think that we are critically countering the rule of exchange-value. In the two essays excerpted here, 'The Mirror of Production' and 'Marxism and the System of Political Economy', Baudrillard argues that 'defining objects as useful, and responding to needs, is the most complete, most internalised expression of abstract economic exchange: its subjective closure.' It is therefore impossible to ground an analysis of exchange or sign value in some foundational use-value: 'exchange-value retrospectively originates and logically closes itself off in use-value. In other words, here the signified "use-value" is still an *effect of the code*, the final precipitate of the law of value.'

Baudrillard clearly was not interested in a nuanced reading of Marx that does justice to the complexities of his theory of value. Instead, he attacked what he saw as a humanist and romantic essentialism that privileges use over exchange in order to show that the former really is an effect of the latter – it has no autonomous existence.

JEAN BAUDRILLARD, 'THE MIRROR OF PRODUCTION'

Reprinted from Jean Baudrillard, *Utopia Deferred: Writings for 'Utopie' (1967-1978)*, New York: Semiotext(e), 2006, pp.105-129. First published in 1972. Translation from the French by Stuart Kendall; amended by Sven Lütticken.

In order to grasp the radicality of political economy, it does not suffice to unmask what is hidden behind the concept of consumption: the anthropology of needs and use-value. We must also unmask everything that hides behind the concept of production, of the mode of production, of productive forces, of relationships of production, etc. All the concepts fundamental to Marxist analysis need to be questioned starting from even from its demand for radical critique and for the transcendence of political economy. What is axiomatic about productive forces, about the dialectical genesis of modes of production from which revolutionary theory springs? What is axiomatic about the generic wealth of man – labour power, about the motor of history, about history itself, which is only 'the production by men of their material life'? 'The first historical act is thus the production of the means to satisfy these needs, the production of material life itself. And indeed this is an historical act, a fundamental condition of all history, which today, as thousands of years ago, must daily and hourly be fulfilled merely in order to sustain human life.'[8]

The liberation of productive forces is confused with the liberation of man: is this a revolutionary watchword or one for political economy? Almost no one has doubted this final evidence, certainly not Marx, for whom men 'begin to distinguish themselves from animals as soon as they begin to *produce* their means of subsistence'.[9] (Why must man's vocation always be to distinguish himself from animals? Humanism is an *idée fixe* that comes to us – it too – from political economy – leave that.) But is existence itself an end for man, an end for which he must find the means? These little innocent phrases are already theoretical ultimatums; the separation of ends and means already constitutes the most ferocious and most naïve postulate about the human species. Man has needs. Does he have needs? Is he sworn to satisfy them? Is he a labour power (through which he separates himself, as means, from his own ends)? Prodigious metaphors of the system that dominates us; a fable of political economy still recounted to generations of revolutionaries, infected even in their political radicality by the conceptual virus of this same political economy.

Critique of Use-value and Labour Power
In the distinction between exchange-value and use-value, Marxism assumes its greatest force but also its weakness. The presupposition of use-value, the hypothesis, beyond the abstraction of exchange-value, of a concrete value, of a human finality of commodities in the moment of their direct relationship of use for a subject, we have seen that this value is only an effect of the system of exchange-value, a concept produced by the system, in which the system completes itself.[10] Far from designating a beyond for political economy, use-value is but the horizon of exchange-value. A radical questioning of the concept of consumption begins on the level of needs and products. *But this critique assumes its full scope in its extension to that other commodity, labour power.* The concept of production then falls under radical critique.

Don't forget that according to Marx himself the revolutionary originality of his theory consists in unleashing the concept of labour power from its status as an exceptional commodity, the insertion of which, in the cycle of production *under the name of use-value* carries the X element, the differential extra value which generates surplus value and the whole process of capital. (Bourgeois economics speculates on simple 'labour' as one factor of production among others in the economic process.)

The history of the use-value of labour power in Marx is complex. Adam Smith attacked the Physiocrats and the Exchangists with the concept of labour. Marx in turn deconstructed abstract social labour (exchange-value) and

---

[8]   Karl Marx and Friedrich Engels, *The German Ideology*, New York: International Publishers, 1947, p.16.
[9]   *Ibid.*, p.7.
[10]   See Jean Baudrillard, *For a Critique of the Political Economy of the Sign* (trans. Charles Levin), St. Louis: Telos Press, 1981.

concrete labour (use-value) in the double concept labour power/commodity. And he insisted on the necessity of maintaining in all their force the two aspects, the articulation of which alone can aid in objectively deciphering the process of capitalist labour. To A. Wagner, who reproached him for having neglected use-value, he responds: '... the *vir obscurus* overlooks the fact that even in the analysis of the commodity I do not stop at the double manner in which it is represented, but immediately go on to say that in this double being of the commodity is represented the *twofold character of the labour* whose product it is: *useful labour*, i.e. the concrete modes of the labours which create use-values, and *abstract labour*, *labour as expenditure of labour power*, irrespective of whatever "useful" way it is expended ... that in the development of the *value form of the commodity*, in the last instance of its money form and hence of *money*, the *value* of a commodity is represented in the *use-value* of the other, i.e. in the natural form of the other commodity; that surplus value itself is derived from *a "specific" use-value of labour power* exclusively pertaining to the latter, etc. etc., thus for me use-value plays a far more important part than it has in economics hitherto, however, that is only ever taken into account where it springs from the analysis of a given economic constellation, not from arguing backwards and forwards about the concepts of words "use-value" and "value".'[11]

It is clear that in this text the use-value of labour, losing its 'naturality', recovers a 'specific' value that is much greater in the *structural* functioning of exchange-value. Also, that in maintaining a kind of dialectical equilibrium between qualitative concrete labour and quantitative abstract labour, Marx – while granting logical priority to exchange-value (the given economic formation), retaining, even in that structure, a kind of concrete precedence, a concrete positivity of use-value – still retains something *of the apparent movement of political economy*. He does not radicalise the schema to the point of reversing this appearance and revealing use-value *as produced by the play of exchange-value*. We have shown this for the products of consumption, it is the same for labour power. The fact of defining objects as useful, and responding to needs, is the most complete, the most internalised expression of abstract economic exchange: its subjective closure. The fact of defining labour power as the source of 'concrete' social wealth is the complete expression of the abstract manipulation of labour power: the truth of capital culminates in this 'evidence' of man as producer of value. Such is the twist by which exchange-value retrospectively originates and logically closes itself off in use-value. In other words, here the signified 'use-value' is still an *effect of the code*, the final precipitate of the law of value. It does not suffice to analyse the operation of the quantitative abstraction of exchange-value *starting from* use-value, one must still make visible the conditions for the possibility of this operation: to understand the production of even the concept of the use-value of labour power, of a specific rationality of productive man. Without this generic definition, no political economy. Therein, in the last instance, lies the foundation of political economy. It is therein as well that one must disrupt it, by unmasking this quantitative – qualitative 'dialectic', behind which the definitive structural institution of the field of value is hidden.

---

[11] Karl Marx, 'Marginal Notes on Adolph Wagner's *Lehrbuch der politischen Oekonomie*' (1879-80), in *Theoretical Practice*, no.5, Spring 1972, pp.51-52.

What is Concrete about Labour: The Quantitative-Qualitative 'Dialectic'
'The quantitative consideration of labour could only come about once it had been universalised during the eighteenth century in Europe. ... Until then, different forms of activity were not comparable in their breadth. ... At first, all tasks presented themselves as diverse qualities.'[12] During the historical epoch of the artisanal mode of production, qualitative labour came to be differentiated in relation to its process, to its product, and to the destination of the product. In the subsequent capitalist mode of production, labour is analyzed under a double aspect: 'While labour which creates exchange-values is *abstract, universal* and *homogeneous*, labour which produces use-value is concrete and special and is made up of an endless variety of kinds of labour according to the way in which and the material to which it is applied.'[13] Here we rediscover the moment of use-value: concrete, differentiated, incomparable. In opposition to the quantitative measure of labour power, labour use-value remains a qualitative potentiality. Neither more nor less. It is specified by its own end, the material that it works, or simply because it is the energetic expenditure of a particular individual at a particular moment. The use-value of labour power is the moment of its actualisation, of the relation of man to the useful expenditure that he possesses – it is basically an act of (productive) *consumption* – and this moment retains, in the general process, all of its singularity. At this level, labour power is incommensurable.

There is a profound enigma in the articulation of Marx's theory: how is surplus labour born? How does the actualisation of labour power, by definition qualitative, come to be 'more' or 'less'? One would have to suppose that the 'dialectical' opposition of the quantitative and the qualitative only expresses an apparent movement. [...]

The 'Generic' Double Face of Man
In fact, the use-value of labour power is no more real than the use-value of products, no more real than the autonomy of the signified and the referent. The same fiction reigns in the orders of production, consumption and signification. Exchange-value makes the use-value of products appear as its anthropological horizon. The exchange-value of labour power makes use-value visible as the originality and concrete finality of the act of labour, as its 'generic' alibi. The logic of signifiers produces 'evidence' of the 'reality' of the signified and of the referent. Throughout, exchange-value makes concrete production, concrete consumption and concrete signification appear as a kind of abstraction, as an abstract distortion. Exchange-value foments this concreteness as its ideological ectoplasm, as its originary phantasm and its surpassing. In this sense, needs, use-value, the referent 'don't exist': they are only concepts produced and projected in a generic dimension by the same development of the system of exchange-value.[14]

In the same way, the double potentiality of man, that of needs and labour power, that 'generic' double face of universal man is only that of man as he is produced by the system of political economy. And productivity is not there at first as a generic dimension, as the human and social seed of all wealth, that one must

[12]   Pierre Naville, *Le nouveau léviathan*, Paris: Riviare, 1954, p.371.
[13]   Karl Marx, *Contribution to a Critique of Political Economy*, New York: International Publishers, 1904, p.33.
[14]   This is not to say that they have *never existed*: another paradox to which we will have to return.

extract from the dross of capitalist relations of production (the eternal empiricist illusion), one must reverse all of this, and see that it is the development of abstract and generalised productivity (the developed form of political economy) that makes the *concept of production* itself visible as movement and generic end of man (or again the concept of man as producer).

In other words, the system of political economy produces not only the individual as labour power sold and exchanged, it produces the concept of labour power as the fundamental human potentiality. More profoundly than in the fiction of the individual freely selling his labour power in the market, the system takes root to the extent that the individual identifies with his labour power and his act of 'transforming nature toward human ends'. In a word, there is not only the quantitative exploitation of man as productive force by the *system* of capitalist political economy, but the metaphysical overdetermination of man as producer by the *code* of political economy.[15] In the final instance, that is how the system rationalises its power. *And in this Marxism aides the capitalist deceit by persuading men that they are alienated by the sale of their labour power, censuring the much more radical hypothesis that they could be alienated as labour power, as the 'inalienable' power of creating value through labour.* [...]

Ethic of Labour; Aesthetics of Play
This logic of material production, this dialectic of modes of production always returns, beyond history, to a generic definition of man as a dialectical being, understandable based on the sole process of the objectification of nature. This is heavy with consequences to the extent that, even through the fortunes of his history, man (whose history is also a 'product') will be ruled by this clear and definitive reason, by this dialectical schema which acts like implicit philosophy. Marx developed it in the *Manuscripts of 1844*, Marcuse revives it in his critique of the economic concept of labour: 'Labour is an ontological concept of human existence as such'. He cites Lorenz von Stein: 'Labour is ... in every way the actualisation of one's infinite determinations through the self-positing of the individual personality [in which the personality itself] makes the content of the external world its own and in this way forces the world to become a part of its own internal world.'[16] Marx: 'Labour is *man's coming-to-be for himself* within the *externalisation* or as *externalised* man ... [that is] the *self-creation* and self-objectification [of man]'.[17] And even in *Capital*: 'So far therefore as labour is a creator of use-value, is useful labour, it is a necessary condition, independent of all forms of society, for the existence of the human race; it is an external nature-imposed necessity, without which there can be no material exchanges between man and nature, and therefore no life.'[18] 'Labour is, in the first place, a process in which both man and nature participate, and in which man of his own accord starts, regulates and controls the material reactions between himself and nature. He opposes himself to nature as one of her own forces setting

---

15   The same for nature: not only the exploitation of nature as productive force, but the overdetermination of nature as referent, as 'objective' reality, by the code of political economy.

16   Herbert Marcuse, 'On the Concept of Labor', *Telos*, no.16, Summer 1973, pp.11-12.

17   Loyd D. Easton and Kurt H. Guddat (ed.), *Writings of the Young Marx on Philosophy and Society*, New York: Anchor, 1969, pp.322, 332.

18   Karl Marx, *Capital*, vol.1, Moscow: Foreign Languages Publishing House, pp.42-43.

arms and legs, head and hands, the natural forces of his body in motion in order to appropriate nature's productions in a form adapted to his own wants.'[19] The dialectical culmination of all this is the concept of nature as 'the inorganic body of man': the naturalisation of man and the humanisation of nature.[20]

On this dialectical basis, Marxist philosophy unfolds in two directions: an ethics of labour, an aesthetics of non-labour. The first across the entirety of bourgeois and socialist ideology – the exaltation of labour as value, as an end in itself, as a categorical imperative. Labour loses its negativity here and stands as an absolute value. But is the 'materialist' thesis of the generic productivity of man far from this 'idealist' sanctification of labour? It is in any case dangerously vulnerable here. Marcuse: 'Insofar as they take the concept of "needs" and its satisfaction in the world of goods as the starting point, all economic theories fail to recognise the full factual content of labour. ... The essential factual content of labour is not grounded in the scarcity of goods, nor in a discontinuity between the world of disposable and utilisable goods and human needs, but, on the contrary, in an essential excess of human existence beyond every possible situation in which it finds itself and the world.'[21] In the name of which he separates play as a secondary activity: 'In the structural sense, within the totality of human existence, labour is necessarily and eternally "earlier" than play.'[22] Labour alone founds the world as objective and man as historical, only labour founds a real dialectic of transcendence and completion. It even justifies metaphysically the burdensome nature of labour. 'In the final analysis, the burdensome character of labour expresses nothing other than a negativity rooted in the very essence of human existence: man can achieve his own self only by passing through otherness: by passing through "externalisation" and "alienation".'[23] I have only cited this purest Christian ethic (and inversely of course: today we see a large contamination of these two points of view on the basis of this transcendence of alienation and this intraworldly asceticism of effort and of the overcoming that Weber located as the radical germ of the capitalist spirit). And also because since the beginning this aberrant sanctification of labour found itself to be the secret vice of Marxist political and economic strategy. Walter Benjamin stigmatised it violently: 'Nothing has so corrupted the German working class as the notion that it was moving with the current. It regarded technological development as the driving force of the stream with which it thought it was moving. From there it was but a step to the illusion that the factory work ostensibly furthering technological progress constituted a political achievement. The old Protestant work ethic was resurrected among German workers in secularised form. The Gotha Program already bears traces of this confusion, defining labor as "the source of all wealth and all culture". Smelling a rat, Marx countered that "the man who possesses no other property than his labor power" must of necessity become "the slave of other men who have made themselves owners". Yet the confusion spread, and soon thereafter Josef Dietzgen proclaimed: "The saviour of modem times is called work. The ... perfecting ... of the labour process constitutes the wealth

---

¹⁹ *Ibid.*, p.177.
²⁰ Engels, always a naturalist, goes on to praise the role play by labour in the transition from ape to man.
²¹ H. Marcuse, 'On the Concept of Labor', p.22.
²² *Ibid.*, p.15.
²³ *Ibid.*, p.25.

which can now do what no redeemer has ever been able to accomplish."'[24] Is this a question of a 'vulgar' Marxism as Benjamin suggests? No less 'vulgar' in the case of the 'strange delusion' Paul Lafargue denounced in *The Right to be Lazy*: 'A strange delusion possesses the working classes of the nations where capitalist civilisation holds its sway.'[25] Apparently orthodox Marxism preaches the liberation of productive forces under the auspices of the *negativity* of labour. But is this not a question, faced with the gospel of labour, of an 'aristocratic' idealism? The other is positivist, and Marxism wants to be 'dialectical', but they have the hypothesis of man's productive vocation in common. If one admits that it raises the purest metaphysics,[26] then the difference between 'vulgar' Marxism and the 'other' would be that of a mass religion and a philosophical theory – which, as we know, is not much. [...]

This *beyond* of political economy called play, non-work or non-alienated labour, is defined as the reign of finality without end. It is in this sense that it is and remains, in the very Kantian sense of the term, an *aesthetic*. With all the bourgeois ideological connotations that this implies. And it is true that the thought of Marx, if it settled its accounts with bourgeois morality, remains defenceless against bourgeois aesthetics, the ambiguity of which is more subtle, but whose complicity with the general system of political economy is also profound. Once again, it is at the heart of its strategy, in the analytic distinction that it makes between the quantitative and the qualitative, that Marxist thought inherits from the aesthetic and humanist virus of bourgeois thought – the concept of the qualitative is burdened with all these finalities, whether the concrete finality of use-value or the endless idealist and transcendental finalities. This is the defect of every notion of play, of liberty, of transparency, of disalienation, the defect of the *revolutionary imagination* insofar as in the ideal type of play, of the free play of human faculties, we are still in the process of repressive desublimation. This sphere of play effectively defines itself as the fulfilment of human rationality, as the dialectical culmination of man's activity, of his incessant objectification of nature and control of his exchanges with it. It presupposes the full development of productive forces, it remains 'mixed up with' the reality principle and the transformation of nature. It can only flourish, Marx says clearly, when based on the reign of necessity. This is to say that, wishing itself beyond labour, but in its *prolongation*, the sphere of play is never only the aesthetic sublimation of its constraints. We are still well within the typically bourgeois problematic of necessity and freedom, the double ideological expression of which has always been, since coming into existence, the institution of a reality principle (repression and sublimation: principle of labour) and its formal surpassing in an ideal transcendence.

Work and non-work: a 'revolutionary' theme. This is undoubtedly the most most subtle form of the aforementioned binary, structural opposition. The end of the end of the exploitation by labour is truly this inverse fascination with non-labour, this inverse mirage of free time (obligated time – free time, full time – empty time: another paradigm that seals the hegemony of the order of time, which is always merely that of production). Non-work is still only the repressive

---

24   W. Benjamin, 'On the Concept of History', *op. cit.*, p.393.
25   Paul Lafargue, *The Right to be Lazy* (trans. C. Kerr), Chicago: Kerr, 1917, p.9.
26   Insofar as it conceives of man as the union of a soul and a body – which took place, as we know, in an extraordinary 'dialectical' flowering during the Christian Middles Ages.

desublimation of labour power – the antithesis that acts as an alternative. Such is the sphere of non-work, even if one does not confuse it immediately with that of leisure and its present bureaucratic organisation, wherein the desire for death and for mortification and its management by social institutions is as powerful as in the sphere of work; even if one envisions it in a radical way that *represents* it as other than the model of a 'total availability', of a 'liberty' for the individual to 'produce' himself as a value, to 'express' himself, to 'liberate' himself as authentic *content* (conscious or unconscious), in short the ideality of time and of the individual as an empty form, to be filled in the end by his freedom. The finality of value is always there. It no longer inscribes itself, as in the sphere of productive activity, in *determined* contents. It is there henceforth as *pure form*, but no less determining. Exactly as the pure institutional form of painting, of art and theatre shines, emptied of its contents, in anti-painting, anti-art, anti-theatre – non-work shines with the pure form of labour. The concept can therefore be fantasised as the abolition of political economy, it is bound to fall back into the sphere of political economy, as a sign – and only a sign – of its abolition. It already escapes the revolutionaries to enter into the programmatic field of the 'new society'. [...]

In the Shadow of Marxist Concepts
Historical Materialism, dialectics, modes of production, labour power: all these concepts by which Marxist theory seeks to shatter the abstract universality of the concepts of bourgeois thought (Nature and Progress, Man and Reason, formal Logic, Labour, Exchange, etc.). Marxism in its turn is in the process of universalising them according to a 'critical' imperialism as ferocious as that of bourgeois thought.

The proposition that a concept is not only an interpretative hypothesis but a translation of the movement of the universe is pure metaphysics. Marxist concepts don't escape this lapse. Thus, by all logic, the concept of history must maintain itself as historical, turn on and clarify itself by abolishing the context that produces it. In place of this, it is transhistorisised, it is redoubled in itself and thereby universalised. Dialectics, in all rigour, should dialectically surpass and annul itself. By radicalizing the concept of production and modes of production at a given moment, Marx made a breach in the social mystery of exchange-value. Thereafter the concept took all of its strategic power from its irruption, by which it deposes political economy from its imaginary universality. But it lost its power, already in Marx's time, by offering itself as a principle of explication. It cancels its 'difference' by universalising itself, returning by the same blow to the form of the dominant code, universality, and to the strategy of political economy. It is not tautological that the concept of history should be historical, the concept of dialectics dialectical, the concept of production itself a product (which is to say judged by a kind of auto-analysis). This simply designates the present, explosive, mortal form of critical concepts. From the moment they assert themselves in the universal, they cease to be analytical: the religion of meaning commences. They become canonical and they enter into the general system's mode of theoretical reproduction. At this moment too – and this is not by chance – they assume their scientific cast (the canonisation of Marxist concepts from Engels to Althusser). They set themselves up to express an 'objective reality'. They become signs: signifiers of a 'real' signified. And if, in the best moments these concepts have been practiced as such, this is to say without taking themselves for reality, nevertheless they have fallen into the *imaginary of the sign*, which is to say into the *sphere of truth*, no longer in the sphere of interpretation, but in that of *repressive simulation.*

From here, they can only evoke one another, in an indefinite metonymic process: man is historical, history is dialectical, dialectics is the process of (material) production, production is the movement of human existence itself, history is that of modes of production, etc. Scientific and universalist, this discourse (this code) becomes immediately imperialist. All these possible societies are summoned to respond. To interrogate Marxist thought to see if societies 'without history' are something other than 'pre'-historic, other than a chrysalis and a larva. The dialectics of the world of production is not yet well developed, but you lose nothing by waiting – the Marxist egg is ready to hatch. The psychoanalytical egg, elsewhere, is also already ready, because everything that we have said of these Marxist concepts goes for the unconscious, repression, Oedipus, etc. This even better: the Bororos are closer to the primary processes than we are.

All of this constitutes the most surprising – and the most reactionary – theoretical aberration. There is *neither mode of production nor production itself* in primitive societies. There is *no dialectic* in primitive societies. There is *no unconscious* in primitive societies. All of these concepts analyse only our societies, regulated by political economy. These concepts have only a kind of boomerang value. If psychoanalysis speaks of the unconscious in primitive societies, should we ask what psychoanalysis represses or what repression produced psychoanalysis itself? When Marxism speaks of the mode of production in primitive societies, should we ask to what extent this concept fails to account for even our historical societies – the reason we export it. And there where all of our ideologues seek to finalise, to rationalise primitive societies according to their own concepts, to encode the primitives, should we ask what obsession makes them perceive this finality, this code blowing up in their faces. In place of exporting Marxism and psychoanalysis (not to mention bourgeois ideology, though on this level there is no difference), bring all of the impact, the entire interrogation of primitive societies to bear on Marxism and psychoanalysis. Maybe then we can shatter this fascination, this auto-fetishism of Western thought, maybe we could escape from a Marxism which has become a specialist in the impasses of capitalism much more than a road to revolution, from a psychoanalysis which has become a specialist in the impasses of libidinal economy much more than in the ways of desire.

Following page: Group Material,
cover of zine produced for the exhibition
'Resistance (Anti-Baudrillard)',
6–28 February 1987, White Columns, New York
Courtesy the artists and White Columns

RESISTANCE

ANTI-BAUDRILLARD

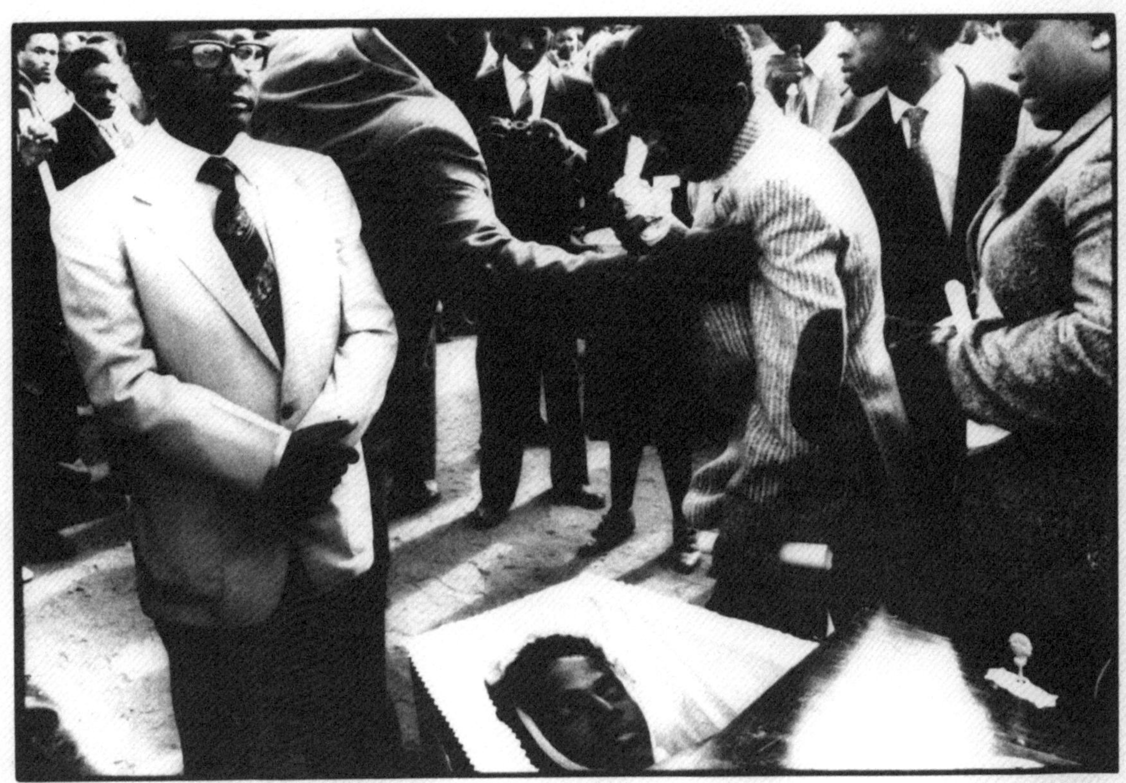

GROUP MATERIAL

JEAN BAUDRILLARD, 'MARXISM AND THE SYSTEM OF POLITICAL ECONOMY'

Reprinted from Jean Baudrillard, *Utopia
Deferred: Writings for* Utopie *(1967-1978)*,
New York: Semiotext(e), 2006, pp.138-41, and
145-46. First published in 1973. Translated
from the French by Stuart Kendall.

The Third Phase of Political Economy

In *The Poverty of Philosophy*, Marx drew up a kind of genealogy of the system of exchange-value:

1. Only what is superfluous to material production is exchanged (in archaic and feudal forms, for example). Vast sectors remain outside the sphere of exchange and of the commodity.

2. The entire volume of 'industrial' material production is alienated in exchange (capitalist political economy).

3. Even what is considered inalienable (shared, but not exchanged): virtue, love, knowledge, consciousness; also falls into the sphere of exchange-value. This is the era of 'general corruption', 'the time when each object, physical or moral, is brought to market as a commodity value, to be priced at its exact value'.

The schema is clear, beyond even what Marx anticipated. Between the first and second phases, the birth of capital, a decisive mutation not only when it comes to the *extension* of the sphere of exchange, but also its repercussions at the level of social relations. Between phases two and three, on the contrary, Marx and Marxism see only a kind of extensive effect. The 'infrastructural' mutation, which locates the mode of production and contemporary social relations, is acquired in phase two. Phase three only represents the 'superstructural' effect in the domain of 'immaterial' values. With Marx, and against him in a way, we think that one must grant this schema all of its analytical force.

There is a decisive mutation between phase two and phase three. It is as revolutionary in relation to phase two as phase two was to phase one. To the third power of the system of political economy, another type of contradiction than that of phase two, which is properly that of capital (and of *Capital*). Anticipated by Marx, this new phase of political economy, which had not yet assumed in his time its full extent, is as quickly neutralised, drawn into the wake of phase two, in terms of the market and of 'mercantile venality'.

Even today the only 'Marxist' critique of culture, of consumption, of information, of ideology, of sexuality, etc., is made in terms of 'capitalist prostitution', which is to say in terms of commodities, exploitation, profit, money, surplus value. These are all characteristic terms of phase two and terms about which one can say (in reverse for the moment) that they now assume their full value, but that they serve only as a *metaphoric reference* when they are transferred to analytic principles in phase three. Even the Situationists, undoubtedly the only ones who attempted to release this new radicality from political economy in the 'society of the spectacle', still refer to this 'infrastructural' logic of the commodity. Their fidelity to the proletariat is logical if, behind spectacular organisation, the exploitation of labour power is still determinant – the spectacle being only an immense connotation of commodities – illogical if the concept of the spectacle is taken *as that of the commodity as it was by Marx in his time*, in all its radicality, as a process of generalised social abstraction of which 'material' exploitation is only a particular phase. In this hypothesis, the form-spectacle is determinant, from it one sets out *as from the most developed structural phase.*[27] This over-turns many perspectives on politics and revolution, the proletariat and class, but take it or leave it. Things have changed in any case. A revolution has taken place in the capitalist mode without our Marxists having wanted to apperceive it. When it comes to the objection that our society is still largely dominated by the logic of the commodity, the objection is valueless. When Marx set himself to analyse capital, capitalist industrial production was still largely in the minority. When he outlined political economy as the determinant sphere, religion was still largely dominant. The decision was never at the quantitative level, but at the level of structural critique.

This mutation concerns the passage from the commodity form to the sign form, from the abstraction of the exchange of material products under the law of general equivalence to the operationalisation of all exchanges under the law of the code. With this passage *to the political economy of the sign*, it is not a question of a simple 'mercantile prostitution' of all values (the completely romantic vision of the celebrated passage from the *Communist Manifesto*, cap-italism trampling all human values, art, culture, labour, etc., to make money: the *romantic critique* of profit). It is a question of the passage of all values to the value of sign exchange, under the hegemony of the code, which is to say of a structure of control and power much more subtle and more totalitarian than that of exploitation. Because the *sign is much more than a connotation of a com-modity*, than a semiological supplement to exchange-value. It is an operational structure around which the quantitative mystery of surplus value appears inoffensive. The meta-ideology [*suridéologie*] of the sign and the generalised operationalisation of the signifier – sanctioned everywhere today by the new master disciplines: structural linguistics, semiology, information theory, and cybernetics, which have replaced good old political economy as the theoretical foundation of the system – this new ideological structure, which plays on the hieroglyphs of the code, is much more illegible than that which plays on produc-tive energy. This manipulation, which plays on the faculty to produce meaning and difference, is more radical than that which acts on labour power. [...]

Demand, which is to say needs, corresponds more and more to a model of simulation. These new productive forces no longer pose a question to the system: they are an anticipated response; the system itself controls their emergence. It can afford the luxury of contradiction and dialectic through the play of signs. It can offer itself all the signs of revolution. Since it produces all the responses, it annihilates the question at the same time. This is only possible through the imposition and the monopoly of the code. This is to say that, however one takes it, one can only respond to the system in its own terms and according to its own laws, answering it with its own signs. The passage to this stage constitutes some-thing other than the end of competition, it signifies that, from a system of pro-ductive forces, of exploitation and profit, as in the competitive system, its logic dominated the time of social labour, we pass to a gigantic operational game of

---

27   Lukács's concept of 'reification' undoubtedly constitutes the only attempt at critical theoretical development between Marx and the Situationists.

questions and responses, a gigantic combinatory wherein all values commutate and exchange according to their operational sign. The monopolistic stage signifies less the monopoly of the means of production (which is never total) than the *monopoly of the code*.

This phase is accompanied by a radical change, in the functioning of the sign, in the *mode of signification*. The goals of prestige and distinction still correspond to a traditional status of the sign, where a signifier refers to a signified, where a forma difference, a distinctive opposition (the cut of clothes, the style of an object) still refers to what we might call the use-value of the sign – to a differential profit, to a lived distinction (signified value). This is still the classical era of signification, with its referential psychology (and philosophy). This is also the *competitive* era in the manipulation of signs. The sign form describes an entirely other organisation: the signified and the referent are abolished to the benefit of a single game of signifiers, a generalised formalisation wherein the code no longer refers to any subjective or objective 'reality', but to its own logic: it becomes its own referent, and the use-value of the sign disappears to the benefit of its commutation and exchange-value alone. The sign no longer designates anything, it reaches its true structural limit, it only refers to other signs. The whole of reality becomes the place of a semiurgical manipulation, of a structural simulation. And since the traditional sign (in linguistic exchange as well) is the object of a conscious investment, of a rational calculation of signifieds, here the code becomes the instance of absolute reference, and at the same time the object of perverse desire.[28]

Baudrillard's critique of dialectical and historical theories, which he chides for their use of binary oppositions, sits oddly with his own reliance on a binary opposition (courtesy of Bataille) between 'primitive' societies of *symbolic exchange*, on the one hand, and capitalist economies of *equivalence*, on the other. 'Symbolic exchange' is Baudrillard's version of the Maussian/Bataillian potlatch: it creates forms of debt and (inter)dependence that can never be settled by any monetary transaction.[36] The rise of capitalism replaced symbolic exchange with relations of equivalence, with exchange-value and, ultimately, sign value. In this regime, use-value is a fiction: a fiction produced by exchange and sign value.

As evidenced by *The Poverty of Philosophy*, which Baudrillard references in 'Marxism and the System of Political Economy', Marx was fully aware that use-value is not a natural given, but is itself historically and socially specific. This applies even to basic means of subsistence. Everybody needs food, but what is deemed a delicacy in one culture may be inedible in another:

Most things have value only because they satisfy needs engendered by estimation. The estimation of our needs may change; therefore the utility of things, which expresses only the relation of these things to our needs, may also change. Natural needs themselves are continually changing. Indeed, what could be more varied than the objects which form the staple food of different peoples![37]

---

28   See Jean Baudrillard, 'Fetishism and Ideology' (1970), in *For a Critique of the Political Economy of the Sign*, (trans. Charles Levin), St. Louis: Telos Press, 1981, pp.88-101.

Baudrillard took this one step further by radicalising 'the schema to the point of reversing this appearance and revealing use-value *as produced by the play of exchange*'. Clearly a brilliant seismograph, Baudrillard's theoretical account of advanced capitalism struck a chord as the 1980s approached. That 'the sign no longer designates anything' is a more totalising statement than anything found in Marx, and it was tailor-made for the Thatcherite/Reaganite art world. The yuppie era's debt-driven world of 'democratised' conspicuous consumption, branded consumer goods, luxury products and lifestyle accoutrements did appear to signal the triumph of the autonomous signifier over the signified. With no viable political alternative to laissez-faire capitalism in sight, Baudrillard seemed to offer the perfect legitimation for an art that fetishised the code, the play of signifiers – an art that took care to produce expensive art objects on this basis. This was the era of Jeff Koons's and Haim Steinbach's commodity art. Baudrillard's work became so dominant in 1980s art discourse that the collective Group Material even staged an exhibition titled 'Resistance (Anti-Baudrillard)' in 1987 at White Columns gallery in New York.

The capitalist production that Bataille reproached for its subservience to utility has by now resulted in a frenzied potlatch of consumerism, a global festival of destruction that seems to boil down to *après nous le déluge*. Better to risk nuclear contamination or deadly smog than to challenge the dogma that economic growth is paramount, even if it is debt-based, irrespective of racking up (social and ecological) debts the global economy cannot pay. Art plays a prominent role in this neoliberal potlatch. In the era of François-Henri Pinault and Roman Abramovich, art is investment (a vehicle for the storage of wealth and the entrenchment of privilege) masquerading as conspicuous consumption. Meanwhile, in an expanding art world many 'cultural workers' are in the vanguard of new forms of exploitation and accumulation, of wealth redistribution. Is it any wonder that the search for intimations of post-capitalist aesthetic practice intensifies? Is it any wonder that – cautions about romantic essentialism and binary thinking notwithstanding – a renewed focus on the uses of art seeks to counter art's status as semiotic exchange-value, as speculative investment?

The Uses of Art

Since the late 1980s, an explosion of biennials and themed and curated shows has provided a thriving ecosystem for a new breed of itinerant, international and nomadic artists to flourish. As funds and opportunities for artists to work with communities became more and more common (being, in some cases, mandated by government policies and funding bodies), so too did a critical scrutiny of the relationships that artists might have with those communities. Questions began to be asked about the long and short-term effects of socially engaged art practice, as well as its sustainability and legacy. Concurrent to this, new forms of socially engaged art practice began to offer neoliberal governmental policy makers an opportunity to bring publicly funded art to an economically measurable audience. The effect of this was an unprecedented level of cultural instrumentalisation, based largely on a statistical fascination with audience participation, which overlapped almost seamlessly with earlier avant-garde rhetorics of social integration and useful art. Within this complex, the idea that art could somehow offer a simple alternative to more established and fixed divisions of labour was lost.

The late 1990s and early 2000s had seen a hype around 'relational aesthetics' – a term introduced by the curator Nicolas Bourriaud to group a number of art practices (including those of Rirkrit Tiravanija, Pierre Huyghe and Dominique Gonzalez-Foerster) that often involved the stating of social relations and situations. Claire Bishop's 2006 *Artforum* article 'The Social Turn: Collaboration and its Discontents' offered a critical alternative. By analysing examples of the instrumentalised uses of socially engaged art (most specifically by New Labour in the UK), Bishop identified what she saw as a corresponding shift toward forms of art criticism that judged art in ethical rather than aesthetic terms. In light of this, Bishop began to deploy Jacques Rancière's writings on aesthetics as a means to rethink the possibility of aesthetics and politics as a contradictory and entwined condition that resides at the heart of artistic production.[38]

The debate on 'social art practice' or 'socially engaged art' has not died down since then. As art and life diverge into a complicit irreducibility, and the avant-garde's utopian dream of uniting art and life becomes realised as commodified nightmare, notions of 'useful art' have cropped up once again. Used polemically by artists, critics and curators, such reclamations of 'usefulness' hint at possibilities for imagining alternative forms of community and citizenship to those currently provided by international financial capital. At first, the return of 'useful art' might seem symptomatic of a regressive relapse into dubious dichotomies (use-value and exchange-value, utility and conspicuous consumption). One would do well to bear in mind cautions against assuming that 'use-value' is merely given. If we want to oppose the destructive manufacturing of needs, then do we not run the risk of returning, like latter-day Veblens, to a puritanical and 'primitivist' image of 'utility'? Can artistic projects that seek to 'make art useful again' escape circular reasoning? In the following essay, John Byrne argues that the concept can have its tactical uses in a situation in which old binaries have collapsed. What was already visible in certain avant-garde movements is once more apparent: in this heteronomous world, notions of usefulness can be deployed to defend and develop forms of relative autonomy.

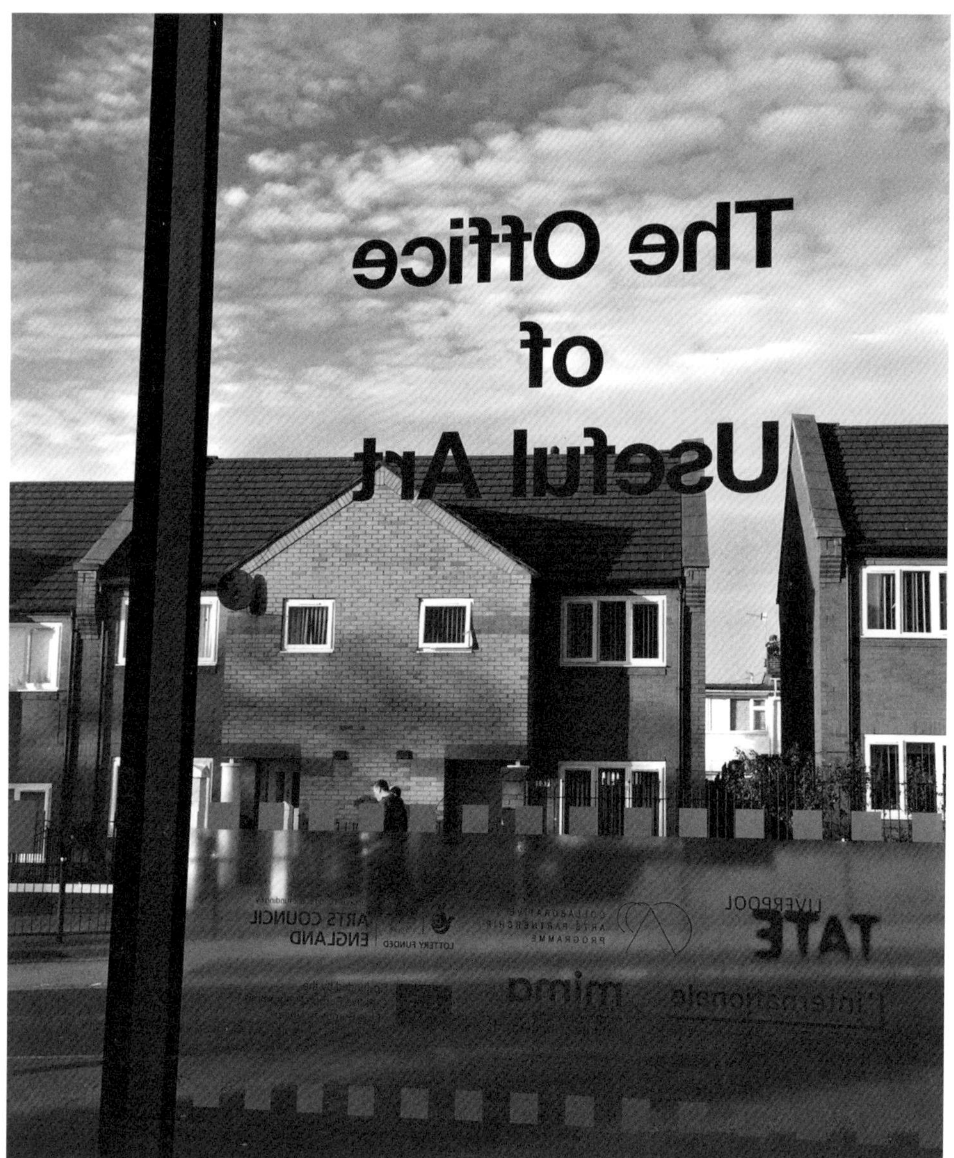

'Office of Useful Art 2015: Localist Worker',
organised by Liverpool John Moores University/
Liverpool School of Art and Design, Middlesbrough
Institute of Modern Art and Tate Liverpool,
Exhibition Research Centre, 2015
Courtesy the Office of Useful Art

JOHN BYRNE, 'SOCIAL AUTONOMY AND THE USE-VALUE OF ART'

This text was written for inclusion in this
reader and first published in *Afterall*, issue 42,
Autumn/Winter 2016, pp.61-69.

The Asociación de Arte Útil (AAU) is the home of an ongoing and propositional
art project instigated by Tania Bruguera. The overall intention of the Asociación
is to produce an international online and offline resource, or toolkit, that brings
together and propagates forms of art practice that seek to have direct and lasting
social, political and economic impact. Begun in 2013, at the Arte Útil Lab at the
Queens Museum of Art in New York, the project has consisted of a series of public programmes, workshops, symposia and events at a number of art museums
and institutions; an online platform with a selected archive-cum-database of
useful art projects and other Arte Útil-related materials; several exhibition-pre-
sentations of the project and its archive; and most recently, an Office of Useful
Art, due to be opened by the Granby Four Streets Community Land Trust in
Liverpool in late 2016.

Underpinning the AAU is a collaboratively developed set of criteria for the
production, distribution and propagation of Arte Útil. Arte Útil projects should:

1. Propose new uses for art within society.
2. Challenge the field within which it operates (civic, legislative, pedagogi-
cal, scientific, economic, etc.).
3. Be 'timing specific', responding to current urgencies.
4. Be implemented and function in real situations.
5. Replace authors with initiators and spectators with users.
6. Have practical, beneficial outcomes for its users.
7. Pursue sustainability whilst adapting to changing conditions.
8. Re-establish aesthetics as a system of *transformation*.[29]

These are also the criteria by which any application for inclusion in the AAU
online resource/archive is considered.[30] At the time of writing, there are over
four hundred entries, including work as familiar as Bauhaus and as diverse as
Theaster Gates's *Dorchester Projects* (2009-ongoing), an artist-led regeneration
of housing in Chicago; Darren O'Donnell's *Haircuts by Children* (2006-07);
Ruben Santiago's *Turning a public toilet into a spa* (2007); and the AHT Group/
Sun Development PTY project 'Violence prevention through urban upgrading
(VPUU)' (2006-ongoing), a holistic attempt to improve living conditions and
reduce violence in the township of Khayelitsha, in Cape Town, South Africa.
The archive also includes projects by Bruguera herself, such as Immigrant

---

[29] These criteria came about as a result of discussions at the Queens Museum, Grizedale
Arts, Cumbria and the Van Abbemuseum, Eindhoven in the run up to the exhibition
'Museum of Arte Útil' at the Van Abbemuseum from 7 December 2013 to 30 March 2014.
See http://museumarteutil.net and http://www.arte-util.org/about/colophon/ (both last
accessed on 19 September 2020).

[30] The AAU archive is currently run by Broadcasting the Archive, an independent
project conceived by Gemma Medina Estupiñán and Alessandra Saviotti, which aims to
'reactivate and mediate the Arte Útil's archive within and beyond the museum's context'.
See http://broadcastingthearchive.tumblr.com (last accessed on 19 September 2020).

Movement International, founded in 2010, conceived as a community space hosted by the Queens Museum and encompassing a diverse range of activities, from public programming, residencies and workshops to language lessons and free legal services, with the ultimate goal of developing 'an international think tank that recognises (im)migrants' role in the advancement of society at large'.[31]

The AAU – the projects that constitute it and its call for an international movement of oppositional artistic strategies – immediately conjures up a familiar landscape of ethical and aesthetic dilemmas. In an art world where artworks are being replaced by experiences, passive audiences are giving way to active 'users' and museums are repurposing themselves as producers of new civic identities, AAU might simply seem to offer one more stark alternative to the established neo-Kantian logics of aesthetic autonomy and disinterested contemplation. Moreover, at first glance it might seem that Arte Útil is barely distinguishable from existing modes of socially engaged art practice, such as Jonas Staal's New World Summit or Ahmet Ögˇüt's Silent University, to give just two recent examples (both also feature in the AAU archive), but I would argue that the AAU represents something more ambitious and far-reaching than the individual projects and practices that fall within its remit. The AAU is nothing less than a radical reorganisation of our relationship to art, artists, museums, galleries and their attendant 'art worlds' as we commonly know them – or knew them – to be.

To this end, the AAU demands an alternative set of descriptive and evaluative terms. For the Museum of Arte Útil, at the Van Abbemuseum, Eindhoven in 2013, theorist Stephen Wright was commissioned to produce a 'Lexicon of Usership', in an attempt to develop terminology more suited to evaluating forms of complex co-production and usership extending well beyond the borders of our current 'museological' understanding of art.[32] The AAU archive is divided into sections such as 'urban development', 'scientific', 'economy' and 'environment', and the entries for specific projects (which can be downloaded as printable pdfs) are categorised in terms of their 'initiators', 'goals', 'users' and 'beneficial outcomes'. In Wright's compendium, the question is posed, wouldn't it be better to simply retire terms like 'author-ship', 'objecthood' and 'autonomy'?[33]

In fact, I would suggest that Arte Útil raises two key and interrelated issues about the changing nature and status of aesthetic autonomy, and that, furthermore, these two issues may uncover an internal and inherited contradiction within contemporary art practice – an as-yet-unresolved contradiction that begins to point beyond the historical impasse of autonomy versus social engagement. If this is the case, then projects such as Arte Útil, and the whole notion of 'useful art', carry with them the means and the necessity to rethink and repurpose the term 'autonomy' in order to reactivate the very possibility of a radical alternative.

---

31 See http://www.queensmuseum.org/immigrant-movement-international (last accessed on 19 September 2020).

32 See Steven Wright, *Towards a Lexicon of Usership*, Eindhoven: Van Abbemuseum, 2013, available at http://www.arte-util.org/tools/lexicon/ (last accessed on 19 September 2020).

33 As alternatives Wright suggests 'emerging concepts' such as 'cognitive surplus'; 'double ontology'; 'Museum 3.0'; 'narratorship (talking art)' and 'repurposing'; and new 'modes of usership' such as 'gleaning', 'hacking', 'piggybacking' and 'poaching'. See *ibid*.

The first and most familiar of the two key issues that are raised by Arte Útil concerns the material (or increasingly immaterial) status of the work of art itself. If art is to resist the status quo, then surely it must provide us with something to resist it with or by? Whether this 'artwork' be a recalcitrant object, a gesture, a process or something else is not at stake here; rather, what is at stake is the cultural investment in the recognisable manifestation of that thing we call 'art'. This concern is historically underpinned by discourses surrounding the relation of aesthetic autonomy to the process of making and craft as possible alternatives to the industrialised and commercialised commodification of mass-produced culture that developed throughout the nineteenth and twentieth centuries. More often than not, these positions developed nostalgic notions of the autonomy of art and valorised handmade artefacts or artworks against items produced through divided, alienated labour and the reification of commodity culture.

The second and more recent of the key issues raised by this notion of useful art concerns *work* – the kind of labour that the work of art has now become (or is becoming). This perhaps more pressing issue has its theoretical underpinnings in the Italian automonism and draws upon a set of concerns regarding the ideological coercion, and subsequent instrumentalisation, of traditionally oppositional discourses within an increasingly globalised neoliberal economy.[34] As the artist Liam Gillick has succinctly put it:

> The accusation … is that artists are at best the ultimate freelance knowledge workers and at worst barely capable of distinguishing themselves from the consuming desire to work at all times, neurotic people who deploy a series of practices that coincide quite neatly with the requirements of neoliberal, predatory, continually mutating capitalism of the every moment. Artists are people who behave, communicate and innovate in the same manner as those who spend their days trying to capitalise every moment and exchange of daily life. They offer no alternative.[35]

If Gillick is right, then we now find ourselves at an increasingly difficult and complex cultural impasse. On the one hand, it becomes increasingly impossible to resist the status quo through any kind of recognisable artistic gesture – material or otherwise – without falling into the trap of a commodified and commercialised art industry. On the other, it is similarly impossible to step outside the framework of the art industry – as a recognisable form of radical gesture or resistance – when any attempt to do so runs the risk of direct complicity with the deregulatory logic of capital. What was once seen to be the pursuit of an alternative artistic lifestyle, the refusal to 'fit in' or to follow the patterns and rhythms of a contracted nine-to-five job, is now the new standard of precarious labour. Any symbolic value in this form of alterity has already been commodified and re-consumed as neoliberal forms of autonomous 'self-management'.

---

34   Editors' Note: See Part Four of this reader, pp.217-57.
35   Liam Gillick, 'The Good of Work', *e-flux journal*, no.16, May 2010, available at http://www.e-flux. com/journal/the-good-of-work/ (last accessed on 19 September 2020).

※

Another way of trying to think through this conundrum, and also of attempting to avoid any collapse into the familiar binary of aesthetics versus politics (however interconnected, intertwined or emplotted they may be), is to re-examine the historical emergence of the idea of useful art itself. The AAU points out that 'Arte Útil in Spanish roughly translates as useful art, but also suggests art as a device or tool'.[36] The term's manifold meaning can be difficult to translate into English, where the very idea of useful art often appears as either an oxymoron or an irrelevance – where art's 'use' is merely a function or addendum of its value as art. (An attitude captured, for instance, in Oscar Wilde's preface to his 1891 novel *The Picture of Dorian Gray*, by the phrase 'All art is quite useless.')[37]

In 1969, Argentinean-born artist Eduardo Costa began a series of artistic interventions titled *Useful Art Works* that were intended to bring modest improvements to daily life in New York. These works – which included, for example, the simple act of buying and replacing missing metal street signs, or, more ambitiously, repainting a subway station on the Flushing Line (a proposal Costa was prevented from completing) – were intended as an attack on the assumption that art and utility were two separate and incompatible spheres. Also in 1969, Mierle Laderman Ukeles – another key figure for Arte Útil – produced her 'Manifesto for Maintenance Art', centred on the invisible and gendered labour that underpins the functioning of culture and its institutions.[38] A washing performance by Ukeles was the closing event for Bruguera's initial Arte Útil Lab at the Queens Museum, conducted with the participation of the institution's director and its maintenance supervisor.[39] Through her subsequent research, Bruguera discovered that the Italian artist Pino Poggi had previously referred to 'Arte Utile'; the intention of which, according to Poggi's 1965 manifesto, is to 'help give the average man a clear grasp of his real problems in life. [...] AU is not limited solely to the precincts of the universities and academies, where the same, small clique of intellectuals constantly embalms the whole with their verbiage'. Instead, 'AU will only exist of the people and for the people in public places, in shopping centres and as street theatre'.[40]

Arte Útil and its 1960s precursors are also embedded, I would contend, within a longer and often overlooked lineage of artistic resistance. To ask when and why the juxtaposition of 'use' and 'art' became problematic is to return to a period before the neo-Kantian architecture of artistic production, distribution and reception, when aesthetics, politics, autonomy and the uses of art all played a role in the production of a new sense of the civic in Europe. In that period, in the late eighteenth and early nineteenth centuries, the idea of useful art had a decisive role in imagining social alternatives to the economic and cultural impact of the Industrial Revolution.

---

[36]   See the 'About' page of the Museum of Arte Útil website: http://museumarteutil.net/about/ (last accessed on 19 September 2020).

[37]   Oscar Wilde, *The Picture of Dorian Gray*, London: Penguin Books, 1985, p.4. EN: The book's preface is reprinted in Part Two of this reader, p.213.

[38]   EN: Mierle Laderman Ukeles's 'Manifesto for Maintenance Art 1969! Proposal for an exhibition "CARE"' is reprinted in Part Four of this reader, pp.247-49.

[39]   The performance is documented at https://vimeo.com/69101898 (last accessed on 19 September 2020).

[40]   Pino Poggi, 'Manifest Arte Utile I' (1965), available at https://www.arte-utile.net/manifestos/manifesto-arte-utile-1/ (last accessed on 19 September 2020).

The growing difficulty in reconciling use or use-value with the alienation of mechanised mass production during this period is perhaps most clearly expressed in the writings of Karl Marx, specifically in his attempt to distinguish between use-value and exchange-value.[41] As Fredric Jameson has recently reminded us, underpinning this distinction is an inherited moral and ethical imperative. Use-value, for Marx, was both qualitative and bodily, a metaphysical imperative regarding the necessity of material and social production.[42] Exchange-value, on the other hand, tended to be equated with the quantitative, as a more abstract function of the mind and soul. This analytical attempt to separate the bodily, material and qualitative from the mental, abstract and quantitative is also familiar from the famous 'base and superstructure' metaphor that Marx employed in his preface to *A Contribution to the Critique of Political Economy* (1859). Here, a real, material and economic base (which Marx suggested could be analysed with the accuracy of science) is seen as the true driving force of history, producing the ideological superstructure of law, politics, ethics and culture.

As we know, the historical consequences of this bifurcation for the role of art in the West have been profound. At one extreme, art and culture came to be seen as little more than a functional reflection of the true economic driving forces of history (with the concomitant assumption that a reading or analysis of culture could provide a key to understanding these material driving forces). At the other extreme, an emerging mentality of art for art's sake saw political and ethical value in this separation, arguing that art and culture should be isolated from the material necessities of everyday life and held within an autonomous, aesthetic field. The political argument for this position was that art and culture had to be protected from the corrupting forces of industrialised capital if they were to remain a viable vehicle through which to imagine any kind of alternative utopian future. This latter position, propagated by Alfred H. Barr, Jr's development of a white-cube museum space (as the most appropriate arena to experience autonomous works of art) and an accompanying historical narrative of isms (underpinned by a commitment to the pursuit of technical radicalism as a viable artistic end in itself) is still largely with us today.

However, in opposition to both of these polarities (art as a mere function of its socio-economic determinants or art as a separate, emancipatory and autonomous field) a more discernibly left-wing lineage emerged, arguing for the value of art and culture as the physical embodiment of non-alienated labour, and for art and craft to be used as a means of protecting the moral and ethical ownership of work and labour against the instrumentalising and brutalising forces of mass production. This tradition, which emphasises craft, design and making – and extends from John Ruskin and William Morris to Constructivism, Bauhaus and beyond – also provides, I would argue, the conceptual framework within which the two seemingly irreconcilable positions of autonomy and heteronomy have traditionally met: the qualitative and ethical bodily function of the work or labour of art that, in turn, underpins the valorisation of authentic labour in

<hr>

[41]   See Karl Marx, *Capital: A Critique of Political Economy, Volume 1* (1867; trans. Ben Fowkes), London: Penguin, 1990, pp.131–38. EN: An excerpt is reprinted in Part Two of this reader, pp.113–18.
[42]   See Fredric Jameson, *Representing Capital: A Reading of Volume 1*, London: Verso, 2014.

art. By insisting on the dialectical codependency of autonomy and heteronomy, and – whether tacitly or explicitly – on the use-value of art as its distinguishing trait, this lineage encompasses both the scale and ambition of AAU today.

❋

Despite recent attempts to think through the complex relationships of autonomy and heteronomy, there remains a tendency to posit any understanding of art's social and political functions in terms of its ability to bridge the gap between art and life.[43] As a result, the flexible and productive relationship involving autonomy, heteronomy and use-value remains a fixed one between irreconcilable though mutually dependent regimes. Put another way: artists might work with communities to produce all manner of ephemeral, temporal and ongoing projects, but it is still expected that we experience the legacy or residue of the activity itself as art, or at least as art as we know it, within and through the existing framework of art world reception (museums, galleries, biennials, websites, books, journals, etc.).

The 2013 exhibition of the Museum of Arte Útil at the Van Abbemuseum was, in part, an attempt to shift some of these received ideas. Visitors were given the choice of either paying a standard entrance fee or gaining free entry by agreeing to be an active 'user' of the show. The Van Abbemuseum itself was proposed as a 'social power plant' – a site of interchange and co-production, where history and art could be collaboratively reused as a means to imagine new forms of civic citizenship. The show's centre was a physical presentation of the Arte Útil online archive; surrounding rooms were organised according to a series of thematics, mixing artworks, documentation and makeshift structures and carrying instructions for the visitor-user on 'what to use and how to use it'.[44] Perhaps inevitably, the exhibition also highlighted its own physical and ideological limitations: when the spaces were activated – through discussions, meetings, presentations, workshops or performances – the potentialities of Arte Útil became accessible and usable; when they were not, the current templates we have for experiencing artworks in galleries and museum spaces – as objectifications of invested artistic labour, whose latent surplus value is waiting to be extracted via the aesthetic experience of spectatorship – began to contradict the manifest intentions of both the AAU and the long-term projects whose legacies were on display.

But there is also another, and perhaps more radical, way of thinking through this conundrum that, I would argue, the project of Arte Útil can help provide. What if we simply accept that the avant-garde dream of uniting art and life has finally come true, as deregulated nightmare? What if we also accept that there is no longer a discernable split between material base and ideological

---

43   For instance, Jacques Rancière posits a metapolitics of aesthetics as a means to illuminate the full complexity and interconnectedness of aesthetic and political debate within the Western canon. See J. Rancière, Politics of Aesthetics: The Distribution of the Sensible (trans. Gabriel Rockhill), London: Continuum, 2004. See also Claire Bishop's Artificial Hells: Participatory Art and the Politics of Spectatorship (London: Verso, 2012), which is more orientated towards objectified forms of resistance as art in gallery spaces

44   See http://museumarteutil.net/about/ (last accessed on 29 September 2020).

superstructure? And what if we can finally agree that art and life have already merged, not as the emancipatory and dialectical resolution of a historical struggle, but as the neoliberal elision of work and leisure through the aestheticisation of labour? If this is the case, then art, as it now exists, provides little more than a commodified cypher of delusional radicality, a semiotised mechanism which now functions, rather like Jean Baudrillard's Disneyland, as a last ideological lie – a mythological guarantee that there still somehow exists a reality beyond art, a discernable material and economic base that art can still be an effective and productive part of. This admittedly bleak scenario would suggest that we have reached a point of cultural saturation, an overlap and integration of previously identifiable political positions, in which left and right ideologies have blended and blurred – a successful occupation of art by life and life by art.

However unpalatable these observations may be, or however discordantly they may jar with our cherished notions of art's ameliorative and reparatory capacity, they would also seem to be the only possible solution for remapping a territory of effective artistic activism under current conditions. And this activist-pragmatist approach, as Bruguera herself outlined at the most recent AAU Summit,[45] should operate at multiple political levels. To be able to talk to institutions of power, let alone to harbour the ambition of changing their systems of operation, the AAU must also be capable of operating at an institutional level. It is not enough to simply point towards a set of seemingly useful purposes that social art projects can engage themselves with – which, for Bruguera, would be to infantilise the concept of Arte Útil. The focus must be on changing existing power structures rather than merely illustrating their current shortcomings through the tried and tested vehicles of art practice. In this way, Bruguera's alignment of the AAU with the mechanisms of various international institutions can be seen as a deliberate and pragmatic attempt to change the way such institutions operate – a kind of activist approach at an institutional level. This process also goes hand in hand with the expansion of an international AAU network that, to some extent, has already begun to grow and govern itself autonomously as a self-regulated user-based resource.

No doubt as a result of these factors, Bruguera displays an ambivalent, and sometimes contradictory, relationship to her own role as artist and/or instigator, on the one hand questioning the use and purpose of the authorial role of the artist within the museum or gallery setting, and on the other openly adopting the 'artist' role as and when it is a useful tool for addressing power. In her own conflictual and well-publicised relationship with the Cuban government, Bruguera's right to be seen as an artist (as well as her official validation as an artist through her participation in major exhibitions, biennales, etc.) provides both a public platform and legal mandate for her voice as well as others' to be publicly heard.

Yet such fluid and contradictory forms of pragmatism may well begin to run counter to the overall concerns of the AAU project. To really provide new models of practice as meaningful alternatives to the current political status quo, the AAU needs to develop a rigorous theory of how it can begin to value the co-production and redistribution of real and existing social knowledge. This

---

45 'Arte Útil Summit 2016', Middlesbrough Institute of Modern Art, 22–25 July 2016. See http://www. arte-util.org/studies/arte-util-summit-2016/ (last accessed on 19 September 2020).

can only be achieved through the development of a truly peer-to-peer online and offline network of collaborating associates, affiliates and active constituents who are willing to test and redefine the legal, moral and ethical limits of reproducing and repurposing existing art-led projects to their own, and each other's, social ends and needs. Such a strategy would depend on a real, rather than symbolic, commitment to the development and co-production of strategies for artistic and social change. And if this is the case, then we may have to confront some of the difficulties in retaining or propagating the current role and function of the 'artist' in our neoliberal society, however useful artists may appear to be in confronting the existing legal systems of power. After all, is it not also in the interests of power to maintain and sustain the existing category of the artist?

In light of this, we might consider AAU's recently established collaboration with the residents of the Granby Four Streets Community Land Trust in Liverpool. The CLT itself evolved out of a twenty-year struggle by residents against attempts by local and national government to depopulate and demolish the local community and its infrastructure. At one point, around 2007, when only five houses on one street (Cairn Street) remained occupied, a group of female residents began to develop forms of everyday resistance and activism by moving their lives onto the street: planting flowers, sitting at tables, redecorating boarded-up buildings and, above all, developing a shared knowledge of housing and property law. The Granby Four Streets CLT, formed in 2011 as a not-for-profit community-interest company and emerging from a grass-roots activism, successfully lobbied and secured assets from the local authority, which they then began to regenerate. Granby Four Streets were recently brought to the attention of the UK media through their collaboration with the London-based architects' collective Assemble to renovate houses in the area with the participation of local residents, a project that won the 2015 Turner Prize.

Yet perhaps much more than Assemble – the de facto recipients of the Turner Prize, who were deemed the 'artists' in this community-based collaboration – it is the example of Granby Four Streets that suggests a model of resistance to current frameworks of instrumentalising totality that does not, as a consequence, do the dirty work of neoliberalism in the name of art. Granby's newfound Office of Useful Art intends to develop ground-up, constituency-led uses of the Asociación's toolkit, providing valuable means to collectively rethink the role of art as socially produced knowledge. After successfully fighting local and national government policy for many years, the Granby residents are well aware of the dangers of instrumentalisation. For them, the AAU offers access to a growing network of resources and institutional links whilst, at the same time, inviting their contributions toward the growth of the Asociación, which is keen to listen to and learn from their wealth of experience. Such active forms of reciprocity are, I would argue, capable of developing beyond the usual experience, in art, of exchange as symbolic gesture. Instead, they indicate the capacity for new forms of oppositional realpolitik, operating as a double ontological proposition – able to function as both, or either, a work of art and/or a radical social proposition for living otherwise.

In this scenario, terms like 'autonomy' once again become useful precisely because they are now, seemingly, so useless. To reject autonomy out of hand, to assume that it is a term that can somehow be jettisoned or retired, is to give too much ground away to a predatory neoliberal logic that is more than capable of rebranding activism for its own needs. Instead, autonomy must be reframed and repurposed as a site of social productivity; a collective struggle to re-complexify and reimagine 'art' as a practice of lived resistance. And the key to this, I would argue, lies in the subtle and self-conscious shift in the terms and conditions of art practice that projects like the AAU both represent and, more importantly, can effect – from a use of art that symbolically imagines alternative possible futures within an existing framework of production and consumption, to a use of art that enables diverse constituencies to reimagine what the work, or labour, of art could be today.

Byrnes's essay draws on a lexicon of useful art terms proposed by theorist and critic Steven Wright, who is urging that the museum move into a new form of relationship with its audience based on active usership (as opposed to the allegedly passive form of 'disinterested aesthetic spectatorship' that has characterised the way in which we have consumed art since Kant). The lexicon enumerates terms that need to be adopted and others that should be jettisoned. As Byrne mentions, one of those terms that Wright would consign to the dustbin of history is *autonomy*. Significant here is Wright's very accurate appraisal of the harm done by the notion of autonomy to our understanding and use of art, which is almost exclusively reliant on one particular use of the term:

> [Autonomous] art came at a cost – one that for many has become too much to bear. The price to pay for autonomy are the invisible parentheses that bracket art off from being taken seriously as a proposition having consequences beyond the aesthetic realm. Art judged by art's standards can be easily written off as, well ... *just art*. Of contemplative value to people who like that sort of thing, but without teeth. Of course autonomous art has regularly claimed to bite the hand that feeds it; but never very hard. To gain use-value, to find a usership, requires that art quit the autonomous sphere of purposeless purpose and disinterested spectatorship. For many practitioners today, autonomous art has become less a place of self-determined experimentation than a prison house – a sphere where one must conform to the law of permanent ontological exception, which has left the autonomous artworld rife with cynicism.[39]

In Wright's terms, autonomy deserves to be forgotten. However, as we have seen, the concept is at its most useful when it is seen to be a complex, contradictory and perplexing historical cypher – and as a site of struggle. Most of the projects and practices Bruguera presented in the Museum of Arte Útil at the Van Abbemuseum are scarcely conceivable without some notion of autonomy – albeit probably not 'the autonomy of art'. A more complex dialectical reading of the term in relation to art no longer uses it as an anachronistic a priori but as a tool in the struggle to find better ways to live. Such a tool is not a sci-fi artefact coming to us from the future. For better or worse, it is shaped by contemporary concerns, desires, fears. It is no wonder that visions of future aesthetic play, or of a useful art to come, are informed by the present conditions they oppose. No future has ever been imagined without profound entanglement in a problematic present and its contradictions.

Notes

1 Théophile Gautier, *Mademoiselle de Maupin: A Romance of Love and Passion*, London: Gibbings & Co., 1899, p.31.

2 Noël Burch, *De la beauté des latrines: pour réhabiliter le sens au cinéma et ailleurs*, Paris: L'harmattan, 2007, p.11.

3 While *Fountain* is a work that undermines traditional conceptions of authorship, and the work came about in a collaborative manner, Duchamp is indeed its main instigator and designing intellect. Among Duchamp's close collaborators in the 'Richard Mutt Affair' were his fellow editors of the zine *The Blind Man*, Beatrice Wood and Henri-Pierre Roché, as well as other members of the Arensberg circle, such as Louise Norton and Joseph Stella. In recent years, some have used a letter Duchamp sent to his sister Suzanne on 11 April 1917, in which he mentions 'a female friend' having sent in *Fountain* to the Society of Independent Artists' exhibition, as a smoking gun proving that Duchamp is not the work's author and that he 'stole' its authorship from Baroness Elsa von Freytag-Loringhoven, another member of the Arensberg circle.

For the record, contemporaneous photo shows *Fountain* in Duchamp's studio, suspended from the ceiling, with some of the other readymades; the photo of *Fountain* by Alfred Stieglitz published in *The Blind Man* shows a label in Norton's handwriting, suggesting that she is the 'female friend' to whom Duchamp referred, playfully using his co-conspirator as a proxy; Duchamp's generosity towards fellow artists, including far less successful ones, is amply documented throughout his life; and it takes a giant leap of the paranoid imagination to assume that those who knew the truth would never have spoken up over the course of many decades.

The 'Baronness Elsa' narrative is a quasi-feminist, pseudo-progressive conspiracy theory. In its selective, decontextualised and slanted reading of a few documents it is structurally identical to other forms of conspiracism - from 'Bacon wrote Shakespeare's plays' (which, ironically, Duchamp's patron Walter Arensberg passionately believed in) to Pizzagate, QAnon and microchips in Covid vaccines.

4 See 'Critical Theory and the Autonomy of Art' in Part Four of this reader, pp.219-25.

5 A note on terminology: Marx's German term *Ware* refers to any product that is offered on the market and has value that derives from human labour-power. The customary English translation of *Ware* is 'commodity'. However, this is a different usage than the one in mainstream liberal economics, where 'commodity' refers only to goods that are sold in bulk and are considered interchangeable and equivalent, irrespective of who produced them - typical examples are raw materials and agricultural products such as grain. This more specific meaning should not be confused with the Marxian sense.

6 David Harvey, *A Companion to Marx's 'Capital'*, London: Verso, 2010, pp.20-25.

7 Karl Marx, *Capital: A Critique of Political Economy, Volume 1* (1867; trans. Ben Fowkes), London: Penguin, 1990, p.131.

8 *Ibid.*, p.1044.

9 J. Ruskin, 'Letter 79: Life Guards of New Life' (18 July 1877), in *Fors Clavigera: Letters to the Workmen and Labourers of Great Britain*, in *The Works of John Ruskin, Library Edition* (ed. E.T. Cook and Alexander Wedderburn), vol.29, London: George Allen, 1907, p.160.

10 *Ibid.*

11 James McNeill Whistler quoted in Linda Merrill, *A Pot of Paint: Aesthetics on Trial in 'Whistler v Ruskin'*, Washington, DC and London: Smithsonian Institution Press, 1992, p.144.

12 See, for example, Beate Söntgen, 'Decorating Charleston Farmhouse', in Sami Khatib et al. (ed.), *Critique: The Stakes of Form*, Zürich: Diaphanes, 2000, pp.139-72.

13 Roger Fry: 'Art in a Socialism, a Lecture', *The Burlington Magazine for Connoisseurs*, vol.29, no.157, April 1916, p.39.

14 Kazimir Malevich, 'Sloth - the Real Truth of Mankind' (1921), in *The Artist, Infinity, Suprematism: Unpublished Writings, 1913-1933* (trans. Xenia Hoffmann), Copenhagen: Borgen Forlag, 1978, pp.73-85. As the editors note, Malevich 'puns on the name of Lenin and *len*' (Russian for sloth) - Lenin, son of sloth, leader of sloth.' *Ibid.*, p.223. His argument can also be traced back to Paul Lafargue's book *The Right to be Lazy* (1883).

15 Leon Trotsky, *Literature and the Revolution* (1923; ed. William Keach, trans. Rose Strunsky) Chicago: Haymarket Books, 2005, pp.146, 158-59.

16 *Ibid.*, p.198. See Part One of this reader, pp.29-99.

17 Lu Märten, 'Proletkult' (1919), in *Formen für den Alltag. Schriften, Aufsätze, Vorträge* (ed. Rainhard May), Dresden: VEB Verlag der Kunst, 1982, pp.43-45.

18 On Productivism, see Maria Gough, *The Artist as Producer: Russian Constructivism in Revolution*, Berkeley: University of California Press, 2005; and Christina Kiaer, *Imagine No Possessions: The Socialist Objects of Russian Constructivism*, Cambridge, MA: MIT Press, 2005.

19 Benjamin H.D. Buchloh, 'From Faktura to Factography', *October*, no.30, Autumn 1984, p.99.

20 See Part Five of this reader, pp.289-352.

21   Nikolaí Taraboukine, 'Pour une théorie de la peinture', in *Le Dernier Tableau: écrits sur l'art et l'histoire de l'art à l'époque du constructivisme russe* (ed. Andrei B. Nakov), Paris: Éditions Champ libre, 1972, p.65.

22   George Maciunas, letter to Tomas Schmit, January 1964, in Emmett Williams and Ann Noël (ed.), *Mr. Fluxus: A Collective Portrait of George Maciunas, 1931-1978*, London: Thames & Hudson, 1997, p.104.

23   There exist different permutations of Kopke's last name; this text sticks to the spelling in the referenced Nul manifesto.

24   Wim Beeren (ed.), *Actie, werkelijkheid en fictie in de kunst van de jaren '60 in Nederland*, Rotterdam: Museum Boijmans Van Beuningen, 1979, p.30. Translated from the Dutch by Sven Lütticken.

25   Oddly enough, this case is missing from the putatively exhaustive 'retrospective of closed exhibitions' in Matthieu Copeland and Balthazar Lovay (ed.), *The Anti-Museum: An Anthology*, Fribourg and London: Fri Art and Koenig Books, 2017. Copeland's chronology starts instead with another neo-Dada gesture, by the Japanese collective Hi Red Center, the 1964 'Great Panorama Exhibition' (alternatively titled 'Closing Event').

26   The strategy of the art strike has been proposed on several occasions since, including, notably, for the years 1990-93 by the 'Neoist' network. For more details, including a contribution by philosopher and media theorist Sadie Plant, see Stewart Home, *The Art Strike Papers*, Stirling: AK Press, 1991.

27   Goran Đorđević, quoted in Branislav Dimitrijević, 'Against Art by Other Means (Goran Đorđević: 1972-1985)', in M. Copeland and B. Lovay (ed.), *The Anti-Museum, op. cit.*, p.282.

28   Theodor W. Adorno, 'Veblen's Attack on Culture' (1941), in *Prisms* (trans. Samuel and Shierry Weber), Cambridge, MA: MIT Press, 1981, p.84.

29   Georges Bataille, 'The Notion of Expenditure' (1933), in *Visions of Excess: Selected Writings, 1927-1939* (trans. and ed. Allan Stoekl), Minneapolis: University of Minnesota Press, 1985, pp.116-29. During the later 1930s, Adorno and Benjamin were concerned by what they regarded as Bataille's descent into irrationalism, but it was Bataille who rescued the papers of Benjamin's *Arcades Project* by hiding them in the Bibliothèque nationale de France after Benjamin's flight from Paris in May 1940.

30   Georges Bataille, *The Accursed Share, Volume II & III: The History of Eroticism and Sovereignty* (1953-54; trans. Robert Hurley), New York: Zone Books, 1991, pp.197-98.

31   Georges Bataille, *Erotism: Death and Sensuality* (trans. Mary Dalwood), San Francisco: City Lights Books, 1986, unpaginated, plate 3.

32   G. Bataille, *The Accursed Share, op. cit.*, p.199.

33   Guy Debord, *In girum imus nocte et consumimur igni* (1978; trans. Ken Knabb), available at http://www.bopsecrets.org/SI/debord.films/ingirum.htm (last accessed on 19 September 2020).

34   Asger Jorn, 'Value and Economy; Critique of the Political Economy and the Exploitation of the Unique' (1962), in *The Natural Order and Other Texts* (trans. Peter Shield), Aldershot, UK: Ashgate, 2002, p.184.

35   Jean Baudrillard, 'The Mirror of Production', in *Utopia Deferred: Writings for Utopie, 1967-1978* (trans. Stuart Kendall), New York: Semiotext(e), 2006, p.112.

36   See Jean Baudrillard, *Symbolic Exchange and Death* (1976; trans. Iain Hamilton Grant), London: Sage, 1993.

37   K. Marx, *The Poverty of Philosophy* (1847; trans. Frida Knight), in *Collected Works of Karl Marx*, vol.6, London: Lawrence & Wishart, 1976, p.117.

38   Claire Bishop, 'The Social Turn: Collaboration and its Discontents', *Artforum*, vol.44, no.6, February 2006, pp.178-83. See also C. Bishop, *Artificial Hells: Participatory Art and the Politics of Spectatorship*, London: Verso, 2012.

39   Stephen Wright, *Toward a Lexicon of Usership*, Eindhoven: Van Abbemuseum, 2013, p.12, available at http://www.arte-util.org/tools/lexicon/ (last accessed on 19 September 2020).

PART THREE:
FROM OBJECT TO FRAME

During the age of Romanticism, art became a somewhat uneasy placeholder for something grander: an unalienated, creative, aesthetic life. In Parts One and Two of this reader we explored a key aspect of modern theory and practice: the promise of 'an aesthetic which is not limited to the sphere of "the artistic"'.[1] Still, the placeholder that was art remained of central importance. On the one hand, many felt the need to defend and insulate the artistic sphere against the 'outside world' – against an industrial and capitalist society seen as fundamentally anti-aesthetic. On the other hand, as art developed into a complex institutionalised field in its own right, the enemy was already within the gates. Today, the art world, as a semi-autonomous sphere, is still part and parcel of a society that perverts the aesthetic *promesse de bonheur* at every moment in its commodified mass culture – while being only too happy to lock away art in its specialised field as a deluxe commodity for the happy few. Part Three will deal with some of the responses to this 'incarceration' of the aesthetic in art, and of art in its own institutional field.

Louise Lawler,
Raphael and Drinking Glass,
gelatin silver print,
43.8 × 55.2cm
Courtesy the artist and Sprüth Magers

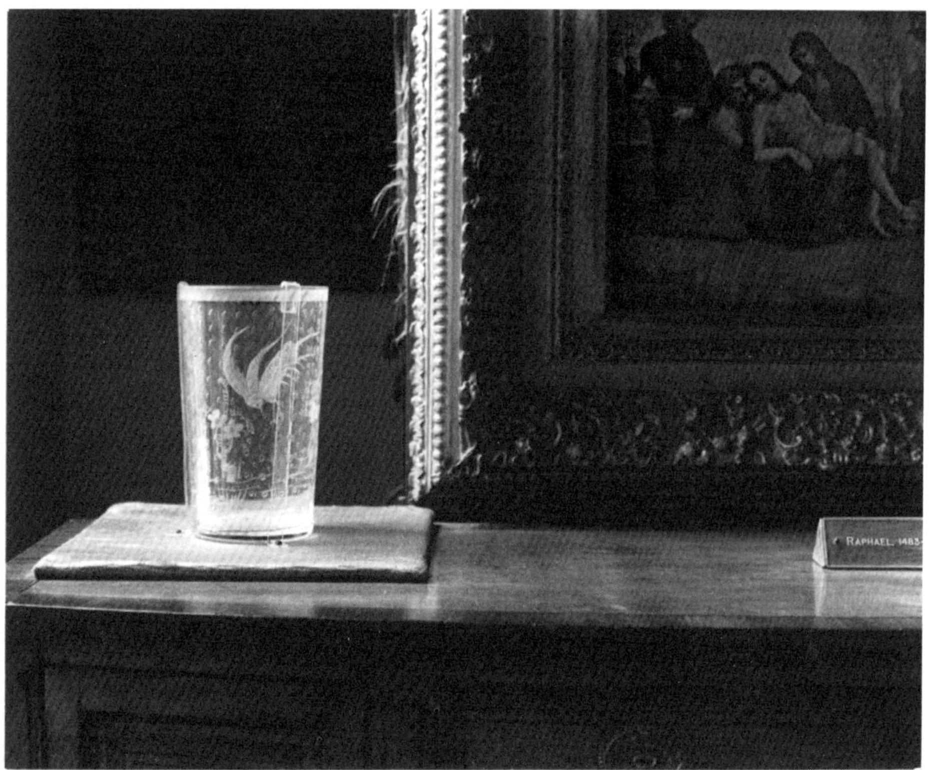

Framing and Reframing

There are a number of conventional – and only seemingly simple – devices that set the artwork apart from its surroundings, and hence from non-art objects. In visual art, these devices include the pedestal (for sculpture) and the frame (for paintings as well as drawings, prints and photographs). In the late nineteenth century, Art Nouveau and Jugendstil sought to turn buildings and interiors into aesthetic ensembles that required no discrete artworks in frames or on pedestals. One crucial figure in Art Nouveau was the German critic and art dealer Julius Meier-Graefe, who co-founded the journals *Pan* in 1895 and *Dekorative Kunst* in 1897 as well as the Paris-based gallery La Maison Moderne in 1899. He would become a champion of post-Impressionist painters such as Paul Cézanne and Vincent van Gogh, and write an influential history of modern art that would win him the admiration of Clement Greenberg and his followers.

The later Meier-Graefe would come to regret his earlier championship of Art Nouveau, which he subsequently came to regard as a doomed attempt to turn back time and overcome 'autonomous' painting:

> In most cases the artist was an undisciplined initiator who ultimately admitted defeat in the face of a floor plan. He sought to revise the history of the last hundred or three hundred years and to restore the *'Gesamtkunstwerk'* in the form of the bourgeois home. This undertaking came to an even more lamentable conclusion than Richard Wagner's phantom. It is certainly agreeable to sit in soberly arranged rooms without plaster caryatids flanking the front door. However, habit makes the influence of such accomplishments evaporate much like one's enjoyment of a sharp trouser crease.[2]

Sardonically, Meier-Graefe noted that many artists

> [abandoned themselves] to the illusion that neatly fitting wallpaper was simply superior to a painting that had not been created for the space in question, and that such wallpaper would also merit the respect accorded to masterpieces. In this interior decoration practice, Rembrandt lost his place in the new dwelling, for his work was held to sully the clear expanse of the wall.[3]

Under those circumstances, it is no surprise that painters from Georges Seurat to Franz von Stuck started paying more attention to the framing of their pictures. After all, the frame was a crucial buffer, but potentially also a mediator, between painting and environment. We see a reflection of this in Georg Simmel's great 1902 essay 'The Picture Frame'. Alongside Max Weber, Simmel was one of the founding fathers of sociology in Germany. The author of a study of the metropolis and mental life as well as of *The Philosophy of Money* (1900), Simmel published essays on a wide range of subjects, including art. In 'The Picture Frame', he takes great care to differentiate between applied art and 'autonomous' art by homing in on the frame. Simmel envisions the artwork that is enclosed by the frame '"to be a whole for itself', as the frame allows the 'island-like position which the work requires vis-à-vis the outer world'.

GEORG SIMMEL, 'THE PICTURE FRAME: AN AESTHETIC STUDY'

Reprinted from *Theory, Culture & Society*, vol.11,
no.1, 1994, pp.11-17. First published in 1902.
Translation from the German by Mark Ritter.

The character of things depends ultimately upon whether they are wholes or parts. Whether an existence, sufficient within itself, closed within itself, is determined only by the law of its own nature or whether it stands as an element within the context of a whole, from which it receives power and meaning – this distinguishes the soul from everything material, the free person from the merely social creature, the moral personality from the person who is held dependent on everything external by sensuous desire. And it separates the work of art from every part of nature. For as a natural existence, each thing is a mere transitional point for continuously flowing energies and materials, comprehensible only from what has preceded it, significant only as an element of the entire natural process. The essence of the work of art, however, is to be a whole for itself, not requiring any relation to an exterior, spinning each of its threads back into its own centre. Insofar as the work of art is that which otherwise only the world as a whole or the psyche can be, a unity of individualities, the work of art closes itself off against everything external to itself as a world of its own. Thus its boundaries mean something quite different from what one calls boundaries in a natural entity. In the case of the natural entity, boundaries are simply the site of continuing exosmosis and endosmosis with everything external; for the work of art they are that absolute ending, which exercises indifference towards and defence against the exterior and a unifying integration with respect to the interior in a *single* act. What the frame achieves for the work of art is to symbolise and strengthen this double function of its boundary. It excludes all that surrounds it, and thus also the viewer as well, from the work of art, and thereby helps to place it at that distance from which alone it is aesthetically enjoyable. The distance of a being from us signifies in everything psychological the unity of this being in itself. For only to the extent to which a being is self-enclosed does it possess that sphere into which no one can penetrate, that existence for itself with which it can protect itself from every other sphere.

Distance and unity, antithesis to us and synthesis within itself are reciprocal concepts; the two prime qualities of a work of art – its inner unity and the fact that it is in a sphere removed from all immediate life – are one and the same, only viewed from two different sides. And only if and because the work of art possesses this self-sufficiency does it have so much to give us; that existence for itself is the preparatory stepping back with which the work penetrates us that much more deeply and fully. The feeling of an undeserved gift with which it delights us originates from the pride of this self-sufficient closure, with which it now nevertheless becomes our own.

.The qualities of the picture frame reveal themselves to be those of assisting and giving meaning to this inner unity of the picture. This commences with such an apparently fortuitous thing as the joints between its sides. The gaze glides inwards on them; by extending them toward their ideal intersection, the eye emphasises the relationship of the picture to its centre from all sides. This unifying effect of the frame joints is visibly strengthened by raising the outer sides of the frame compared with the inner sides, so that the four sides form converging planes. From the same motivation, however, a now common form appears to me to be completely reprehensible, namely, the raising of the inner frame sides so that the frame slopes downwards to the outside. Since the gaze, like bodily movement, moves more easily from higher to lower than vice versa, so in this way the gaze is unavoidably led outwards away from the picture, and the coherence of the picture is subjected to a centrifugal dispersal.

The fact that the frame side is enclosed by two mouldings serves the closing function more than it does the synthetic one. In this way, the entire ornamentation or the profiling of the frame runs like a stream between two banks. And it is precisely this which favours that island-like position which the work of art requires vis-à-vis the outer world. It is therefore of the greatest importance that the design of the frame makes possible this continuous flowing of the gaze, as if it always flowed back into itself. That is why the frame, through its configuration, must never offer a gap or a bridge through which, as it were, the world could get in or from which the picture could get out – as occurs, for instance, when the picture's content extends into the frame, a fortunately rare mistake, which completely negates the work of art's autonomous being and thereby the significance of the frame.

The self-enclosing flow of the frame does not mean, however, that the frame's ornamentation itself must run parallel to its setting. On the contrary, precisely in order to emphasise clearly the flow of the frame, which makes the picture into an island, the lines of the ornamentation must deviate strongly, perhaps even perpendicularly, from this parallelism. All lines placed obliquely to the frame's side form blockages to that flow within it whose power and movement, felt by us aesthetically, are heightened and made clear by overcoming such barriers. The entire formation of the frame's ornamentation is controlled by the impression of flowing and closing in on itself, through which it emphasises the separation of the picture from all that surrounding it, so that every separating line is justified to the extent to which it helps to raise that impression to its maximum. The same reason renders intelligible the long-proven practice of giving the smaller picture a broader and, at all events, a more dynamically effective frame. For the danger in this case is that the picture may blend into the simultaneously viewed surroundings; it may not stand out with sufficient independence and therefore must be countered with stronger means of demarcation than is the case with the very large picture, which fills out a considerable portion of the field of vision for itself. Since the latter need not fear any competition from its surroundings with regard to the independent significance of its impression, it can be content with a minimally framed boundary.

The ultimate purpose of the frame proves the unacceptability of the cloth frame which turns up from time to time; a piece of material is felt to be part of a much more extensive material, there is no inner reason why the pattern is cut off at this particular point, it refers by itself to an unlimited prolongation – the cloth frame thus lacks the sense of boundary justified by the form and cannot therefore bound anything else. In the case of unpatterned materials, where this lack of closure and ability to serve as a boundary is less prominent, the mere softness of the boundary and of the entire material effect in general already suffices to produce the same deficiency. The material is lacking an organic structure of its own, which is why wood retains such an effective and yet modest closure within itself – something that is sorely missed in the case of imitation wood frames, whereas it becomes tangible in carved gilded frames, despite the coating. For the latter does not hide the slight irregularities of craftwork, which make its organic liveliness superior to all the exactness of the machine.

This principle, if properly understood, explains why, in more or less tasteful milieus, one no longer finds photographs from nature in frames. The frame is suited only to structures with a closed unity, which a piece of nature never possesses. Any excerpt from unmediated nature is connected by a thousand spatial, historical, conceptual and emotional relationships with everything that surrounds it more or less closely, physically or mentally. Only artistic form severs these threads and, as it were, ties them inwardly back together. Around the piece of nature, which we instinctively feel to be a mere part in the context of the greater whole, the frame is therefore contradictory and violent for the same reason that the inner vital principle of the work of art tolerates and even promotes it.

Another fundamental misunderstanding from which the frame suffers is a derivative of modern sins in furniture. The principle that furniture is a work of art has disposed of a great deal of poor taste and dreary banality, but its rights are not as positive and unlimited as favourable prejudice for it would lead one to believe. The work of art is something for itself, whereas furniture is something for us. The work of art may be as individual as it wishes, as the sensualisation of a spiritual unity: while hanging in our room, it does not disturb our acquaintances, since it has a frame, that is, since it is like an island in the world that waits until one approaches it and which one can as well pass by and overlook. In the case of the piece of furniture, we make contact with it constantly, it intervenes in our life and thus has no right to exist for itself. Many a modern piece of furniture appears degraded when one sits on it, since it is the direct expression of individual artistry; its form seems to cry out for a frame, and standing in a room without one it oppresses the human being, who, with his or her individuality, is after all supposed to be the main concern and furniture merely the background. When one hears the individuality of the piece of furniture being preached everywhere, this represents a hypertrophy of the modern sense of individuality. The same error in rank ordering occurs if one wishes to grant the frame an aesthetic value of its own by figurative ornamentation, by the independent appeal of the colour, by design or symbolism, all of which make it into the expression of a self-sufficient artistic idea. All of this displaces the subordinate position of the frame with respect to the picture. Just as the frame for a soul can only be a body, but not itself a soul, so a work of art which exists for its own sake cannot emphasise and support the autonomous existence of another such work: the resignation required to this end rules out existing as art.

Like furniture, the frame should possess no individuality, but rather a style. Style is an unburdening of the personality, the replacement of individual intensification by a broader general entity. Thus, whereas an object of the applied arts immediately places in the foreground of consciousness the issue as to its particular style, we tend to ask this question much less often in the presence of a work of art; indeed, in the case of the greatest works of art, their style is really of no significance to us. Here, the individual aspect completely outshines that general aspect which we call style, and which the individual object shares with countless others. The subdued and calming quality that emanates from all strictly stylised objects resides in this supra-individual character. In the works of humanity, style takes a middle position between the uniqueness of the individual soul and the absolute universality of nature. This is the reason why people surround themselves with stylised objects in their cultural milieu, which separates them from the merely natural world, and this is why style and not individualisation is the proper principle of life for the frame of a work of art, which repeats the relationship of the psyche to the world in its relationship to the environment.

If, then, the aesthetic position of the frame is determined as much by a certain indifference as by those energies of its forms, whose uniform flow characterises it as the mere border guard of the picture, then it is precisely very old frames which seem to contradict this. Here the sides are often constructed as pillars or columns which support a cornice or a gable, such that each part and the whole is more differentiated and significant than in the case of a modern frame, any of whose four sides can be substituted for one another. By virtue of this heavy architectonics, through the division of labour-like interdependence of its elements, the inner coherence of the frame is of course elevated in the extreme. In so doing, however, it takes on an organic life and a weightiness of its own which enter into a degrading competition with its existence as a mere frame. This may have been justified as long as the inner artistic unity of the picture, which holds it together and closes it off against the external world, was still not experienced sufficiently strongly. Whenever a picture served the purposes of divine worship, whenever it was drawn into religious experience, whenever it addressed the intelligence of the viewer directly through banderoles or other such interpretations, then extra-artistic spheres were taking control of it and threatening to break through its formal artistic unity. This is counteracted by the dynamism of the architectonic frame, whose mutually referential components create an impenetrably strong connection – and thereby a boundary. The more the work of art rejects such relationships that transcend it, the more it can forego the powers of the frame, which disavow their own subordinate function by their own organic liveliness.

The fact that, compared with the architectonic frame, the modern frame, with the much more mechanical and schematic character of its four equal sides, represents a progress, integrates the frame into a far-reaching principle of cultural development. The latter by no means always leads the individual element from a mechanistic-external form to an organically animated and autonomously more meaningful form. On the contrary, whenever the spirit organises the material of existence into ever more extensive and ever higher designs, then innumerable objects that had previously led a self-enclosed life representing an idea of their own are degraded to merely mechanically effective, specific elements of larger constellations; only the latter are now bearers of the idea, whereas the former have become mere means, whose autonomous existence is meaningless. This is the relationship of the medieval knight to the soldiers of a modern army, of the independent craftsman to the factory worker, of the enclosed community to the city in a modern state, of household self-sufficient production to labour within the financial and global economic organisation of the market. From out of the coexisting, mutually independent and self-sufficient entities there grows an all-embracing structure to which, as it were, each gives up their soul, their existence for themselves, in order to regain a meaning for their existence only as mechanically functioning elements of that structure. Thus the mechanical uniform design of the frame, meaningless in comparison with architectonic or other 'organic' forms, indicates that the relationship between the picture and its surrounds has only now been understood and adequately expressed as a whole. The apparently higher spirituality of the intrinsically meaningful frame only proves the lesser degree of spirituality in the understanding of the whole to which it belongs.

The work of art is in the actually contradictory position of being supposed to form a unified whole with its surroundings, whereas it is itself already a whole. In this way, it repeats the general difficulty of life that the elements of totalities nevertheless lay claim to being autonomous totalities themselves. It is evident what an infinitely delicate consideration of the advancing and retreating, of the energies and arrestments of the frame is necessary if it is to solve the problem in the visual sphere of mediating between the work of art and its milieu, separating and connecting – the task which has its analogy in the historical realm, in which the individual and society mutually wear one another down.

Installation view, Hans Haacke,
Manet-PROJEKT '74,
Wallraf-Richartz Museum, Cologne, 1974

Opposite page: Hans Haacke,
Manet-PROJEKT '74 (detail)

Both images courtesy
Hans Haacke/VG Bild-Kunst

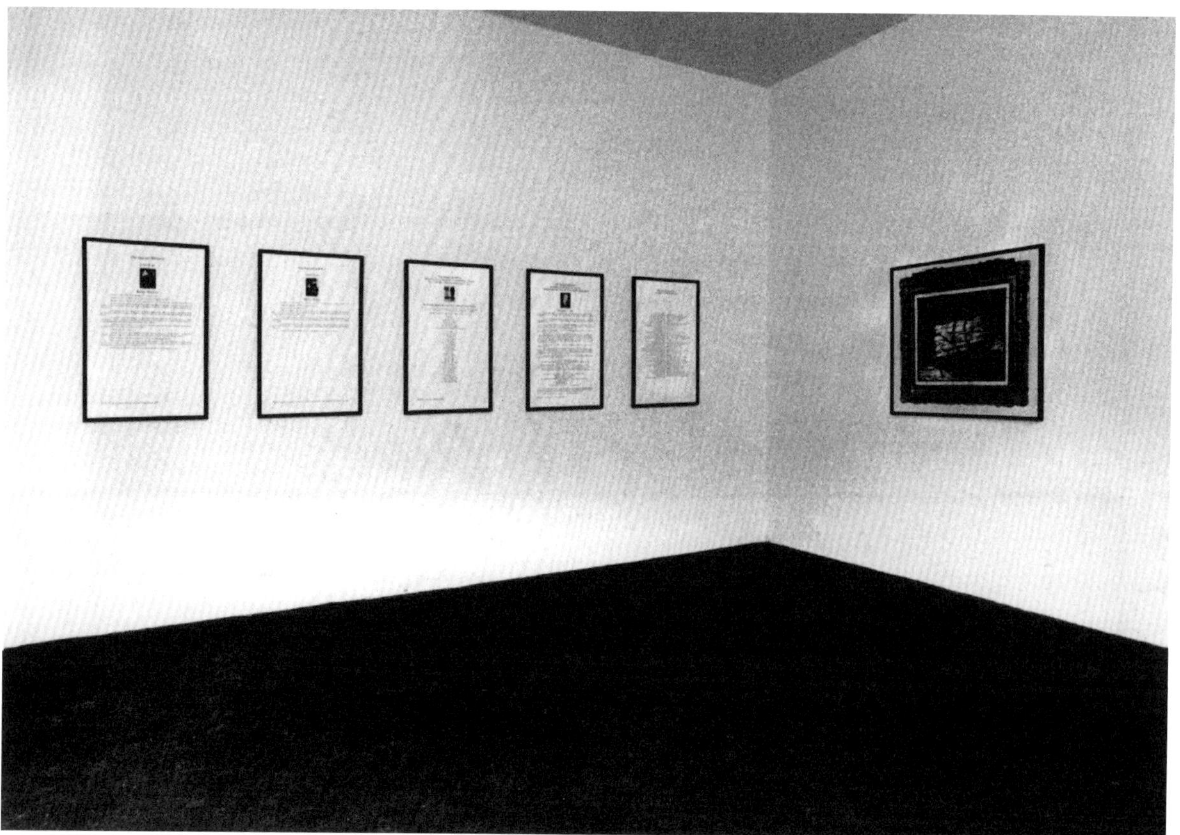

Das Spargel-Stilleben
erworben durch die Initiative des
Vorsitzenden des Wallraf-Richartz-Kuratoriums

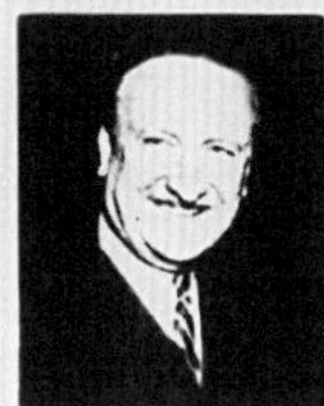

Hermann J. Abs

Geboren 1901 in Bonn. – Entstammt wohlhabender katholischer Familie. Vater Dr. Josef Abs, Rechtsanwalt und Justizrat, Mitinhaber der Hubertus Braunkohlen AG. Brüggen, Erft. Mutter Katharina Lückerath.

Abitur 1919 Realgymnasium Bonn. – Ein Sem. Jurastudium Universität Bonn. – Banklehre im Kölner Bankhaus Delbrück von der Heydt & Co. Erwirbt internationale Bankerfahrung in Amsterdam, London, Paris, USA.

Heiratet 1928 Inez Schnitzler. Ihr Vater mit Georg von Schnitzler vom Vorstand des IG. Farben-Konzerns verwandt. Tante verheiratet mit Baron Alfred Neven du Mont. Schwester verheiratet mit Georg Graf von der Goltz. – Geburt der Kinder Thomas und Marion Abs.

Mitglied der Zentrumspartei. – 1929 Prokura im Bankhaus Delbrück, Schickler & Co., Berlin. 1935-37 einer der 5 Teilhaber der Bank.

1937 im Vorstand und Aufsichtsrat der Deutschen Bank, Berlin. Leiter der Auslandsabteilung. – 1939 von Reichswirtschaftsminister Funk in den Beirat der Deutschen Reichsbank berufen. – Mitglied in Ausschüssen der Reichsbank, Reichsgruppe Industrie, Reichsgruppe Banken, Reichswirtschafts-kammer und einem Arbeitskreis im Reichswirtschaftsministerium. – 1944 in über 50 Aufsichts- und Verwaltungsräten großer Unternehmen. Mitgliedschaft in Gesellschaften zur Wahrnehmung deutscher Wirtschaftsinteressen im Ausland.

1946 für 6 Wochen in britischer Haft. – Von der Alliierten Entnazifizierungsbehörde als entlastet (5) eingestuft.

1948 bei der Gründung der Kreditanstalt für Wiederaufbau. Maßgeblich an der Wirtschafts-planung der Bundesregierung beteiligt. Wirtschaftsberater Konrad Adenauers. – Leiter der deutschen Delegation bei der Londoner Schuldenkonferenz 1951-53. Berater bei den Wiedergutmachungsver-handlungen mit Israel in Den Haag. 1954 Mitglied der CDU.

1952 im Aufsichtsrat der Süddeutschen Bank AG. – 1957-67 Vorstandssprecher der Deutschen Bank AG. Seit 1967 Vorsitzender des Aufsichtsrats.

Ehrenvorsitzender des Aufsichtsrats:
Deutsche Überseeische Bank, Hamburg – Pittler Maschinenfabrik AG, Langen (Hessen)
Vorsitzender des Aufsichtsrats:
Dahlbusch Verwaltungs-AG, Gelsenkirchen – Daimler Benz AG, Stuttgart-Untertürkheim –
Deutsche Bank AG, Frankfurt – Deutsche Lufthansa AG, Köln – Philipp Holzmann AG, Frankfurt –
Phoenix Gummiwerke AG, Hamburg-Harburg – RWE Elektrizitätswerk AG, Essen –
Vereinigte Glanzstoff AG, Wuppertal-Elberfeld – Zellstoff-Fabrik Waldhof AG, Mannheim

Ehrenvorsitzender:
Salamander AG, Kornwestheim – Gebr. Stumm GmbH, Brambauer (Westf.) –
Süddeutsche Zucker-AG, Mannheim
Stellvertr. Vors. des Aufsichtsrats:
Badische Anilin- und Sodafabrik AG, Ludwigshafen – Siemens AG, Berlin-München
Mitglied des Aufsichtsrats:
Metallgesellschaft AG, Frankfurt
Präsident des Verwaltungsrats:
Kreditanstalt für Wiederaufbau – Deutsche Bundesbahn

Großes Bundesverdienstkreuz mit Stern, Päpstl. Stern zum Komturkreuz, Großkreuz Isabella die Katholische von Spanien, Cruzeiro do Sul von Brasilien. – Ritter des Ordens vom Heiligen Grabe. – Dr. h.c. der Univ. Göttingen, Sofia, Tokio und der Wirtschaftshochschule Mannheim.

Lebt in Kronberg (Taunus) und auf dem Bentgerhof bei Remagen.

For Simmel, the picture frame was an essential device for ensuring that the artwork stood out as an 'autonomous totality'. Precisely for that reason, the frame was deconstructed and demolished by various avant-gardes and neo-avant-gardes. Kazimir Malevich noted acerbically that to the 'intelligentsia … picture frames are more readable than paintings'.[4] As in the case of the artist's *Black Square* of 1915, where the painted shape echoes the edges of the painting, much modernist painting reflects the shape of the canvas formally, for instance in grid structures. Such grids internalise the frame, while the actual frame is now often abandoned in favour of paintings hung directly on the wall.[5]

As art divested itself of conventional markers of aesthetic difference, the exhibition space itself increasingly became the primary frame. Stripped of its nineteenth-century accoutrements (wooden panels, coloured fabrics) by modernist curators during the early twentieth century, the exhibition space became a supposedly neutral framework: the white cube. However, as Brian O'Doherty notes in his 1986 book *Inside the White Cube* (which collects a series of essays going back to 1976), far from being a mere container for artworks, this white space is transformative and enables certain forms of art in the first place.[6] In the 1960s and 1970s, artists increasingly worked directly with this space as their primary medium. While O'Doherty's essays purport to address the 'ideology of the gallery space' in a critical manner, they are profoundly ambivalent. He seems to revel in the white cube's transformative, aestheticising power, and largely refrains from discussing art projects that happened outside the white cube (no Fluxus here, for instance).[7] For him, there may be life outside the white cube, but certainly not art.

The white cube is never a purely formal or spatial affair; it is also the physical manifestation of more intangible frames. Around 1970, institutional frameworks became the focal point for artists such as Michael Asher, Marcel Broodthaers, Daniel Buren, Hans Haacke, Robert Smithson and Mierle Laderman Ukeles – we shall return to Ukeles later.[8] These artists were later identified as the 'first wave' of institutional critique – a term that only started to get currency in the mid-1980s.[9] Here we are dealing, then, not with physical picture frames, but with methods of institutional, economical and ideological framing – a complex of conditions that artists have both analysed and challenged.

A 1975 publication on Haacke's work is titled *Framing and Being Framed*; in the previous year he had published a statement stressing that artists, their supporters and their enemies 'participate jointly in the maintenance and/or development of the ideological make-up of their society. They work within that frame, set the frame and are being framed.'[10] The use of the framing metaphor by artists such as Buren and Haacke paralleled developments in the social sciences – from Gregory Bateson's 1955 theory of 'the play frame', determining when an activity is seen as play rather than as an act of aggression, to Erving Goffman's 1974 book *Frame Analysis*, a more fully developed account of the ways in which social actors contextualise and conceptualise situations and events.[11]

In a text from 1985, the critic and art historian Craig Owens both looked back and expanded on the 'frame analysis' of early institutional critique. Owens is one of a number of art historians and critics associated with the journal *October* who, in the late 1970s and 1980s, did much to theorise and canonise institutional critique, in turn providing an important impetus for younger practitioners. Owens's 1987 essay 'From Work to Frame, or Is There Life after "The Death of the Author"?' begins by quoting Smithson's statement in a 1972 interview with Bruce Kurtz:

Paintings are bought and sold. The artist sits in his solitude, knocks out his paintings, assembles them, then waits for someone to confer the value, some external source. *The artist isn't in control of his value.* And that's the way it operates. [...] Whatever a painting goes for at Parke-Bernet is really somebody else's decision, not the artist's decision, so there's a division, on the broad social realm, the value is separated from the artist, *the artist is estranged from his own production.*[12]

Owens notes that Smithson made these remarks when artists such as Buren and Broodthaers had already developed the key aspects of their practices, and that he was possibly inspired by them. He continues:

Having thus contradicted a deeply entrenched, distinctly modern view of artistic labour as non-alienated labour, Smithson predicted [to Kurtz] that artists would become increasingly involved in an analysis of the forces and relations of artistic production: 'This is the great issue, I think it will be the growing issue, of the seventies: the investigation of the apparatus the artist is threaded through.'

The investigation of the apparatus the artist is threaded through indeed turned out – in the practices of Marcel Broodthaers, Daniel Buren, Michael Asher, Hans Haacke and Louise Lawler, as well as writings by such artists as Martha Rosler, Mary Kelly and Allan Sekula (among others) – to be the main preoccupation of art in the '70s.[13]

Owens's theoretical references include Jacques Derrida's work on the *parergon*, or the para-work that cannot be neatly separated from the 'work':

Who is free to define, manipulate and, ultimately, to benefit from the codes and conventions of cultural production? These questions shift attention away from the work and its producer and onto its *frame* – the first, by focussing on the *location* in which the work of art is encountered; the second, by insisting on the *social* nature of artistic production and reception. Sometimes the postmodernist work insists upon the impossibility of framing, of ever rigorously distinguishing a text from its context (this argument is made repeatedly in Jacques Derrida's writings on visual art[1]); at others, it is *all* frame (Allan McCollum's plaster painting 'surrogates'). More often than not, however, the 'frame' is treated as that network of institutional practices (Foucault would have called them 'discourses') that define, circumscribe and contain both artistic production and reception.[14]

In the work of the artists discussed by Owens, the 'displacement from work to frame' is articulated in various ways. Louise Lawler, for instance, presented 'arrangements' of works by other artists, and took on positions such as that of an installation photographer or graphic designer. Daniel Buren used his own deliberately anonymous or impersonal work – vertical stripes in various colours, on varying supports, but always 8.7 centimetres wide – to foreground the museum or gallery as the fundamental support or framework of art. Buren was as critical of object-based art as he was of

---

[1] See 'Parergon' and 'Restitutions of the truth in pointing', in Jacques Derrida, *The Truth in Painting* (trans. Geoff Bennington and Ian McLeod), Chicago: University of Chicago Press, 1987. For a broader account of the impossibility of distinguishing text from context, see Jacques Derrida, 'Signature, Event, Context', in *Margins of Philosophy* (trans. Alan Bass), Brighton: The Harvester Press, 1982.

attempts to 'abandon the museum' or 'leave the art world'; there was no escape, as the museum became more progressively 'generalised'. As Owens puts it: '[The] "missing parts" of a 1975 installation at the Museum of Modern Art in New York - the (imaginary) sections of Buren's work "concealed" by a staircase - were posted on billboards in SoHo, thereby reminding viewers that these two parts of the city were already connected by the art economy.'[15]

Or, in Buren's own words: 'To pretend to escape from these limits is to reinforce the prevailing ideology which expects enterta

inment from the artist. Art is not free, the artist does not express himself freely (he cannot). Art is not the prophecy of a free society. Freedom in art is the luxury/privilege of a repressive society.'[16] In his essay 'Critical Limits' (1970), Buren argues that while art had significantly rid itself of conventional limiting or framing devices such as stretchers and canvas (and of course, picture frames), this only meant that frames or 'limits' were becoming more insidious, taking new and increasingly intangible forms. The frame is now both concealed and omnipresent.

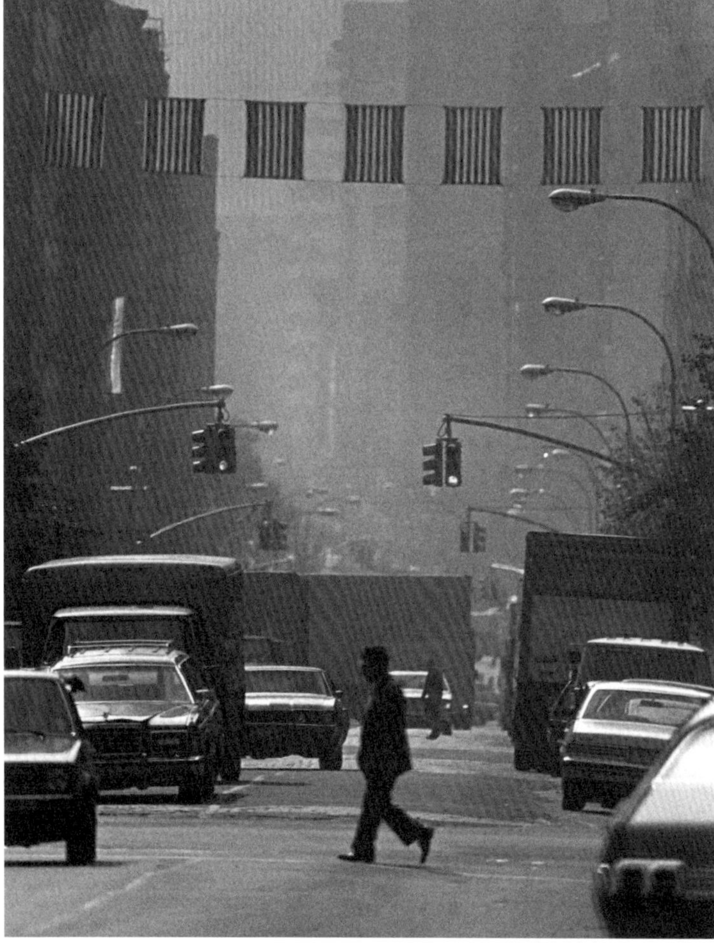

Photo-souvenir of Daniel Buren's, *Within and Beyond the Frame* (detail) in situ outside of John Weber Gallery, New York, October 1973
© DB-ADAGP Paris
Courtesy the artist

DANIEL BUREN, 'CRITICAL LIMITS'

Reprinted from Daniel Buren, *Five Texts*,
New York and London: John Weber Gallery
and Jack Wendler Gallery, 1973, pp.43-50
with accompanying diagrams. First published
in 1970 by Yvon Lambert, Paris. Translated
from the French by Laurent Sauerwein, revised
by Olivia Fairweather and Jack Cox.

The following text, which results from the practice of work that is specifically, exclusively TO BE SEEN,[2] is only the demonstration, presentation of this work and not its theory. At a push, the text may be considered to be an illustration of the work in question. It is dictated by this proposition and not by an abstract and purified image of any particular future. It is no doubt didactic.

In the explanations of the diagrams that follow, I have no qualms in using terms such as 'stretcher', 'canvas', 'paint', even though these materials are no longer in general use, having been eliminated by successive generations of avant-gardes since the beginning of the century.

Today, paradoxically, since these means were abandoned without due regard either to the necessities that brought them into use in the first place, or to the implications of such necessities in the resulting product (the work), an analysis of those very works that eliminated them without questioning their basis cannot ignore their continual presence. It is precisely the pathological ignorance of the artist that allows him to keep on saying/doing the same thing – in other words regressing – while giving the appearance of change and novelty.

I will therefore use this terminology in spite of its anachronistic resonance. Their material disappearance having in no way corresponded to an understanding of their meaning, we can observe that their traces are still in evidence today.

The material absence of these means (stretcher, canvas, paint) even sharpens their earlier meanings through their current ersatz forms.

The above considerations serve only as a warning concerning the terminology used in this text. I will, however, attempt a comparison.

In the classical meaning of these terms we have a canvas stretched on a stretcher which it covers and hides, thus already producing a front (*recto*) and a back (*verso*). But the work is not complete since the blank surface of the canvas remains to be covered (concealed) by paint. At this point we have a stretcher concealed by a canvas – a first step in ignoring the verso – and a canvas masked by paint. This painting remains to be defined: it 'tells' both a story and the history of painting. It is the mask of painting.

All painting, all art, is based among other things on the unconditional acceptance of the above fundamental facts.

---

[2] When we use (and insist on) words such as 'view', 'to see', 'visible', they are to be understood in a wide sense, never referring exclusively to sight or the eye as an independent organ, which would be mechanistic and absurd. SEEING and LOOKING are actions which make it possible to apprehend our work. Without them it could not exist – as opposed to other works (so-called Conceptual) which claim no need for visibility. A proposal can be 'to be seen', of course, but without forgetting that there can be no sight without thought.

The emotional power produced by any stretched canvas (Christ on the Cross) is so strong that one will find the same (religious) process in thousands of works (icons) produced since the beginning of the century, which, however, very seldom resort to the use of canvas, stretcher or paint. Let's consider Minimal Art: we notice a desire to use raw material which a priori has no front or back (a steel plate, a wooden plank ...). This material is transformed into a box, cube or simple parallelepiped - thus immediately creating a recto and verso, a visible side (the body) and a hidden one (the soul). The visible side is itself sometimes covered (masked) in favour of a colour, a varnish, a metallisation. The resulting object can be defined as typically idealistic, since one pretends to ignore what is really at stake - the above-mentioned fundamental conditions - revealing through its contradictions its failure to raise the question of art, a question which is totally ignored.

We will see, with the help of diagrams, that this object itself only exists, can only be seen, in relation to the Museum/Gallery that contains it, a Museum/Gallery in view of which it was produced and to which no particular attention is paid.

The stretcher, the canvas and the paint have been eliminated, but in fact what is produced is their exact image, an image that itself only exists in relation to the single viewpoint from which it is seen/made, this viewpoint being in turn ignored as a matter of course.

And yet, outside this context, supposedly neutral since one does not think about it, the work, considered timeless, beyond limits, even pure and neutral, simply falls apart. We will attempt to briefly indicate the various processes of artistic camouflage in relation to the works themselves as much as to their outsides (their contexts).

Only knowledge of these successive frames/limits and their importance can enable the work/product such as I conceive it to situate itself in relation to these limits and subsequently to unmask and reveal them.

I. CANCELLING DISCOURSES
(ART AS IT IS PERCEIVED)

Here, the painted object, or any object (ready-made) captures all interest and relegates to minimal importance, or even completely masks, its very condition for existing as an object perceived as an art object or work of art. It acts like the tree hiding the forest. The work of art appears in all its strength. It is supreme. It is truly the exception to the rule that in overcoming all difficulties, and attaining full freedom, nourishes the prevailing ideology. It functions as a security valve for the system, an image of freedom in the midst of general alienation, a bourgeois concept, supposedly beyond all criticism, natural, above and beyond all ideology.

Art as it presents itself to us under the manifold form of the 'pure masterpiece' refuses to reveal its underlying 'supports', 'frames' or 'limits'.

The simple ignorance of these limits or the wish to mask them has an equally simple but essential consequence: as soon as one reveals these limits (see Diagrams 1.2, 2.2, 3.2) the whole discourse on art as it has hitherto flourished is cancelled out.

Diagram 1.1: Any painting (what is painted) first cancels out, masks its support (the canvas, paper, wood ...) which itself permanently conceals one of its sides, its verso (and consequently its stretcher). When we speak of illusion in painting we refer on the one hand to what is effectively being shown (an artist's style, his ability to 'transform' the reality of the world into a partial vision, etc.), but we also and above all refer to the illusion created by the process of hiding the reality of the painting itself: how is it made, how is it painted, why, for whom, on what, with what, etc. This painting, in cancelling out its own process obviously also cancels out its point of view (the Museum/Gallery) passing the latter off as a neutral, subtending frame that doesn't affect the content/work. The importance of the Museum/Gallery, even its interest, is reduced to a minimum so that the idealist discourse can develop seamlessly. Diagram 1.1 shows that in relation to the various components that are present, the Museum/Gallery is only minimally in play. As for the cultural limits (CL), they hardly appear, so thoroughly does art present itself as the message of the eternal, especially if it comes in the latest style.

Diagram 2.1: In the case of a ready-made or neutral or pure object (cf. Minimal Art, certain Pop Art works, Conceptual Art, New Realism, etc.), the support, the stretcher, painting (in the sense of coloured pigments) have generally disappeared. But here again the whole discourse is based on what is being exhibited and that only, as if the place of visibility were of no importance. One will notice in this diagram that because certain components have disappeared, the Museum/Gallery and the 'cultural limits' appear closer to the realm of 'art' and start becoming more difficult to hide. (We will see further on, in Diagram 2.2, that M and CL are privileged by the 'mysterious' disappearance of S and C.)

Nevertheless, they are still considered as pursuing an indifferent existence. It is true that the basic preoccupations in this case lie elsewhere and that the aim is to 'solve' the problem of painting by unveiling its own reality (as if this problem could be 'solved'), *by replacing art with its opposite.* This is the birth of the ready-made, in other words, the radical (i.e. 'petit-bourgeois') negation of art in favour of the object ('reality') such as it is (cf. 'Standpoints' in Studio International).[3] The failure stems from the basic ignorance of the two other components involved, namely 'Museum/Gallery' and 'Cultural Limits'. It is a complete failure, as the unforeseen apparition of these two frameworks will suddenly disclose all the other components that were believed to have been conjured away.

Diagram 3.1: Here it is the Museum/Gallery and the Cultural Limits that the artist will attempt to make disappear. Their presence has indeed become cumbersome. *Initially,* the artist simply dismisses them. He does his thing, gives a pretty speech, free at last, outside! He thus recreates with other means (earth, stones, water, words, branches or by transporting museum 'paintings' to vacant lots) certain worn-out forms of traditional painting and pretends to breathe new life into what has died. And so we see the unashamed return of the ego, the anecdote, naturalism, kitsch, Romanticism and all such similar nineteenth-century notions which the twentieth century keeps on carting around. In this instance, the Museum/Gallery is masked in a different manner than in Diagrams 1.1 and 2.1. One radicalises (see 'petit-bourgeois' above) and simply crosses it off the map just as the ready-made 'cancelled-out' painting. Below, it will be shown that in *a second stage* (see Diagram 3.2) all this nicely reintegrates the museum and its cultural framework, to the great joy of the gaping onlookers, astounded once more at having been transported to such a distance. The bourgeois values of freedom and escape are thus preserved thanks to the joint efforts of art and its so-called revolutionary avant-garde.

II. WHAT REALLY GOES ON
(ART WHERE IT TAKES PLACE)

The Museum/Gallery is not the neutral place one would like us to believe it is, but rather the single viewpoint where a work is seen and in the final analysis the single viewpoint in view of which the work is made. In order not to be taken into consideration or in order to be considered as natural/a matter of course, the Museum/Gallery becomes the mythical/distorting framework of everything that goes into it.

Diagram 1.2: We see the various frames and media as they are included in one another in the reality of their situation.

In what is really going on, the roles are not those that we were led to believe (see Diagrams 1.1, 2.1, 3.1). The Museum/Gallery has become the general frame, container of all art as it exists. It is at once the centre and the backdrop of art, at once its figure and its ground. *The Museum/Gallery becomes the common*

---

[3]   Editors' Note: Daniel Buren, 'Standpoints' (1971), in *Five Texts, op. cit.*, pp.28-41.

revelator to all forms of art. Art appears as the product of two limits that did not seem to concern it: the Museum/Gallery and the cultural limits. Art depends on those limits precisely because it avoided situating itself in relation to them, and those very limits consequently become the pivot of creation. Their ignored yet ever returning presence makes these frameworks both art's point of departure and its point of arrival.

The frames M and CL contain and subordinate P, which itself, as in Diagram 1.1, cancels out S and C.

Diagram 2.2: Here the painting, or object, or ready-made, for all that the problem of the 'support' (stretcher-canvas) has been solved, are themselves only legible because they are inscribed within the framework of the Museum/Gallery, which totally encompasses them. 'Painting-object-ready-made' (P, O, RM) do not exist outside the Museum/Gallery. The container of the Museum/Gallery is bypassed only in the case of Diagram 3.1 and we will see both how and what ultimately comes of this.

Diagram 3.2: In Diagram 1.2, the Museum/Gallery container encloses all art in the classical complexity of its terms (LC, P, S, C). The same container M appears even more as the usual comfortable haven in Diagram 2.2. One sees it receiving a discourse (O, RM, even P) whose magic (the extravagant disappearance of traditional pictorial components) only depends on the necessary acceptance of the place of discourse, i.e. the Museum/Gallery. Diagram 3.2 shows what goes on in reality when those who (see Diagram 3.1), having perceived the limits imposed by the Museum/Gallery, attempt to escape it. Obviously they choose 'radicality', the radicality which dispenses them from thinking and ends up supplying the Museum/Gallery with the alibi it needed to justify its claim for openness.

The procedure through which the ready-made wished to believe it had broken away from P (art) is put to use in the same way by Land Art, Conceptual Art, etc. (LA, CA, etc.) in their attempts to break away from M. The bypassing of the limit M as proof of sublimation (a 'solution'). We could simply call this *escapism*.

The attempt is doubly reactionary: an individual search for greater freedom achieved in a return to nature that is constituted by the imposed, double illusion of the disappearance of the object and the Museum/Gallery.

> Now the object continues to exist and as an appropriated object, even if it is no longer an object to 'take home'. The work, the product, remains nevertheless and in a more totalitarian way than ever as *an appropriated object, the appropriation of an idea or of nature in the purest colonialist style.* As for the Museum/Gallery, its usual comforting, host function is reaffirmed since it imposes itself as the only possible exhibitor of the work (LA, CA, etc.) that has pretended to escape from it. Besides, the cultural limits in their general and in their particular forms ('society' and the media, respectively) have reached a decisive level of intensity: to ignore them as limits is necessary to the survival of art, at least in its most advanced avant-garde.

In parallel with the flight from Museums/Galleries, whose stubborn presence we have otherwise observed, we note, in fact, a rather widespread flight from the urban environment. Doubtless, the limit formed by culture, as represented by the city and urban society, has been perceived. And obviously, as is the case at every stage in the process, as soon as a frame, a limit, is perceived as such, in art, one rushes to evade them. In order to do this, one takes off for the country, maybe even for the desert, and sets up one's easel there. But it is no longer a matter of applying paint to canvas as if it were an emanation from the landscape. The conquest is now made directly on nature itself. One flees the city to spread the plague through the countryside. This remark is not intended to defend nature but to denounce the cowardly vanity of the country aesthete. That said, in relation to art and its limits, the fleeing artist cheats no more nor less than his coreligionists in years past. In doubt, we will simply say that it has not been proven that anybody should be held responsible for his own stupidity.

Detail of Diagram 1.1: *Diagram 1.3*: In this diagram, a detail of Diagram 1.1, P refers to anything painted, whatever the motif, the idea, the style or the justifications. In all cases, the 'support' (canvas or other) on which this painting is made is covered up and cancelled out. P therefore masks S, which in turn masks C. This results in the creation of a recto and a verso. *The history of art (of forms) is the history of 'rectos'.* The history of 'versos' (reality), the same plus the same plus the same … is yet to be made. This problem of the 'non-reversibility' of art is one of the many raised by art as question. To emphasise only this is to give art a new form and not to question it.

Detail of Diagram 2.1: This diagram, which should be Diagram 2.3, cannot be represented, as the work (RM or O) exists only as directly linked (aesthetically and culturally speaking) to the Museum/Gallery/Support. In Diagrams 2.1 and 2.2, detail and whole are indissociable.

Detail of Diagram 3.1: This detail can be anything as its only criteria is *exoticism*. Land Art and Conceptual Art use all the symbols, even the most hackneyed.
Diagram 3.3 is not represented.

III. CRITICAL WORK
(THE LIMITS OF MY WORK - THE POINTS OF VIEW - WHAT IS ATTEMPTED)

Diagram A.2: In this diagram, detail of Diagram A.1, P is shown by concealing only part of S, S is transformed by P, P and S are both linked and different. As for C, it is visible since the verso of P is accepted as possible and an integral part of the whole. C can be used or not as long as its presence or its absence is made obvious. Similarly, the verso can be used as recto (P partially covering S) or left unused. Either way, it will appear either as a verso that can be used as a recto or, already used, as a recto, or as a verso according to its particular and indifferent use.

The 'painting' thus presented reveals in itself its own process and limits, i.e. its contradictions.

It must subsequently be placed in its context (whatever it may be) to appear as it is, i.e. in relation to 'the rest': within a frame, a boundary, delimiting a situation (see Diagram A.1).

Its context is not necessarily the Museum or the Gallery in as much as it appears as something painted no matter where it is located. In this sense, and in order to question this 'painted thing', it becomes necessary to analyse its behaviour in all places. Indeed, even if the painting in question reveals its own process itself, *it can never be seen or be visible in itself.*

The place where it is perceived thus determines its very existence (see Diagram A.1).

Diagram B.1: In this diagram, PC (pasted paper) plays the role of the 'painting' or P previously described (see Diagram A.2). The support/canvas of Diagrams A.1 and A.2 become the very walls of the Museum/Gallery. Here the work and its support, the support and the work are revealed literally.

Here, what we call the work (PC) cannot be seen (exist) and only really exists together with its support (whatever it may be): NS, while at the same time, the support exists with or without the work. PC therefore defines and reveals its own immediate limits. In the case of Diagram B, the work (PC) reveals the role of M, exposes its function as a frame/limit for the work in the first instance and then whatever (without exception) appears in it (see Diagram B.2). This is also true of my work (paint applied to pre-striped canvases) as shown in Diagram A.1.

Diagram C.1: Here P or PC is shown outside the usual places of exhibition and therefore outside of M. This can be the walls of the city, of the subway, a highway, any urban place of any place where some kind of social life exists (which excludes the oceans, the deserts, the Himalayas, the Great Salt Lake, virgin forests and other exotic places, all invitations for artistic safaris).

Where the work is shown, it shatters (or masters) the limits of M, i.e. the single viewpoint from which a work is generally seen, and reveals the new limits of its location. (Given the nature of the work and its very existence, it is not a matter of 'reproducing' in the Museum/Gallery – when it is used – what is done on the outside, since the same proposal is indifferently used outside or inside, both in places that are artistically defined and those that are not.) It is for this reason that the work in question, when it is placed outside the Museum/Gallery, *shatters the limits inherent to these places.* The work being identical (and yet always different) inside or outside, *it is no longer essential to one or the other.* It is the dialectic engendered by this practice that shows, in this particular case, that the limits of the Museum/Gallery as the only framework for a work of art are shattered.

The new and different frames in which the work is placed reveal, little by little, the work itself. This practice shows, among other things, that the 'frame' each time revealed (the street wall, the Museum/Gallery wall, the billboard, the subway...) 'frames' nothing.

The work is moved off centre, dissipates, *making it impossible for the eyes to apprehend it as a whole*, at the very moment when *it is only when it is seen that it exists.*

The multiplicity of different viewpoints dissolves the notion of property. They do not constitute a directed visit. At the very least the limit of the visit, if it is possible to visit this work, is that *it can be made in any direction. The exhibition/ presentation of the work is thus decentred and reversible just as 'painting'* (see Diagram A) *is both recto and verso.*

The work, confined, limited, always the same and yet non-identical, appears actually different at each moment because it reveals its limits. An 'exhibition' in different locations (viewpoints) prevents, at the least, an all-encompassing (possessive) apprehension of the whole. This whole allows itself to be seen only bit by bit. The whole is fragmented but each fragment is the whole. One must also remember that if the 'frame' where the work is shown is different (and revealed) each time, the work itself (visibly) changes each time: *the outer form is never the same, the colour is always different.* These constant 'differences' with the aim of arriving at the same, are what we call 'repetitions'.

Finally, in Diagram C.1, the strictest and until now most camouflaged limit clearly appears: the cultural limit. This is the most encompassing frame; it contains all forms, every action runs up against it. It is the limit of *knowledge.*

In Diagrams 1.1, 2.1, 3.1, CL is reduced to a strict minimum. (Particular) art would like to include its own culture whereas it is (general) art that is part of culture.

In Diagrams 1.2 and 2.2, CL appears as the silent frame that reinforces the formal frame M, and becomes more of a concern in the process described in Diagram 3.2.

In Diagrams A, B and C, CL takes its real place as the container enclosing the entire question of art. The work which is then carried out inside CL in Diagrams A, B and C has no proper place, i.e. other than revealing each time both its limits and itself (location). Priority can be given successively to one or the other of these aspects (limits) according to the particular analysis desired.

The cultural limit must be brought into question just like the others; it is the inescapable and expandable constraint of all discourse. *This container limits to its measured norms the very discourse we attempt to establish.* This limit is stringent but *it exists*, and to reject it (not to take it into account) or pretend to ignore it is to idealise.

Its enveloping power is particularly perceptible in Diagram C.1, as here we place ourselves definitively outside the screen/barrier – without hope of returning – formed by the Museum/Gallery itself, as a defined cultural area. In so doing, the cultural limit, which also allows for this discourse for instance, clearly appears as the background of the work itself (of all works) in the same way as in Diagram A.1 and especially B.1; the Museum/Gallery appears clearly, and is revealed as being the 'canvas' or the 'frame' within which whatever is shown there is inscribed/painted/drawn.

It becomes obvious that to *limit art's discourse to a single one of its elements* – P. in relation to S., or S. in relation to C., or S. in relation to M., etc – *is to continue art's usual practice,* with some tackling the problem of material, others the continual question of what it is to consider the work in itself, as if it included everything that was to be said or done. This is to consider the work as a closed system shielded from contingency. Those who consider the work itself, what is inscribed in it or what is hidden in it, as the only important question, forgetting the place where it is shown for instance, confine themselves to partial questions that always lead to acceptable solutions (i.e. art history).

Any discourse of this kind can only be considered regressive.

All the points raised by our proposal are mutually conditioned.

To ignore a single one is to ignore all of them.

It is not a matter of solving such and such a specific problem. It is a matter of showing clearly the problems which arise and trying, insofar as it is possible, not to give undue importance to any single one. *Only practice/theory can bring these problems to light.*

In this sense, we consider our work as *essentially critical.* The work is critical of its own processes, revealing its own contradictions, a process which also indicates the position of each of the elements taken into consideration, and this each time the work is presented in an order that is not pre-established.

Following Diagrams A.1, B.1, and C.1, it can be said that 'painting' is only able to appear when its processes, its support(s) and its various points of view are brought to light. This, without favouring one element over another, but by locating it, as precisely as possible, in relation to the whole.

Once painting and its discourse have been returned to their proper place, as a partial problem, as one part of the entire question of art, they can in this way *appear* truly and for the first time.

Painting becomes visible when it does not affect the gaze. Schemas I, II, and III show to what extent art is contained within precise and definite limits, limits that are generally unperceived, or hidden, or simply eliminated.

Schema I shows the idealist discourse as it is practiced. Schema II reveals what Schema I would like to hide, and Schema III indicates the practice of my own work and what that practice reveals about the work. Within Schema III, Diagram B.1 reveals what might pass unnoticed to a careless eye in Diagram A.1.

To pretend to escape from these limits is to reinforce the prevailing ideology which expects entertainment from the artist. Art is not free, the artist does not express himself freely (he cannot). Art is not the prophecy of a free society. Freedom in art is the luxury/privilege of a repressive society.

All art, whichever it may be, is exclusively political. What is called for *is the analysis of the formal and cultural limits* (and not one or the other) within which art exists and struggles.

These limits are many and of different intensities. Although the prevailing ideology and its associated artists try in every way to camouflage them, and although it is too early - the conditions have not met - to blow them up, the time has come to *unveil* them.

Daniel BUREN,
October, 1970.

I. CANCELLING DISCOURSES
(Art as it is perceived)

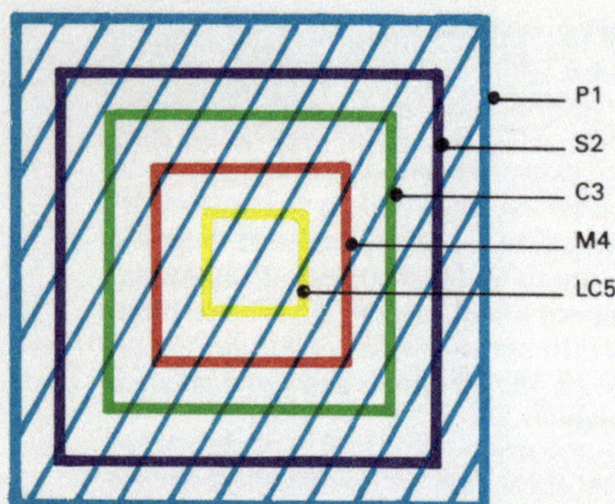

Diag. 1.1

The numbers after the letters (S2) indicate the places, in order of importance, of the different limits or frames.

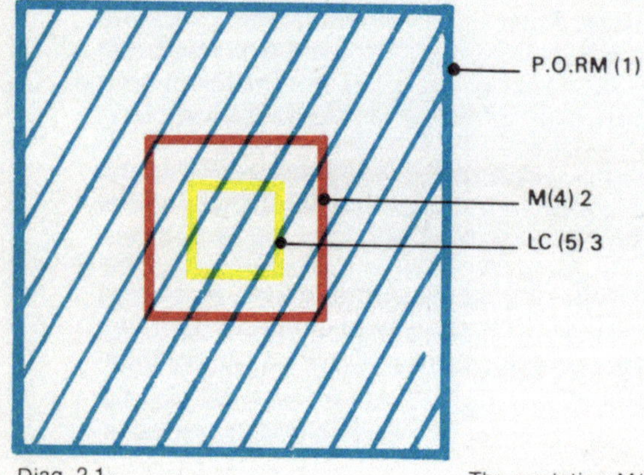

Diag. 2.1

The quotation M(4) 2 indicates the previous plan in parentheses (see diagram 1) and the new one.

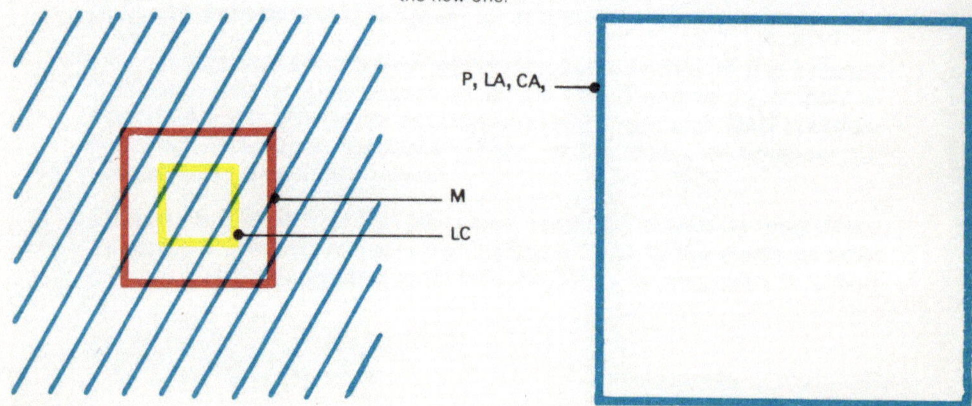

Diag. 3.1

The color of the hatching (blue) corresponds to the frame/limit which cancels out the others.

LEGEND

- **C** : Stretcher, verso (back)…
- **S** : Support: canvas/wall/store windows…
- **M** : Museum/Gallery/any defined artistic place.
- **LC** : Cultural Limits/Knowledge. In general (the period) and in particular (media such as TV, newspapers…)
- **O** : Object - Sculpture - Environment - Arte Povera - Technological Art…
- **RM** : Ready-Made.
- **LA** : Land Art - Happening.
- **CA** : Concept Art.
- **P** : Painting (in the sense of what one paints, i.e. on canvas/stretcher or directly on walls, stones, trees…)

II. WHAT REALLY GOES ON
(Art where it takes place)

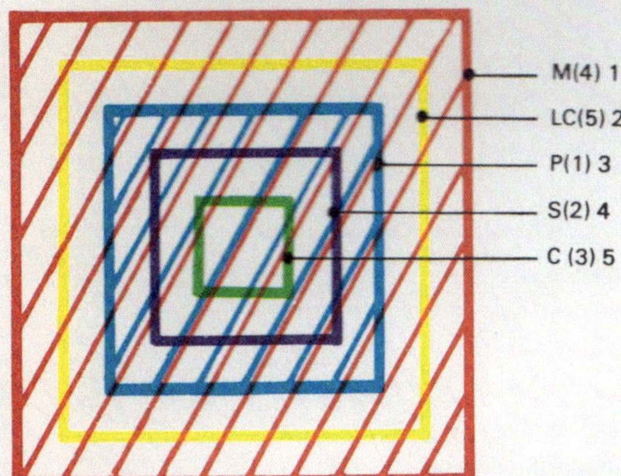

Diag. 1.2

The number in paren-
theses indicates the
place occupied in dia-
gram 1.

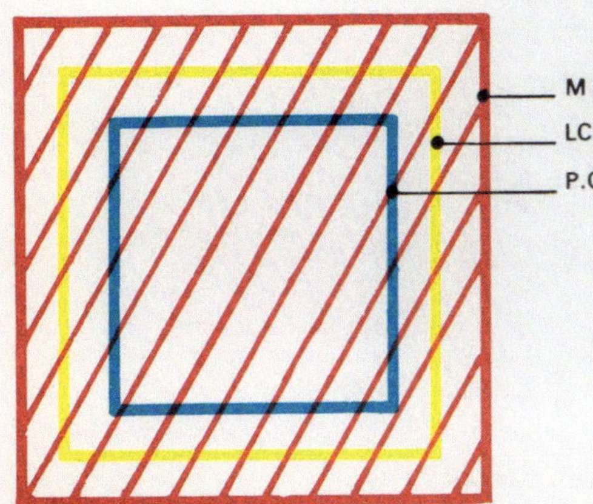

Diag. 2.2

The numbers in paren-
thesis indicate the
places occupied in
diagram 2.1.

LEGEND

The red hatching indicates that M is the
real limit (single viewpoint) of everything
that takes place within it. However, P always
cancels out C and S. The blue hatching
therefore remains.

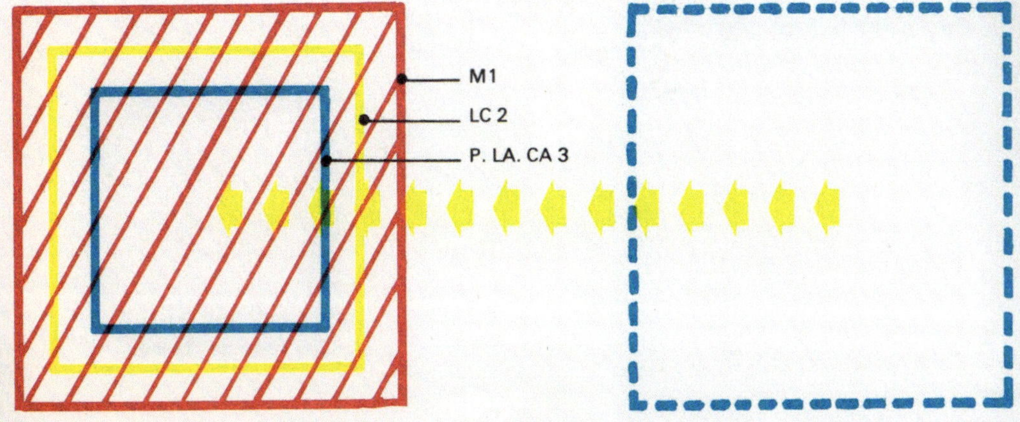

Diag. 3.2

III. CRITICAL WORK
(The limits of our work — the points of view — what is attempted)

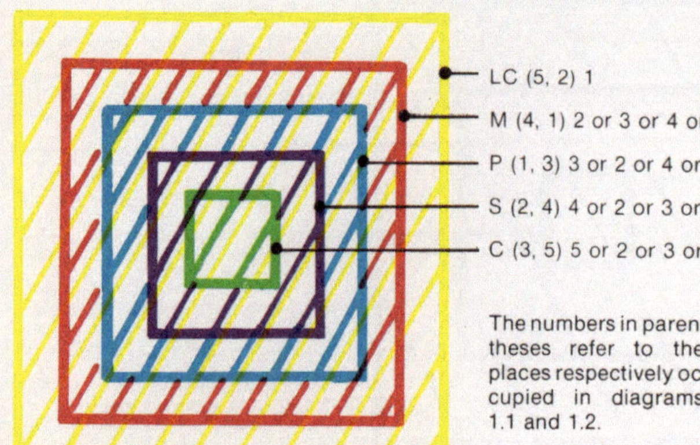

Diag. A.1

The numbers in parentheses refer to the places respectively occupied in diagrams 1.1 and 1.2.

Only LC keeps the first place. M, P, S, and C can take different places depending on which constant of art one emphasizes.

With the exception of LC, the frames/limits reveal themselves in turn. Their importance being equal, their differences are visible depending on what point of view is chosen.

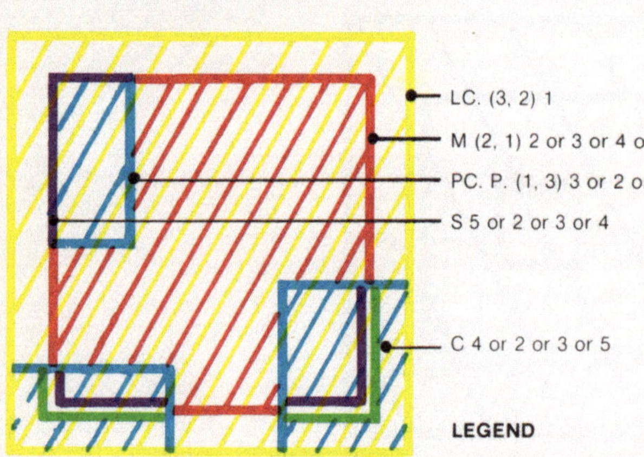

Diag. B.1

The numbers in parentheses refer to the places respectively occupied in diagrams 2.1 and 2.2.

LEGEND

● NS : New support or frame (x) other than a place defined *a priori* as artistic, and different every time.
● PC : Pasted papers (vertical stripes white and colored alternately).
Dotted lines: broken limits of M.

Diag. C

DETAILS FROM SOME DIAGRAMS

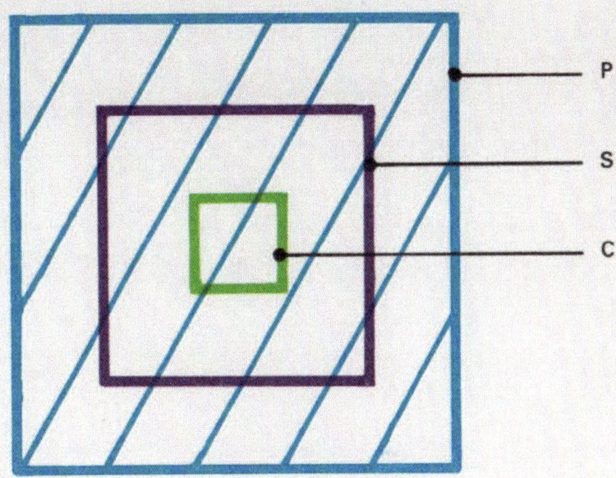

Diag. 1.3

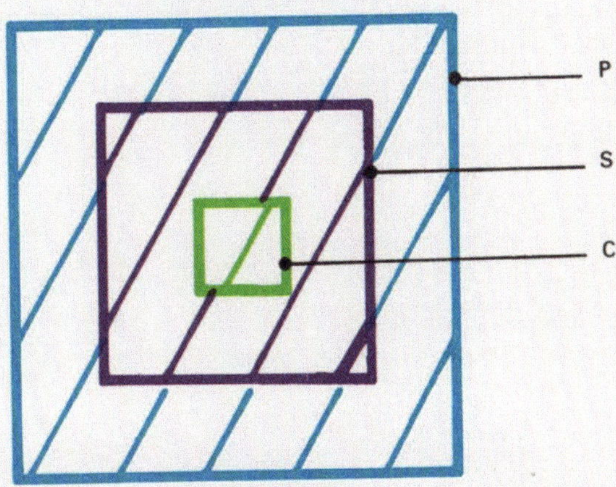

Diag. A.2

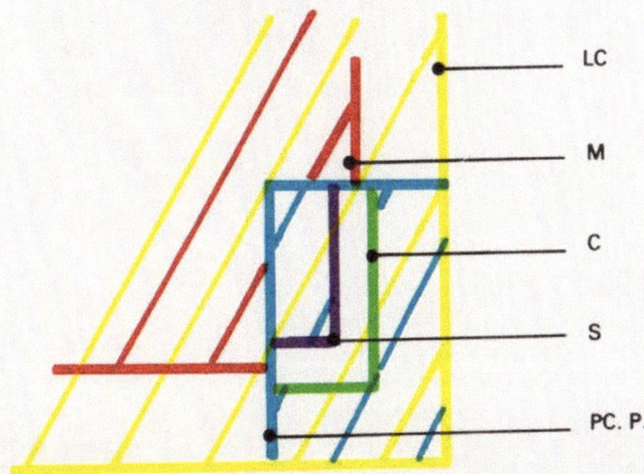

Diag. B.2

The diagrams can be read in these ways:

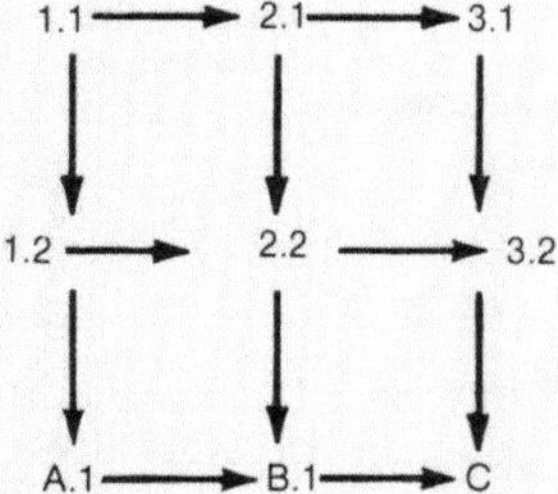

N.B. — The different diagrams are only here to help our demonstration. It is obvious that they are by nature approximate and incomplete. To consider them as "formal/rigid truths" would be pure fantasy on the part of the reader.

In his work, Buren intervenes in art's frames in a somewhat abstract manner. Early projects such as the 1975 MoMA piece foreground the mutual dependency of art institutions and their environments in concise and elegant ways, but without directly addressing the social and economic antinomies and conflicts inherent in most of these frameworks. More recently, Buren has operated in additional frameworks. His 2013 designs for a Louis Vuitton catwalk show and advertising campaign were brilliant in terms of form and colour; whether it still makes sense for this practice to be termed institutional critique is another matter. Has the re-framer himself been well and truly framed? Does this commission present an intervention into the blurring of art and fashion through a framework of heteronomous creative industries hodgepodge? But then, what does such an intervention do? The blindingly obvious does not need revealing, so the work's value (whatever it may be) must lie in something other than an old-school critical laying-bare.

Haacke's practice makes the case that 'the artist cannot express himself freely' in much more specific terms. Conceived on the occasion of the 'PROJEKT '74' show at the Wallraf-Richartz Museum in Cologne, Haacke's *Manet–PROJEKT '74* (1974) consists of a framed reproduction of Édouard Manet's *Bunch of Asparagus* (1880) – including its own frame – from the museum's collection and a series of panels that delve into the work's biography. Owned by the German-Jewish artist Max Liebermann before World War II, the Manet painting was bought after the war by the Wallraf-Richartz Kuratorium under the oversight of chairman Hermann Josef Abs, who, during the Nazi era, held a high position at Deutsche Bank. The listing of such facts was too much information for the museum, which suppressed *Manet–PROJEKT '74*; Haacke and Buren then pasted copies of Haacke's panels onto Buren's striped walls in the same show; these were then ripped off by management during the night.[17]

Autonomy in an Exploding Field

With Hans Haacke's work, the institutional framework is already conceived as an open system that is not contained by any one building. As Andrea Fraser puts it, 'the "institution" engaged by Haacke can best be defined as the network of social relations between [various spaces, places, people and things that make up the art field]'.[18] It is the fact that museums are embedded in larger structures that makes them profoundly political, as noted in an essay written by Haacke in the mid-1980s. In the same text he characterises museums as 'managers of consciousness' (in reference to Hans Magnus Enzensberger's notion of the 'consciousness industry'):

> Every museum is perforce a political institution, no matter whether it is privately run or maintained and supervised by governmental agencies. Those who hold the purse strings and have the authority over hiring and firing are, in effect, in charge of every element of the organisation, if they choose to use their powers. While the rule of the boards of trustees of museums in the United States is generally uncontested, the supervisory bodies of public institutions elsewhere have to contend much more with public opinion and the prevailing political climate. It follows that political considerations play a role in the appointment of museum directors. Once they are in office and have civil service status with tenure, such officials often enjoy more independence than their colleagues in the United States, who can be dismissed from one day to the next, as occurred with Bates Lowry and John Hightower at the Museum of Modern Art within a few years' time. But it is advisable, of course, to be a political animal in both settings. Funding, as much as one's prospect for promotion to more prestigious posts, depends on how well one can play the game.
>
> Directors in private US museums need to be attuned primarily to the frame of mind represented by the *Wall Street Journal*, the daily source of edification of the board members. They are affected less by who happens to be the occupant of the White House or the mayor's office, although this is not totally irrelevant for the success of applications for public grants. In other countries the outcome of elections can have a direct bearing on museum policies. Agility in dealing with political parties, possibly even membership in a party, can be an asset. The arrival of Margaret Thatcher in Downing Street and of François Mitterrand at the Élysée noticeably affect the art institutions in their respective countries. Whether in private or in public museums, disregard of political realities, among them the political needs of the supervising bodies and the ideological complexion of their members, is a guarantee of managerial failure.[19]

Haacke's analysis was published in the catalogue for his 1986 exhibition 'Unfinished Business' at the New Museum in New York; the same volume includes an essay by Fredric Jameson that is among the first to use 'institutional critique' to define this kind of practice – following a 1985 article by Fraser on Louise Lawler, 'In and Out of Place'.[20] In 'Hans Haacke and the Cultural Logic of Postmodernism', Jameson defines Haacke's work as bringing together two distinct genealogies.

FREDRIC JAMESON, 'HANS HAACKE AND THE CULTURAL LOGIC OF POSTMODERNISM'

Reprinted from *Hans Haacke: Unfinished Business* (exh. cat.; ed. Brian Wallis), New York and Cambridge, MA: The New Museum and MIT Press, 1986, pp.38-41, 46, 48-50.

> The logic of Haacke's works and their sense of necessity can be accounted for, at least initially, by the confluence in them of two powerful 'traditions' which emerge from the 1960s: the preoccupation with the whole issue of the autonomy of art and culture (something which only becomes intense after that autonomy is objectively problematised), and the inflection of the critique of ideology in the direction of institutions (I will call this institutional critique or institutional analysis).

Jameson's text was published during the heyday of the discourse on postmodernism. For Jameson, postmodernism had to be understood as 'the cultural logic of late capitalism', which calls into question two meanings of the concept of autonomy: the autonomy of aesthetic experience (foregrounded by Rancière) and of art as a semi-autonomous social sphere (analysed by sociologists from Weber to Bourdieu).

> The question of the autonomy of the aesthetic and of culture, the argument that culture exists somehow outside of and above the experience of daily life, provides one of the privileged entry points into any discussion of postmodernism. If we begin with this issue, then, we immediately recognise that it can be staged on at least two levels. In other words, the concept of 'autonomy' can be understood either as characterising aesthetic experience as such, or it can be taken to designate the placement of the sphere of culture within social life and 'society'. In both of these areas, Haacke's work has something instructive, perhaps even exemplary, to tell us; but it is important to keep the two kinds of issues distinct initially, even if later on we want to explore the determinations that bind those two issues together (these determinations will be found to emerge most dramatically in a third area, that of *ideologies* of the aesthetic and of culture).

The relationship between aesthetic experience and institutionalised art had always been complex, but the increasing 'aestheticisation' of postmodern consumer culture and the commodification of art brought this problem into renewed focus:

> [A] prodigious expansion of commodity logic or of commodification in general has begun to colonise the very utopian realm of the aesthetic itself. ... [Culture] and the work of art can no longer be thought of as a zone beyond the teleological and the basely practical. The work of the Frankfurt School clearly marks the great moment of radical doubt and self-consciousness of aesthetic philosophy. Already it had begun to question its own nature and existence in a profoundly historical fashion. The limits of the theories of the Frankfurt School for us today

are drawn by their desperate attempt to rescue a diminished, but even more intense and utopian, place for some last surviving 'authentic' – noncommodified and 'high modernist' – artistic production, an attempt whose historical failure the emergence of postmodernism signals in a more than symptomatic way. [...]

[Both] of these ways of framing the problem of the autonomy of art – as the phenomenological experience of the 'work' or as the socially given space of culture itself – inevitably develop consequences which seem to turn on a third and rather different matter, which is that of aesthetic ideology or value. What is in our time the *value* of the aesthetic – of reception as well as production? Indeed, what is the point (political or otherwise) of culture itself in the first place?

In answering these questions, Jameson situates Haacke's work by noting that there are two forms of 'demystification':

> The demystification of aesthetic ideology begins in the realm of superstructures, which it positions and defamiliarises by designating a putative functional relationship to the base. So, for example, a particular aesthetic gives itself as a philosophically coherent theory in its own right, but becomes more problematical when we interrogate that theory socially and when we become aware of the various functions (class legitimation, status, socially symbolic praxis or whatever) which it fulfils and which then seem to have little enough to do with the overt content of the aesthetic itself. Analysis in terms of base, however, begins with institutions, such as the museum, to which superstructural or ideological effects are attributed. These two analytical movements are symmetrical, but rarely coincide; to achieve a satisfying mediation between the study of aesthetic ideologies and the analysis of the institutions that produce or reproduce them is a complicated activity whose terms are never given in advance and which always seem to involve a dialectical leap of some kind.

One can question Jameson's use of the Marxian categories of base and superstructure and debate whether the institutions of art would not themselves be part of the superstructure, rather than the productive base; perhaps the point is precisely that this questionable dichotomy really breaks down when dealing with an art world that is so fully developed and corporatised as the one Haacke is concerned with. We will return to this question in Part Four. Nonetheless, the distinction between the two forms of critique (institutional and ideological) is an important one. Jameson goes on to argue that Haacke's 'solution' to the confluence of these two genealogies (the problematisation of the autonomy of the aesthetic and the critique of institutions) is to 'transform the "extrinsic" determinants of art into the "intrinsic" content of a new artistic text', and continues:

> Haacke's way of handling this problem is exemplary (although perhaps inimitable) because of the particular mapping and totalising representations which he dramatises in a situation in which not only the concept of totalisation but also its politics had seemed to have been rendered archaic. For Haacke's installations

recreate the process of totalisation by acknowledging the power and existence
of the micro-public or institution (rather than by attempting, in traditional
realistic or 'representational' ways, to elude or short-circuit it). These proper
names, these patrons, are very specifically the trustees of the particular cultural
institution where the work is shown – so that to make of them the theme and
subject of a particular artistic 'text' is to reinvent in a new and heightened, dialectically transformed practice of 'auto-referentiality'. But that they should also
be linked in various systematic ways to corporations active in the perpetuation
of apartheid in South Africa or to multinationals contributing to the overthrow
of Allende in Chile, for example, moves us beyond 'culture' and its autonomy.
Rather it poses an imperative of totalisation of an equally new type, one which
does not draw on a received idea or pre-existent category of the 'ruling class',
yet which makes its reinvention – in a socially and globally far more complex
situation – indispensible.

With work such as Haacke's, art takes a sociological turn. Pierre Bourdieu's sociology
of art became a point of reference for Haacke and Buren, and especially for younger
practitioners such as Fraser. An early reference to Bourdieu can be found in Martha
Rosler's belligerent 1979 essay 'Lookers, Buyers, Dealers, and Makers: Thoughts on
Audience', in which the artist insists that:

> While cultural myth actively claims that art is a human universal – transcending
> its historical moment and the conditions of its making, and above all the class
> of its makers and patrons – and that it is the highest expression of spiritual and
> metaphysical truth, high art is patently exclusionary in its appeal, culturally
> relative in its concerns, and indissolubly wedded to big money and 'upper-class'
> life in general.[21]

In his 1986 essay on Haacke, Jameson references 'Bourdieu's trenchant critique of
ideologies of autonomy':

> Bourdieu unmasks *all* of the theories of cultural value (autonomous or otherwise)
> as so much Sartrean bad faith in the service of class activities and class praxis of
> a non-aesthetic nature (some of Haacke's works – for example, the *Visitors' Polls*
> or the *Residence Profiles*[4] – perform analogous operations, with suggestively
> different results: since in these installations, no pre-existing aesthetic 'pleasure'
> is present to be demystified, the focus shifts from the destruction of categories
> of 'taste' and 'art', as in Bourdieu, to the attempt to grasp and 'map' the social
> system that subtends them). The values of high art (or modernism), then, become
> merely the disguises of behaviour by which aesthetes of a given period seek to
> distinguish themselves from business and from labour.[22]

---

4   Editors' Note: Between 1969 and 1973, Haacke conducted a variety of polls among
gallery and museum visitors, the earliest of which was *Gallery-Goers' Birthplace and
Residency Profile, Part 1.* In a sense, the online poll that accompanied the 2019-20
exhibition 'Hans Haacke: All Connected' at the New Museum in New York can be seen as
a belated realisation of Haacke's proposal for an automated poll in Jack Burnham's 1970
exhibition 'Software – Information Technology: Its Meaning for Art' at the Jewish
Museum in New York, which fell through because of technical difficulties.

Although one might assume that a sociology of art would concern itself above all with the 'institutional base', in fact some of Bourdieu's most relevant and influential work deals primarily with the ideology of the aesthetic, though always as embodied and performed by subjects with specific habitus and occupying a particular position in the cultural field.[23] Bourdieu's book *Distinction: A Social Critique of the Judgment of Taste* (1979) focusses in particular on taste and artistic autonomy as means of distinction and as a way of legitimising elites:

> The denial of lower, course, vulgar, venal, servile – in a word, natural – enjoyment, which constitutes the sacred sphere of culture, implies an affirmation of the superiority of those who can be satisfied with the sublimated, refined, disinterested, gratuitous, distinguished pleasures forever closed to the profane. That is why art and cultural consumption are predisposed, consciously and deliberately or not, to fulfil a social function of legitimating social differences.[24]

Installation view, Hans Haacke,
Documenta Besucherprofil
(*Documenta Visitors' Profile*), 1972

Opposite page: Hans Haacke,
Guggenheim Museum Visitors' Profile,
1971, unrealised questionnaire

Both images courtesy
Hans Haacke/VG Bild-Kunst

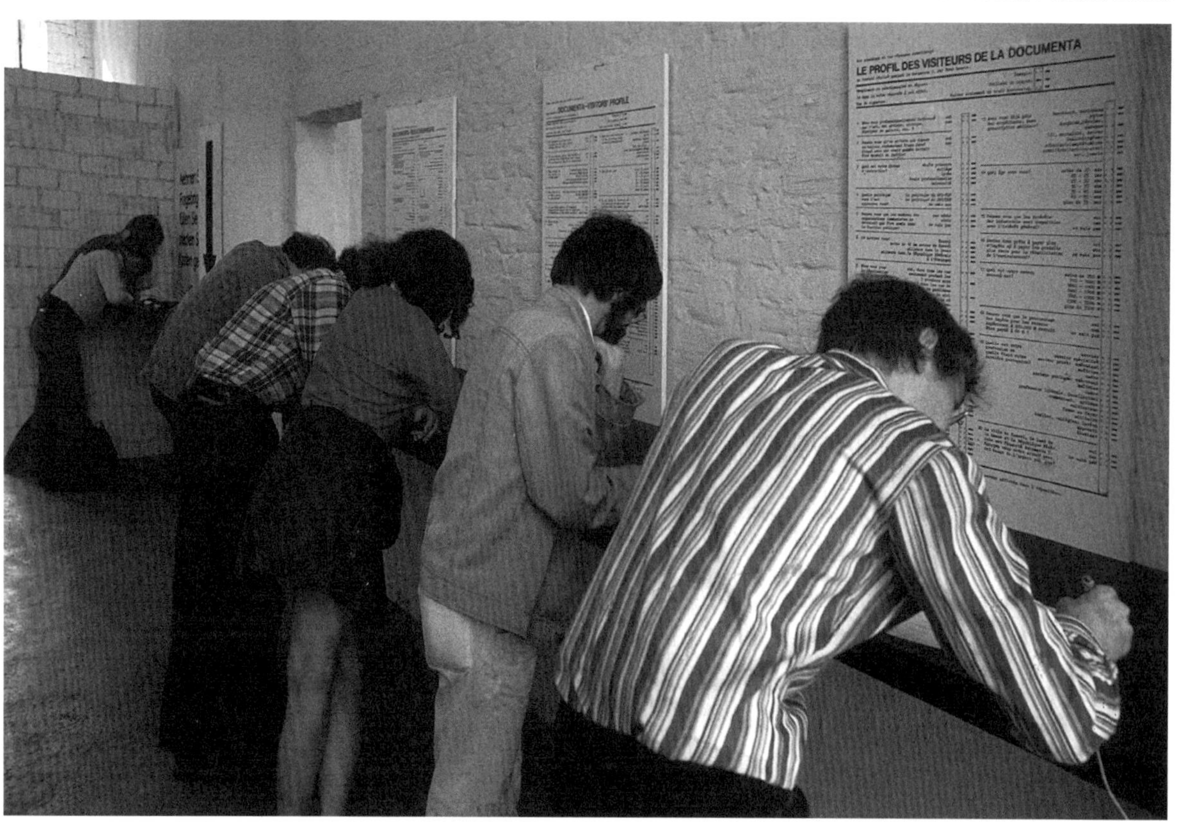

These questions are and your answers will be part of

Hans Haacke's VISITORS' PROFILE

a work in progress during the Haacke exhibition at the

Guggenheim Museum.

____

Please fill out the questionnaire and drop it into the box on

the white round table near the windows on the Museum's ground

floor. Do not sign your name.

1) Do you have a professional interest in art,
   e.g. artist, student, critic, historian, etc?
   _______   _______
    yes   no

2) Is the use of the American flag for the expression
   of political beliefs, e.g. on hard-hats and in
   dissident art exhibitions a legitimate exercise
   of free speech?
   _______   _______
    yes   no

3) How old are you?
   ____
    years

4) Should the use of marijuana be legalized,
   lightly or severely punished?
   _________   _______   ________
   legalized   lightly   severely
                         punished

5) What is your marital status?
   _______   ______   ________   _________
   married   single   divorced   separated

              ____
              widowed

6) Do you sympathize with Womens' Lib?
   _______   _______
    yes   no

7) Are you male, female?
   _______   _______
    male   female

8) Do you have children?
   _______   _______
    yes   no

9) Would you mind busing your child to integrate
   schools?
   _______   _______
    yes   no

10) What is your ethic background?
    ____

11) Assuming you were Indochinese, would you
    sympathize with the present Saigon regime?
    _______   _______
     yes   no

12) In your opinion is the moral fabric of this
    country strengthened or weakened by the US
    involvement in Indochina?
    _____________   ________
    strengthened   weakened

13) What is your religion?
    ____

14) Do you think the interests of profit-
    oriented business usually are compatible
    with the common good of the world?
    _______   _______
     yes   no

15) What is your annual income (before taxes)?
    $__________

16) In your opinion are the economic difficulties
    of the US mainly attributable to the Nixon
    Administration's policies?
    _______   _______
     yes   no

17) Where do you live?
    _______   _______   _______
     city   county   state

18) Do you think the defeat of the SST was a step
    in the right direction?
    _______   _______
     yes   no

19) Are you enrolled in or have you graduated
    from college?
    _______   _______
     yes   no

20) In your opinion should the general orientation
    of the country be more or less conservative?
    _______   _______
     more   less

Your answers will be tabulated later today together with the
answers of all other visitors of the exhibition. Thank you.

Bourdieu's *The Rules of Art* (1992) traces the emergence of a relatively autonomous field of modern art in nineteenth-century France, with a focus on literature rather than visual art. Authors such as Gustave Flaubert pitted themselves against mass-market fiction by using artistic strategies that provided little immediate income but high 'symbolic capital', ensuring the longevity of their works.

> The degree of autonomy of a field of cultural production is revealed to the extent that the principle of external hierarchisation there is subordinated to the principle of internal hierachisation: the greater the autonomy, the more the symbolic relationship of forces is favourable to producers who are the most independent of demand.[25]

There is a familiar myth of modern art with a basis in social reality: the great artist lives in poverty and obscurity while smart artistic hucksters charm the rich, but ultimately the work of the latter will fade and the more 'autonomous' artists will be redeemed. This means that their works can be used by successive generations of early, middle and late adaptors for symbolic distinction and the 'affirmation of superiority'. While Bourdieu did not necessarily reduce art to such social functions, he was, much like artists such as Haacke, suspicious of those ideologies of autonomy that serve to obfuscate art's ongoing instrumentalisation.

Genealogies of institutional critique usually distinguish between a 'first generation' (Haacke, Buren et al.) and a 'second' (Fraser, Renée Green, Christian Philipp Müller). Sometimes a third and even fourth wave are posited, though the fact that important artists such as Rosler and Lawler - who started to make an impact during the mid- to late 1970s - fall between generations should make one cautious of attaching too much importance to such a model. Often, the first generation is presented as having sought or maintained critical distance from the institution, thus externalising it, while the second acknowledged its own involvement in the institution, and focussed more on subjectivity as being itself shaped by institutional structures and processes - analogous to Foucault's work on power as not external to the subject but inscribed in and producing it.

While this is far too schematic and reductive concerning first-generation practices such as Haacke's, it is true that with Fraser and others the focus on subjectivation and on the artist's self-implication increased. In the process, the definition of the crucial concept of the 'institution' became both more precise and more general. Fraser argues against understanding the 'institution' in terms of a limited number of organisations and spaces; instead, we should move towards 'a conception of it as a social field'. Thus it is ultimately the whole field that constitutes the institution, and we all embody and perform it in various ways.

> Every time we speak of the 'institution' as other than 'us', we disavow our role in the creation and perpetuation of its conditions. [...] It's not a question of being against the institution. It's a question of what kind of institution we are, what kind of values we institutionalise, what forms of practice we reward and what kinds of rewards we aspire to. Because the institution of art is internalised, embodied and performed by individuals, these are the questions that institutional critique demands we ask, above all, of ourselves.[26]

For her artistic and theoretical practice, Fraser has taken cues from artists such as Haacke and Lawler; the latter's use of a variety of media, strategies and positions within the art field was the subject of Fraser's first important essay, from 1985.[27] While most well-known for her photographs of artworks in private and public collections, Lawler has also intervened in the frameworks of the art field through the use of various forms of printed matter and understated events – she refuses to be reduced to a 'signature style'.

The theoretical positions Fraser has engaged with include Bourdieu; psychoanalysts such as Sigmund Freud and Jacques Lacan; and Wilfred Bion, whose work considers group relations. In an essay first published in 2012 and since revised, 'Autonomy and Its Contradictions', Fraser revisits and develops some of her earlier work on the subject of autonomy, asking whether certain conceptions of artistic autonomy and critique serve defensive functions (in psychological terms) by disowning and expelling bad parts from 'the boundaries of the ideally autonomous field, practice or self'.

Installation views, Helmut Draxler and Andrea Fraser, *Services: The Conditions and Relations of Service Provision in Contemporary Project Oriented Artistic Practice*, Kunstraum der Leuphana Universität Lüneburg, 1994
Photo: Michael Schindel
Courtesy Kunstraum der Leuphana Universität Lüneburg

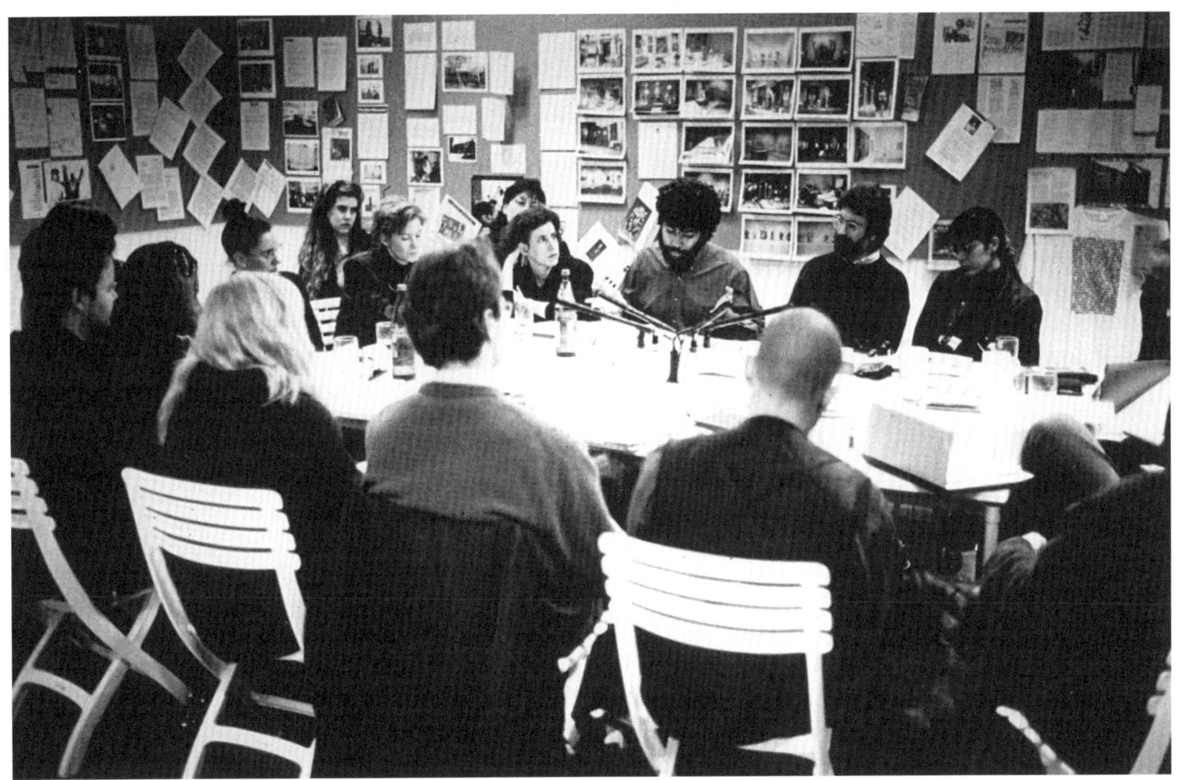

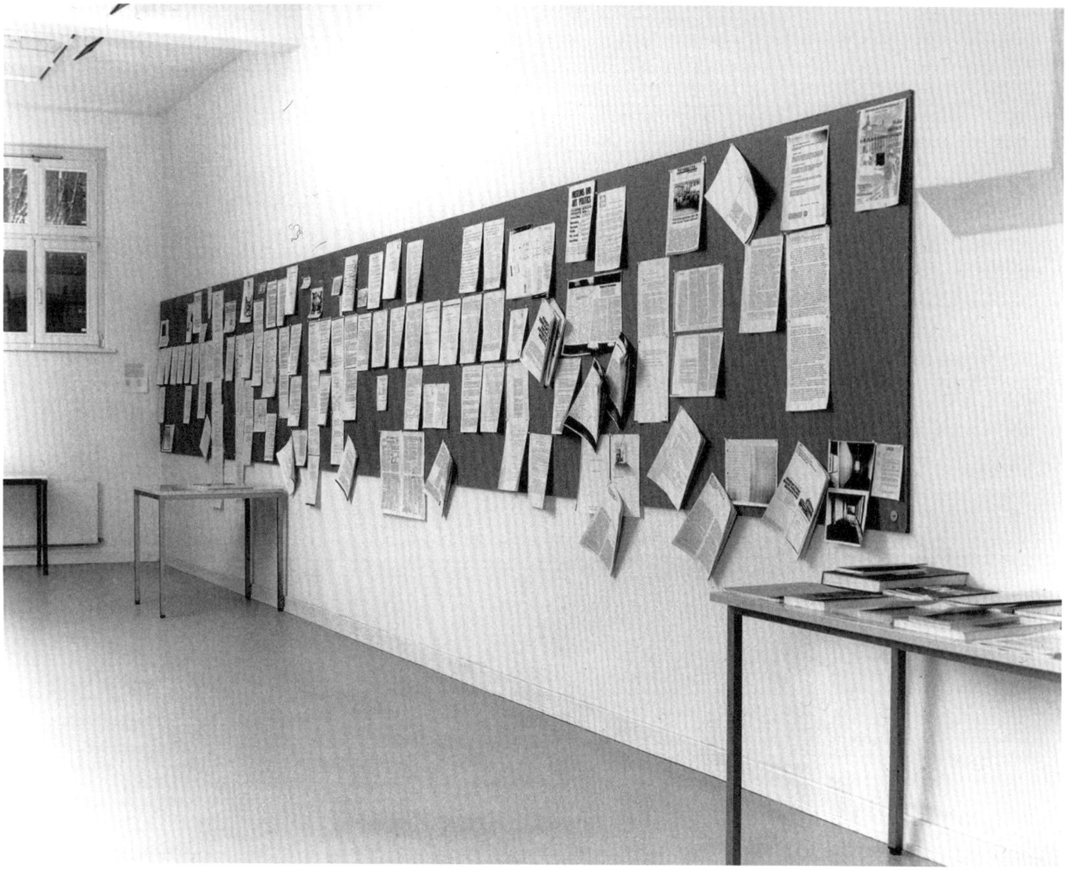

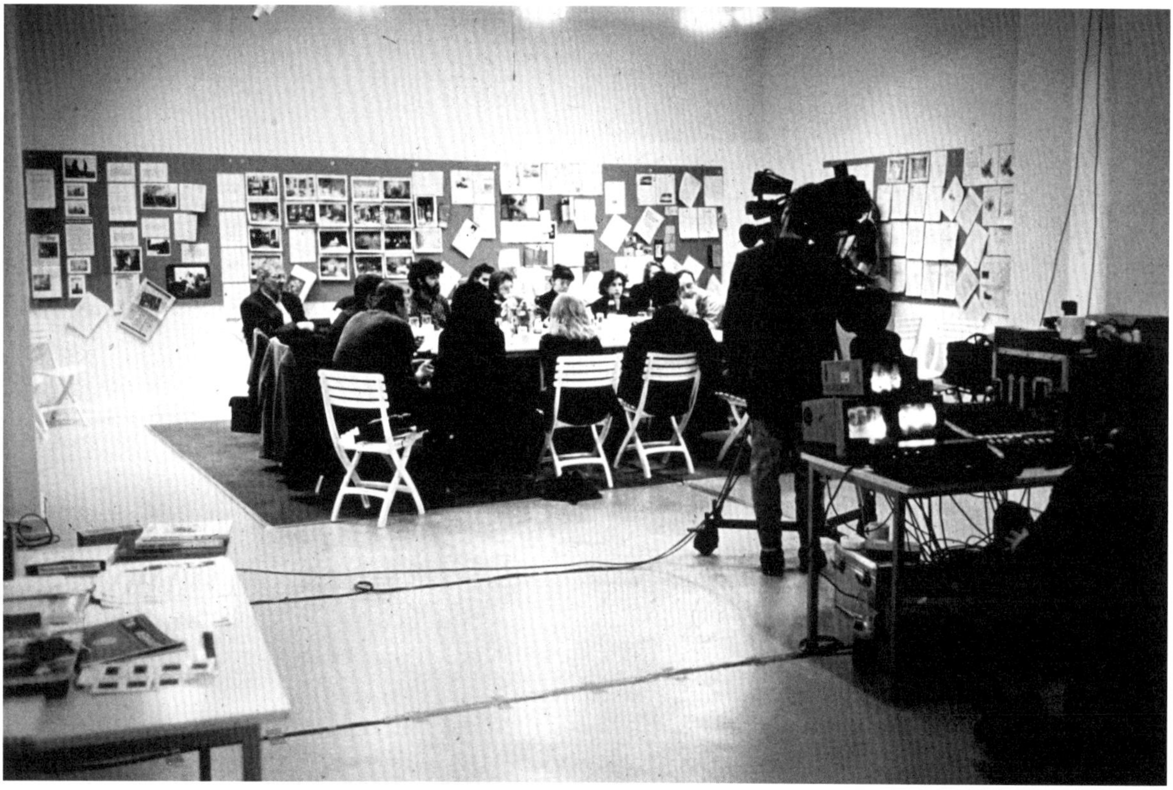

ANDREA FRASER, 'AUTONOMY AND ITS CONTRADICTIONS'

2015 revised version of essay originally
published in *Open!*, no.23, 2012, pp.106-15.

I began my 1996 essay 'What's Intangible, Transitory, Mediating, Participatory, and Rendered in the Public Sphere, Part II' by enumerating four different aspects or 'dimensions' of artistic autonomy. First, I listed the 'aesthetic dimension', including 'the freedom of artworks from rationalisation with respect to specific use or function, whether moral, economic, political, social, material or emotional'. Second, the 'economic dimension', which emerged with 'the relatively anonymous bourgeois market and, with it, the artistic commodity; the consequent separation of sites of production and consumption and, with it, the separation of production from the demands it meets or satisfies in the places and processes of consumption'. Third, the 'social dimension', the autonomy of art as a field which, like the autonomy of other fields, in Pierre Bourdieu's analysis, is a condition of its 'capacity to impose "its own norms on both the production and the consumption of its products" and to exclude norms and criteria dominant in other fields – especially the economic and political fields'. And, finally, the 'political dimension', which I frame in terms of 'the freedom of speech and conscience and the right to dissident opinion'.[5]

My characterisation of the 'aesthetic' and 'political' dimensions of autonomy in that essay are perhaps particularly in need of elaboration, and I would now also add to this list what might be described, broadly, as the psychological dimension of autonomy (which I will return to in the second half of this essay). However, I still believe that any meaningful and productive discussion of artistic autonomy must include a clear articulation of which aspects of autonomy – these or others – are at issue, and how these aspects of autonomy are interrelating. The challenge is not only that discussions of autonomy often blur these different aspects, but that these different dimensions of autonomy often function in contradiction to each other.

Bourdieu: Artistic Autonomy and the Aesthetic Disposition
Bourdieu has been central to the development of my thinking about artistic autonomy and its contradictions. Bourdieu himself, to my knowledge, only used the term 'autonomy' to describe what I would call the social dimension of artistic autonomy. He develops his theory of relatively autonomous social fields in the context of 'The Field of Cultural Production, or: the Economic World Reversed' and other essays from the 1970s and 80s, which he later revised into the book *The Rules of Art*. Interestingly, he rarely uses the term in *Distinction: A Social Critique of the Judgment of Taste*, even while he engages those aspect of art that are often central to discussions of autonomy in art discourse: what I would call the aesthetic dimension of artistic autonomy, such as traditions of disinterestedness, distancing and freedom from rationalisation with respect to specific functions. He engages these aspects of art in terms of the 'aesthetic disposition',

<hr>

5   Andrea Fraser, 'What's Intangible, Transitory, Mediating, Participatory, and Rendered in the Public Sphere, Part II' (1996), in *Museum Highlights: The Writings of Andrea Fraser* (ed. Alexander Alberro), Cambridge, MA: MIT Press, 2005, p.56.

but never 'autonomy'. However, clear links are to be found between these two aspects of his analysis of culture, particularly in the homology between the social conditions of the relative autonomy of the artistic field and the social conditions of the formation of the aesthetic disposition, both of which he links to the negation of economic and, perhaps more broadly, material interests, needs and forms of determination.

For Bourdieu, of course, all social fields are 'relatively autonomous' – otherwise, they would not exist or be recognisable *as fields* (he says somewhere that a completely heteronomous field would be, rather, an 'apparatus'). The relative autonomy of all fields, from this perspective, is contingent upon their capacity to 'impose their own norms and sanctions' within their sphere and to exclude external or competing norms, values, etc. In this sense, to say that fields are 'relatively autonomous' is not just to say that they are never completely autonomous, but also that they are autonomous *only* relative to other fields. What is particular to cultural fields as they developed in the West, in Bourdieu's analysis, is their tendency not only to exclude but also to negate and even invert economic values specifically. With artistic fields this is then linked – although usually only implicitly in Bourdieu's work – to specifically aesthetic traditions of disinterestedness, the conditions of which, in his analysis of the aesthetic disposition, are also characterised by a negation of the economic. In the case of the aesthetic disposition, however, Bourdieu's emphasis shifts from the negation of economic values to the negation of economic and material determination more broadly, particularly in the form of need, and of the uses and functions that serve need. Because the disposition and also the capacity to distance material and especially economic necessity is usually afforded by means of economic resources, the 'aesthetic disposition' is predisposed to manifest economic privilege. The 'aesthetic disposition' is thus 'the paradoxical product of negative economic conditioning' in that it manifests the economic conditions that determine it precisely by negating economic conditioning and determination.[6]

This is where artistic autonomy becomes particularly problematic. It is at this juncture that one finds the homology between, on the one hand, the freedom from economic (and other forms of) rationality, which, in left traditions, has been won by artists through sacrifice and struggle, and, on the other, the freedom from economic rationality that is a byproduct of economic privilege. And it is here that one finds the structural logic of the objective collusion between avant-garde artists and economic elites that is performed in the art market and bourgeois art institutions *despite* the apparent social and even political opposition between these positions.[7] It is extremely important to recognise that this is a matter of collusive homologies and not of the kind of co-optation that many avant-garde traditions have made it out to be. From there we might begin

---

6   Pierre Bourdieu, *Distinction: A Social Critique of the Judgment of Taste* (trans. Richard Nice), Cambridge, MA: Harvard University Press, 1984, p.55.
7   Within the structure of this homology it also often seems that avant-garde negations of instrumentality are felt most acutely not by those in power and against whom they may be manifestly addressed, but by those who do experience themselves as subject to this instrumentality. I encountered this quite directly in my project with the Generali Foundation, a corporate art programme, where the autonomy performed by the artists and curators seemed to be experienced by employees as no more than a particularly arbitrary and violent manifestation of managerial power, stripped of the economic rationality that governed their own working lives and provided that power with legitimacy.

to be able to reflect more honestly and productively on what it is in our field, our practices and even our politics that serves to reproduce these structures.

The Critique of Artistic Autonomy Revisited
Looking back over the past century of avant-garde practice, it is difficult to avoid the conclusion that efforts by artists to reject the privilege, elitism and idealism associated with the aesthetic disposition have often led not to an emancipatory gain but to the development of even more rarefied cultural forms. For example, the rejection of specialised modes of artistic production and reception – commonly associated with the 'de-skilling' of Minimalism but in fact ongoing throughout the twentieth century – most often ended up producing aesthetic forms that are even more obscure and demanding than the craft-based competencies eschewed in 'de-skilling.' A similarly bitter irony can be found in cultural activist and culturally engaged political positions that seem to slide into an aestheticisation of politics, or that reject artistic vanguardism only to replace it with a political – and often also intellectual – vanguardism that is no less demanding of cultural capital and competence, no less lifestyle determined and no more egalitarian, except perhaps in rhetoric.

From this vantage point, many of the developments that have been identified with the critique of artistic autonomy, or at least some of the privileged forms of production and consumption associated with that autonomy, also can be seen to have been motivated more by a frustration with the limits imposed by artistic autonomy than by radical egalitarian impulses. The 'specific principle of legitimacy' of relatively autonomous fields in which producers produce for the recognition and evaluation of other producers – institutionalised in mechanisms such as peer review – tends to generate increasingly specialised forms of production and consumption. While these mechanisms and the highly specialised discourses and practices they produce are more or less accepted in the sciences, in cultural fields they have been decried as elitist, obscure and cut off from the culture of everyday life. However, one can see in pop art traditions, as well as in the more recent vogue of all things participatory, a hunger by artists and art institutions for larger audiences and wider influence – an aim in which radical democratic rhetoric and corporate populism, if not marketing, often seem to merge all too seamlessly.

Another example of this may be found in activist and productivist positions that perform a protest against art's traditional lack of function, material impact and use-value, but have led to an instrumentalisation or bureaucratisation of art – most problematically, not only by artists but by public and other institutional funders. The expansion of these positions in and since the 1990s clearly has coincided with what is sometimes called the instrumental turn in cultural policy in the US as well as Europe, when the end of the cold war, European integration and globalisation led to the collapse of traditional rationales for public subsidy in the West, such as national prestige and regional competition (although these seemed to have gained ground in the East), and as neoliberalism trampled on social democratic public goods.

I ran up against these tendencies quite directly in the 1990s, when I was focussed on working through a model of art making as service provision. By the mid-90s I felt that most forms of artistic autonomy were just too problematic and contradictory to defend, except perhaps for the political dimension of artistic autonomy, which I identified with free speech rights above all and which are not specifically artistic. However, as I learned in the course of studying art censorship battles in 1999–2000, even this form of autonomy may be reduced to a kind of artistic or professional privilege in the context of culture wars, as an 'artistic freedom' specifically if not exclusively that artists and art institutions rarely defend as political principle or civil right. The reduction of free speech to an artistic privilege is one of the most vicious forms of symbolic violence produced by such art controversies – and one in which the art field often seems to collude with conservative forces, despite their apparently opposed positions.[8]

Despite these contradictions, however, I believe that the autonomy of cultural and perhaps especially educational institutions must be defended, above all in their traditions of self-governance and self-regulation, peer review and freedom from market criteria as well as immediate rationalisation in the service of social uses, economic values and political interests. This is particularly pressing in the sciences, where research and practice is increasingly market-directed and 'inconvenient' facts come under immediate political attack. In our contemporary political and economic context, any critique of the professional or expert privilege historically associated with these forms of autonomy runs the risk of colluding with the right-wing populists who have so successfully identified class hierarchy with educational and cultural rather than economic capital and who are intent on destroying anything that gets in the way of their political agenda.

In this context, we must also take care that the constructions and claims of artistic autonomy, as well as those emerging from the theoretical field with which the art world has become so closely identified, do not serve to weaken the autonomy of other cultural fields, and perhaps ultimately, even of the artistic field itself. I am thinking of formulations that reach for a kind of pure autonomy, a kind of pure freedom, and in which avant-garde practices are identified with radical political practices, such as anarchist traditions and Autonomia. I am also thinking of formulations that identify artistic autonomy as an essential property of the aesthetic, rather than as an historically specific social form. Such formulations have appeared, for example, in debates about artistic research and requirements for art practice PhDs, as arguments that artists should not be required to write book-length dissertations or to formulate an explicit research methodology. Such requirements, the arguments often go, constitute an attack on artistic autonomy and the subjection of art to the criteria of academic fields. But such arguments themselves constitute an attack on the autonomy of academic fields, which is also based on the capacity of those fields to impose their own norms and sanctions within their sphere. Surely, if artists were as autonomous as these formulations claim, they would not be pursuing academic doctorates in the first place. In this case it begins to look very much like some of the most apparently radical formulations of artistic autonomy are in fact only the most expedient. Again, we find an objective collusion between 'radical' artistic positions and political and market forces that see academic standards only as impediments to the exploitation of academic fields as instruments of specific political and economic aims.

---

[8]   See Andrea Fraser, 'A "Sensation" Chronicle', *Social Text*, no.67, Summer 2001; reprinted in A. Fraser, *Museum Highlights, op. cit.*, pp.179–211.

Critical Practice, Negation and the Psychological Dimension of Autonomy
For artists invested in critical practice, one of the most challenging aspects of
artistic critique may be its relationship to the conditions and contradictions of
artistic autonomy. Historically and discursively, critical art practice is unthinkable without at least some form of autonomy – even if one of the primary objects
of artistic critique has been artistic autonomy itself. The capacity of art to negate
or invert the values and principles of hierarchisation dominant in other fields
is linked to the autonomy of art as a social field. The freedom of artists to question and challenge is linked not only to politically autonomy and free speech
rights, but also to the practical and economic autonomy of artists as independent
producers who control our own labour and its products. But then again there is
also the link between critical art practice and the aesthetic dimension of artistic autonomy: traditions of disinterestedness, distancing and freedom from
rationalisation with respect to specific functions; the 'aesthetic disposition' that
Bourdieu analyses as 'the paradoxical product of negative economic conditioning', and that manifests the economic conditions that determine it precisely by
negating economic conditioning and determination.[9] This link can be found
most clearly in the distancing that is a basic feature of both the aesthetic disposition (in the form of disinterestedness, etc.) and critical art practices (in the operation of estrangement that may be found in almost all critical art strategies).[10]

This distancing may be the most problematic feature of both critical art
practice and many formulations of artistic autonomy. Developing on Bourdieu's
scattered references to 'negation in a Freudian sense', I have considered this
distancing as functioning through an operation of negation that may be more
defensive than dialectical. Bourdieu himself seems to vacillate on the character
of this negation a great deal. Sometimes he links artistic autonomy to 'a bad faith
denial of the economic', with all its intimations of moral failing and fraud. At
other times he links negation to the social conditions of art as a relatively autonomous field, which he defended vigorously with his anti-neoliberal activism. And,
in language that parallels many formulations of artistic critique and evokes the
operations of psychoanalysis, he links negation to art's capacity to achieve a
'partial anamnesis of deep and repressed structures'.[11]

In many ways, the complexity of negation in Bourdieu's analysis mirrors
its complexity in Freud's. Freud begins his essay 'Negation' (1925) by introducing
negation as a mechanism of defence. However, although he describes negation as
a form of denial, it is a denial that nevertheless also represents a partial lifting
of repression. Here he makes a key distinction between idea and affect: with negation, something may be thought but only negatively, as an idea that is rejected
and dismissed: it may be admitted to consciousness as an idea, but is nevertheless distanced from the self affectively. Freud goes on to identify negation as a
condition of the development of intellectual functions, symbolisation and even
of thought. According to Freud, all intellectual judgment has its origins in these
fundamental alternatives: "'I should like to eat this", or "I should like to spit it

---

9   P. Bourdieu, *Distinction*, *op. cit.*, p.55.

10   Here I would distinguish critical from political art and cultural activism, which
often do not rely on such forms of distancing.

11   Pierre Bourdieu, *The Rules of Art: The Structure and Genesis of the Literary Field*
(trans. Susan Emanuel), Palo Alto, CA: Stanford University Press, 1992, pp.3-4.

out"; and ... "I should like to take this into me and keep that out of me."[12] From this point of view, writes Freud, 'What is bad, what is alien to the ego and what is external are, to being with, identical.'[13] This leads Freud to link negation to the division of inside and outside: whether the idea or affect is owned and accepted or whether it is split off, expelled, projected or otherwise disowned – first of all, by locating it outside of the boundaries of the self. In this way, negation also appears to be one of the primary mechanisms through which this self is constituted, by way of these boundaries, as autonomous – we could even say, as a kind of autonomous field. And it is also from this basic operation that develops the distinction between what Melanie Klein would call the internal psychic reality of phantasy and the external reality of things, as judgment seeks to determine whether an object taken in and fed on in phantasy can be 're-discovered' again in the external world.

Is it possible to distinguish, in practice, between defensive negation and critical negation? Can there be a 'critical' distancing that is not also a defensive disowning? Consideration of the defensive function of negation has led me is to consider substituting the term 'analysis' for 'critique', or at least to advocate for a necessary step following critique. If critique is a moment of defensive negation that nevertheless allows a repressed idea to make its way to consciousness – but only as split off and disowned – then we still need a second step that allows for a recognition and reintegration of that idea and our affective connection to it. Such a second step might be called analysis, and I would hope that such analysis might finally lead us out of the reproduction and expansion of contradictions in which art seems perpetually trapped.[14]

Psychoanalytic understanding may also help us rethink the relationship between artistic critique and autonomy. Autonomy is also a much-debated term in the field of psychoanalysis. Jacques Lacan's rejection of the Cartesian *cogito* and of the autonomous ego postulated in ego psychology, his theorisation of the autonomous I as Imaginary, and the theory of ideology developed by Louis Althusser inspired by these formulations have been central to the development of critical practice since the 1970s as well as to many other Marxist as well as feminist critiques of the autonomous subjects produced by and for capitalist and patriarchal institutions.

In psychoanalytic perspectives rooted in the work of Klein, Wilfred Bion and object-relations theory, 'autonomy' figures most prominently as an unconscious phantasy of agency, often linked to infantile omnipotence. Autonomy in these frameworks is opposed neither to instrumentality and heteronomy nor to Symbolic subjectivation, but rather to dependency. Like negation, this phantasy of agency also serves a defensive function, but one that is initially necessary for psychic survival and development. It protects the infant from the anxiety associated with the frustration, privation, discomfort and potential losses that go along helplessness and dependency, as well as from the dis-integrating trauma

[12]   Sigmund Freud, 'Negation' (1925), in *The Standard Edition of the Complete Psychological Works of Sigmund Freud*, vol.19 *(1923-1925): The Ego and the Id and Other Works* (trans. and ed. James Strachey in collaboration with Anna Freud), London: The Hogarth Press, 2001, p.237.
[13]   *Ibid.*
[14]   I attempted to develop this idea further in 'From Critique to Analysis', presented at 'Phantasm and Politics #8 – The Art of the Phantasm', Hebbel am Ufer, 6-7 June 2014.

threatened by the external world as such – overwhelming, impinging and determining – whether that external world is physically or only narcissistically injurious. In these perspectives, the tenacity and rigidity of that unconscious phantasy of autonomy and agency often appears as a key factor in the development of psychopathology.[15]

D.W. Winnicott, however, posits infantile omnipotence not as phantasy but a developmentally necessary stage in which infants *experience* a magical control over the world. He describes this as an 'area of omnipotence' created not only by infantile belief but also by adult collusion: sustained above all by 'primary maternal preoccupation' and the adaptive care provided by the adult world. In Winnicott's theory of the transitional stage, infants are gradually and necessarily 'failed' by this adaptive environment: gradually exposed to their own dependency on and determination by the external and pre-existing world. This phase is eased by 'transitional objects': objects of emotional investment that are both found and made, both inside and outside, both subjective and objective, and that belong both to internal reality and external reality. Through this transitional stage, the infant passes from magical relating to introjected internal objects to manual relating to objects that are outside the self: 'not-me' objects 'which the individual has decided to recognise (with whatever difficulty and even pain)'. The 'truly external ... is outside magical control. To control what is outside one has to *do* things, not simply to think or to wish.'[16] It is in this transitional stage – not in the external object-relating of *doing* – that Winnicott identifies the location of cultural experience. In this, Winnicott seems to agree with Freud who, in his 'Formulations on the Two Principles of Mental Functioning' (1911), famously suggests that art brings about a reconciliation of fantasy and reality in a particular way: artists turn away from reality to fantasy, but then find a way to return from fantasy back to reality by moulding fantasy into a new kind of reality. Artists do this, according to Freud, without 'creating real alterations in the outer world'. Instead, he suggests, fantasy is realised through the recognition and collusion of others who share the artist's dissatisfaction with reality, which itself is part of reality.

Clearly, Bourdieu read Freud. We know from a few citations that he read Klein. I am convinced that he also read Winnicott. In *Distinction*, Bourdieu describes 'the suspension and removal of economic necessity' and the 'objective and subjective distance' from determination that characterises the aesthetic disposition and links this to 'a child's relation to the world'. In what sounds very much like a reference to infantile omnipotence, he adds parenthetically that 'all children start life as baby bourgeois, in a relation of magical power over others and, through them, over the world'.[17]

From these psychoanalytic perspectives, the question is not whether artistic autonomy is only a figment of artistic narcissism and grandiosity or an objective social structure. From a Freudian or Kleinian perspective, the question might be whether constructions of artistic autonomy, and perhaps also those of

---

[15]   See, for example, D.W. Winnicott, 'The Use of an Object', *International Journal of Psycho-Analysis*, vol.50 no.4, pp.711–16, 1969.
[16]   D.W. Winnicott, 'Playing: A Theoretical Statement', in *Playing and Reality*, London: Tavistock Publications, 1971, p.40.
[17]   P. Bourdieu, *Distinction*, op. cit., p.54.

critique, serve defensive functions through mechanisms of negation, splitting, externalisation, idealisation and omnipotence (among others) that ward off external demands and impingement as well as affectively experienced and invested conflicts, social or psychological, by disowning the bad parts of ourselves and expelling them beyond the boundaries of the ideally autonomous field, practice or self. Such defensive constructions of autonomy would only serve to reproduce those conflicts, like symptoms and perhaps especially as contradictions, and to protect them from potentially transformative engagement. From the perspective suggested by Winnicott, the question might be whether constructions of autonomy and aesthetic repudiations of dependencies and determinisms serve anachronistic needs for magical control that effectively disable us from the power we seek in the external world – except perhaps through the collusion of those with power in that world.

Or, can constructions of artistic autonomy enable a working-through of those conflicts? Might the artistic frame, like the analytic frame (with which it has parallels), enable the re-framing of familiar patterns of existing, relating, thinking, behaving and, especially, judging and thus also for new relationships and new experiences to emerge? Or can constructions of artistic autonomy be seen as a transitional space through which the potential trauma represented by the pre-existing and overdetermining world can be negotiated in a process of development and potential transformation?

From these psychoanalytic perspectives, transformative autonomy and agency can only develop with an acceptance of dependency and determinisms: with the capacity to tolerate the anxiety provoked by dependency and with a loosening of the defensive mechanisms we employ to manage that anxiety, to nurse the tremendous insult to our narcissism constituted by the pre-existing world and to put off the difficult, often painful and only marginally achievable task of making changes to our psychic and social realities. And I would like to imagine that this form of autonomy would also finally allow us to escape those collusive homologies with economic privilege and the not-so-magical power of the adult bourgeoisie.

That meaningful autonomy can only develop from 'an acceptance of dependency and determinisms' should not be construed to mean that any and all determinism is just fine and dandy. Institutional critique only 'accepts' certain constraints and determinisms in the sense of accepting a challenge; that is, it engages with them. Of course, over the past forty years or so the 'field' of contemporary art changed and expanded rather drastically, creating new forms of heteronomous determination. Fraser herself has noted elsewhere that the contradictions of the art world are intensifying, and that 'the diversity and complexity brought about by art-world expansion itself makes it perilous to generalise about [various new forms of critique and contestation in art]. While I believe that we can still speak of "the art world" as a singular field, this expansion has led to the growth and coalescence of increasingly distinct artistic subfields, each defined by particular economies as well as configurations of practices, institutions and values.'[28] The 'frame', as Fraser puts is, has been 'transformed in the process'.[29] The field of art indeed appears to have become an archipelago, and some of the subfields may be closer to, for instance, certain forms of theory or activism.

As much as Bourdieuan classicists would like to maintain as still valid the rather linear mechanism of art's valuation that he analysed, this increasingly appears as a doubtful theoretical venture.

On the surface, everything would appear the be the same as it ever was. On the one hand, there are sensationally successful artists, popular with the yacht set, who don't have much symbolic capital among the editors of this reader and their ilk. On the other hand, there are those artists who don't reap the fruits of the art market of the recent gilded age, and who might therefore be expected to be today's 'autonomous' artists *à la* Manet or van Gogh. They have symbolic capital but not much of a market; this market will no doubt emerge in the future, proving that the Bourdieu model still works. However, there is no guarantee that the linear succession posited by this model (autonomous avant-garde artists whose success will grow over time until they are canonical) will keep occurring. What if the current fragmentation of the art world into subfields with rather different sets of criteria persists? Perhaps today's critical alternatives will remain just that, eking out a marginal existence in various counter-canons without ever becoming hegemonic.

If there is an ever-greater interest in transversal practices that refuse to abide by strict divisions between relatively autonomous fields, this can be seen as one of the major consequences of the fragmentation process that is currently underway. Why not forge connections with forms of practice outside of what used to be 'the art world'? One notable theorist of such an approach is Gerald Raunig, who, in a critical response to Fraser's 2005 essay 'From the Critique of Institutions to an Institution of Critique', argues:

> In her account, all possible forms of institutional critique are ultimately limited to a critique of the 'institution of art'[18] and its sub-institutions. Invoking Bourdieu, she writes:

>> [J]ust as art cannot exist outside the field of art, we cannot exist outside the field of art, at least not as artists, critics, curators, etc. And what we do outside the field, to the extent that it remains outside, can have no effect within it. So if there is no outside for us, it is not because the institution is perfectly closed, or exists as an apparatus in a 'totally administered society', or has grown all-encompassing in size and scope. It is because the institution is inside of us, and we can't get outside of ourselves.[19]

Although there seems to be an echo of Foucault's concept of self-government here, there is no indication of forms of escaping, shifting, transforming. Whereas for Foucault the critical attitude appears simultaneously as 'partner' and as 'adversary' of the arts of governing, the second part of this specific ambivalence vanishes in Andrea Fraser's depiction, yielding to a discursive self-limitation that barely permits reflection on one's own enclosure. Against all the evidence that art – and not only critical art – over the whole twentieth century produced effects that went beyond the restricted field of art, she plays a worn-out record: art is and

---

[18]   Peter Bürger, *Theory of the Avant-Garde* (trans. Michael Shaw), Minneapolis: University of Minnesota Press, 1984, p.12.

[19]   Andrea Fraser, 'From the Critique of Institutions to an Institution of Critique' (2005), in John C. Welchman (ed.), *Institutional Critique and After*, Zurich: JRP Ringer, 2006, pp.130-31.

remains autonomous, its function limited to its own field. 'With each attempt to evade the limits of institutional determination, to embrace an outside, we expand our frame and bring more of the world into it. But we never escape it.'[20]

Yet exactly this kind of construction is refused in Foucault's concept of critique, the critical attitude: instead of inducing the closure of the field with theoretical arguments and promoting this practically, thus carrying out the art of governing, a different form of art should be pushed at the same time which leads to *escaping the arts of governing*. And Foucault is not the only one to introduce these new non-escapist terms of escape. Figures of flight, of dropping out, of betrayal, of desertion, of exodus, these are the figures that several authors advance as poststructuralist, non-dialectical forms of resistance in refusal of cynical or conservative invocations of inescapability and hopelessness.[30]

Raunig quotes Fraser to the effect that 'we are trapped in our field', but he obscures the context of this striking phrase in her essay: 'However, the fact that we are trapped in our field does not mean that we have no effect on, and are not affected by, what takes place beyond its boundaries. Once again, Haacke may have been the first to understand and represent the full extent of the interplay between what is inside and outside the field of art.'[31] This contradicts Raunig's assertion that Fraser presents the institution as 'perfectly closed', and art as having no possible effects outside its field. More generally, Raunig has a point: there are indeed plenty of moments when institutional critique becomes all too wilfully self-limiting, when a form of sociological reductionism kicks in and the institutional dimension of the 'field' of art is fetishised, and when the 'revealing' of the antinomies and aporias of this field – and one's position(s) within it – becomes the all too narrow horizon of critical practice.

Against such a reductionist fallacy, it is important to bring the other dimensions of autonomy listed by Fraser back into play, including the 'aesthetic dimension'. The latter should not be equated with limited, modernist conceptions of 'the autonomy of art'. Recalling the discussion in Part One of this reader, we could argue that the aesthetic is the dialectic of the quasi-autonomous appearance of art and its problematisation. In this sense, a Haacke piece examining the various entanglements of a Manet painting is not an 'anti-aesthetic' comment on this artwork. It is, on the contrary, a further aesthetic potentialisation of Manet's work. Insofar as it can be termed aesthetic, art can never be content with the 'actually existing' institutional field. This is as true today as in the 1970s – but the sprawl and balkanisation of the art world has eroded, or at least severely complicated, the distinction between art and non-art, and between art-immanent practice and transgression.

In Marina Vishmidt's words, institutional critique has 'soldered artists and institutions together in an increasingly half-hearted *tableau vivant* of autonomy'.[32] Fraser has summarised her own take on the 'tragedy' of institutional critique as follows: 'I don't believe that art can exist outside of the field of art, but I also don't believe that art can exist inside the field of art.'[33] However, as inside and outside become ever less clearly defined, and as the relative autonomy of the field is undermined by its ever more direct integration in the financial sector, new pockets of autonomy pop up here and there. Perhaps what is needed is what Vishmidt has termed an *infrastructural critique* that goes beyond the 'loyal criticism' of institutions by seeking to use and develop organisational infrastructures:

---

20   *Ibid.*, p.131.

'Infrastructure', like 'institution', is used here in a moderately flexible way but chiefly to signal a view of the art institution as a site of resources – material and symbolic – and that calls for an opportunist deployment for the sake of furthering all sorts of projects rather than the loyal criticism attendant on 'institutional critique' in its established version. In this light, the construction of institutions may be, at the same time, a practice of institutional and infrastructural critique, depending on whether the institution is mainly intended to critically reassess or renew working conditions and visibility in the space of art or has other ambitions.[34]

Protest view, Decolonize This Place,
'9 Weeks of Art and Action',
Whitney Museum of American Art,
New York, 2019
Photo: William Powhida

See p.284 of this reader for more images of
'9 Weeks of Art and Action'

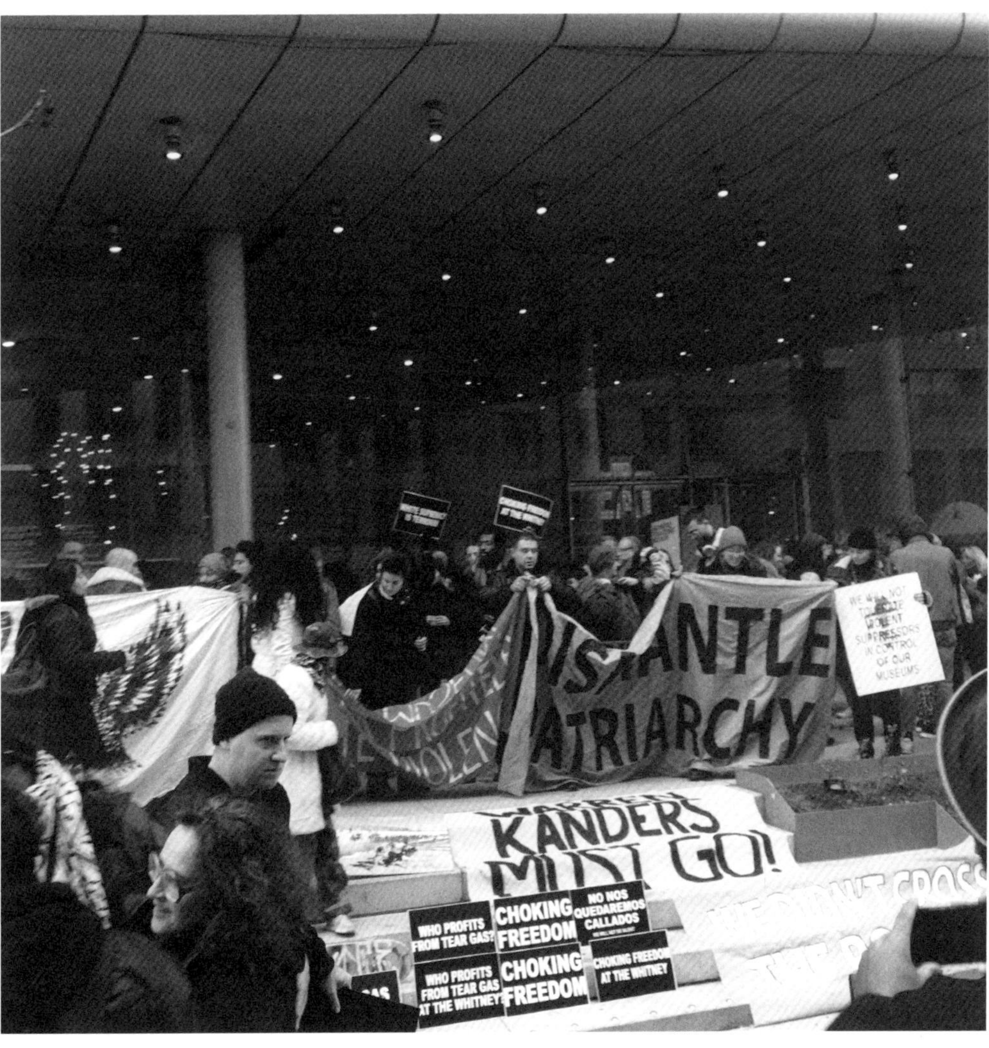

Notes

1   Hans Magnus Enzensberger, 'Constituents of a Theory of the Media', *New Left Review*, vol.1, no.64, November-December 1970, p.25.

2   Julius Meier-Graefe, *Entwicklungsgeschichte der modernen Kunst*, expanded 2nd ed., vol.3, Munich: Piper, 1915, p.641. Translated from the German by Helen Ferguson.

3   *Ibid.*

4   Kazimir Malevich, 'Perelom', *Anarkhiia*, no.77, 5 June 1918, p.4; cited in Margarita Tupitsyn, *Malevich and Film*, New Haven, CT: Yale University Press, 2002, p.17.

5   See Rosalind E. Krauss, 'Grids', in *The Originality of the Avant-Garde and Other Modernist Myths*, Cambridge, MA: MIT Press, 1986, pp.8-22.

6   See Brian O'Doherty, *Inside the White Cube: The Ideology of the Gallery Space* (1986), expanded edition, Berkeley: University of California Press, 1999.

7   Dieter Lesage and Ina Wudtke, *Black Sound White Cube. Die Ideologie des Ausstellungsraums*, Vienna: Löcker, 2011, pp.11-13.

8   See 'Reproduction' in Part Four of this reader, pp.243-55.

9   An early use of the term 'institutional critique' can be found in Mel Ramsden's essay 'On Practice' (*The Fox*, vol.1, no.1, 1975, p.69), but this was a somewhat isolated case. In the mid-1980s the term started to be used by Andrea Fraser and Fredric Jameson, and it would come to play an important role in Benjamin H.D. Buchloh's writing.

10   Hans Haacke, 'All the "Art" that's Fit to Show' (1974), in Alexander Alberro and Blake Stimson (ed.), *Conceptual Art: A Critical Anthology*, Cambridge, MA: MIT Press, 1999, p.304.

11   See Gregory Bateson, 'A Theory of Play and Fantasy' (1955), in *Steps to an Ecology of Mind*, Chicago: University of Chicago Press, 1972, pp.177-93; Erving Goffmann, *Frame Analysis: An Essay on the Organization of Experience*, Cambridge, MA: Harvard University Press, 1974.

12   Bruce Kurtz, 'Conversation with Robert Smithson on April 22nd 1972', in *The Writings of Robert Smithson* (ed. Nancy Holt), New York: New York University Press, p.200; cited in Craig Owens, 'From Work to Frame, or, Is There Life After "The Death of the Author"?', in *Beyond Recognition: Representation, Power, and Culture*, Berkeley: University of California Press, 1992, p.122. Emphasis in original.

13   C. Owens, 'From Work to Frame', *op. cit.*, pp.122-23.

14   *Ibid.*, p.126.

15   *Ibid*, p.129.

16   Daniel Buren, 'Critical Limits' (trans. by Laurent Sauerwein, revised by Olivia Fairweather and Jack Cox), *Five Texts*, New York and London: John Weber Gallery and Jack Wendler Gallery, 1973, p.52.

17   See Hans Haacke, 'Manet-PROJEKT '74', in *Hans Haacke: Framing and Being Framed, 7 Works 1970-75* (ed. Kasper Koenig), Halifax and New York: The Press of the Nova Scotia College of Art and Design and New York University Press, 1975, pp.70-94.

18   Andrea Fraser, 'From the Critique of Institutions to an Institution of Critique' (2005), in John C. Welchman (ed.), *Institutional Critique and After*, Zurich: JRP Ringer, 2006, p.129.

19   Hans Haacke, 'Museums, Managers of Consciousness', in *Hans Haacke: Unfinished Business* (exh. cat.; ed. Brian Wallis), New York and Cambridge, MA: The New Museum and MIT Press, 1986, pp.66-67. Haacke's essay was delivered as a talk at the annual meeting of the Art Museum Association of Australia in Canberra, 30 August 1983, and published with minor alterations in *Art in America*, vol.72, no.2, February 1984.

20   See Andrea Fraser, 'In and Out of Place' (1985), in *Museum Highlights: The Writings of Andrea Fraser* (ed. Alexander Alberro), Cambridge, MA: MIT Press, 2005, pp.17-27.

21   Martha Rosler, 'Lookers, Buyers, Dealers, and Makers: Thoughts on Audience' (1979), in *Decoys and Disruptions: Selected Writings, 1975-2001*, Cambridge, MA: MIT Press, 2004, p.12.

22   Fredric Jameson, 'Hans Haacke and the Cultural Logic of Postmodernism', in *Hans Haacke: Unfinished Business*, *op. cit.*, p.45.

23   Bourdieu once defined habitus (one of his key concepts) as 'the durably installed generative principle of regulated improvisations [that] produces practices which tend to reproduce the regularities immanent in the objective conditions of the production of their generative principle, while adjusting to the demands inscribed as objective potentialities in the situation, as defined by the cognitive and motivating structures making up the habitus.' Pierre Bourdieu, *Outline of a Theory of Practice* (trans. Richard Nice), Cambridge: Cambridge University Press, 1977, p.78.

24   Pierre Bourdieu, *Distinction: A Social Critique of the Judgement of Taste* (1979; trans. Richard Nice), London: Routledge & Kegan Paul, 1986, p.7.

25   Pierre Bourdieu, *The Rules of Art: Genesis and Structure of the Literary Field* (1992; trans. Susan Emanuel), Palo Alto, CA: Stanford University Press, 1996, p.217.

26   A. Fraser, 'From the Critique of Institutions to an Institution of Critique', *op. cit.*, p.133.

27   See A. Fraser, 'In and Out of Place', *op. cit.*

28   Andrea Fraser, 'There's No Place Like Home', in *Whitney Biennial 2012* (exh. cat.), New York: Whitney

Museum of American Art, 2012, p.29.

29   A. Fraser, 'From the Critique of Institutions to an Institution of Critique', *op. cit.*, p.131.

30   Gerald Raunig, 'Instituent Practices: Fleeing, Instituting, Transforming', in G. Raunig and Gene Ray (ed.), *Art and Contemporary Critical Practice: Reinventing Institutional Critique*, London: MayFly, 2009, p.6.

31   A. Fraser, 'From the Critique of Institutions to an Institution of Critique', *op. cit.*, p.132.

32   Marina Vishmidt, 'Beneath the Atelier, the Desert: Critique, Institutional and Infrastructural', in Tom Holert and Maria Hlavajova (ed.), *Marion von Osten: Once We Were Artists*, Utrecht and Amsterdam: BAK, basis voor actuele kunst and Valiz, 2017, p.119.

33   Andrea Fraser, 'Why Does Fred Sandback's Work Make Me Cry?' (2004), in *Andrea Fraser: Texts, Scripts, Transcripts*, Cologne: Museum Ludwig and Walther König, 2013, p.89.

34   M. Vishmidt, 'Beneath the Atelier, the Desert', *op. cit.*, p.222.

PART FOUR:
SOCIAL AUTONOMY AND THE LABOUR OF ART

To a significant extent, institutional critique was a response to the rampant commodification of contemporary art in the 1960s and 1970s. While the art world of that period was almost quaint by more recent standards, the rise of corporate sponsors and private collectors resulted in an unprecedented influx of cash. If art is a mere plaything for capitalists, revolving around a specific type of exclusive and unique fetish – as distinct from more regular commodities – then what exactly is art's relation to other commodities? And how does artistic and cultural labour work compare to other forms of labour?

Critical artists responded to cult of the art object by pioneering a different kind of artistic and cultural practice: project-based work dependent on fees rather than sales (though for many practitioners of institutional critique, the two were not mutually exclusive). In the 1993-94 working group and exhibition project *Services: The Conditions and Relations of Service Provision in Contemporary Project Oriented Artistic Practice*, Andrea Fraser and Helmut Draxler investigated the model of the service industry and its relevance for project-based art practice as an alternative to the production of commodity objects. However, art as service – or, to use a different vocabulary, as immaterial labour – is hardly free from commodification as such. Artistic work and 'art workers' themselves are still subject to commodification, and to precarisation and exploitation.

If contemporary capitalism puts a premium on cognitive and creative work without necessarily giving this work the form of wage labour, this suggests that we need to reconsider the commodification of art not in light of Marxian orthodoxy but of twenty-first-century capitalism's ongoing structural transformations. To this end, this section focusses on texts from the last two decades that take up or engage with two important strands of theoretical practice: first, Marxian 'Critical Theory' (as exemplified by Adorno); and second, that of Italian Operaismo and Autonomia. Whereas the former reflects on 'autonomous' art as a critical if compromised practice under the conditions of the capitalist culture industry, the latter posits forms of collective autonomous practice in and against capitalism – manifesting themselves in ways that are not containable by the frames of institutionalised and commodified art.

Critical Theory and the Autonomy of Art

In recent decades, the role of commodification in art has been re-examined by British Marxists such as Peter Osborne and Stewart Martin, for whom Adorno remains the crucial theorist in this context. Adorno noted that the appearance of the artwork's autonomy is possible only because of 'the concealment of the labour that went into it'.[1] This remark was aimed at Richard Wagner as a precursor of the modern culture industry. Like Wagner's staged phantasmagorias, Hollywood films try very hard to obfuscate the various forms of specialist labour that go into them – so as to not hinder our enjoyment of what we know to be an illusion.

But modernist art, which Adorno defended against the culture industry, is hardly exempt from the logic of the commodity fetish – and Adorno never claimed it was. On the contrary, modernist art was profoundly informed by the commodity; its autonomy was wrested from an engagement with heteronomy. In his 2007 essay 'The Absolute Artwork Meets the Absolute Commodity', titled after an Adorno quotation, Martin seeks to excavate the productive core of his account of the commodified modern artwork.

STEWART MARTIN, 'THE ABSOLUTE ARTWORK MEETS THE ABSOLUTE COMMODITY'

Reprinted from *Radical Philosophy*, no.146,
November-December 2007, pp.18, 17.

The implicit argument here is that, within a society in which commodification is dominant, everything that is external to this commodification becomes marginal, liable to be socially irrelevant or merely yet-to-be-commodified. This predicament recommends an alternative, immanent critique: the generation of art's autonomy from *out of* commodification; the refusal of commodification by a subversive mimesis of it: 'Only by immersing its autonomy in society's *imagerie* can art surmount the heteronomous market. Art is modern art through mimesis of the hardened and alienated.'[1]

Therefore, we need to grasp the extremely contradictory sense of this claim that 'the absolute artwork converges with the absolute commodity'.[2] The idea of the absolute artwork turns out to be far from what its post-Kantian proponents, from Schelling to Novalis, might have anticipated. Rather than an alternative to the world of commodification, it is revealed to be a product of it. 'Pure art', 'l'art pour l'art', is revealed to be an ideology, a fetish; not just in the general sense that it conceals the social determinations of art, but in the specific sense that it conceals them by virtue of the same logic as that of the fetishised commodity. But in doing so, the artwork insists on itself as something that is autonomous and that

---

[1] Theodor W. Adorno, Aesthetic Theory (1970; trans. Robert Hullot-Kentor, ed. Gretel Adorno and Rolf Tiedemann), London: Althone Press, 1997, p.21.
[2] *Ibid.*

therefore cannot be reduced to its commodification. Art establishes its autonomy against commodification, despite being constituted by it. The commodification of the world leaves art increasingly embattled and unable to affirm any content except itself, while, in so reducing itself, it also follows the logic of commodification all the more. Pure art's ignorance of its entwinement with commodification is ideological insofar as it denies or misconceives it. But the objection to capitalism's reduction of everything to exchange-value criticises the lie, implicit in the commodity, that exchange-value is the only possible value.

We can already see how this conception of autonomous art is distinguished from the typical positions of contemporary cultural and art theory. For Adorno, autonomous art is both a commodity and not, both destroyed by *and* a product of capitalism, both its critique *and* its ideology. The artwork is presented as a contradiction produced by capitalism. Commodification is a condition of possibility of autonomous art as well as a condition of its impossibility.

In this text, Martin argues that Adorno plays one form of illusion (that of the commodity object as fetish, as sensuous presence) against another (the illusion of the autonomy of the value-form). What makes the modernist artwork valid and valuable is precisely that it is an 'emphatically fetishised commodity, which is to say that it is a sensuous fixation of abstraction'.[2] Martin uses this dialectical conception against theories that effectively posit that art was once autonomous, but that commodification came and spoiled it. From an Adornian vantage point, it is clear that

autonomous art is *not* outmoded by its commodification, but is rather a contradictory product of it: namely, that autonomous art is both produced by *and* destroyed by capitalist culture, both its ideology *and* its critique. This may appear like an intensified dilemma. But if art's autonomy is a produced, and reproduced, contradiction of developed capitalist culture, then it remains a vital form through which this culture can be resisted and criticised. And in times and places where commodification has become a pervasive form of social life, such an immanent critique is essential. Nonetheless, the aim of grasping this antinomy of art and commodification here is not to dissolve it, philosophically, but to comprehend why and how it is coterminous with capitalist culture, and thereby to orient critical practice to this end.

But what is the value of a critical practice that remains forever bound to what it critiques? Such is the fate of immanent critique unless it opens up a collective horizon and generates practices that push the systemic contradictions articulated to a breaking point. Osborne raises this issue in his 2012 essay 'Theorem 4. Autonomy: Can It Be True of Art and Politics at the Same Time?', which historicises Adorno's aesthetic to a greater extent than Martin's essay, both in order to make a case for Adorno's specificity and incisiveness, and to point out his limitations.

PETER OSBORNE, 'THEOREM 4. AUTONOMY: CAN IT BE TRUE OF ART AND POLITICS AT THE SAME TIME?'

Reprinted from *The Postconceptual Condition:
Critical Essays*, London: Verso, 2018, pp.65, 66-67,
and 70-72.

The autonomy of art is not – as it is often thought to be – a freedom of art from social determination. Historically (so the familiar story goes, and Bourdieu tells it quite well in *The Rules of Art*), the autonomous work required the production of a special social space in which it can be received as autonomous from the standpoint of its art-character. This first requires, of course, famously, the development of a market in art (the commodification of the artwork), and second, the transformation of art-institutional spaces into spaces of exhibition for autonomous art. The social history is familiar. From the standpoint of the concept of autonomous art, however, the by-now-well-established dialectical point is that autonomous art requires (ideally) the social determination of a space *free from social determinations of meaning based on non-artistic functions.* Separation. Artistic autonomy is thus – in part – a social form, an institutional form, as Peter Bürger famously argued, taking his cue from Adorno.

In his essay, Osborne further historicises Adorno's analysis of the art commodity by relating it back to Kant and Schiller, as well as forward to more recent theorists.

Adorno subjects the social concept of autonomous art to the history of capitalism. The is the distinctiveness and rigour of his critical art history. The history of modern art thus becomes for him, in large part, the history of art's relationship to/struggle with the commodity form – a dimension as absent from Rancière's account of the aesthetic *regime* of art as it is from much Autonomia and post-Autonomia writing on art activism.

But what are the 'autonomous determinations' enabled by this social form? At this point, we need to refer back to Schiller's taking up of Kant's philosophy of practical reason into his attempt to supplement Kant's aesthetic with an 'objective' concept of beauty.

The first half of 'Theorem 4' of Kant's *Critique of Practical Reason* reads as follows:

> *Autonomy* of the will is the sole principle of all moral laws and of duties in keeping with them; *heteronomy* of choice, on the other hand, ... is instead opposed to the principle of obligation and to the morality of the will [i.e. to all universality, PO] ... the sole principle of morality consists in independence from all matter of the law (namely from a desired object) and at the same time in the determination of choice through the mere form of giving universal law that a maxim must be capable of. That independence, however, is freedom in the *negative* sense, whereas this *lawgiving of its own* on the part of pure and, as such, practical reason

is freedom in the *positive* sense. Thus, the moral law expresses nothing other than the *autonomy* of pure practical reason, that is, freedom.[3]

This is not the autonomy of 'the subject' – note – but the autonomy of 'pure practical reason' itself, or the autonomy of pure reason in its practical deployment, as Kant describes it, transcendentally. The subject's relation to the causality of this freedom, whose act it *is*, is problematic.

If Kant's philosophy attempted to define and safeguard 'man's freedom as a rational being', as Herbert Marcuse put it, then Osborne points out that the autonomy of the Kantian subject does in fact not belong to that subject, but to practical reason, to the free will. Can this said to be *the subject's* free will if Kant has completely abstracted and split up the subject, so that no connection with lived reality remains? After an excursus on Schiller's *Kallias Letters* (1793) – where Schiller, in a more Kantian vein than in his slightly later *Aesthetic Education*, defines beauty not as an actual synthesis of freedom and necessity in the form of the play drive, but as a mere appearance of freedom – Osborne returns to Adorno and post-Adornian aesthetic politics. Here he acknowledges the limitations of Adorno's conception of art while simultaneously emphasising its strengths:

This is a great strength of Adorno's position: despite his personal artistic preferences, his position refuses the red herring of having simply to choose between monolithically conceived blocs of 'autonomous art' and anti-institutional 'avant-garde activism'. First, because the relationship is structurally dialectical; and second, because *the institution changes* in response to this dialectic. Contra Bürger, the issue is thus not anti-art-institutionalism as such, but *socially alternative modes* of the institutionalisation of art (which was the problematic of the productive phase of the Soviet experience in the first place).

This leads to the limits of this conception of autonomous art – namely, its basis in the analogical application of Kant's concept of autonomy: autonomy of the will in its 'positive' guise as *self-determining universal form*.

The Limits of Adorno and Art Activism Alike
The conceptual and political limits of Adorno's conception of autonomous art derive from the individualistic assumptions behind Kant's application of the concept of pure rational will. Adorno's notion of autonomy continues to pertain to *individual subjects*; autonomous art thus provides no more than an immanent criticism of liberal capitalist societies, through which it figures the possibility of a free *individual* praxis.

Now, Adorno's is not a 'straight' Kantianism, to be sure, but a certain kind of Marxian one. He is a Marxian Kantian. He thinks that the development of capitalism has destroyed/demobilised collective subject formation, leaving a retreat to individual freedom the sole remaining progressive option. But this does not get around the conceptual issue that for him *the artwork images the*

---

[3]   Immanuel Kant, *Critique of Practical Reason* (1788; trans. and ed. Mary J. Gregor), Cambridge: Cambridge University Press, 1996, p.166.

political freedom of the ideal liberal individual: this is its 'enigmatic', subject-like, singular object status. Despite the historical argument, the political limitation remains the result of a conceptual limitation. The question is: *is this a limitation of Adorno's thought*, or *an inherent limitation on the critical functioning of autonomous art in capitalist societies?*

As Osborne suggests, the practice of modern(ist) art and theory does not amount to any collective project. Art imagines freedom for a critical yet complicit individual. It is in this way that the artwork as aesthetic fetish transmutes its social heteronomy into aesthetic autonomy. The artwork ultimately exists not to reveal the truth about the commodity, but to wrest a semblance of freedom from heteronomy.

On the Schillerian argument that both Adorno and Rancière appear to accept, autonomy appears most adequately, albeit only analogically, in the artwork, because it *cannot appear in the world*, directly, in practice itself – since freedom in the form of *pure* practical reason is *alienated from life*. Those who believe the contrary, however – that freedom does appear directly politically in a movement (Autonomia and post-Autonomia political movements, for example) – believe that it can do so only through *withdrawal* ('exodus') from the existing capitalistic form of the social. And they conceive of this relationship, politically, primarily negatively (although they rarely acknowledge this fact): freedom as negative freedom – *autonomy from* ... economic determinations, capital, the state, the party, etc. – as the social condition of positive freedom, despite the latter's usually *ontological* construal. Yet, in an ironic mimesis of the autonomous work of art, such *autonomy from* – or separation from – prevailing forms of social practice makes the exercise of any such positive freedom *impotent*; impotence famously being the price of autonomous art's criticality. Political autonomy, in the Autonomia tradition, is thus not so much the negation of the autonomy of the artwork as its ironic political mimesis. It is thus *critically* redeemable primarily only as art – an art more strictly *autonomous* than the *political* art, the *heteronomy* of which it aims to radicalise. Such is the dialectics of activism and art in the politics of Autonomia.

To put it more formally: Theorem 4 – Kant's concept of autonomy – cannot be true of art (analogically) and politics (directly) at the same time. It is in the historical contradiction between art and politics that the truth of autonomy lies.

Osborne's criticism of autonomist positions can here be read as a counterpoint to Gerald Raunig's autonomist critique of Fraser's own institutional immanence.[3] Do the politics of Italian Autonomia as a movement ultimately amount not so much to 'the negation of the autonomy of the artwork as its ironic political mimesis', as Osborne suggests? And is the end result a kind of aestheticised activism? Autonomia, which grew out of the Italian Operaismo (Workerism) movement during the 1970s, has had a significant impact on recent social movements including Occupy Wall Street, via theorists such as Antonio Negri and Raunig himself. If autonomist organising has an element of 'exodus' from broken institutional structures, as Osborne formulates it, its strategies cannot be reduced to withdrawal. Precisely by responding to – and perhaps even generating – breakdowns, Autonomia foregrounded contemporary labour as an aesthetic and political problem.

As noted, Adorno argued that an artwork's autonomy is predicated on 'the concealment of the labour that went into it'.[4] This is precisely where Italian Operaismo parted ways with Adorno. Raniero Panzieri, a transitional figure whose journal *Quaderni Rossi* functioned as the crucial incubator of Operiasmo in the early 1960s, criticised Adorno for remaining fixated on the level of consumption, on the commodity fetish rather than on the labour that produced it.[5] Operaists insisted on the primacy of labour and of workers' resistance in the historical development of capitalism and aimed at forging a movement of true workers' autonomy, distinct from and against co-opted trade unions.[6]

The curator and critic Marco Scotini has described the growth of the Autonomia movement in Italy from the Potere Operaio movement of the late 1960s:

> For Autonomia, it is clear that the trade unions are an inner institute of capitalist dynamics and, therefore, an instrument for negotiating the selling price of the workforce. Here the new, avant-garde forms of organising labour begin to emerge not only outside the trade union movement, but mainly as an alternative to it, developing a radical and destructive criticism of trade unionism. At the same time, the concept of 'class composition' has radically shifted the focus of the working class to one of social self-composition in which the different cultural, political and imaginary elements produced by social work merge. As Toni Negri asserts: 'With the end of the Potere Operaio (Workers' Power) movement, the origin of the councils and the crisis of organised political groups, the first autonomous assemblies emerged in the factories.'[4]
>
> The major incentive for their birth came not only from a complex series of political issues that emerged within the framework of the struggles, but more specifically from the Fiat factory conflict of 1972–1973, which gave rise to the complex political grouping of workers known as the Mirafiori Party. The activity of the autonomous labour assemblies spread rapidly from Turin, as the movement made contact with emerging political student groups and autonomous collectives that were being established in many of the proletarian areas of towns and cities, giving life to a large and informal network of social struggles in schools and factories that, due to the groupings involved and their composition, can be identified as the birth of the Autonomous Zone.[5]

It took five more years before the fateful 1977, when the movement reached its culmination, having effectively disseminated its notions of autonomous behaviour en masse. If, in the 1960s, 'labour autonomy' (*autonomia operaia*) was an expression initially related to forms of contractualism and trade unionism, by 1973, the expression began to mean something different, something larger. The struggle for self-organisation transcended trade union control and a prescribed political logic. The events of 1973 in the Mirafiori district of Turin spawned new, more radical meanings of the expression *autonomia operaia*. It came to mean that workers and the supportive proletarian community could establish their own social terms of exchange, production and cohabitation,

---

[4]   Antonio Negri, cited in Marco Scotini, 'Autonomy', in Atlas of Transformation (ed. Zbyněk Baladran and Vít Havránek), Zurich: JRP Ringier, 2010, p.70.

[5]   See Nanni Balestrini, L'orda d'oro, Milan: Feltrinelli, 2003; and Sylvere Lotringer and Christian Marazzi, Autonomia: Post-Political Politics, New York: Semiotext(e), 2007.

independent of the state justice – autonomous of the laws that govern shifts, working hours and private ownership. The autonomy principle now acquired its full etymological meaning: proletarian society defines its own laws even in a region that was under the state's military occupation.[7]

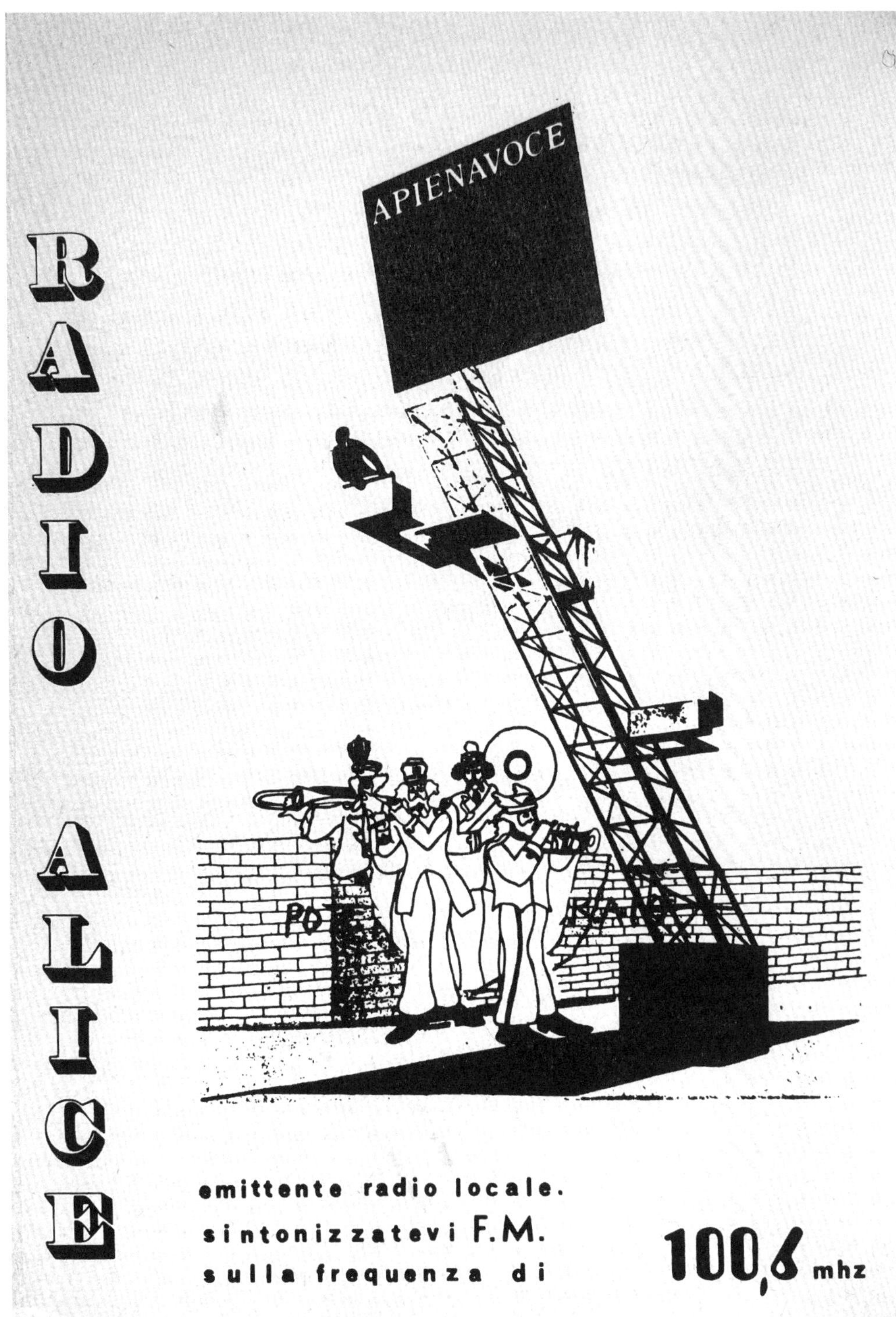

Autonomy of the Political?

In insisting on the primacy of labour and of workers' resistance in the historical development, Operaism sought to counter the appearance of an 'autonomy of capital'. Marx had polemically and ironically noted that 'in the circulation M-C-M [money-commodity-money] both the money and the commodity function only as different modes of existence of value itself', which 'is constantly changing from one form into the other, without becoming lost in this movement; it thus becomes transformed into an automatic subject'.[8] The notion of the 'automatic subject' of value, as constituted by the circulation of capital, has been taken up in Germany in particular by authors intent on forging a Marxian critique of value.[9] However, for Operaists it was crucial to assert that from a historical point of view there could be no real automatism here; any specific iteration of the M-C-M cycle has to be seen in the context of capital's responses to forms of refusal, of workers' autonomy.

Much of the heritage of Operaism was later transmitted outside of Italy by Antonio Negri and by autonomist thinkers affiliated with him. Alongside Mario Tronti, Negri had been one of the key Operaist theorists and organisers; however, their positions are far from identical. In his 2008 book *The Project of Autonomy*, Pier Vittorio Aureli argues that the Negrian understanding of autonomy differs crucially from Tronti's conception of workers' action as constituting an 'autonomy of the political'. Aurelli argues that for the Operaism of the 1960s, 'the possibility of autonomy was not a generic claim of autonomy *from*, but rather a more audacious and radical claim of autonomy *for*. This autonomy for consisted of a bid by the workers to construct a source of power alternative to the one established and maintained by capitalism.'[10] The central role of the organised working-class vanguard, Aureli posits, is jettisoned in the Negrian focus on post-workerist, spontaneous, anarchic-multitudinous forms of action.

Previous page:
Flyer for Radio Alice,
Bologna, 1976-77

PIER VITTORIO AURELI, *THE PROJECT OF AUTONOMY: POLITICS AND ARCHITECTURE WITHIN AND AGAINST CAPITALISM*

Reprinted from *The Project of Autonomy: Politics and Architecture within and against Capitalism*, New York: Temple Hoyne Buell Center and Princeton Architectural Press, 2008, pp.9-11.

What I wish to argue here is that the most legitimate theoretical consequence of Operaism was Tronti's notion of the autonomy of the political: the discovery of an autonomous dimension of political power within the tradition of the working class.[6] Operaism conceived this project as a conscious 'heresy' that made sense within the tradition of the working-class movement. For the Autonomia groups during the 1970s and 1980s, it became a way to translate the rising crisis of the workers as a relevant political subject through an imaginary escalation of workers' power. In this situation, in which, as Tronti said, 'the red sky of the working class's sunset was misunderstood as the red sky of the dawn',[7] the main target of Autonomia and the site of its struggle became not so much the fight against capitalism as a subtle attack on the institutions of the Left as the emblematic elements of social and cultural retardation within the highly advanced trajectory of capitalism.

This is why the theoretical contribution of Autonomia, which was less original in its conception (since it was inherited from Operaism), turned out to be so creative. This creativity served to elevate the subjects of the political struggle culturally, but it often devolved into mystification. As part of this process of cultural elevation, social semantics and the invention of new terms played an important role. In the Autonomist lexicon, the industrial mass worker of the 1960s became the 'social worker' of the 1970s; finally, in the 1990s and 2000s, he turned into the 'multitude'. Under such transformations, capitalism appeared bit by bit to abandon its paternalistic intentions to be a state plan on the model of the post-World War II welfare state and to take on the trappings of a more sophisticated form of command, the high-tech and extra-state Empire. Yet while the Autonomists succeeded – following Operaism's *modus operandi* of the working class – in establishing a convincing and fascinating narrative to explain why capitalism had changed and evolved into its present form, it was more difficult for them to explain the reasons the subject struggling against the Empire of capitalism had moved, and continued to move, forward. If, according to Negri and Hardt, the multitude's impetus for emancipation was a product of the very biopowers that constituted the deep infrastructure of Empire, what kind of *telos* constituted the autonomy of this subject from the logic of power that subjugated it?

The answer that the Autonomists, and more recently Negri and Hardt, proposed to this question often coincided with the imperative of production seen through (or concealed by) suggestive concepts, at times romantic, at times futuristic, such as their insistent science of desire. This was the trigger for individual *cupiditas* unrestricted by any (political) limitations and the manipulation of human life seen as a victory over traditional distinctions between human and

---

[6]   See Mario Tronti, *L'Autonomia del politico*, Milan: Feltrinelli, 1977.

[7]   Interview with Mario Tronti, in Guido Borio, Francesca Pozzi and Gigi Roggero (ed.), *Gli operaisti*, Rome: Derive a Approdi, 2005, p.281.

animal, human and machine. But is it not this *modus vivendi* of the human subject that capitalism currently fully invests, transforming human labour into its most efficient productive force? Does not the reproduction of capital occur in our minds as a psychological process of 'objectification' of desire, individualism and subjectivity itself? In this sense, the argument of the Autonomists still depended on the logic of capitalism, which in its deepest essence is the stimulus for the unlimited desire of production supported by the mastery of technological development as a way to create and re-create the conditions of its own reproduction. Autonomy was thus *de facto* transformed by the Autonomists into its opposite: heteronomy. The workers in turn – the collective subject exploited by capitalism though its transformation into paid labour and thereby expropriated not simply of its own product but of its prerogatives over production (that is, the decision whether to produce) – became the fancy 'multitude'.

It is within this context of political opportunism that the legacy of Autonomia in the 1970s has recently been celebrated, while the project of autonomy prior to the 1970s has been overlooked. The multitude became a subject that was seen as existing in a state of pseudo-anarchic hypercreativity rather than as a making political decisions to limit, frame and form the need for production (and thereby the conditions of consumption). Thus, if the project of autonomy in its original meaning of a grand and radical reconstruction of the political subject – one that not only resisted capitalism but demanded power over it – could not avoid the collapse of Communism, in the 1970s and 1980s it became a postpolitical practice. Autonomy became a way neither to master nor to resist capitalism but instead to transform it by means of a very sophisticated hermeneutics of its cultural effects, and within the highly progressive perspective of the development of forces that were supposed to be its antagonist.

In his autobiography, Tronti himself has credited 'Toni Negri's influence' with a transition from early Operaist publications that 'took themselves to be critically inside the workers' movement' to later initiatives that were 'grounded more in self-organisation' and 'placed themselves dangerously against the movement.'[11] While the political efficacy of later 'Negrist' autonomism can certainly be scrutinised, it is questionable if Tronti's traditional concept of 'the movement' and of 'the (Communist) Party' had much to offer by the late 1960s. As the Dutch sociologist Merijn Oudenampsen summarises the debate:

> The foundations of the idea of the autonomy of the political are to be found in the very core of the Operaist tradition, the idea that workers' struggle drives history and not capitalist development, hence the primacy of political action. Tronti's conception of politics departed in significant ways from what he termed 'vulgar Marxism': taking from Max Weber and Carl Schmitt the idea of political struggle as a clash of values and identities, rather than the Marxist idea of class struggle based on social contradictions. When this position was taken to its logical extreme, the autonomy of the political became the pretext for Tronti's return to the bosom of the Italian Communist Party.

Negri has been a persistent critic of Tronti's line, which he rightly equated with 'the ideology of Historic Compromise'. Therefore it is no surprise that we read in *Empire* that 'any notion of the autonomy of the political' has disappeared, and that 'the notion of politics as an independent sphere' has 'very little room to exist' in our present situation where 'consensus is determined more significantly by economic factors'.[8] Negri instead, opts for the other extreme, where the political is completely subsumed in the economic. Hence the absence of an outside, the collapse of the distinction between public and private, hence Empire as a ghostlike, ubiquitous and centreless phenomenon, the struggle as immanent to the capitalist mode of production and the university as a factory that produces commodities.[12]

In such an 'immanentist' approach, the construction of moments and zones of autonomy only became all the more pressing, but it could not depend on any pre-existing autonomy of the political, as guaranteed by the proletariat as the sole revolutionary subject. For some of its theorists, this project was closely connected to Gilles Deleuze and Félix Guattari's rejection of party politics and embrace of minoritarian movements. In 1985, Guattari and Negri co-authored a book – first translated into English under the title *Communists Like Us* and later republished as *New Lines of Alliance, New Spaces of Liberty* – that maps various movements of the 1970s as results of a 'collective self-making', asserting that 'Revolutionary struggles have never "targeted" to this extent the theoretical definition and the practical realisation of an orientation resting intrinsically on collective subjectivation and implying, in consequence, the destruction of all ideologies of an external vanguard. Autonomy has never appeared with more force as a primary objective.'[13]

This, to be sure, is no longer the autonomy 'of art', but Autonomia has had a significant impact on artistic as well as activist practice. This impact reached a peak around and just after the turn of the millennium. With its focus on subjectivity, on the refusal of work and the flexibilisation of labour, the following essay on 'the meaning of autonomy today' by the Italian autonomist Franco 'Bifo' Berardi – who was close to Guattari – gives a good sense of the latter-day appeal and use-value of 1970s autonomist theory and practice.

---

[8]   Antonio Negri and Michael Hardt, *Empire*, Cambridge, MA and London: Harvard University Press, p.307.

FRANCO 'BIFO' BERARDI, 'WHAT IS THE MEANING OF AUTONOMY TODAY?'

Reprinted from Franco 'Bifo' Berardi, *Precarious Rhapsody: Semiocapitalism and the Pathologies of the Post-Alpha Generation*, London, New York, NY and Port Watson: Minor Compositions, 2009, pp.74–83. Translated from the Italian by Arianna Bove, Erik Empson, Michael Goddard, Giuseppina Mecchia, Antonella Schintu and Steve Wright.

I do not intend to give a historical account of the movement called Autonomia, but I want to understand its peculiarity through an overview of some concepts like refusal of work, and class composition. Journalists often use the word 'Operaismo' to define a political and philosophical movement which surfaced in Italy during the 1960s. I dislike this term absolutely, because it reduces the complexity of social reality to the mere datum of the centrality of the industrial workers in the social dynamics of late modernity.

The origin of this philosophical and political movement can be identified in the works of Mario Tronti, Romano Alquati, Raniero Panzieri and Toni Negri, and its central focus can be seen in the emancipation from the Hegelian concept of subject.

In place of the historical subject inherited from the Hegelian legacy, we should speak of the process of becoming subject. Subjectivation takes the conceptual place of subject. This conceptual move is very close to the contemporary modification of the philosophical landscape that was promoted by French post-structuralism. Subjectivation in the place of subject. That means that we should not focus on identity, but on the process of becoming. This also means that the concept of social class is not to be seen as an ontological concept, but rather as a vectorial concept.

In the framework of autonomous thought the concept of social class is redefined as an investment of social desire, and that means culture, sexuality, refusal of work. In the 1960s and 1970s the thinkers who wrote in magazines like *Classe Operaia* and *Potere Operaio* did not speak of social investments of desire: they spoke in a much more Leninist way. But their philosophical gesture produced an important change in the philosophical landscape, from the centrality of the worker identity to the decentralisation of the process of subjectivation.

Félix Guattari has always emphasised the idea that we should not talk of subject, but of 'processus de subjectivation'. From this perspective we can understand what the expression refusal of work means.

Refusal of work does not mean so much the obvious fact that workers do not like to be exploited, but something more. It means that capitalist restructuring, technological change and the general transformation of social institutions are produced by the daily action of withdrawal from exploitation, of the rejection of the obligation to produce surplus value and to increase the value of capital by reducing the value of life. I do not like the term 'Operaismo', because of the implicit reduction to a narrow social reference (the workers, *operai* in Italian), and I would prefer to use the word 'compositionism' The concept of social composition, or 'class composition' (widely used by the group of thinkers we are talking about), has much more to do with chemistry than with the history of society.

I like this idea that the place where social phenomena occur is not the solid, rocky historical territory of Hegelian descent, but a chemical environment where culture, sexuality, disease and desire fight and meet and mix and continuously change the landscape. If we use the concept of composition, we can better understand what happened in Italy in the 1970s, and we can better understand what autonomy means: not the constitution of a subject, not the strong identification of human beings with a social destiny, but the continuous change of social relationships, sexual identification and de-identification, and the refusal of work. Refusal of work is actually generated by the complexity of social investments of desire.

In this view autonomy means that social life does not depend only on the disciplinary regulation imposed by economic power, but also depends on the internal displacement, shifts, settlings and dissolutions that are the process of the self-composition of living society; struggle, withdrawal, alienation, sabotage and lines of flight from the capitalist system of domination.

Autonomy is the independence of social time from the temporality of capitalism.

This is the meaning of the expression *refusal of work*. It means quite simply: I don't want to go to work because I prefer to sleep. But this laziness is the source of intelligence, of technology, of progress. Autonomy is the self-regulation of the social body in its independence and in its interaction with the disciplinary norm.

There is another side of autonomy, which has been scarcely recognised so far. The process of the becoming autonomous of workers away from their disciplinary role has provoked a social earthquake which triggered capitalist deregulation. The deregulation that entered the world scene in the Thatcher-Reagan era can be seen as the capitalist response to the autonomisation from the disciplinary order of labour. Workers demanded freedom from capitalist regulation, then capital did the same thing, but in a reverse way. Freedom from state regulation has become economic despotism over the social fabric. Workers demanded freedom from the lifetime prison of the industrial factory. Deregulation responded with the flexibilisation and the fractalisation of labour.

The autonomy movement of the 1970s triggered a dangerous process, a process which evolved from the social refusal of capitalist disciplinary rule to capitalist revenge, which took the form of deregulation, freedom of the enterprise from the state, destruction of social protections, downsizing and externalisation of production, cutback of social spending, de-taxation and, finally, flexibilisation.

The movement of autonomisation did, in fact, trigger the destabilisation of the social framework resulting from a century of pressure on the part of the unions and of state regulation. Was it a terrible mistake that we made? Should we repent the actions of sabotage and dissent, of autonomy, of refusal of work which seem to have provoked capitalist deregulation? Absolutely not.

The movement of autonomy actually forestalled the capitalist move, but the process of deregulation was inscribed in the coming capitalist post-industrial development and was naturally implied in the technological restructuring and in the globalisation of production.

There is a close relationship between refusal of work, informatisation of the factories, downsizing, outsourcing of jobs and the flexibilisation of labour. But this relationship is much more complex than a cause-and-effect chain. The process of deregulation was inscribed in the development of new technologies allowing capitalist corporations to unleash a process of globalisation. A similar process happened in the media field, during the same period.

Think about the free radio stations in the 1970s. In Italy at that time there was a state-owned monopoly, and free broadcasting was forbidden. In 1975-76 a group of media activists began to create small free radio stations like Radio Alice in Bologna. The traditional left (the PCI and so on) denounced those media activists, warning about the danger of weakening the public media system, and opening the door to privately owned media. Should we think today that those people of the traditional statist left were right? I don't think so, I think they were wrong at that time, because the end of the state-owned monopoly was inevitable, and freedom of expression is better than centralised media. The traditional statist left was a conservative force, doomed to defeat as they desperately tried to preserve an old framework which could no longer last in the new technological and cultural situation of the post-industrial transition.

We could say much the same about the end of the Soviet Empire and of so-called 'real socialism'.

Everybody knows that Russian people were probably living better twenty years ago than today, and the ostensible democratisation of Russian society has so far mostly been the destruction of social protections, and the unleashing of a social nightmare of aggressive competition, violence and economic corruption. But the dissolution of the socialist regime was inevitable, because that order was blocking the dynamic of the social investment of desire, and because the totalitarian regime was obstructing cultural innovation. The dissolution of the communist regimes was inscribed in the social composition of collective intelligence, in the imagination created by the new global media and in the collective investment of desire. This is why the democratic intelligentsia and dissident cultural forces took part in the struggle against the socialist regime, although they knew that capitalism was not paradise. Now deregulation is savaging the former Soviet society, and people are experiencing exploitation and misery and humiliation at a point never reached before, but this transition was inevitable and in a sense it has to be seen as a progressive change. Deregulation does not mean only the emancipation of private enterprise from state regulation and a reduction of public spending and social protection. It also means an increasing flexibility of labour.

The reality of labour flexibility is the other side of this kind of emancipation from capitalist regulation. We should not underestimate the connection between refusal of work and the flexibilisation which ensued.

I remember that one of the strong ideas of the movement of autonomous proletarians during the 1970s was the idea 'precariousness is good'. Job precariousness is a form of autonomy from steady regular work, lasting an entire life. In the 1970s many people used to work for a few months, then to go away for a journey, then back to work for a while. This was possible in times of almost full employment and in times of egalitarian culture. This situation allowed people to work in their own interest and not in the interest of capitalists, but quite obviously this could not last forever, and the neoliberal offensive of the 1980s was aimed to reverse this balance of forces.

Deregulation and the flexibilisation of labour have been the effect and the reversal of the worker's autonomy and it is not only for historical reasons that we should try to grasp this. If we want to understand what has to be done today, in the age of fully flexibilised labour, we have to understand how the capitalist takeover of social desire could happen.

Cognitive labour and recombinant capital
During the last decades, the informatisation of machinery has played a crucial role in making labour flexible, fostering the immateriality of production.

The introduction of the new electronic technologies into the production cycle opened the way for the creation of a global network of info-production, deterritorialised, delocalised, depersonalised. The subject of work can be increasingly identified with the global network of info-production.

The industrial workers had been refusing their role in the factory and gaining freedom from capitalist domination. However, this situation drove the capitalists to invest in labour-saving technologies and also to change the technical composition of the work process, in order to expel the well-organised industrial workers and to create a new organisation of labour which could be more flexible.

The increasing intellectual and immaterial nature of labour is one side of the social change in production forms. Planetary globalisation is the other face. Immateriality and globalisation are subsidiary and complementary. Globalisation does indeed have a material side, because industrial labour does not disappear in the post-industrial age, but migrates towards the geographic zones where it is possible to pay low wages and regulations are poorly implemented.

In the last issue of the magazine *Classe Operaia*, in 1967, Mario Tronti wrote: the most important phenomenon of the next decades will be the development of the working class on a global planetary scale. This intuition was not based on an analysis of the capitalist process of production, but rather on an understanding of the transformation in the social composition of labour. Globalisation and informatisation could be foretold as an effect of the refusal of work in the Western capitalist countries.

During the last two decades of the twentieth century we have witnessed a sort of alliance between recombinant capital and cognitive work. What I call recombinant are those sections of capitalism which are not closely connected to a particular industrial application, but can be easily transferred from one place to another, from one industrial application to another, from one sector of economic activity to another and so on. The financial capital that takes the central role in politics and in the culture of the 1990s may be called recombinant. The alliance of cognitive labour and financial capital has produced important cultural effects, namely the ideological identification of labour and enterprise. The workers have been induced to see themselves as self-entrepreneurs, and this was not completely false in the dotcom period, when the cognitive worker could create his own enterprise, just investing his intellectual force (an idea, a project, a formula) as an asset. This was the period that Geert Lovink has defined as 'dotcommania' in his remarkable book *Dark Fiber* (2002).[9]

What was dotcommania? Due to mass participation in the cycle of financial investment in the 1990s, a vast process of self-organisation of cognitive

---

[9]   Editors' Note: Geert Lovink, *Dark Fiber: Tracking Critical Internet Culture*, Cambridge, MA and London: MIT Press, 2002.

producers got underway. Cognitive workers invested their expertise, their knowledge and their creativity, and found in the stock market the means to create enterprises. For several years, the entrepreneurial form became the point where financial capital and highly productive cognitive labour met. The libertarian and liberal ideology that dominated the (American) cyberculture of the 1990s idealised the market by presenting it as a pure environment. In this environment, as natural as the struggle for the survival of the fittest that makes evolution possible, labour would find the necessary means to valorise itself and become enterprise. Once left to its own dynamic, the reticular economic system was destined to optimise economic gains for everyone, owners and workers, also because the distinction between owners and workers would become increasingly imperceptible when one enters the virtual productive cycle. This model, theorised by authors such as Kevin Kelly and transformed by *Wired* magazine into a sort of digital liberal, scornful and triumphalist *Weltanschauung*, went bankrupt in the first couple of years of the new millennium, together with the new economy and a large part of the army of self-employed cognitive entrepreneurs who had inhabited the dotcom world. It went bankrupt because the model of a perfectly free market is a practical and theoretical lie. What neoliberalism supported in the long run was not the free market, but monopoly. While the market was idealised as a free space where knowledges, expertise and creativity meet, reality showed that the big groups of command operate in a way that is far from being libertarian, but instead introduces technological automatisms, imposing itself with the power of the media or money, and finally shamelessly robbing the mass of shareholders and cognitive labour.

In the second half of the 1990s a real class struggle occurred within the productive circuit of high technologies. The becoming of the web has been characterised by this struggle. The outcome of the struggle, at present, is unclear. Surely the ideology of a free and natural market turned out to be a blunder. The idea that the market works as a pure environment of equal confrontation for ideas, projects, the productive quality and the utility of services has been wiped out by the sour truth of a war that monopolies have waged against the multitude of self-employed cognitive workers and against the slightly pathetic mass of micro-traders.

The struggle for survival was not won by the best and most successful, but by the one who drew his gun – the gun of violence, robbery, systematic theft, of the violation of all legal and ethical norms. The Bush-Gates alliance sanctioned the liquidation of the market, and at that point the phase of the internal struggle of the virtual class ended. One part of the virtual class entered the techno-military complex; another part (the large majority) was expelled from the enterprise and pushed to the margins of explicit proletarianisation. On the cultural plane, the conditions for the formation of a social consciousness of the cognitariat are emerging, and this could be the most important phenomenon of the years to come, the only key to offer solutions to the disaster.

Dotcoms were the training laboratory for a productive model and for a market. In the end the market was conquered and suffocated by the corporations, and the army of self-employed entrepreneurs and venture micro-capitalists was robbed and dissolved. Thus a new phase began: the groups that became predominant in the cycle of the net economy forge an alliance with the dominant group of the old economy (the Bush clan, representative of the oil and military industry), and this phase signals a blocking of the project of globalisation. Neoliberalism produced its own negation, and those who were its most enthusiastic supporters become its marginalised victims.

With the dotcom crash, cognitive labour has separated itself from capital. Digital artisans, who felt like entrepreneurs of their own labour during the 1990s, are slowly realising that they have been deceived, expropriated, and this will create the conditions for a new consciousness of cognitive workers. The latter will realise that despite having all the productive power, they have been expropriated of its fruits by a minority of ignorant speculators who are only good at handling the legal and financial aspects of the productive process. The unproductive section of the virtual class, the lawyers and the accountants, appropriate the cognitive surplus value of physicists and engineers, of chemists, writers and media operators. But they can detach themselves from the juridical and financial castle of semiocapitalism, and build a direct relation with society, with the users. Maybe then the process of the autonomous self-organisation of cognitive labour will begin. This process is already underway, as the experiences of media activism and the creation of networks of solidarity from migrant labour show.

We needed to go through the dotcom purgatory, through the illusion of a fusion between labour and capitalist enterprise, and then through the hell of recession and endless war, in order to see the problem emerge in clear terms. On the one hand lies the useless and obsessive system of financial accumulation and privatisation of public knowledge, the heritage of the old industrial economy. On the other hand, productive labour is being increasingly inscribed in the cognitive functions of society: cognitive labour is starting to see itself as a cognitariat, building institutions of knowledge, of creation, of care, of invention and of education that are autonomous from capital.

Fractal time and social pathology

In the net economy flexibility has evolved into a form of the fractalisation of labour. Fractalisation means the fragmentation of time-activity. The worker does not exist anymore as a person. He is just the interchangeable producer of micro-fragments of recombinant semiosis which enters into the continuous flux of the network. Capital is no longer paying for the availability of the worker to be exploited for a long period of time; no longer paying a salary covering the entire range of economic needs of a working person. The worker (a mere machine possessing a brain that can be used for a fragment of time) is paid for his punctual performance. The working time is made fractal and cellular. Cells of time are on sale on the net, and the corporation can buy as many as it needs. The cellular phone is the tool that best defines the relationship between the fractal worker and recombinant capital.

Cognitive labour is an ocean of microscopic fragments of time that can be fragmented and recombined. The cellular phone can be seen as the assembly line of cognitive labour. What used to be the autonomy and the political power of the workforce has become the total dependence of cognitive labour on the capitalist organisation of the global network, because time has been fragmented and made flexible in a fractal recombinant way. Where there used to be a refusal of work we find today a total dependence of emotions and thought on the flow of information. And the effect of this is a sort of nervous breakdown that strikes the global mind and provoked what we have called the dotcom-crash.

The dotcom-crash and the crisis of financial mass-capitalism can be viewed as an effect of the collapse of the economic investment of social desire. I use the word 'collapse' in a sense that is not metaphorical, but rather a clinical description of what is going on in the Western mind. I use the word 'collapse' in order to express a real pathological crash of the psychosocial organism. What we have seen in the period following the first signs of economic crash, in the first months of the new century, is a psychopathological phenomenon, the collapse of the global mind. I see the present economic depression as the side effect of a psychic depression. The intense and prolonged investment of desire and of mental and libidinal energies in labour has created the psychic environment for the collapse which is now manifesting itself in the field of economic recession, in the field of military aggression and of a suicidal tendency.

The attention economy has become an important subject during the first years of the new century. Virtual workers have less and less time for attention, they are involved in a growing number of intellectual tasks, and they have no more time to devote to their own life, to love, tenderness and affection. They take Viagra because they have no time for sexual preliminaries. Cellular communication has made possible a total occupation of the lifetime of workers. Its effect is the nervous pathology of the social relationship. The symptoms of it are quite evident: millions of boxes of Prozac sold every month, the epidemic of attention deficit disorders among youngsters, the diffusion of drugs like Ritalin to school children and the spreading epidemic of panic.

The scenario of the first years of the new millennium seems to be dominated by a veritable wave of psychopathic behaviour. The suicidal phenomenon is spreading well beyond the borders of Islamic fanatic martyrdom. Since the World Trade Center bombings, suicide has become the crucial political act on the global political scene.

Aggressive suicide should not be seen as a mere phenomenon of despair and aggression, but has to be seen as the declaration of the end. The suicidal wave seems to suggest that humankind has run out of time, and despair has become the prevalent way of thinking about the future.

So what? I have no answer. All we can do is what we are actually doing already: the self-organisation of cognitive work is the only way to go beyond the psychopathic present. I don't believe that the world can be governed by reason. The utopia of Enlightenment has failed. But I think that the dissemination of self-organised knowledge can create a social framework containing infinite autonomous and self-reliant worlds.

The process of creating the network is so complex that it cannot be governed by human reason. The global mind is too complex to be known and mastered by subsegmental localised minds. We cannot know, we cannot control, we cannot govern the entire force of the global mind. But we can master the singular process of producing a singular world of sociality. This is autonomy today.

Berardi's text, or at least aspects of its prose, would seem to bear out Osborne's critique of the 'exodus' rhetoric employed by Autonomists. However, this is not an abstract break with a social system. Not remaining on the level of the atomised Kantian subject, or even its Adornian incarnation, this critique takes the form of a widely felt and shared discontent with the contradictions that (de)form the subject, leading to the self-organisation of cognitive work as a way out of a toxic present. This, then, is an immanent exodus.

While Berardi's prose has struck a chord in artistic milieus, it ultimately leaves the reader as empty-handed as Adorno's most Byzantine dictums – that is, when it comes to the question of *what is to be done*. The question remains whether the turn against Tronti and the party model has not led to an impoverishment of leftist politics, as Jodi Dean, for one, has argued. The disenchantment with social-democratic or Moscow-style communist parties is said to have led the left into a cul-de-sac of autonomist spontaneism, unable to build on any achievements or to aim for long-term goals. The party form, then, returns once more to the fore. Dean writes:

> The vision of a multitude of incommunicable struggles theorised by Hardt and Negri and held up in appeals to democracy replaces the antagonism of class struggle with pluralisation, creativity and becoming, thereby flattening and immediatising the terrain of struggle. [...]
>
> The new cycle of struggles has demonstrated the political strength that comes from collectivity. Common names, tactics and images are bringing the fragments together, making them legible as many fronts of one struggle against capitalism. [...]
>
> The party suggests itself as a mode of association appropriate to such as process.[14]

Event view, 'Autonomy Conference', Berlin, 1995,
with text 'Autonomy is self-determined dependency',
reproduced in *Autonomie-Kongreß der undogmatischen
linken Bewegungen: Standpunkte – Provokationen – Thesen*,
Münster: Unrast Verlag, 1996

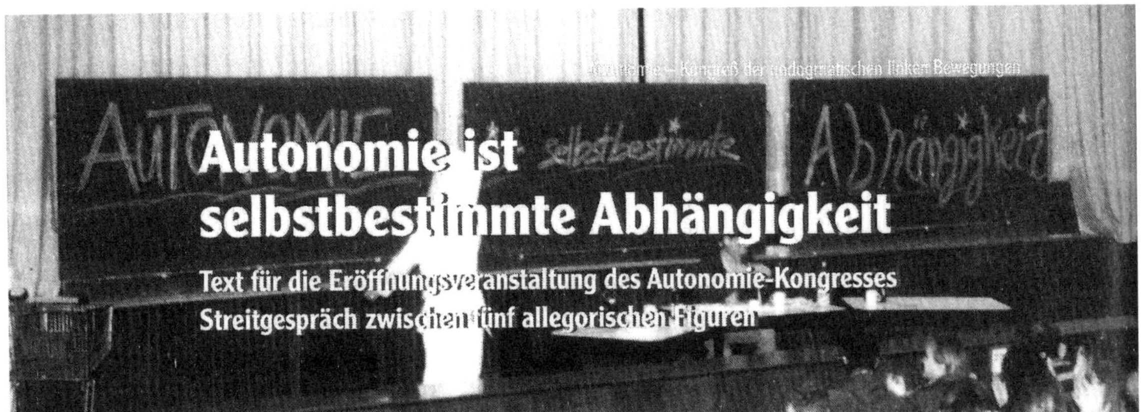

Autonomist Genealogies

In line with Autonomia, later movements from alter-globalism to Occupy Wall Street have insisted on autonomy not as a property of the subject, but as 'collective adventure' produced by transversal connections and groupings.[15] As in activism, (post-)Operaist and Autonomist theory has met with growing appreciation in certain sections of the art world. In Germany, for instance, debates on social and political autonomy in the post-68 'Sponti' milieu were informed by the developments in Italy. In 1975, writing in the inaugural issue of the journal *Autonomie*, Thomas Schmid noted that the old Bolshevik concept of the revolutionary avant-garde was broken, and that new forms of organisation were needed.[16] Schmid – who would move steadily to the right, and ended up working for the German equivalent of Rupert Murdoch's publishing empire, Springer – praised Italian Operaism for stimulating spontaneous and autonomous actions by workers and students, which ultimately created an understanding of autonomous self-organisation that went much beyond classic left-wing ideas of workers' autonomy.

Via *Autonomie* and other channels – such as the translations churned out by the Merve publishing house – Autonomist theory reached artists and intellectuals as well as activists in Germany. One outcome of this was the alternative (counter-)art fair Messe 2*ok*, organised in Cologne in 1995 by a group of artists that included Alice Creischer, Andreas Siekmann and Dierk Schmidt. In the publication that documents the 'fair', Creischer and Siekmann interview the activist and author Imma Harms about the German *autonome Szene*, a militant milieu of squatters and protesters known in the media mostly through its aggressive 'black bloc' faction at demonstrations and riots.[17] The interview references an 'Autonomy Congress' organised by participants in this scene in Berlin during Easter 1995.

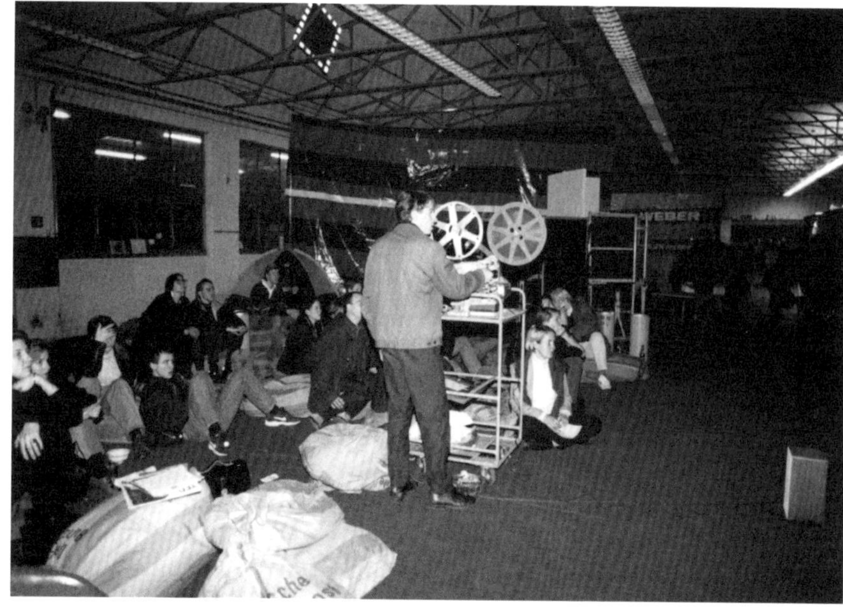

Messe 2*ok*, Cologne,
10–14 November, 1995
Courtesy Andreas Siekmann

See pp.268–69 of this reader
for more images

ALICE CREISCHER AND ANDREAS SIEKMANN, INTERVIEW WITH IMMA HARMS

Reprinted from, 'Keine Kontakte...', in *Messe 2ok: ÖkonoMiese Machen*, Cologne and Berlin: Permanent Press, 1996, pp.12, 39. Translated from the German by Helen Ferguson.

Alice: You asked about our motivation for this interview. There were two points: At the Autonomy Congress we liked the mode of organisation and the running order, above all the working groups on structural issues, such as the Eastern Europe working group, or the one on autonomy and militancy, because they were flexible and could be linked to other points. We also liked the way that presentations were limited to a kind of short introductory facilitation, so that an open discussion developed fairly quickly. We had the impression, too, that the Congress was more akin to a working meeting than a manifestation of various positions. Those who were not insiders in the politicised scene, as was our case, could nonetheless gain access to the debate.

All of that was an inspiration for us to try out similar forms for the Messe *2ok* fair. However, proposals along these lines, such as those in our initial concept papers, were hardly ever put into practice – perhaps also because the frames of reference were entirely different. The Autonomy Congress was nonetheless often cited at Messe *2ok*.

There is a further point that interests us too, namely the attempt to compare two concepts of autonomy that have both become more or less discredited: artistic and political autonomy ...

In the interview, Harms sketches the development of the German autonomist scene in the 1970s, including the post-68 Sponti movement, squats and anti-nuclear protests.

Imma: In their heyday the autonomists were not really bothered about theory. [...] As spontaneity gradually faded away as a tenable concept, the theoretical foundations, which did also exist, albeit to a limited degree, assumed greater importance again: Detlef Hartmann's book *Leben als Sabotage* [Life as Sabotage, 1981], *Autonomie* (a 1970s journal), Karl Heinz Roth's *Die »andere« Arbeiterbewegung* [The 'Other' Workers' Movement, 1974], theoretically inclined members of the Italian Autonomia movement, which was an anti-trade-union Operaist movement in the factories.

The discussion goes on to address the 'balancing act' involved in 'viewing oneself simultaneously as a subject with agency and as part of a structure':

Andreas: And what does that mean for political practice?

Imma: Moving away from a culture of grievances to a politics of taking action. In other words, in each instance shifting the focus of the question – not 'How can

I convince an adversary to stop doing certain things?', but rather 'What can I do to ensure the adversary simply *cannot do* certain things any longer?' When you talk about the Kunstakademie Düsseldorf, there really is a difference between Beuys simply declaring that everyone is actually an artist and his actually getting everybody into the school by occupying the administration.

Alice: Here the onus is on Messe 2*ok* to justify the decision not to act 'autonomously' in this case, and instead deliberately choosing to react to the event from the outside – that is, to organise our project during Art Cologne. This was the way that we aimed to turn the counterpart, to which you inevitably have to relate, into a matter of general concern that everyone would have to take a stance on, so that the object of criticism doesn't fade from view and the critical working-through cannot be delegated to single individuals.

Here, the interconnections between Autonomist organising and institutional critique become evident. If the latter has been identified with individual artistic practices that are invited to respond critically to an institutional context, there are also more collaborative and collective constellations. These range from activist groups and movements putting pressure on institutions, such as the Art Workers' Coalition, Guerrilla Girls or Decolonize This Place, to art spaces that seek to foster different modes of production and exchange. Andrea Fraser, who has a long-standing interest in group psychology, has been part of several such initiatives, including the Orchard exhibition space in New York, which was in turn a continuation of Colin de Land's American Fine Arts, which had been far more than a regular gallery for those involved.[18]

Such alternative institutions were crucial in Cologne as well as in New York. Cologne in 1995 was something of a hotbed of institutional critique thanks to Galerie Christian Nagel, alternative spaces such as the Friesenwall, and the magazine *Texte zur Kunst*. This is the milieu that gave rise to Messe 2*ok*, and the fair's publication contains a text by Stefan Römer – at the time a frequent contributor to *Texte zur Kunst* – that states: 'Art that is viewed as an object-based expression by an individual is subject to a process of ontologisation, which, in terms of its value-creation, reproduces existing capitalist practice and only rarely leads to an individualistic disruption of this practice.'[19] Of course, 'capitalist practice' was itself changing, its Western version becoming less industrial and Fordist and more cognitive and 'culturalised'. All of this contributed to making autonomy once more a pressing issue.

The Italian Operaists and Autonomists had been the first to accord a central role to Marx's notion of the 'general intellect', as developed in a tantalising passage of his *Grundrisse* (1857-58), which argues that capitalist technology makes knowledge directly part of the productive forces. In other words, you can't have modern industry without vast reserves of technical and social knowledge.[20] Building on this, some of the post-Operaists and Autonomists proceeded to craft new and controversial conceptual tools. The notion of immaterial labour, as developed by Maurizio Lazzarato and Antonio Negri, was both descriptive and prescriptive: it described 'creative' professions at the forefront of capitalist development and exploitation, and made it possible to theorise or fantasise about artistic and cultural practice as a potential site of resistance, along the lines of industrial labour in an earlier age.

MAURIZIO LAZZARATO, 'IMMATERIAL LABOR'

Available at http://frontdeskapparatus.com/
wp/wp-content/uploads/2012/10/Immateri-
al-Labor-Maurizio-Lazzarato.pdf (last accessed
on 19 September 2020). First published in 1997.
Translated from the Italian by Paul Colilli and
Ed Emery.

A significant amount of empirical research has been conducted concerning the new forms of the organisation of work. This, combined with a corresponding wealth of theoretical reflection, has made possible the identification of a new conception of what work is nowadays and what new power relations it implies.

An initial synthesis of these results – framed in terms of an attempt to define the technical and subjective-political composition of the working class – can be expressed in the concept of *immaterial labour,* which is defined as the labour that produces the informational and cultural consent of the commodity. The concept of immaterial labour refers to *two different aspects* of labour. On the one hand, as regards the 'informational content' of the commodity, it refers directly to the changes taking place in workers' labour processes in big companies in the industrial and tertiary sectors, where the skills involved in direct labour are increasingly skills involving cybernetics and computer control (and horizontal and vertical communication). On the other hand, as regards the activity that produces the 'cultural content' of the commodity, immaterial labour involves a series of activities that are not normally recognised as 'work' – in other words, the kinds of activities involved in defining and fixing cultural and artistic standards, fashions, tastes, consumer norms and, more strategically, public opinion. Once the privileged domain of the bourgeoisie and its children, these activities have since the end of the 1970s become the domain of what we have come to define as 'mass intellectuality'. The profound changes in these strategic sectors have radically modified not only the composition, management and regulation of the workforce – the organisation of production – but also, and more deeply, the role and function of intellectuals and their activities within society.

The 'great transformation' that began at the start of the 1970s has changed the very terms in which the question is posed. Manual labour is increasingly coming to involve procedures that could be defined as 'intellectual', and the new communications technologies increasingly require subjectivities that are rich in knowledge. It is not simply that intellectual labour has become subjected to the norms of capitalist production. What has happened is that a new 'mass intellectuality' has come into being, created out of a combination of the demands of capitalist production and the forms of 'self-valorisation' that the struggle against work has produced. The old dichotomy between 'mental and manual labour', or between 'material labour and immaterial labour', risks failing to grasp the new nature of productive activity, which takes this separation on board and transforms it. The split between conception and execution, between labour and creativity, between author and audience, is simultaneously transcended within the 'labour process' and reimposed as political command within the 'process of valorisation'.

Even aside from the question of its analytical cogency, the notion of immaterial labour has retained a certain vanguardist sex appeal that accounts for much of its traction in contemporary art. It could be seen as the leftist counterpart to neoliberal buzzwords such as 'the creative industries' and 'the creative class', which have been designed by policy intellectuals to be not so much descriptive as performative: they are used by governments and city councils to restructure economies and cities, privileging certain 'creative groups' while continuing to marginalise the old working class as well as low-income migrants (who are distinguished from desirable, high-income 'expats').[21] The notion of immaterial labour, of course, was designed by left-wing intellectuals to have a different kind of agency: to allow for the analysis of proliferating forms of precarity and for the forging of new alliances in the form of a new multitude that points both beyond the traditional working class and against the 'creative class' beloved by policymakers.

The concept of the multitude will be explored in Part Six of this reader; for now, we merely note that the post-Operaist concept of immaterial labour appears to complete the transition from art as commodity-object to art as labour – which is to say, to a different kind of commodity. In this sense, the project- or service-based work that emerged with institutional critique could be seen as part of the vanguard of commodification – and having critical potential precisely because of that. The Adornian dual character of the artwork as autonomous and as *fait social* returns in full swing, but takes on different forms, and explodes Adorno's conceptual framework. Labour is no longer concealed, but rather becomes itself the subject of 'sensuous fixation'. In this shift from fetish object to artistic labour, from artwork to art-as-work, labour is no longer concealed and sublated in the commodity fetish, but is itself foregrounded as a commodity whose value appears to indeed obey fetishist whims.

In a disintegrating field staffed by precarious workers, the question is not whether some theorem can be true for art and politics at the same time. An economic, social and intellectual imperative. Artists, curators and critics collaborate in various constellations with others inside and outside what remains of the frame; this collaboration can be pragmatic and aimed at economic survival, or it can be activist and aimed against the overall framework. The results can be artistic or political to varying degrees. Perhaps not much of this amounts to well-behaved 'productive labour' resulting in 'genuinely capitalist' commodities. If so, it is because these categories themselves are in crisis. As economic growth falters, culture becomes the exemplary zone of exception where absurd profits are mirrored by precarity and self-exploitation.[22]

Reproduction

Not everybody was convinced of the use-value of Operaist and Autonomist concepts. When Lazzarato and Negri appeared at the 2008 Tate Modern symposium 'Art and Immaterial Labour', co-organised by Peter Osborne, the anarchist and anthropologist David Graeber – who would become a key actor in the Occupy Wall Street movement – criticised these thinkers' receptions within this artistic framework in a fairly savage text that focusses on the problems of the notion of immaterial labour.

DAVID GRAEBER, 'THE SADNESS OF POST-WORKERISM'

Reprinted from David Graeber, *Revolutions in Reverse: Essays on Politics, Violence, and Imagination*, London, New York, and Port Watson: Minor Compositions, 2011, pp.87-88, 90-91.

The notion of immaterial labour can be disposed of fairly quickly. In many ways it is transparently absurd.

The classic definition, by Maurizio Lazzarato, is 'the labour that produces the informational and cultural content of the commodity' – the 'informational content' referring to the increasing importance in production and marketing of new forms of 'cybernetics and computer control', while the second, the 'cultural content', refers to the labour of 'defining and fixing cultural and artistic standards, fashions, tastes, consumer norms and, more strategically, public opinion', which, increasingly, everyone is doing all the time. On the one hand, 'immaterial workers' are 'those who work in advertising, fashion, marketing, television, cybernetics and so forth', on the other, we are all immaterial workers, insofar as we are disseminating information about brand names, creating subcultures, frequenting fan magazines or web pages or developing our own personal sense of style. As a result, production – or, at least in the sense of the production of the *value* of a commodity, what makes it something anyone would wish to buy – is no longer limited to the factory but is dispersed across society as a whole, and becomes impossible to measure.

To some degree this is just a much more sophisticated Leftist version of the rise of the service economy, etc., but there is also a very particular history, which goes back to dilemmas in Italian workerism in the '70s and '80s. On the one hand, there was a stubborn Leninist assumption – promoted, for instance, by Toni Negri – that it must always be the most 'advanced' sector of the proletariat that makes up the revolutionary class. Computer and other information workers were the obvious candidates here. But the same period saw the rise of feminism and the Wages for Housework movement, which put the whole problem of unwaged, domestic labour on the political table in a way that could no longer simply be ignored. The solution was to argue that computer work and housework were really the same thing. Or, more precisely, were becoming so: since, it was argued, the increase of labour-saving devices meant that housework was becoming less and less a matter of simple drudgery, and more and more itself a matter of managing fashions, tastes and styles.

The result is a genuinely strange concept, combining a kind of frenzied postmodernism with the most clunky, old-fashioned Marxist material determinism.

Graeber does not deny that in its 'clunky' manner, the notion of immaterial labour does pinpoint real transformations in the economy and in society:

Obviously all this is not to say that nothing has changed in recent years. It's not even to say that many of the connections being drawn in the immaterial labour argument are not real and important. Most of these, however, have been identified, and debated, in feminist literature for some time, and often to much better effect. Donna Haraway, for example, was already discussing the way that new communication technologies were allowing forms of 'home work' to disseminate throughout society in the '80s. To take an obvious example: for most of the twentieth century, capitalist offices have been organised according to a gendered division of labour that mirrors the organisation of upper-class households: male executives engage in strategic planning while female secretaries were expected to do much of the day-to-day organisational work, along with almost all of the impression-management, communicative and interpretive labour, mostly over the phone. Gradually these traditionally female functions have become digitised and replaced by computers; this creates a dilemma, though, because the interpretive elements of female labour (figuring out how to ensure no one's ego is bruised, that sort of thing) are precisely those that computers are *least* capable of performing. Hence the renewed importance of what the post-workerists like to refer to as 'affective labour'. This in turn effects how phone work is reorganised, now, as globalised, but also as largely complementary to software, with interpretive work aimed more at the egos of customers than (now invisible) male bosses. The connections are all there. But it's only by starting from long-term perspectives that one can get any clear idea what's really new here, and this is precisely what the postmodern approach makes impossible.

This last example brings us to my second point, which is that very notion that there is something that can be referred to as 'immaterial labour' relies on a remarkably crude, old-fashioned kind of Marxism. Immaterial labour, we are told, is labour that produces information and culture. In other words, it is 'immaterial' not because the labour itself is immaterial (how could it be?) but because it *produces* immaterial things. This idea that different sorts of labour can be sorted into more material and less material categories according to the nature of their product is the basis for the whole conception that societies consist of a 'material base' (the production, again, of wheat, socks and petrochemicals) and 'ideological superstructure' (the production of music, culture, laws, religion, essays such as this). This is what's allowed generations of Marxists to declare that most of what we call 'culture' is really just so much fluff, at best a reflex of the really important stuff going on in fields and foundries.

All such conceptions ignore what is to my mind probably the single most powerful, and enduring insight of Marxist theory: that the world does not really consist (as capitalists would encourage us to believe) of a collection of discrete objects that can then be bought and sold, but of actions and processes. This is what makes it possible for rich and powerful people to insist that what they do is somehow more abstract, more ethereal, higher and more spiritual, than everybody else. They do so by pointing at the products – poems, prayers, statutes, essays or pure abstractions like style and taste – rather than the process of making such things, which is always much messier and dirtier than the products themselves. So do such people claim to float above the muck and mire of ordinary profane existence. One would think that the first aim of a materialist approach would be to explode such pretensions – to point out, for instance, that just as the *production* of socks and silverware involves a great deal of thinking and imagining, so is the production of laws, poems and prayers an eminently material process. And indeed most contemporary materialists do, in fact, make this point. By bringing in terms like 'immaterial labour', authors like Lazzarato and Negri, bizarrely, seem to want to turn back the theory clock to somewhere around 1935.

Regardless of whether one considers Graeber's critique of Negri and Lazzarato to be entirely fair, one of his main points is in synch with the feminist revaluation of domestic, reproductive and affective labour in the context of contemporary art. Never mind the programmers, curators and jet-setting artists: what about those who make those professions possible? What about those who enable their productivism by maintaining the infrastructure, and by taking care of the reproduction of life itself?

In this framework, Mierle Laderman Ukeles's 'maintenance' projects of the late 1960s and early 1970s have taken on renewed importance. Ukeles has focussed on female reproductive (and often unpaid) labour. Her cleaning performances in art institutions put a feminist spin on institutional critique, foregrounding not so much corporate sponsorship as the museum's – and society's – dependence on disavowed female labour. The artist's 1969 manifesto on 'maintenance art' provides the theoretical and ideological underpinnings for her practice.

Following page: Photograph used on
front and back covers of *Heresies:
A Feminist Publication on Art and Politics*,
no.7, 'Women Working Together', 1979,
later reproduced on the front cover of
the zine *LABOUR*, 2011 edited by
Melissa Gordon and Marina Vishmidt

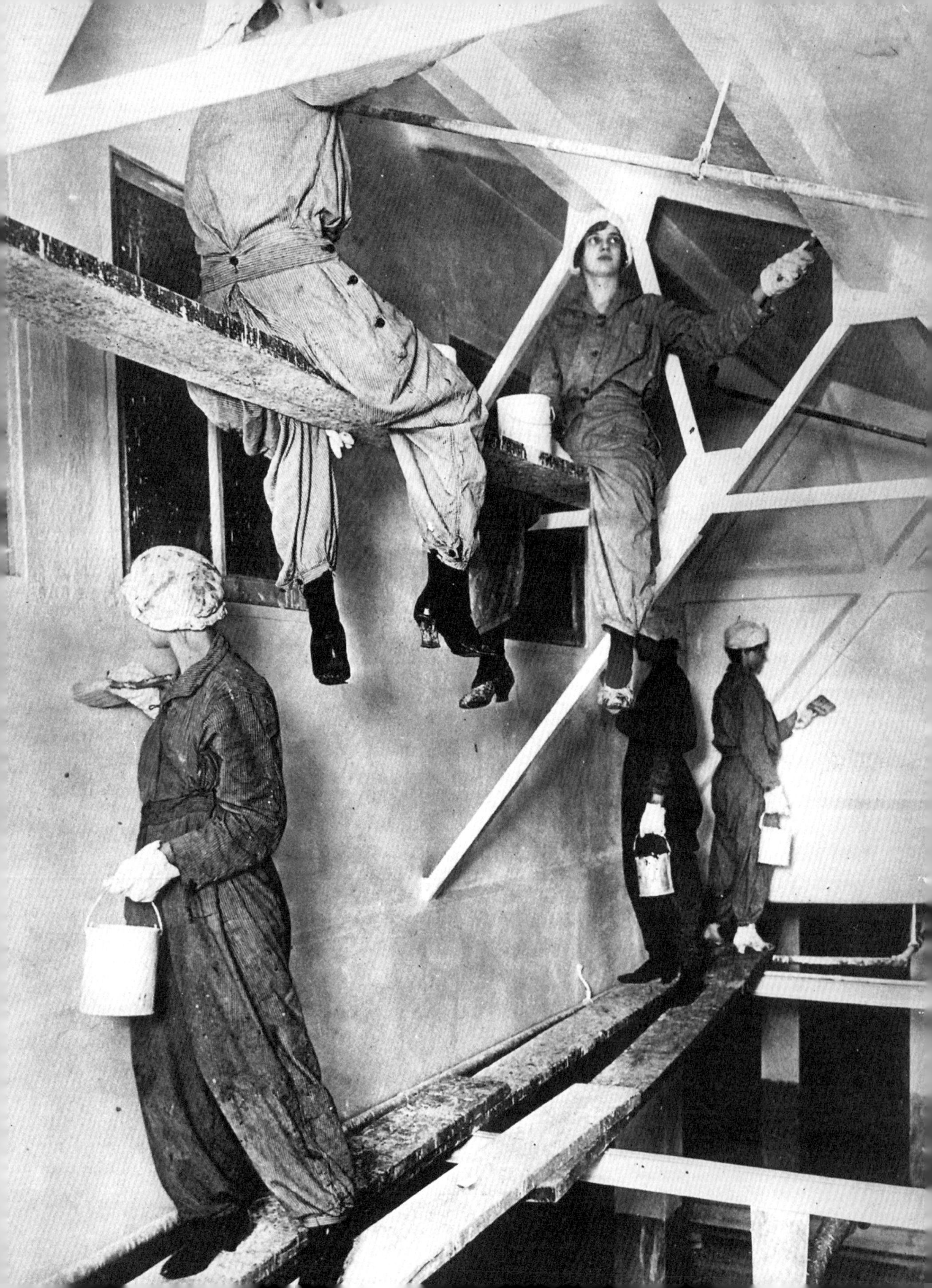

MIERLE LADERMAN UKELES, 'MANIFESTO FOR MAINTENANCE ART 1969! PROPOSAL FOR AN EXHIBITION "CARE"'

Reprinted from Binna Choi and Maiko Tanaka
(ed.), *Grand Domestic Revolution Handbook*, Utrecht
and Amsterdam: Casco and Valiz, 2014, pp.134-37.

I. IDEAS

A.   The Death Instinct and the Life Instinct:

The Death Instinct: separation; individuality; Avant-Garde par excellence; to follow one's own path to death - do your own thing; dynamic change.

The Life Instinct: unification; the eternal return; the perpetuation and MAINTENANCE of the species; survival systems and operations; equilibrium.

B.   Two basic systems: Development and Maintenance. The sourball of every revolution: after the revolution, who's going to pick up the garbage on Monday morning?

Development: pure individual creation; the new; change; progress; advance; excitement; flight or fleeing.

Maintenance: keep the dust off the pure individual creation; preserve the new; sustain the change; protect progress; defend and prolong the advance; renew the excitement; repeat the flight;

show your work - show it again
keep the contemporaryartmuseum groovy
keep the home fires burning

Development systems are partial feedback systems with major room for change.
Maintenance systems are direct feedback systems with little room for alteration.

C.   Maintenance is a drag; it takes all the fucking time (lit.)
The mind boggles and chafes at the boredom.
The culture confers lousy status on maintenance jobs = minimum wages, housewives = no pay.

clean your desk, wash the dishes, clean the floor, wash your clothes, wash your toes, change the baby's diaper, finish the report, correct the typos, mend the fence, keep the customer happy, throw out the stinking garbage, watch out don't put things in your nose, what shall I wear, I have no sox, pay your bills, don't litter, save string, wash your hair, change the sheets, go to the store, I'm out of perfume, say it again – he doesn't understand, seal it again – it leaks, go to work, this art is dusty, clear the table, call him again, flush the toilet, stay young.

D. Art:

Everything I say is Art is Art. Everything I do is Art is Art. 'We have no Art, we try to do everything well.' (Balinese saying)

Avant-garde art, which claims utter development, is infected by strains of maintenance ideas, maintenance activities and maintenance materials.
Conceptual & Process art, especially, claim pure development and change, yet employ almost purely maintenance processes.

E. The exhibition of Maintenance Art, 'CARE', would zero in on pure maintenance, exhibit it as contemporary art, and yield, by utter opposition, clarity of issues.

II. THE MAINTENANCE ART EXHIBITION: 'CARE'
Three parts: Personal, General and Earth Maintenance.

A. *Part One: Personal*

I am an artist. I am a woman. I am a wife. I am a mother. (Random order).

I do a hell of a lot of washing, cleaning, cooking, renewing, supporting, preserving, etc. Also, up to now separately I 'do' Art.

Now, I will simply do these maintenance everyday things, and flush them up to consciousness, exhibit them, as Art. I will live in the museum and I customarily do at home with my husband and my baby, for the duration of the exhibition. (Right? or if you don't want me around at night I would come in every day) and do all these things as public Art activities: I will sweep and wax the floors, dust everything, wash the walls (i.e. 'floor paintings, dust works, soap-sculpture, wall-paintings'), cook, invite people to eat, make agglomerations and dispositions of all functional refuse.

The exhibition area might look 'empty' of art, but it will be maintained in full public view.

MY WORKING WILL BE THE WORK

B.   *Part Two: General*

Everyone does a hell of a lot of noodling maintenance work. The general part of
the exhibition would consist of interviews of two kinds.

   1.   Previous individual interviews, typed and exhibited.

   Interviewees come from, say, 50 different classes and kinds of occupations
   that run a gamut from maintenance 'man', maid, sanitation 'man', mail
   'man', union 'man', construction worker, librarian, grocerystore 'man',
   nurse, doctor, teacher, museum director, baseball player, sales'man', child,
   criminal, bank president, mayor, moviestar, artist, etc., about:

      - what you think maintenance is;
      - how you feel about spending whatever parts of your life you spend on
      maintenance activities;
      - what is the relationship between maintenance and freedom;
      - what is the relationship between maintenance and life's dreams.

   2.   Interview Room - for spectators at the Exhibition:

   A room of desks and chairs where professional (?) interviewers will
   interview the spectators at the exhibition along same questions as typed
   interviews. The responses should be personal.

   These interviews are taped and replayed throughout the exhibition area.

C.   *Part Three: Earth Maintenance*

Everyday, containers of the following kinds of refuse will be delivered to the
Museum:

      - the contents of one sanitation truck;
      - a container of polluted air;
      - a container of polluted Hudson River;
      - a container of ravaged land.

Once at the exhibition, each container will be serviced:

      purified, de-polluted, rehabilitated, recycled and conserved

by various technical (and/or pseudo-technical) procedures either by myself or
scientists.

These servicing procedures are repeated throughout the duration of the
exhibition.

Ukeles developed her maintenance practice at a moment of intense feminist activity in the art world, politics and academia. This also saw a contestation of the male (and white) canon of art history. In a classic 1971 essay, art historian Linda Nochlin took the question 'Why have there been no great women artists?' – usually asked by men to suggest that women are simply not capable of achieving artistic genius – as the basis for a serious inquiry into the conditions under which 'artistic greatness' can emerge. 'What if Picasso had been born a girl? Would Senor Ruiz have paid as much attention or stimulated as much ambition for achievement in a little Pablita?'[23] One conclusion from her inquiry was that

> art is not a free, autonomous activity of a super-endowed individual, 'influenced' by previous artists, and more vaguely and superficially, by 'social forces', but rather, that the total situation of art making, both in terms of the development of the art maker and in the nature and quality of the work of art itself, occur in a social situation, are integral elements of this social structure, and are mediated and determined by specific and definable social institutions, be they art academies, systems of patronage, mythologies of the divine creator, artist as he-man or social outcast.[24]

Feminism thus foregrounds the structural conditions that make possible autonomy as an exceptional privilege. Ukeles's artistic focus on 'lowly' and feminised maintenance had its theoretical and activist counterpart in the international Wages for Housework campaign, started in 1972 by feminists from the milieu of Autonomia, in Italy and elsewhere – Mariarosa Dalla Costa, Silvia Federici, Selma James and others. At stake was the unremunerated nature of housework, which placed women in a dependent position. In arguing that the value of commodities, including labour-power itself, is determined by the amount of labour socially necessary to produce them, Marx acknowledged the time necessary for maintaining and reproducing the labour-power of the workforce. Overall, however, Marxism has failed to do justice to the sphere of reproduction as integral to the production process in general, and thus has been complicit in women's relegation to the domestic sphere as a supposedly extra-economic supplement.

In the 1940s, the American feminist Mary Inman launched a fierce debate in the American Communist Party by insisting that 'under capitalism, housewives' work, in a majority of cases, is necessary to the process of producing and distributing commodities' and is thus productive labour.[25] In the founding documents of the Wages for Housework campaign, such as Dalla Costa and James's *The Power of Women and the Subversion of the Community* (1972), we again see an insistence that housework is productive.[26] This was an important point of departure for Federici's theoretical work, yet (in spite of her praise for Dalla Costa and James) Federici came to see the analytical and political value of the distinction between productive and reproductive labour – even while arguing that the reproduction of labour-power 'must be simultaneously a production and valorisation of desired human qualities and capacities'.[27] Federici developed an account of reproductive work under capitalism as being valuable precisely insofar as it is treated as an immanent exception: 'capitalism is a production system that depends structurally on non-contractual and unpaid work'.[28]

Since those first debates, Wages for Housework has become a key reference for new generations of artists, activists and theorists. In their joint book *Reproducing*

Autonomy (2016), Kerstin Stakemeier and Marina Vishmidt place themselves in the Autonomist feminist lineage of Dalla Costa, arguing that reproductive labour is a privileged site of contestation:

> What *is* 'reproduction'? How has it been conceived across the various traditions of Marxist theory and political aesthetics in the latter part of the twentieth century up to the present? Is it only a form of 'preservational' labour, which, unlike production, is restricted to the *maintenance* of what already exists; and, if so, would it not have a *more* and not *less* distant relationship to political autonomy than the category of production? Can we continue to believe that reproduction under capitalism is primarily a problem for feminist politics, or has the concept now acquired new dimensions? And, once again, if it's possible to show that it has acquired such dimensions, what ramifications would this expansion of the domain of reproduction have for feminism itself, conceived in materialist terms as the practical rejection of the forms of gendered domination specific to contemporary capitalist societies – with gender abolition as its horizon?[29]

Stakemeier and Vishmidt are both art theorists, and their book was published by Mute, a London-based publishing platform for critical art and media theory. This is not some hijacking of art by politics or activism; rather, it is a consequence of living and working within a cultural sphere where the value of commodities and services are out of joint, and which is crucially dependent on unpaid intern work, as well as unpaid and paid reproductive labour. With women increasingly having been incorporated into the workforce, life in the metropolis depends to a significant extent on a disavowed shadow world of paid domestic labour, often performed by immigrants (though this rarely takes the form of a wage relationship, and still falls outside strict definitions of productive labour). The superstructure meets the base, as both the latter and the former are dominated by flexible and precarious jobs – which is not to say that these forms of precarity are equivalent. In fact, 'flexible' curators and artists often hire domestic workers who may be in a vastly more (legally) precarious position. In consequence, various artistic-activist practices have collaborated with groups of domestic workers.[30] This has also contributed to a greater awareness of intersections of gender and race, as these forms of labour are often delegated to women of colour. Françoise Vergès has noted that 'In the 1970s, as white feminists denounced the boredom and invisibility of unpaid housework, the movement to recruit racialised women for cleaning/caring accelerated.'[31] While Western feminists were at times too focused on their status of victims of oppression to take note of this, or to reflect on the legacy and persistence of colonialism, Wages for Housework has arguably developed tools that allow contemporary theorists, activists and artist to challenge the outsourcing of necessary but disavowed work to the most vulnerable and precarized of lives.

In her solo-authored section of *Reproducing Autonomy*, Stakemeier stresses the crucial step taken by Marx: in standing Hegel's idealist dialectics 'on its head', Marx placed primacy not on some autonomous unfolding of spirit (or on its secularised cognate, capital), but rather on autonomy as a particular material and social process and practice.

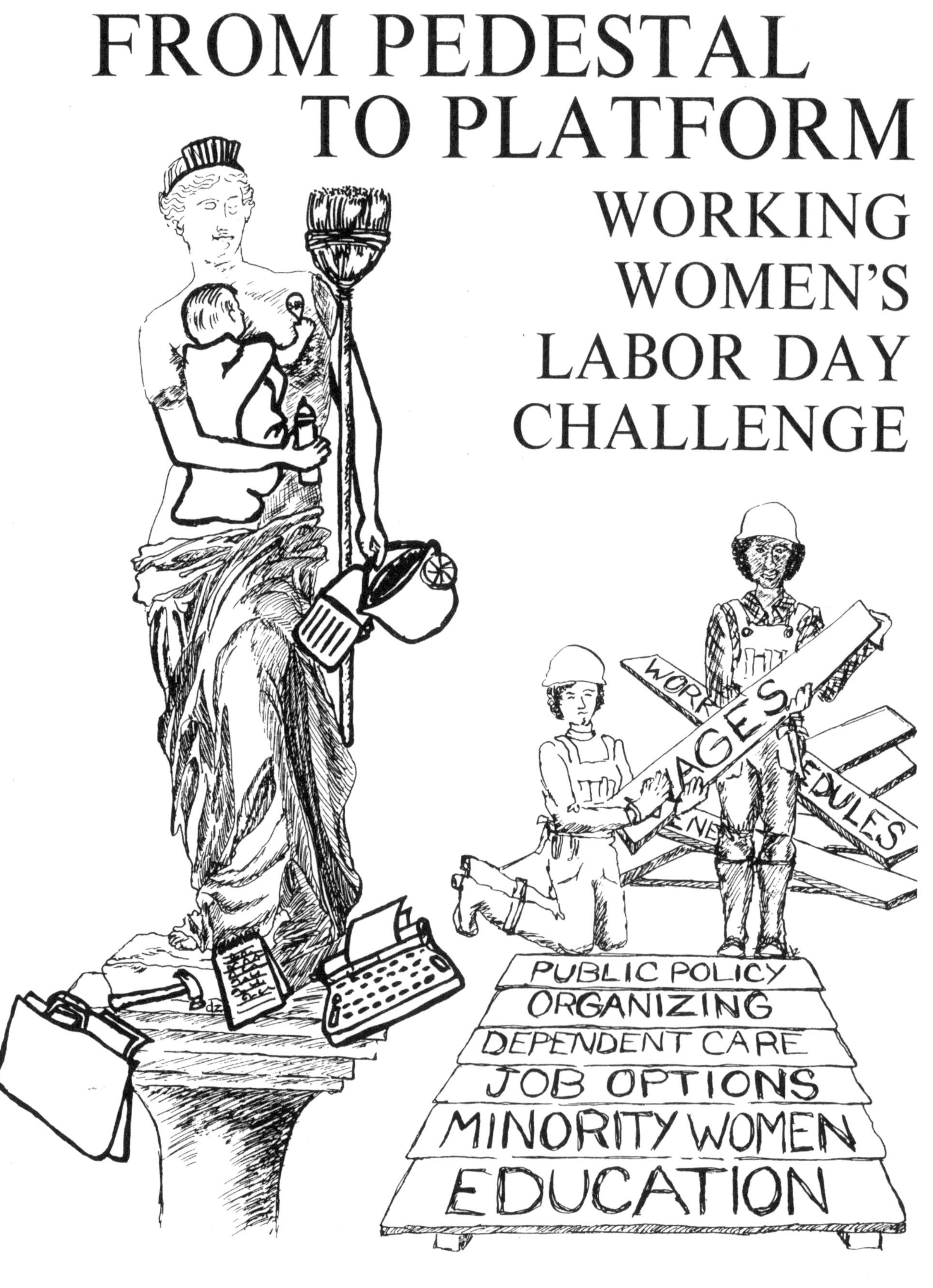

FROM PEDESTAL
TO PLATFORM
WORKING
WOMEN'S
LABOR DAY
CHALLENGE
WORK
WAGES
EDULES
PUBLIC POLICY
ORGANIZING
DEPENDENT CARE
JOB OPTIONS
MINORITY WOMEN
EDUCATION

KERSTIN STAKEMEIER, '(NOT) MORE AUTONOMY'

Reprinted from Kerstin Stakemeier and
Marina Vishmidt, *Reproducing Autonomy:
Work, Money, Crisis and Contemporary Art*,
London: Mute Publishing, 2016, pp.17, 20-22, 13.

In understanding the emanation of capital's seemingly immaterial totality as a violent, historical and material process, Marx enables a critical understanding of autonomy as a process no longer primarily intellectual but consisting instead of ongoing materialisations: processes of integration, functionalisation, separation, exclusion and destruction.

Returning to the context of 1960s Operaismo, Stakemeier stresses that the same point was made with great force by Mario Tronti:

In Tronti's *Operaismo*,[10] autonomy appears as a position to be wrought from the disintegrated status of individual work as abstract labour. Where Adorno discerns intellectual labour as that realm of capitalist life that has not yet been fully subsumed under capital, Tronti presents autonomy as a necessarily tactical category of material labour. 'The autonomy of the political', he writes, 'proves to be a utopia, if considered as a directly capitalistic political project; it is the very last of bourgeois ideologies; it becomes sustainable, maybe, only as a labour claim'.[11] For Tronti, the autonomy of the political is a bourgeois operation obscuring the immanently economic nature of the political. Where Adorno locates autonomy in the realm of the aesthetic to construct a maximal distance from the reproductive brutalities of capital, Tronti argues that autonomy cannot be won at any distance from the production process but can be anticipated only as an autonomisation from within divided labour. Otherwise, autonomy within capital is, according to Tronti, nothing less than its driving force, because it is where labour 'appears to be an autonomous inner power of capital' that capital thrives.[12]

Tronti's reconstruction of autonomy as a category immanent to capital lays out the ground for an understanding of autonomy beyond its modern fate as a dialectically bound figure of emancipation and regression. As I intend to understand it here, he offers a reconstruction of autonomy as a figure of immanence and affirmation: not so much of capital as *against* it. Tronti's orientation toward the primacy of autonomisations in material praxis turns theoretical reflections upon autonomy upside down. Autonomy is once again brought into

[10]   For an introduction to the history of Autonomia, see Sylvère Lotringer and Christian Marazzi (ed.), *Autonomia: Post-Political Politics*, Los Angeles: Semiotext(e), 1980; and Steve Wright, *Storming Heaven: Composition and Struggle in Italian Autonomist Marxism*, London: Pluto Press, 2002.

[11]   Mario Tronti, cited in Dario Gentili, 'The Autonomy of the Political in the Italian Tradition (Tronti, Negri, Cacciari)', in Nathaniel Boyd, Michele Filippini and Luisa Lorenza Corna (ed.), *The Autonomy of the Political: Concept, Theory, Form*, Maastricht: Jan van Eyck Academie, 2012, p.13.

[12]   Mario Tronti, 'Fabrik und Gesellschaft [La fabbrica et la società]', *Quaderni Rossi*, no.2, 1962. Editors' Note: An English-language translation of this text is available at https://operaismoinenglish.files.wordpress.com/2013/06/factory-and-society.pdf (last accessed on 19 September 2020).

process. In analogy to Marx's understanding of capital as a negative *Weltgeist*, autonomy here fulfils the Hegelian argument against autonomy: it is systematically rendered as a merely formal, subjective but necessary step within the fulfilment of the *Weltgeist* – that is, of capital. Thus, it returns as an affirmative figure of capital, but, as Tronti demonstrates, where this claim to autonomy is transposed into a category of a praxis against this actualised *Weltgeist*, it can develop self-affirming forms of material life that strive for the abolition of labour and capital alike.[13]

While Tronti focusses his discussion exclusively on the classical Marxist political subject, the worker, this transposition might also be – and was, in fact – refigured in other realms of capitalist life. The relocation of autonomy from a deficient developmental step of a subjective conclusion within capital to a transposed subjective emblem developed beyond and against it brings autonomy's aesthetic and political uses once again into closer proximity. Such an immanent understanding of autonomy repudiates the capitalistic distinction between art and life as an inadequate circumscription of subjective praxis from which nothing is to be won – and that under current conditions seems increasingly nostalgic. … As Gilles Deleuze suggests, it denies the representative meaning of autonomy within bourgeois societies by strengthening its practical meaning; intervening into the relentless (re)production of capitalist totalities, it tries to traverse the institutionalisations of art and life alike. The subjectivism for which Hegel disregarded the figure of autonomy herein becomes its individuating potential.

This individuation has not least been attempted by feminist theoreticians like Silvia Federici and Mariarosa Dalla Costa, who, coming out of the Operaismo movement, demanded that autonomy be affirmed as a category of reproductive work. Their insistence on the productive character of the privatised, invisible and – in Marx's sense – unproductive forms of reproductive work in the household enacted such a transposition: the transposition of a struggle for autonomy *into* a social realm deemed heteronomous. This is precisely what Helke Sander addressed in 1968 … when she declared that the political struggle for autonomy could not be achieved by displacing heteronomy into specific sectors of life.[14] Gisela Dischner's similar attack … on the social distinction of the 'sphere of reproduction' and the 'sphere of production' implicates art within this process.[15] She suggests understanding artistic processes as a potentially general factor of individuation, one that can enhance a more integrated conception of subjective development, counteracting not only the social exclusiveness of artistic actions … but also the insinuation of the distinction of production and reproduction into the process of subjective individuation.[16]

---

[13]   *Ibid.*

[14]   Speech of Helke Sander, 'Aktionsrat zur Befreiung der Frau', at 'Delegiertenkonferenz des Sozialistischen Deutschen Studentenbundes', Frankfurt, 13 September 1968.

[15]   Gisela Dischner, 'Sozialisationstheorie und materialistische Ästhetik', in Chris Bezzel (ed.), *Das Unvermögen der Realität. Beiträge zu einem anderen materialistischen Ästhetikum*, Berlin: Wagenbach, 1974, p.99.

[16]   See Andrea Fraser's contribution to the Autonomy Project, suggesting that autonomy, understood in psychological terms, might be read as a 'defence function': A. Fraser, 'Autonomy and Its Contradictions', *Open!*, no.23, 2012, pp.106-15. EN: Reprinted in Part Three of this reader, pp.203-10.

Autonomy, then, is never an aestheticist *l'art-pour-l'art* autonomy from labour, just as it cannot be the autonomy of (male) industrial wage labour from (feminine) reproductive labour. Both of these 'autonomies' delude themselves by turning a blind eye to their material basis. Or, as Stakemeier puts it at one point in her essay:

> Autonomy in art is no longer modern and its modern forms, far from being the remnants of a lost ideal, are stabilising heteronomies whenever they are simply imported into our present. In modern times, autonomy was an abstraction from the reproduction of life, preconditioning the realm of art as one marked by a subjective excess of expression; in contemporary times, autonomy is a concretion, an individuation that designates specific figurations within life. Its excess is one *of* life.

Autonomy is a surplus raher than the subtraction of a specialisation from the mesh of life. It is not artistic *or* activist, aesthetic *or* political, but their clashing and enmeshing in lived and collaborative praxis. However, the art world has frequently betrayed the promise of 'a more integrated conception of subjective development'. In recent years, the #MeToo movement has revealed a systemic failure to hold powerful male figures accountable for sexual harassment and abuse; the cards have continued to be stacked against the Pablitas. Art can hardly be said to have been in the vanguard of this more general social reckoning, with the residual myth of the male genius having provided oh so convenient cover. From Instagram accounts and petitions to offline assemblies and protests, a new wave of activism has emerged that functions as feminist institutional critique by way of networked autonomous self-organisation.

Notes

1   Theodor W. Adorno, *In Search of Wagner* (trans. Rodney Livingstone), London: Verso, 2005, p.72.

2   Stewart Martin, 'The Absolute Artwork Meets the Absolute Commodity', Radical Philosophy, no.146, November-December 2007, p.23.

3   See 'Autonomy in an Exploding Field' in Part Three of this reader, pp.194-213.

4   T.W. Adorno, *In Search of Wagner*, op. cit., p.72.

5   Raniero Panzieri, 'Relazione sul neocapitalismo', in *La Ripresa del Marxismo-Leninismo in Italia*, Milan: Sapere Edizioni, 1972, p.212; cited in Pier Vittorio Aurelli, *The Project of Autonomy: Politics and Architecture within and against Capitalism*, New York: Temple Hoyne Buell Center and Princeton Architectural Press, 2008, p.27.

6   The best general introduction to Operaismo in English remains Steve Wright, *Storming Heaven: Class Composition in Italian Autonomist Marxism*, London: Pluto Press, 2017.

7   Marco Scotini, 'Disobedient Images; Autonomia and the Politics of Representation', *Open!*, 17 November 2013, http://www.onlineopen.org/disobedient-images (last accessed on 19 September 2020).

8   Karl Marx, *Capital: A Critique of Political Economy, Volume I*, trans. Ben Fowkes (London: Penguin, 1990), p.255.

9   See, for instance, Hans-Georg Bensch and Frank Kuhne (ed.), *Das automatische Subjekt bei Marx. Studien zum 'Kapital'*, Lüneburg: Gesellschaftswissenschaftliches Institut Hannover, 1998. In recent art theory, see, for instance, Kerstin Stakemeier, 'Art as Capital - Art as Service - Art as Industry: Timing Art in Capitalism', in Beatrice von Bismarck, Rike Frank, Benjamin Meyer-Krahmer, Jörn Schafaff and Thomas Weski (ed.), *Timing: On the Temporal Dimension of Exhibiting*, Berlin: Sternberg Press, 2014, pp.15-38.

10   P.V. Aureli, *The Project of Autonomy*, op. cit., p.12.

11   Mario Tronti, 'Our Operaismo', *New Left Review*, no. 73 (January-February 2012), p.138.

12   Merijn Oudenampsen, 'On the Autonomy of the Political and the Poverty of Theory', presentation at 'What is Autonomia Today', Amsterdam, 19 May 2011, available at http://merijnoudenampsen.org/2013/05/07/on-the-autonomy-of-the-political-and-the-poverty-of-theory/ (last accessed on 19 September 2020)

13   Félix Guattari and Antonio Negri, *New Lines of Alliance, New Spaces of Liberty* (trans. Michael Ryan, Jared Becker, Arianna Bove and Noe Le Blanc), London, New York and Port Watson: Minor Compositions and Autonomedia, 2010, pp.64-65. The book was first published in French as *Les nouveaux espaces de liberté* (Paris: Nouvelles editions Lignes, 1985), and in English as *Communists Like Us* (New York: Semiotext(e): 1990).

14   Jodi Dean, *Crowds and Party*, London: Verso, 2016, pp.24-25.

15   See B. Holmes, 'Artistic Autonomy and the Communication Society', *op cit*., p.548.

16   Thomas Schmid, 'Facing Reality: Organisation kaputt', *Autonomie*, no.1, 1975, October, pp.16-35.

17   With its violent actions during the 2017 protests against the G20 summit in Hamburg, the 'black bloc' managed to create mass hysteria against the 'autonomous scene' and 'the radical left' - and by extension the entire left. In the German media, this was a gift to conservative politicians in an election year.

18   See Jeannine Tang, Ann E. Butler and Lia Gangitano (ed.), *The Conditions of Being Art: Pat Hearn Gallery & American Fine Arts, Co.*, Brooklyn, NY: Dancing Foxes Press, 2018.

19   Stefan Römer, 'Die Autonomie der Kunst oder die Kunst der Autonomen. "Kunst bleibt politik"', in *Messe 2ok: ÖkonoMiese machen*, Cologne and Berlin: Permanent Press, 1996, p.42. Translated from the German by Helen Ferguson.

20   Karl Marx, *Grundrisse: Foundations of the Critique of Political Economy (Rough Draft)* (1857-58; trans. Martin Nicolaus), London: Penguin Books, 1992, p.708. See also Hans-Jürgen Krahl, 'Produktion und Klassenkampf' (1970), in *Konstitution und Klassenkampf. Zur historischen Dialektik von bürgerlicher Emanzipation und proleratischer Revolution*, Frankfurt: Neue Kritik, 2008, pp.392-414. Tribute is paid to Krahl, a student of Adorno, in Franco 'Bifo' Berardi, *The Soul at Work: From Alienation to Autonomy* (trans. Francesca Cadel and Giuseppina Mecchia), New York: Semiotext(e), 2009, pp.58-70.

21   The notion of the 'creative industries' emerged in policy in the 1990s, most famously with UK Prime Minister Tony Blair's establishment of a Creative Industries Task Force, in 1997. The concept of the 'creative class' was introduced in Richard Florida, *The Rise of the Creative Class: And How It's Transforming Work, Leisure, Community and Everyday Life*, New York: Perseus Book Group, 2002. For a critique, see, for instance, Martha Rosler, 'Culture Class: Art, Creativity, Urbanism', part 2, *e-flux journal*, no.23, March 2011, available at http://www.e-flux.com/journal/culture-class-art-creativity-urbanism-part-ii/ (last accessed on 19 September 2020).

22   See Sven Lütticken, 'The Coming Exception: Art and the Crisis of Value', *New Left Review*, no.99, May-June 2016, pp.111-36.

23   Linda Nochlin, 'Why Have There Been No Great Women Artists?' (1971), in *Women, Art, and Power and Other Essays*, New York and London: Routledge, 2018, 155.

24   *Ibid.*, p.158.

25   Mary Inman, *In Women's Defense*, Los Angeles: The Committee to Organize the Advancement of Women, 1940, p.136.

26   Mariarosa Dalla Costa and Selma James, *The Power of Women and the Subversion of the Community*, Bristol: Falling Wall Press, 1972. See also Silvia Federici's 1975 essay "Wages against Housework," in *Revolution at Point Zero: Housework, Reproduction, and Feminist Struggle*, Oakland, CA: PM Press/Autonomedia, 2012, pp.15-22.

27   Silvia Federici, 'The Reproduction of Labor Power in the Global Economy and the Unfinished Feminist Revolution' (2008), in *ibid.*, p.99.

28   Louise Toupin interview with Silvia Federici in *Wages for Housework: A History of an International Feminist Movement*, London: Pluto Press, 2018, p.242. The importance of Federici's exchange with German scholar Maria Mies for her mature work should also be noted here.

29   Kerstin Stakemeier and Marina Vishmidt, 'Reproducing Autonomy', in *Reproducing Autonomy: Work, Money, Crisis and Contemporary Art*, London: Mute Publishing, 2016, pp.56-55.

30   For instance, the cleaning interventions by the ASK! (Actie Schone Kunsten) collective as part of Casco's 'living research' *Grand Domestic Revolution*.

31   Françoise Vergès. 'Capitalocene, Waste, Race, and Gender', in *e-flux journal*, no.100, May 2019, available at https://www.e-flux.com/journal/100/269165/capitalocene-waste-race-and-gender/ (last accessed on 19 September 2020).

PLATES

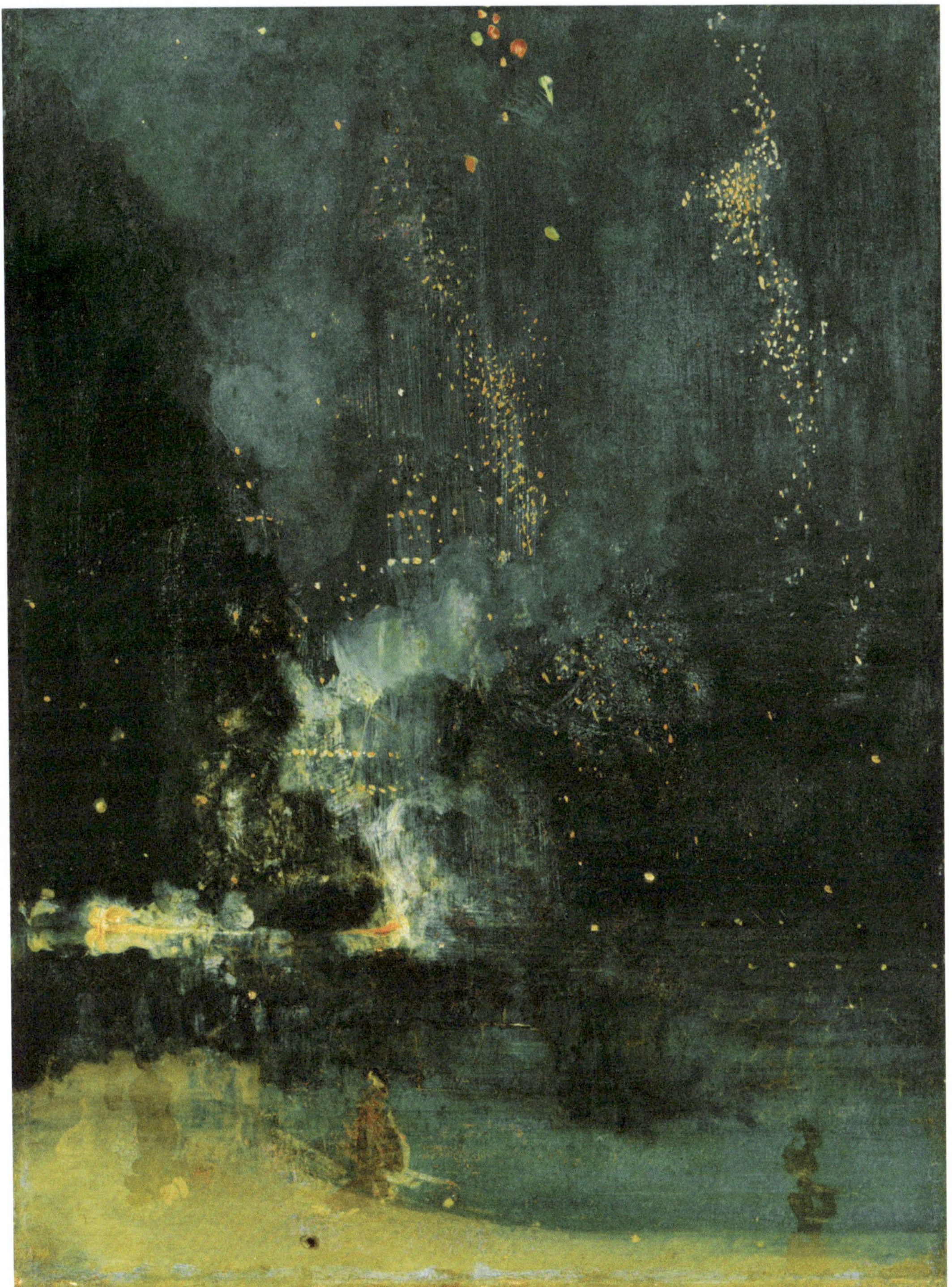

James Abbott McNeill Whistler,
Nocturne in Black and Gold, the Falling Rocket, 1875,
oil on panel, 60.3 × 46.7cm
Courtesy Detroit Institute of Arts

See pp.120-21 of this reader for a discussion of
John Ruskin's criticisms of this painting

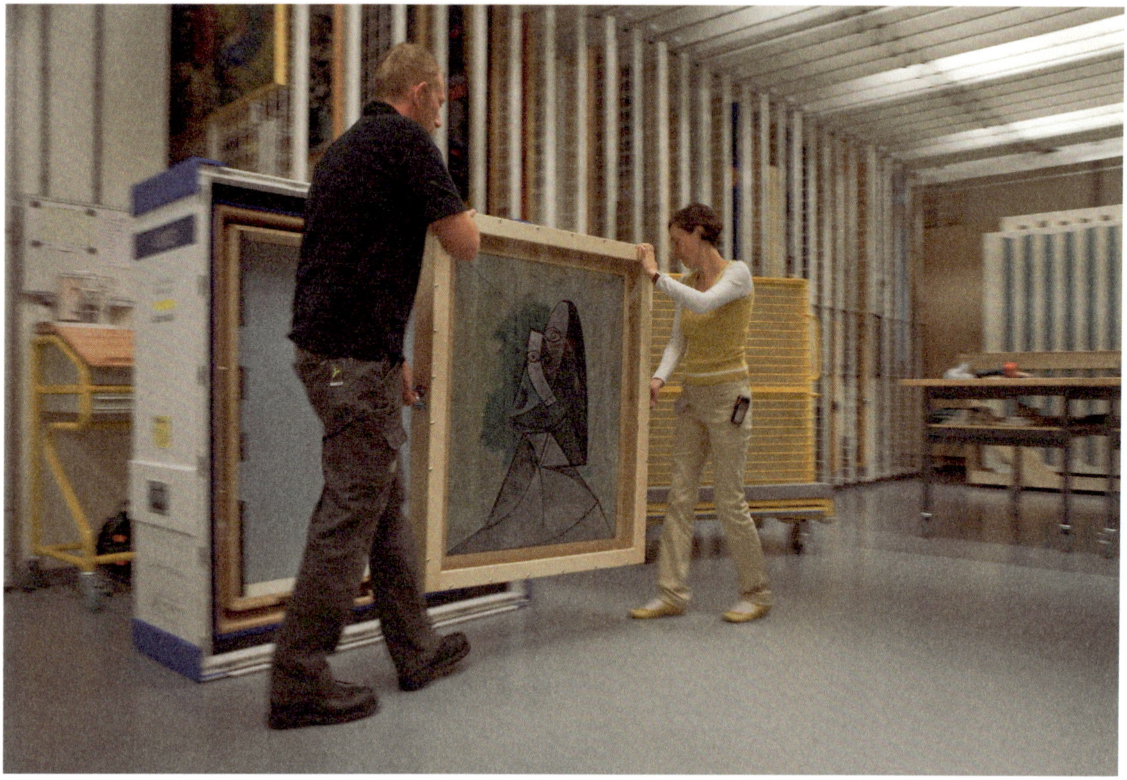

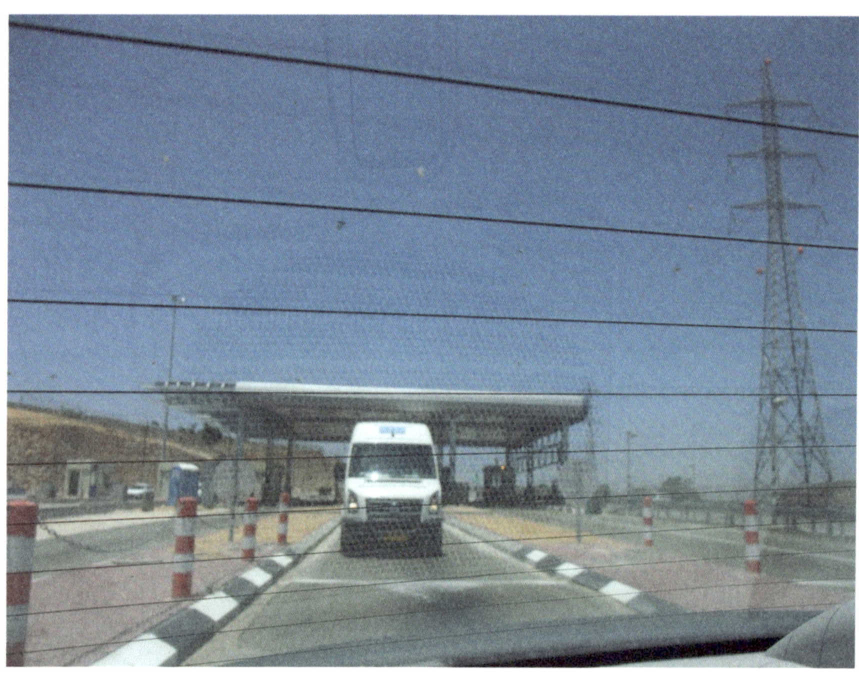

Various views,
Picasso in Palestine, 2011,
showing the preparation,
transportation of Pablo
Picasso's *Buste de Femme*,
1943, from the Van
Abbemuseum, Eindhoven
to its exhibition at the
International Art Academy
Palestine, Ramallah
Photo: Perry van Duijnhoven
(above), Khaled Jarrar (left
and opposite page, below)
and Sander Buyck (opposite
page, above)
Courtesy Van Abbemuseum,
Eindhoven

See p.21 of this reader for
a discussion of *Picasso in
Palestine*

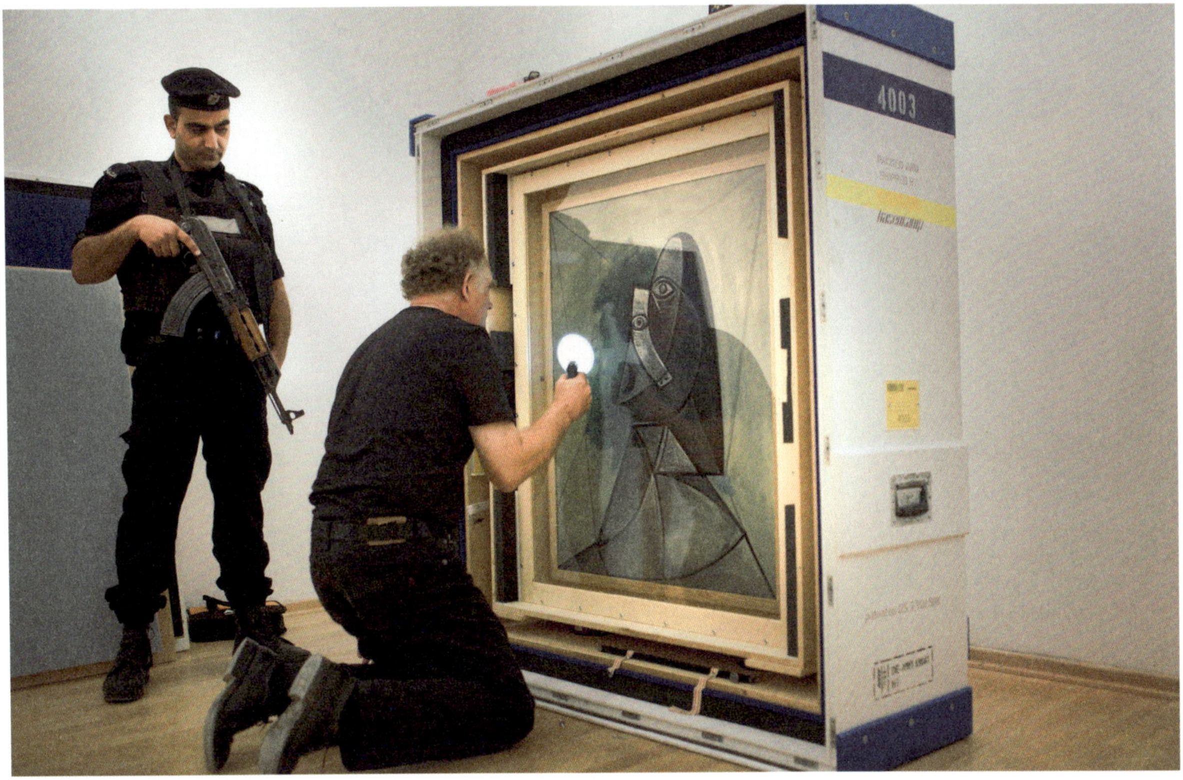

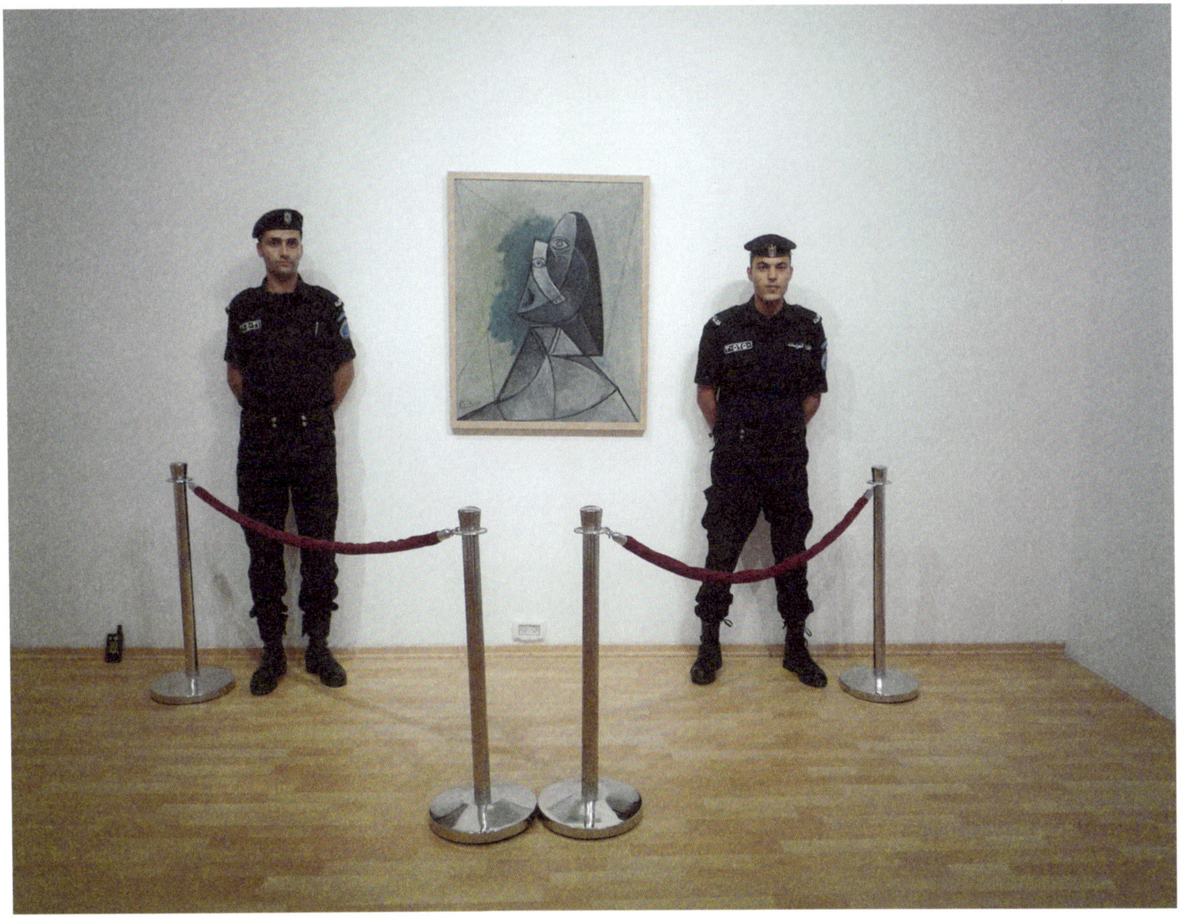

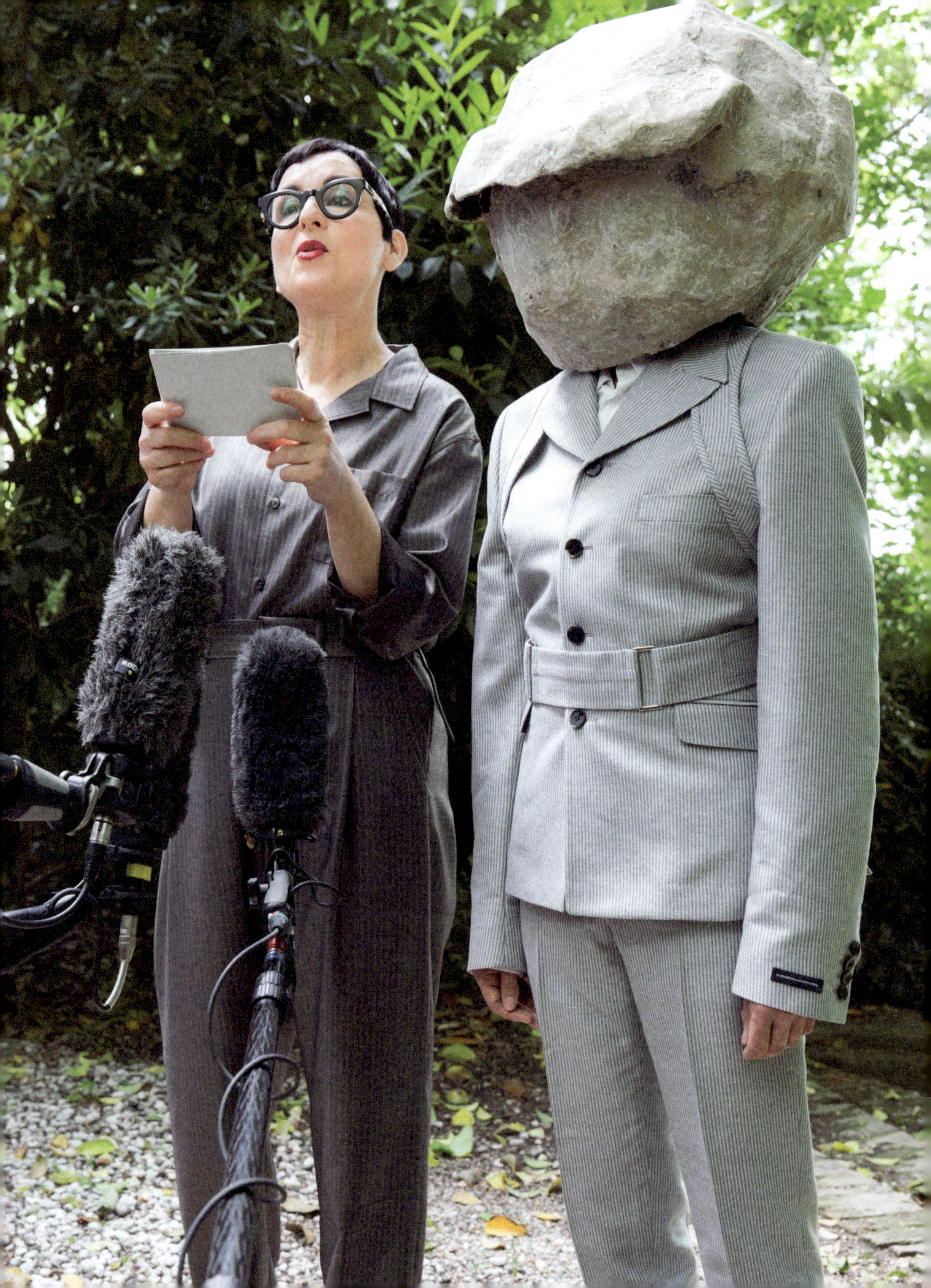

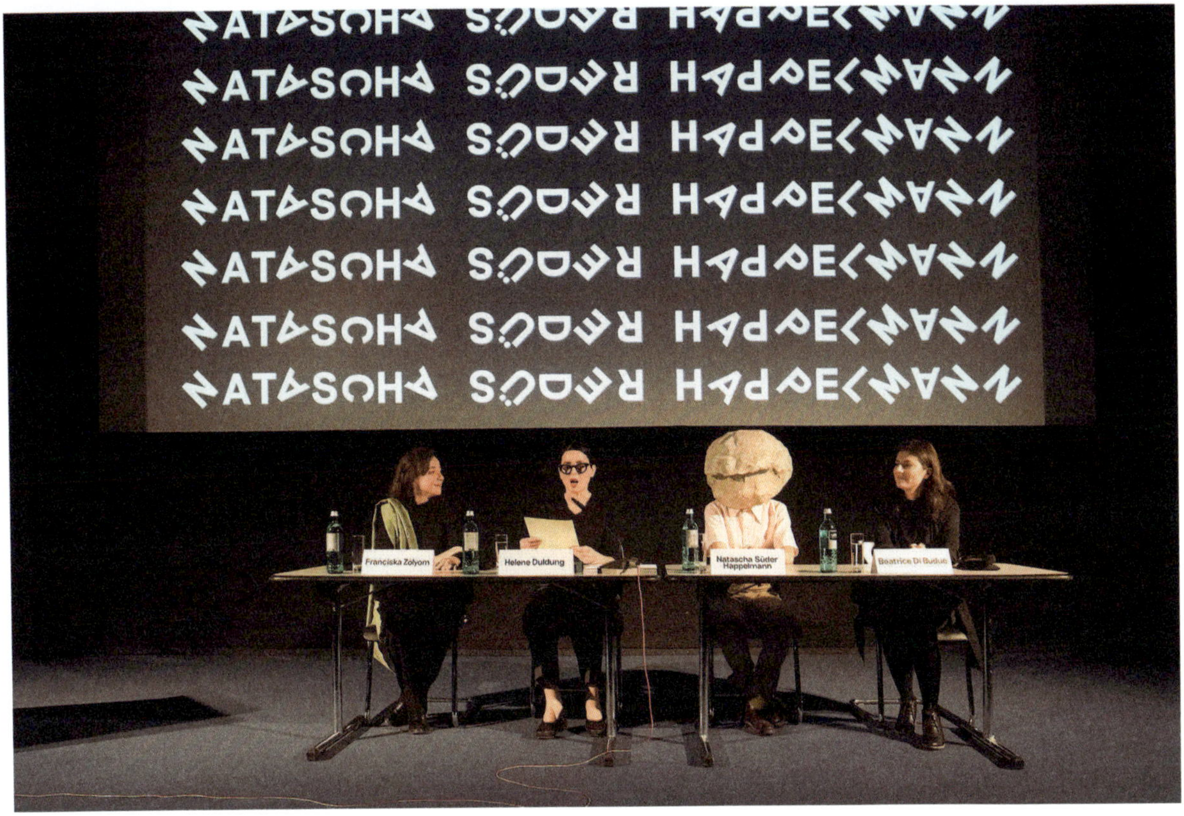

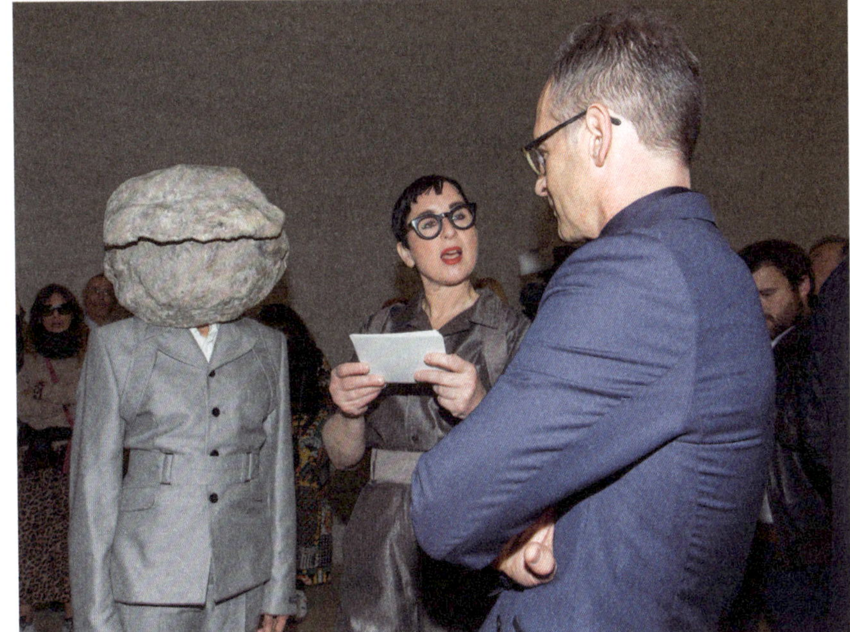

Helene Duldung and others at opening of presentation by Natascha Süder Happelmann (pseudonym of Natascha Sadr Haghighian), German Pavilion, 58th Venice Biennale, 2019
Photo: Jasper Kettner
Courtesy Natascha Sadr Haghighian and Galerie für Zeitgenössische Kunst, Leipzig

See pp.262-63 of this reader for more images and pp.348-50 for Natascha Sadr Haghighian, 'Dear Artfukts, Look at My Curve'

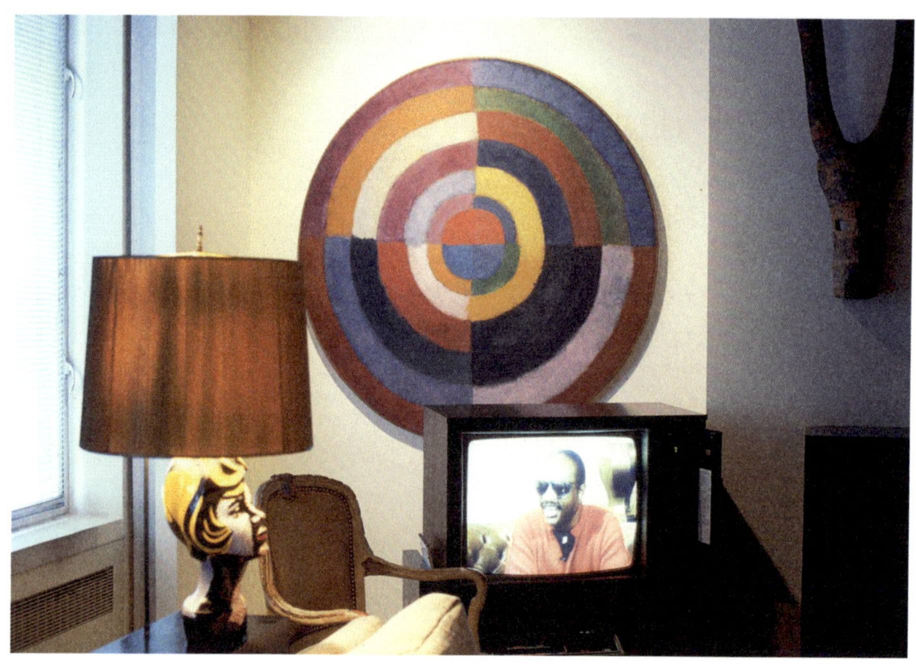

Louise Lawler,
(Stevie Wonder) Living Room Corner, Arranged by Mr. & Mrs. Burton Tremaine Sr., New York City (detail), 1984/1985, silver dye bleach print with title as text on mat, 46.4 × 60.3cm

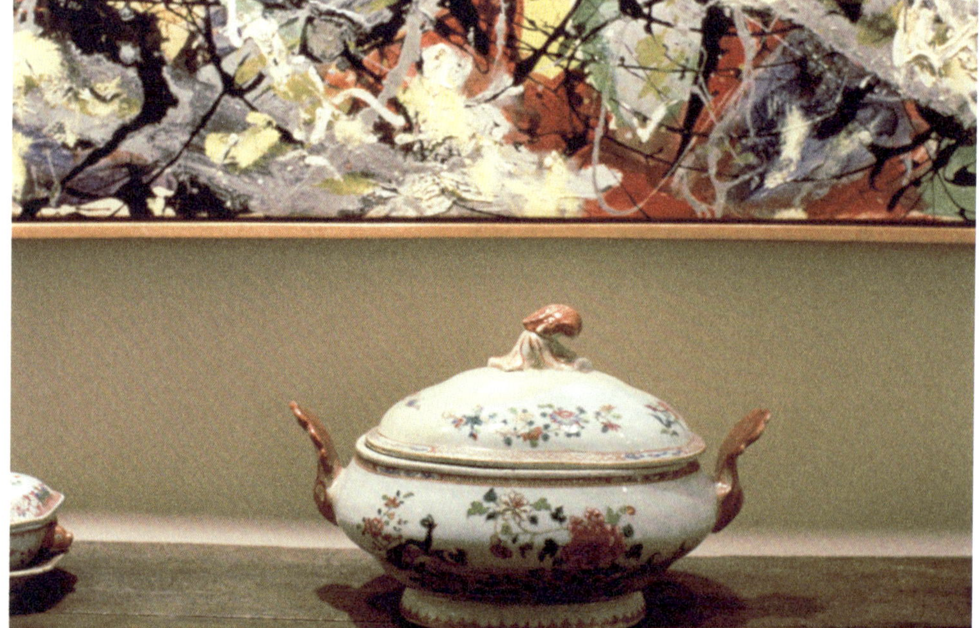

Louise Lawler,
Pollock and Tureen, 1984, silver dye bleach print, 71.1 × 99.1cm

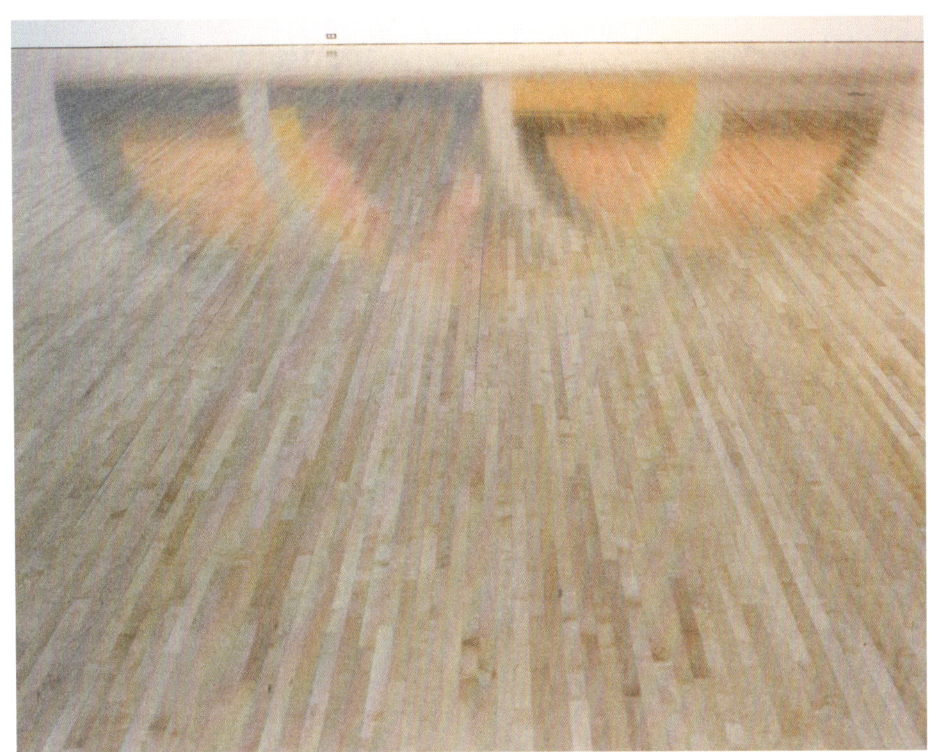

Louise Lawler,
How Many Pictures, 1989,
silver dye bleach print,
122.1 × 157.2cm

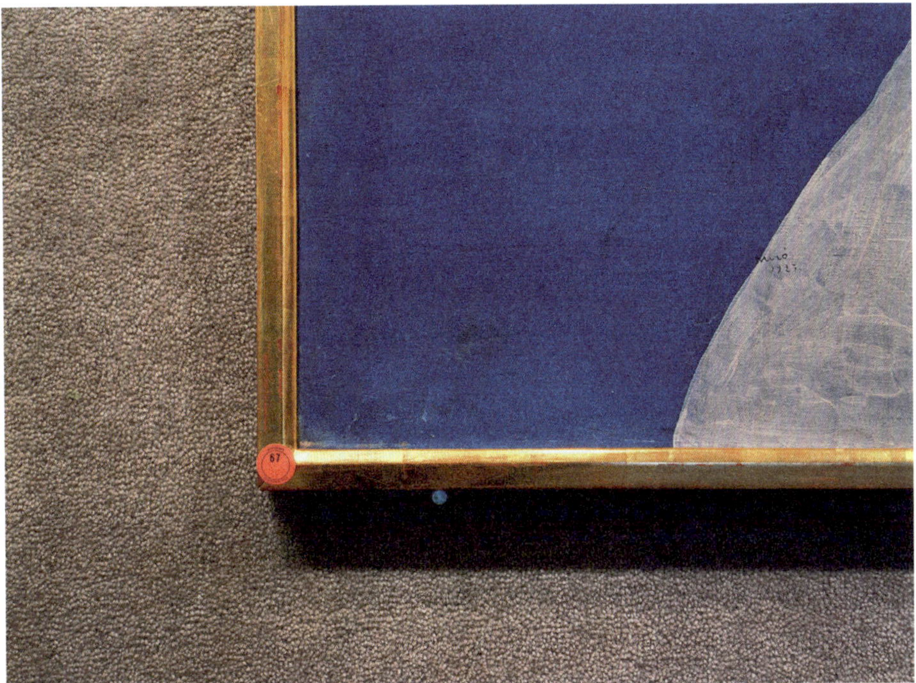

Louise Lawler,
Blue Nail, 1990,
silver dye bleach print,
101.6 × 127cm

All images courtesy the
artist and Sprüth Magers

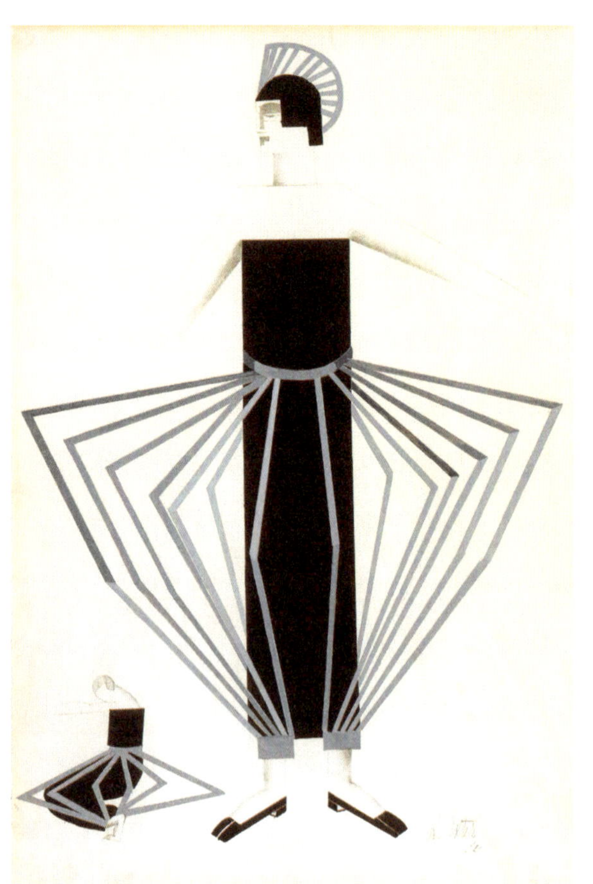

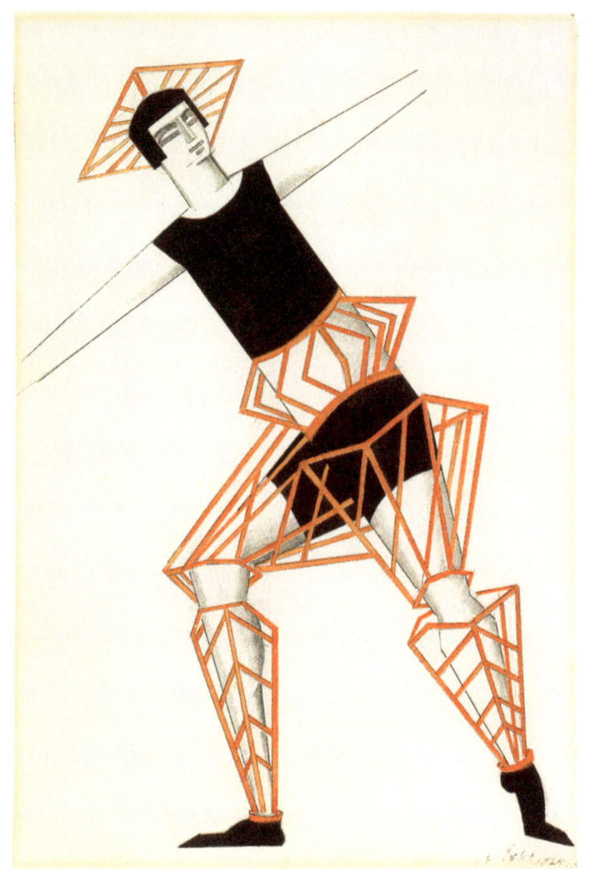

Above: Alexandra Exter,
costume designs for
Aelita: Queen of Mars, 1924,
goauche, ink and graphite on paper
Courtesy McNay Art Museum

Right: Liubov Popova, cover for
fashion magazine *Leto*, 1924,
collage and gouache on paper

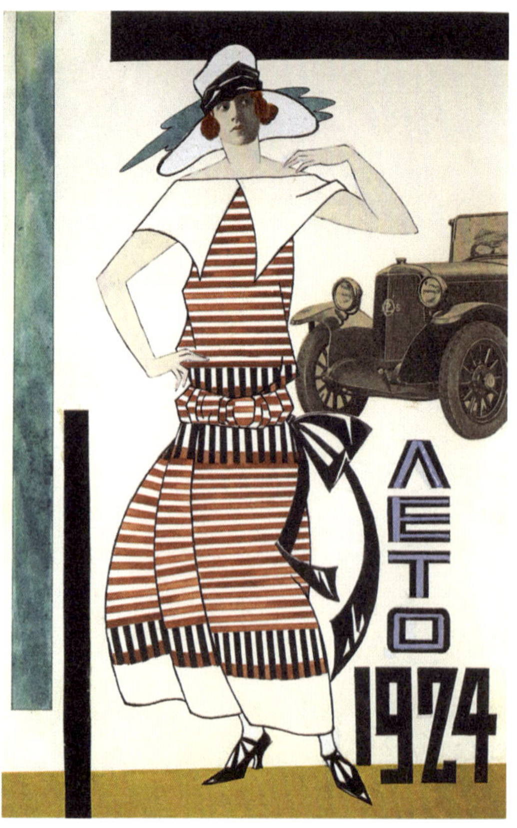

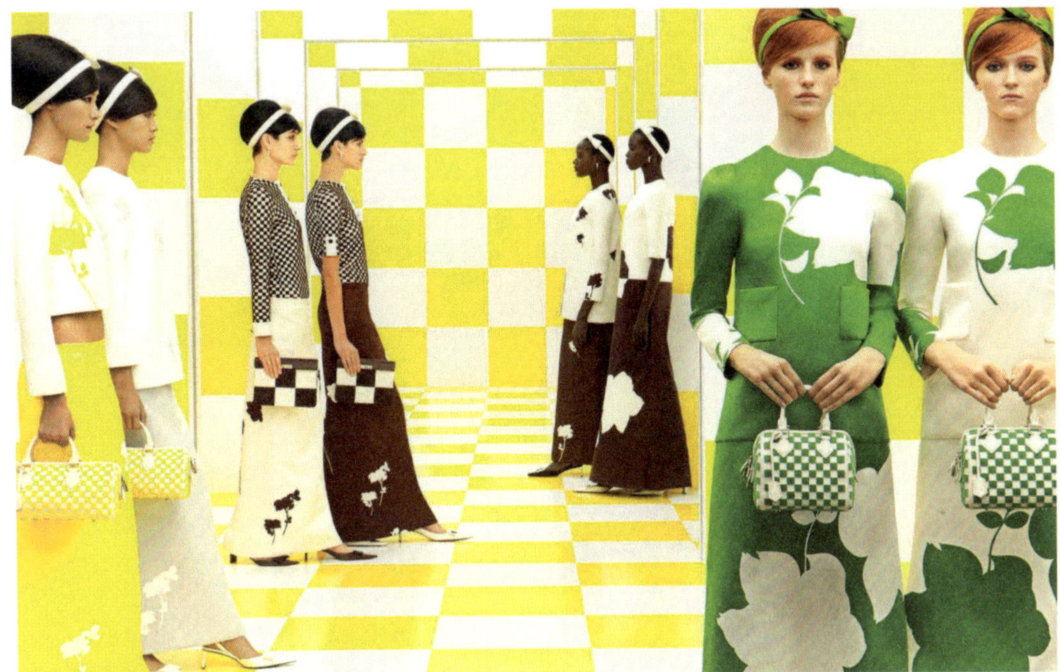

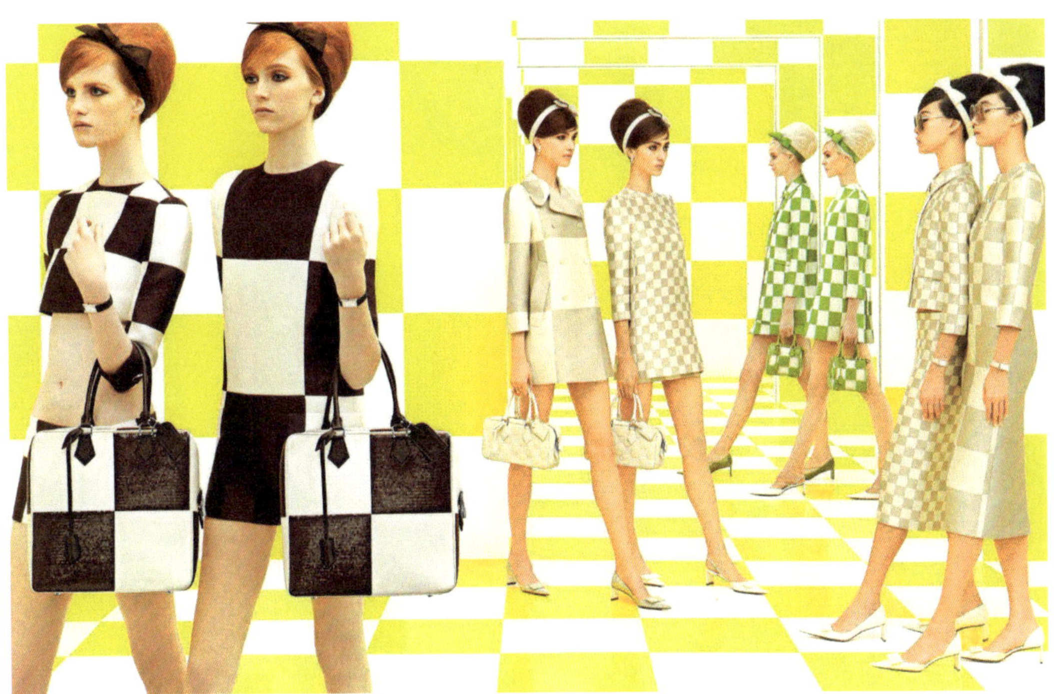

Louis Vuitton advertising campaign, Spring 2013, featuring set design by Daniel Buren

See pp.179-92 of this reader for Daniel Buren, 'Critical Limits'

See pp.239–40 of this reader for Alice
Creischer and Andreas Siekmann,
Interview with Imma Harms

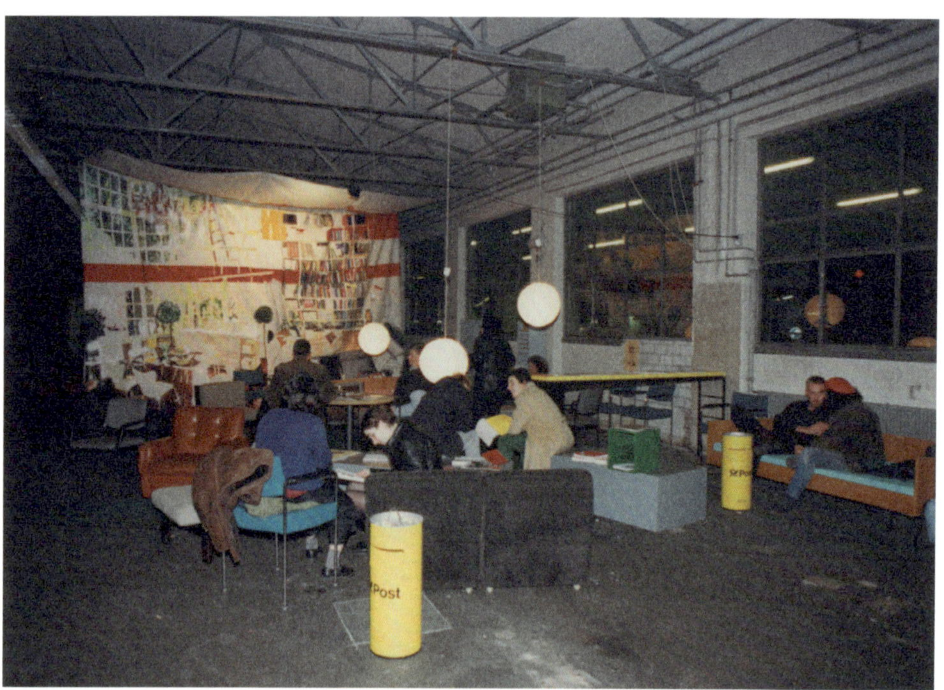

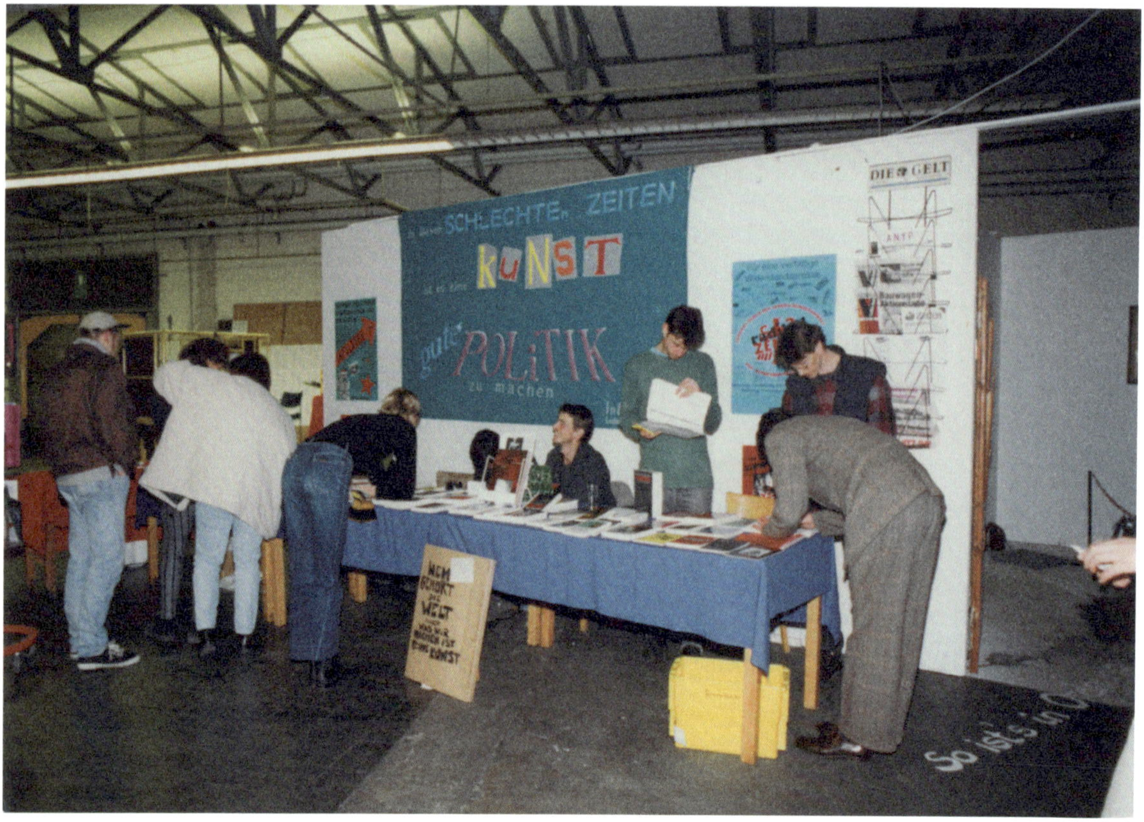

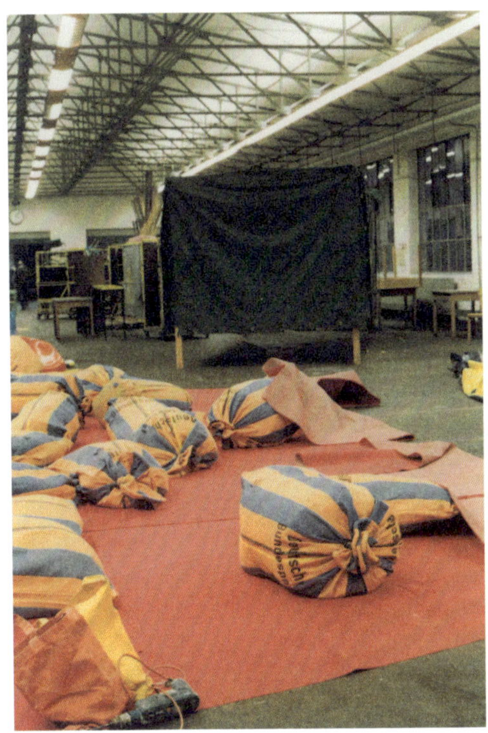

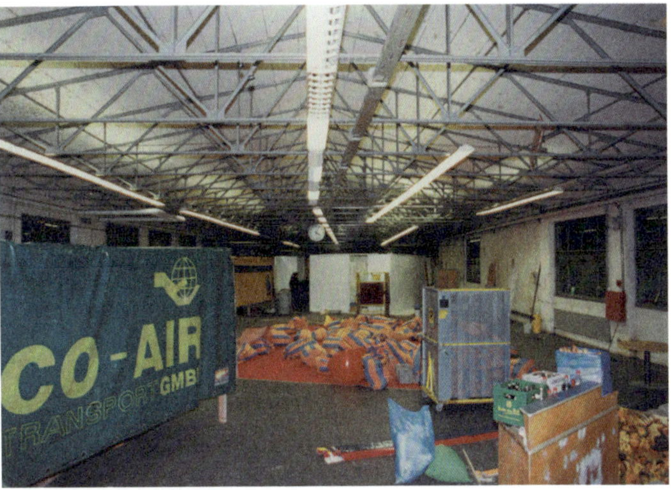

CO - AIR
TRANSPORT GMBH

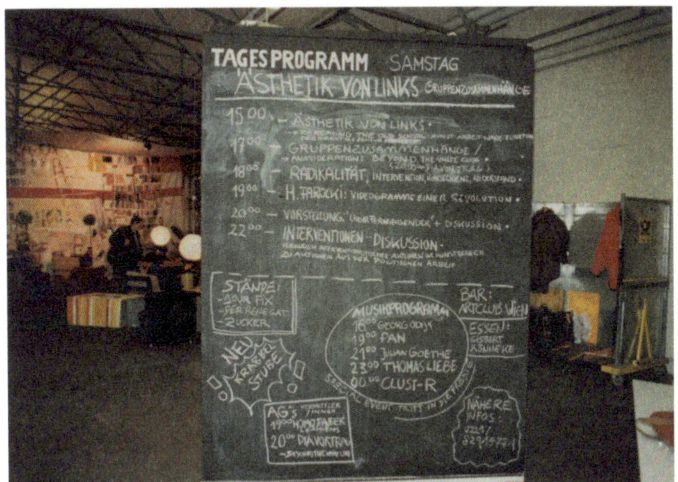

TAGESPROGRAMM   SAMSTAG
ÄSTHETIK VON LINKS GRUPPENZUSAMMENHÄNGE
15.00 — ÄSTHETIK VON LINKS
17.00 — GRUPPENZUSAMMENHÄNGE /
18.00 — RADIKALITÄT, INTERVENTION, KONSEQUENZ, WIDERSTAND
19.00 — H. FAROCKI: VIDEOGRAMME EINER REVOLUTION
20.00 — VORSTELLUNG: "UNDERGROUND" + DISKUSSION
22.00 — INTERVENTIONEN - DISKUSSION -
STÄNDE:
BAR:
ARTCLUB WIEN
MUSIKPROGRAMM
16.00 GEORG ODIJK
19.00 PAN
21.00 JUAN GOETHE
23.00 THOMAS LIEBE
00.00 CLUST-R
ESSEN:
GISBERT KÖNNEKE
NEU KRANKEL STUBE
AG's
DIAVORTRAG
NÄHERE INFOS:

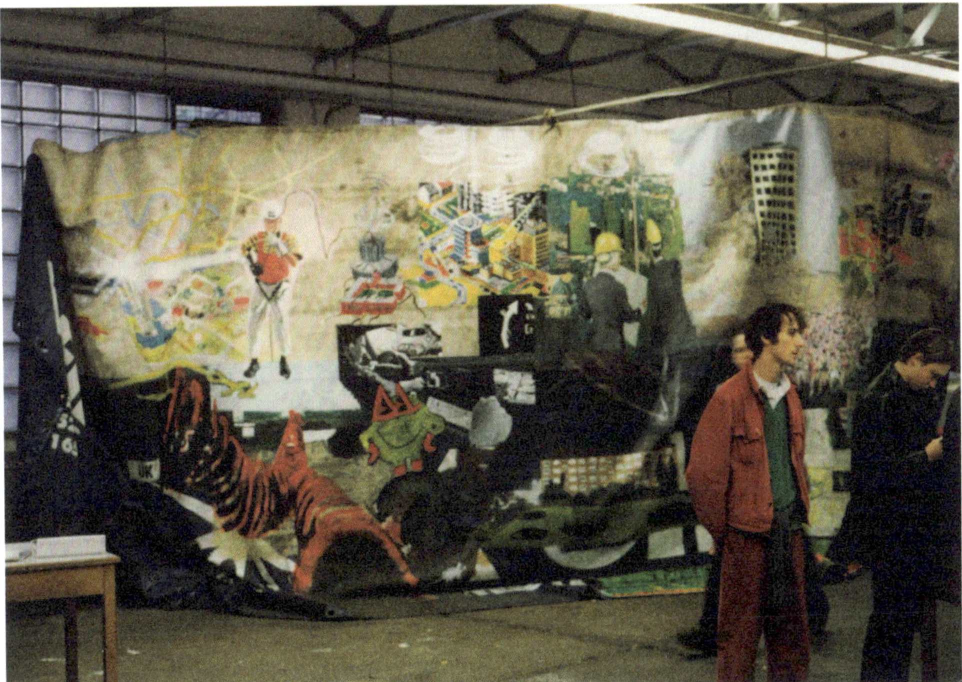

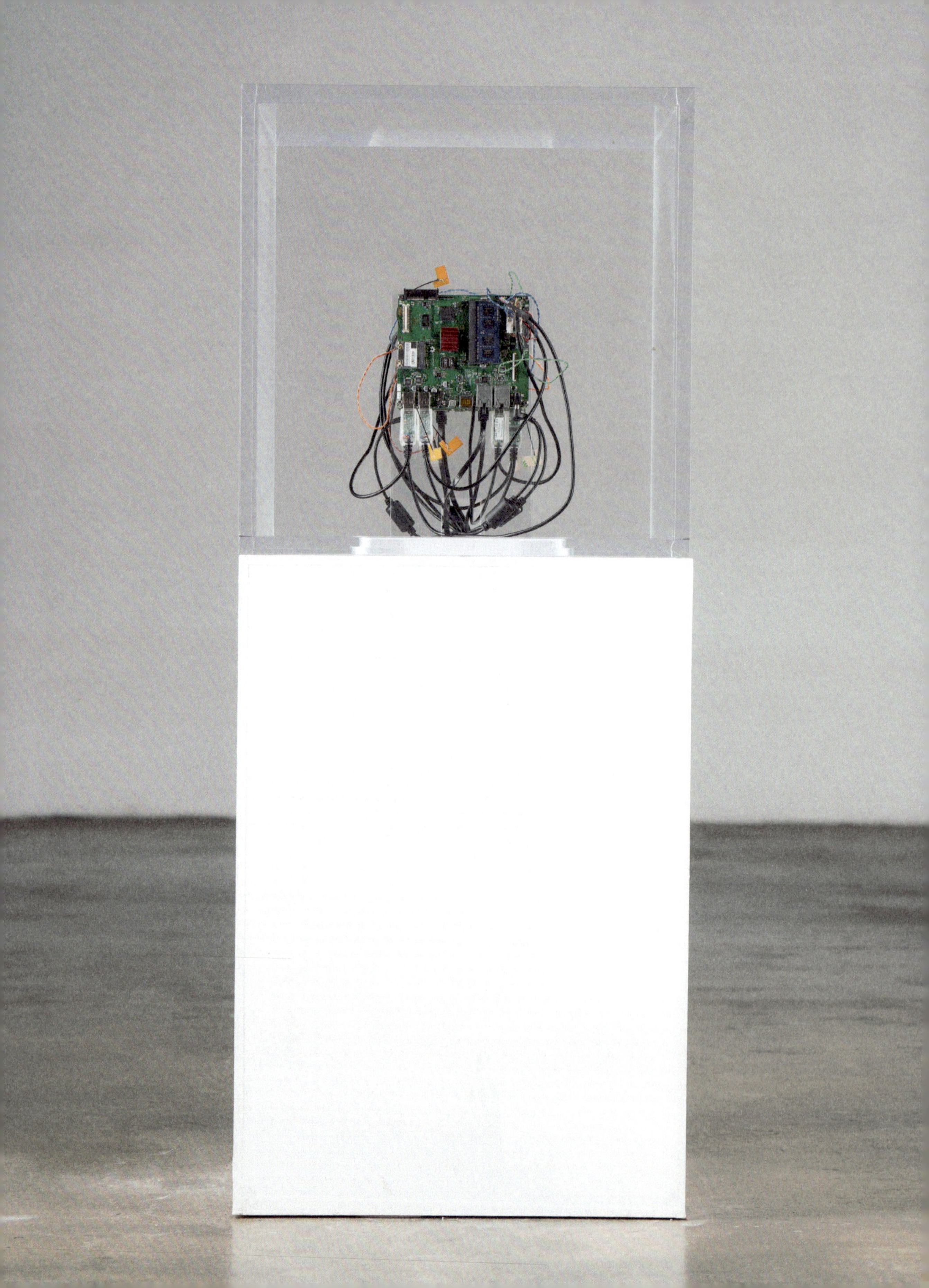

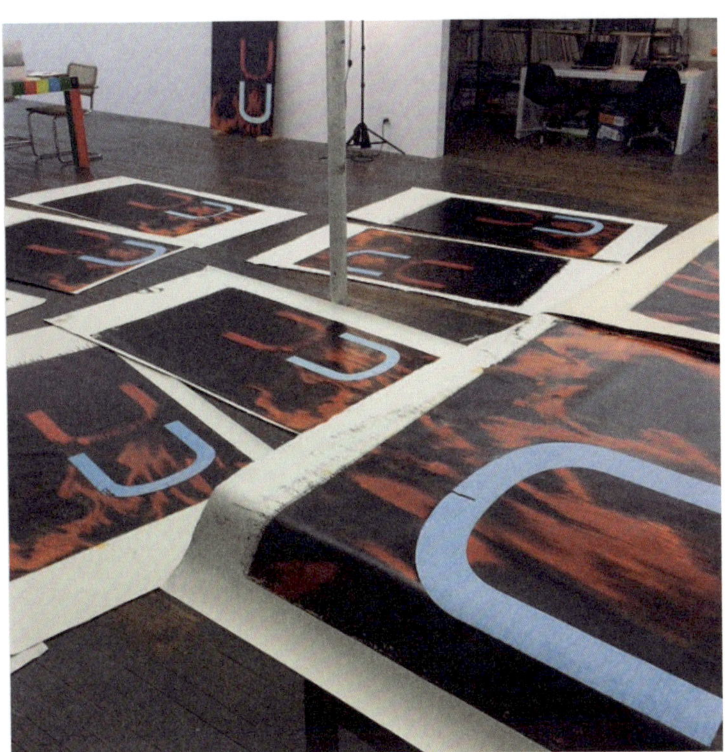

Above: Instagram post by
Wade Guyton (using the
moniker burningbridges38),
8 May 2014

Below: Wade Guyton,
Untitled, 2005,
Epson UltraChrome inkjet
on linen, 142.2 × 91.4cm

Both images courtesy the artist
and Petzel, New York

See pp.290-91 of this reader for a
discussion of this intervention

Opposite page:
Trevor Paglen, *Autonomy Cube*, 2015,
Plexiglass cube, computer components,
49.8 × 49.8 × 49.8cm
Courtesy the artist

See p.346 of this reader for a discussion
of *Autonomy Cube*

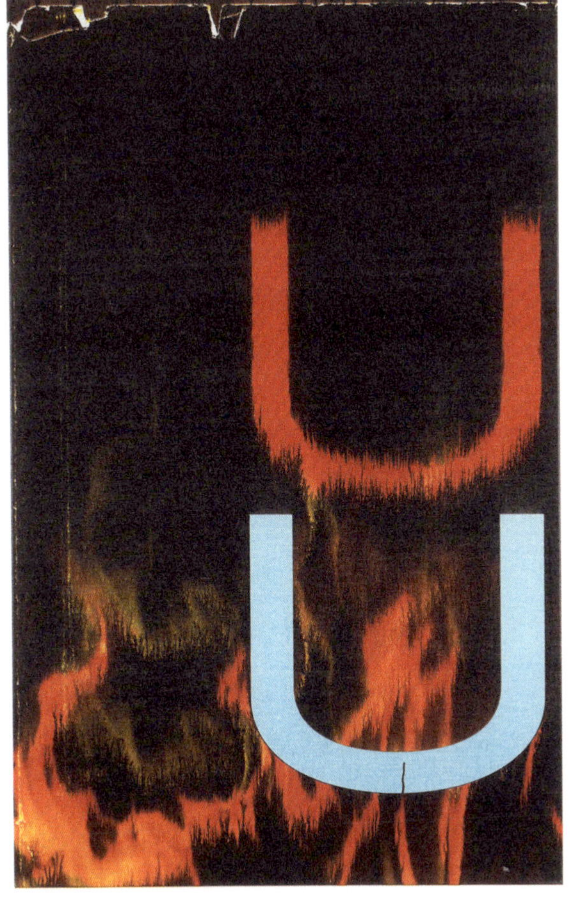

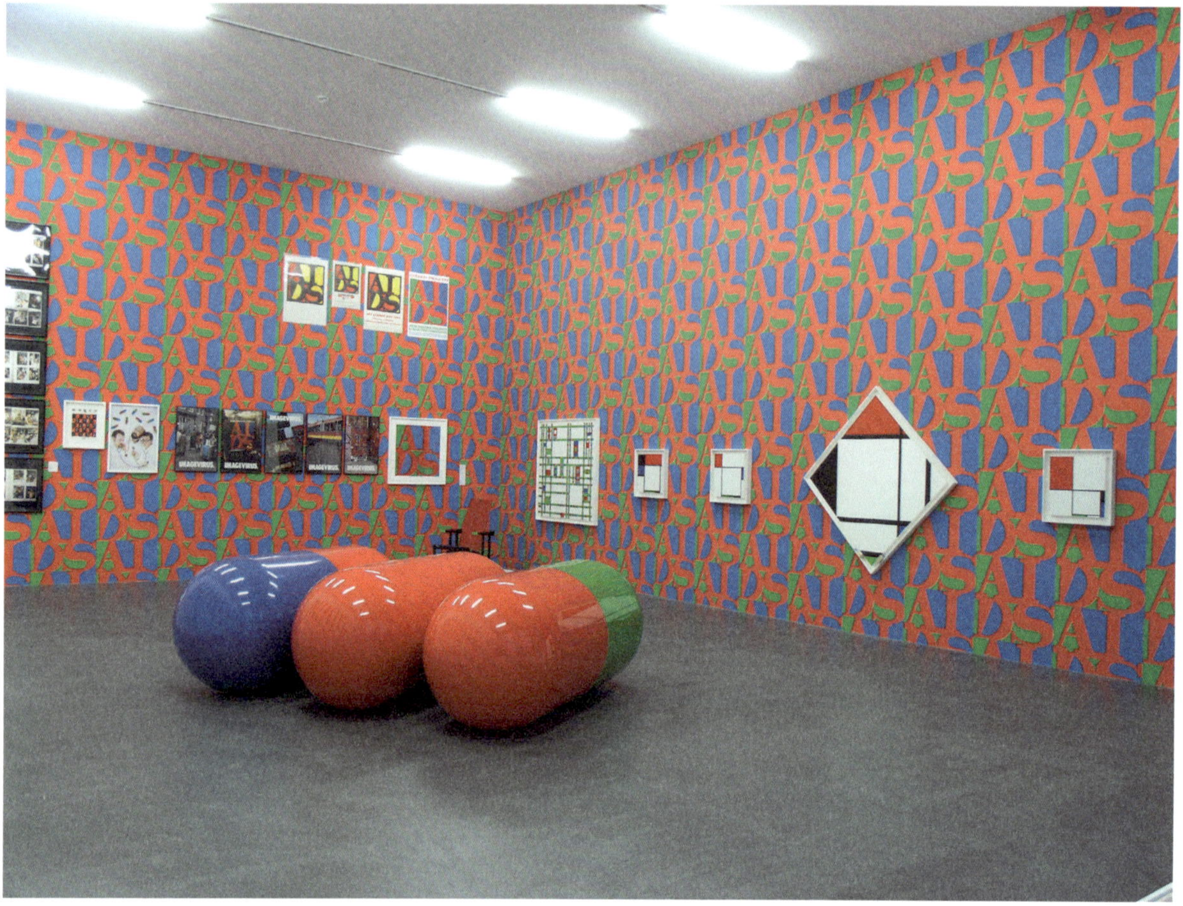

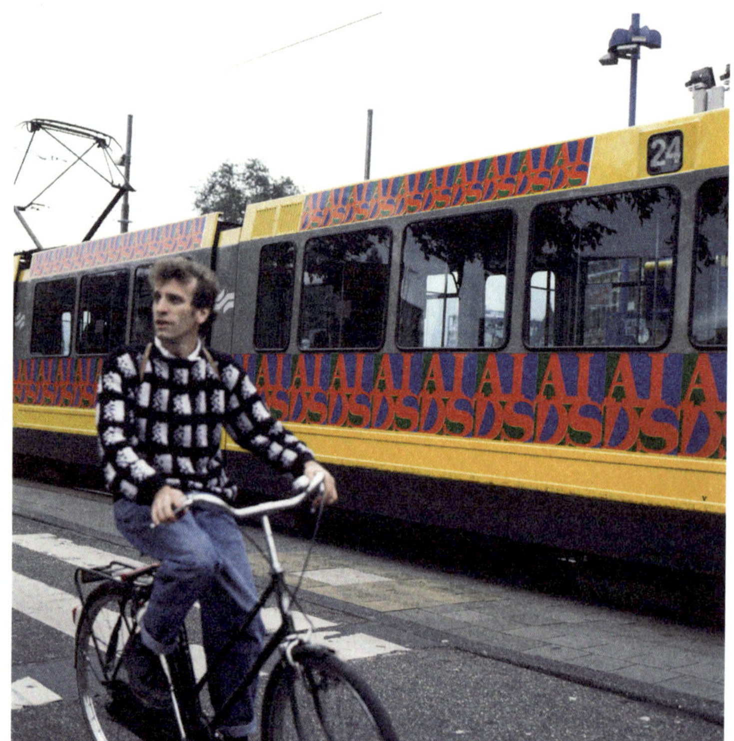

Above: Installation view,
General Idea,
AIDS Wallpaper, 1990, *Infe©ted
Mondrian* and *Infe©ted Rietveld*,
Kunsthalle Zürich, 2006
Photo: Stefan Altenberger
Courtesy the artists and Kunsthalle
Zürich

Below: General Idea, *AIDS*, 1990,
silkscreened vinyl affixed to
Amsterdam tram as part of the
conference 'Art Meets Science and
Spirituality in a Changing Economy',
Stedelijk Museum
Courtesy the artists

Above: General Idea, *Imagevirus (Hamburg)*, 1991, chromogenic print, 76 × 50.4cm

Below: General Idea, *Imagevirus (New York Subway)*, 1991, chromogenic print, 76 × 50.4cm

Both images courtesy the artists

See pp.332–33 of this reader for a discussion of General Idea and *Imagevirus*

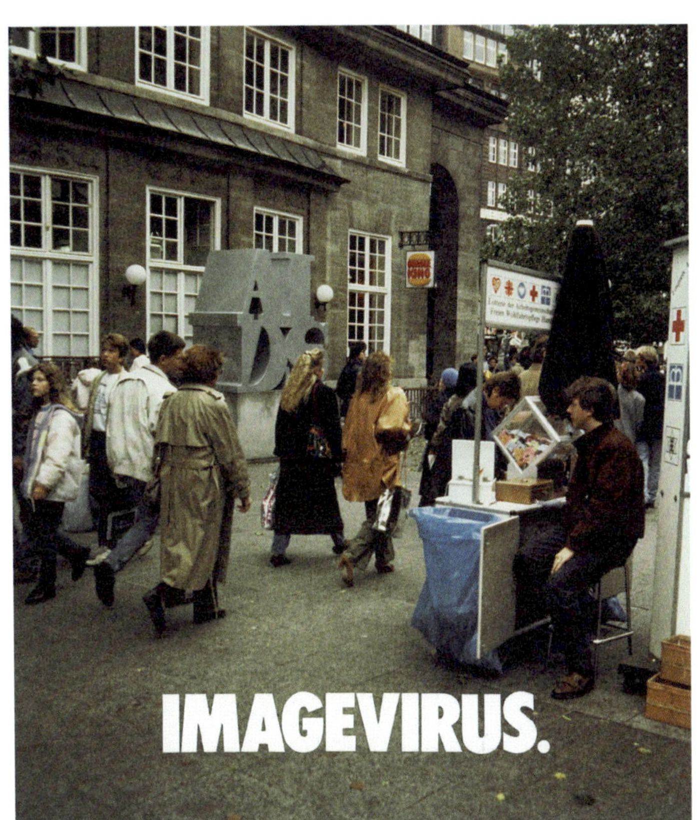

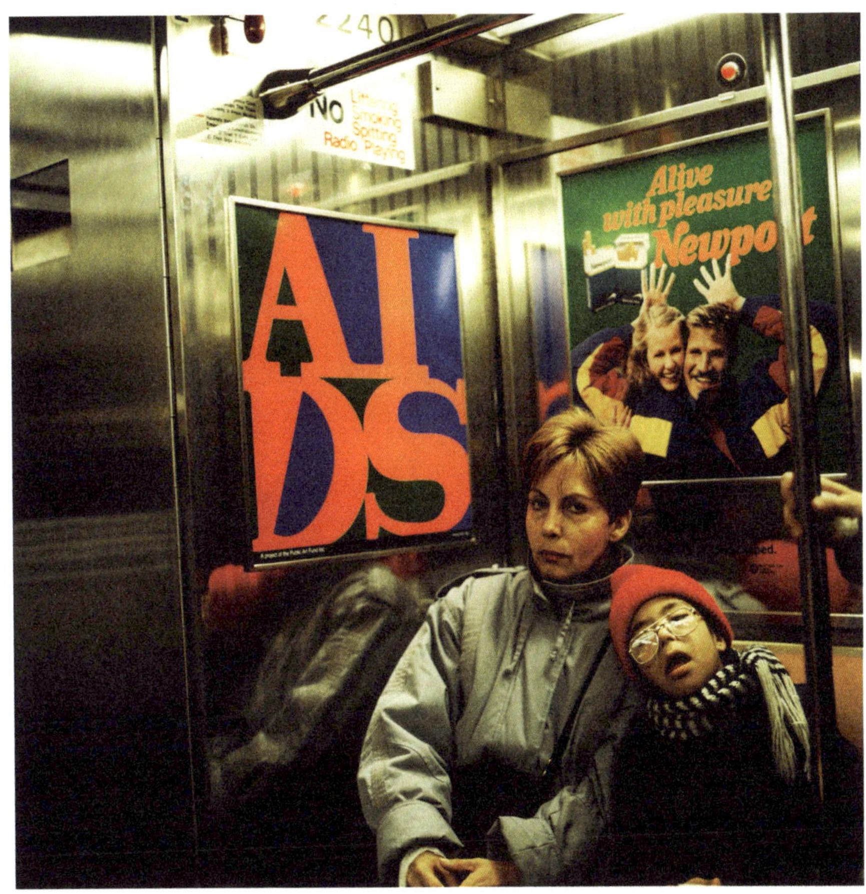

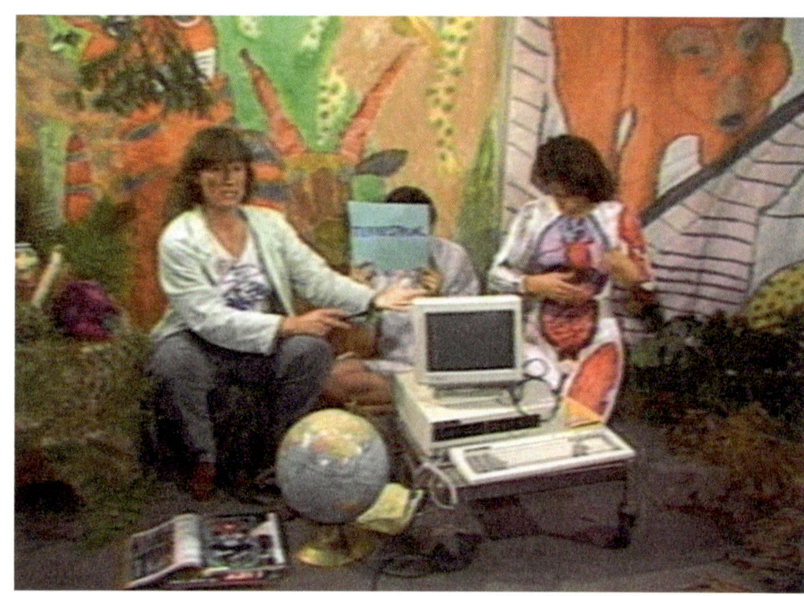

Stills from Donna Haraway
with Paper Tiger Television,
*Donna Haraway Reads 'The
National Geographic' on
Primates*, 1987, colour video
with sound, 28min
Courtesy Paper Tiger Television

See pp.344–46 of this reader
for Donna Haraway, 'A Cyborg
Manifesto'

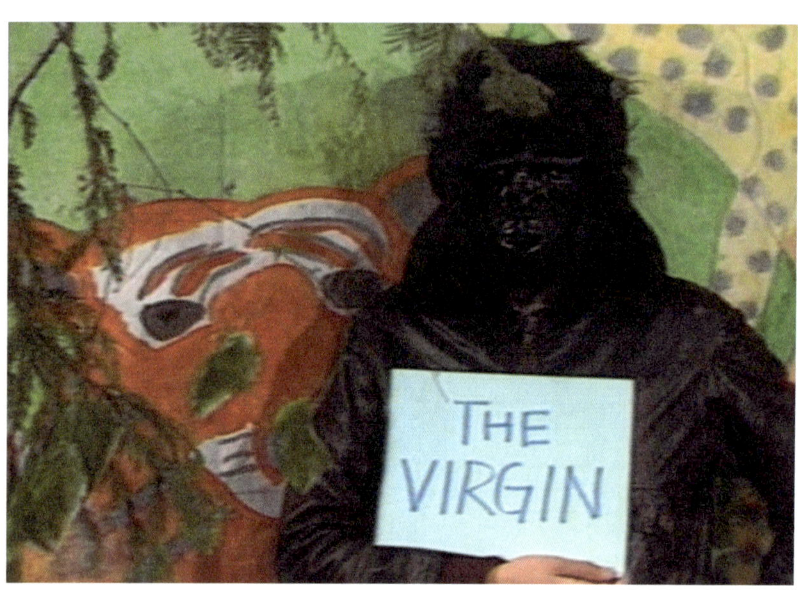

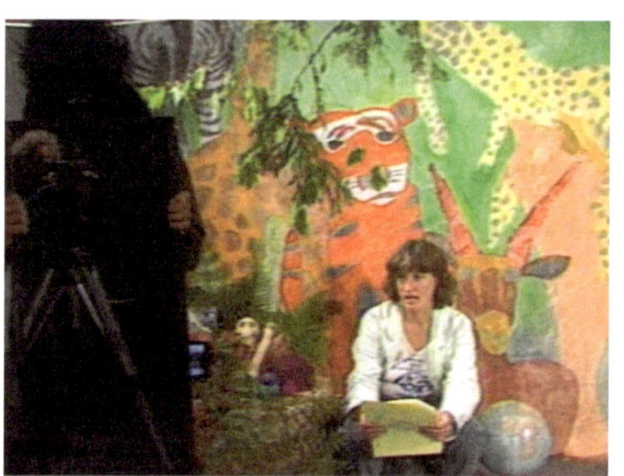

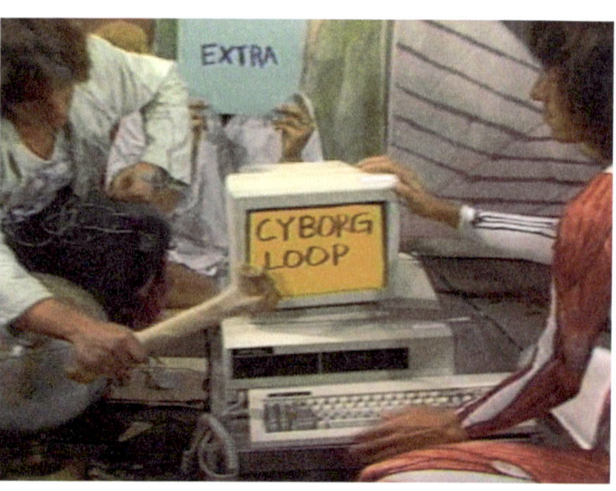

Stills from Nathalie Magnan,
Internautes, 1995,
colour video with sound,
13min

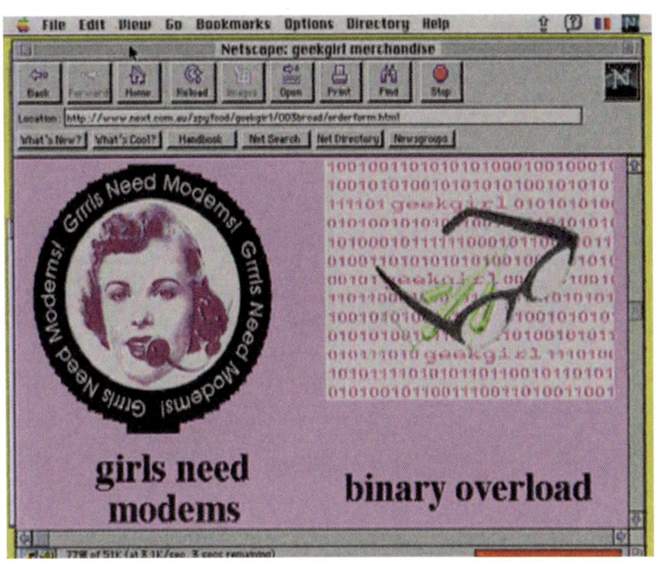

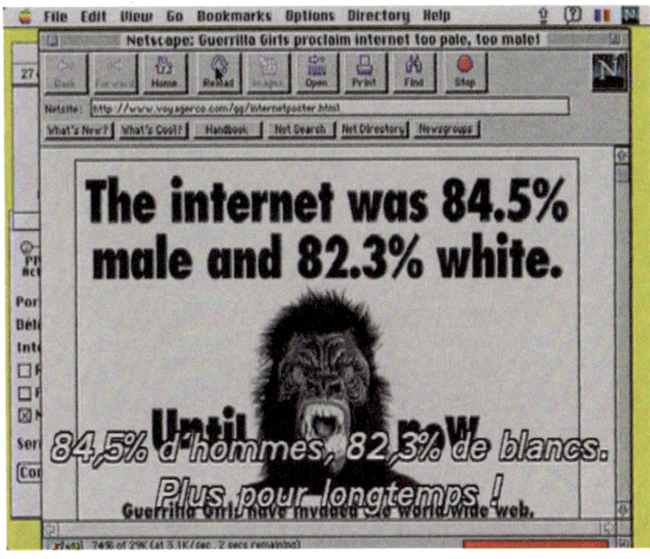

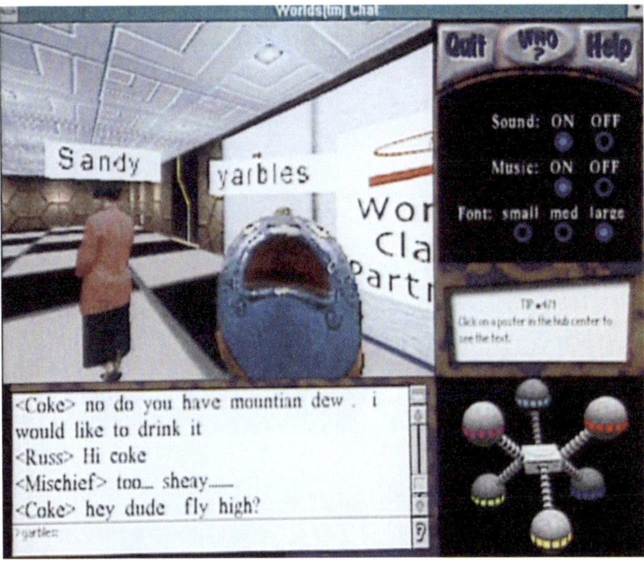

Stills from Martha Rosler with
Paper Tiger Television, *Born to be Sold:
Martha Rosler Reads the Strange Case of
Baby S/M or $M*, 1988,
colour video with sound, 35min
Courtesy Paper Tiger Television

Opposite page: Stills from DIVA TV, *Like a Prayer*,
1990, colour video with sound, 26min
Courtesy DIVA TV/Catherine Gund

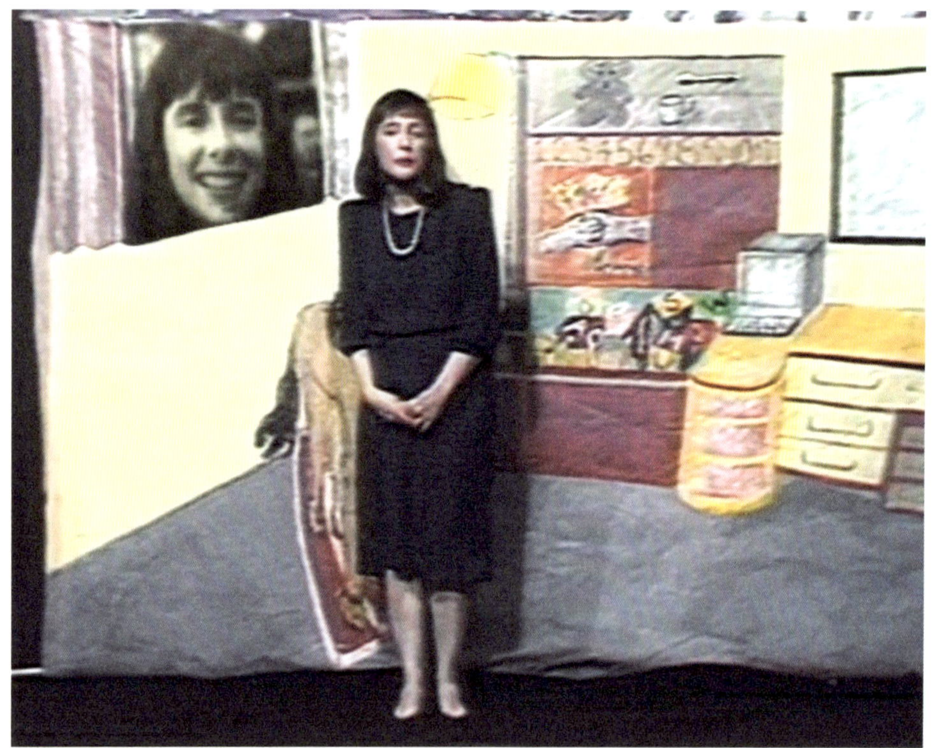

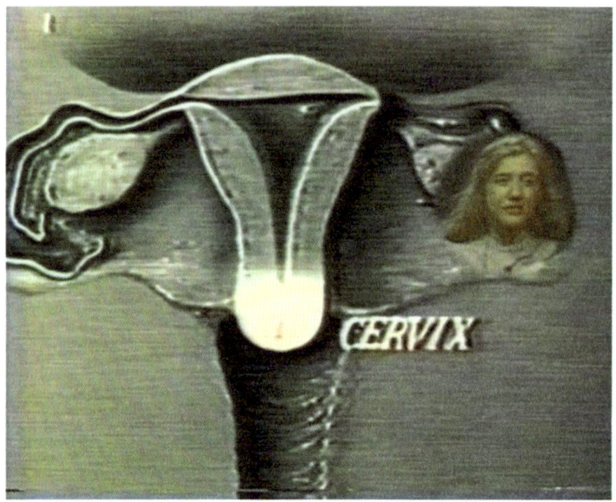

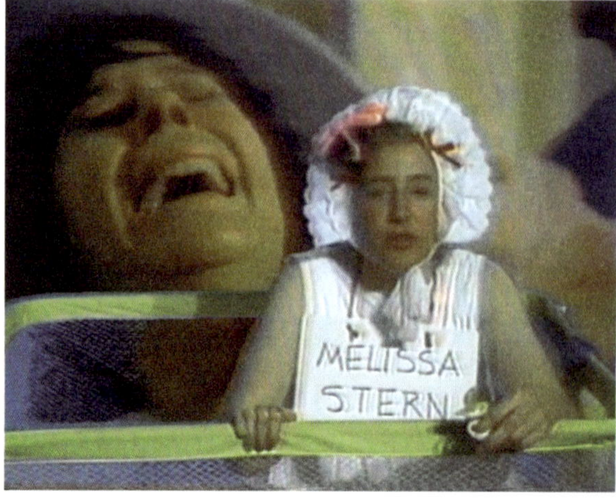

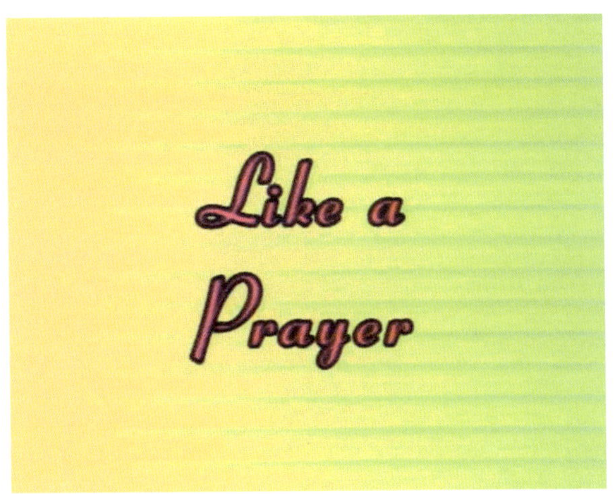

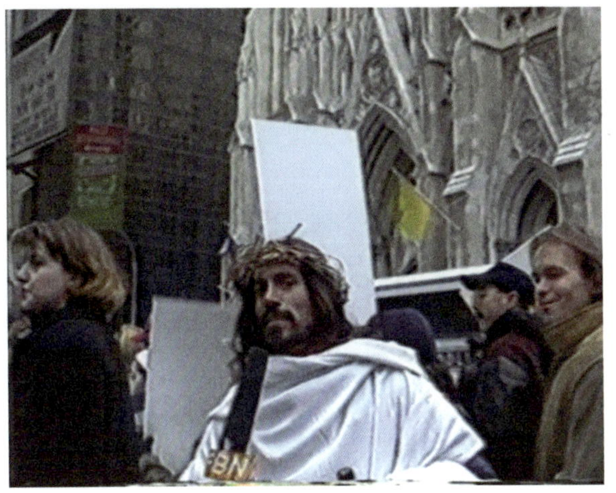

FOR WHAT IT IS:

A POWERFUL, WEALTHY
CORPORATION LOBBYING
TO TURN MORALITY INTO
MEDICINE, AND
RELIGION INTO
POLITICAL POLICY.

THEY CANNOT IMPOSE
THEIR MORALITY ON
PEOPLE WHO DO NOT
SHARE THEIR DOCTRINE.

THIS VIOLATES FREEDOM
OF RELIGION.

CHURCH LEADERSHIP
MUST BE RECOGNIZED

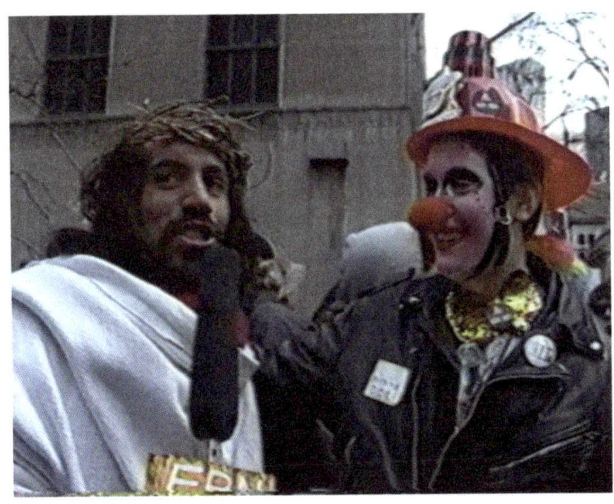

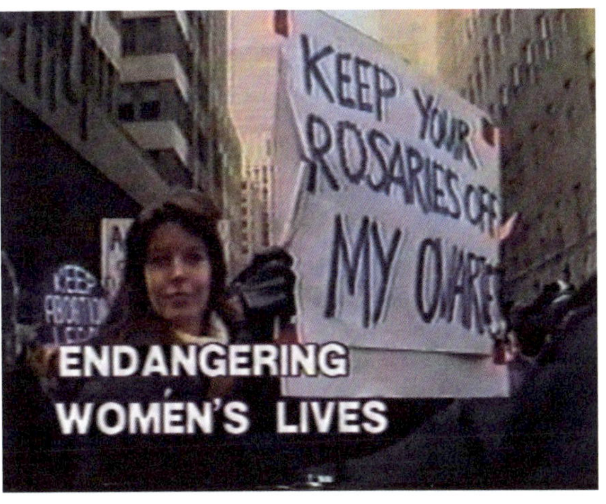

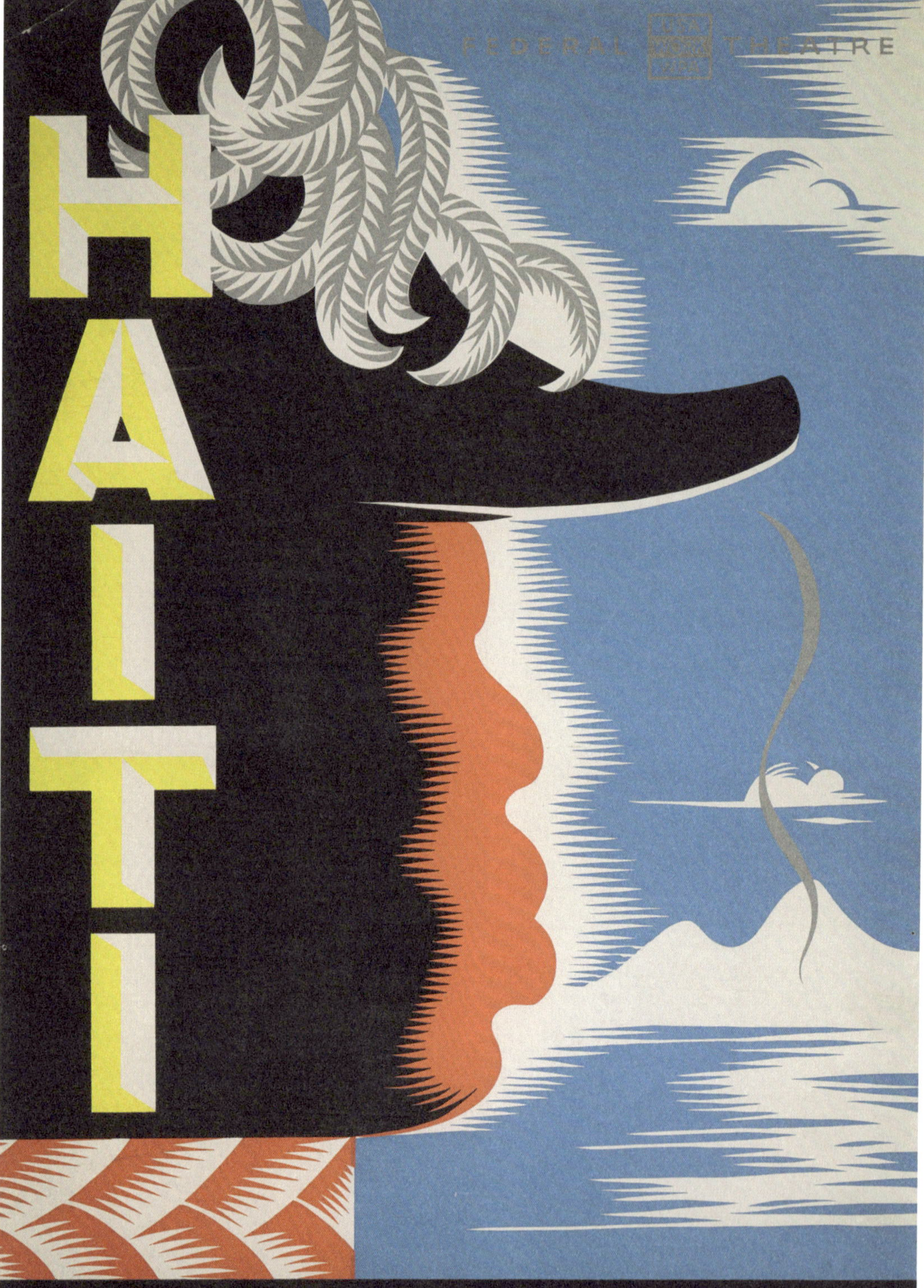

FEDERAL THEATRE
HAITI
A DRAMA OF THE BLACK NAPOLEON
By William Du Bois
LAFAYETTE THEATRE
SEVENTH AVE. AT 131st ST.

Opposite page: Vera Bock,
poster for W.E.B. Du Bois's
*Haiti: A Drama of the Black
Napoleon*, Lafayette Theater,
New York, 1938

Above: Piet Zwart, Untitled
(portrait of Anton de Kom),
1934, photomontage on paper
© DACS 2022
Courtesy Gemeentemuseum
Den Haag

Below: Detail of 100 Guilder note
issued in 1986 by the Central
Bank of Suriname

See pp.367–68 of this reader
for a discussion of Piet Zwart
and Anton de Kom

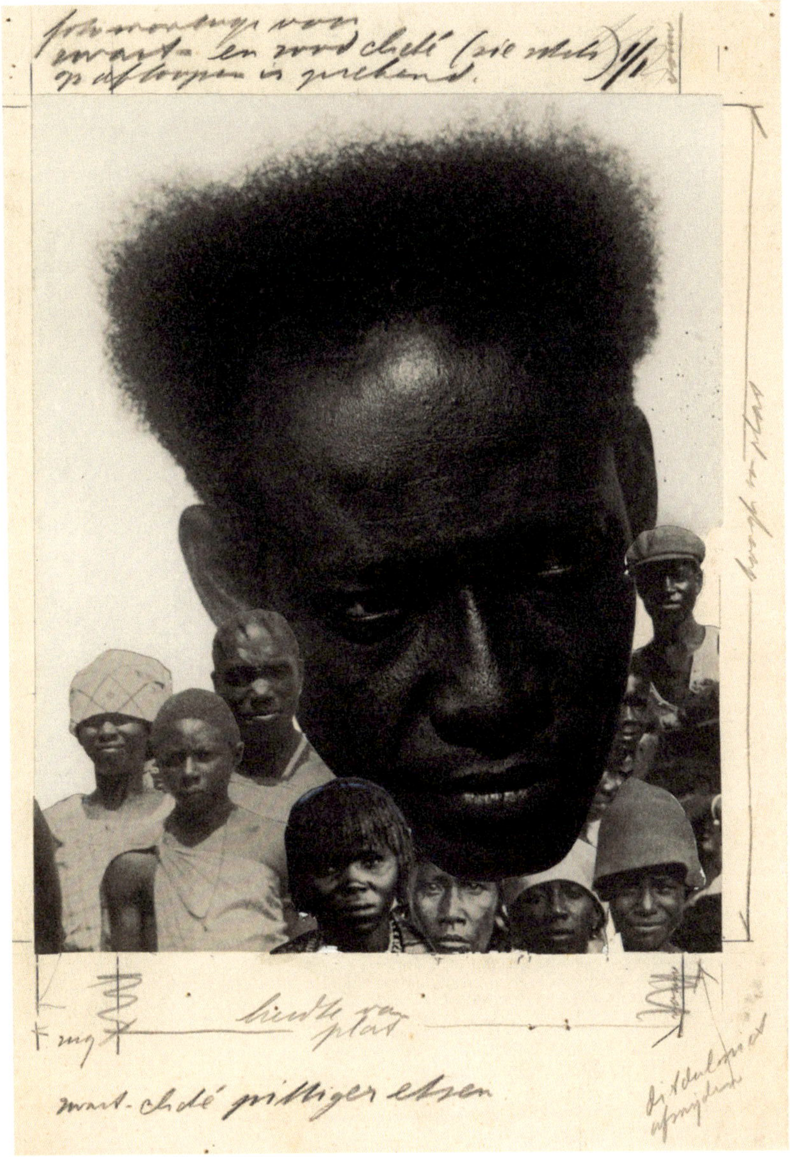

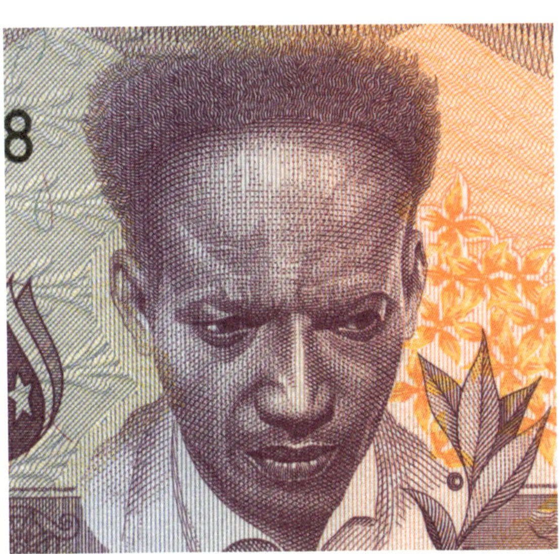

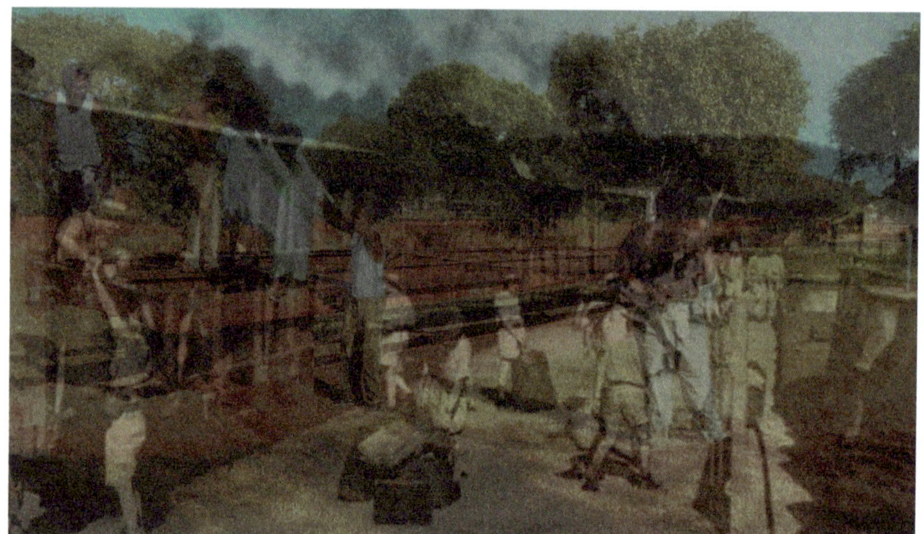

Stills from Karrabing Film Collective, *Night Time Go*, 2017, colour film with sound, 31min

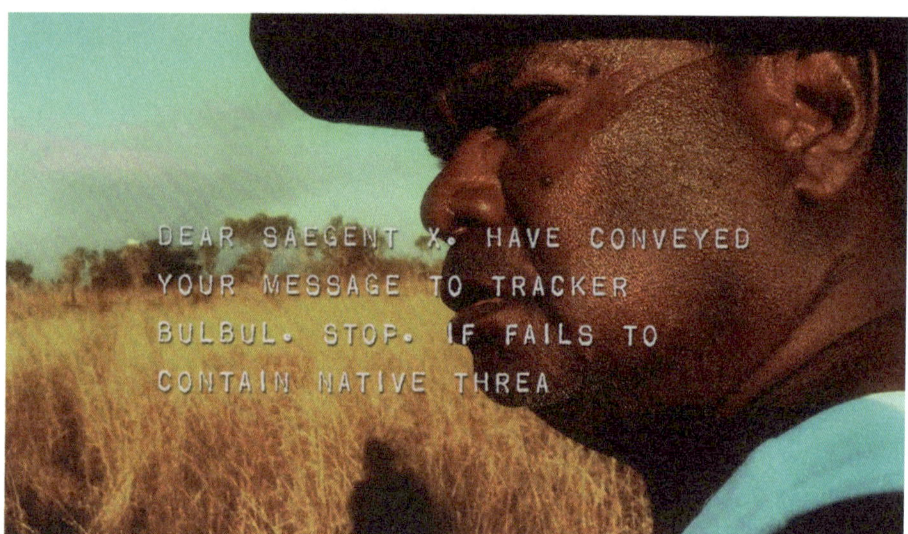

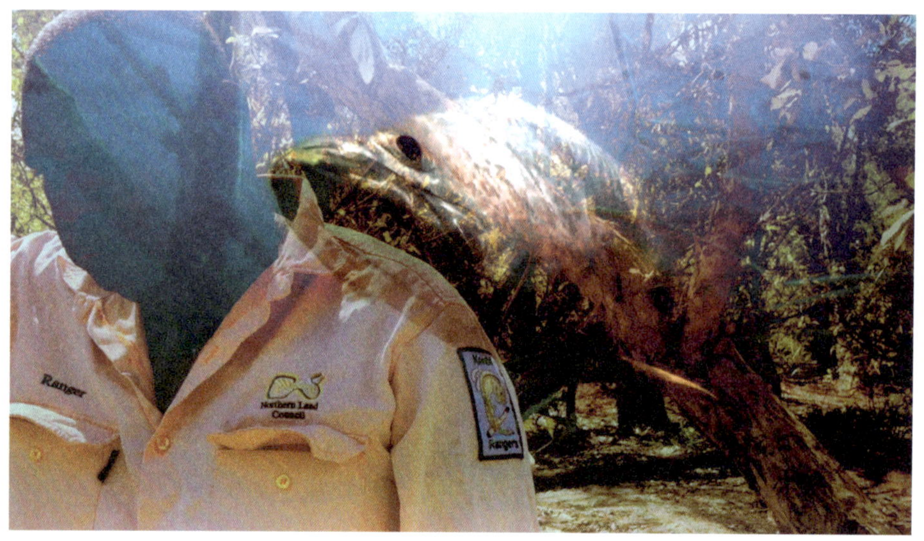

Still from Karrabing Film Collective, *The Jealous One*, 2017, colour film with sound, 29min

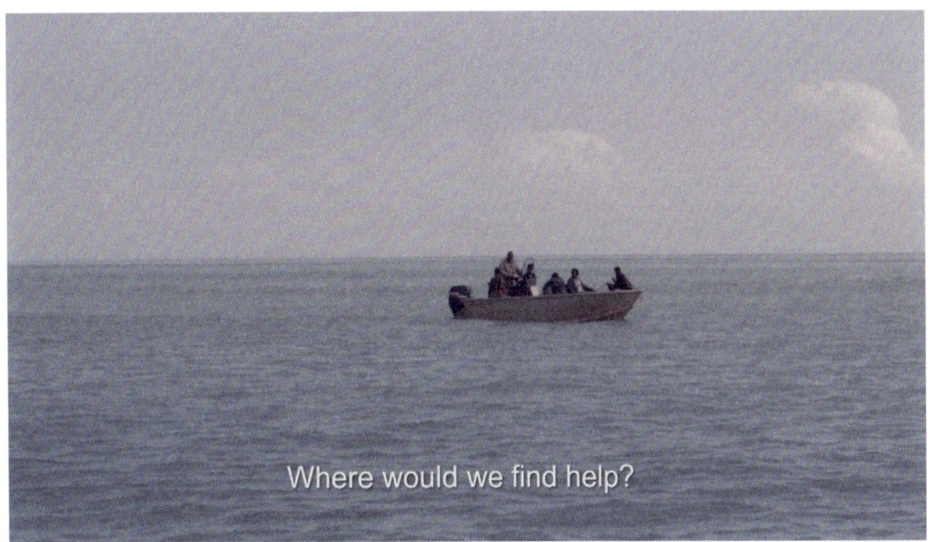

Still from Karrabing Film Collective, *When the Dogs Talked*, 2014, colour film with sound, 34min

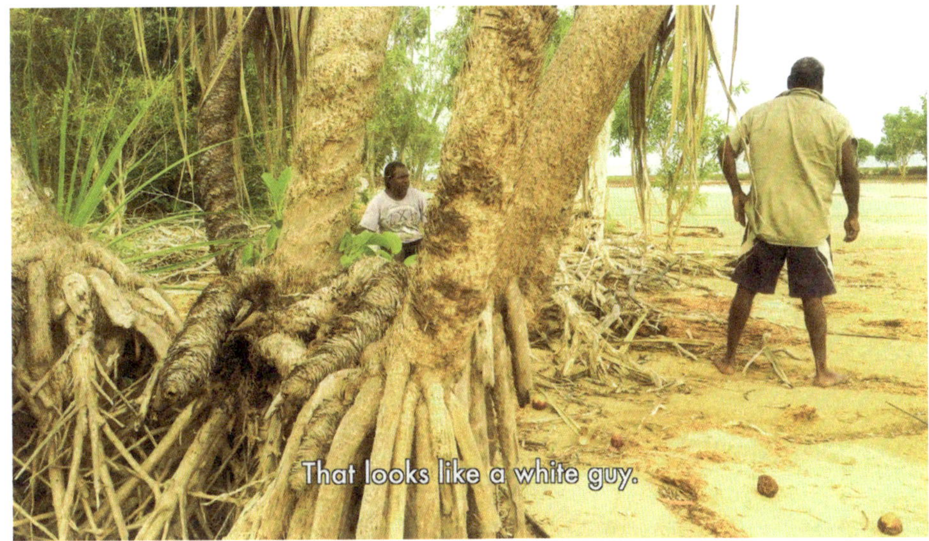

Stills from Karrabing Film Collective, *Wutharr, Saltwater Dreams*, 2016, colour film with sound, 29min

All images courtesy the artists

See pp.371–77 of this reader for Elizabeth Povinelli, 'The Ends of Humans: Anthropocene, Autonomism, Antagonism, and the Illusions of Our Epoch'

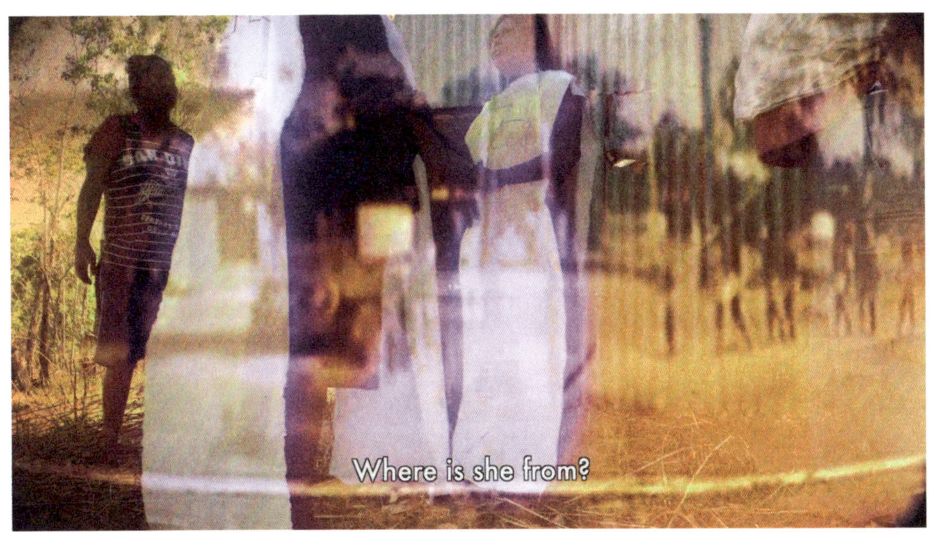

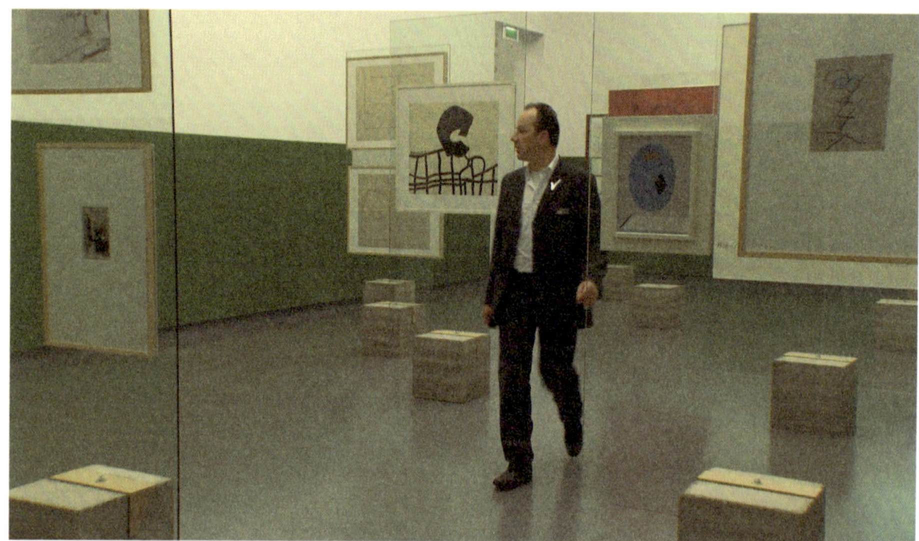

Stills from Chto Delat,
*Museum Songspiel: The
Netherlands 20XX*, 2011,
colour video with sound,
25min 36sec
Courtesy the artists
and KOW, Berlin

See p.420 of this reader
for a discussion of
*Museum Songspiel: The
Netherlands 20XX*

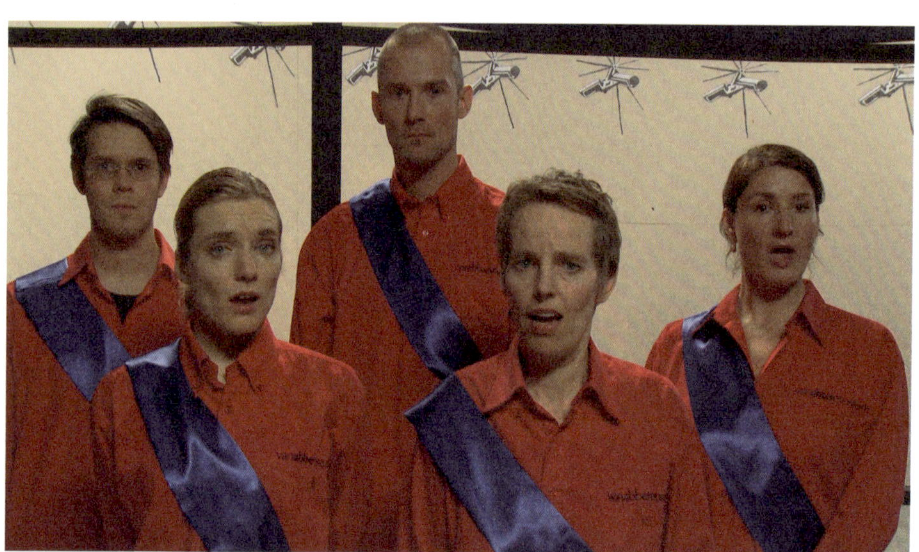

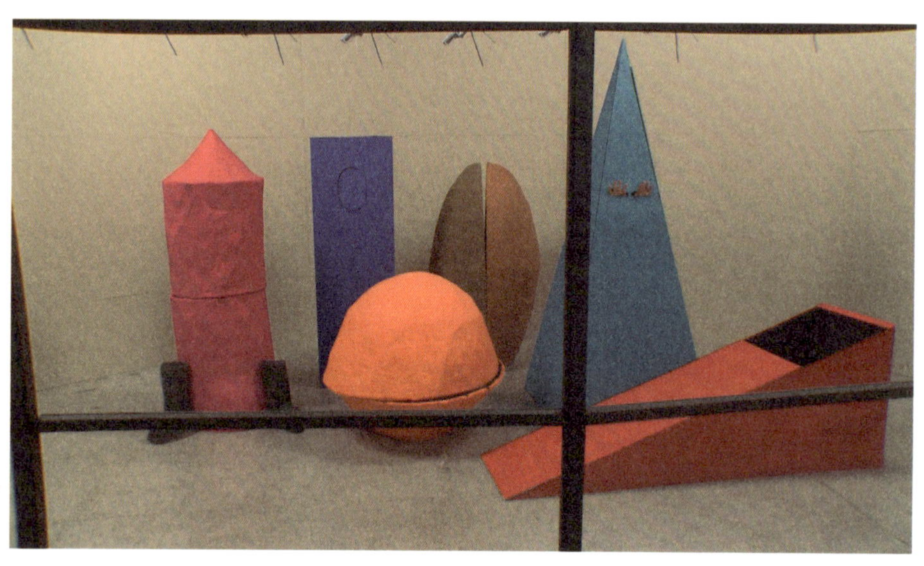

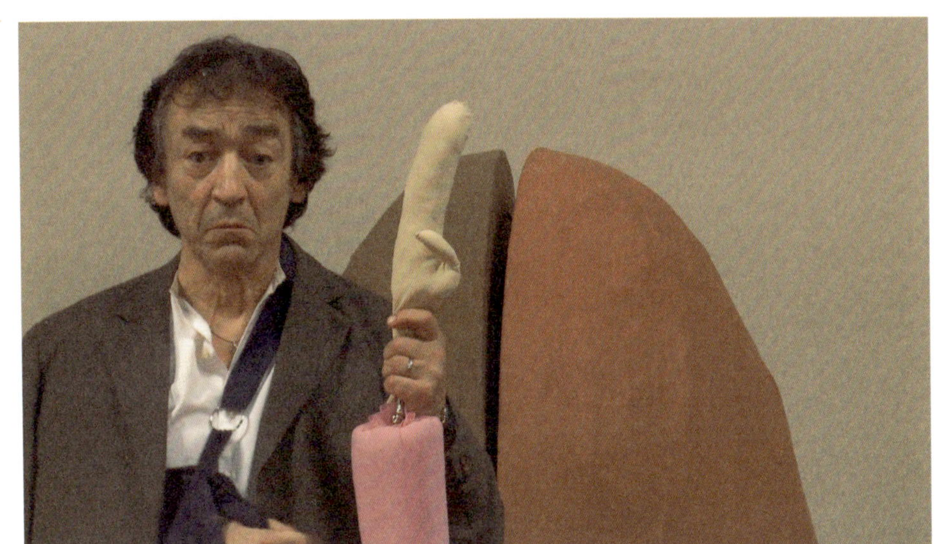

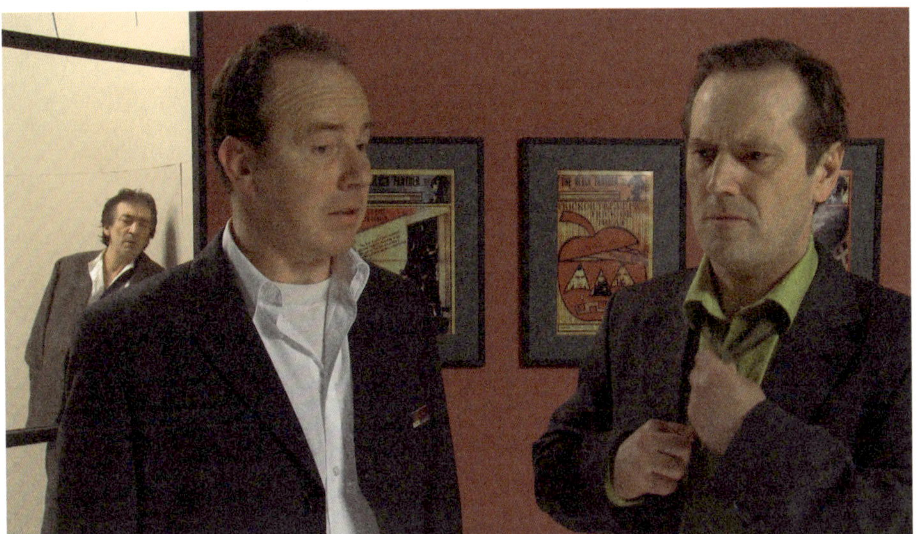

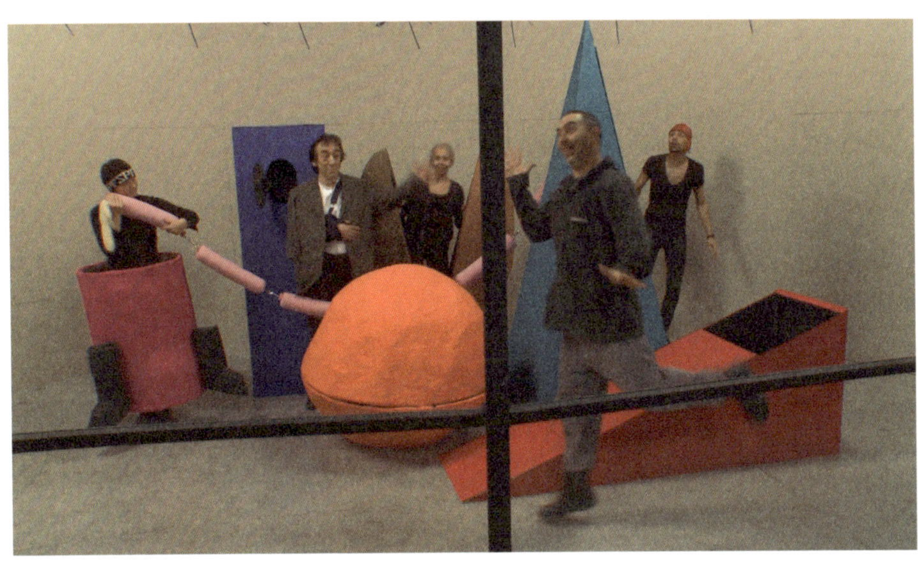

Protest views,
Decolonize This Place,
'9 Weeks of Art and Action',
Whitney Museum of
American Art,
New York, 2019
Photo: William Powhida

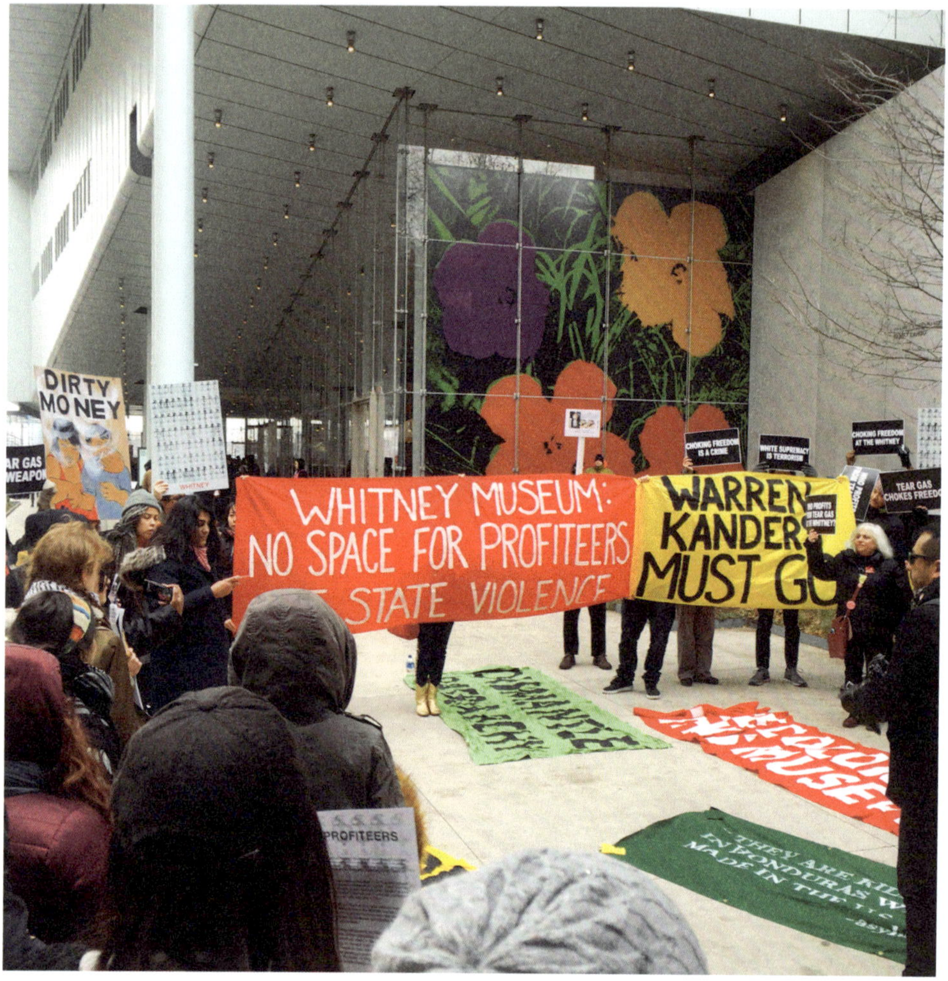

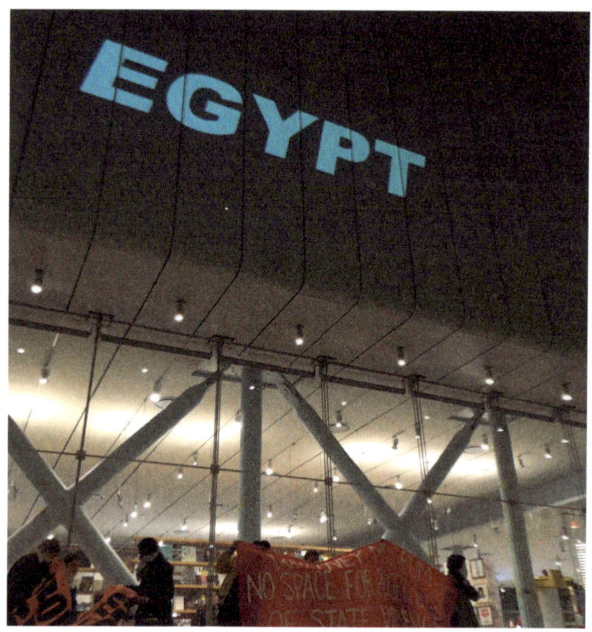

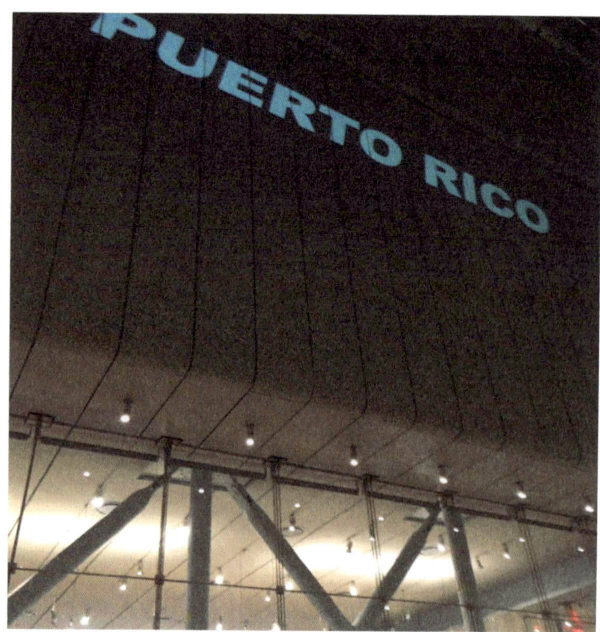

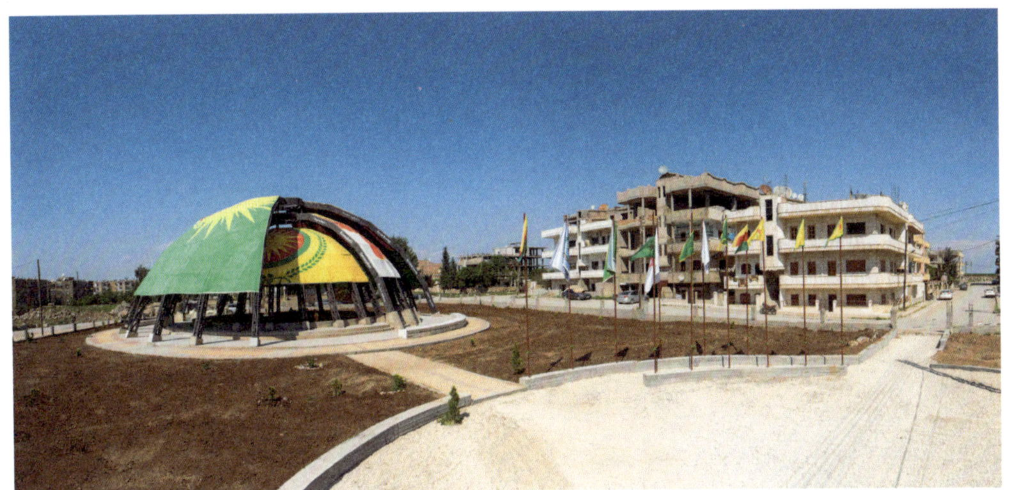

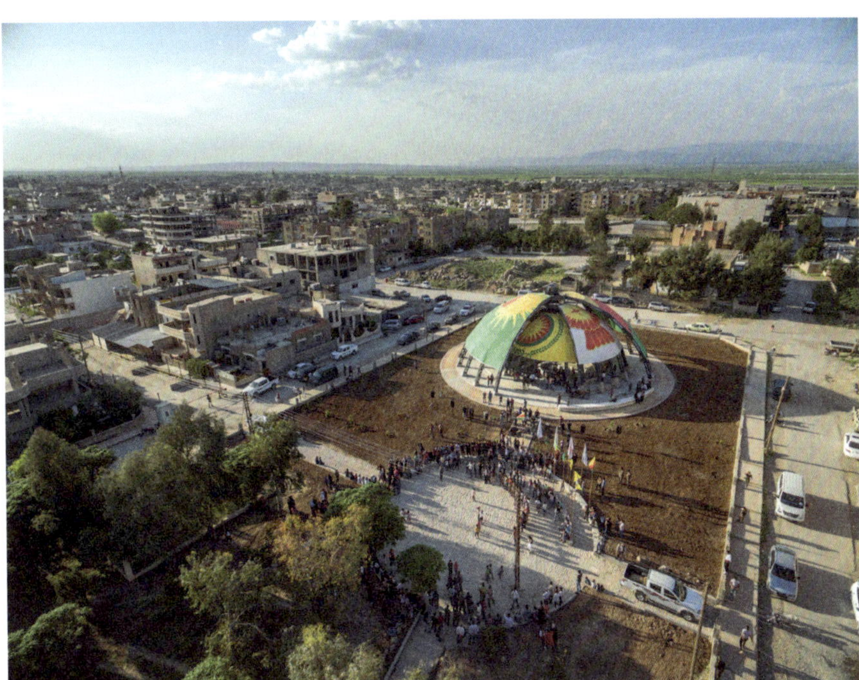

Site views, *New World Summit, Rojava*, organised by Jonas Staal, 2015–18

See pp.404–09 of this reader for 'Living Without Approval: Dilar Dirik Interviewed by Jonas Staal'

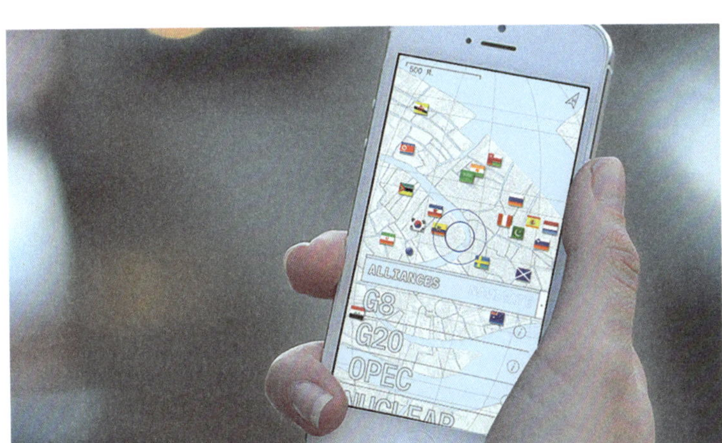

Jonas Staal, *Ideological Guide to the Venice Biennale*, 2013, smartphone app

All images courtesy the artist

See p.398 of this reader for Stephen Wright, 'The Autonomy Archipelago'

Stills from Hito Steyerl,
Liquidity Inc., 2014,
colour video with sound and
architectural environment
Courtesy the artist, Andrew Kreps
Gallery, New York and Esther
Schipper, Berlin

See pp.419-20 of this reader for
Hito Steyerl, 'Duty-Free Art'

Opposite page: Paul Chan,
Weatherman Sez, colour screenprint
on paper, 55.3 × 43.7cm
Courtesy the artist

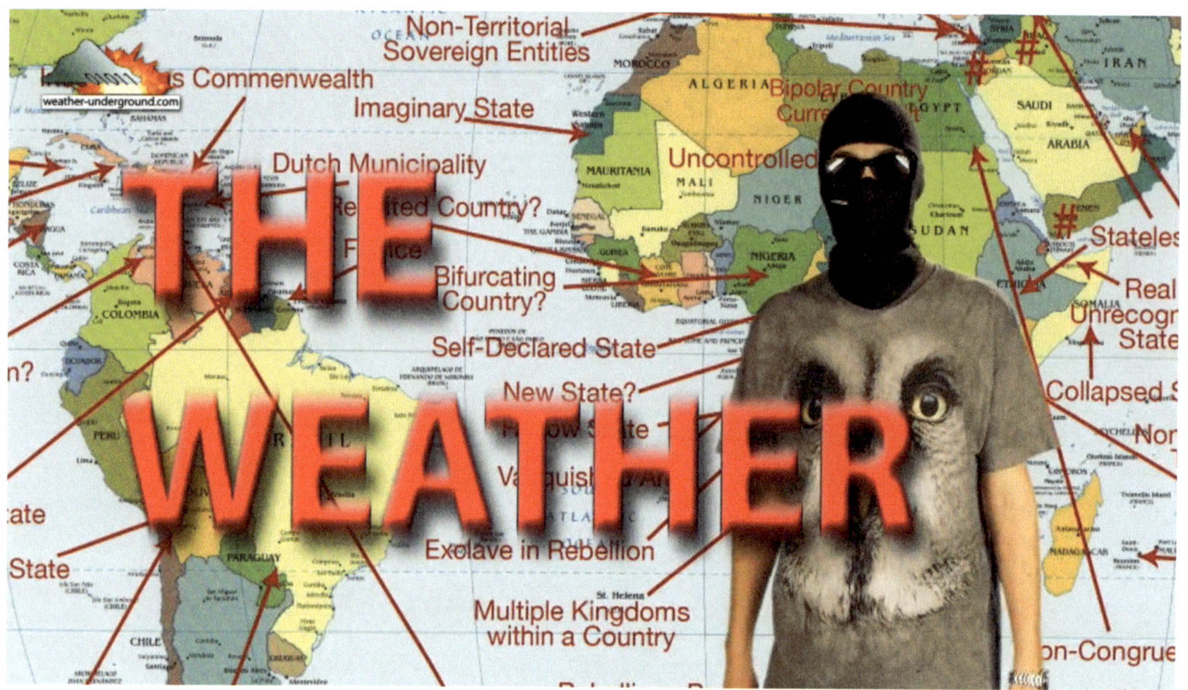

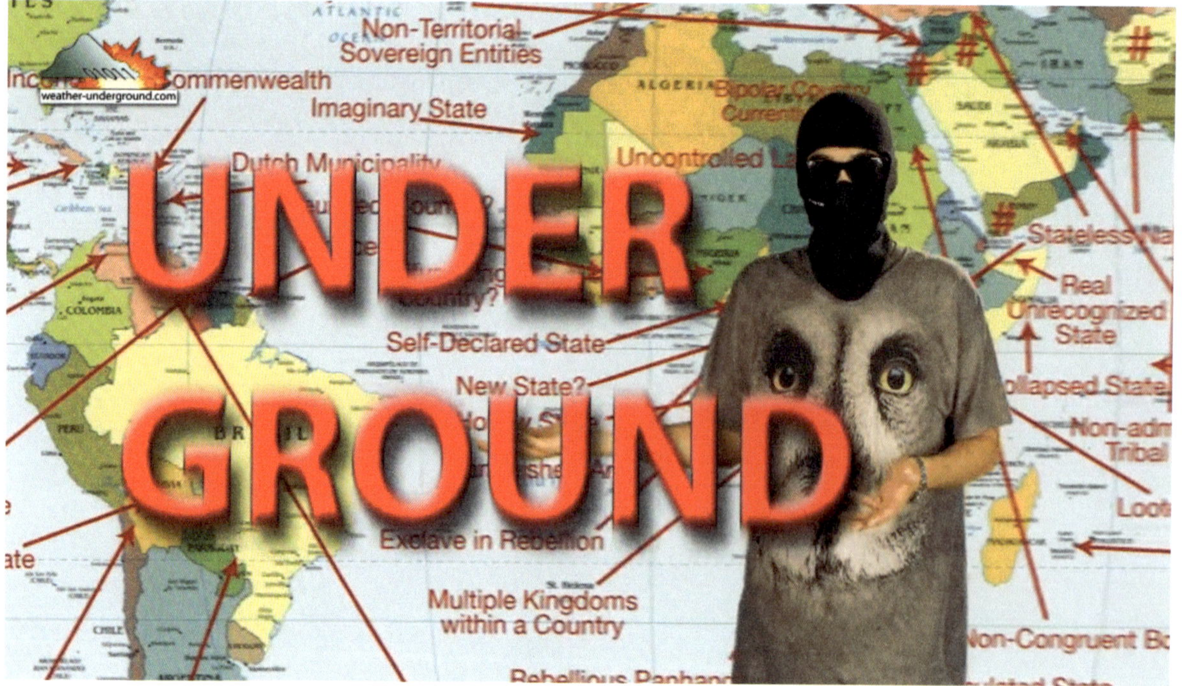

WEATHERMAN SEZ

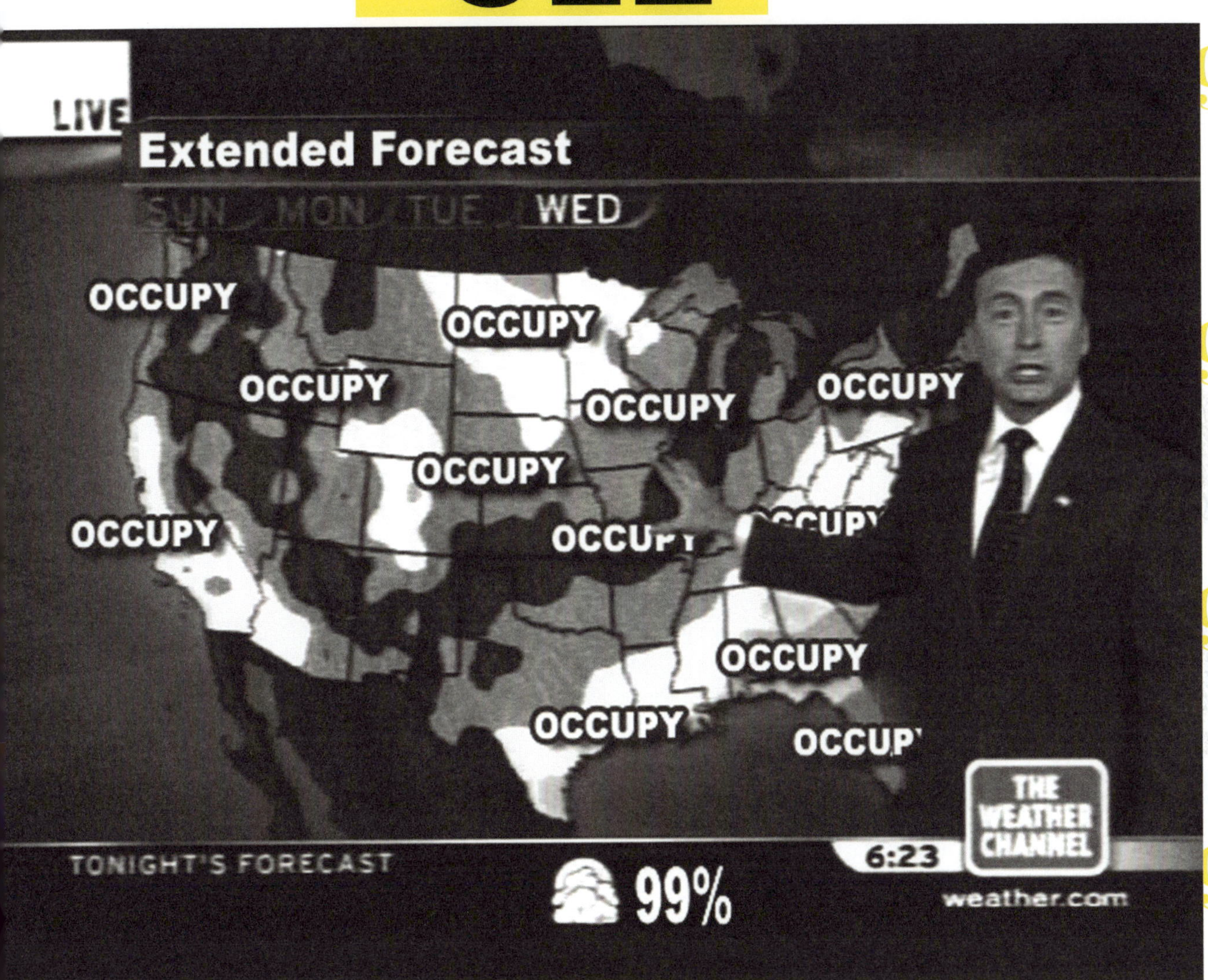

SEZ WEATHERMAN

PART FIVE:
AUTONOMEDIA

In Parts Three and Four, we traced a shift from object to frame and from the artwork as commodity to artwork as artistic labour, as service. This does not mean that artistic activity has become magically 'dematerialised'. It is clear that the senses and the activity in Marx's 'human sensuous activity' (his definition of *praxis*) can never be purely human. To be human is to be always already mediated and alienated. As the media theory collective Bilwet (aka ADILKNO, whose members included Geert Lovink and Arjen Mulder) put it in the 1990s, 'media = the human + the alien'.[1] Media alienate, exteriorise; it's what they do. But in doing so, they also humanise; they propel individuation. In a period of unprecedented technological integration, these properties of media technologies have only been exacerbated.

The artwork was never just 'an object'. It was always an object that came with the conventions - or broke with the conventions - of an artistic discipline such as sculpture, painting or print-making. Modern aesthetics thus involved not just a dialectic of art and life, but also a dialectic of art and the individual arts; a dialectic that, so Adorno argued, could ultimately never be resolved.[2] Romantic attempts to merge all the arts into a total work of art, or *Gesamtkunstwerk*, regarded the separation between the different arts as a manifestation of an alienating division of labour and culture of specialisation; the total work of art was not just supposed to be a synthesis of the arts, but also a re-integration of this re-synthesised art into the community.

By contrast, modernists valued the specifics of individual artistic mediums and emphasised their autonomy in order to safeguard the autonomy of art from life. It was, in fact, in the context of modernist aesthetic theory in the 1930s and 1940s that the notion of the medium received its first sustained attention, before the rise of 'media theory' as a field in the 1960s. If one searches for 'medium' and 'media' in nineteenth-century publications, one mostly finds treatises on optics and spiritualism; and even in 1912, in his important article 'The Esthetic Significance of the Motion Picture', published in the review *Camera Work*, Sadakichi Hartmann wavered between film as 'popular amusement' and as a 'fine art', nowhere deploying the term *medium*.[3]

In the 1960s, as Marshall McLuhan was establishing his fame as a media-theory guru, the authority of modernist critics such as Clement Greenberg was challenged by new forms of 'intermedia' art and practices that were *generic* visual art. This type of art was no longer anchored in specific arts and their media, such as painting or sculpture. It was not so much that all the arts were merged into Art, but rather that they were all incorporated into contemporary visual art, which could now incorporate photography, film, music, performance and any and all admixtures of those. In the process, visual art became the exemplary or paradigmatic form of Art.[4]

Institutional critique's move from work to frame reflects this shift: working with the institutional framework is, by definition, a 'generic' approach to contemporary art, beyond conventional and specific media. Of course, artists still engage with specific mediums and their histories - but rarely in the sense of a purist reduction of a medium to a single essence, or material or technical 'base'. Intermedial layerings abound, particularly as even traditional artistic media have become contingent on contemporary technology.

In 2014, Wade Guyton posted photos on Instagram of what appeared to be dozens of extra prints of a 'painting' that were practically identical to a work by him that was about to be sold at auction by Christie's - with its projected value being related, of course, to its perceived uniqueness. However, as fellow artist Greg Allen noted on his blog, Guyton's move could hardly be expected to undermine his auction results:

Guyton's own Instagram photo [shows that] the *Times* (and Christie's themselves) had already made him the poster child for anxiety marketing for an auction that was actually full of guarantees and third-party pre-bids. If Guyton really wanted to destabilise his market, he could just pull a Cady Noland and demand the auction house remove his name from a work. This did not happen. Instead he reaffirmed the central element of his practice: that his paintings are each machine-printed renderings of infinitely reproducible digital files, whose uniqueness derives from the circumstances of their production. And record resale prices continued apace. [...]

Guyton: it's the little differences. And those are precisely what is lost when paintings are seen one at a time, in auction catalogues, art fair slideshows and drifting by in infinite Instagram scrolls. Guyton's inky black paintings cast a harsh light on the impoverished experience of art-as-shoppertainment, of paintings decontextualised from the artist's practice and the flow in which they were conceived, and remerchandised as, well, merchandise. Paintings remain ruthlessly efficient units of exchange even though they're often no longer optimal units of aesthetic experience. That divergence marks what's lost when painting becomes nothing more than, as Ben Davis's timely quote[1] of John Berger puts it, 'a celebration of private property'.[5]

Allen quotes from an essay by John Kelsey in a catalogue on Guyton, titled *Black Paintings* (2011), about works which – like the painting sold at Christie's – originate as computer files:

> What this work displays is the difference between sending information and receiving aesthetic objects in the gallery, or what happens when 'black' moves from desktop to printer to museum, and whatever is lost along the way. The monochrome is a record of circulation. As it is copied and communicated, discrepancies are produced. And these are what now stand in for painting.[6]

On the one hand, then, Guyton's extra prints could be seen as an attempt to undermine the speculative market for his works and their reduction to fetishised private property; on the other, arguments such as Kelsey's suggest that he may just have been supplying the market with more of the not-quite-the-same, with fascinating variations, nuances or just glitches. Either way, the distributed existence of Guyton's art, between digital files and materialised forms, throws conventional understandings of what constitutes a medium into question.

The role of technology is more crucial than ever in what has been identified as a post-media age in which all materials have been remediated as digital. If Greenberg focussed on the autonomy of artistic media to define and defend the autonomy of art, what are the possibilities of current media for autonomist practices that go against the autonomy of technology? How can its 'monopoly on autonomy' be countered?[7]

---

1   Editors' Note: Ben Davis, 'Ways of Seeing Instagram', *artnet*, 24 June 2014, available at https://news.artnet.com/art-world/ways-of-seeing-instagram-37635 (last a accessed on 19 September 2020).

Modernism and Media

There was a theory of media before 'media theory' came to be a recognised field in the 1960s and 1970s through the impact of Marshall McLuhan. In art theory, various authors have debated the properties, possibilities and limitations of the various *arts* – or of the various *artistic mediums*, as we would now say. In 1766, the German Enlightenment dramatist and theorist Gotthold Ephraim Lessing published *Laocoön: An Essay on the Limits of Painting and Poetry*, in an attempt to differentiate valid artistic strategies in literature (as a time-based art) from those in visual art. The latter, according to Lessing, is all about physical beauty; therefore a sculpture showing the priest Laocoön being killed by giant snakes should not show his face distorted in agony – which is something that the poet can describe, but the visual artist should not depict.

Nineteenth-century theorists such as Robert Prutz, as discussed in Part One, credited Lessing with having created a theoretical basis for 'the autonomy of art'. In the twentieth century, theorists of autonomy also had recourse to Lessing's *Laocoön*. When Rudolf Arnheim tried to come to terms with sound film in his 1938 essay 'A New Laocoön', the Lessingian project of defining the properties of the arts and of defending their limits was inflected by the rise of new technological media and the culture industry. Clement Greenberg's 'Towards a Newer Laocoon' (1940) followed hot on the heels of Arnheim's essay; here Greenberg adopts the term *medium* to better differentiate between artistically valid use of a medium on the one hand, and the mass media on the other:

> Purity in art consists in the acceptance, willing acceptance, of the limitations of the medium of the specific art. [...]
>
> The arts, then, have been hunted back to their mediums, and there they have been isolated, concentrated and defined. It is by virtue of its medium that each art is unique and strictly itself. To restore the identity of an art the opacity of its medium must be emphasised.[8]

While Lessing had inaugurated a powerful critical tradition, many opposed such rigid distinction and separation between media. In the mid-nineteenth century, the composer Richard Wagner mounted perhaps the most elaborate theoretical challenge to Lessing. Wagner's romantic striving for totality and for the integration of artistic media in a total work of art reflects the socialist ideals of his youth, leading up to his participation in the Revolution of 1849 (alongside Mikhail Bakunin). For Wagner as a Romantic socialist (who would go on to become a reactionary and anti-Semitic ideologue), Lessing's differentiations between the arts were unhelpful, although Lessing's status in Germany meant that Wagner was careful not to attack him directly:

> When Lessing laboured in his 'Laocöon' to discover and map out the bounds of Poetry and Painting, he had in his eye that poetry which was already mere description (*Schilderei*). He starts from lines of comparison and demarcation which he draws between the plastic group portraying the scene of Laocöon's death-struggle, and that description of the same scene as sketched by Virgil in his 'Aeneid', an epos written for dumb reading. Though in the course of his inquiry

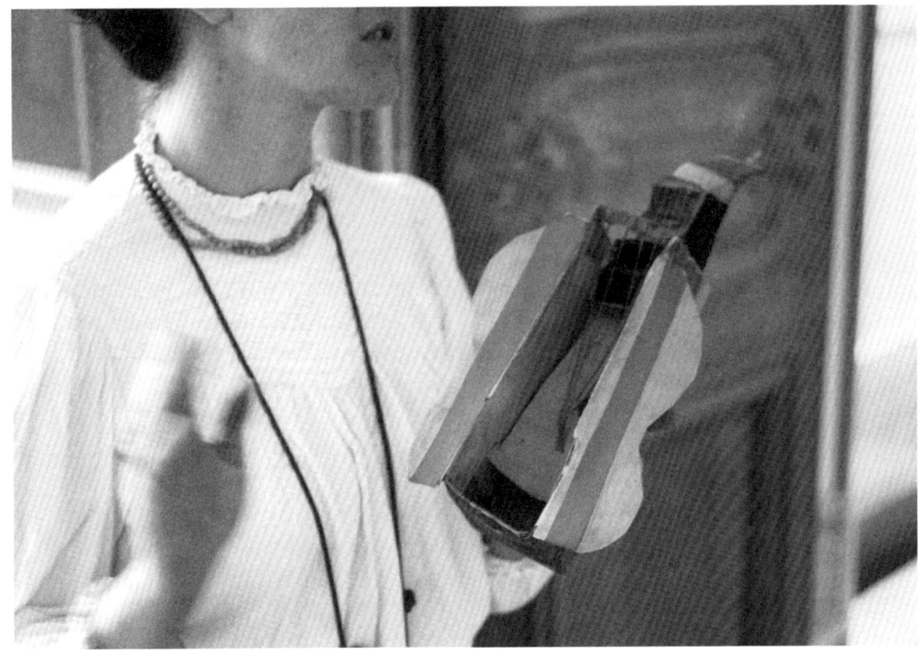

Lessing touches on Sophocles, again he has only in mind the literary Sophocles, such as alone exists *for us*; or, if he takes into his purview the poet's Tragic Artwork in all its life of actual performance, he instinctively places it outside any comparison with the works of Sculpture or Painting: since not the living Tragic Artwork is bounded as against these plastic arts, but *these*, compared with *that*, find in their straitened natures their necessary bounds. Wherever Lessing sets up limits and boundaries for Poetry, he does not mean the *dramatic Artwork* directly brought before the senses by physical performance, that Artwork which sums in itself each factor of the plastic arts, in highest potence such as it alone can reach, and by its power has first brought to these their higher potentiality of artistic life; but he means the exiguous phantom of this Artwork, the narrating, depicting, literary poem, appealing to the imagination and not the senses – the form in which that force of imagination has been turned into the virtual performer, toward which the poem merely acts as stimulus.

Such an *artificial* art, 'tis true, can only produce an effect at all by the exactest observance of boundaries and limits, since she must be ever on her watch to guard the unlimited force of imagination – which has here to play the performer's role *in place of her* – from any bewildering digression, and thus to guide it to the one fixed point at which she can display her purposed object as definitely and distinctly as possible. But it is to the force of imagination alone that all the egoistically severed arts address themselves; and especially the Plastic art, which can only bring into play the weightiest moment of Art, namely *motion*, by appealing to the Phantasy. All these arts *merely suggest*: an *actual representation* would to them be possible only could they parley with the universality of man's artistic receptivity, could they address his entire sentient (*sinnlichen*) organism, and not his force of imagination; for the true Artwork can only be engendered by an advance from imagination into actuality, i.e. physicality (*Sinnlichkeit*).[9]

Wagner, then, opposed the 'artificial arts' with his ideal of a unified work of art that would also have a different social function than that of a specialist modern commodity that was the property of art dealers, impresarios and critics. In contrast, the *Gesamtkunstwerk* supposedly formed an organic whole with 'the people' conceived as a community – *Gemeinschaft* – rather than an anonymous modern public. That the development of the art market and art criticism in the nineteenth century ran parallel to a partial emancipation of Jews across Europe, and that many promoters and critics of the 'artificial arts' were Jewish, was fuel for Wagner's anti-Semitism.

A key concept for Wagner was *myth*, which he glorified as a great unifier, as a force that could heal the rifts of modern society. Myth can be seen in media-theoretical terms. Its natural medium is allusive, poetical rather than conceptual; a 'tone-speech' that is midway between music and language, and thus lays the foundation for the total work of art, which draws all artistic media into its orbit.

> Greek Tragedy is the artistic embodiment of the spirit and contents of Greek Mythos. As in this Mythos the widest-ranging phenomena were compressed into closer and ever closer shape, so the Drama took this shape and re-presented it in the closest, most compressed of forms. The view-in-common of the essence of things, which in Mythos had condensed itself from a view of Nature to a view of Men and morals, here appeals in its distinctest, most pregnant form to the most universal receptive-force of man; and thus steps, as Art-work, from Phantasy into reality. [...]
>
> If, then, we wish to define the Poet's work according to its highest power thinkable, we must call it *the – vindicated by the clearest human Consciousness, the new-devised to answer the beholdings of an ever-present Life, the brought in Drama to a show the most intelligible – the Mythos.* [...]
>
> Tone-speech is the beginning and end of Word-speech: as the *Feeling* is beginning and end of the Understanding, as *Mythos* is beginning and end of History, the *Lyric* beginning and end of Poetry. The mediator between beginning and middle, as between the latter and the point of exit, is *the Phantasy.*[10]

To return to the twentieth century, and specifically to the interwar period; in his important 'Essay on Wagner' (written in 1938, published in its entirety in 1952), Adorno attacks the composer's attempt to forge a *Gesamtkunstwerk* as reactionary in trying to do away with the borders between media and to forge a 'false identity' that disregards the divergent historical development of the different senses and media, and that pretends to overcome the modern division of labour.

Like Greenberg, Adorno was convinced that modern differentiation and specialisation could not simply be wished away. In fact, a Wagnerian work creates a mere semblance of pre-modern organic unity; a phantasmagoria, as Adorno puts it in his analysis. When the grail in Wagner's *Parsifal* (1882) 'magically' lights up, this is in fact due to electrical light, which turns it into the ultimate commodity fetish, apparently endowed with a kind of autonomous agency. The result is a technological spectacle that does indeed, Adorno suggests, prefigure cinema:

Technological intoxication is generated from the fear of a sobriety that is all too close at hand. Thus we see that the evolution of opera in the direction of the autonomous sovereignty of the artist is intertwined with the origins of the culture industry. Nietzsche, in his youthful enthusiasm, misidentified the artwork of the future: it enacts the birth of film from the spirit of music.[11]

Adorno spent the years around World War II in exile in New York (where the Institute for Social Research, the institutional embodiment of the Frankfurt School, had entered into an affiliation with Columbia University) and in Los Angeles. Around 1945, he was deeply involved with the Institute's massive sociological research project on anti-Semitism, which was supported by the American Jewish Committee (AJC). For collating its data, the Institute used rooms provided by the AJC – on the same office floor as the AJC's magazine, *Commentary*, where Clement Greenberg was an editor. Institute members and *Commentary* staffers mingled freely, and *Commentary* gave the Frankfurt School some early exposure in the US. Greenberg later recalled seeing 'eye to eye on a lot' with Adorno.[12]

However, Adorno took a more nuanced view than Greenberg of the relationship between specific arts and art in general. He characterised modern art as being marked by a fraught dialectic of the specific and the general, of modernist fetishisation of specific artistic media on the one hand and romantic and avant-garde attempts to combine, blend and synthesise them into 'art' in general on the other, and both tendencies pose dangers of aesthetic impoverishment and regression.[13] Greenberg, by contrast, sided fully with the specific – stressing again and again that all authentic modern art homes in on the medium's specific and unique characteristics (e.g. the 'flatness' of the picture plane in painting, and movement in film). Whereas German authors such as Adorno and Benjamin mostly wrote about the 'materials' or the *Mittel* (means) of art, Greenberg much more consistently applied the Latin term *medium* to denote the material basis of each art.[14] Truth to the medium could now be used to differentiate between art and kitsch, between Picasso and Normal Rockwell, between the avant-garde's 'pure' films and Hollywood.

Greenberg's 'Avant-Garde and Kitsch' (1939) was published in the Trotskyist journal *Partisan Review* at a moment when the political horizon could hardly have been darker – Stalinism entrenched in the Soviet Union, Nazism triumphant in Europe.[15] In Greenberg's opposition of the avant-garde art and kitsch, the latter term does not so much refer to the homespun variety (garden gnomes and the like) as it does to industrially produced kitsch: Hollywood, illustrated magazines, Tin Pan Alley songs, but also Stalinist and fascist cultural production. In other words, Greenberg's text analyses the dialectic of avant-garde art and what Adorno and Max Horkheimer would soon dub the *culture industry*.

Greenberg's later writings would increasingly become dogmatic and schematic, and all too compatible with Cold War attempts to present modern art as 'free' in the most abstract and general way possible. Early on, in 'Avant-Garde and Kitsch', Greenberg was still analysing the dialectic of autonomy and heteronomy in modern art and culture in a way that approaches Adorno's writings, although the emphasis on the transmutation of avant-garde activity into art for art's sake anticipates his later stance.

CLEMENT GREENBERG, 'AVANT-GARDE AND KITSCH'

Reprinted from *Clement Greenberg: The Collected
Essays and Criticism*, vol.1, *Perceptions and
Judgments, 1939-1944* (ed. John O'Brian),
Chicago: The University of Chicago Press, 1986,
pp.5-22. First published in 1939.

One and the same civilisation produces simultaneously two such different things as a poem by T.S. Eliot and a Tin Pan Alley song, or a painting by Braque and a *Saturday Evening Post* cover. All four are on the order of culture, and ostensibly, parts of the same culture and products of the same society. Here, however, their connection seems to end. A poem by Eliot and a poem by Eddie Guest – what perspective of culture is large enough to enable us to situate them in an enlightening relation to each other? Does the fact that a disparity such as this within the frame of a single cultural tradition, which is and has been taken for granted – does this fact indicate that the disparity is a part of the natural order of things? Or is it something entirely new, and particular to our age?

The answer involves more than an investigation in aesthetics. It appears to me that it is necessary to examine more closely and with more originality than hitherto the relationship between aesthetic experience as met by the specific – not the generalised – individual, and the social and historical contexts in which that experience takes place. What is brought to light will answer, in addition to the question posed above, other and perhaps more important questions.

I

A society, as it becomes less and less able, in the course of its development, to justify the inevitability of its particular forms, breaks up the accepted notions upon which artists and writers must depend in large part for communication with their audiences. It becomes difficult to assume anything. All the verities involved by religion, authority, tradition, style, are thrown into question, and the writer or artist is no longer able to estimate the response of his audience to the symbols and references with which he works. In the past such a state of affairs has usually resolved itself into a motionless Alexandrianism, an academicism in which the really important issues are left untouched because they involve controversy, and in which creative activity dwindles to virtuosity in the small details of form, all larger questions being decided by the precedent of the old masters. The same themes are mechanically varied in a hundred different works, and yet nothing new is produced: Statius, mandarin verse, Roman sculpture, Beaux-Arts painting, neo-republican architecture.

It is among the hopeful signs in the midst of the decay of our present society that we – some of us – have been unwilling to accept this last phase for our own culture. In seeking to go beyond Alexandrianism, a part of Western bourgeois society has produced something unheard of heretofore: avant-garde culture. A superior consciousness of history – more precisely, the appearance of a new kind of criticism of society, an historical criticism – made this possible. This criticism has not confronted our present society with timeless utopias, but has soberly examined in the terms of history and of cause and effect the antecedents, justifications and functions of the forms that lie at the heart of every society. Thus our present bourgeois social order was shown to be, not an eternal, 'natural' condition of life, but simply the latest term in a succession of social orders. New perspectives of this kind, becoming a part of the advanced intellectual conscience of the fifth and sixth decades of the nineteenth century, soon were absorbed by artists and poets, even if unconsciously for the most part. It was no accident, therefore, that the birth of the avant-garde coincided chronologically – and geographically, too – with the first bold development of scientific revolutionary thought in Europe.

True, the first settlers of bohemia – which was then identical with the avant-garde – turned out soon to be demonstratively uninterested in politics. Nevertheless, without the circulation of revolutionary ideas in the air about them, they would never have been able to isolate their concept of the 'bourgeois' in order to define what they were *not*. Nor, without the moral aid of revolutionary political attitudes would they have had the courage to assert themselves as aggressively as they did against the prevailing standards of society. Courage indeed was needed for this, because the avant-garde's emigration from bourgeois society to bohemia meant also an emigration from the markets of capitalism, upon which artists and writers had been thrown by the falling away of aristocratic patronage. (Ostensibly, at least, it meant this – meant starving in a garret – although, as we will be shown later, the avant-garde remained attached to bourgeois society precisely because it needed its money.)

Yet it is true that once the avant-garde had succeeded in 'detaching' itself from society, it proceeded to turn around and repudiate revolutionary as well as bourgeois politics. The revolution was left inside society, a part of that welter of ideological struggle which art and poetry find so unpropitious as soon as it begins to involve those 'precious' axiomatic beliefs upon which culture thus far has had to rest. Hence it developed that the true and most important function of the avant-garde was not to 'experiment', but to find a path along which it would be possible to keep culture *moving* in the midst of ideological confusion and violence. Retiring from public altogether, the avant-garde poet or artist sought to maintain the high level of his art by both narrowing and raising it to the expression of an absolute in which all relativities and contradictions would be either resolved or beside the point. 'Art for art's sake' and 'pure poetry' appear, and subject matter or content becomes something to be avoided like a plague.

It has been in search of the absolute that the avant-garde has arrived at 'abstract' or 'nonobjective' art – and poetry, too. The avant-garde poet or artist tries in effect to imitate God by creating something valid solely on its own terms, in the way nature itself is valid, in the way a landscape – not its picture – is aesthetically valid; something *given*, increate, independent of meanings, similars or originals. Content is to be dissolved so completely into form that the work of art or literature cannot be reduced in whole or in part to anything not itself.

But the absolute is absolute, and the poet or artist, being what he is, cherishes certain relative values more than others. The very values in the name of which he invokes the absolute are relative values, the values of aesthetics. And so he turns out to be imitating, not God – and here I use 'imitate' in its Aristotelian sense – but the disciplines and processes of art and literature themselves. This is the genesis of the 'abstract'.[2] In turning his attention away from subject matter

<hr>

[2] The example of music, which has long been an abstract art, and which avant-garde poetry has tried so much to emulate, is interesting. Music, Aristotle said curiously enough, is the most imitative and vivid of all arts because it imitates its original – the state of

of common experience, the poet or artist turns it in upon the medium of his own craft. The nonrepresentational or 'abstract', if it is to have aesthetic validity, cannot be arbitrary and accidental, but must stem from obedience to some worthy constraint or original. This constraint, once the world of common, extroverted experience has been renounced, can only be found in the very processes or disciplines by which art and literature have already imitated the former. These themselves become the subject matter of art and literature. If, to continue with Aristotle, all art and literature are imitation, then what we have here is the imitation of imitating. To quote Yeats:

> Nor is there singing school but studying
> Monuments of its own magnificence.

Picasso, Braque, Mondrian, Miró, Kandinsky, Brancusi, even Klee, Matisse and Cézanne derive their chief inspiration from the medium they work in.[3] The excitement of their art seems to lie most of all in its pure preoccupation with the invention and arrangement of spaces, surfaces, shapes, colours, etc., to the exclusion of whatever is not necessarily implicated in these factors. The attention of poets like Rimbaud, Mallarmé, Valéry, Éluard, Pound, Hart Crane, Stevens, even Rilke and Yeats, appears to be centred on the effort to create poetry and on the 'moments' themselves of poetic conversion, rather than on experience to be converted into poetry. Of course, this cannot exclude other preoccupations in their work, for poetry must deal with words, and words must communicate. Certain poets, such as Mallarmé and Valéry,[4] are more radical in this respect than others – leaving aside those poets who have tried to compose poetry in pure sound alone. However, if it were easier to define poetry, modern poetry would be much more 'pure' and 'abstract'. As for the other fields of literature – the definition of avant-garde aesthetics advanced here is no Procrustean bed. But aside from the fact that most of our best contemporary novelists have gone to school with the avant-garde, it is significant that Gide's most ambitious book is a novel about the writing of a novel, and that Joyce's *Ulysses* and *Finnegans Wake* seem to be, above all, as one French critic says, the reduction of experience to expression for the sake of expression, the expression mattering more than what is being expressed.

That avant-garde culture is the imitation of imitating – the fact itself – calls for neither approval nor disapproval. It is true that this culture contains within itself some of the very Alexandrianism it seeks to overcome. The lines quoted

----

the soul – with the greatest immediacy. Today this strikes up as the exact opposite of truth, because no art seems to us to have less reference to something outside itself than music. However, aside from the fact that in a sense Aristotle may still be right, it must be explained that ancient Greek music was closely associated with poetry, and depended upon its character as an accessory to verse to make its imitative meaning clear. Plato, speaking of music, said: 'For when there are no words, it is very difficult to recognise the meaning of the harmony and rhythm, or to see that any worthy object is imitated by them.' As far as we know, all music originally served such an accessory function. Once, however, it was abandoned, music was forced to withdraw into itself to find a constraint or original. This is found in the various means of its own composition and performance.

[3]   I owe this formulation to a remark made by Hans Hofmann, the art teacher, in one of his lectures. From the point of view of this formulation, Surrealism in plastic art is a reactionary tendency which is attempting to restore 'outside' subject matter. The chief concern of a painter like Dalí is to represent the processes and concepts of his consciousness, not the processes of his medium.

[4]   See Valéry's remarks about his own poetry.

from Yeats referred to Byzantium, which is very close to Alexandria; and in a sense this imitation of imitating is a superior sort of Alexandrianism. But there is one most important difference: the avant-garde moves, while Alexandrianism stands still. And this, precisely, is what justifies the avant-garde's methods and makes them necessary. The necessity lies in the fact that by no other means is it possible today to create art and literature of a high order. To quarrel with necessity by throwing about terms like 'formalism', 'purism', 'ivory tower' and so forth is either dull or dishonest. This is not to say, however, that it is to the *social* advantage of the avant-garde that it is what it is. Quite the opposite.

The avant-garde's specialisation of itself, the fact that its best artists are artists' artists, its best poets, poets' poets, has estranged a great many of those who were capable formerly of enjoying and appreciating ambitious art and literature, but who are now unwilling or unable to acquire an initiation into their craft secrets. The masses have always remained more or less indifferent to culture in the process of development. But today such culture is being abandoned by those to whom it actually belongs – our ruling class. For it is to the latter that the avant-garde belongs. No culture can develop without a social basis, without a source of stable income. And in the case of the avant-garde, this was provided by an elite among the ruling class of that society from which it assumed itself to be cut off, but to which it has always remained attached by an umbilical cord of gold. The paradox is real. And now this elite is rapidly shrinking. Since the avant-garde forms the only living culture we now have, the survival in the near future of culture in general is thus threatened.

We must not be deceived by superficial phenomena and local successes. Picasso's shows still draw crowds, and T.S. Eliot is taught in the universities; the dealers in modernist art are still in business, and the publishers still publish some 'difficult' poetry. But the avant-garde itself, already sensing the danger, is becoming more and more timid every day that passes. Academicism and commercialism are appearing in the strangest places. This can mean only one thing: that the avant-garde is becoming unsure of the audience it depends on – the rich and the cultivated.

Is it the nature itself of avant-garde culture that is alone responsible for the danger it finds itself in? Or is that only a dangerous liability? Are there other, and perhaps more important, factors involved?

II

Where there is an avant-garde, generally we also find a rear-guard. True enough – simultaneously with the entrance of the avant-garde, a second new cultural phenomenon appeared in the industrial West: that thing to which the Germans give the wonderful name of *Kitsch*: popular, commercial art and literature with their chromeotypes, magazine covers, illustrations, ads, slick and pulp fiction, comics, Tin Pan Alley music, tap dancing, Hollywood movies, etc., etc. For some reason this gigantic apparition has always been taken for granted. It is time we looked into its whys and wherefores.

Kitsch is a product of the industrial revolution which urbanised the masses of Western Europe and America and established what is called universal literacy.

Prior to this the only market for formal culture, as distinguished from folk culture, had been among those who, in addition to being able to read and write, could command the leisure and comfort that always goes hand in hand with cultivation of some sort. This until then had been inextricably associated with literacy. But with the introduction of universal literacy, the ability to read and write became almost a minor skill like driving a car, and it no longer served to distinguish an individual's cultural inclinations, since it was no longer the exclusive concomitant of refined tastes.

The peasants who settled in the cities as proletariat and petty bourgeois learned to read and write for the sake of efficiency, but they did not win the leisure and comfort necessary for the enjoyment of the city's traditional culture. Losing, nevertheless, their taste for the folk culture whose background was the countryside, and discovering a new capacity for boredom at the same time, the new urban masses set up a pressure on society to provide them with a kind of culture fit for their own consumption. To fill the demand of the new market, a new commodity was devised: *ersatz* culture, kitsch, destined for those who, insensible to the values of genuine culture, are hungry nevertheless for the diversion that only culture of some sort can provide.

Kitsch, using for raw material the debased and academicised simulacra of genuine culture, welcomes and cultivates this insensibility. It is the source of its profits. Kitsch is mechanical and operates by formulas. Kitsch is vicarious experience and faked sensations. Kitsch changes according to style, but remains always the same. Kitsch is the epitome of all that is spurious in the life of our times. Kitsch pretends to demand nothing of its customers except their money – not even their time.

The precondition for kitsch, a condition without which kitsch would be impossible, is the availability close at hand of a fully matured cultural tradition, whose discoveries, acquisitions and perfected self-consciousness kitsch can take advantage of for its own ends. It borrows from it devices, tricks, stratagems, rules of thumb, themes, converts them into a system, and discards the rest. It draws its life blood, so to speak, from this reservoir of accumulated experience. This is what is really meant when it is said that the popular art and literature of today were once the daring, esoteric art and literature of yesterday. Of course, no such thing is true. What is meant is that when enough time has elapsed the new is looted for new 'twists', which are then watered down and served up as kitsch. Self-evidently, all kitsch is academic; and conversely, all that's academic is kitsch. For what is called the academic as such no longer has an independent existence, but has become the stuffed-shirt 'front' for kitsch. The methods of industrialism displace the handicrafts.

Because it can be turned out mechanically, kitsch has become an integral part of our productive system in a way in which true culture could never be, except accidentally. It has been capitalised at a tremendous investment which must show commensurate returns; it is compelled to extend as well as to keep its markets. While it is essentially its own salesman, a great sales apparatus has nevertheless been created for it, which brings pressure to bear on every member of society. Traps are laid even in those areas, so to speak, that are the preserves of genuine culture. It is not enough today, in a country like ours, to have an inclination towards the latter; one must have a true passion for it that will give him the power to resist the faked article that surrounds and presses in on him from the moment he is old enough to look at the funny papers. Kitsch is deceptive. It has many different levels, and some of them are high enough to be dangerous to the naïve seeker of true light. A magazine like the *New Yorker*, which is fundamentally high-class kitsch for the luxury trade, converts and waters down a great deal of avant-garde material for its own uses. Nor is every single item of kitsch altogether worthless. Now and then it produces something of merit, something that has an authentic folk flavour; and these accidental and isolated instances have fooled people who should know better.

Kitsch's enormous profits are a source of temptation to the avant-garde itself, and its members have not always resisted this temptation. Ambitious writers and artists will modify their work under the pressure of kitsch, if they do not succumb to it entirely. And then those puzzling borderline cases appear, such as the popular novelist, Simenon, in France, and Steinbeck, in this country. The net result is always to the detriment of true culture in any case.

Kitsch has not been confined to the cities in which it was born, but has flowed out over the countryside, wiping out folk culture. Nor has it shown any regard for geographical and national-cultural boundaries. Another mass product of Western industrialism, it has gone on a triumphal tour of the world, crowding out and defacing native cultures in one colonial country after another, so that it is now by way of becoming a universal culture, the first universal culture ever beheld. Today the native of China, no less than the South American Indian, the Hindu, no less than the Polynesian, have come to prefer to the products of their native art, magazine covers, rotogravure sections and calendar girls. How is this virulence of kitsch, this irresistible attractiveness, to be explained? Naturally, machine-made kitsch can undersell the native handmade article, and the prestige of the West also helps; but why is kitsch a so much more profitable export article than Rembrandt? One, after all, can be reproduced as cheaply as the other.

In his last article on the Soviet cinema in the *Partisan Review*,[5] Dwight Macdonald points out that kitsch has in the last ten years become the dominant culture in Soviet Russia. For this he blames the political regime – not only for the fact that kitsch is the official culture, but also that it is actually the dominant, most popular culture, and he quotes the following from Kurt London's *The Seven Soviet Arts*: ' ... the attitude of the masses both to the old and new art styles probably remains essentially dependent on the nature of the education afforded them by their respective states'. Macdonald goes on to say: 'Why after all should ignorant peasants prefer Repin (a leading exponent of Russian academic kitsch in painting) to Picasso, whose abstract technique is at least as relevant to their own primitive folk art as is the former's realistic style? No, if the masses crowd into the Tretyakov (Moscow's museum of contemporary Russian art: kitsch), it is largely because they have been conditioned to shun "formalism" and to admire "socialist realism".'

In the first place it is not a question of a choice between merely the old and merely the new, as London seems to think – but of a choice between the bad, up-to-date old and the genuinely new. The alternative to Picasso is not Michelangelo, but kitsch. In the second place, neither in backward Russia nor in the advanced West do the masses prefer kitsch simply because their governments condition them toward it. Where state educational systems take the trouble to mention art, we are told to respect the old masters, not kitsch; and yet we go and hang

---

5   Note from John O'Brian: *Partisan Review*, Winter 1939. Greenberg wrote to Macdonald about the article shortly after it was published, in a letter dated 9 February 1939. Several ideas raised in the letter are discussed at greater length here.

Maxfield Parrish or his equivalent on our walls, instead of Rembrandt and Michelangelo. Moreover, as Macdonald himself points out, around 1925, when the Soviet regime was encouraging avant-garde cinema, the Russian masses continued to prefer Hollywood movies. No, 'conditioning' does not explain the potency of kitsch.

All values are human values, relative values, in art as well as elsewhere. Yet there does seem to have been more or less of a general agreement among the cultivated of mankind over the ages as to what is good art and what bad. Taste has varied, but not beyond certain limits; contemporary connoisseurs agree with the eighteenth-century Japanese that Hokusai was one of the greatest artists of his time; we even agree with the ancient Egyptians that Third and Fourth Dynasty art was the most worthy of being selected as their paragon by those who came after. We may have come to prefer Giotto to Raphael, but we still do not deny that Raphael was one of the best painters of his time. There has been an agreement then, and this agreement rests, I believe, on a fairly constant distinction made between those values only to be found in art and the values which can be found elsewhere. Kitsch, by virtue of a rationalised technique that draws on science and industry, has erased this distinction in practice.

Let us see, for example, what happens when an ignorant Russian peasant such as Macdonald mentions stands with hypothetical freedom of choice before two paintings, one by Picasso, the other by Repin. In the first he sees, let us say, a play of lines, colours and spaces that represent a woman. The abstract technique – to accept Macdonald's supposition, which I am inclined to doubt – reminds him somewhat of the icons he has left behind him in the village, and he feels the attraction of the familiar. We will even suppose that he faintly surmises some of the great art values the cultivated find in Picasso. He turns next to Repin's picture and sees a battle scene. The technique is not so familiar – as technique. But that weighs very little with the peasant, for he suddenly discovers values in Repin's picture that seem far superior to the values he has been accustomed to find in icon art; and the unfamiliar itself is one of the sources of those values: the values of the vividly recognisable, the miraculous and the sympathetic. In Repin's picture the peasant recognises and sees things in the way in which he recognises and sees things outside of pictures – there is no discontinuity between art and life, no need to accept a convention and say to oneself, that icon represents Jesus because it intends to represent Jesus, even if it does not remind me very much of a man. That Repin can paint so realistically that identifications are self-evident immediately and without any effort on the part of the spectator – that is miraculous. The peasant is also pleased by the wealth of self-evident meanings which he finds in the picture: 'It tells a story.' Picasso and the icons are so austere and barren in comparison. What is more, Repin heightens reality and makes it dramatic: sunset, exploding shells, running and falling men. There is no longer any question of Picasso or icons. Repin is what the peasant wants, and nothing else but Repin. It is lucky, however, for Repin that the peasant is protected from the products of American capitalism, for he would not stand a chance next to a *Saturday Evening Post* cover by Norman Rockwell.

Ultimately, it can be said that the cultivated spectator derives the same values from Picasso that the peasant gets from Repin, since what the latter enjoys in Repin is somehow art too, on however low a scale, and he is sent to look at pictures by the same instincts that send the cultivated spectator. But the ultimate values which the cultivated spectator derives from Picasso are derived at a second remove, as the result of reflection upon the immediate impression left by the plastic values. It is only then that the recognisable, the miraculous and the sympathetic enter. They are not immediately or externally present in Picasso's painting, but must be projected into it by the spectator sensitive enough to react sufficiently to plastic qualities. They belong to the 'reflected' effect. In Repin, on the other hand, the 'reflected' effect has already been included in the picture, ready for the spectator's unreflective enjoyment.[6] Where Picasso paints *cause*, Repin paints *effect*. Repin predigests art for the spectator and spares him effort, provides him with a shortcut to the pleasure of art that detours what is necessarily difficult in genuine art. Repin, or kitsch, is synthetic art.

The same point can be made with respect to kitsch literature: it provides vicarious experience for the insensitive with far greater immediacy than serious fiction can hope to do. And Eddie Guest and the *Indian Love Lyrics* are more poetic than T.S. Eliot and Shakespeare.

III

If the avant-garde imitates the processes of art, kitsch, we now see, imitates its effects. [...]

In a stable society that functions well enough to hold in solution the contradictions between its classes, the cultural dichotomy becomes somewhat blurred. The axioms of the few are shared by the many; the latter believe superstitiously what the former believe soberly. And at such moments in history the masses are able to feel wonder and admiration for the culture, on no matter how high a plane, of its masters. This applies at least to plastic culture, which is accessible to all. [...]

It is a platitude that art becomes caviar to the general when the reality it imitates no longer corresponds even roughly to the reality recognised by the general. Even then, however, the resentment the common man may feel is silenced by the awe in which he stands of the patrons of this art. Only when he becomes dissatisfied with the social order they administer does he begin to criticise their culture. Then the plebeian finds courage for the first time to voice his opinions openly. Every man, from the Tammany alderman to the Austrian house painter, finds that he is entitled to his opinion. Most often this resentment toward culture is to be found where the dissatisfaction with society is a reactionary dissatisfaction which expresses itself in revivalism and puritanism, and latest of all, in fascism. Here revolvers and torches begin to be mentioned in the same breath as culture. In the name of godliness or the blood's health, in the name of simple ways and solid virtues, the statue-smashing commences.

IV

Returning to our Russian peasant for the moment, let us suppose that after he has chosen Repin in preference to Picasso, the state's educational apparatus comes along and tells him that he is wrong, that he should have chosen Picasso – and shows him why. It is quite possible for the Soviet state to do this. But things being

---

6   T.S. Eliot said something to the same effect in accounting for the shortcomings of English Romantic poetry. Indeed the Romantics can be considered the original sinners whose guilt kitsch inherited. They showed kitsch how. What does Keats write about mainly, if not the effect of poetry upon himself?

as they are in Russia – and everywhere else – the peasant soon finds the necessity of working hard all day for his living and the rude, uncomfortable circumstances in which he lives do not allow him enough leisure, energy and comfort to train for the enjoyment of Picasso. This needs, after all, a considerable amount of 'conditioning'. Superior culture is one of the most artificial of all human creations, and the peasant finds no 'natural' urgency within himself that will drive him toward Picasso in spite of all difficulties. In the end the peasant will go back to kitsch when he feels like looking at pictures, for he can enjoy kitsch without effort. The state is helpless in this matter and remains so as long as the problems of production have not been solved in a socialist sense. The same holds true, of course, for capitalist countries and makes all talk of art for the masses there nothing but demagogy.[7]

Where today a political regime establishes an official cultural policy, it is for the sake of demagogy. If kitsch is the official tendency of culture in Germany, Italy and Russia, it is not because their respective governments are controlled by philistines, but because kitsch is the culture of the masses in these countries, as it is everywhere else. The encouragement of kitsch is merely another of the inexpensive ways in which totalitarian regimes seek to ingratiate themselves with their subjects. Since these regimes cannot raise the cultural level of the masses – even if they wanted to – by anything short of a surrender to international socialism, they will flatter the masses by bringing all culture down to their level. It is for this reason that the avant-garde is outlawed, and not so much because a superior culture is inherently a more critical culture. (Whether or not the avant-garde could possibly flourish under a totalitarian regime is not pertinent to the question at this point.) As a matter of fact, the main trouble with avant-garde art and literature, from the point of view of fascists and Stalinists, is not that they are too critical, but that they are too 'innocent', that it is too difficult to inject effective propaganda into them, that kitsch is more pliable to this end. Kitsch keeps a dictator in closer contact with the 'soul' of the people. Should the official culture be one superior to the general mass-level, there would be a danger of isolation.

Nevertheless, if the masses were conceivably to ask for avant-garde art and literature, Hitler, Mussolini and Stalin would not hesitate long in attempting to satisfy such a demand. Hitler is a bitter enemy of the avant-garde, both on doctrinal and personal grounds, yet this did not prevent Goebbels in 1932–33 from strenuously courting avant-garde artists and writers. When Gottfried Benn, an Expressionist poet, came over to the Nazis he was welcomed with a great

---

[7]   It will be objected that such art for the masses as folk art was developed under rudimentary conditions of production – and that a good deal of folk art is on a high level. Yes it is – but folk art is not Athene, and it's Athene whom we want: formal culture with its infinity of aspects, its luxuriance, its large comprehension. Besides, we are now told that most of what we consider good in folk culture is the static survival of dead formal, aristocratic cultures. Our old English ballads, for instance, were not created by the 'fold', but by the post-feudal squirearchy of the English countryside, to survive in the mouths of the folk long after those for whom the ballads were composed had gone on to other forms of literature. Unfortunately, until the machine age, culture was the exclusive prerogative of a society that lived by the labour of serfs or slaves. They were the real symbols of culture. For one man to spend time and energy creating or listening to poetry meant that another man had to produce enough to keep himself alive and the former in comfort. In Africa today we find that the culture of slave-owning tribes is generally much superior to that of the tribes that possess no slaves.

fanfare, although at that very moment Hitler was denouncing Expressionism as *Kulturbolschewismus* [Cultural Bolshevism]. This was at a time when the Nazis felt that the prestige which the avant-garde enjoyed among the cultivated German public could be of advantage to them, and practical considerations of this nature, the Nazis being skilful politicians, have always taken precedence over Hitler's personal inclinations. Later the Nazis realised that it was more practical to accede to the wishes of the masses in matters of culture than to those of their paymasters; the latter, when it came to a question of preserving power, were as willing to sacrifice their culture as they were their moral principles; while the former, precisely because power was being withheld from them, had to be cozened in every other way possible. It was necessary to promote on a much more grandiose style than in the democracies the illusion that the masses actually rule. The literature and art they enjoy and understand were to be proclaimed the only true art and literature and any other kind was to be suppressed. Under these circumstances people like Gottfried Benn, no matter how ardently they support Hitler, become a liability; and we hear no more of them in Nazi Germany.

We can see then that although from one point of view the personal philistinism of Hitler and Stalin is not accidental to the roles they play, from another point of view it is only an incidentally contributory factor in determining the cultural policies of their respective regimes. Their personal philistinism simply adds brutality and double-darkness to policies they would be forced to support anyhow by the pressure of all their other policies – even were they, personally, devotees of avant-garde culture. What the acceptance of the isolation of the Russian Revolution forces Stalin to do, Hitler is compelled to do by his acceptance of the contradictions of capitalism and his efforts to freeze them. As for Mussolini – his case is a perfect example of the *disponsibilité* of a realist in these matters. For years he bent a benevolent eye on the Futurists and built modernistic railroad stations and government-owned apartment houses. One can still see in the suburbs of Rome more modernistic apartments than almost anywhere else in the world. Perhaps Fascism wanted to show its up-to-dateness, to conceal the fact that it was a retrogression; perhaps it wanted to conform to the tastes of the wealthy elite it served. At any rate Mussolini seems to have realised lately that it would be more useful to him to please the cultural tastes of the Italian masses than those of their masters. The masses must be provided with objects of admiration and wonder; the latter can dispense with them. And so we find Mussolini announcing a 'new Imperial style'. Marinetti, Chirico et al., are sent into the outer darkness, and the new railroad station in Rome will not be modernistic. That Mussolini was late in coming to this only illustrates again the relative hesitance with which Italian Fascism has drawn the necessary implications of its role.

Capitalism in decline finds that whatever of quality it is still capable of producing becomes almost invariably a threat to its own existence. Advances in culture, no less than advances in science and industry, corrode the very society under whose aegis they are made possible. Here, as in every other question today, it becomes necessary to quote Marx word for word. Today we no longer look toward socialism for a new culture – as inevitably as one will appear, once we do have socialism. Today we look to socialism *simply* for the preservation of whatever living culture we have right now.

Greenberg's essay once again underlines that the term *avant-garde* was closely associated with leftist thought and praxis – with the idea of a revolutionary vanguard that would realise political and social progress by forging an emancipatory collective subject. As we have also seen, the role of art in this project remained ambiguous and somewhat precarious. Here Greenberg nominally still subscribes to the Trotskyist version of this agenda, but his analysis of the fraught relationship between the political and artistic avant-gardes already amounts to a defence of art for art's sake. It is hence not surprising that he would later prefer the term *modernism*, which was less politically charged, and reference Kant rather than Hegel and Marx.

During the Cold War, Greenberg moved steadily to the right, becoming a 'hawk' with ties to the CIA-backed Congress for Cultural Freedom.[16] His defence of the autonomy of art as being grounded in medium-specificity also served as a rejection of the political aspects of the historical avant-garde – the Constructivist, Dadaist and Surrealist practices whose political aspects were put on the agenda once more by theorists and artists during the late 1960s and early 1970s. This re-politicised avant-garde was clearly at odds with modernism as Greenberg defined it in his 1960 essay 'Modernist Painting' – which was originally written for the Voice of America, a US radio station that served as a Cold War propaganda machine.[17]

> The essence of Modernism lies, as I see it, in the use of characteristic methods of a discipline to criticise the discipline itself, not in order to subvert it but in order to entrench it more firmly in its area of competence. Kant used logic to establish the limits of logic, and while he withdrew much from its old jurisdiction, logic was left all the more secure in what there remained to it.
>
> The self-criticism of Modernism grows out of, but is not the same thing as, the criticism of the Enlightenment. The Enlightenment criticised from the outside, the way criticism in its accepted sense does; Modernism criticises from the inside, through the procedures themselves of that which is being criticised.[18]

One should not consider *avant-garde* and *modernism* to be mutually exclusive categories; rather, they are different ways of conceptualising the aesthetic. Many movements and practices can be shown to have both 'modernist' and 'avant-garde' traits. The Dutch De Stijl movement, for instance, emphasised the purity of various artistic means/media while also dreaming of their reintegration in the service of a grand redesign of society, of urban life.

To remain in Holland during the late 1920s and early 1930s: in this period, the Dutch Filmliga organisation sought to defend the artistic 'purity' of film against the corrupting influence of narrative and sentimental commercial cinema; while some films shown by the Filmliga are abstract and thus best seen in a modernist framework, others challenge this framework. The Filmliga screened Soviet films such as Sergei Eisenstein's *Staroye i noveye* (*The General Line*, 1929),[19] and while Eisenstein's use of montage could certainly be valued for formal(ist) reasons, his films were not intended to be valued as self-contained formal masterpieces. They had an agitprop function. Filmliga member Joris Ivens started out as a film-maker with formal studies such as *De brug* (*The Bridge*, 1928) and *Regen* (*Rain*, 1929), but his political radicalisation and embrace of communism meant that for him, too, filmic means were soon no longer an end in themselves. The following section from Menno ter Braak's 'Absolute Film' (1931), in which Ter Braak eviscerates Fritz Lang's two-part film *Die Nibelungen* (*The Nibelungs*, 1924), represents the formalist/modernist tendency in the Filmliga.

MENNO TER BRAAK, 'ABSOLUTE FILM'

Reprinted from Menno ter Braak, *Verzameld werk. Deel 2* (ed. M. van Crevel, H.A. Gomperts and G.H.'s-Gravesande), Amsterdam: G.A. van Oorschot, 1950, pp.525-27. Translated from the Dutch by Juliette Huygen.

Upon viewing Fritz Lang's *Nibelungen* film again in the year 1930, one is astounded that such a flawed and in many aspects even mendacious work was capable of convincing so many minds of the justification of this new form of imagination, even those minds who had originally been hostile to the idea of film as art. Lang's film is like a Wagnerian opera in its conventional staging of a nineteenth-century theatre and its lack of the allure of theatrical reality. The film even adheres to such an opera's considerable length, necessitating two breaks for snacks, thus leaving the audience exhausted and brooding over the ephemerality of affect by the time they leave the room. Fritz Lang, once the idol of cinephile Germany, now appears to be dead and buried. His ill fate was to be born as an artist before film was born as a medium that is entirely independent and can be pure and beautiful by its own means.

At the same time, if one watches one of the countless all-talkies reel off at one of London's cinema centres in the year 1930, in which gentlemen and detectives unfurl dialogues, audibly mount stairs, slam doors, refuse offers of whisky and violate life in general, one wonders if Fritz Lang is not in fact immortal, dead and buried though he might be. One wonders if the Wagnerian opera of the screen was not grounded in mightier instincts than was originally surmised, and if the purity of art is of any relevance to the economically significant industry that is film. After all, it doesn't matter that Siegfried had to be killed by Hagen of Tronje before the kitchen master showed up, and thus could not roar about the injustice that befell him, whereas the most insignificant murder committed somewhere in the criminal underworld is now accompanied by loud bangs. Appearances notwithstanding, the all-talkie is continuing the tradition of the *Nibelungen* by essentially functioning as a friendly shelter for actors, rather than as a film. If one regards these two examples of moving photography from an 'absolute' point of view, no difference in valuation is possible: both have no filmic value and both hang in between all forms of art [*kunstgenres*] one can think of, without striving for unity, for simplicity. They are like the first automobiles, which cherished no other ambition than to function as carriages without horses.

Ter Braak contrasts the majority of Lang's 'Wagnerian' film with its one-minute semi-abstract insert animated by the film-maker Walter Ruttmann, which signifies a dream by Kriemhild, the female protagonist. For Ter Braak, this animation is a blissful manifestation of 'absolute film':

In the middle of the operatic proceedings, with sovereign disregard for the scenic backgrounds and the skilful actors, a wisp of poetry emerges. Its beauty is as indescribable as the nuance of a beautiful tonal articulation. Though the delight is only momentarily, it is all the more intense within its withered and desiccated surroundings. A dream, a dream by Kriemhild, is what this play of motion is supposed to signify. Though this is possible in principle, Lang's theatrical Kriemhild is hardly capable of dreaming up such free and ephemeral apparitions! A dream of untainted ineffable forms, of black and white morphing into large and threatening birds, is all this unexpected minute leaves behind. Five years ago, people regarded this animation, rather than the *Nibelungen* itself, as a mere curiosity. The five years that have passed have reversed the roles; Kriemhild's fondly remembered dream, this one minute, annihilates Fritz Lang's entire pathetic oeuvre. For alas, it was not Lang that was responsible for this fleeting fragment, but someone who was a complete unknown in 1925: Walter Ruttmann.

Although Lang did not base his film on Wagner's opera cycle *Der Ring des Nibelungen*, Ter Braak clearly saw a Wagnerian impulse in Lang's aesthetic, which strove towards operatic theatricality rather than medium-specific purity. For Ter Braak, Lang's *Nibelungen* was a fatally misguided attempt to create a cinematic *Gesamtkunstwerk*. In a moralising rather than theoretically and politically grounded manner, the critic thus articulated reservations to the culture industry's products that were similar to those Adorno and Greenberg would voice late in the 1930s and 1940s.

Still from Fritz Lang's
*The Nibelungs, Part One:
Siegfried*, 1924

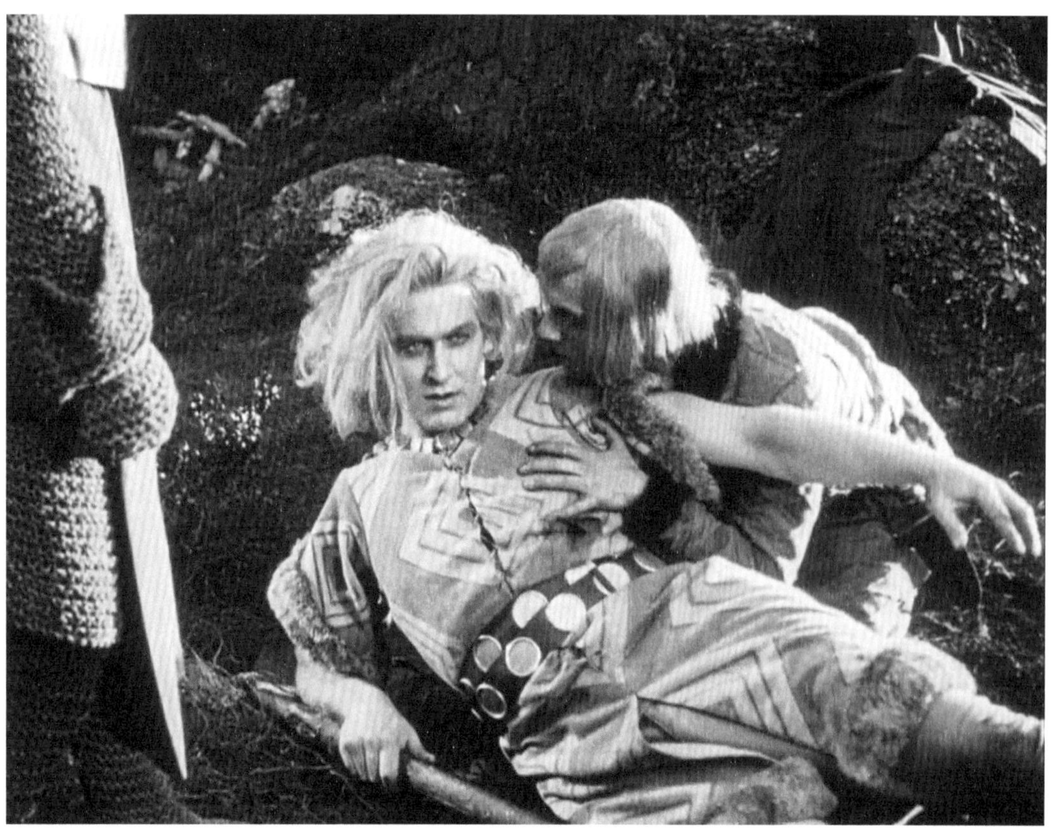

From Culture Industry to Activated Spectators

Though the Institute for Social Research kept a base in New York, during the 1940s Adorno spent much time in Los Angeles, where Horkheimer (the Institute's director) had relocated for health reasons. It was here that the pair wrote the *Dialectic of Enlightenment*, which introduces the notion of the *culture industry*, subjecting it to a grim and total critique. The proximity of Hollywood filtered more directly into another book, *Composing for the Films* (1947), which Adorno co-authored with the composer Hanns Eisler – a long-time associate of Bertolt Brecht, who, like Eisler, attempted to land jobs in Hollywood while in exile during the Nazi era. The first US and UK editions of the *Composing for the Films* were published under Eisler's name alone, presumably to protect Adorno from McCarthyite investigations for associating with Eisler, a 'known communist'.

The book is fascinating for several reasons. Firstly, the chapters on the 'sociological aspects' and the 'aesthetic aspects' of film music contain a succinct analysis of the fate of art in the culture industry, and a good introduction to Adorno's analysis of the contradictions of autonomy. Adorno makes it clear that there is no 'autonomous history of art', as if art throughout the centuries had developed according to an art-immanent logic. However, there is a history of art's relative autonomy, and in the culture industry the artist (in this case, the film composer) is asked to throw overboard whatever degree of autonomy their art had developed in modernism (Schoenberg being the paradigmatic figure for Adorno). If, in Adorno's famous turn of phrase, art's double character is both autonomous and 'social fact' (*fait social*), in Hollywood only the latter tended to remain, as elements of 'genuine' low entertainment and high art were both amalgamated into the bad compromise of mass culture.

Secondly, with Eisler as co-author Adorno does examine options for film music that would presumably not be 'high modernist' *à la* Schoenberg but would function as entertainment and yet be different from Hollywood schlock. Eisler's Brechtian avant-garde notion of montage is the decisive factor here: rather than trying to cover up the 'insurmountable heterogeneity' of media, film music should instead exacerbate it in the manner of certain 'movie revues'.

THEODOR W. ADORNO AND HANNS EISLER,
COMPOSING FOR THE FILMS

Reprinted from *Composing for the Films*, London:
The Althone Press, 1994, pp.45-54, 62-65, 71-79.
First published in 1947. Reproduced with minor
amendments.

Chapter Four
Sociological Aspects

In his painstaking and informative study, *Film Music*,[8] Kurt London has collected the data of the history of motion-picture music. It would be superfluous to repeat the facts here; however, it is pertinent to inquire whether the historical approach is applicable to motion-picture music; and to analyse the significance of the developmental phases outlined by London. One can hardly speak of a genuine history of motion-picture music, even in the dubious sense in which this term is generally used: that is, to imply that any form of art has an autonomous history. Up until now motion-picture music has not developed according to its own laws and has hardly taken cognisance of problems and solutions posed by the nature of its own material. The changes it has undergone relate to some extent to methods of mechanical reproduction and to some extent represent ill-considered, clumsy and backward attempts to pander to the imagined or actual taste of the public. While it is reasonable to speak of a qualitatively progressive development, for instance, from Edison's apparatus to the modern sound picture, it would be naïve to speak of a roughly corresponding artistic development from the *Kinothek* to the musical scores of modern sound tracks.

The haphazard development of cinema music is comparable to that of the radio or of the motion picture itself. It is first of all a question of personnel. In the early days of the amusement industry, owners and directors were the same persons. Experts were used far less than in the older industries, either in the administration as a whole or in the individual production groups, and as a result a pioneer spirit of incompetence prevailed. What is true of motion pictures and the radio also holds true for motion-picture music: the artistic level of these media was determined by those who first entered the field, attracted by the commercial prospects of the new ventures. Motion-picture music, however, suffers from a particular handicap: from the very beginning it has been regarded as an auxiliary art not of first-rank importance. In the early days it was entrusted to anyone who happened to be around and willing – often enough to musicians whose qualifications were not such as to permit them to compete in fields where solid musical standards still obtained. This created an affinity between inferior 'hack' musicians, busybodies and motion-picture music.

In order to understand the personnel problem of cinema music, some more general reflections on the sociology of the musician may be appropriate. The whole realm of musical performance has always had the social stigma of a service for those who can pay. The practice of music is historically linked with the idea of selling one's talent, and even one's self, directly, without intermediaries, rather than selling one's labour in its congealed form, as a commodity;

---

[8]   Kurt London, *Film Music*, London: Faber & Faber, 1936, pp.50-61.

and through the ages the musician, like the actor, has been regarded as closely akin to the lackey, the jester or the prostitute. Although musical performance presupposes the most exacting labour, the fact that the artist appears in person, and the coincidence between his existence and his achievement, together create the illusion that he does it for fun, that he earns his living without honest labour, and this very illusion is readily exploited.

Before the jazz age, most people used to look with contempt at a musician who led a dance orchestra. This deprecating glance is the rudiment of an attitude that has to some extent shaped the social character of musicians. In the early bourgeois era musicians were called in from the servants' quarters, where even Haydn had to take his meals, and were subject to the laws of competition. But the taint of social outcasts still clings to them. Even the austere chamber-music player sometimes assumes the posture of an obsequious and resentful headwaiter who hopes for a tip. Even he still takes note of the ladies and gentlemen of the audience, and ingratiates himself by the sweetness of his playing and the smoothness of his manners. His turned-up coat collar, the violin under his arm and the studied carelessness of his appearance remind his audience of his colleagues of the café, from whose ranks he has often come.[9]

Some of the best qualities of musical reproduction, its spontaneity, its sensuousness, its aspect of vagrancy opposed to settled orderliness – in short, everything that is good in the much-abused notion of the itinerant musician – is reflected in the popular picture of the gypsy. If this picture were eradicated, musical performance, too, would probably come to an end, just as, if complete technical rationalisation were achieved and if music could really be 'drawn' rather than written down in symbols, the function of the interpreter, the intermediary, would merge with that of the composer who 'produces' music.

At the same time, the habit of rendering 'service' – in Germany, orchestra players speak of *Abenddienst*, evening service – has left ominous marks on musicians. Among these is the mania to please, even at the price of self-humiliation, manifested in a thousand ways that range from over-elegant dress to zealous pandering to what the audience wants. This conformism of professional musicians shackles modern composition even more than the passivity of the concertgoers. There remains also a very special and anachronistic kind of envy and malice, and a fondness for intrigue, the disreputable heritage of a profession only superficially adjusted to competitive conditions. It is such archaic features that fit paradoxically into the trend of musical mass culture, which does away with competition, while still needing the old-fashioned gypsy-like traits as an added attraction. A servility both coquettish and impudent is useful for ensnaring the customer; intrigue and the irresistible urge to deceive one's colleagues, often combined with insincere 'comradeship', harmonise with the more pragmatic role of business. The musicians in control have a spontaneous understanding of the aims and practices of the amusement industry. In fact, the latecomer industry of motion pictures has not rid itself of the pre-capitalist elements of musicianship, the social type of the *Stehgeiger*,[10] despite its apparent

---

9   Flaubert described this type as early as the middle of the nineteenth century: 'The singer Lagardy had a beautiful voice, more temperament than intelligence, more pathos than feeling. He was both a genius and a charlatan, and in his nature there was as much of a barber as of a toreador' (*Madame Bovary*).

contradiction to industrial production and the artistic incompetence of its outspoken representatives. On the contrary, this 'irrational' type itself has been given a monopolistic position in the streamlined set-up. The industry, out of deepest kinship, has attracted him, preferred him to all musicians with objective tendencies, and made him a permanent institution. He has been regimented like other sham elements of a former spontaneity. The cinema exploits the barber aspect of his personality as a Don Juan, and his headwaiter functions as a troubadour *de luxe*, and occasionally even gives him the role of a bouncer to keep undesirable elements out. Its musical ideal is *schmaltz* in a chrome metal pot. But since the regimentation of the gypsy musician deprives him of the last vestiges of spontaneity which the inexorable technical and organisational machinery has already undermined, objectively nothing is left of the itinerant musician except a few bad mannerisms of performance.

Under these circumstances, it is preposterous to use words such as 'history' with reference to an apocryphal branch of art like motion-picture music. The person who around 1910 first conceived the repulsive idea of using the Bridal March from *Lohengrin* [by Richard Wagner, first performed in 1850] as an accompaniment is no more of a historical figure than any other second-hand dealer. Similarly, the prominent composer of today who, under the pretext of motion-picture requirements, willingly or unwillingly debases his music earns money, but not a place in history. The historical processes that can be perceived in cinema music are only reflections of the decay of middle-class cultural goods into commodities for the amusement market. At most, one can say that music has parasitically shared in the progress of the technical resources and the growing wealth of the motion-picture industry. It would be ludicrous to claim that motion-picture music has really evolved, either in itself or in its relation to other motion-picture media.

Musical Administration

This does not mean that motion-picture music has stood still. On the contrary, the economic might of the industry has set a tremendously dynamic machinery in motion. There is a constant stream of improvements of all kinds: new composers, new ideas in the sense of gadgets, marketable tricks that are sufficiently different from earlier ones to be conspicuous, yet not different enough to offend established habits. But what is true of all mass cultural advances under the prevailing system is true in this instance, too: ostentatious spending has increased, and the mode of presentation, the technique of transmission in the broadest sense, from acoustical accuracy to the psycho-technical treatment of the audience, has been improved in direct proportion to the capital invested, but nothing essential has changed in the music itself, its substance, its material, its function as a whole, or in the quality of the compositions. There has only been a streamlining of the façade. The progress is one of means, not of ends.

There is a striking disproportion between the tremendous improvement in the technique of recording, on which all the miracles of this technique are spent, and the music itself, either indifferent or borrowed without taste or logic from the stock of clichés. Formerly the movie theatre pianist thumped out the *Lohengrin* Bridal Chorus in the semi-darkness; today, after the extermination

---

10   The violinist who stands while he conducts a café orchestra, the other members remaining seated.

of the pianist, the Bridal Chorus, or its made-to-order equivalent, is projected in neon lights of a hundred different colours, but it is still the old Bridal Chorus, and the moment it resounds everyone knows that lawful wedded bliss is being glorified. The triumphant procession from the *Kinothek* to the movie palace has really been marking time.

If there is such a thing as a historical phase of motion-picture music, it is marked by the transition of the industry from more or less important private capitalistic enterprises to highly concentrated and rationalised companies, which divide the market among themselves and control it, although they fondly imagine that they are obeying its laws. This transition was accomplished before the development of pictures with sound, according to Kurt London, between 1913 and 1928. It might be placed in the early twenties, when the first big movie palaces were built, when the custom of the 'opening night' was deliberately grafted on the cinema in a strenuous effort to make it a social event, and when *de luxe* 'super-productions' were first promoted with the aid of extensive national and international advertising. The musical equivalent of these innovations was the replacement of the inconspicuous little group of musicians, such as is used in cafés, by the symphony orchestras of the great moving-picture theatres.

The full-fledged and quantitatively pretentious scores composed for the last silent pictures were essentially the same as those composed later for sound pictures. They merely had to be recorded, as it were, and synchronised with the speaking parts. Kurt London comments on this stage:

> Finally, in the last few years of the silent film period, the big cinema palaces were served by orchestras which, composed, as they were, of 50–100 musicians, put to shame many a medium-sized city orchestra. Parallel with this development, a new career for conductors offered itself: they had to lead the cinema orchestra and select the illustrative music. Prominent men often filled these posts with salaries which more often than not exceeded those of an opera conductor.[11]

The term 'prominent' as used here does not express real artistic accomplishments, but is part of the grandiloquent phraseology affected by all advertising in the entertainment industry, with its insincere slogan that nothing is too good for the public. This kind of prominence is determined by the fabulous salaries paid to those whom the publicity agencies elect to build up – the prominence of Radio City [in New York], the Pathé Theater in Paris or the Ufapalast am Zoo in Berlin. It belongs to the realm that Siegfried Kracauer called *Angestelltenkultur*,[12] culture of the white-collar workers, of supposedly high-class entertainment, accessible to recipients of small pay checks, yet presented in such a way that nothing seems too good or too expensive for them. It is a pseudo-democratic luxury, which is neither luxurious nor democratic, for the people who walk on heavily

---

11   K. London, *Film Music*, op. cit., p.43.
12   Siegfried Kracauer, *Die Angestellten. Aus dem neuesten Deutschland*, Frankfurt: Frankfurter Societäts-Druckerei, 1930. Translator's Note: *Die Angestellten* appeared more recently as volume five of Kracauer's *Schriften* (Frankfurt: Suhrkamp, 1971). Editors' Note: An English-language translation by Quentin Hoare of this has since appeared under the title *The Salaried Masses: Duty and Distraction in Weimar Germany* (London: Verso, 1998).

carpeted stairways into the marble palaces and glamorous castles of moviedom
are incessantly frustrated without being aware of it. This kind of opulence, manifested, for instance, in submersible and floodlighted monster orchestras, marks
the beginning of a development that has left behind it all the obvious naïveté of
the old amusement park, but raised the technique of the barker to the point of
anonymous yet all-embracing practice.

This development, however, is not merely a quantitative one. The careful
planning and sumptuous presentation of motion-picture music has changed its
social purpose. Its inflated power and dimensions ostentatiously and directly
demonstrate the economic power behind it. Its rich display of colours masks the
monotony of serial productions. Its excessive ebullience and optimism enhance
its universal advertising appeal. Music thus becomes one of the departments of
cultural industry.

The administrative element was inherent in cinema music from the very
beginning. The time beater who selected the pieces, the editor of the *Kinothek* and
the arranger have always thumbed through the treasury of traditional music as
through a stick of standard goods, and chosen what best suited their purpose.
The summary way in which they handled the cultural riches at their disposal,
utilising 'Asleep in the Deep' [by Arthur J. Lamb and Henry W. Petrie, 1897]
or the fate theme of *Carmen* [by Georges Bizet, 1875] according to the circumstances, was always that of the bureaucrat who finally divests works of art of all
their meaning and brings them down to the status of auxiliary means designed
to produce a predetermined effect. Today this attitude has become all-pervasive.
It is as though the process of rationalisation of art and the conscious command
of its resources were diverted by social forces from the real purpose of art, and
directed merely toward 'making friends and influencing people'. Progress has
become perverted into calculating the audience's reactions, and the result is a
combination of third-rate entertainment, maudlin sentimentality and boastful
advertisements of what is going to be shown.

In earlier motion-picture music, bureaucratic manipulation was mitigated
by overt barbarism – then no fiction of taste invested the mutilated melodies with
the glamour of intellectual achievement, and no highly complicated machine
put itself between the music and its effect on the public. The pianist who played
'Asleep in the Deep' when the ship went down on the silent screen, coloured in
brown or green for the occasion, and even the small orchestra that pandered to
the maharajah's favourite wife by playing an exotic medley when she walked
down the stairs, were doubtless also employees free from any artistic scruples;
but they understood their audiences and were not too different from them; they
were not completely subjected to their superiors, and still had in them something
of the ribaldry and lust for adventure that characterised the county fairs in which
the moving-picture theatres originated. It is this 'illegitimate', still impromptu
and anarchistic element that motion pictures as big business drove out of their
music. And it is this 'purge' that is called progress, and doubtless *is* progress as far
as wealth of resources and planning of their distribution is concerned. But such
progress is of dubious value. Since its streamlining, cinema music has become a
helpless victim of culture without becoming one whit more cultured than it was
before it attained respectability. Its progress consists only in the fact that trash
was taken out of its humble hiding place and set up as an official institution. [...]

To establish aesthetic principles of cinema music is as dubious an enterprise as to write its history. Up until now all attempts at an aesthetic analysis of motion pictures and radio, the two most important media of the cultural industry, have been more or less formalistic. The rule of big business has fettered the freedom of artistic creation, which is the prerequisite for a fruitful interaction between form and content; and a concrete aesthetics must necessarily refer to such an interaction. Because of the vulgar materialism of the content of motion pictures entirely alien to art, aesthetic considerations about them so far had to dodge the whole issue of content. That is why they have only been abstract. They have dealt predominantly with technicalities such as the laws of movement or colour, the sequence, the cutting, or with vague categories such as 'the inner rhythm'. Although the criteria derived from such analyses can to some extent circumscribe the framework of *métier* within a given production, they are completely insufficient to determine whether the product is good or bad. It is possible to imagine a motion picture – and this applies to its music as well – which conforms to all these criteria, upon which an enormous amount of conscientious labour and expert knowledge has been spent, and which is nevertheless utterly devoid of any real value, because the falseness and emptiness of the underlying conception have degraded the formal achievements into merely technical ingredients.

Quite apart from the detrimental influence of commercialism, aesthetic analyses of the motion picture easily become inadequate because it is rooted less in artistic wants than in the fact that in the twentieth century optical and acoustic technic reached a definite stage, which is essentially unrelated, or related only very indirectly, to any possible aesthetic idea. An attempt to formulate the aesthetic laws of the Greek tragedy, for instance, might be based on concrete social and historical factors, such as the symbolic rites of the Greek religion, the sacrifice, the trial, the primitive family conflicts, and the dawning critical attitude toward mythology. To attempt anything of this kind with regard to the motion picture would be puerile. Its connection with the developmental tendencies of dramatic or novelistic art is defined only by the fact that it takes for granted and assimilates these traditional forms, that is to say, reproduces them with some modifications dictated by requirements of technic or social conformity. Its potentialities are far more closely connected with those of photography and electrical sound developments. These media, however, have evolved entirely outside the domain of aesthetics, and aesthetic principles in relation to them are so insubstantial that they need not even be challenged. The possible contribution of these fields to the aesthetics of the motion picture is about the same as that of the physical theory of contrasting colours to the art of painting, or that of overtones to music.

Hence caution is particularly advisable with regard to pseudo-aesthetic considerations in the functionalist style, such as were popular in Germany in the name of the principle of *Materialgerechtigkeit,* or adequacy to the given material. With regard to the most essential instrument in cinema music – the microphone – the experience of the radio showed long ago that the creation of compositions 'adequate' to the microphone led in practice to an unjustifiable oversimplification of musical language.

So-called adjustment to such supposedly objective material conditions fetters musical imagination, generally for the sake of that kind of popularity which is the main concern of the motion-picture industry. The postulate of adequacy to the material would make sense only if it referred to the musical material in the proper meaning of the term, namely, to the tones and their relationships, not to extraneous and relatively accidental recording technics. A truly functional procedure would consist in adapting the microphone to the requirements of the music, not vice versa. Even in architecture, which is practiced with a tangible material, the term functional would not be applied to a structure that is adapted to the nature of the trucks and cranes that serve for transporting the building material, but rather to one that is adopted to the nature of the available building material and the end of the whole. The microphone is a means of communication, not of construction. Incidentally, the progress of recording technics has today made speculations on aesthetic limitations of that sort obsolete.

Even more dubious are speculations that seek to develop laws from the abstract nature of the media as such, for instance from the relation between optical and phonetical data in terms of the psychology of perception. At best this results in the ornamental applied-art duplicate of the 'abstract' picture. The antidote to commercialism in motion pictures is not the foundation of sects which dwell, let us say, on the affinity between certain colours and sounds and which mistake their obsessions for *avant-garde* ideas. Arbitrarily established rules for playing with the kaleidoscope are not criteria of art. If artistic beauty is derived exclusively from the material of the given art, it is degraded to the level of nature, but does not thereby acquire natural beauty. An art that aims at the geometrical purity, perfect proportions and regularity of natural objects infects beautiful forms, if they are still beautiful at all, with the reflexive element that inevitably dissolves natural beauty. For the latter, 'in connection with the abstract unity of form and the simplicity and purity of the sensuously perceived material' is 'owing to their abstraction, lifeless, and afford no truly actual unity; because for such unity we require ideal subjectivity which natural beauty always lacks, even in its perfect appearance'.[13] [...]

Montage

The application of the principle of montage to motion-picture music would help to make it more adequate to the present development phase, to begin with, simply because those media have been evolved independently of each other, and the modern technic by which they are brought together was not generated by them, but by the emergence of new facilities for reproduction. Montage makes the best of the aesthetically accidental form of the sound picture by transforming an entirely extraneous relation into a virtual element of expression.[14]

The direct merging of two media of such different historical origins would not make much more sense than the idiotic movie scripts in which a singer

---

[13]   G.W.F. Hegel, *Aesthetics: Lectures on Fine Art*, vol. 1 (trans. T.M. Knox), Oxford: Oxford University Press, 2010, p.142.

[14]   '[T]wo film pieces of any kind, placed together, inevitably combine into a new concept, a new quality, arising out of that juxtaposition.' Sergei Eisenstein, *The Film Sense* (trans. and ed. Jay Leyda), New York: Meridian Books, 1957, p.4. This applies not only to the clash of heterogeneous pictorial elements, but also to that of music and picture, particularly when they are not assimilated to each other.

loses his voice and then regains it in order to supply a pretext for exhausting all the possibilities of photographed sound. Such a synthesis would limit motion pictures to those accidental cases in which both media somehow coincide, that is to say, to the domain of synaesthesia, the magic of moods, semi-darkness and intoxication. In brief, the cinema would be confined to those expressive contents which, as Walter Benjamin showed, are basically incompatible with its technological reproducibility. The effects in which picture and music can be directly united are inevitably of the type that Benjamin calls 'auratic'[15] – actually they are degenerated forms of the 'aura', in which the spell of the here and now is technically manipulated.

There can be no greater error than producing pictures of which the aesthetic ideas are incompatible with their technical premises, and which at the same time camouflage this incompatibility. In the words of Benjamin,

> It is revealing that even today especially reactionary authors look in the same direction for the significance of film – finding, if not actually a sacred significance, then at least a supernatural one. In connection with Max Reinhardt's film version of *A Midsummer Night's Dream* [1935], Werfel comments that it was undoubtedly the sterile copying of the external world – with its streets, interiors, railway stations, restaurants, automobiles and beaches – that had prevented film up to now from ascending to the realm of art. 'Film has not yet realised its true purpose, its real possibilities. ... These consist in its unique ability to use natural means to give incomparably convincing expression to the fairylike, the marvellous, the supernatural.'[16]

Such magical pictures would be characterised by the tendency to fuse the music and the picture and to avoid montage as an instrument for the cognition of reality. It is hardly necessary to stress the artistic and social implication of Werfel's program – pseudo-individualisation achieved by industrial mass production.[17] It would also mark a retrogression from the achievements of modern music, which has freed itself from the *Musikdrama*, the programmatic school and synaesthesia, and is working with might and main at the dialectical task

---

15   '[W]hat withers in the age of the technological reproducibility of the work of art is the latter's aura'. The aura is '[a] strange tissue of space and time: the unique apparition of a distance, however near it may be. To follow with the eye – while resting on a summer afternoon – a mountain range on the horizon or a branch that casts its shadow on the beholder is to breathe the aura of those mountains, of that branch'. The aura is 'bound to his presence in the here and now. There is no facsimile of the aura'. Walter Benjamin, 'The Work of Art in the Age of Its Technological Reproducibility: Second Version' (trans. Edmund Jephcott and Harry Zohn), in *The Work of Art in the Age of Its Technological Reproducibility, and Other Writings on Media* (ed. Michael W. Jennings, Brigid Doherty and Thomas Y. Levin), Cambridge, MA: The Belknap Press of Harvard University Press, 2008, pp.23, 23, 31. EN: This and subsequent quotes have been amended to the E. Jephcott and H. Zohn translation.
16   Citing Franz Werfel, 'Ein Sommernachtstraum: Ein Film Von Shakespeare und Reinhardt', in *Neues Wiener Journal*, cited in *Lu*, 15 November 1935. EN: W. Benjamin, 'The Work of Art', *op. cit.*, p.29.
17   Eisenstein is aware of the materialistic potentialities of the principle of montage: the juxtaposition of heterogeneous elements raises them to the level of consciousness and takes over the function of theory. This is probably the meaning of Eisenstein's formulation: 'Montage has a realistic significance when the separate pieces produce, in juxtaposition, the generality, the synthesis of one's theme' (S. Eisenstein, *The Film Sense, op. cit.*, p.30). The real achievement of montage is always interpretation.

of becoming unromantic while preserving its character of music. The sound picture without montage would amount to a 'selling out' of Richard Wagner's idea – and his work falls to pieces even in its original form.

Aesthetic models of genuine motion-picture music are to be found in the incidental music written for dramas or the topical songs and production numbers in musical comedies. These may be of little musical merit, but they have never served to create the illusion of a unity of the two media or to camouflage the illusionary character of the whole, but functioned as stimulants because they were foreign elements, which interrupted the dramatic context, or tended to raise this context from the realm of literal immediacy into that of meaning. They have never helped the spectator to identify himself with the heroes of the drama, and have been an obstacle to any form of aesthetic empathy.

It has been pointed out above that today's cultural industry unwittingly carries out the verdict that is objectively pronounced by the development of the art forms and materials. Applying this law to the relation between pictures, words and music in the films, we might say that the insurmountable heterogeneity of these media furthers from the outside the liquidation of romanticism which is an intrinsic historical tendency within each art. The alienation of the media from each other reflects a society alienated from itself, men whose functions are severed from each other even within each individual. Therefore the aesthetic divergence of the media is potentially a legitimate means of expression, not merely a regrettable deficiency that has to be concealed as well as possible. And this is perhaps the fundamental reason why many light-entertainment pictures that fall far below the pretentious standards of the usual movie seem to be more substantial than motion pictures that flirt with real art. Movie revues usually come closest to the ideal of montage, hence music fulfils its proper function most adequately in them. Their potentialities are wasted only because of their standardisation, their spurious romanticism and their stupidly super-imposed plots of successful careers. They may be remembered if the motion picture is ever emancipated from the present-day conventions.

However, the principle of montage is suggested not merely by the intrinsic relation between pictures and music and the historical situation of the mechanically reproduced work of art. This principle is probably implied in the need that originally brought pictures and music together and that was of an antithetic character. Since their beginning, motion pictures have been accompanied by music. The pure cinema must have had a ghostly effect like that of the shadow play – shadows and ghosts have always been associated. The magic function of music that has been hinted at above probably consisted in appeasing the evil spirits unconsciously dreaded. Music was introduced as a kind of antidote against the picture. The need was felt to spare the spectator the unpleasantness involved in seeing effigies of living, acting and even speaking persons, who were at the same time silent. The fact that they are living and non-living at the same time is what constitutes their ghostly character, and music was introduced not to supply them with the life they lacked – this became its aim only in the era of total ideological planning – but to exorcise fear or help the spectator absorb the shock.[18]

---

[18]   Kurt London makes the following illuminating remark: 'It [motion-picture music] began not as a result of any artistic urge, but from the dire need of something which would drown the noise made by the projection. For in those times there was as yet no

Motion-picture music corresponds to the whistling or singing child in the dark. The real reason for the fear is not even that these people whose silent effigies are moving in front of one seem to be ghosts. The captions do their best to come to the aid of these images. But confronted with gesticulating masks, people experience themselves as creatures of the very same kind, as being threatened by muteness. The origin of motion-picture music is inseparably connected with the decay of spoken language, which has been demonstrated by Karl Kraus. It is hardly accidental that the early motion pictures did not resort to the seemingly most natural device of accompanying the pictures by dialogues of concealed actors, as is done in the Punch and Judy shows, but always resorted to music, although in the old horror or slapstick pictures it had hardly any relation to the plots.

The sound pictures have changed this original function of music less than might be imagined. *For the talking picture, too, is mute.* The characters in it are not speaking people but speaking effigies, endowed with all the features of the pictorial, the photographic two-dimensionality, the lack of spatial depth. Their bodiless mouths utter words in a way that must seem disquieting to anyone uninformed. Although the sound of these words is sufficiently different from the sound of natural words, they are far from providing 'images of voices' in the same sense in which photography provides us with images of people.

This technical disparity between picture and word is further accented by something much more deep-lying – the fact that all speech in motion pictures has an artificial, impersonal character. The fundamental principle of the motion picture, its basic invention, is the photographing of motions. This principle is so all-pervading that everything that is not resolved into visual motion has a rigid and heterogeneous effect with regard to the inherent law of the motion-picture form. Every movie director is familiar with the dangers of filmed theatre dialogues; and the technical inadequacy of psychological motion pictures partly derives from their inability to free themselves from the dominance of the dialogue. By its material, the cinema is essentially related to the ballet and the pantomime; speech, which presupposes man as a self, rather than the primacy of the gesture, ultimately is only loosely superimposed upon the characters.

Speech in motion pictures is the legitimate heir to the captions; it is a roll retranslated into acoustics, and that is what it sounds like even if the formulation of the words is not bookish but rather feigns the 'natural'. The fundamental divergences between words and pictures are unconsciously registered by the

---

sound-absorbent walls between the projection machine and the auditorium. This painful noise disturbed visual enjoyment to no small extent. Instinctively cinema proprietors had recourse to music, and it was the right way, using an agreeable sound to neutralise one less agreeable.' K. London, *Film Music*, op. cit., p.28. This sounds plausible enough. But there remains the question, why should the sound of the projector have been so unpleasant? Hardly because of its noisiness, but rather because it seemed to belong to the uncanny sphere which anyone who remembers the magic lantern performances can easily evoke. The grating, whirring sound actually had to be 'neutralised', 'appeased', not merely muted. If one reconstructed a cinema booth of the type used in 1900 and made the projector work in the audience room, more might be learned about the origin and meaning of motion-picture music than from extensive research. The experience in question is probably a collective one akin to panic, and it involves the flash-like awareness of being a helpless inarticulate man given over to the power of a mechanism. Such an impulse of feeling that something may befall a man even if he be 'many'. This is precisely the consciousness of one's own mechanisation.

spectator, and the obtrusive unity of the sound picture that is presented as a complete reduplication of the external world with all its elements is perceived as fraudulent and fragile. Speech in the motion picture is a stopgap, not unlike wrongly employed music that aims at being identical with the events on the screen. A talking picture without music is not very different from a silent picture, and there is even reason to believe that the more closely pictures and words are coordinated, the more emphatically their intrinsic contradiction and the actual muteness of those who seem to be speaking are felt by the spectators. This may explain – although the requirements of the market supply a more obvious reason – why the sound pictures still need music, while they seem to have all the opportunities of the stage and much greater mobility at their disposal.

Eisenstein's theory regarding movement can be appraised in the light of the foregoing discussion. The concrete factor of unity of music and pictures consists in the gestural element. This does not refer to the movement or 'rhythm' of the motion picture as such, but to the photographed motions and their function in the picture as a whole. The function of music, however, is not to 'express' this movement – here Eisenstein commits an error under the influence of Wagnerian ideas about the *Gesamtkunstwerk* and the theory of aesthetic empathy – but to release, or more accurately, to justify movement. The photographed picture as such lacks motivation for movement; only indirectly do we realise that the pictures are in motion, that the frozen replica of external reality has suddenly been endowed with the spontaneity that it was deprived of by its fixation, and that something petrified is manifesting a kind of life of its own. At this point music intervenes, supplying momentum, muscular energy, a sense of corporeity, as it were. Its aesthetic effect is that of a stimulus of motion, not a reduplication of motion. In the same way, good ballet music, for instance Stravinsky's, does not express the feelings of the dancers and does not aim at any identity with them, but only summons them to dance. Thus, the relation between music and pictures is antithetic at the very moment when the deepest unity is achieved.

The development of cinema music will be measured by the extent to which it is able to make this antithetic relation fruitful and to dispel the illusion of direct unity. The examples in the chapter on dramaturgy were discussed in reference to this idea. As a matter of principle, the relation between the two media should be made much more mobile than it has been. This means, on the one hand, that standard cues for interpolating music – as for background effect, or in scenes of suspense or high emotion – should be avoided as far as possible and that music should no longer intervene automatically at certain moments as though obeying a cue. On the other hand, methods that take into account the relation between the two media should be developed, just as methods have been developed that take into account the modifications of photographic exposures and camera installations. Thanks to them, it would be possible to make music perceptible on different levels, more or less distant, as a figure or a background, over-distinct or quite vague. Even musical complexes as such might be articulated into their different sound elements by means of an appropriate recording technique.

Furthermore it should be possible to introduce music at certain points without any pictures or words, and at other points, instead of gradually concluding the music or cautiously fading it out, to break it off abruptly, for instance at a change of scenery. The true muteness of the talking picture would thus be revealed and would have to become an element of expression. Or the picture might be treated as a musical theme, to which the actual music would serve as a mere accompaniment, consisting of musical base figures without any leading voice.

Conversely, music might be used to 'outshout' the action on the screen, and thus achieve the very opposite of what is demanded by conventional lyricism. This latter possibility was effectively exploited in the orchestrion scene of *Algiers*, where the noise of the mechanical instrument deafened the cries of mortal fear. However, even here the principle of montage was not fully applied, and the old prejudice that the music must be justified by the plot was respected.

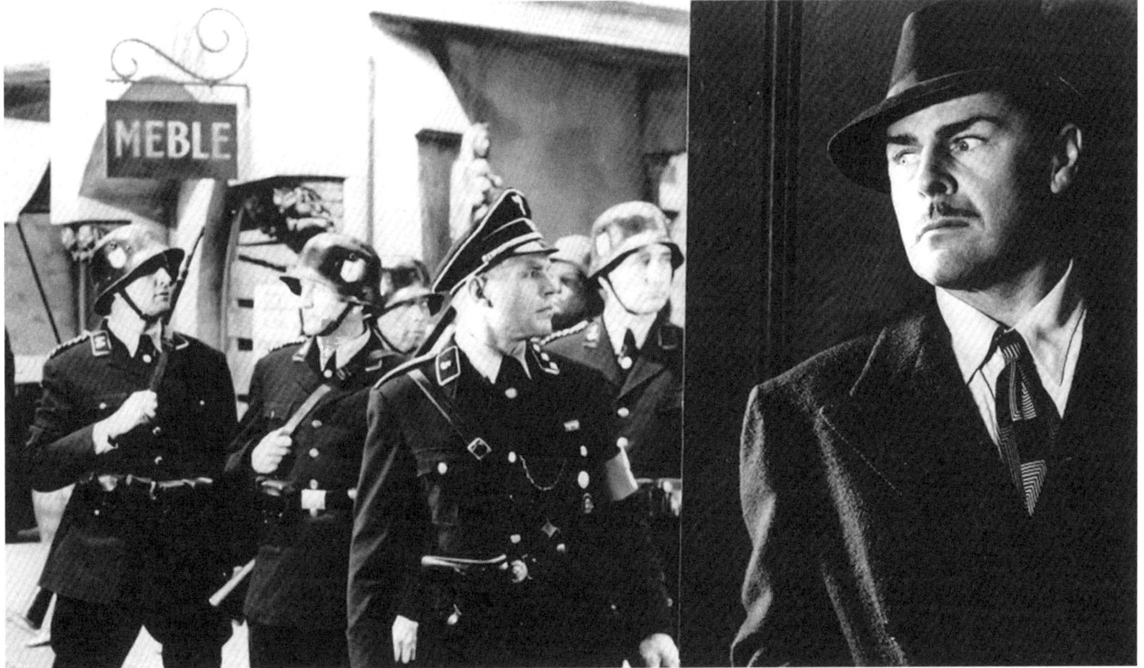

Promotional image
for Fritz Lang's
Hangmen Also Die!, 1943

Productivist Media-Activism Against Modernism

Composing for the Films is fascinating in part because it is a somewhat uneasy marriage between Adorno's Alexandrian modernism and Eisler's Brechtian productivism. In many ways, Eisler's aesthetic was closer to Benjamin's, which emphasised the emancipatory potential of new media, especially film – whereas Adorno stressed the overwhelming problems of these media insofar as they were part of the culture industry. As he made known in their private correspondence, Adorno was highly sceptical of the claims, such as the following, put forward by Benjamin in 'The Work of Art in the Age of Its Technological Reproducibility':

> It is inherent in the technology of film, as of sports, that everyone who witnesses these performances does so as a quasi-expert. Anyone who has listened to a group of newspaper boys leaning on their bicycles and discussing the outcome of a bicycle race will have an inkling of this. In the case of film, the newsreel demonstrates unequivocally that any individual can be in a position to be filmed. But that possibility is not enough. *Any person today can lay claim to being filmed.* This claim can best be clarified by considering the historical situation of literature today.[20]

In some ways, the 'The Work of Art' essay is an extension – with a focus on film and literature – of Benjamin's 1934 lecture to a left-wing audience in Paris, 'The Author as Producer', which dealt primarily with literature.

WALTER BENJAMIN, 'THE AUTHOR AS PRODUCER'

Reprinted from *New Left Review*, vol.1, no.62, July-August 1970, pp.83-89. First published in 1934. Translated from the German by John Heckman.

You recall how Plato treats the poets in his projected State. In the interest of the community, he does not allow them to live there. He had a high idea of the power of poetry. But he considered it destructive, superfluous – in a perfect community, needless to say. Since then, the question of the poet's right to exist has not often been stated with the same insistence; but it is today. Certainly it has rarely been posed in this *form*. But you are all more or less familiar with it as the question of the poet's autonomy: his freedom to write whatever he may please. You are not inclined to accord him this autonomy. You believe that the current social situation forces the poet to choose whom his activity will serve. The bourgeois writer of popular stories does not acknowledge this alternative. So you show him that even without admitting it, he works in the interests of a particular class. An advanced type of writer acknowledges this alternative. His decision is determined on the basis of the class struggle when he places himself on the side of the proletariat. But then his autonomy is done for. He directs his energies toward what is useful for the proletariat in the class struggle. We say that he espouses a *tendency*.[19]

For Benjamin, a work of art should no longer be seen as some kind of semi-autonomous reflection of its time and of the productive relations, but as directly standing in those relations:

When it examined a work of art, materialist criticism was accustomed to ask how that work stood in relation to the social relationships of production of its time. That is an important question. But also a very difficult one. The answer to it is not always unambiguous. Thus I would now like to suggest a question which lies closer at hand. A question which is somewhat more modest, which is less encompassing, but which seems to me to have a better chance of being answered. Namely, instead of asking: what is the relationship of a work of art to the relationships of production of the time? Is it in accord with them, is it reactionary or does it strive to overthrow them, is it revolutionary? – in place of this question, or in any case before asking this question, I would like to propose another. Before I ask: how does a literary work stand in relation *to* the relationships of production of a period, I would like to ask: how does it stand *in* them? This question aims directly at the function that the work has within the literary relationships of production of a period. In other words, it aims directly at a work's literary *technique*.[20] [...]

It will certainly be in line with your thinking if I now, only apparently without transition, go on to quite concrete literary problems. Russian ones. I should like to call your attention to Sergei Tretyakov and to the model of the 'operative' writer which he has defined and embodied.[21] This operative writer presents the clearest example of the functional relation which always exists, in any circumstances, between correct political tendency and a progressive literary technique. Of course it is only one example: I am keeping others in reserve. Tretyakov distinguishes the operative writer from one who gives information. His mission is not to report, but to struggle; he does not play the role of spectator, but actively intervenes. He defines his task through the statements he makes about his activity. At the time of the total collectivisation of agriculture, in 1928, when the slogan 'writers to the kolkhozy (collective farms)' was launched,

---

19   Translator's Note: Benjamin uses the word *Tendenz* throughout to mean the general direction a writer or his work takes, whether political or literary. It combines the notions of political line or group with literary school or movement.

20   TN: Benjamin uses the word *Technik* to denote the aesthetic technique of a work, but with considerable scientific and manufacturing connotations. Thus it is also close to 'technology' – the technical means by which a work is produced, its means of production.

21   TN: Sergei Tretyakov (1892-1939?) was a famous Soviet playwright and futurist. He was a leading participant in the Moscow group which produced the journals *Lef* and *Novy Lef*. His most important plays, produced in collaboration with Meyerhold and Eisenstein, were *Gas Masks* (1924), *Listen Moscow* (1924) and *Roar China* (1930). His views on newspapers were published in a collective volume edited by Chuzak in 1929, entitled *The Literature of Fact*, which also included contributions by Brik and Shklovsky. Attacking those who demanded 'Red Tolstoys', he wrote: 'There is no need for us to wait for Tolstoys, because we have our own epics. Our epics are the newspapers.' Tretyakov was purged about 1937. The date of his death shortly thereafter is unknown.

Tretyakov left for the 'Communist Lighthouse' commune and during two lengthy stays there undertook the following tasks: calling mass meetings, collecting money to pay for tractors, persuading individual peasants who worked alone to enter the kolkhoz, inspecting reading rooms, creating wall-newspapers and editing the kolkhoz newspaper, being a reporter for Moscow papers, introducing radio and travelling movies. It is not surprising that the novel *Master of the Fields*,[22] which Tretyakov wrote after his stay, had a substantial influence on the further formation of agricultural collectives.

In this essay, Benjamin redefines 'literature' along Productivist lines. Literature is now no longer locked in the domain of belles-lettres but has its basis in the popular press and its activist transformation.

Thus I hope I have shown that the portrayal of the author as a producer must be derived from the press. For the press, at least the Russian press, makes us acknowledge that the powerful process of transformation of which I spoke before goes beyond not only the conventional separations between genres, between writer and poet, between the scholar and the populariser, but it also forces us to re-examine the separation between author and reader. The press is the most authoritative instance of this process and therefore any study of the author as a producer must deal with it.

But we cannot remain at that point. For as yet the newspapers of Western Europe are not a suitable instrument of production in the hands of the writer. They still belong to capital.

Aside from Soviet practices, the main inspiration for Benjamin in this text is Brecht, who himself took many cues from the Soviet avant-garde:

Brecht elaborated the concept of 'functional transformation' (*Umfunktionierung*) for the transformation of the forms and instruments of production by a progressive intelligentsia – interested in the liberation of the means of production and thus useful in the class struggle. He was the first to formulate for intellectuals this far-reaching demand: do not simply transmit the apparatus of production without simultaneously changing it to the maximum extent possible in the direction of socialism.

---

[22] Editors' Note: Benjamin makes references Tretyakov's *Feld-Herren: Der Kampf um eine Kollektiv-Wirtschaft* (Master of the Fields: The Struggle for a Collective Economy, Berlin: Malik Verlag 1931). The back cover of the book indicates that it is a translation of Tretjakov's Приказываем Земле, although further publication details could not be found. For more on Benjamin's relation to Tretyakov, see Gerald Raunig, *Art and Revolution: Transversal Activism in the Long Twentieth Century*, New York: Semiotext(e), 2007, pp.163-69.

In 'The Work of Art' essay, Benjamin applies his analysis of the transformation of literary labour to film:

> All this can readily be applied to film, where shifts that in literature took place over centuries have occurred in a decade. In cinematic practice – above all, in Russia – this shift has already been partly realised. Some of the actors taking part in Russian films are not actors in our sense but people who portray *themselves* – and primarily in their own work process. In Western Europe today, the capitalist exploitation of film obstructs the human being's legitimate claim to being reproduced. The claim is also obstructed, incidentally, by unemployment, which excludes large masses from production – the process in which their primary entitlement to be reproduced would lie. Under these circumstances, the film industry has an overriding interest in stimulating the involvement of the masses through illusionary displays and ambiguous speculations.[21]

Benjamin claims that in contrast to modernist painting such as Picasso's, film can inspire 'progressive' responses from non-specialists.[22] It is non-elitist and progressive, as long as its potential is not wilfully curtailed. For years, these theses languished in obscurity, but in the 1960s the text's visibility and renown increased. As editor of his late friend's work, Adorno did much to publish Benjamin's writings after the War, but he was wary of the avant-garde rhetoric of the 'Work of Art' essay, and at the end of the 1960s complained about its 'overbearing popularity' (*penetrante Beliebtheit*).[23] Adorno's own analysis of the culture industry was a staple of left-wing media critique, yet it was also challenged by the resurgent interest in Benjamin and in Brecht. [24] In contrast to Adorno and Horkheimer's totalising indictments, these authors had emphasised the capacity of industrial media – radio, but also the press and film – for becoming two-way rather than one-way channels. Instead of being consumers, workers could become producers and seize the means of production.

In art, modernist media essentialism quickly became discredited during this period. In 1965, Fluxus artist Dick Higgins introduced the notion of intermedia, claiming that much of the best work falls in between established media. Indeed, new forms such as environments, happenings and events could hardly be encompassed by a Greenbergian framework.

> Much of the best work being produced today seems to fall between media. This is no accident. The concept of the separation between media arose in the Renaissance. The idea that a painting is made of paint on canvas or that a sculpture should not be painted seems characteristic of the kind of social thought – categorising and dividing society into nobility with its various subdivisions, untitled gentry, artisans, serfs and landless workers – which we call the feudal conception of the Great Chain of Being. This essentially mechanistic approach continued to be relevant throughout the first two industrial revolutions, just concluded, and into the present era of automation, which constitutes, in fact, a third industrial revolution.[25]

This pleasantly potted history echoes McLuhan's pronouncements on the advent of a culture of linearity, segmentation and specialisation in the Renaissance, occasioned by the invention of print and linear perspective and having shattered the more unitary world of the Middle Ages. By contrast, Higgins's opening line seems to ironically mimic Greenberg's apodictic statements in what constitutes the 'best' art of the present – which for Higgins is a very different type of art than for Greenberg.

> Part of the reason that Duchamp's objects are fascinating while Picasso's voice is fading is that the Duchamp pieces are truly between media, between sculpture and something else, while a Picasso is readily classifiable as a painted ornament. Similarly, by invading the land between collage and photography, the German John Heartfield produced what are probably the greatest graphics of our century, surely the most powerful political art that has been done to date.
>
> The ready-made or found object, in a sense an intermedium since it was not intended to conform to the pure medium, usually suggests this, and therefore suggests a location in the field between the general area of art media and those of life media.[26]

According to Higgins, there is no need to put the urinal back in the bathroom, for the ready-made is already a bridge between art and life.[27] If this pronouncement can be regarded as naïve from a later vantage point, after the seemingly definitive institutionalisation of the ready-made, it nonetheless remains significant that Higgins here proposes a different interpretation than that of 'Duchamp turning an everyday item into an artwork'. Here, at a moment when the ready-made was about to be museified, Higgins values precisely its indeterminacy, its capacity to mix up categories and transgress frameworks, at least temporarily. This is the importance of intermedia, which shows its political potential in John Heartfield's photo-graphic Productivism.

Like Higgins, Nam June Paik was a member of Fluxus. His work, too, sought a way out of modernism and its focus on the essence of (traditional) artistic media; he found one escape route in video. Though he has been canonised as 'the father of video art', the point was not to merely develop a new medium for art, not merely a new specialism. Rather, video was supposed to be an intermedium capable of traversing and transforming different fields. A McLuhan-influenced essay Paik published in 1970 in the *Radical Software* journal stresses video's potential for education in the 'paperless society' to come:

> America has 5,000 colleges, which require 20,000 philosophy teachers. The shortage of qualified teachers of philosophy is acute, especially at the junior community college level. This discipline cannot profit much from automatic devices or computerised quiz machines. The supreme act of 'Philosophieren' requires a total involvement of the whole personality. Therefore new information techniques such as videotape, film, audio devices, loop techniques, non-linear printing techniques, light art, stroboscope, medical electronics, brain wave transmissions, brain wave transmission should be used for the total conveyance of great philosophers' messages, and for the stimulation of students' own 'Philosophieren' and maybe for the preparation of post-McLuhan, non-linear, possibly more iconographic and totally involved 22nd-century philosophy. If philosophy wants to recover the hegemony which it held for centuries, the students of philosophy proper should also be exposed to today's electronic situation, instead of to parchment philology.[28]

A more orthodox Marxist-Brechtian-Benjaminian note is sounded by Hans Magnus Enzensberger in his widely and internationally discussed 1970 essay 'Constituents of a Theory of the Media'. In this text, the German writer and critic complains that the left's ignorance of the media has allowed them to fall into the hands of mystics and obscurantists.

HANS MAGNUS ENZENSBERGER, 'CONSTITUENTS OF A THEORY OF THE MEDIA'

Reprinted from *New Left Review*, vol.1, no.64, November-December 1970, pp.27-28, 20-21.

That the Marxist Left should argue theoretically and act practically from the standpoint of the most advanced productive forces in their society, that they should develop in depth all the liberating factors immanent in these forces and use them strategically, is no academic expectation but a political necessity. However, with a single great exception, that of Walter Benjamin (and in his footsteps, Brecht), Marxists have not understood the consciousness industry and have been aware only of its bourgeois-capitalist dark side and not of its socialist possibilities. An author like Georg Lukács is a perfect example of this theoretical and practical backwardness. Nor are the works of Horkheimer and Adorno free of a nostalgia which clings to early bourgeois media.

Recalling Benjamin, Enzensberger argues that in fundamental ways, the 'new media' in fact represent an implicit challenge to capitalism:

The new media are egalitarian in structure. Anyone can take part in them by a simple switching process. The programmes themselves are not material things and can be reproduced at will. In this sense the electronic media are entirely different from the older media like the book or the easel painting, the exclusive class character of which is obvious. Television programmes for privileged groups are certainly technically conceivable - closed-circuit television - but run counter to the structure. Potentially the new media do away with all educational privileges and thereby with the cultural monopoly of the bourgeois intelligentsia. This is one of the reasons for the intelligentsia's resentment against the new industry. As for the 'spirit' which they are endeavouring to defend against 'depersonalisation' and 'mass culture', the sooner they abandon it the better. [...]

The new media are orientated towards action, not contemplation; towards the present, not tradition. Their attitude to time is completely opposed to that of bourgeois culture which aspires to possession, that is, to extension in time, best of all, to eternity. The media produce no objects that can be hoarded and auctioned. They do away completely with 'intellectual property' and liquidate the 'heritage', that is to say, the class-specific handing-on of non-material capital.

In the late 1960s and 1970s, many heeded such calls for the abandonment of traditional authorship in favour of a more egalitarian, collective mode of working. Artists embraced media such as video for activist practices, founding media collectives that sought to produce and distribute in alternative ways, transforming subjectivity and the nature of work and collaboration in the process: Marxist and feminist film collectives, for instance, but also groups that used the newly affordable medium of video. Particularly in the US context, video groups and magazines such as *Radical Software* were often marked by the countercultural or hippie ethos markedly seen in the do-it-yourself ideology of the California-based *Whole Earth Catalog* (published every several months between 1968–72), with its 'access to tools' slogan.

Cover image of *Filmkritk*, June 1976,
co-edited by Harun Farocki and
dedicated to activist video

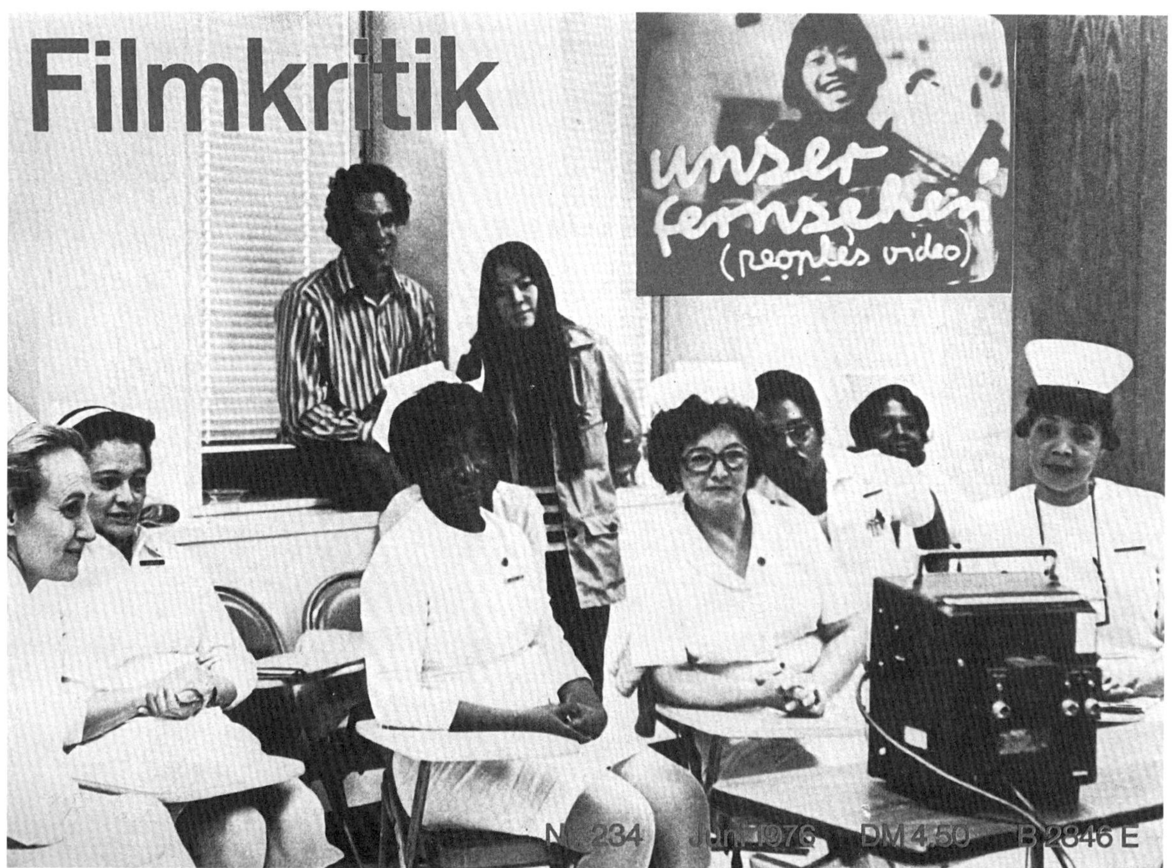

Autonomedia

The new collectivism was not limited to artists and activists focussing on 'new media' such as video and television. A case in point is the New York branch of (the originally British group) Art & Language, which included Joseph Kosuth, who had famously transformed visual art into a series of linguistic-analytical propositions *on* art, as in his canvas-sized dictionary definitions. Kosuth argued that visual art's essence was by no means formal, but could only be articulated on a conceptual level; rather than being a collection of specific arts, contemporary art became 'art in general' (or generic art, as Thierry de Duve put it).[29] No longer bound by formal or medium-specific constraints, conceptual work often incorporated 'new' media (for art) such as print and typography, photography and video. Kosuth was thus a harbinger of the 'post-medium condition' that art historian Rosalind Krauss was to later diagnose.[30]

By the mid-1970s, the discussions in Art & Language had moved on from the nature of art to the *functioning* of art and artists in society. Dictionary definitions were no longer deemed enough, and Art & Language in New York engaged in ulti-mately destructive discussions about individual and collective authorship. Should members abandon their solo careers, and should group activities be 'artistic' or move more fully in an activist and political direction? The New York group's media platform was the journal *The Fox*, and for its third and final issue Mel Ramsden chronicled the group's fractious discussions. Using the pen name Peter Benchley (borrowed from the author of the 1974 novel *Jaws*), Ramsden documented the debate in great detail but protected the perhaps-not-so-innocent by giving them all the names of tropical fish.[31] In this passage, 'Oscellatus' (Kosuth) proposes working in a truly collective manner for a number of months to see if and how that works.

PETER BENCHLEY [MEL RAMSDEN],
'THE LUMPEN-HEADACHE'

Reprinted from *The Fox*, no. 3, 1976, pp. 33-34.

Oscellatus: It's about testing the water in a certain way. Seeing how it actually will function because some of us will have certain fears about it being coercive but one won't know until one fucking tries.

Pongo Pongo: Of course it's coercive!

Oscellatus: Leave it to you to say it.

[...]

Jarbua: Socialism, it seems to me, is to provide the conditions of individual free-dom, not to provide the conditions of mob rule ... There can't be any individual freedom under capitalism because of the nature of the social coercion. Now if there can be individual freedom under socialism, I think there can, and that's why people are working toward socialism …

Bellica: The whole point of capitalism *is* that you *are* an individual.

Jarbua: But because you're not an individual in the sense of a super-star (you're) an individual in the sense of having the freedom to challenge the institutions.

Pongo Pongo: Jarbua, can I say something, this *is* fucking coercive.

Jarbua: Of course it is.

Pongo Pongo: It is coercive. I don't need outside people to convince me that those points of unity point towards socialism. I watch my relationships with Punkay, Bellica, Hypostomous, with Puntius Stigma and Oscellatus all deteriorate under capitalist conditions, market penetration. *This* is a way to fix those relations.

Oscellatus: Then let's see what problems come up with this that might be equally strong but of a different character, we won't know until we try.

Pongo Pongo: Yeah, but what use is it to say that in order to get away from the flood waters you have to build a bridge but if you build a bridge there 'might' be worse problems on the other side. You have no choice. We have no choice. We have to go on.

Oscellatus: That's all I'm saying.

Pongo Pongo: Of course it could be a disaster.

Oscellatus: Exactly. So I was suggesting a transitional period. So let's just talk amongst ourselves and talk that out…

[…]

Clarius: What do we think about a transition period? How would it operate?

Pongo Pongo: I think two weeks is plenty of time.

Oscellatus: Two weeks? Puntius Stigma said six months.

Art & Language never actually made 'the transition' and eventually disintegrated into warring factions – one of which, a small core in the UK, continued to use the name for their artistic and theoretical practice. However, many other self-organised groups (perhaps less invested in their artistic careers) developed different forms of subjectivation and collaboration in a more sustained manner. Often what tied such groups together was no mere abstract rejection of 'the system' but a shared subjectivity on the basis of identity. In the place of Marxist Productivism, micropolitical forms of artistic and media activism proliferated. Here one can think of feminist collectives

such as the London Women's Film Group (established in 1972) and *Heresies* journal
(founded in New York in 1977). The practice of General Idea – a group hailing from
Vancouver, whose queer conceptualism was networked internationally – embraced
not just a variety of media (print matter, video and performance) but also of alternative forms of life. Among General Idea's media and platforms was the long-running
FILE Megazine, first published in 1972, which devoted issues to topics such as glamour and sexual transgression.[32]

An interest in different forms of subjectivation and new social formations is also
what drove Félix Guattari's interest in media practices and his involvement with the
'free radio' movement in Italy during the late 1970s – in particular Radio Alice in
Bologna, with which Franco 'Bifo' Berardi was involved.[33] One could say that in texts
such as his essay 'Popular Free Radio' (1978) Guattari recasts some of Enzensberger's
concerns in micropolitical and autonomist terms.

FÉLIX GUATTARI, 'POPULAR FREE RADIO'

Reprinted from Neil Strauss and Dave Mandl
(ed.), *Radiotext(e)*, New York: Semiotext(e), 1993,
pp.85–86. Translated from the French by David
Sweet.

The evolution of the means of mass communication seems to be going in two
directions:
- toward hyper-concentrated systems controlled by the apparatus of state,
  of monopolies, of big political machines with the aim of shaping opinion
  and of adapting the attitudes and unconscious schemas of the population
  to dominant norms;
- toward miniaturised systems that create the possibility of a collective
  appropriation of the media, that provide real means of communication, not
  only the 'great masses', but also to minorities, to marginalised and deviant
  groups of all kinds.

On the one hand: always more centralisation, conformism, oppression; on the
other, the perspective of a new space of freedom, self-management, and the fulfilment of the singularities of desire. [...]

It was possible right away to conceive of technical equipment for the kind
of production and consumption that was adapted to 'group subjects' and not to
subjugated groups. But with capitalist and state decision-makers lacking any
interest in such an orientation, it is the people 'of means' (*moyen lourd*) that have
triumphed. And today one has a tendency to base the legitimacy of this choice on
the nature of things, on the 'natural' evolution of the technology.

With Free Radio, we find ourselves before the same type of technicopolit-
ical problem. But here, because of the confrontation with power, it's the people
'of lesser means' (*moyens pauvre*) who assert themselves as if by necessity. In
fact, at the present stage, the only way to resist the jamming and the searches is
by multiplying the number of transmitters and my miniaturising the material
in order to minimise the risks. (This daily guerrilla warfare of the airwaves is

perfectly compatible with the kind of public airing that takes place whenever the balance of powers is poised for it: public broadcasts, national holidays, etc.)

But the point the organisers of the popular Free Radio stations particularly emphasise is that the totality of technical and human means must permit the establishment of a veritable feedback system between the listeners and the broadcast team: whether through direct intervention by phone, through opening studio doors, through interviews or making programmes on cassettes by listeners, etc. The Italian experience, in this regard, shows us the immense field of new possibilities that is opened in this way; in particular, the experience of the Bologna group that organised Radio Alice and the journal *A Traverso*. We realise here that radio constitutes but one element at the heart of an entire range of communication means, from daily, informal encounters in the Piazza Maggiore to the newspaper – via billboards, mural paintings, posters, leaflets, meetings, community activities, celebrations, etc.

In this text, we see the question of the medium becoming one of collective and transversal media activism, because modern media allow for other forms of production than the top-down, one-way model. Around 1970s, authors such as Enzensberger or Alexander Kluge and Oskar Negt still thought they could build on traditional notions of the proletariat in their conceptualisations of radical media practice and of a 'proletarian counterpublic sphere'.[34] For Guattari, in line with Autonomia in Italy, this was no longer realistic. The development of counter-media remained the goal, but such 'autonomedia' (as the name of a Brooklyn-based publishing collective has it) would have to be autonomous from orthodox Marxist party politics.

From the mid-1980s on, the AIDS crisis became a pressing concern for several groups, amongst them General Idea, which transformed Robert Indiana's iconic *LOVE* (1965) into an AIDS logotype, or 'imagevirus'.[35] Group Material and AIDS-activist collectives such as ACT UP and Gran Fury used diverse media for their projects, from publications and exhibitions to video activism and community television. The artist Gregg Bordowitz, infected with HIV, wrote 'Picture a Coalition' (1987) while being active in Testing the Limits, a video collective within ACT UP.

Imagine a screening. In a local community centre a consumer VCR deck and a TV set sit on a table. Representatives from the various communities affected by AIDS sit in front of the TV. They watch a video composed of interviews with each of them. They see themselves pictured in relation to one another as they sit next to one another.

Consider this screening. It presents both means and ends for the video AIDS activist. The AIDS movement, like other radical movements, creates itself as it attempts to represent itself. Video puts into play the means of recognising one's place within the movement in relation to that of others in the movement. Video has the potential to render the concerted efforts – as yet unimagined – between groups. The most significant challenge to the movement is coalition building, because the AIDS epidemic has engendered a community of people who cannot afford *not* to recognise themselves as a community and to act as one.

[...] I am a member of the gay community and a member of the AIDS community. Furthermore, I am a gay member of the AIDS community, a community that

Still from DIVA TV,
Like a Prayer,
1990, colour video
with sound, 26min
Courtesy DIVA TV/
Catherine Gund

See p.277 of this reader
for more images

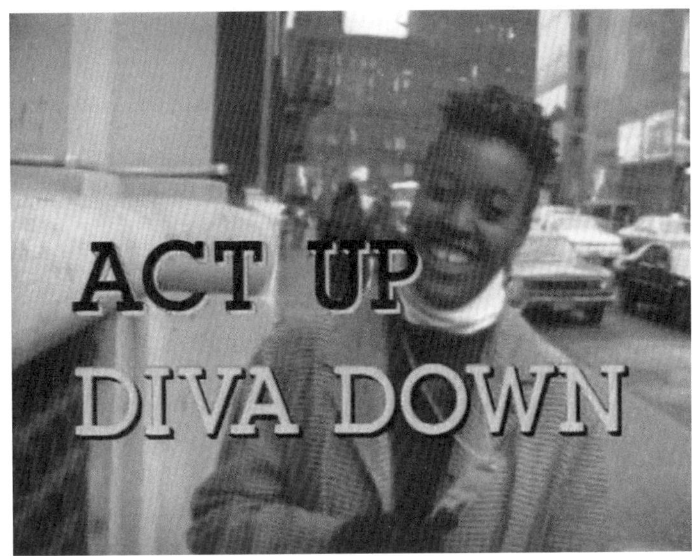

> some will establish by force, for no other end but containment, toward no other end but repression, with no other end but our deaths – a community that must, instead, establish *itself* in the face of this containment and repression. We must proudly identify ourselves as a coalition.[36]

If this scenario invokes a kind of communal home video, the AIDS activists also used local cable television. In 1985, Bordowitz had attended the Whitney Independent Study Program (together with Andrea Fraser), and his AIDS activism can also be seen as a form of engagement with institutional frames: a form of 'desertion' into new media, alternative modes of distribution, but without the grand avant-garde gesture of 'leaving the art world'. Artist-activists used all available institutions and media, from video and cable TV, posters and inserts in the press to exhibitions and academic journals; for instance, Group Material curated an exhibition on the AIDS crisis at the Dia Art Foundation in New York and art historian Douglas Crimp edited an issue of *October* (to which Bordowitz contributed 'Picture a Coalition').[37] Such practices can be seen as extended and intensified forms of institutional critique, though they were mostly excised from institutional critique's emerging canon.[38]

In 1990, at the peak of the AIDS crisis, feminist critical theorist Nancy Fraser coined the term 'subaltern counterpublic'. Fraser and others, such as the literary critic and cultural theories Michael Warner, argued that women, workers, LGBTQ communities and people of colour have historically responded to their marginalisation by forming their own 'subaltern counterpublics', using whatever means and media were available for their collective self-formation and self-organisation.[39] Certain forms of AIDS activism can be seen in those terms; using art-world institutions and other media to build and maintain a counterpublic. However, as Bordowitz has stressed, this counterpublic was a coalition, a montage of different constituencies. If a counterpublic is not to become a mere exercise in self-ghettoisation, the element of transversality is of crucial importance; the forging of connections and coalitions with others who may not have the same profile.

By the mid-1990s, the media activism and theory of the previous two decades were reformatted for the digital age. Informed by (post-)punk, the Amsterdam squatting scene and its burgeoning hacker culture, by Guattarian autonomedia and AIDS activism, a number of artists and organisers in Amsterdam gathered around what they called 'tactical media'. Shaped by Amsterdam's public access cable channels and influenced by video and TV activists and artists from New York (such as Paper Tiger Television) to Eastern Europe and West Africa, these *Next 5 Minutes* festivals started in 1993 with a focus on 'tactical television'. The de Certeau–derived opposition between the tactical and the strategic was, in this context, intended as a displacement of the opposition between mass-media broadcasting and small-scale 'narrowcasting'; tactical practices could use cable channels but also infiltrate network television.

By the second edition in 1996, the burgeoning Amsterdam hacker scene had created its own internet provider, XS4ALL, and the focus of *Next 5 Minutes* shifted to digital activism under the general moniker 'tactical media'. In the following 1997 essay-cum-manifesto, David Garcia and Geert Lovink – two key players in this scene – present a theoretical summary of tactical media.

DAVID GARCIA AND GEERT LOVINK, 'THE ABC OF TACTICAL MEDIA'

Available at http://www.nettime.org/Lists-Archives/nettime-l-9705/msg00096.html (last accessed on 19 September 2020). First published in 1997. The text is here provided as posted on the Nettime mailing list, including stylistic irregularities, to acknowledge new modes of production, distribution and reception that emerged in the 1990s; only minor amendments have been made to spelling for the sake of consistency.

Tactical Media are what happens when the cheap 'do it yourself' media, made possible by the revolution in consumer electronics and expanded forms of distribution (from public access cable to the internet) are exploited by groups and individuals who feel aggrieved by or excluded from the wider culture. Tactical media do not just report events, as they are never impartial they always participate and it is this that more than anything separates them from mainstream media.

A distinctive tactical ethic and aesthetic that has emerged, which is culturally influential from MTV through to recent video work made by artists. It began as a quick and dirty aesthetic although it is just another style it (at least in its camcorder form) has come to symbolize a verite for the 90's.

Tactical media are media of crisis, criticism and opposition. This is both the source their power, ('anger is an energy' : John Lydon), and also their limitation. their typical heroes are; the activist, Nomadic media warriors, the pranxter, the hacker,the street rapper, the camcorder kamikaze, they are the happy negatives, always in search of an enemy. But once the enemy has been named and vanquished it is the tactical practitioner whose turn it is to fall into crisis. Then (despite their achievements) its easy to mock them, with catch phrases of the right, 'politically correct' 'Victim culture' etc. More theoretically the identity politics, media critiques and theories of representation, that became the foundation of much western tactical media are themselves in crisis. These ways of thinking are widely seen as, carping and repressive remnants of an outmoded humanism.

To believe that issues of representation are now irrelevant is to believe that the very real life chances of groups and individuals are not still crucially affected by the available images circulating in any given society. And the fact that we no longer see the mass media as the sole and centralized source of our self definitions might make these issues more slippery but that does not make them redundant.

Tactical media a qualified form of humanism. A useful antidote to both, what Peter Lamborn Wilson described, as 'the unopposed rule of money over human beings'. But also as an antidote to newly emerging forms of technocratic scientism which under the banner of post-humanism tend to restrict discussions of human use and social reception.

What makes Our Media Tactical? In 'The Practice of Every Day Life' De Certueau analysed popular culture not as a 'domain of texts or artefacts but rather as a set of practices or operations performed on textual or text like structures'. He shifted the emphasis from representations in their own right to the 'uses' of representations. In other words how do we as consumers use the texts and artefacts that surround us. And the answer, he suggested, was 'tactically'. That is in far more creative and rebellious ways than had previously been imagined. He described the process of consumption as a set of tactics by which the weak make use of the strong. He characterized the rebellious user (a term he preferred to consumer) as tactical and the presumptuous producer (in which he included authors, educators, curators and revolutionaries) as strategic. Setting up this dichotomy allowed him to produce a vocabulary of tactics rich and complex enough to amount to a distinctive and recognizable aesthetic. An existential aesthetic. An aesthetic of Poaching, tricking, reading, speaking, strolling, shopping, desiring. Clever tricks, the hunter's cunning, maneuvers, polymorphic situations, joyful discoveries, poetic as well as warlike. Awareness of this tactical/strategic dichotomy helped us to name a class of producers of who seem uniquely aware of the value of these temporary reversals in the flow of power. And rather than resisting these rebellions do everything in their power to amplify them. And indeed make the creation of spaces, channels and platforms for these reversals central to their practice. We dubbed their (our) work tactical media.

Tactical Media are never perfect, always in becoming, performative and pragmatic, involved in a continual process of questioning the premises of the channels they work with. This requires the confidence that the content can survive intact as it travels from interface to interface. But we must never forget that hybrid media has its opposite its nemesis, the Medialen Gesamtkunstwerk. The final program for the electronic Bauhaus.

Of course it is much safer to stick to the classic rituals of the underground and alternative scene. Bu tactical media are based on a principal of flexible response, of working with different coalitions, being able to move between the different entities in the vast media landscape without betraying their original motivations. Tactical Media may be hedonistic, or zealously euphoric. Even fashion hypes have their uses. But it is above all mobility that most characterizes the tactical practitioner. The desire and capability to combine or jump from one media to another creating a continuous supply of mutants and hybrids. To cross boarders, connecting and re-wiring a variety of disciplines and always taking full advantage of the free spaces in the media that are continually appearing because of the pace of technological change and regulatory uncertainty.

Although tactical media include alternative media, we are not restricted to that category. In fact we introduced the term tactical to disrupt and take us beyond the rigid dichotomies that have restricted thinking in this area, for so long, dichotomies such as amateur Vs professional, alternative Vs mainstream. Even private Vs public.

Our hybrid forms are always provisional. What counts are the temporary connections you are able to make. Here and now, Not some vaporware promised for the future. But what we can do on the spot with the media we have access to. Here in Amsterdam we have access to local TV, digital cities and fortresses of new and old media. In other places they might have theater, street demonstrations, experimental film, literature, photography. Tactical media's mobility connects it to a wider movement of migrant culture. Espousedby the proponents of what Nie Ascherson described as the stimulating pseudo science of Nomadism. 'The human race say its exponants are entering a new epoch of movement and migration. The subjects of history once the settled farmers and citizens, have become the migrants, the refugees the gastarbeiters, the asylum seekers, the urban homeless.' [...]

But capital is also radically deterritorialized. This is why we like being based in a building like De Waag, an old fortress in the center of Amsterdam. We happily accept the paradox of *centers* of tactical media. As well as castles in the air, we need fortresses of bricks and mortar, to resist a world of unconstrained nomadic capital. Spaces to plan not just improvise and the possibility of capitalizing on acquired advantages, has always been the preserve of 'strategic' media. As flexible media tacticians, who are not afraid of power, we are happy to adopt this approach ourselves.

Following Donald Trump's election victory and speculation about the role played by alt-right media activism (meme wars) in his campaign, proponents of tactical media such as Garcia and Lovink found themselves wondering what had gone wrong. Tactical media activism had been turned into a neo-fascist weapon, aimed not at self-emancipation but at the subjugation of citizens and denizens. We've gone from Walter Benjamin to Steve Bannon and his ghoulish progeny.

Event views, *Next 5 Minutes 2: Tactical Media*, Amsterdam and Rotterdam, 18-21 January 1996. Photo: Jan Sprij. Courtesy V2_, Lab for Unstable Media, Rotterdam

Opposite page, above: Performance view, Critical Art Emsemble, *The Matter of Media*, 1996

Opposite page, below: 'Media in the Diaspora' panel with Sivam Krishnapillai (centre) and Krzysztof Wodiczko (right)

Following page, below: David Garcia

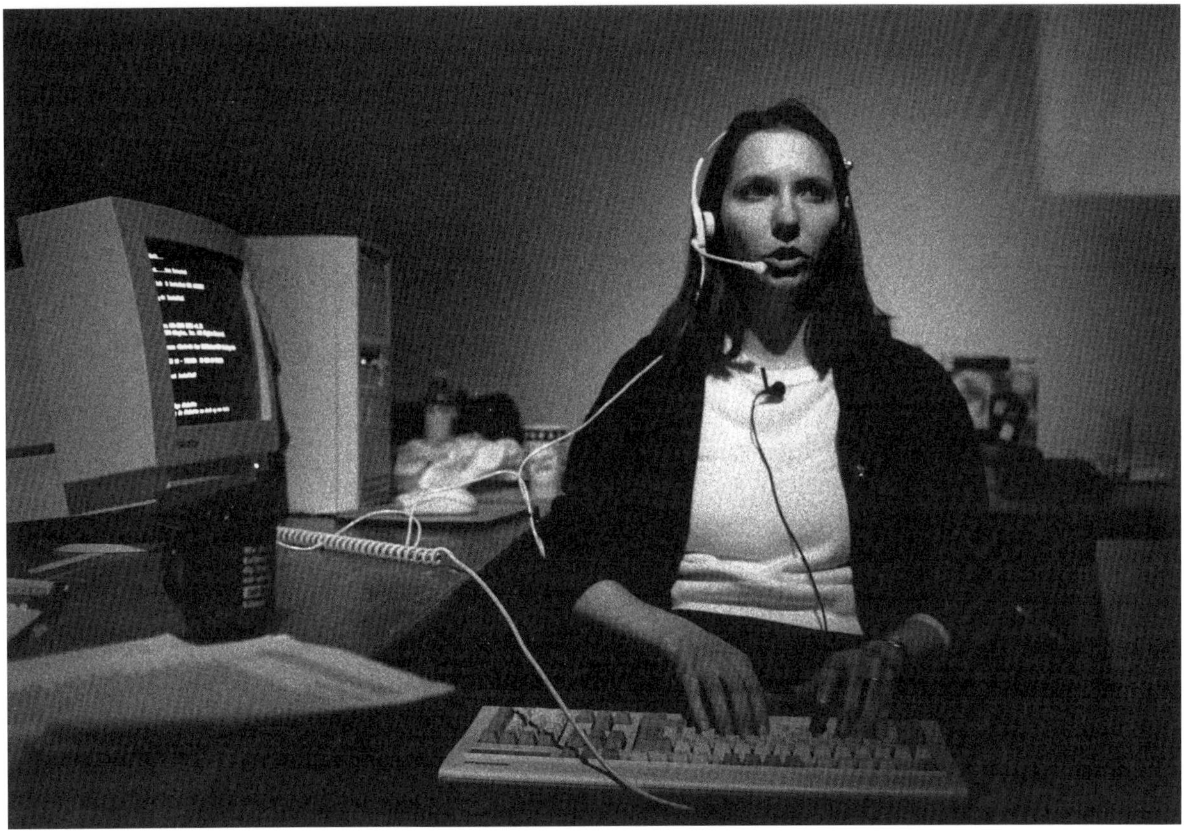

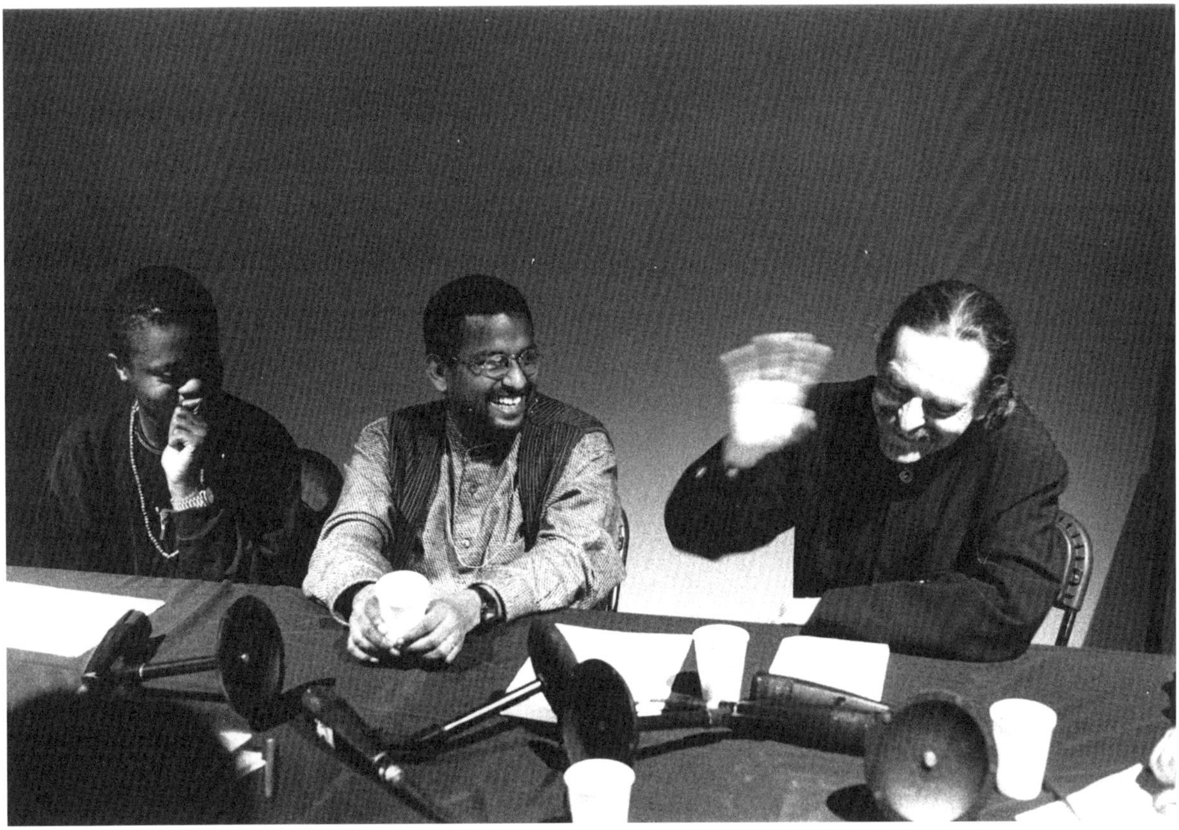

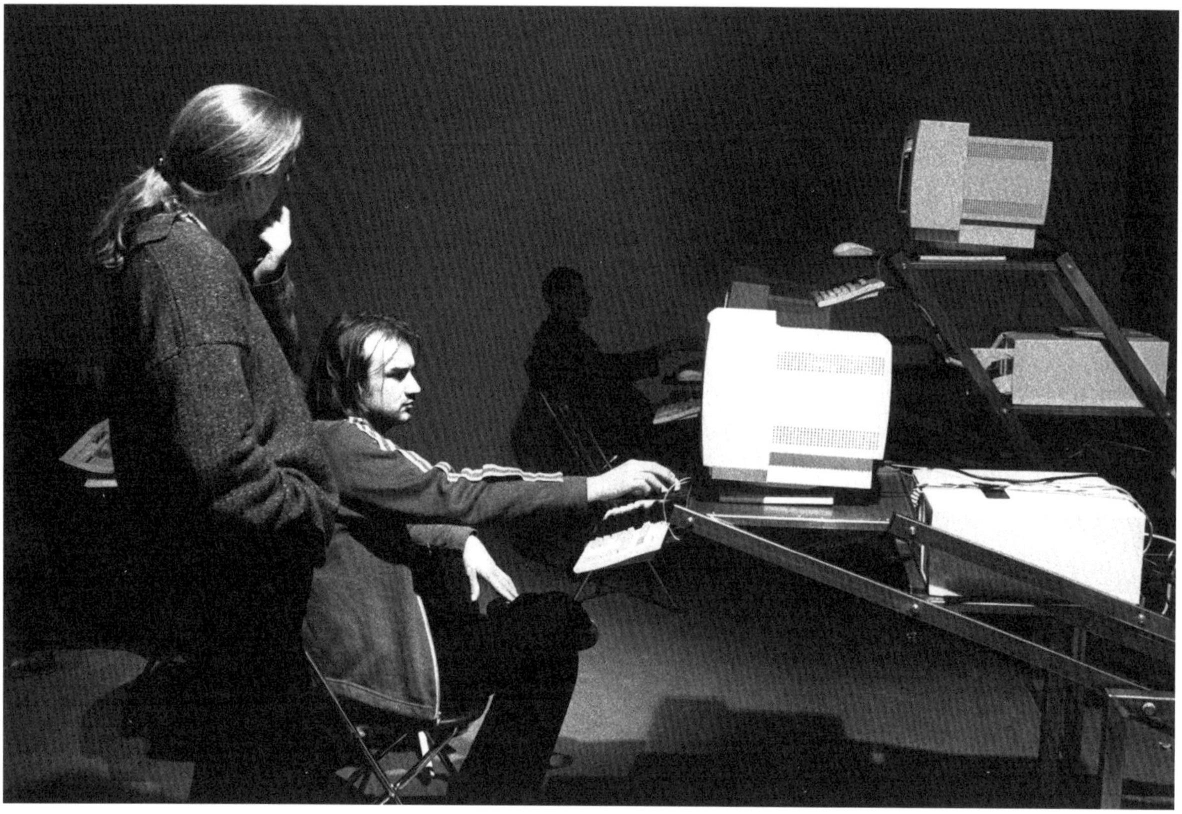

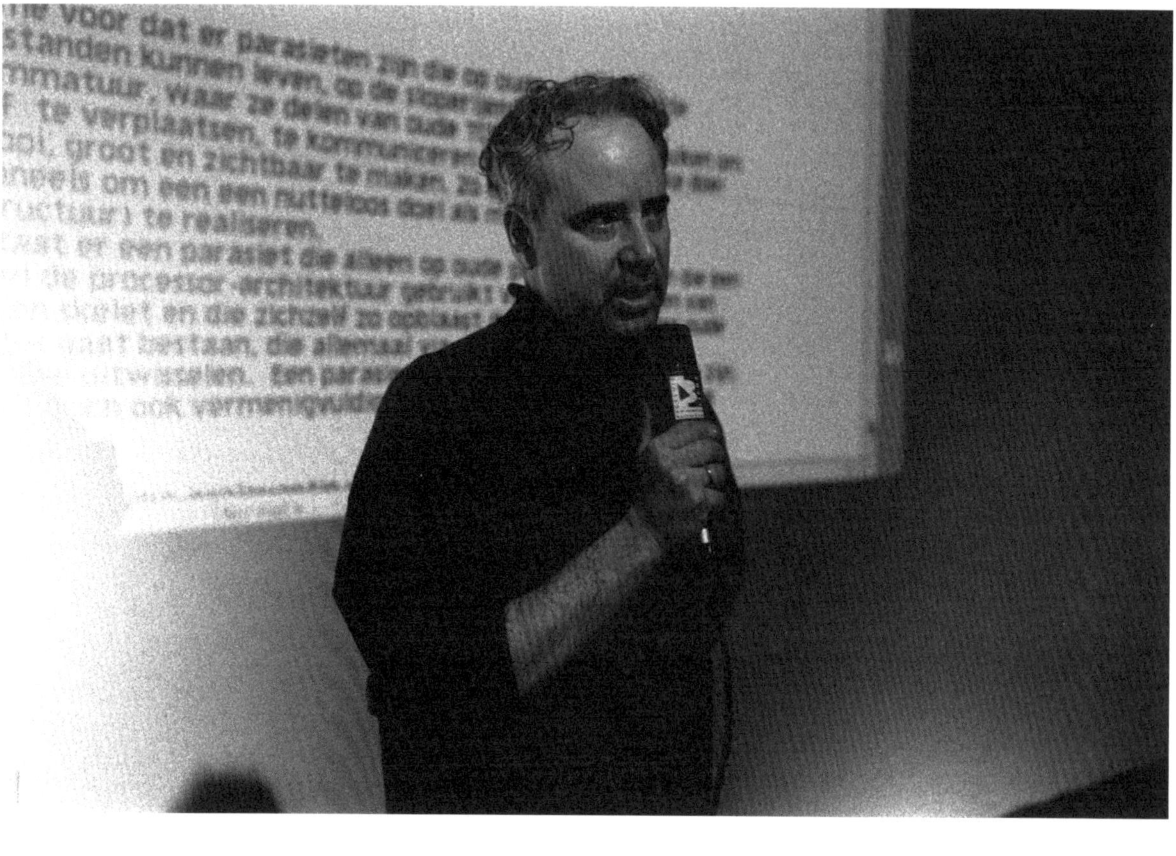

tie voor dat er parasieten zijn die op
standen kunnen leven, op de ...
mmatuur. Waar ze delen van oude
te verplaatsen, te kommunicer
ol, groot en zichtbaar te maken. Ze
nneels om een een nutteloos doel als
ructuur) te realiseren.
aat er een parasiet die alleen op oude
die processor-architektuur gebruikt
n skelet en die zichzelf zo optiaal
waart bestaan, die allemaal
enwisselen. Een para
en ook vermenigvuldi

Autonomy of Technology, Autonomy of Capital

In the case of tactical media, we are no longer dealing with the autonomous (individual or class) subject, with autonomous art or with semi-autonomous social fields, but rather with a collective practice within the heteronomy of networked capitalism – always splitting off, seceding, to create autonomous zones in the interstices.

The modernist emphasis on materials and media could itself be seen as a salutary (if limited and compromised) rejection of the modern subject's autocratic sway over the world. As material or technological substrata, media confront their users with their own 'objective' conditions and affordances. The object is the subject's obstreperous counterpart, appearing to resist assimilation to instrumental reason – making it 'non-identical', in Adorno's parlance. However, precisely as the subject's neat polar opposite, the object is identified and reappropriated by reason and made productive in the form of vacuum cleaners or smartphones. For Adorno, the object is 'the positive face of the non-identical', or, in other words, 'a terminological mask'.[40] It gains a false, illusory autonomy, as per the Marxian analysis of commodity fetishism: 'the primacy of the object notwithstanding, the thingness of the world is also illusory. It tempts the subject to ascribe to the things themselves the social conditions of their production. This is elaborated in Marx's chapter on the fetish.'[41]

In its fetish character, the commodity appears as a thing endowed with an autonomous life. For Adorno, as we have discussed, the artwork was the site in which such commodity fetishism could be mimetically transformed and made aesthetically reflexive. But was the modernist artwork (that exceptional object, that über-fetish) not ultimately compromised precisely by its dependence on a subject that used art to avail itself of some illusory shred of mastery in the guise of critical engagement with media and materials? In the following text from 2003, the American theorist and activist Brian Holmes raises the question of what happens 'if you truly abandon the notion that an object, by its distinction from all others, can serve as a mirror for an equally singular and independent subject'.

BRIAN HOLMES, 'ARTISTIC AUTONOMY AND THE COMMUNICATION SOCIETY'

Reprinted from *Third Text*, vol.18, no.6, 2004, pp.547-48, 551-52.

Why talk about autonomy when the major thrust of experimental art in the 1960s and 1970s was to undermine the autonomous work? This is the question that always arises when you speak with those for whom the academic discourses of the 1950s still seem to matter. Indeed, the university careers to be made by refuting Greenberg, by deconstructing the harmonious totality of the white male Kantian subject, by critiquing the closure of the artistic frame, are seemingly infinite. And the same holds for the description of the paradoxes that invariably arise when mechanically reproduced works or recorded slices of everyday life are presented in the auratic, singularising spaces of the museum. But one sometimes wonders if the members of the art establishment, while seemingly obsessed with these transgressions of a very old status quo, are in fact not afraid to draw the most basic conclusions from their own ideas. For if you truly abandon the notion that an object, by its distinction from all others, can serve as a mirror for an equally singular and independent subject, then the issue of autonomy becomes a deep existential problem. Because for those without a substitute identity, for those without a passionate belief in their blackness, their whiteness, their Jewishness, their Muslimness, their Communistness, their Britishness or whatever, the condition of existence in the communication society – that is, the awareness that one's own mental processes are intimately traversed or even determined by a ceaseless flux of mediated images and signs – is at first deeply anguishing, then ultimately anaesthetising, as basic structures of the ego dissolve and the postmodern 'waning of affect' sets in.[23] We always work beneath the pall of this postmodern anaesthetic.

No doubt there are thousands of very exciting ways to make artworks where the question of autonomy is not at issue. But there is some doubt as to whether any of these ways of art-making could be called political. Does politics, in the democratic sense at least, not presuppose that one is somehow able to make a free decision? That one is not blindly driven by a determining, heteronomous force? What does it mean to make an artistic decision? And what happens when that decision is collective? How can the sensible world – that is, the world composed by the senses, the intellect and the expressive imagination – be reshaped according to what the artist François Deck would call a 'strategy of freedom'?

---

[23]   Fredric Jameson, *Postmodernism, or, the Cultural Logic of Late Capitalism*, Durham, NC: Duke University Press, 1991, especially this passage: 'The end of the bourgeois ego, or monad, no doubt brings with it the end of the psychopathologies of that ego – what I have been calling the waning of affect. But it means the end of much more … the liberation, in contemporary society, from the older *anomie* of the centred subject may also mean not merely a liberation from anxiety but a liberation from every other kind of feeling as well, since there is no longer a self present to do the feeling.' *Ibid.*, p.15. But Jameson's limit has been never to ask about the possible invention of other kinds of feeling, or of a process of individuation detached from the 'bourgeois ego'.

If 'the condition of existence in the communication society' is that 'one's own mental processes are intimately traversed or even determined by a flood of mediated images and signs', then clearly dreams of an 'autonomy of art' safeguarded by art-world institutions are as oneiric and insufficient as the increasingly ritualised, generic and rearguard actions of certain balaclava-clad political autonomists. Based in Paris at the time of this 2004 essay, Holmes points to some (minor but promising) forms of French media activism that are not content with the ghettoisation of autonomy:

> On Saturday, 18 October 2003, a group of part-time performers broke into a prime-time broadcast called 'Star Academy'. They seized the microphone to announce the demands of the movement and unfurled a banner reading: 'Shut off your TVs'. It was not an isolated event: innumerable broadcasts, ministerial speeches and film sets have been interrupted. Just a week before the Star Academy action, a networked movement had arisen to deface the advertisements that pollute the public space of the Metro. Thousands of ads were destroyed over a period of a several months. These insurgencies constitute a live reflection on our collective fictions, on the instituted imaginary of the current neoliberal system.[24] And such symbolic violence, practiced collectively in the open air and raised to a level of engaged reflection on what we want our society to become, is a more interesting collaboration than anything I see in the museums. If we want to regain any chance at a democracy, we must make the production of the collective imaginary into an issue, by derailing or deconstructing certain communications machines, while building others and adapting the existing ones to meet new needs.

Behind autonomist media practices is the spectre of the autonomy of the nonhuman, or the autonomy of the inhuman: an autonomy that is located anywhere but on the part of human agency. If Adorno tried to counter subject-centrism with an insistence on the autonomy of the object, in networked capitalism autonomy appears to lie neither with objects nor individual subjects nor collectives but with finance and technology – with digital techno-finance. Like secularised offspring of the Kantian will, this technological telos imposes its imperative. Autonomy appears to have become well and truly post-human – this is autonomy as automatism, usually presented to the populace as an objective imperative, usually in the form of 'saving the economy' or 'saving the banks' or 'saving the Euro' because 'there are no alternatives'.

The seeming autonomy-as-automatism of value production reaches new heights partly due to the synthesis of technology and finance. Jameson has argued that finance capital has been marked by a further autonomisation vis-à-vis industrial capitalism, just as the postmodern play of 'autonomised fragments' goes beyond the relative autonomy of modernist forms. Finance capital brings into being 'a play of monetary entities that need neither production (as capital does) nor consumption (as money does), which supremely, like cyberspace, can live on their own internal metabolisms and circulate without any reference to an older type of content'; this also manifests itself in 'a new cultural realm or dimension that is independent from the former real world'.[42]

---

[24]   For further information, see *Multitudes*, no. 17, Summer 2004, special issue on 'Intermittence dans tous ses états', as well as the article 'Stopub', *Multitudes*, no. 16, Spring 2004, both available at https://www.multitudes.net/ (last accessed on 19 September 2020).

Such pronouncements on the autonomy of finance enter into a coalition with statements on the autonomisation of technology. In the 1970s it was commonplace for Marxist critics of capitalist 'communication' to assert that 'in the universe of fetishes, the communications media appear to be endowed with autonomy, "a will and mind of their own"', which was to be countered with steps 'towards an autonomous cultural production' by 'the popular classes'.[43] Such media-operaism seems quaint now that we are dealing with a techno-economic system that is constantly spawning new products and tools that demand an instant reschooling of the subject, which has to keep up with developments to shore up its own precarious illusion of subjective autonomy.

As the American art historian and critic Jonathan Crary has noted, the 'idea of technological change as quasi-autonomous, driven by some process of auto-poesis or self-organisation' is now ubiquitous.[44] Technoscience merges with finance capital to form an imposed sense of capitalist technoscience as automaton, as unstoppable juggernaut. Of course, in its very autonomisation from the social, techno-financial capitalism keeps producing social problems – and ecological problems. If this form and degree of autonomisation is extremely problematic, the answer cannot be to try to resuscitate old notions of the autonomous subject. The point that needs to be made is that this subject was always already conditioned by its heteronomy.

The late French philosopher Bernard Stiegler has argued this in the context of his work on the *pharmakon* – a term taken from Plato, referring to a medium such as writing as being both poison *and* medicine. The human subject was always conditioned by 'alien' media technologies that produced forms of subjectivation; not just writing but also speech itself.

> Without doubt it is in fact this *autos*, which only claims to constitute itself *in law* [*en droit*] by positing its *absolute autonomy* as a principle, is *in fact* never *constituted* other than through the accidentality of a *pharmakon* that is absolutely empirical, that is, heteronomic – 'autonomy' always having its *provenance* (and this would be a fact that could never be *opposed* to a right) in a primary heteronomy, autonomy being therefore always *relative*. This relative autonomy is a *relational* autonomy, and relational autonomy (which is also to say, dialogical autonomy)[25] *composes* with heteronomy; it plays creatively with transitional space, as one could also say.[45]

Stiegler is critical of Adorno and Horkheimer for failing to grasp the true *pharmakological* dialectic of media; their diagnosis of the culture industry acknowledges only the poisonous aspect. This does not mean that Stiegler sugarcoats grave political issues. Rather, he analyses which forms of individuation and of (social) 'transindividuation' specific media and their current use allow for, and which ones they sabotage. In his remarks on the contemporary digital *pharmakon*, Stiegler stresses the dangers of a situation in which processes of transindividuation have been outsourced to Facebook and Twitter.

> To generate metadata is also of course to grammatise and vice versa, since each is to meta-categorise. The production of metadata happens, therefore, in all the fields of grammatised transindividuation. The powers that be take control of

---

[25] In the Bakhtinian sense that also contaminates Platonic dialectic.

the circuits of transindividuation – and all the forms of knowledge – through the hegemonic production of this metadata. [...]

The problem is that the *exploitation* of *collaborative metadata* is not itself collaborative in any way, and it is never made the object of a critical scrutiny through which these collaboratively transindividuated knowledges would become precisely critical knowledges. That is, they are not coupled with the processes of psychosocial individuation through which *deep attention* is produced.

This concerns at once a general organology and a cultural therapeutic, that is, the forming and organisation of the care and attention through which a particular kind of social existence is developed.

The entire organology of the contemporary social web is constructed to smooth out the diachronies and singularities of psychic individuals in order to aggregate them through relational technologies with the aim of unilaterally controlling the fruits of the collaborative production of metadata. But this situation is absolutely contingent. It can and indeed must be transformed by an organological invention that puts into motion critical collaborative instruments. In particular, these should permit the formation of collaborative spaces of discussion which produce conflicts and critical debates that are made formally explicit in and through transindividuation.[46]

A Platonic or Adornian rejection of certain media hardly seems like a viable option today (if it ever was). We are quasi-objects, hybrids, assemblages both physical and mental. In this situation, to conceive of certain media as intrinsically progressive or revolutionary in specific political terms is as problematic as regarding them as autonomous juggernauts that follow an intrinsic logic hardwired into them. It is true that the development of technology in 'actually existing capitalism' can appear frighteningly autonomous, as the feminist theorist Donna Haraway puts it in a striking passage of her 'A Cyborg Manifesto' (1985).

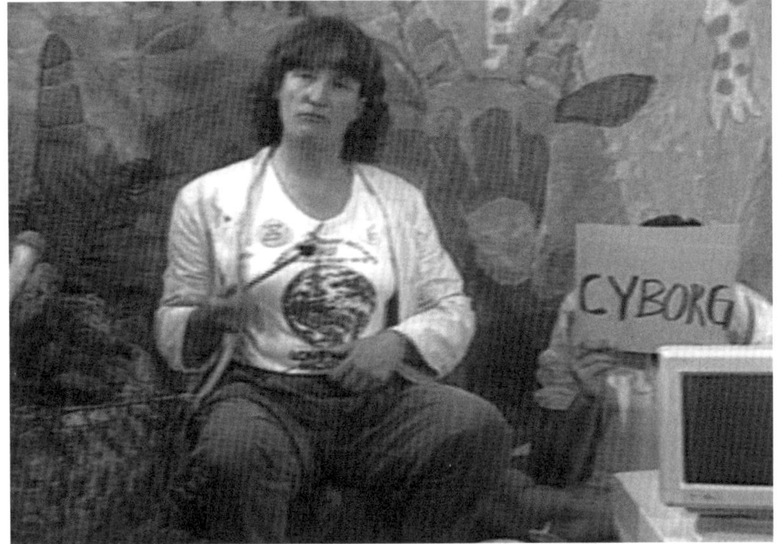

Still from Donna Haraway with Paper Tiger Television, *Donna Haraway Reads 'The National Geographic' on Primates*, 1987, colour video with sound, 28min
Courtesy Paper Tiger Television

See p.274 of this reader for more images

DONNA J. HARAWAY, 'A CYBORG MANIFESTO'

Reprinted from Donna J. Haraway, *Simians,
Cyborgs, and Women: The Reinvention of Nature*,
New York: Routledge, 1991, pp.149, 152, 174-75.
First published in 1985.

> Pre-cybernetic machines could be haunted; there was always the spectre of the ghost in the machine. This dualism structured the dialogue between materialism and idealism that was settled by a dialectical progeny, called spirit or history, according to taste. But basically machines were not self-moving, self-designing, autonomous. They could not achieve man's dream, only mock it. They were not man, an author to himself, but only a caricature of that masculinist reproductive dream. To think they were otherwise was paranoid. Now we are not so sure. Late twentieth-century machines have made thoroughly ambiguous the difference between natural and artificial, mind and body, self-developing and externally designed, and many other distinctions that used to apply to organisms and machines. Our machines are disturbingly lively, and we ourselves frighteningly inert.

Here 'our machines' effectively realise one of the 'emplotments' of modern art: the autonomous life of art has become the autonomous life of technoscience. Of course, this autonomy of technoscience is ultimately relative, as it is both a product of and a contributor to (a co-producer of) contemporary capitalism. Under neoliberalism, 'the market' itself is usually presented as an autonomous system that must not be tampered with, even though the partial realisation of such an autonomous financial market does in fact require political will and legislation ('deregulation'); and today's financial market is of course unthinkable without networked digital technology.

When trading is largely delegated to algorithms, to 'black boxes' that can act much faster than humans, this can result in a 'flash crash', the result of feedback that has spun out of control. Meanwhile, in art we have 'algorithmic collecting' and websites whose 'content' only serves to gather user data and build up profiles that are the real commodity these sites traffic in. Every choice you make on such sites – presumably as subject, as agent, expressing your individuality – serves to define your position as a more or less exchangeable node in the network. The network is the real subject. You are in the network, part of the assemblage.

Haraway's 'Cyborg Manifesto' attempts to forge an 'ironic political myth' aimed against the long-standing Western tendency to relegate women and people of colour to the realm of nature, depriving them of subjecthood. In contrast to earlier feminists, Haraway does not aim to elevate woman to subjecthood; her agency is instead the agency of a posthuman assemblage.

> A cyborg is a cybernetic organism, a hybrid of machine and organism, a creature of social reality as well as a creature of fiction. Social reality is lived social relations, our most important political construction, a world-changing fiction. The international women's movements have constructed 'women's experience', as well as uncovered or discovered this crucial collective object. This experience is a fiction and fact of the most crucial, political kind. Liberation rests on the

construction of the consciousness, the imaginative apprehension, of oppression, and so of possibility. The cyborg is a matter of fiction and lived experience that changes what counts as women's experience in the late twentieth century. This is a struggle over life and death, but the boundary between science fiction and social reality is an optical illusion.

Stating that her cyborg myth 'is about transgressed boundaries, potent fusions and dangerous possibilities', Haraway criticises feminists and socialists alike for clinging to 'deepened dualisms of mind and body, animal and machine, idealism and materialism'.[47] Returning to the analysis of the aesthetic regime in Part One of this reader, we might say that Haraway's project is a quintessentially aesthetic one. She pushes the autocritique of modern thought to the point where the imperialist subject of pure thought becomes so entangled with the sensuous and the technological that it loses itself in a polymorphous assemblage beyond binary conceptions of gender.

It is patently clear that modern conceptions of the autonomous subject often carried a mass of unacknowledged connotations. Insofar as the subject was rational and self-legislating, shaping his own destiny, it was indeed a he: a white, bourgeois male. People of colour, workers and women all fell short of the ideal of subjecthood, as did gender non-conforming people. From legal restrictions to systemic violence, being deemed heteronomous came at a cost, and could be deadly. To early Haraway readers like tactical media artist and cyberfeminist Nathalie Magnan, who made *Donna Haraway Reads the 'National Geographic' of Primates* with Paper Tiger Television in 1987, it was obvious that her cyborg figure implied a queering of the subject.

The cyborg's self-fashioning is crucially dependent on various technological pharmaka. While Haraway sounds warning notes about our 'frighteningly lively' machines, overall she stresses the emancipatory potential of becoming-cyborg. One of her most compelling and concrete passages concerns women of colour:

Contrary to orientalist stereotypes of the 'oral primitive', literacy is a special mark of women of colour, acquired by US black women as well as men through a history of risking death to learn and to teach reading and writing. Writing has a special significance for all colonised groups. Writing has been crucial to the Western myth of the distinction between oral and written cultures, primitive and civilised mentalities, and more recently to the erosion of that distinction in 'postmodernist' theories attacking the phallogocentrism of the West, with its worship of the monotheistic, phallic, authoritative and singular work, the unique and perfect name.[26] Contests for the meanings of writing are a major form of contemporary political struggle. Releasing the play of writing is deadly serious. The poetry and stories of US women of colour are repeatedly about writing, about

---

26   See Jacques Derrida, *Of Grammatology* (trans. Gayatari C. Spivak), Baltimore: John Hopkins University Press, 1976, especially Part 2; Claude Lévi-Strauss, *Tristes Tropiques* (trans. John Russell), New York: Criterion, 1961, especially 'A Writing Lesson'; Henry Louis Gates, 'Writing "Race" and the Difference It Makes', in the special issue 'Race', Writing, and Difference' of *Critical Inquiry*, vol.12, no.1, 1985, pp.1-20; Douglas Kahn and Diane Neumaier (ed.), *Cultures in Contention*, Seattle: Real Comet, 1985; Walter Ong, *Orality and Literacy: The Technologization of the World*, New York: Methuen, 1982; and Cheris Kramarae and Paula Treichler, *A Feminist Dictionary*, Boston: Pandora, 1985.

access to the power to signify; but this time that power must be neither phallic nor innocent. Cyborg writing must not be about the Fall, the imagination of a once-upon-a-time wholeness before language, before writing, before Man. Cyborg writing is about the power to survive, not on the basis of original innocence, but on the basis of seizing the tools to mark the world that marked them as other.

The tools are often stories, retold stories, versions that reverse and displace the hierarchical dualisms of naturalised identities. In retelling origin stories, cyborg authors subvert the central myths of origin of Western culture. We have all been colonised by those origin myths, with their longing for fulfilment in apocalypse. The phallogocentric origin stories most crucial for feminist cyborgs are built into the literal technologies – technologies that write the world, biotechnology and microelectronics – that have recently textualised our bodies as code problems on the grid of C³I. Feminist cyborg stories have the task of recoding communication and intelligence to subvert command and control.

To be human is to be a 'prosthetic god', as Freud once put it in *Civilisation and Its Discontents* (1930) – to be deeply dependent on technology.[48] The present publication could not have been produced without devices ranging from glasses to laptops, cameras to design software, and indeed the human brain itself; as theorists from the nineteenth century to the present have stressed, the human body, including the brain, is the product of evolutionary self-design. But if 'the human is permanently suspended between being the cause and the effect, between designing living systems and being designed through them', the question remains what the role of human agency is within today's cyborg assemblages.[49]

Since aesthetic practice and theory are always engaged with the heteronomous conditions of autonomy, political activism that challenges the reduction of humans to involuntary data producers retains an aesthetic dimension. This aspect is brought to the fore in a project such as *Autonomy Cube*, first realised in 2014, by Trevor Paglen: a pseudo-Minimalist sculpture that gives people in its vicinity Wi-Fi access via the Tor network.[50] It also serves as a Tor relay itself, thus helping to maintain this anonymising network. But the 'darknet' is no mere hacker haven: in 2015, after the Paris attacks, the Anonymous splinter group GhostSec started to target ISIS sites on Tor, replacing one site with an ad for that quintessential contemporary *pharmakon*, Prozac.[51]

The *Autonomy Cube* recalls Haacke's early work *Condensation Cube* (1965), which contained a layer of water that generated more or less condensation on the inside of the Plexiglas volume depending on the temperature in the gallery space. This exercise in 'system aesthetics' revealed the seemingly self-contained modernist or Minimalist artwork to be responsive to heteronomous climatic conditions. With the *Autonomy Cube*, the microclimate of the white cube is itself shown to be anything but a closed system; the art space being part of a networked information economy, meaningful autonomy has to be wrested from these networked structures of control-by-communication and information mining as a new form of economic extractivism. The work could actually be read in medium-specific terms – the medium in question being the human, as material that is perpetually data-mined.

Yesterday's subject is today's object. While humans are mined for information, artworks once again parade in galleries like so many quasi-subjects, as artist Nairy Baghramian notes:

In the past few years, the status of the work of art has risen beyond that of mere autonomous existence to the point where works are sometimes treated like quasi-subjects capable of autonomous thinking. From a philosophical point of view, this is an interesting state-condition. In practice, however, the consequence is that this autonomous, thinking work begins to take action by itself as well. [...] One sometimes gets the impression that a work of art can speak, live and even outlive the artist and hence also artistic discourse. I believe that this work-turned-subject is a monster. [...]

The tendency of the artwork to be turned into a subject is further promoted by the growing silence of the artist-subject, who thereby threatens to turn him or herself into a self-mystifying object. [...]

We should ... take a critical look at the fact that, these days, artworks have actually returned to a status of autonomy they held until the 1960s. Consider that had they retained this status to begin with, there would have been no institutional critique and no debate on aesthetic experience in general.[52]

Is it enough to defend well-known definitions of subjecthood against the onslaught of quasi-subjects and networked cyborgs? Is a defence of autonomy necessarily a defence of the subject? In her essay 'Dear Artfukts, Look at My Curve' (2013) artist Natascha Sadr Haghiaghian responds to Baghramian's plea for a restoration of the critical subject.

Dear Artfukts,

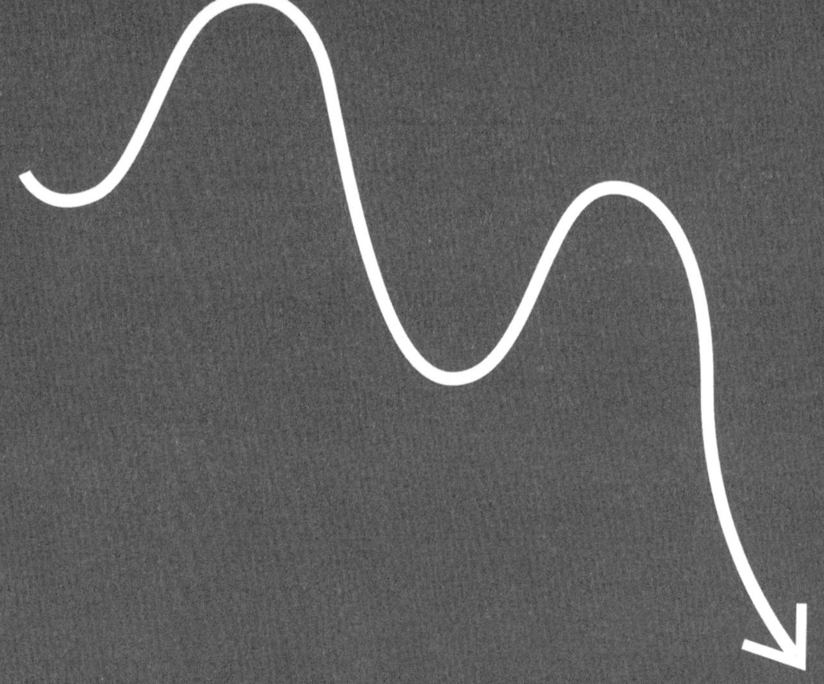

Look at
My Curve

NATASCHA SADR HAGHIGHIAN, 'DEAR ARTFUKTS, LOOK AT MY CURVE. A REPORT TO AN ACADEMY'

Reprinted from *9 Artists* (exh. cat.), Minneapolis:
Walker Art Center, 2013, pp.11-12, 9-10.

With the evidence at hand, one could say that Baghramian is claiming a dead duck. Then again, she is advocating for the subject's agency, an agency that has come like so many other emancipatory enablements through and by struggle. And, similar to such discussions within feminism or labour struggle, the political question is raised of whether letting go of such achievements uncontested might be a huge mistake?

But what if the question is wrong and the struggle with the borders of inclusion/exclusion, powerful/disenfranchised, subject/object just does not hold, does not do it any longer? If the quest is still for agency and sovereignty and rights – and I believe it is – maybe the agents, the territories, the movements have changed and so strategies have to change too. Surely claiming subjecthood did create a feeling of integrity, a wholeness of a specific kind but, as in the very idea of solidarity, this integrity often exceeds the limits of our own body, our own voice, our own movements.

Sadr Haghighian's essay was occasioned by her finding out about her profile on the website ArtFacts.net, which deploys an algorithm to rank contemporary artists. Looking at the (falling) graph that showed the trajectory of her career, Sadr reflects on the complicated relationship between this seemingly autonomous quasi-object and her sub-subjecthood.

One aspect of the magic I am detecting in my relation with the graph could be described as the participation of the name in the thing named, or the participation of the image in the thing it depicts. It is the magic of language, as Walter Benjamin describes it. The word participates in the object via the magical attributes of the name, wherein the name tries to become the object. It's a process of participation of the name in the object rather than a relation in which the name represents the object.

I detect this very same magic in my encounter with the graph. I don't identify with what the image represents but I participate in it as much as it participates in me, drawing on its character and power as it draws on my character and power. The curve and I are entangled in a mimetic dance, imitating and becoming one another. Our shapes submerge into one amorphous thing as we interact, and in this process of participation I am not a subject looking at an object that represents me.

Hito Steyerl refers to this concept of participation when she suggests that we side with the object instead of the subject in the struggle over representation.[27] She notes that the striving for full subjecthood in most emancipatory movements

---

[27]   See Hito Steyerl, 'A Thing Like You and Me', *e-flux journal*, no.15, April 2010, available at https://www.e-flux.com/journal/15/61298/a-thing-like-you-and-me/ (last accessed on 19 September 2020).

– with its promise of autonomy, sovereignty and agency – has lost attraction to some degree after encountering implicit subjectification to power relations. The empowerment that comes with subjecthood is in practice often complex and full of conflict. The subject finds itself enmeshed in a social and political fabric of relations with other subjects, reproducing patterns of exclusion, oppression or discrimination. While we figured out this complication, we also discovered that objects also actually have agency and seem to act with some autonomy. But Steyerl does not suggest that we identify with what the object represents and enter another subject-object relation. Instead, she points toward a concept of identifying with the thing itself, of participating in the object. It is an approach to participation as the absence of relation. Subject and object merge in this process, wherein the subject is first of all a subject of knowledge and not necessarily always a person. Looking at me and the graph, I realise that participation does enact a different magic than the one inherent in relation. From this perspective, the struggle over representation seems strangely outdated.

So now we side with things instead of subjects, transgressing the border between us and stuff. First, we discover that things have agency, that objects might be sovereign and act autonomously without us subjects making them do so, or rather without our being able to control them, as there are multiple forces at work. Then we learn that 'the thing and the knowing being', as Benjamin phrases it, are not necessarily different entities but instead are 'relative unities of reflection' participating in knowledge.[28] It does seem contradictory that while the object can act autonomously, the subject cannot know of that object but can only participate in it. It creates a sensation of blindness, a feeling of not knowing where one stands, where one is positioned. It does match the feeling of being sucked up by the cloud.

My graph is a manifestation from, of and in the cloud. But what is the cloud? It does not seem to be an object of the kind we know, neither is it a subject. It is as much fact as it is fiction. As much as it is an empty envelope of parameters and subroutines, it is also a formation of multiple voices, enacting the formats the envelope provides. This enactment constantly exceeds the envelope; the envelope responds by constantly changing, adapting and mimicking the movements, the voices and the bodies that enact it. The cloud is not representing anything. It just exists as a mimetic machine that constantly renders realities. I am part of the cloud. My movements, my voice, my body are linked to this machine, whether I choose to actively participate in it or not, and I am unable to clearly distinguish agents and agencies in this process.

But wait, my dear artfukts, all this goes beyond my graph acting autonomously, and confuses me profoundly. Let's go back to that desire to overcome representation and side with the object. In my case, we were looking at an image of me – a curve – acting independently, without me doing anything or at least without me controlling it.

28   Walter Benjamin, 'The Concept of Criticism in German Romanticism', in *Selected Writings*, vol.1, *1913-1926* (ed. Marcus Bullock and Michael W. Jennings), Cambridge, MA: The Belknap Press of Harvard University Press, 2004, p.146.

We began Part Five by restaging the historical dialogue between the modernist emphasis on medium-specificity and the avant-garde focus on the revolutionary or activist potential of new media. Both strands have continued to morph and interact – with recent theories of autonomist media clearly indebted to the avant-garde genealogy, at times with an admixture of modernist emphasis on the specific properties of (new) media. However, in recent theoretical and artistic responses to the pervasiveness of digital technology, the modernist autonomy of the medium and the seemingly independent 'life of forms' – so dear to formalist art history and criticism – return in spectral guise as digital automatism and the mining of the human object.

Sadr Haghighian's essay evokes both feminist criticisms of the objectification of the female body and decolonial critiques of the reduction of subaltern and enslaved Others to the status of things – and the contemporary algorithmic continuation of such racial objectification. An example of the latter would be facial recognition and 'emotion detection' software that has its racial bias inbuilt, to mention but the tip of the iceberg. In 'surveillance capitalism', predictive power is money, and humans can only become predictable when profiled.[53] With every click we make, or every time our phone gets ransacked by spyware, we contribute to making more valuable profiles that can be used by corporations or state agencies to target us – as voters, consumers, bad investments or potential threats.

Sadr Haghiaghian's angry missive to 'artfukts' is a kind of political-formalist criticism that is both bitingly funny and strangely affecting. The artist (who changed her name to Natascha Süder Happelmann upon representing Germany at the 2019 Venice Biennale, in a sardonic response to a widespread German inability to spell her name) is writing back as a fragile human to a machine for which she is a resource to be mined for surplus. Her decision to use the form of a letter seems defiantly anachronistic. There is hope in such tactical anachronism, in such an insistence that talking or writing back still matters. Whether that hope is illusory remains to be seen. With the onset of the COVID-19 pandemic, self-isolating cultural workers (and many others) handed themselves and their selves over to social media platforms more fully than ever before. Who or what is looking at our curves? Can there be other ways of becoming cyborg? How to generate data in relative autonomy, rather than under conditions of neofeudal digital serfdom? How to even begin to envisage a socialisation or collectivisation of social media platforms?[54]

Notes

1   'Media = mens + alien.' Bilwet, *Media-Archief*, Amsterdam: Ravijn, 1992, p.81. Translated from the Dutch by Sven Lütticken.
2   Theodor W. Adorno, 'Art and the Arts' (1967), in *Can One Live after Auschwitz? A Philosophical Reader* (ed. Rolf Tiedemann), Palo Alto, CA: Stanford University Press, 2003, pp.368-87. See Part One of this reader, pp.29-99.
3   Sadakichi Hartmann, 'The Esthetic Significance of the Motion Picture', *Camera Work*, no.38, 1912, pp.19-21, available online at http://www.photocriticism.com/members/archivetexts/relatedsubjects/hartmann/hartmannmovies.html (last accessed on 19 September 2020).
4   Helmut Draxler suggested this at the symposium 'Aber etwas fehlt. But something's missing', Museum Moderner Kunst Stiftung Ludwig, Vienna, 5 December 2015.
5   Greg Allen, 'It's the Little Differences', 24 June 2014, greg.org [blog], http://greg.org/archive/2014/06/24/its_the_little_differences.html (last accessed on 19 September 2020.
6   John Kelsey, '100%', cited in *ibid.*
7   Tiqqun, *The Cybernetic Hypothesis* (trans. Robert Hurley), South Pasadena: Semiotext(e), 2020, p.167 For the complete text, see John Kelsey, *Rich Texts: Selected Writing for Art* (ed. Daniel Birnbaum and Isabelle Graw), Berlin: Sternberg Press, 2010, pp.15-22.
8   Clement Greenberg, 'Towards a Newer Laocoon' (1940), in *Clement Greenberg: The Collected Essays and Criticism*, vol.1, *Perceptions and Judgments, 1939-1944* (ed. John O'Brian), Chicago: University of Chicago Press, 1986, p.32.
9   Richard Wagner, *Opera and Drama* (trans. William Ashton Ellis), Lincoln: University of Nebraska Press, 1995, pp.119-20.
10   *Ibid.*, pp.155, 220, 224. Emphasis in the original.
11   See Theodor W. Adorno, *In Search of Wagner* (1938/52; trans. Rodney Livingstone), London: Verso, 2005, p.96. The translation has been adapted by the editors of this reader on the basis of the German. Starting with its title, *In Search of Wagner* (*Versuch über Wagner* should be *Essay on Wagner*) is a low point in the murky field of translations of Adorno into English. When fragments from Adorno's Wagner book were published in the *Zeitschrift für Sozialforschung* in 1939 ('Fragmente über Wagner', vol.8, pp.1-49), the chapter from which this passage stems was only summarised briefly; presumably he later reworked it somewhat for publication in 1952 and incorporated the term *culture industry*, which was first used in the *Dialectic of Enlightenment*.
12   Saul Ostrow, 'Clement Greenberg: The Last Interview' (1994), in *Late Writings* (ed. Robert C. Morgan), Minneapolis: University of Minnesota Press, 2003, p.235. On the Institute for Social Research, the AJC and *Commentary*, see also Thomas Wheatland, *The Frankfurt School in Exile*, Minneapolis: University of Minnesota Press, 2009, pp.227-63, esp. pp.253-54. It should be noted that in the mid-1940s, the AJC and *Commentary* were still much more progressive than they would become in later years, when many of the New York intellectuals associated with *Commentary* morphed into neoconservatives and the AJC became intent on tarring all criticisms of Israel with the brush of anti-Semitism.
13   See T.W. Adorno, 'Art and the Arts', *op. cit.*, pp.368-87.
14   Reflecting the rise of media theory and media studies as fields of research, in 2002 Suhrkamp Verlag published a Walter Benjamin collection titled *Medienästhetische Schriften*.
15   See also Part One of this reader, pp.29-99.
16   Greenberg's membership of the American Committee for Cultural Freedom, was meant, at least in part, to make the Congress for Cultural Freedom (CCF) look less like a CIA front. In 1952, the Committee became an embarrassment to the CIA and the CCF when it refused to condemn Senator Joseph McCarthy, whose anti-communist crusade extended to all artistic and intellectual life that did not fit his Rockwellian idea of America - including the modern art and discourse sponsored at the CIA's behest by the Congress in Western Europe so as to position the US as enlightened leader of the free world. Greenberg was among the hardliners on the Committee who refused to support a condemnation of McCarthy. See Stonor Saunders, *The Cultural Cold War*, New York: The New Press, 2013, pp.198-204.
17   See Francis Frascina, 'Institutions, Culture, and America's 'Cold War Years': The Making of Greenberg's "Modernist Painting"', *Oxford Art Journal*, vol.26, no.1, 2003, pp.69-97.
18   Clement Greenberg, 'Modernist Painting', in *Clement Greenberg: The Collected Essays and Criticism*, vol. 4, *Modernism with a Vengeance, 1957-1969* (ed. John O'Brian), p.85.
19   Elsewhere translated as *Old and New*.
20   Walter Benjamin, 'The Work of Art in the Age of Its Technological Reproducibility: Second Version' (1936; trans. Edmund Jephcott and Harry Zohn), in *The Work of Art in the Age of Its Technological Reproducibility, and Other Writings on Media* (ed. Michael W. Jennings, Brigid Doherty and Thomas Y. Levin), Cambridge, MA: The Belknap Press of Harvard University Press, 2008, p.33. For more information on the different versions of Benjamin's essay, and particularly the second version translated and reproduced here, which he considered his *Ur*-text, see Miriam Bratu Hansen, 'Room-for-Play: Benjamin's Gamble with Cinema', *October*, vol.109, Summer 2004, pp.3-45. For more on Benjamin's use of the suffix *-keit*, see Samuel Weber, *Benjamin's -abilities*, Cambridge, MA: Harvard University Press, 2008.
21   W. Benjamin, 'The Work of Art', *op. cit.*, p.34.
22   *Ibid.*, p.36.

23   Theodor W. Adorno, *Ästhetische Theorie*, Frankfurt a.M.: Suhrkamp Verlag, 1970, p.89. In Robert Hullot-Kentor's English-language translation of *Aesthetic Theory*, elsewhere cited in this book, he renders 'die Simplifizierung, die dann der Reproduktionsarbeit zu ihrer penetranten Beliebtheit verhalf' as 'the simplification that made the essay on reproduction so popular' (p.76). While Hullot-Kentor's *Aesthetic Theory* is one of the best Adorno translations, something is lost here: Adorno's visceral annoyance at the success of Benjamin's essay, as encapsulated in the adjective *penetrant* (which can be rendered as 'obtrusive', 'annoying', 'obnoxious' or 'overbearing').

24   In the fascinating, episodic late essay 'Filmtransparente' (1966), Adorno not only shows that he kept up to speed with 1960s film, but also acknowledges the ideological content of films is not necessarily swallowed hook, line and sinker by viewers – thus providing an opening for an analysis of the reception and appropriation of films. Translated by Thomas Y. Levin as 'Transparencies on Film', *New German Critique*, no.24/25, Autumn 1981/Winter 1982, pp.199-205. One factor in Adorno's relative willingness during the later 1960s to engage with recent developments in film and film theory was no doubt a dialogue with his young associate, Alexander Kluge. See A. Kluge with Martin Weinmann, *Neonröhren des Himmels*, booklet of DVD box set *Sämtliche Kinofilme*, Frankfurt a.M.: Zweitausendeins, 2007, pp.107-08.

25   Dick Higgins, 'Intermedia' (1965), in *foew&ombwhnw: a grammar of the mind and a phenomenology of love and a science of the arts as seen by a stalker of the wild mushroom*, New York: Something Else Press, 1969, p.11.

26   *Ibid.*, p.17.

27   See artist Tania Bruguera's proposal for putting Duchamp's urinal back in the bathroom, in Part Two of this reader, pp.102-03.

28   Nam June Paik, 'Expanded Education for the Paperless Society', *Radical Software*, no.1, Spring 1970, p.7.

29   See Thierry de Duve, *Kant After Duchamp*, Cambridge, MA: MIT Press, 1996, pp.244-48.

30   See Rosalind Krauss, *'A Voyage on the North Sea': Art in the Age of the Post-Medium Condition*, London: Thames & Hudson, 1999, p.10. In these lectures, Krauss opposes this condition in the name of a new understanding of medium-specificity.

31   Mel Ramsden confirmed his authorship in an email to Sven Lütticken, 17 September 2013.

32   These are the Fall 1975 and Fall 1979 issues, respectively. On *FILE Megazine*, see Gwen Allen, *Artists' Magazines: An Alternative Space for Art*, Cambridge, MA: The MIT Press, 2011, pp.147-73.

33   See Part Four of this reader, pp.217-57.

34   See Oskar Negt and Alexander Kluge, *Public Sphere and Experience: Toward an Analysis of the Bourgeois and Proletarian Public Sphere* (1972; trans. Peter Labanyi, Jamie Owen Daniel and Assenka Oksiloff), Minneapolis: University of Minnesota Press, 1983, p.xlvi.

35   At the time, General Idea's *Imagevirus* project was not well received by many New York AIDS activists, Bordowitz amongst them; see Gregg Bordowitz, *General Idea: Imagevirus*, London: Afterall Books, 2010.

36   Gregg Bordowitz, 'Picture a Coalition', *October*, vol.43, Winter 1987, pp.182-96, p.195.

37   The Dia exhibition on AIDS was part of the multipart project *Democracy: A Project by Group Material* (1987-89). Bordowitz's 'Picture a Coalition', cited above, was featured alongside contributions by Leo Bersani, Martha Gever, Sander L. Gilman, Carol Leigh, Paula A. Treichler, Simon Watney and others in the 'AIDS: Cultural Analysis/Cultural Activism' issue of the journal *October* (vol. 43, Winter 1987).

38   An attempt to redress this was the 2014 exhibition 'Take It or Leave It: Institution, Image, Ideology', curated by Johanna Burton and Anne Ellegood at the Hammer Museum, Los Angeles.

39   See Nancy Fraser, 'Rethinking the Public Sphere: A Contribution to the Critique of Actually Existing Democracy', *Social Text*, no.25/26, 1990, pp.56-80; and Michael Warner, *Publics and Counterpublics*, New York: Zone Books, 2002.

40   Theodor W. Adorno, *Negative Dialectics* (trans. E.B. Ashton), London: Routledge, 1990, p.192. Translation amended by this book's editors. For an analysis of Adorno's concept of reification, building out of his critique of identity thinking and in distinction from that of Lukács and Benjamin, see Gillian Rose, *The Melancholy Science: An Introduction to the Thought of Theodor W. Adorno*, London: Verso, 2014, pp.35-66.

41   *Ibid.*, pp.189-90. Translation amended by this book's editors.

42   Fredric Jameson, 'Culture and Finance Capital', *Critical Inquiry*, vol.24, no.1, Autumn 1997, p.265.

43   Armand Mattelart, 'Communication Ideology and Class Practice' (Chile, 1971), in A. Mattelart and Seth Siegelaub (ed.), *Communication and Class Struggle: 1. Capitalism, Imperialism*, New York and Bagnolet: International General and IMMRC, 1979, p.116. The 1970s also saw the publication of a media study about the trope of autonomous technology: Langdon Winner, *Autonomous Technology: Technics-out-of-Control as a Theme in Political Thought*, Cambridge, MA: MIT Press, 1977.

44   Jonathan Crary, *24/7: Late Capitalism and the Ends of Sleep*, London: Verso, 2013, p.36.

45   Bernard Stiegler, *What Makes Life Worth Living; On Pharmacology* (trans. Daniel Ross), Cambridge: Polity Press, 2013, p.41. Emphasis in the original.

46   Bernard Stiegler, 'Relational Ecology and the Digital Pharmakon', *Culture Machine*, vol.13, 2002, pp.14-15.

47   Donna J. Haraway, 'A Cyborg Manifesto', *Simians, Cyborgs, and Women: The Reinvention of Nature*, New York: Routledge, 1991, p.154.

48   Sigmund Freud, 'Das Unbehagen in der Kultur' (1930), in *Das Unbehagen in der Kultur und andere Schriften*, Frankfurt: Fischer, 1994, p.57. In contrast to the dominant English-language translation of Freud's *Prothesengott* as 'prosthetic God', a lowercase 'god' would seem to be called for here.

49   Beatriz Colomina and Mark Wigley, *Are We Human? Notes on an Archaeology of Design*, Zurich: Lars Müller, 2016, pp.56-57.

50   Originally co-credited to the hacker Jacob Appelbaum, the *Autonomy Cube* is now credited to Paglen alone.

In 2016, Appelbaum was accused of sexual assault.

51   Samuel Gibbs, 'Anonymous swaps ISIS propaganda site for Prozac ad in trolling fight', *The Guardian*, 26 November 2015, available at http://www.theguardian.com/technology/2015/nov/26/anonymous-swaps-isis-propaganda-site-for-prozac-ad-in-trolling-fight (last accessed 19 September 2020).

52   Nairy Baghramian, 'Le Mépris', *Texte zur Kunst*, no.87, September 2012, p.110.

53   Shoshana Zuboff, *The Age of Surveillance Capitalism: The Fight for a Human Future at the New Frontier of Power*, London: Profile Books, 2019.

54   Recently, Jonas Staal and lawyer Jan Fermon launched their Collectivize Facebook campaign at https://collectivize.org/ (last accessed 19 September 2020).

PART SIX:
ANOTHER AUTONOMY IS POSSIBLE

On Friday, 18 September 2015, the *New York Times International Weekly* (produced by the *New York Times* as a supplement for foreign 'host' newspapers) boasted the front-page headline 'Spread of West's Values Now Appears Uncertain'. Rarely does a dominant ideology manifest itself in such a hilariously inept manner; usually its technicians are less clumsy. That a newspaper which supported the 2003 US-led invasion of Iraq – based on falsified evidence of weapons of mass destruction – would come around to the conclusion that the neo-imperial project of the 'spread of the West's values' *now* appears uncertain is one thing. Another is the jingoistic use of the notion of 'the West's values' itself in a newspaper headline (as opposed to in a speech by a certain kind of politician). The full article confirms that we are correct to infer that these values are democracy, human rights and so on – essentially a conveniently packaged Enlightenment, supposedly universal yet still copyrighted by 'the West'.

The Enlightenment was haunted by slavery. In 1776, when Thomas Jefferson incorporated the phrase 'all men are created equal' into the Declaration of Independence, this did not have immediate consequences for any slaves he personally owned. Thus, the universalism of the Enlightenment was a severely qualified one. On the one hand, it held the promise of equality and subjecthood for all, irrespective of race or gender. In the UK, the abolitionist cause continued to gain momentum in the years after American independence, fuelled by books such as John Gabriel Stedman's *The Narrative of a Five Years Expedition against the Revolted Negroes of Surinam* (1796), which paints a grim picture of slavery in the Dutch South American colony. William Blake's *A Negro Hung Alive by the Ribs to a Gallows*, published as an illustration in Stedman's account, remains a haunting image of the human reduced to bare life, snuffed out without second thought. However, even among well-meaning liberals, colonised peoples were usually cast in the role of the Other – at times celebrated for their vitality and mystery, but always fundamentally excluded.

The American Revolution did not emancipate the former colonies' slaves, and some historians have argued that it was designed explicitly against this 'threat'.[1] The logical conclusion of the *Declaration of the Rights of Man and of the Citizen*, authored by the French Constituent Assembly in 1789 and inspired largely by Jefferson and the Declaration of Independence, would have been that slavery had to be abolished – at least, if one accepted that non-whites were fully human, which apologists of slavery routinely denied. Many of the rights defined in the 1789 French declaration were effectively restricted to men (the only proper *citoyens*), and the text avoided any mention of slavery – even though its emphasis on the universality of basic human rights would soon help to inspire slave uprisings and revolutions in the Caribbean. Building on the recent scholarship of Thomas Keenan and Lynn Hunt, Eyal Weizman notes of the two conjoined declarations that their

> ongoing dissemination and influence was precisely due to the fact that they did not define or fix what they meant by 'human'. Yet its meaning in practice tended to exclude foreigners, landless, slaves and women. In these cases the biological threshold of the human obviously did not overlap with the effective threshold of rights or the law, which the ongoing struggle for human rights aims to make overlap.[2]

Kant's *Critique of the Power of Judgment* was published the year after the French declaration. We have seen that for Kant, aesthetic judgement held out the promise of becoming a fully rounded subject that can bridge the worlds of freedom and the senses, of the autonomous will and the world. We have also noted that one of Kant's examples concerns a 'primitive' Other, a naïf who does not have the required disinterestedness to arrive at this aesthetic state of grace: the Iroquois chief who has no eye for the beauties of Paris, and is only interested in its culinary attractions. Let us return to this passage, first visited in Part One:

> The satisfaction that we combine with the representation of the existence of an object is called interest. Hence such a satisfaction always has at the same time a relation to the faculty of desire, either as its determining ground or else as necessarily interconnected with its determining ground. But if the question is whether something is beautiful, one does not want to know whether there is anything that is or that could be at stake, for us or for someone else, in the existence of the thing, but rather how we judge it in mere contemplation (intuition or reflection). If someone asks me whether I find the palace that I see before me beautiful, I may well say that I don't like that sort of thing, which is made merely to be gaped at, or, like the Iroquois sachem, that nothing in Paris pleased him better than the cookshops; in true **Rousseauesque** style I might even vilify the vanity of the great who waste the sweat of the people on such superfluous things; finally I could even easily convince myself that if I were to find myself on an uninhabited island, without any hope of ever coming upon human beings again, and could conjure up such a magnificent structure through my mere wish, I would not even take the trouble of doing so if I already had a hut that was comfortable enough for me. All of this might be conceded to me and approved; but that is not what is at issue here. One only wants to know whether the mere representation of the object is accompanied with satisfaction in me, however indifferent I might be with regard to the existence of the object of this representation. It is readily seen that to say that it is **beautiful** and to prove that I have taste what matters is what I make of this representation in myself, not how I depend on the existence of the object. Everyone must admit that a judgment about beauty in which there is mixed the least interest is very partial and not a pure judgment of taste. One must not be in the least biased in favour of the existence of the thing, but must be entirely indifferent in this respect in order to play the judge in matters of taste.[3]

Here, the 'sachem' reveals himself to be unworthy of true subjecthood through his adherence to self-interest and immediate use-value. The concluding part of this reader on art and autonomy, then, is about the sachem's return into the picture, like a Freudian return of the repressed; it is about the agency of those whom Enlightenment thought deemed heteronomous, and thus relegated to dependency on more or (usually) less benevolent tutelage.

For much of modernity, non-Western peoples were seen as pre-rational – that is, below the threshold of true subjecthood. In Denise Ferreira da Silva's terminology, a white 'transparent I' of reason produced its counterpart in the form of an 'affectable I' that was its dark Other.[4] Various emancipatory movements have effectively tried to include ever more people in the first category: they have demanded that full subjecthood and legal personhood be accorded to people of colour as well as to women. While many successes along these lines are to be noted – partial successes that must be defended in the current climate, with its triumphant neofascist movements – one could argue that the fundamental mechanism has always remained intact. We may seek to make the category of the subject more encompassing, but when it is a privileged status that has to be awarded or won, does this not also mean that its counterpart keeps being re-produced, as failed subjects, just as Western interventions keep producing 'failed states'?

If you want to know about autonomy, engage with those considered heteronomous. While the property-owning male bourgeois is supposed to be the model of autonomous subjecthood, lessons about autonomy are more likely to be learned among non-propertied workers, among women. If autonomy is supposed to be a 'Western achievement' or a 'Western value', then run for the hills. Or rather, run for the hinterlands of the Global West, towards the Global South – the sites of extraction and naked exploitation, of neo-slavery, of exported violence and ecological destruction. The question, then, as Kerstin Stakemeier and Marina Vishmidt put it, is once more:

> Who is the subject of autonomy? According to the dictates of liberal common sense, autonomy is a political concept referring to free individuals represented by their freely elected governments. From this perspective, slaves as subjects lacking in legal rights are heteronomous, while modern proletarians thrown into the industrial reserve army of labour and forced to eke out a life in the teeth of the workfare programmes of the modern state are autonomous. The autonomy of the worker is a consequence of his or her legal status as a free and equal subject party to non-binding wage labour contracts. The upshot of this peculiar definition is that autonomy is deprived of any meaningful relationship to what Marx called 'sensuous human practice', the most common form of which, in Marx's day as well as in ours, is patently *unfree*, compulsory, fragmented and physically and psychologically damaging labour.[5]

There can be no doubt that the field of aesthetic theory and practice was profoundly implicated in this production of racialised and dehumanised subalterns. As suggested by Kant's imaginary sachem, aesthetic theory proliferated representations of objectified Others, while art provided plenty of examples of exoticising – or just plain racist – depictions of such sub-subjects, who could be objects of aesthetic delectation but who were too enmired in brute sensuality to be aesthetic subjects themselves.[6] Such objectification, in turn, has provided a point of departure for the political aesthetics of black radicalism, from Aimé Césaire and Édouard Glissant to Fred Moten. Césaire took cues from Marx and Lukács to characterise enslavement as *chosification* (rendered in English as *reification* or *thingification*).[7] More recently, in his book on the aesthetics of the black radical tradition, Moten insists that: 'The history of blackness is testament to the fact that objects can and do resist.'[8]

Cover of programme
for W.E.B. Du Bois's *Haiti:
A Drama of the Black Napoleon*,
Daly's Theatre, 63rd Street,
New York, c.1938

See p.278 of this reader
for another image

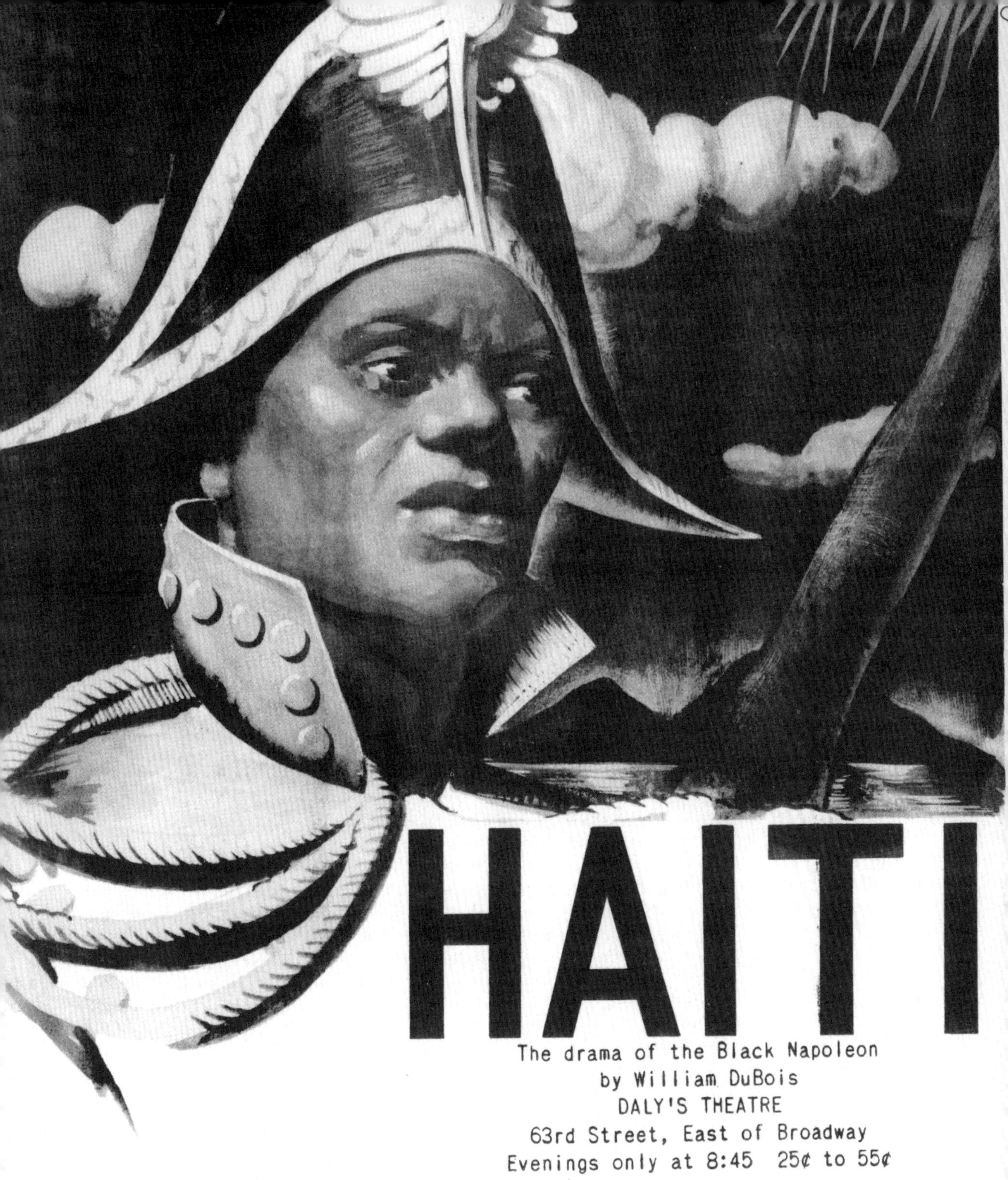

HAITI
The drama of the Black Napoleon
by William DuBois
DALY'S THEATRE
63rd Street, East of Broadway
Evenings only at 8:45   25¢ to 55¢

For theatre parties at special low rates, call GRamercy 7-7800, Extension 56

"A splendid production... tense, gripping drama." --WORLD-TELEGRAM

"A roaring melodrama. Rex Ingram gives a rattling good performance."--TIMES

"An exciting play on an exciting Negro theme." --HERALD TRIBUNE

A presentation of the Federal Theatre
A division of the Works Progress Administration

Decolonise Autonomy

One way in which Enlightenment thought cast doubt on the ability of colonised Others to achieve fully autonomous subjecthood was through the notion of 'fetishism', which posited that Africans worshipped random objects, projecting their subjectivity onto them without being able to recognise that these objects did not actually contain some magical, spiritual essence. In contrast to Christian artworks, these fetishes were not active transformations of matter by the subject precisely because subjectivity remained external to the fetishes; they showed that these cultures had not yet achieved any degree of mastery over the heteronomy of matter. Introduced by the eighteenth-century writer Charles de Brosses, the concept of fetishism also appears in Hegel's *Lectures on the Philosophy of Religion* of 1832 (rather than his lectures on art):

> The Negroes have an endless multitude of divine images which they make into their gods or their 'fetishes' (a corrupted Portuguese term). The nearest stone or butterfly, a grasshopper, a beetle and the like – these are their Lares – indeterminate, unknown powers that they have made themselves; and if something does not work out or some unhappiness befalls them, then they throw this fetish away and get themselves another.
>
> The use of charms and fetishes among these peoples does, of course, lead to the representation of a power outside of empirical consciousness, or of the will and passion of the living and the dead; but this power is set forth only as something external and sensible, and remains completely within the caprice of those who have raised things of this sort to such power.[9]

The fetish was thus disparaged as a mere means to an end, proof of its magical-utilitarian nature and its inability to constitute art. Nonetheless, Hegel's discussion of the fetish had an aesthetic component: as a confused projection of subjectivity on an object, the fetish functions as failed art in Hegel's system. Some early twentieth-century artists came to see the fetish as *more* aesthetic than the West's all-too-harmonious-and-regulated works of art. These artists' 'discovery' of tribal art was enabled by the fact that much of it had been plundered or otherwise extracted from tribal cultures in Africa, the Americas and Oceania, and stored away in museums – to be specific, in ethnographic museums, which were separate from art museums.

Nonetheless, the German-American anthropologist Franz Boas published scholarly essays in which he took the art of indigenous American and Inuit peoples highly seriously as art – the art of 'primitive peoples', to be sure, but no less important for that.[10] At the same time, Edward S. Curtis was photographing indigenous American life and artefacts, and artists and critics started appreciating African tribal art – certain German Expressionists, the Cubists, the German critic Carl Einstein and Marius de Zayas, a Mexican-born member of the Alfred Stieglitz circle in New York. De Zayas proudly claimed that his 1914 exhibition of African tribal art at the 291 Gallery was the first time that such works were unapologetically exhibited as art.[11] But what did such aesthetic appreciation of tribal artefacts mean? Some, like the theorist Ariella Azoulay, stress the complicity of such appreciation with the very imperialist plunder that led to the accumulation of artefacts from colonised regions in Western museums and their eventual valuation as Art.[12] However, there may be a danger in suggesting such complicity can only ever be *total*. The question is if and when *difference makes a difference*, even under compromised circumstances.

'Unlearning imperialism' has been, and continues to be, a lengthy and fitful process. In the early twentieth century, a formal appreciation of 'primitive' artworks' bold designs was often paired with romantic-primitivist fantasies of authenticity. Although admirers of tribal art such as André Breton and Tristan Tzara were far from immune to the suggestion that such works exist outside of history, as the products of 'static' societies without any progress or development, they were nonetheless opponents of colonialism. As the Surrealist movement came to ally itself with communism in the late 1920s, anti-imperialist and anti-colonial agitation moved to the forefront. In collaboration with the international organisations Ligue universelle pour la défense de la race noire (Universal League for the Defence of the Black Race) and the League Against Imperialism, the Surrealists organised 'La Vérité sur les colonies' as a counterstatement to the Paris Exposition Coloniale of 1931.[13] Here, they polemically turned the tables on Western conceptions of African Otherness: the exhibition contained a display of kitsch figurines labelled 'European fetishes', including a Madonna and a black child holding a dish for collecting money – a prop of the Catholic missionary work. The division between enlightened, autonomous subjects and benighted fetish-worshipers was tenuous at best, and the conjunction of the term 'fetish' with money here recalls Marx's polemical analysis of the commodity as fetish.[14] The Surrealists were, of course, also interested in Freud's 1927 account of sexual fetishism.[15] 'Primitive' fetishes, sexual fetishes and (obsolete) commodity fetishes could all be deployed to attack Western rationalism.

The League Against Imperialism was founded on the initiative of the communist publisher and agitator Willi Münzenberg (for whose publications John Heartfield made most of his most famous photomontages). It effectively served as a front organisation for the Comintern – which is to say, for the Soviet Union. In the late 1920s and 1930s, Moscow sought to align class struggle in the industrialised world with anti-racist and anti-colonial struggles. Though the relation between the categories of class and race remained a bone of contention, communism seemed like the one serious and radical emancipatory movement to a new generation of black Caribbean anti-colonialist and anti-imperialist writers and intellectuals, amongst them C.L.R. James, Aimé Césaire and the lesser-known Anton de Kom. They often studied or worked in the imperial centres of the West, and they all explored the relevance of the Marxist analysis of the capitalist economy's relentless appropriation and exploitation of natural resources and workers for an anti-colonial critique of the violent reduction of human beings to mere commodities.

In his magisterial 1938 study *The Black Jacobins: Toussaint L'Ouverture and the San Domingo Revolution*, James recounts the 1791–1804 slave uprising that started in present-day Haiti in parallel to the French Revolution. Inspired by the universalist principles of the French Revolution and led by Toussaint L'Ouverture, slaves would overthrow the French colonial regime and the institution of slavery. It was in Haiti that the ideology of universal human rights became, at least to some extent, lived practice – due to the enslaved's own initiative, not French benevolence. In claiming their agency and enacting their autonomy, the Haitian slaves revealed both the lie and the promise of 'Western values' by prying them from the hands of the white Westerners who were loudly (pro)claiming them. In Paris, the National Assembly finally abolished slavery in 1794. However, the situation in the colonies remained murky, and under Napoleon the military effort to 'restore order' intensified. Napoleon revoked the law abolishing slavery in 1802, and Toussaint was arrested and left to die in a prison in France before Haiti finally gained its independence in 1804 – an independence that would be blighted by crippling debt, as France demanded massive compensation for the loss of 'its' colony.[16]

Around the time of the publication of *The Black Jacobins*, the Russian-born philosopher Alexandre Kojève was lecturing in Paris on the philosophy of Hegel, in particular the master–slave dialectic in the *Phenomenology of Spirit* plays a crucial role.[17] Rather than dealing with any concrete historical forms of slavery or servitude, Hegel's master–slave dialectic is a philosophical fable in which two forms of consciousness encounter each other, with each subject being the other's object.[18] Their conflict is dialectically 'resolved' when the loser agrees to be the other's servant or slave instead of being killed. Kojève interpreted this dialectic as the basis of all history.

Susan Buck-Morss has argued that Hegel's account of subjectivity and the master–slave dialectic, for all its abstract distancing from social and historical specificity, was in fact profoundly marked by his knowledge of slavery, slave revolts and revolutions. In restoring the sociopolitical context of Hegel's work, Buck-Morss emphasises tell-tale phrases that seem to acknowledge the slave-industrial complex in the Caribbean, such as the following, from his lectures in the philosophy of right: 'if I have someone whipped, it does not damage that person's freedom'.[19] However, Hegel integrated his knowledge (via the media of the day) of actual slavery and resistance to it into a mode of philosophical speculation that did not dwell on the details of actual life and struggle.

> As spectator via the press (newspaper names like *Spectator* and *Observer* were common),[1] Hegel achieved glimpses of a global perspective, viewing the uprising of the slaves of Saint-Domingue as a manifestation of *universal* freedom, the realisation of which he saw as the very structure and meaning of history. Once Hegel had grasped this meaning, however, he demonstrated little patience with the mere matter of empirical history, dismissing it as 'lazy existence' (*faule Existenz*).[2] Concept took precedence over content, and attention to historical facts was overwhelmed by Hegel's enthusiasm for the philosophical system itself.[20]

Likewise, disregarding colonialism and actual slavery in favour of the philosophical system, in the 1930s Kojève turned Napoleon – who had reintroduced slavery! – into a heroic figure who had spread Enlightenment values throughout Europe and thereby established the 'universal and homogenous state'. Without any evidence to back this up, Kojève claimed that Hegel himself had interpreted Napoleon's victory at the 1806 Battle of Jena as spelling the triumph of universal reason and the end of the master-slave dialectic: the 'end of history'. As citizens, people were now neither masters nor slaves. Though this narrative was in fact Kojève's own invention, he successfully passed it off as authentic Hegel.

Although James's real immersion in Hegel would only take place in the 1940s as a consequence of his close collaboration with the Marxist Raya Dunayevskaya, *The Black Jacobins* effectively already analyses the Haitian revolution as a real-world example of the master–slave dialectic – restoring agency to the actual enslaved

---

1   Such names were common in colonial newspapers (for example, the Saint-Domingue *L'Observateur colonial*) as well as in Europe.

2   For a critique of Hegel's dismissal of 'lazy existence', see Theodor W. Adorno, *Negative Dialectics* (trans. E.B. Ashton), London: Routledge, 1990, p.8.

subjects whose actions were neutralised in Hegel's writings even as the latter were informed by them. Following Buck-Morss, we can say that while it is important to study Hegel's half-acknowledged debt to the Caribbean slave revolt, at least as important is the later appropriation (one could perhaps say *re*appropriation) of his thought by twentieth-century Afro-Caribbean thinkers.

> [We] need to consider not only Hegel's Haiti, but Haiti's Hegel, that is, the Afro-Caribbean reception of Hegel that claims him as their own. [Nick] Nesbitt has traced this legacy through the work of Aimé Césaire, whose influential conception of *negritude*, referring to the African diaspora's self-understanding based on 'a common experience of subjugation and enslavement', considers the slave's self-liberation in the Haitian Revolution as 'emblematic'.[3] Césaire recalled to Nesbitt personally his youthful excitement in discovering Hyppolite's new translation of Hegel's *Phenomenology* (1941): 'When the French translation of the *Phenomenology* first came out, I showed it to [Léopold Sédar Senghor, later to become president of Senegal], and said to him: "Listen to what Hegel says, Léopold: to arrive at the Universal, one must immerse oneself in the Particular!"'[4] Césaire understood that the truly productive, 'universal' experience of reading Hegel is not through a summary of the total and totalising system, but through the liberation that one's own imagination can achieve by encountering dialectical thinking in its most concrete exemplification.[21]

While Hegel himself had tended to abstract from the particulars of the Caribbean slave revolt, the descendants of those slaves could nonetheless use the tools his dialectical thought provides in order to analyse and challenge the colonial status quo. Césaire turned the tables on the colonial regime and its dehumanisation of the non-Western Other. In his *Discourse on Colonialism* (first published in 1950), Césaire argues in stark terms that the coloniser is above all dehumanising himself. In a controversial move, Césaire polemically argues that Nazi genocide followed quite logically from colonial brutality and extermination.

---

[3] Cited in Nick Nesbitt, *Voicing Memory: History and Subjectivity in French Caribbean Literature*, Charlottesville: University of Virginia Press, 2003, p.21. Nesbitt discusses Hegel's *Phenomenology* with Césaire's 1963 play *La Tragédie du roi Christophe*, as putting together Yoruba/Vodou and Hegelian philosophies of history, see *ibid.*, p.143.
[4] *Ibid.*, p.120.

AIMÉ CÉSAIRE, *DISCOURSE ON COLONIALISM*

Reprinted from *Discourse on Colonialism*,
New York: Monthly Review Press, 2000, pp.36,
38–41, 52. First published in 1950/1955.
Translated from the French by Joan Pinkham.

[What the Christian bourgeois] cannot forgive Hitler for is not *the crime* itself, *the crime against man*, it is not *the humiliation of man as such*, it is the crime against the white man, the humiliation of the white man, and the fact that he applied to Europe colonialist procedures which until then had been reserved exclusively for the Arabs of Algeria, the 'coolies' of India, and the 'niggers' of Africa. [...]

Who protests? No one, so far as I know, when M. Albert Sarraut, the former governor-general of Indochina, holding forth to the students of the Ecole Coloniale, teaches them that it would be puerile to object to the European colonial enterprises in the name of 'an alleged right to possess the land one occupies, and some sort of right to remain in fierce isolation, which would leave unutilised resources to lie forever idle in the hand of incompetents'.

And who is roused to indignation when a certain Rev. Barde assures us that if the goods of this world 'remained divided up indefinitely, as they would be without colonisation. They would answer neither the purposes of God nor the just demands of the human collectivity'?

Since, as his fellow Christian, the Rev. Muller, declares: 'Humanity must not, cannot allow the incompetence, negligence and laziness of the uncivilised peoples to leave idle indefinitely the wealth which God has confided to them, charging them to make it serve the good of all.'

No one.

I mean not one established writer, not one academic, not one preacher, not one crusader for the right and for religion, not one 'defender of the human person'.

And yet, through the mouths of the Sarrauts and the Bardes, the Mullers and the Renans, though the mouths of all those who considered – and consider – it lawful to apply to non-European peoples 'a kind of expropriation for public purposes' for the benefit of nations that were stronger and better equipped, it was already Hitler speaking!

What am I driving at? At this idea: that no one colonises innocently, that no one colonises with impunity either; that a nation which colonises, that a civilisation which justifies colonisation – and therefore force – is already a sick civilisation, a civilisation which is morally diseased, which irresistibly, progressing from one consequence to another, one denial for another, calls for its Hitler, I mean its punishment.

Colonisation: bridgehead in a campaign to civilise barbarism, from which there may emerge at any moment the negation of civilisation, pure and simple.

Elsewhere I have cited at length a few incidents culled from the history of colonial expeditions. [...]

For my part, if I have recalled a few details of these hideous butcheries, it is by no means because I take a morbid delight in them, but because I think that these heads of men, these collections of ears, these burned houses, these Gothic invasions, this streaming blood, these cities that evaporate at the edge

of the sword, are not to be so easily disposed of. They prove that colonisation, I
repeat, dehumanises even the most civilised man; that colonial activity, colonial
enterprise, colonial conquest, which is based on contempt for the native and justified by that contempt, inevitably tends to change him who undertakes it; that
the coloniser, who in order to ease his conscience gets into the habit of seeing the
other man as *an animal*, accustoms to treating him like an animal, and tends
objectively to transform *himself* into an animal. It is this result, this boomerang
effect of colonisation that I wanted to point out.

While mounting a defence of pre-conquest tribal society as being not only ante-capitalist
but properly anti-capitalist and communist, Césaire the dialectician stresses that:

It is not a dead society that we want to revive. We leave that to those who go in for
exoticism. Nor is it the present colonial society that we wish to prolong, the most
putrid carrion that ever rotted under the sun. It is a new society that we must create, with the help of all our brother slaves, a society rich with all the productive
power of modern times, warm with all the fraternity of olden days.

As Homi K. Bhabha argues in a 2006 text referencing Toussaint and James, various
forms of subaltern agency – the agency of people who are or were the subaltern Others
of the Western subject and state – raise questions about the very fabric of modernity
and contemporaneity, which he conceptualises as disjunctive rather than homogenous. We are not dealing with some empty geometric space covering the globe and
inhabited by disembodied subjects defined by their access to universal rationality and
their citizenship. Both the space and the time that we share (or refuse to share) are
messy, fractured – far more political and more aesthetic than the United Nations, the
World Bank or most NGOs would have it.

The ethnocentric limitations of Foucault's spatial sign of modernity become
immediately apparent if we take our stand, in the immediate post-revolutionary
period, in San Domingo with the Black Jacobins, rather than Paris. What if the
'distance' that constitutes the meaning of the Revolution as sign, the signifying
lag between event and enunciation, stretches not across the Place de la Bastille or
the Rue des Blancs-Monteaux, but spans the temporal difference of the colonial
space? What if we heard the 'moral disposition of mankind' uttered by Toussaint
L'Ouverture for whom, as C.L.R. James so vividly recalls, the signs of modernity,
'liberty, equality, fraternity … What revolutionary France signified was perpetually on his lips, in public statements, in his correspondence, in the spontaneous
intimacy of private conversation.'[5] What do we make of the figure of Toussaint
– James invokes Phedre, Ahab, Hamlet – at the moment when he grasps the tragic
lesson that the moral, *modern* disposition of mankind, enshrined in the sign of
the Revolution, only fuels the archaic racial factor in the society of slavery? What
do we learn from that split consciousness, that 'colonial' disjunction of modern

---

5   C.L.R. James, *The Black Jacobins: Toussaint L'Ouverture and the San Domingo Revolution* (second edition, revised), New York: Vintage Books, 1989, pp.290. [Editors' Note: This
quote has been updated to reflect the current edition.]

times and colonial and slave histories, where the reinvention of the self and the remaking of the social are strictly out of joint?

These are the issues of the catachrestic, postcolonial translation of modernity. They force us to introduce the question of subaltern agency, into the question of modernity: what is this 'now' of modernity? Who defines this present from which we speak? This leads to more challenging questions: *What is the desire of this repeated demand to modernise? Why does it insist, so compulsively, on its contemporaneous reality, its spatial dimension, its spectatorial distance?* What happens to the sign of modernity in those repressive places like San Domingo, where progress is only heard (of) and not 'seen', is that it reveals the problem of the disjunctive moment of its utterance: the space which enables a postcolonial contra-modernity to emerge.[22]

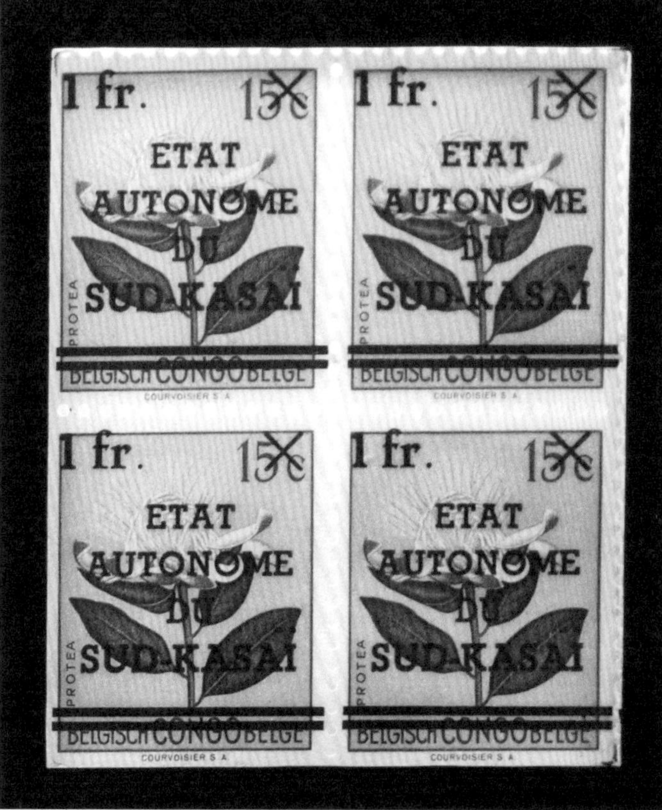

Otolith Group, *Statecraft* (detail), 2014, postage stamps issued by the Autonomous State of South Kasai on card

Autonomy and Sovereignty

Colonial powers would sometimes accord a relative 'autonomy' or 'self-government' to countries or regions while making sure that they remained under their control. In his 1934 book *We Slaves of Suriname*, Anton de Kom eviscerates the entire history of Dutch rule in Suriname, which functioned as a Caribbean plantation economy on the Latin American mainland – slavery was only banned by the Dutch masters in 1863. De Kom, who was arrested in Suriname in 1933 and deported to Holland without trial, unmasks this colony's status within the kingdom of the Netherlands. Similar to the French, the Dutch have used the term *autonomie* to refer to what the British historically called 'self-government'. (Even today, Britain still has self-governing colonies such as Bermuda and Gibraltar.) De Kom exposes Suriname's autonomous status as a sham in a passage on 'The Nature of Autonomy':

> Why this indignation against a few governors? Why don't we remember the fact that in 1866 the enlightened Dutch nation already gave Suriname that which others are still yearning and aching for: 'autonomy, the holy right of self-determination for the population!'
>
> Let us not rejoice too soon; let us not be blinded by a name, as though the 'Labour Council'[6] were the same thing as a 'workers' council' [*arbeidersraad*]. In other words: let us not be placated by words but first question what the autonomy of Suriname truly looks like.[23]

As can be gauged from his reference to workers' councils, De Kom moved in communist circles, particularly those of the Dutch writers' and photographers' collective Links Richten. Avant-garde designer and photographer Piet Zwart, who was loosely affiliated with Links Richten, designed the cover of De Kom's book. The fact that the latter was written in Dutch, rather than in a more 'successful' imperialist language such as English or French, may account for its lack of international renown.

The results of De Kom's examination of Surinamese autonomy were predictably grim, as was his assessment of the perpetuation of quasi-slavery in the form of 'contract labour'. Particularly affected were the Indonesian labourers (Indonesia being another Dutch colony) who were imported to work on plantations, as well as Creole ex-slaves:

> Let there be no misunderstanding; Surinamese people are certainly not opposed to a truly free immigration of labourers and poor farmers to a prosperous Suriname. Our country is rich and large enough to provide many with prosperity, provided that we have a good administration. We are willing to bestow equal rights to Indonesians as to all workers in addition. However, we oppose the exploitation of the need and misery of Indonesians by making them sign contracts under false pretences – contracts that undermine the wage and working conditions of Suriname and maintain the old slave mentality.[24]

---

6   Editors' Note: A reference to an advisory council created by the Dutch government, known as Hoge Raad van Arbeid.

In line with authors such as De Kom, James or Césaire, the anti-colonial movements of the twentieth century roundly rejected relative 'autonomy' and instead demanded full *sovereignty*. The concept of sovereignty commonly refers to authority over a territory and society. Kings are sovereigns; the *French Declaration of the Rights of Man and of the Citizen* insists that not monarchs but nations are sovereign, and it is a liberal-democratic commonplace to note that 'the people are the sovereign'. Former colonies attain sovereignty when becoming independent, leaving the status of 'autonomous zone' within the empire behind them.

During the 1930s, Georges Bataille was lauding tribal cultures precisely because their members were not subject to modern conceptions of the subject as a putatively autonomous yet disciplined and productive member of society. In this, they were sovereign, in his understanding of the term: 'The sovereignty *I* speak of has little to do with the sovereignty of States, as international law defines it. I speak in general of an aspect that is opposed to the servile and the subordinate. [...] What distinguishes sovereignty is the consumption of wealth, as against labour and servitude, which produce wealth without consuming it.'[25] Putting a different spin on Kojève's interpretation of the master-slave dialectic, Bataille notes that the beggar can be as close to sovereignty as the nobleman, while 'the bourgeois is voluntarily the most far removed'.[26] Tribal, premodern societies side with sovereignty; the bourgeois, capitalist world makes do with an instrumentalist, impoverished autonomy.

Today, sovereignty has returned in a decolonial context as territorial sovereignty against the nation-state. This is true especially of indigenous movements in settler colonial states such as the US and Australia (and indeed Israel). Settler colonialism is specific in that its basis is not predominantly the extraction of resources (including human resources in the form of slaves) by a relatively small colonial elite, but on settlement of the land by colonisers who displace and sometimes eradicate local populations – and who often ended up demanding and achieving a degree of autonomy or full independence from the motherland. Today, indigenous populations in settler colonial states assert their autonomy (or right to self-determination) and claim territorial sovereignty over their traditional lands. As Rachel O'Reilly and Danny Butt argue, this makes for a problematic montage with the local version of global artistic and political discourse:

> Today, art as a marker of the 'cultured' free citizen gives way to a massified 'inclusive' artistic infrastructure that imbricates human and financial capital in ever-larger circuits of labour and life. The large-scale art event's geographic reach of included practitioners and audiences; its openness to 'public' participation and education programmes; and the art industry's overall 'expansion' – occurs by way of a secessionist class of artistic managers whose financial and knowledge-sharing infrastructures are underwritten by industries that profit from the strict policing of the border between legitimate and illegitimate subjects. We see this most explicitly in the case of mandatory detention of asylum seekers, but we can also see this at work in the attacks on indigenous sovereignty through mining and governmental reoccupations such as the Northern Territory intervention. [...]
>
> In Australia, heritages of mostly English-language but globally reconfigured discourses of aesthetic and political autonomy hover next to the specificity and intractable complexity of indigenous self-determination. The proximity of these reduce the settler left's openness to any deep understanding of and literacy in the juxtapolitical nuances of autonomy as differentially enacted modes and crafts of

survivance. In other words, the failure to engage indigenous autonomy prevents the settler colonial cultural worker from dealing materially enough with the political economic registers and dispossessions in our own practices.[27]

While it is understandable that, in settler states, the discussion of sovereignty has returned to the fore as *indigenous sovereignty*, the theorist Jared Sexton has suggested that decolonial movements should side precisely with the *unsovereign*.[28] The unsovereign is Ferreira da Silva's 'affectable I': the sub-subject that has historically been deemed impure and unreasonable.

Likewise, the anthropologist Elizabeth A. Povinelli has aired severe doubts about the progressive and emancipatory potential of the notions of sovereignty and autonomy. Povinelli is the sole non-Aboriginal member of the Karrabing Film Collective, whose work informs her analysis in the 2017 essay 'The Ends of Humans: Anthropocene, Autonomism, Antagonism, and the Illusions of Our Epoch'. If one could call Karrabing's practice a form of indigenous autonomism, Povinelli would argue that such a label comes with too many old illusions. In the sections of the following essay on 'the autonomy of the wastelands' and 'toxic sovereignty', she unpacks the problems of these notions in the Australian settler colonial context – even while taking cues from autonomist theory, specfically Berardi's take on Autonomia under post-Fordist semiocapitalism.[29]

ELIZABETH POVINELLI, 'THE ENDS OF HUMANS: ANTHROPOCENE, AUTONOMISM, ANTAGONISM, AND THE ILLUSIONS OF OUR EPOCH'

Reprinted from *South Atlantic Quarterly*, vol.116, no.2, April 2017, pp.298-99, 302-08.

In *semiocapital*, affective-informational loops are oriented toward the capture of different spheres of human knowledge and the immanent desires of subjects. And insofar as it is effective in this capture, semiocapital pushes beyond labour power into soul power – not merely a consumption of human labour but a pneumaphagia, a spirit-eater.

If autonomism is to succeed in this new climate, Berardi argues, it must work to rewire the multitude of positions within the working assemblage of cognitive capital and discover the new antagonisms that define contemporary time. For Berardi, the contemporary antagonism pivots on the soul, for it is the human soul semiocapital commodifies. Thus the aim of revolution must be the liberation of the soul from the labour of capital. When that is the aim, the Left's definition of workers also changes. Once autonomism liberates the Left from semiocapital's pneumaphagia, new subjects of work and workers emerge. Workers are not merely the precarious labourers within the Silicon knowledge factories but all the dispersed and fragmented nodes within and across which information-desire is being produced, elaborated, amplified, distributed and consumed. This vast assemblage includes geologists, geneticists, biochemists, miners, software coders, biocircuitry, computer algorithms, massive data-storage facilities, air conditioners, satellites, human fingers and rare-earth-based screens, legislation for appropriating gas and minerals, ships and ship canals and the teaming life and toxicities carried and discharged in their ballast that cross territories, sink into soils and are ingested in drinking water. All existence is turned into abstract labour and oriented to the accumulation of informational capital.[7] [...]

The Autonomy of the Wastelands
The autonomous soul that Berardi and others seek to defend from semiocapitalism's assault is, in other settler colonial spaces, not merely an illusionary construct but a weapon of the enlightened liberal state in its constant manoeuvring against indigenous people. And where *autonomy from* late liberal settler governance does emerge it is nothing like the autonomy that some within the autonomist movement imagine. Let's start with autonomy as weaponry of settler colonialism, namely, the *autological subject*. The imaginary of the autological subject pivots on a miraculous enclosure of a human self-defined by nothing but his or her historical unfolding of desire. Autological subjects make their history. The sense and drama of this imaginary form of subjectivity is always contrasted to the *genealogical society* – societies in which matters of the heart and labours of life are defined by preexisting collectively constraining restrictions on individual risk and exploration. We can think of these two imaginary forms of sociality as companion species defined by their different social tense – on the one side we find any account of the actual freedoms and justices of the autological subject endlessly deferred to an unreachable future, and on the other we find the genealogical society relegated to the frozen landscapes of past perfect. The normative orientation of the autological subject is said to be the open future – its desire is to endlessly unfold in myriad and unimpeded creative gestures and explorations. Its sovereignty rests in the more or less self-determining individual. But to make this unfolding a universal historical form of subjectivity and governance, this subject must make other forms and arrangements of existence radically different from itself and historically retrograde. The autological subject demands that the genealogical society be its opposite; namely, the genealogical society is past perfect, and its sovereignty must rest in its ability to determine the truth of the individual.

The imaginary dialectic of the autological subject and genealogical society co-evolved in the vicious landscapes of liberal imperialism and became an invasive species in settler colonialism. Everywhere liberalism went this fantasy went with it, such that sovereignty likewise came to be bifurcated – the coloniser claiming that its form of sovereignty was based on the subject's autonomy (within limits) and that the sovereignty of the colonised was based on genealogy (various forms of a dominated social order). For many critical race and indigenous theorists such as Denise Ferreira da Silva[8] and Aileen Moreton-Robinson,[9]

7   See Melinda Cooper, *Life as Surplus: Biotechnology and Capitalism in the Neoliberal Era*, Seattle: University of Washington Press, 2008; Nikolas Rose, *The Politics of Life Itself: Biomedicine, Power, and Subjectivity in the Twenty-First Century*, Princeton, NJ: Princeton University Press, 2006; and Kaushik Sunder Rajan, *Biocapital: The Constitution of Postgenomic Life*, Durham, NC: Duke University Press, 2006.
8   Denise Ferreira da Silva, *Toward a Global Idea of Race*, Minneapolis: University of Minnesota Press, 2007.
9   Aileen Moreton-Robinson, *The White Possessive: Property, Power, and Indigenous Sovereignty*, Minneapolis: University of Minnesota Press, 2015.

the struggle is to find a mode of belonging outside these Western imaginaries.[10] What would we know differently if we read the history of autonomy from the perspective of settler liberal colonialism? For Moreton-Robinson, indigenous relations to land are not defined by autonomy as signified by a settler notion of sovereign possession of or over oneself, another or a place. Instead, they are forms of 'ontological belonging'.[11] Likewise, Glen Coulthard has more accurately described the shuttle between violent settler dispossession and a subtler, quieter form of subjective and spatial dislocation, a form of ongoing and relentless appropriation of indigenous lands.[12] For Coulthard, 'it is a profound misunderstanding to think of land or place as simply some material object of profound importance to Indigenous cultures (although it is this too); instead it ought to be understood as a field of relationships of things to each other'.[13]

In the first stage of the invasion of Australia, Europeans attempted to subsume the myriad indigenous forms of human and land co-belonging into, first, a colonial and, second, a national identity. As the settler invasion proceeded, the invasive species consumed whatever fuelled its ongoing expansion, uprooting, burning and killing whatever did not. Some indigenous people and their lands resisted the genocide as the invasive species built camps to function as 'the pillow of a dying race'.[14] Many within the invasive species argued that massive exterminations of indigenous forms of life were a tragic but natural process by which the old withered in the face of the new. It was not murder but history. After all, how can one murder what is already in the past? The invasive species was simply bringing a retarded space into its proper time. Autological sovereignty was the natural future of genealogical sovereignty. Settler genocide was simply a means of speeding up the process.

But indigenous forms of existence refused to be yet another fantastical version of the settler projection of the genealogical society. They refused to go away, to die or to let (their) history (have) happen(ed). From the 1950s through the 1970s, radical Red Power, Black Power, anticolonial and new social movements refused paternalistic liberal imperialism and settler colonialism. In other words, anticolonial movements were turning back imperial Europe just as workerist strategies were refusing the left unionist/capital convergence. Berardi's insight that working-class struggles precede and prefigure the unfolding formations and strategies of capital is useful here. Just as capital was forced to *respond* to the tactics of the radical Left, so the settler state was forced to respond to the demands of an indigenous uprising. Thus a new settler tactic emerged in the 1970s. The settler state would not kill indigenous people or let

---

[10]   See also Audra Simpson, *Mohawk Interruptus: Political Life across the Borders of Settler States*, Durham, NC: Duke University Press, 2014.

[11]   A. Moreton-Robinson, *The White Possessive, op. cit.*, p.4.

[12]   Glen Coulthard, *Red Skin, White Masks: Rejecting the Colonial Politics of Recognition*, Minneapolis: University of Minnesota Press, 2014. See also Taiaiake Alfred, *Wasáse: Indigenous Pathways of Activism and Freedom*, Toronto: University of Toronto Press, 2005; and Patrick Wolfe, *Traces of History: Elementary Structures of Race*, London: Verso, 2016.

[13]   Glen Coulthard, 'Place against Empire: Understanding Indigenous Anti-Colonialism', *Affinities*, vol.4, no.2, p.79.

[14]   Unlike in the Jim Crow American South, the one-drop rule pertained to white blood, such that 'one drop' of white blood was justification for removing children from their parents. See G.C. Bolton, 'Aborigines in Social History: An Overview', in Ronald M. Berndt (ed.), *Aboriginal Sites, Rights, and Resource Development*, Perth: University of Western Australia Press, 1982, pp.59-81.

them die comfortably, if they agreed to a toxic form of sovereignty. The first mode is primarily known under the name of self-determination and cultural recognition. In Australia, from the mid-1970s through the mid-2000s, the federal Aboriginal Lands Rights Act exemplified this new state tactic. The Lands Rights Act granted indigenous groups in the Northern Territory the right to lay claim over their own lands provided (a) that these lands had not already been alienated over the long course of settler colonisation and (b) that the claimants fit a narrow anthropological and legal definition of the 'traditional'. A series of legislative documents was written that offered land and recognition to indigenous people if they agreed to be 'traditional'. In other words a form of past-oriented being-in-the-present was carved into settler governance – the state-backed indigene would be past perfect, and its sovereignty must rest in its ability to determine the truth of the individual. Every action of the indigenous person and group would be assessed and valued relative to these temporal and sovereign disciplines.[15] Each failure to conform to these sovereign temporal regimes would shift more land to the side of the invading species, narrowing the range of indigenous manoeuvre. If indigenous people accepted these terms, they would be given back the lands that capital and the state never wanted in the first place. There in state and capital wastelands, history could be autonomous because the freehold was over the wastelands of settler history. The form of property invented to justify as a gift the giving of what had not yet been taken was called 'Aboriginal freehold tenure'.

The rights that indigenous groups received from the state were never intended to make indigenous worlds the norm. Neither the invasive state nor capital suddenly or fundamentally altered how they related to lands and peoples on the basis of what indigenous people told them. Extractive capital, for instance, did not suddenly become obligated to an indigenous analysis of the unalterable co-constitution of various forms of existence. Instead, the rights the state gave indigenous people were meant to provide a means of cleansing the national history of its shameful past and providing authorised indigenous groups a means of attaching a small spigot to the larger pipeline of settler late liberal capital. It should not be surprising then that by the 2000s, mining on Aboriginal land in the Northern Territory of Australia alone contributed more than $1 billion a year to the territory's economy and accounted for 80 per cent of its income.[16] Four hundred and thirty-two indigenous land agreements stretched across two hundred mining operations. This détente held until the mid-2000s. But by the 2000s, in the long shadow of the global financial crisis and China's great hunger for raw minerals, indigenous people were not willing to hand over even more land. The state and capital realised that they had made a mistake. All those machines and clouds, all that desire captured and manipulated by the attunement of the positive and negative atomic charges that allow fingertips to communicate to copper or indium tin oxide wires on large and small screens, then stored and manipulated across ever-larger arrays of big data, all the ways that all institutions of intelligence shift to accommodate their

---

[15] See Larry Nesper, *The Walleye War: The Struggle for Ojibwe Spearfishing and Treaty Rights*, Lincoln: University of Nebraska Press, 2002.

[d] See Central Land Council, 'Making agreements on Aboriginal land: Mining and development', 2016, available at https://www.clc.org.au/index.php?/articles/info/mining-and-development (last accessed on 19 September 2020).

dominion (universities shifting from the arts and humanities to the quantitative informational sciences): all this depended on commoditised minerals and gases found in what were thought to be the great wastelands of the nation.

But strong binaries can always be flipped. In 2007, the conservative federal government fanned the flames of panic about the sexual assault of Indigenous children on remote communities in order to pass the Northern Territory National Emergency Response (NTNER), claiming that a set of unsubstantiated assaults were caused by Indigenous sexual traditions.[17] Among other measures, NTNER allowed the federal government to seize Indigenous lands and open them to mining. Whereas traditions had once been good for the nation, now they were bad. The conservative state, their allies in extractive capital and indigenous social politics, did not dispute that indigenous sovereignty existed. Instead, they agreed that it existed as a past perfect, individually constraining power. This is why indigenous people had to be liberated from their own sovereign form. Indigenous individuals had to become autonomous to indigenous sovereignty. So much for the autonomy of Aboriginal freehold – and the hundreds of indigenous land agreements with various mining operations. What was made visible for those for whom it had not been visible before was that the sovereign autonomy of indigenous rights had always had a temporal asterisk attached to it. It was always a toxic asset. What had not already been despoiled became so. And I mean what had not been already despoiled – the lands reserved for the state-sanctioned autonomy of history were not necessarily pristine deserts but asbestos dumping grounds, nuclear test lands, medical experiments and chemical contaminations.[18]

Toxic Autonomy

If we examine semiocapital and anthropogenic climate change from within the many indigenous worlds under assault by the anthropogenic effects of mining and climate, a new form of indigenous autonomy emerges. But, as I noted above, this new form of autonomy challenges the romance of the autonomous soul, replacing it with a more literal form of toxic sovereignty. Take, for example, the second Karrabing Film Collective project, *Windjarrameru, The Stealing C*nt$* [2015]. *Windjarrameru* tells the story of a group of young indigenous men hiding in a chemically contaminated swamp after being falsely accused of stealing two cartons of beer, while all around them miners are wrecking and polluting their land.[19] It is not a documentary film, and it cuts across fiction and nonfiction to produce, what Martina Angelotti has called a factional dimension of truth.[20] For instance, throughout the film are numerous background signs to the main

---

17   Jon Altman, 'Arguing the Intervention', *Journal of Indigenous Policy*, no.14, 2013, pp.1-146.

18   See, for instance, Warwick Anderson, *The Cultivation of Whiteness: Science, Health, and Racial Destiny in Australia*, Durham, NC: Duke University Press, 2006; and Jon Donnison, 'Lingering impact of British nuclear tests in the Australian outback', BBC News, 31 December 2014, available at https://www.bbc.co.uk/news/world-australia-30640338 (last accessed on 19 September 2020).

19   For more information about the Karrabing Film Collective, see Martina Angelotti, 'Karrabing Film Collective: An Interview', *Domus*, 18 December 2015, available at https://www.domusweb.it/en/interviews/2015/12/18/visible_award_2015_the_karrabing_film_collective.html (last accessed on 19 September 2020).

20   *Ibid.*

action of the film – two large, dry branches with 'Stop poison' painted on them; an old, large corrugated water tank with a placard attached stating, 'Warning radiation'; and, at the turnoff to the swamp, a large sign on which is written, 'Danger, asbestos, cancers and lung disease hazard, authorized personnel only, respirators and protective clothing are required at all times'. We created the first two signs ('Stop poison' and 'Radiation area') and placed them on or near already existing historical infrastructures. The large corrugated water tank on which we affixed the sign 'Warning radiation' is, we believe, a leftover part of an illegal nonindigenous squatter dwelling. It sits alongside a group of large concrete and metal structures from the Wagait Battery built in 1944 to defend Darwin from Japanese air assaults in World War II.[21] The sign 'Danger, asbestos …' has a real, factual existence. It refers to the antenna field and compound, located on the far north-western side of the Cox Peninsula. The antenna field and compound were built in 1942 after the Royal Australian Air Force commandeered American equipment. The antenna field was placed next to Charles Lighthouse, built in the late 1800s and the location of forced indigenous labour throughout the early twentieth century.

Which parts of this world are fact or fiction emerges, however, in the practice of making these films. In the film narrative, three police chase the young indigenous men up to a barbed wire fence, where they capture one of them, while the others escape into a contaminated area. The police asked the young man they've grabbed who placed the sign 'Stop poison' at the edge of the fence. The clear implication is that this is an act of illegal signage. After shooting the scene, the Karrabing emerged from the scrub to find two non-fictional police, who confronted them and asked if they had entered illegally or altered signage in the area. To defuse the situation they introduced the real police to the fictional police and joked about which of them seemed more authentic. But curious why the real police were interested in where the film crew was filming, some of the Karrabing went online. There they found a Federal Department of Finance document ('Cox Peninsula Remediation Project', December 2014) submitted to the Parliamentary Standing Committee on Public Works. When studying the maps within this report, the members realised that the toxic field was much bigger than they had known. And, indeed, they had been shooting within it. But they and other members of their family had also hunted, collected fruit and camped within this same toxic area. They learned that water wells in a primarily European community that hugs the coast north of the Radio Australia receiver are periodically tested, but no testing is done of the broader aquifer system regularly used by Karrabing and other indigenous residents on the peninsula. Suddenly, fictional signs became real signs of what many knew but systematically hid from those for whom not knowing had the greatest impact.

But it is not only indigenous worlds that are analysing anthropogenic toxicity and its effects on a new form of immanent being. Black, brown and indigenous lands, cities, and neighbourhoods have long struggled to analyse being in the space of extractive capital as it came, took and left a differentially distributed toxosphere of refuse.[22] We have a rich aesthetics of these sites. [...]

---

[21] See Tim Owens and Shelley James, 'The History, Archaeology, and Material Culture', *Australasian Historical Archaeology*, no. 31, pp. 92–98.

[22] Rob Nixon, *Slow Violence and the Environmentalism of the Poor*, Cambridge, MA: Harvard University Press, 2011.

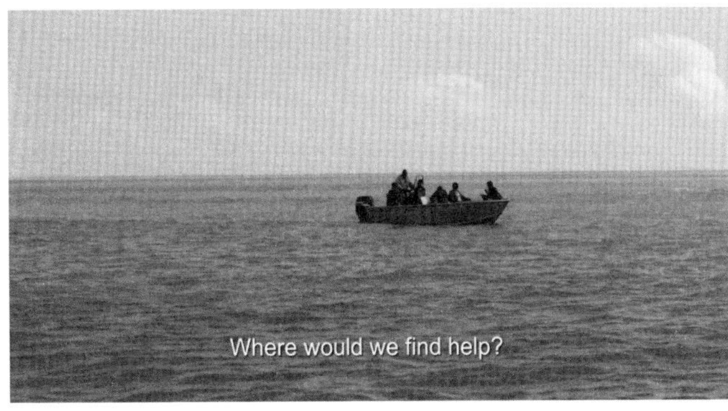

Still from Karrabing Film Collective,
When the Dogs Talked, 2014,
colour film with sound, 34min
Courtesy the artists

See pp.280–81 of this reader for
more images

But what they learn from all of these fictional and nonfictional endeavours is that anthropogenic toxins do not obey the settler colonial spatial technology of a barbed wire fence or the concept of a border. They seep through and corrode. They make use of, but do not oppose. They extinguish, but are not antagonistic in the sense of creating two actively opposing forces. They are inside and outside. They are poisonous according to degree or strength, wiring and unwiring bodies and regions rather than simply silencing them. *They* are not because they are everywhere. Like Moreton-Robinson and Coulthard, Karrabing members do not simply divorce their being from their lands even as their lands, the ancestral beings within them, and they themselves are being recomposed by these toxicities. Instead, in these spaces of utter settler despoilment a new form of sovereignty emerges, a new form of pure autonomy from the capture of capital and state – a toxic autonomy. Throughout their films the Karrabing explore how to be with themselves and other existences within a place as the state and capital flee the areas they have plundered – the areas they, as invasive species, now fear to enter. But the Karrabing are also not naïve about what forms of entangled existence this toxic autonomy produces. This is because film-making is an activity that allows the Karrabing to analyse their world and in this sense is an act of 'survivance'. Gerald Vizenor notes that 'survivance is an active sense of presence, the continuance of native stories, not a mere reaction, or a survivable name' and that 'native survivance stories are renunciations of dominance, tragedy and victimry' even as they reject the fabulous imaginaries of the settler's romantic Aboriginal.[23] For Karrabing, survivance does not mean the survival of the world as it is, or as the settler invasion has conceived it.

[...] But politics after anthropogenic climate change and toxicity will need to grapple with a world without autonomy or antagonists yet extraordinarily hostile to some regions of existence. The illusions of our epoch are the autonomous and antagonistic. Other illusions may be better suited. Viruses, gassings, toxins – these are the names we give to manners of appearing and spreading; tactics of diverting the energies of arrangements of existence in order to extend themselves; strategies of copying, duplicating and lying dormant even as they continually adjust to, experiment with and test their circumstances; manoeuvres to confuse and level every difference that emerges between regions while carefully taking advantage of the minutest aspects of their differentiation.

---

23   Gerald Vizenor, *Manifest Manners: Narratives on Postindian Survivance*, Lincoln: University of Nebraska Press, 1999, p.11.

Postcolonial Autography

Is another autonomy possible? Is there not an urgent need for forms of self-articulation beyond the expropriating violence of the imperialist 'autological subject' as defined by Povinelli? Such self-writing, or autography, is not the same as the self-assertion of a rights-holding, property-owning bourgeois subject; it may in fact involve aesthetic strategies that undermine this subject's alleged autonomy, and it includes the right to self-differ and become other.

The now-legendary exhibition 'Magiciens de la Terre' (1989) was an import-ant catalyst in the burgeoning debate about 'global art' in the late 1980s and early 1990s. The curator Jean-Hubert Martin seemed to include non-Western artists 'not as worldly subjects, as global artists, but as mediums tied to the ground, magicians of the earth'.[30] This was another version of the distinction between allographic modern subjects and genealogical societies tied to the past, as decried by Povinelli. One of the most prominent participants in the 'Magiciens' debates and in the budding discourse on global art was the critic Thomas McEvilley. In 1995, Olu Oguibe attacked him for an interview with the artist Ouattara, in which McEvilley had presumed to speak in the name of the African artist, robbing him of his subjecthood:

> Autonomy. Self-articulation. Autography. These are contested territories where the contemporary African artist finds herself locked in a struggle for survival, a struggle against displacement by the numerous strategies of regulation and surveillance which today characterise Western attitudes towards African art. Within the scheme of their relationship with the West, it is forbidden that African artists should possess the power of self-definition, the right to authority. It is for-bidden that they should enunciate outside the gaze and free of the interventionist powers of others. And it is this contestation of their complete subjectivity and their right to co-legislate patterns of interaction which we find in McEvilley's interview with Ouattara.[31]

Whether one agrees or disagrees with Oguibe's assessment is not the issue here. What matters in the present context is that he actualises a crucial trope of African and Caribbean anti-colonial discourse: the fight of black people to be recognised as subjects rather than treated as subhuman or as slave commodities. Furthermore, in terms of self-articulation and autography he stresses that this project is as aesthetic as it is political; such self-fashioning goes far beyond the demand to finally partake in certain 'universal' rights of man. People of colour have, after all, been dehumanised precisely by being relegated to an anti-aesthetic netherworld of darkness, base sensu-ality and sexuality, and intellectual inferiority.

In the following essay, the Cameroon-born and Paris-educated philosopher Achille Mbembe engages with this history *and* with the potential for other histo-ries to be written. Mbembe visits the Enlightenment and its legacy, characterising the African independence projects of the post-War period in terms of a dialectic of *sovereignty* (defined here as Africans' desire to shape their own destiny) and *auton-omy* (their desire to 'belong to themselves in the world'). Autonomy and sovereignty here stop being Manichean opposites and become complementary and complicit.

However, such emancipatory promises of these appropriated notions of sovereignty and autonomy have not been fulfilled.

Mbembe calls for a focus on 'the disparate, and often intersecting, practices through which Africans *stylise* their conduct and life can account for the thickness of which the African present is made'; self-writing and self-fashioning become vehicles for an autonomy that does not necessarily lay claim to that name. Rather than creating a heroic subject or wallowing in abject, object-like victimhood, Mbembe's contemporary African writes and performs an embodied self that will not get trapped in identitarianism.

ACHILLE MBEMBE, 'AFRICAN MODES OF SELF-WRITING'

Reprinted from *Public Culture*, vol.14, no.1,
Winter 2002, pp.239-73. First published in 2001.
Translated from the French by Steven Rendall.

The only subjectivity is time.
– Gilles Deleuze, *Cinema 2: The Time-Image*

Over the past two centuries, intellectual currents have emerged whose goal has been to confer authority on certain symbolic elements integrated into the African collective *imaginaire*. Some of these trends have gained a following, while others have remained mere outlines. Very few are outstanding in richness and creativity, and fewer still are of exceptional power.

At the intersection of religious practices and the interrogation of human tragedy, a distinctively African philosophy has emerged. But governed though it has been, for the most part, by narratives of loss, such meditation on divine sovereignty and African people's histories has not yielded any integrated philosophico-theological inquiry systematic enough to situate human misfortune and wrongdoing in a singular theoretical framework.[24] Africa offers nothing comparable, for example, to a German philosophy that from [Martin] Luther to [Martin] Heidegger has been based not only on religious mysticism but also, more fundamentally, on the will to transgress the boundary between the human and the divine. Nor is there anything comparable to Jewish Messianism, which, combining desire and dream, confronted almost without mediation the problem of the absolute and its promises, pursuing the latter to its most extreme consequences in tragedy and despair, while at the same time treating the uniqueness of Jewish suffering as sacred at the risk of making it taboo.[25] It is true that, following

---

[24]   See, for example, Fabien Eboussi Boulaga, *Christianisme sans fétiche: Révélation et domination*, Paris: Présence africaine, 1981; Jean-Marc Ela, *Le cri de l'homme africain: Questions aux chrétiens et aux églises d'Afrique*, Paris: L'Harmattan, 1980, and *Ma foi d'africain*, Paris: Karthala, 1985; and Valentin Y. Mudimbe, *Tales of Faith: Religion as Political Performance in Central Africa*, London: Athlone, 1997.

[25]   See Gershom Scholem, *Aux origines religieuses du judaïsme laïque: De la mystique aux Lumières* (ed. Maurice Kriegel), Paris: Calmann-Lévy, 2000; Yitzhak F. Baer, *Galout:*

the examples of these two metanarratives, contemporary African modes of writing the self are inseparably connected with the problematics of self-constitution and the modern philosophy of the subject. However, there the similarities end.

Various factors have prevented the full development of conceptions that might have explained the meaning of the African past and present by reference to the future, but chief among them may be named historicism. The effort to determine the conditions under which the African subject could attain full selfhood, become self-conscious, and be answerable to no one else soon encountered historicist thinking in two forms that led it into a dead end. The first of these is what might be termed *Afro-radicalism*, with its baggage of instrumentalism and political opportunism. The second is the burden of the metaphysics of difference (*nativism*).[26] The first current of thought – which liked to present itself as 'democratic', 'radical' and 'progressive' – used Marxist and nationalist categories to develop an *imaginaire* of culture and politics in which a manipulation of the rhetoric of autonomy, resistance and emancipation serves as the sole criterion for determining the legitimacy of an authentic African discourse.[27] The second current of thought developed out of an emphasis on the 'native condition'. It promoted the idea of a unique African identity founded on membership of the black race.

Fundamental to both currents of thought are three historical events, broadly construed: slavery, colonisation and apartheid. A particular set of canonical meanings has been attributed to these three events. First, on the level of individual subjectivities, there is the idea that through the processes of slavery, colonisation and apartheid, the African self has become alienated from itself (*self-division*). This separation is supposed to result in a loss of familiarity with the self, to the point that the subject, having become estranged from him- or herself, has been relegated to a lifeless form of identity (*objecthood*). Not only is the self no longer recognised by the Other; the self no longer recognises itself.[28]

L'imaginaire de l'exil dans le judaïsme (trans. Marc de Launay), Paris: Calmann-Lévy, 2000; Hannah Arendt, *The Jew as Pariah: Jewish Identity and Politics in the Modern Age*, New York: Grove, 1978; and Sylvie Anne Goldberg, *La Clepsydre: Essai sur la pluralité des temps dans le judaïsme*, Paris: Albin Michel, 2000.

[26] To be sure, the two currents of thought adhere to no single theory of identity, politics or culture. For different critiques, see Amady A. Dieng, *Hegel, Marx, Engels et les problèmes de l'Afrique noire*, Dakar: Sankoré, 1978; Bogumil Jewsiewicki, *Marx, Afrique et Occident: Les pratiques africanistes de l'histoire marxiste*, Montreal: McGill University, Centre for Developing-Area Studies, 1985; and Valentin Y. Mudimbe, *The Idea of Africa*, Bloomington: Indiana University Press, 1994, pp.41-46. See also V.Y. Mudimbe, *Parables and Fables: Exegesis, Textuality, and Politics in Central Africa*, Madison: University of Wisconsin Press, 1991, pp.166-91. It can further be argued that in its attempt to reconceptualise the problem of the subject, African feminism does not fundamentally alter the dominant African Marxist, nationalist or nativist understandings of subjectivity or concepts of human intentionality. See, for example, Amina Mama, Ayesha Imam and Fatou Sow (ed.), *Engendering African Social Sciences*, Dakar: CODESRIA, 1997; and Ifi Amadiume, *Re-inventing Africa: Matriarchy, Religion, and Culture*, London: Zed, 1997.

[27] This approach contrasts with the politics of black radical activity in the United States during the twentieth century. In the latter case, attempts were made to organically conjoin Marxism and Black Nationalism, to develop a praxis that would attend to both *class* and *race* in promoting social transformation. See, for example, Cedric J. Robinson, *Black Marxism: The Making of the Black Radical Tradition*, Chapel Hill: University of North Carolina Press, 2000; and Brent Hayes Edwards, 'The "Autonomy" of Black Radicalism', *Social Text*, no.67, 2001, pp.1-12.

[28] Whether discussing it under the term *alienation* or *deracination*, it is francophone criticism that has most fully conceptualised this process. See, in particular, Frantz

The second canonical meaning has to do with property. According to the dominant narrative, the three events have led to dispossession, a process in which juridical and economic procedures have led to material expropriation. This was followed by a unique experience of subjection characterised by the falsification of Africa's history by the Other, which resulted in a state of maximal exteriority (*estrangement*) and deracination. These two phases – the violence of falsification and material expropriation – are said to be the main components of African history's uniqueness and of the tragedy that is at its foundation.[29]

Finally, there is the idea of historical degradation: slavery, colonisation and apartheid are supposed to have plunged the African subject not only into humiliation, debasement and nameless suffering but also into a zone of nonbeing and social death characterised by the denial of dignity, heavy psychic damage and the torment of exile.[30] These three fundamental elements of slavery, colonisation and apartheid are said to serve as a unifying centre of Africans' desire to know themselves, to recapture their destiny (*sovereignty*), and to belong to themselves in the world (*autonomy*).

By following the model of Jewish reflection on the phenomena of suffering, contingency and finitude, these three meanings might have been used as a starting point for a philosophical and critical interpretation of the apparent long rise toward nothingness that Africa has experienced all through its history. Theology, literature, film, music, political philosophy and psychoanalysis would have had to be involved as well. But such a synthesis did not occur.[31] In reality, the production of the dominant meanings of these events was itself colonised by the two ideological currents introduced above – the one instrumentalist, the other nativist – that claim to speak in the name of Africa as a whole.[32]

Fanon, *Black Skin, White Masks* (trans. Charles Lam Markmann), New York: Grove, 1967; Hamidou Kane, *L'aventure ambiguë*, Paris: Julliard, 1961; and Fabien Eboussi Boulaga, *La crise du Muntu: Authenticité africaine et philosophie*, Paris: Présence africaine, 1977, and *Christianisme sans fétiche, op. cit.*

[29]   This is particularly applicable to English-language studies of Marxist political economy, anthropology or history. Sometimes these also rely on nationalist and dependentist theses. See, for example, Claude Aké, *A Political Economy of Africa*, Harlow, UK: Longman, 1981; Walter Rodney, *How Europe Underdeveloped Africa*, Washington DC: Howard University Press, 1981; and, on a more general level, Samir Amin, *Le développement inégal: Essai sur les formations sociales du capitalisme périphérique*, Paris: Editions de Minuit, 1973.

[30]   On the problematics of slavery and reparation, see J.F. Ade Ajayi, 'The Atlantic Slave Trade and Africa' and 'Pan-Africanism and the Struggle for Reparation', in Toyin Falola (ed.), *Tradition and Change in Africa: The Essays of J.F. Ade Ajayi*, Trenton, NJ: Africa World Press, 2000. For a more subtle and sophisticated interpretation of slavery and its impact, see Orlando Patterson, *Slavery and Social Death: A Comparative Study*, Cambridge, MA: Harvard University Press, 1982; and, on 'dispersion' as seen from the other side of the Atlantic, Paul Gilroy, *The Black Atlantic: Modernity and Double Consciousness*, Cambridge, MA: Harvard University Press, 1993.

[31]   To be sure, attempts have occasionally been made at such a project. Apartheid has been the subject of constant biblical interpretation. See, among others, Allan Boesak, *Black and Reformed: Apartheid, Liberation, and the Calvinist Tradition: Sermons and Speeches*, New York: Orbis, 1984; and Desmond Tutu, *Hope and Suffering*, Grand Rapids, MI: Eerdmans, 1984. Colonisation has also been the subject of such interpretations. See, for example, Oscar Bimwenyi-Kweshi, *Discours théologique négro-africain: Problème des fondements*, Paris: Présence africaine, 1981; and J.-M. Ela, *Le cri de l'homme africain, op. cit.*, and *Ma foi d'Africain, op. cit.*

[32]   See, for example, Thandika Mkandawire and Charles C. Soludo, *Our Continent, Our Future: African Perspectives on Structural Adjustment*, Trenton, NJ: Africa World Press, 1999.

In the remarks that follow, I examine these two currents of thought and draw out their weaknesses. Throughout this discussion, I propose ways out of the dead end into which they have led reflection on the African experience of self and the world. Against the arguments of critics who have equated identity with race and geography, I show how current African imaginations of the self are born out of disparate but often intersecting practices, the goal of which is not only to settle factual and moral disputes about the world but also to open the way for *self-styling*. By emphasising historical contingency and the process of subject formation, my aim is to reinterpret subjectivity as time.

The Instrumentalist Paradigm: Primal Fantasies

The current of thought marked above as Marxist and nationalist is permeated by the tension between voluntarism and victimisation. It has four main characteristics. First of all, it exhibits a lack of self-reflexivity and an instrumental conception of knowledge and science, in the sense that neither is recognised as autonomous. They are useful only insofar as they are mobilised for service in partisan struggle.[33] To this partisan struggle is attributed an intrinsic moral significance, since it is alleged to oppose revolutionary liberation to the forces of conservatism.[34]

The second characteristic is a mechanistic and reified vision of history. Causality is attributed to entities that are fictive and wholly invisible, but are nevertheless said to determine, ultimately, the subject's life and work. According to this point of view, the history of Africa can be reduced to a series of subjugations, narrativised in a seamless continuity. African experience of the world is supposed to be determined, a priori, by a set of forces – always the same ones, though appearing in differing guises – whose function is to prevent the blooming of African uniqueness, of that part of the African historical self that is irreducible to any other.

As a result, Africa is said not to be responsible for the catastrophes that are befalling it. The present destiny of the continent is supposed to proceed not from free and autonomous choices but from the legacy of a history imposed upon Africans – burned into their flesh by rape, brutality and all sorts of economic conditionalities.[35] The African subject's difficulty in representing him- or herself as the subject of a free will is supposed to proceed from this long history of subjugation. This construction of history leads to a naïve and uncritical attitude with regard to so-called struggles for national liberation and to social movements; an emphasis on violence as the privileged avenue for self-determination;

---

[33] See, for example, Jacques Depelchin, 'African Anthropology and History in the Light of the History of FRELIMO', *Contemporary Marxism*, no.7, 1983, pp.69-88.

[34] This tendency took shape during the last quarter of the twentieth century in ideological production issuing not only from national institutions, such as the University of Dar-es-Salaam (Tanzania), but also from regional ones, such as the Southern African Political Economy Series (SAPES) Trust, based in Harare (Zimbabwe), and continental ones, such as the Council for the Development of Social Science Research in Africa (CODESRIA), based in Dakar (Senegal). For a theorisation, see C. Aké, *Social Science as Imperialism: The Theory of Political Development*, Ibadan: Ibadan University Press, 1982, and *Revolutionary Pressures in Africa*, London: Zed, 1978.

[35] See the ideological criticisms of structural adjustment programmes and the continuous conceptual dependence on a developmentalist paradigm in T. Mkandawire and Adebayo Olukoshi (ed.), *Between Liberalization and Oppression: The Politics of Structural Adjustment in Africa*, Dakar: CODESRIA, 1995.

the fetishisation of state power; the disqualification of the model of liberal democracy; and the populist and authoritarian dream of a mass society.[36]

The third characteristic is a desire to destroy tradition and the belief that authentic identity is conferred by the division of labour that gives rise to social classes, the proletariat – urban or rural – playing the role of the universal class par excellence.[37] The dictum that the working class is the only practical agency that can engage in universal emancipatory activity results in the denial of any possible multiplicity of foundations for the exercise of social power.[38]

Finally, this Marxist-nationalist school of thought relies on an essentially *polemical* relationship to the world, a relationship based on a troika of rhetorical rituals. The first ritual contradicts and refutes Western definitions of Africa and Africans by pointing out the falsehoods and bad faith they presuppose. The second denounces what the West has done (and continues to do) to Africa in the name of these definitions. And the third provides ostensible proofs that – by disqualifying the West's fictional representations of Africa and refuting its claim to have a monopoly on the expression of the human in general – are supposed to open up a space in which Africans can finally narrate their own fables. This is to be accomplished through the acquisition of a language and a voice that cannot be imitated because they are, in some sense, authentically Africa's own.[39]

Yet what might appear to be the apotheosis of voluntarism is here accompanied by a lack of philosophical depth and, paradoxically, a cult of victimisation. Philosophically, the Hegelian thematics of identity and difference, as classically exemplified in the master-bondsman relationship, is surreptitiously reappropriated by the ex-colonised. In a move that replicates an unreflexive ethnographic practice, the ex-colonised assigns a set of pseudohistorical features to a geographical entity which is itself subsumed under a *racial name.* The features and the name are then used to identify or make possible the recognition of those who, by virtue of possessing those features or bearing that name, can be said to belong to the racial collectivity and the geographical entity thus defined. Under the guise of 'speaking in one's own voice', then, the figure of the 'native' is reiterated. Boundaries are demarcated between the native and the non-native Other; and on the basis of these boundaries, distinctions can then be made between the authentic and the inauthentic.

In the critique that follows, I will be arguing (1) that such nationalist and Marxist narratives of the African self and the world have been superficial; (2) that as a consequence of this superficiality, the formulations of self-government and autonomy they engender are founded, at best, on a thin philosophical base;

---

[36]   On social movements, see Mahmood Mamdani and Ernest Wamba-dia-Wamba (ed.), *African Studies in Social Movements and Democracy*, Dakar: CODESRIA, 1995. On the populist critique of liberal democracy, see C. Aké, *The Feasibility of Democracy in Africa*, Dakar: CODESRIA, 2000; and Issa G. Shivji, *The Concept of Human Rights in Africa*, London: CODESRIA, 1989, and *Fight My Beloved Continent: New Democracy in Africa*, Harare: SAPES Trust, 1988.
[37]   See, for example, M. Mamdani (ed.), *Uganda: Studies in Labour*, Dakar: CODESRIA, 1996; Issa G. Shivji, *Class Struggles in Tanzania*, London: Heinemann, 1976.
[38]   One recent example is M. Mamdani, *Citizen and Subject: Contemporary Africa and the Legacy of Late Colonialism*, Princeton, NJ: Princeton University Press, 1996. See also Mamdani, *Politics and Class Formation in Uganda*, New York: Monthly Review Press, 1976.
[39]   See, for example, Paul Tiyambe Zeleza, *A Modern Economic History of Africa*, vol.1, *The Nineteenth Century*, Dakar: CODESRIA, 1993, and *Manufacturing African Studies and Crises*, Dakar: CODESRIA, 1997.

and (3) that their privileging of victimhood over subjecthood is derived, ultimately, from a distinctively nativist understanding of history – one of history
as sorcery.

Self-affirmation, autonomy and African emancipation – in the name of
which the right to selfhood is claimed – are not new issues. As the Atlantic slave
trade came to an end in the middle of the nineteenth century, doubts among
Europeans regarding Africans' ability to govern themselves – that is, according
to Hegel, to control their predatory greed and their cruelty[40] – gained impetus.
These doubts were connected with another, more fundamental doubt that was
implicit in the way modern times had resolved the complex general problem of
alterity and the status of the African sign within this economy of alterity. Both
Western philanthropic movements and the African intelligentsia of the times
responded to this doubt from within the paradigm of the Enlightenment.[41]

The Legacy of the Enlightenment
To draw out the political implications of these debates, I should perhaps first
remark the project, central to Enlightenment thought, of defining human
nature in terms of its possession of a generic identity. The rights and values to be
shared by all are derived from this identity, universal in essence. It is identical
in each human subject because it has reason at its centre. The exercise of reason
endows individuals with not only liberty and autonomy, but also the ability to
conduct life in accordance with moral principles and an idea of the good. The
thing to note here is that outside this circle, there is no place for a politics of the
universal. And for European thinkers of the period of abolition, the question
was indeed whether Africans were to be situated inside or outside the circle –
that is, whether they were human beings like all others. In other words: Could
we find among Africans the same human person, merely disguised by different
designations and forms? Could we consider Africans' bodies, languages, works
and lives as products of human activity, as manifesting a subjectivity – that is,
a consciousness like our own – that would allow us to consider each of them,
taken individually, as another self (*alter ego*)? The Enlightenment's response to
these questions can be traced through three distinct intellectual moments with
distinct political implications.

An initial set of answers suggested that Africans be kept within the limits of their presupposed ontological difference. This school of Enlightenment
thought – as exemplified by positions taken by Hegel and Kant – identified in
the African sign something unique, and even indelible, that separated it from
all other human signs. The best testimony to this specificity was the black body,
which was supposed not to contain any sort of consciousness and to have none of

---

[40]   See G.W.F. Hegel, *The Philosophy of History* (trans. John Sibree), Buffalo, NY: Pro-
metheus, 1991, pp.91-99.

[41]   To be sure, Enlightenment discourse on race was not univocal. Nevertheless, it can
be said that, for the most part, its thinkers joined in debate on common discursive terrain.
As Paul Gilroy shows, the extensive debate as to whether 'Negroes' should be accorded membership in the human family was central to the formation of the modern episteme. See P.
Gilroy, 'Race Ends Here', in *Ethnic and Racial Studies*, vol.21, no.5, 1998, pp.838-47. See
also S. Buck-Morss, 'Hegel and Haiti', *Critical Inquiry*, vol.26, no.4, 2000, pp.821-65; and,
more generally, Emmanuel Chukwudi Eze (ed.), *Race and Enlightenment: A Reader*, Cambridge, MA: Blackwell, 1997.

the haracteristics of reason or beauty.[42] Consequently, it could not be considered a body composed of flesh like one's own because it belonged solely to the order of material extension and of the object doomed to death and destruction. It is this centrality of the body in the calculus of political subjection that explains the importance assumed, in the course of the nineteenth century, by theories of the physical, moral and political regeneration of blacks and, later on, of Jews.

According to this darker side of the Enlightenment, Africans developed unique conceptions of society, of the world and of the good that they did not share with other peoples. It so happened that these conceptions in no way manifested the power of invention and universality peculiar to reason. Nor did Africans' representations, lives, works, languages or actions – including death – obey any rule or law whose meaning they could, on their own authority, conceive or justify. Because of this radical difference, it was deemed legitimate to exclude them, both de facto and de jure, from the sphere of full and complete human citizenship: they had nothing to contribute to the work of the universal.[43]

A significant shift occurred with the advent of the formal, state-directed colonisation of Africa in the late nineteenth century. While the principle of ontological difference persisted, the concern for self-determination became connected with the imperative to 'become civilised'. A slight slippage thus was introduced within the old economy of alterity. The thesis of nonsimilarity was not repudiated, but it was no longer based solely on the emptiness of the sign as such. The sign was given a name: *custom*. If Africans were different kinds of beings, that was because they had an identity of their own. This identity was not to be abolished. On the contrary, difference was to be inscribed within a distinct institutional order, a native order forced to operate within the fundamentally inegalitarian and hierarchised colonial framework. In other words, difference was recognised, but only insofar as it implied inequalities that were, moreover, considered natural to the extent that it justified discrimination and, in the most extreme cases, segregation.[44]

Later, the colonial state went on to use this concept of custom – that is, the thesis of nonsimilarity, in a revised edition – as a mode of government in itself. Specific forms of knowledge were produced for this purpose; such was the case of statistics and other methods of quantification, as deployed in censuses and various other instruments like maps, agrarian surveys and racial and tribal

---

[42]   On the centrality of the body in Western philosophy and its status as the ideal unit of the subject, the site of the recognition of his or her identity, see Maurice Merleau-Ponty, *Phénoménologie de la perception*, Paris: Gallimard, 1945, pp.81-234. On the 'weight' of the body of the colonised, see F. Fanon, *Black Skin, White Masks, op. cit.*, pp.110-13.

[43]   On this point and the preceding discussion, cf. Olivier Le Cour Grandmaison, *Les citoyennetés en Révolution, 1789-1794*, Paris: Presses universitaires de France, 1992; Pierre Pluchon, *Nègres et Juifs au XVIIIe siècle: Le racisme au siècle des lumières*, Paris: Tallandier, 1984; Charles de Secondat, Baron de Montesquieu, *De l'esprit des lois*, Paris: Garnier-Flammarion, 1979; Voltaire, *Oeuvres complètes*, Paris: Imprimerie de la Société littéraire et typographique, 1785; and Immanuel Kant, *Observations on the Feeling of the Beautiful and Sublime* (trans. John T. Goldthwait), Berkeley: University of California Press, 1965.

[44]   The most fully realised institutional form of this economy of alterity was the system of apartheid, in which the hierarchies were biological in nature. A less extreme version was 'indirect rule', a not very onerous form of domination which, in the British colonies, made it possible to exercise authority over natives with few soldiers by making use of the natives' passions and vices. Cf. Lucy Philip Mair, *Native Policies in Africa*, London: Routledge, 1936; Frederick John Dealtry, Baron Lugard, *The Dual Mandate in British Tropical Africa*, London: Blackwood and Sons, 1980.

studies.[45] Their objective was to canonise difference and to eliminate the plurality and ambivalence of custom.[46] There was a paradox to this process of reification. On the one hand, it looked like recognition. But on the other, it constituted a moral judgement, because ultimately, custom was only made specific the better to indicate the extent to which the world of the native, in its naturalness, failed to correspond with our own – that it was, in short, not part of our world, and thus could not serve as the basis for a praxis of living together in a civil society.

The third approach offered by the Enlightenment had to do with the politics of assimilation. Here, a comparison with the Jewish experience is worth making. Just as with the figure of the 'blacks', the invocation of the figure of the Jews as an archetypal Other to the West was central to the Enlightenment notion of *Bildung* (the formative process by which the individual moves toward autonomy). Jews were perceived as the negation of the Enlightenment's promise of an emancipation through the use of reason. In principle, the concept of assimilation was based on the possibility of an experience of the world common to all human beings – or, rather, on the possibility of such an experience as premised on an *essential similarity* among human beings. But this world common to all human beings, this similarity, was not supposed to have been given a priori to all.

The black, especially, had to be *converted* to it. This conversion was the condition for his being perceived and recognised as a fellow human being and for his otherwise indefinable humanity to enter representation. Once this condition was met, the project of assimilation could proceed, with the recognition of an African individuality distinct from generic tribal identities. African subjects could have rights and enjoy them, not by virtue of their subordination to the rule of custom, but by reason of their status as autonomous individuals capable of thinking for themselves and exercising reason, the peculiarly human faculty.[47]

To recognise this individuality – that is, this ability to imagine goals different from those imposed by custom – was to do away with difference. The latter had to be erased or annulled if Africans were to become like us, if they were henceforth to be considered as alter ego. Thus, the essence of the politics of assimilation consisted in desubstantialising and aestheticising difference, at least for

---

⁴⁵ See Arjun Appadurai, 'Number in the Colonial Imagination', in *Modernity at Large: Cultural Dimensions of Globalization*, Minneapolis: University of Minnesota Press, 1996. For a study of the appropriation of these techniques by postcolonial elites, see Thongchai Winichakul, *Siam Mapped: A History of the Geo-Body of a Nation*, Honolulu: University of Hawai'i Press, 1994.

⁴⁶ This was done notwithstanding the fact that 'custom' varied radically from place to place. As was the case elsewhere, 'custom' became the trope for social order in African societies thought to be outside of history, devoid of individuals. It could, from the colonial moment on, be reproduced through the force of law. On similar experiences in a different part of the colonised world, see Nicholas B. Dirks, 'The Policing of Tradition: Colonialism and Anthropology in Southern India', *Comparative Studies in Society and History*, vol.39, no.1, 1997, pp.182-212.

⁴⁷ In practice, the new subjects created by the politics of assimilation were cast as homogeneous reproductions of the metropolitan subject. Christopher Miller rightly states that the 'theory and practice of assimilation stressed continuity with the metropolitan country and the reproduction of "her" values, while ignoring or denying the truly profound break that colonial subjects were experiencing in relation to their own cultures'. C. Miller, *Nationalists and Nomads: Essays on Francophone African Literature and Culture*, Chicago: University of Chicago Press, 1998, p.122. As Fanon makes clear, race would remain the barrier between the *assimilé* and Frenchness; the amount of Frenchness available to the colonised would be restricted by biology. See F. Fanon, *Black Skin, White Masks, op. cit.*, chapter 5.

a category of natives (*les évolués*) whose conversion and 'cultivation' made them suitable for citizenship and the enjoyment of civil rights. Assimilation thus inaugurated a passage from custom into civil society, but by way of the civilising mill of Christianity and the colonial state.[48]

During the nineteenth-century conjuncture of abolition and the advent of formal colonialism, when African criticism first took up the question of self-craft in terms of self-government and self-imaging, it inherited these three moments, but did not subject them to a coherent critique. On the contrary, subscribing to the programme of emancipation and autonomy, it accepted, for the most part, the basic categories then used in Western discourse to account for universal history.[49] The notion of 'civilisation' was one of these categories. It authorised the distinction between the human and the nonhuman – or the not-yet-sufficiently human that might become human if given appropriate training.[50] The three vectors of this process of domestication were thought to be conversion to Christianity, the introduction of a market economy and the adoption of rational, enlightened forms of government.[51] In reality, it was less a matter of understanding what led to servitude and what servitude meant than of postulating, in the abstract, the necessity of liberating oneself from foreign rule.

To be sure, African thinkers took seriously the challenge of colonial disruption. Seeking to be their own masters, they at times interrogated the moralities of colonial modernity in vernacular accents. At other times, they sought to capture the material benefits of colonial rule for their own advantage. Leaders of resistance at one moment in history, many shuttled between principled options and dubious alliances. Following a 'zigzag line of a hundred tacks', most inhabited the ambiguous and largely uncharted zones of dependence.[52] In their polemical use of the West's ideas, they imported new concepts and discursive models 'in order to defend new frontiers of locality' and to tame what they perceived as modernity's threats. In the process, they invented a narrative of liberation built round the dual temporality of a glorious – albeit fallen – past (tradition) and a redeemed future (nationalism).[53]

But for the first modern African thinkers, liberation from servitude was equivalent above all to acquiring formal power. The basic moral and philosophical question – that is, how to renegotiate a social bond corrupted by commercial relationships (the sale of human cargoes), the violence of endless wars and the

---

48 Even when the postulate of equality among human beings was admitted, colonisation was sometimes justified in the name of 'civilisation'. See, among others, Alexis de Tocqueville, *De la colonie en Algérie*, Brussels: Editions Complexe, 1988. On the ambiguities of French assimilation policies, see Alice L. Conklin, *A Mission to Civilize: The Republican Idea of Empire in France and West Africa, 1895-1930*, Palo Alto, CA: Stanford University Press, 1997.

49 See for comparison the essays in Henry S. Wilson (ed.), *Origins of West African Nationalism*, London: Macmillan – St. Martin's Press, 1969.

50 See, for example, Marie Jean Antoine Nicolas de Caritat, Marquis de Condorcet, 'Réflexions sur l'esclavage des nègres', in *Oeuvres*, Paris: Firmin-Didot, 1849.

51 See Edward W. Blyden, *Christianity, Islam and the Negro Race*, Edinburgh: Edinburgh University Press, 1967.

52 See Shula Marks, *The Ambiguities of Dependence in South Africa: Class, Nationalism, and the State in Twentieth-Century Natal*, Johannesburg: Ravan, 1986.

53 See Jomo Kenyatta, *Facing Mount Kenya: The Tribal Life of the Gikuyu*, London: Secker and Warburg, 1938; and John Lonsdale, 'Jomo Kenyatta, God, and the Modern World', in Jan-Georg Deutsch, Peter Probst and Heike Schmidt (ed.), *African Modernities: Entangled Meaning in Current Debate*, Oxford: James Currey, 2002, pp.31-66.

catastrophic consequences of the way in which power was exercised – was considered secondary. African criticism did not assume as its primary task a political and moral philosophical reflection on the nature of the internal discord that led to the slave trade and colonial domination. Still less did it concern itself with the modalities of reinventing a being-together in a situation in which, with regard to the philosophy of reason that it claimed to espouse, all the outward appearances of a possible human life seemed to be lacking, and what passed for politics had more to do with the power to destroy and to profit than with any kind of philosophy of life or reason.

To be sure, in the post-World War II period, African nationalisms came to replace the concept of 'civilisation' with that of 'progress'. But they did so the better to endorse the characteristic teleologies of the times.[54] Such was the case of Marxism.

In Marx's narrative, both the subject and the telos of history are known. In this tradition, the ultimate frontier of history is a commodity-free society. To decommodify economic and social relationships entails the abolition of the power of the market and the collapse of the distinction between state and society. Such processes, and the ensuing formation of new relations of production, may involve a coercive logic or even terror. The latter may be mobilised as a means to facilitate the passage of history. As for Marx's subject, he or she exists wholly as a mere reflection and effect of material production. Revolutionary violence is conceived as a force of cohesion, the purpose of which is to produce a moral refashioning of the subject, a transformation of his or her consciousness as well as material condition.

In Marx's narrative, both the subject and the telos of history are known. In this tradition, the ultimate frontier of history is a commodity-free society. To decommodify economic and social relationships entails the abolition of the power of the market and the collapse of the distinction between state and society. Such processes, and the ensuing formation of new relations of production, may involve a coercive logic or even terror. The latter may be mobilised as a means to facilitate the passage of history. As for Marx's subject, he or she exists wholly as a mere reflection and effect of material production. Revolutionary violence is conceived as a force of cohesion, the purpose of which is to produce a moral refashioning of the subject, a transformation of his or her consciousness as well as material conditions.[55]

If, in the Western experience, Marx's theory equated modernisation with modernity and was conceived as a science, the same narrative in the African context soon became associated with politics as a sacramental practice. As such,

---

[54] In later modernity, Western philosophical criticism has begun moving away from some of the most radical Enlightenment propositions. See Jürgen Habermas, *The Philosophical Discourse of Modernity: Twelve Lectures* (trans. Frederick Lawrence), Cambridge, MA: MIT Press, 1987.

[55] Karl Marx, *Capital, A Critique of Political Economy*, vol.1 and 3 (trans. Ben Fowkes and David Fernbach, respectively), Harmondsworth, England: Penguin, 1976 and 1981. On violence, see Leon Trotsky, *Terrorism and Communism: A Reply to Karl Kautsky*, 2nd ed., Ann Arbor: University of Michigan Press, 1961. For critiques, see Maurice Merleau-Ponty, *Humanism and Terror: An Essay on the Communist Problem* (trans. John O'Neill), Boston: Beacon Press, 1969; and Hannah Arendt, *La crise de la culture; Huit exercices de pensée politique* (*Between Past and Future: Eight Exercises in Political Thought*) (trans. Patrick Lévy), Paris: Gallimard, 1972, pp.28-57.

politics required the total surrender of the individual to a utopian future and to the hope of a collective resurrection that, in turn, required the destruction of everything that stood opposed to it. Embedded within this conception of politics as pain and sacrifice was an entrenched belief in the redemptive function of violence. As an offering of one's life on the public altar of the revolution, violence could be expiatory or substitutive. It could also imply self-sacrifice – in which case the logic of sacrifice was linked with that of the gift. Expiatory, substitutive or self- sacrificial, violence was deployed – and death unleashed – in the name of a Marxist telos. Murder itself was commuted and concealed through ascription to a final moral truth, while the proof of virtue and morality lay in pain and suffering.[56]

The possibility of a properly philosophical reflection on the African condition having been set aside, only the question of raw power remained: Who could capture it? How was its enjoyment legitimated? In justifying the right to sovereignty and self-determination and in struggling to wrest power from the colonial regime, two central categories were mobilised: on one hand, the figure of the African as a victimised and wounded subject, and on the other, the assertion of the African's cultural uniqueness.[57] Both required a profound investment in the idea of race and a radicalisation of difference itself.

At the heart of the postcolonial paradigm of victimisation, we find a reading of the self and the world as a series of conspiracies. Such conspiracy theories have their origins in both Marxist and indigenous notions of agency.[58] In African history, it is thought, there is neither irony nor accident. We are told that African history is essentially governed by forces beyond Africans' control. The diversity and the disorder of the world, as well as the open character of historical possibilities, are reduced to a spasmodic, unchanging cycle, infinitely repeated in accord with a conspiracy always fomented by forces beyond Africa's reach. Existence itself is expressed, almost always, as a stuttering. Ultimately, the African is supposed to be merely a castrated subject, the passive instrument of the Other's enjoyment. Under such conditions, there can be no more radical utopian vision than the one suggesting that Africa disconnect itself from the world – the mad dream of a world without Others.

This hatred of the world at large (which also marks a profound desire for recognition) and this paranoid reading of history are presented as a 'democratic', 'radical' and 'progressive' discourse of emancipation and autonomy – the foundation for a so-called politics of Africanity.[59] Rhetoric to the contrary, however, the neurosis of victimisation fosters a mode of thought that is at once xenophobic, racist, negative and circular. In order to function, this logic needs superstitions.

[56]   See, for instance, the texts collected in Aquino de Bragança and Immanuel Wallerstein (ed.), *The African Liberation Reader*, London: Zed, 1982.

57   See Nnamdi Azikiwe, *Renascent Africa*, London: Cass, 1969; Kwame Nkrumah, *I Speak of Freedom: A Statement of African Ideology*, London: Heinemann, 1961; and Amilcar Cabral, *Revolution in Guinea: Selected Texts*, New York: Monthly Review Press, 1970.

58   This is especially the case with respect to notions of witchcraft. See Peter Geschiere, *The Modernity of Witchcraft: Politics and the Occult in Postcolonial Africa* (trans. P. Geschiere and Janet Roitman), Charlottesville: University Press of Virginia, 1997.

59   See Archie Mafeje, 'Africanity: A Combative Ontology', *CODESRIA Bulletin*, no.1, 2000, pp.66-71. For different views, see, in the same issue, Wambui Mwangi and André Zaiman, 'Race and Identity in Africa: A Concept Paper', pp.61-63; Fabien Eboussi Boulaga, 'Race, Identity, and Africanity', pp.63-66; and Mahmoud Ben Romdhane, 'A Word from a Non-Black African', pp.74-75.

It has to create fictions that later pass for real things. It has to fabricate masks that are retained by remodelling them to suit the needs of each period.

The course of African history is said to be determined by the combined action of a diabolical couple formed by an enemy – or tormentor – and a victim. In this closed universe, in which 'making history' consists of annihilating one's enemies, politics is conceived of as a *sacrificial process*, and history, in the end, is seen as participating in a great *economy of sorcery*.[60]

The Prose of Nativism

[...] The next item to consider is tradition and the privileged place it occupies in this nativist current of thought. The starting point here is the claim that Africans have an authentic culture that confers on them a peculiar self irreducible to that of any other group. The negation of this self and this authenticity would thus constitute a mutilation. On the basis of this uniqueness, Africa is supposed to reinvent its relationship to itself and to the world, to own itself and to escape from the obscure regions and the opaque world (the 'Dark Continent') to which history has consigned it. Because of the vicissitudes of history, Africans are supposed to have left tradition behind them. Whence the importance, in order to recover it, of moving backward, which is the necessary condition for overcoming the phase of humiliation and existential anguish caused by the historical debasement of the continent.

The emphasis on establishing an 'African interpretation' of things, on creating one's own schemata of self-mastery, of understanding oneself and the universe, of producing endogenous knowledge have all led to demands for an 'African science', an 'African democracy', an 'African language'.[61] This urge to make Africa unique is presented as a moral and political problem, the reconquest of the power to narrate one's own story – and therefore identity – seeming to be necessarily constitutive of any subjectivity. Ultimately, it is no longer a matter of claiming the status of alter ego for Africans in the world, but rather of asserting loudly and forcefully their alterity.

It is this alterity that must be preserved at all costs. In the most extreme versions of nativism, difference is thus praised, not as the symptom of a greater universality, but rather as the inspiration for determining principles and norms governing Africans' lives in full autonomy and, if necessary, in opposition to the world. Softer versions leave open the possibility of 'working toward the universal' and enriching Western rationality by adding to it the 'values of

---

60   This is something that the vernacular language fully recognises, but that the Marxist lexicon nevertheless prevents African intellectuals from naming as such. See, for example, Ernest Wamba-dia-Wamba, 'Mobutisme après Mobutu: Réflexions sur la situation actuelle en République Démocratique du Congo', *Bulletin du CODESRIA*, no.3-4, 1998, pp.27-34.
61   On these debates, see Julius Nyerere, *Ujamaa: Essays on Socialism*, London: Oxford University Press, 1968; Kwasi Wiredu, *Cultural Universals and Particulars: An African Perspective*, Bloomington: Indiana University Press, 1996, and 'How Not to Compare African Thought with Western Thought', in Ivan Karp and D.A. Masolo (ed.), *African Philosophy as Cultural Inquiry*, Bloomington: Indiana University Press, 2000, pp.187-214; Paulin Hountondji (ed.), *Endogenous Knowledge: Research Trails*, Dakar: CODESRIA, 1997; Kwame Gyekye, *African Cultural Values: An Introduction*, Philadelphia: Sankofa, 1996, and *Tradition and Modernity: Philosophical Reflections on the African Experience*, New York: Oxford University Press, 1997; and Ngugi wa Thiong'o, *Decolonising the Mind: The Politics of Language in African Literature*, London: James Currey, 1986.

black civilisation', the 'genius peculiar to the black race'. This is what Léopold Sédar Senghor calls *le rendez-vous du donner et du recevoir* (the meeting point of giving and receiving), one of the results of which is supposed to be the *métissage* of cultures.

Since the nineteenth century, those who maintain that Africans have their own cultural identity, that there is a specific African autochthony, have sought to find a general denomination and a place to which they could anchor their prose. The geographical place turns out to be a tropical Africa, bounded as a thoroughly fictional realm in opposition to the phantasmatic anatomy invented by Europeans and echoed by Hegel and others.[62] Somehow, the disjointed members of this imaginary polis must be glued back together. The dismembered body of the continent's history is therefore reconstituted in the light of myth. An attempt is made to locate Africanity in a set of specific cultural characteristics that ethnological research is expected to provide. Nationalist historiography sets out in quest of the missing remainder in ancient African empires and in pharaonic Egypt.[63]

In the prose of nativism (as well as in some versions of the Marxist and nationalist narratives), a quasi-equivalence is established between race and geography. Cultural identity is derived from the relationship between the two terms, geography becoming the privileged site at which the (black) race's institutions and power are supposed to be embodied.[64] Pan-Africanism in particular defines the *native* and the *citizen* by identifying them with black people. In this mythology, blacks do not become citizens because they are human beings endowed with political rights, but because of two particularistic factors: their colour and a privileged autochthony. Racial and territorial authenticity are conflated, and Africa becomes the land of black people. Since the racial interpretation is at the foundation of a restricted civic relatedness, everything that is not black is out of place, and thus cannot claim any sort of Africanity. The spatial body, the racial body and the civic body are thenceforth one, each testifying to an autochthonous communal origin by virtue of which everyone born of the soil or sharing the same colour or ancestors is a brother or a sister. [...]

Self, Polis and Cosmopolis

So where are we today? What ways of imagining identity are at work and what social practices do they produce? What has happened to the tropes of victimisation, race and tradition?

First, I must note that the thematics of anti-imperialism is exhausted. This does not mean, however, that the pathos of victimisation has been transcended. The anti-imperialist debate was in fact revived during the 1980s and 1990s in the form of a critique of structural adjustment programmes and neoliberal

---

[62]   See G.W.F. Hegel's geography of Africa in *Philosophy of History*, op. cit.

[63]   See Joseph Ki-Zerbo, *Histoire de l'Afrique noire d'hier à demain*, Paris: Hatier, 1972; Cheikh Anta Diop, *L'unité culturelle de l'Afrique noire: Domaines du patriarcat et du matriarcat dans l'antiquité Classique*, Paris: Présence africaine, 1959; Théophile Obenga, *L'Afrique dans l'antiquité: Egypte pharaonique, Afrique noire*, Paris: Présence africaine, 1973.

[64]   Ironically, we find the same impulse and the same desire to conflate race with geography in the racist writings of white settlers in South Africa. For details, see J.M. Coetzee, *White Writing: On the Culture of Letters in South Africa*, New Haven, CT: Yale University Press, 1988.

conceptions of the state's relation to the market.[65] In the interim, however, the ideology of Pan-Africanism was confronted by the reality of national states that, contrary to received wisdom, turned out to be less artificial than had been thought. A more significant development has been an emerging junction between the old anti-imperialist thematics – 'revolution', 'anticolonialism' – and the nativist theses. Fragments of these imaginaires are now combining to oppose globalisation, to relaunch the metaphysics of difference, to re-enchant tradition and to revive the utopian vision of an Africanity that is coterminous with blackness.

The thematic of race has also undergone major shifts. The extreme case of South Africa (and other settler colonies) has long led people, both in the West and Africa, to think that the polar opposition between blacks and whites summed up by itself the whole racial question in Africa. However, the repertoires on the basis of which the imaginaires of race and the symbolism of blood are constituted have always been characterised by their extreme variety. At a level beyond that of the simple black/white opposition, other racial cleavages have always set Africans against each other. And here may be enumerated not only the most visible – black Africans versus Africans of Arab, South Asian, Jewish or Chinese ancestry – but also a range of others that can attest to the panoply of colours and their annexation to projects of domination: black Africans versus Creoles, Lebanese-Syrians, Métis, Berbers, Tuaregs, Afro-Brazilians and Fulanis; Amharas versus Oromos; and Tutsis versus Hutus, to give some representative examples.

In fact – no matter what definition one gives of the notion – the racial unity of Africa has always been a myth. But this myth is currently imploding under the impact of internal (as well as external) factors connected with African societies' linkages to global cultural flows. For even if inequalities of power and access to property remain (not to mention racist stereotypes and violence), the category of *whiteness* no longer has the same meanings as it did under colonialism or apartheid. Although the 'white condition' has not reached a point of absolute fluidity that would detach it once and for all from any citation of power, privilege and oppression, it is clear that the experience of Africans of European origin has taken on ever more diverse aspects throughout the continent. The forms in which this experience is imagined – not only by whites themselves, but also by others – are no longer the same. This diversity now makes the identity of Africans of European origin a contingent and situated identity.[66] [...]

Conclusion

Attempts to define African identity in a neat and tidy way have so far failed. Further attempts are likely to meet the same fate as long as criticisms of African imaginations of the self and the world remain trapped within a conception of identity as geography – in other words, of time as space. From that conflation has resulted a massive indictment of the twin notions of universalism and

---

[65]   See, for example, T. Mkandawire and C.C. Soludo, *Our Continent, Our Future, op. cit.*

[66]   See, for example, Ian Smith, *The Great Betrayal: The Memoirs of Ian Douglas Smith*, London: Blake, 1997; Eugene De Kock and Jeremy Gordin, *A Long Night's Damage: Working for the Apartheid State*, Saxonwold, South Africa: Contra, 1998; and Antjie Krog, *Country of My Skull*, Johannesburg: Random House, 1998. More generally, see Sarah Nuttall, 'Subjectivities of Whiteness', *African Studies Review*, vol.44, no.2, 2001, pp.115-40.

cosmopolitanism, and in their place a celebration of autochthony – that is, a construction of the self understood in terms of both victimhood and mutilation. One of the major implications of such an understanding of time and subjectivity is that African thought has come to conceive politics either along the lines of a recovery of an essential but lost nature – the liberation of an essence – or as a sacrificial process.

To be sure, there is no African identity that could be designated by a single term or that could be named by a single word or subsumed under a single category. African identity does not exist as a substance. It is constituted, in varying forms, through a series of practices, notably *practices of the self.*[67] Neither the forms of this identity nor its idioms are always self-identical. Rather, these forms and idioms are mobile, reversible and unstable. Given this element of play, they cannot be reduced to a purely biological order based on blood, race or geography. Nor can they be reduced to custom, to the extent that the latter's meaning is itself constantly shifting.[68] But by now, the all-too-familiar and clichéd rhetoric of nonsubstantiality, instability and indetermination is just one more inadequate way to come to grips with African imaginations of the self and the world.[69] It is no longer enough to assert that only an African self-endowed with a capacity for narrative synthesis – that is, a capacity to generate as many stories as possible in as many voices as possible – can sustain the discrepancy and interlacing multiplicity of norms and rules characteristic of our epoch.

Perhaps one step out of this quandary would be to reconceptualise the notion of time in its relation to memory and subjectivity.[70] Because the time we live in is fundamentally fractured, the very project of an essentialist or sacrificial recovery of the self is, by definition, doomed. Only the disparate, and often intersecting, practices through which Africans *stylise* their conduct and life can account for the thickness of which the African present is made.

Mbembe's idea(l) of self-stylisation as an aesthetic-political practice is a clear rejoinder to essentialist takes on blackness or Africanness – whether they posit a triumphant postcolonial subject or one perpetually ensnared in trauma and victimhood. Against monolithic conceptions of (national or ethnic) subjecthood, Mbembe proposes open-ended processes of subjectivation and hybridisation. Such self-becoming is always also self-overcoming; a practice of becoming other, becoming manifold .

---

[67] See T.K. Kiaya, 'Crushing the Pistachio: Eroticism in Senegal and the Art of Ousamane Ndiaye Dago', *Public Culture*, vol.12, no.3, 2000, pp.707-20, and 'Les plaisirs de la ville: Masculinité, féminité et sexualité à Dakar, 1997-2000', *African Studies Review*, vol.44, no.2, 2001, pp.71-85. See also Dominique Malaquais, *Anatomie d'une arnaque: Feymen et feymania au Cameroun*, Les études du CERI, no.77, Paris: Centre d'Etude et de Recherches Internationales, 2001.

[68] See for comparison Carolyn Hamilton, *Terrific Majesty*, Cambridge, MA: Harvard University Press, 1998.

[69] See AbdouMaliq Simone, 'The Worldling of African Cities', *African Studies Review*, vol.44, no.2, 2001, pp.15-41; Mamadou Diouf, 'The Senegalese Murid Trade Diaspora and the Making of a Vernacular Cosmopolitanism', *Public Culture*, vol.12, no.3, 2000, pp.679-702; and Janet MacGaffey and Rémy Bazenguissa-Ganga, *Congo-Paris: Transnational Traders on the Margins of the Law*, Oxford: James Currey, 2000.

[70] See Achille Mbembe, *On the Postcolony*, Berkeley: University of California Press, 2001; and James Ferguson, *Expectation of Modernity: Myths and Meanings of Urban Life on the Zambian Copperbelt*, Berkeley: University of California Press, 1999.

In the process, the subject as lifelong exercise in self-stylisation will also often be the object of forces beyond its control. What of the impact not only of 'global cultural flows', but of global economic flows and of the resulting disparities and conflicts? After all, the cultural flows mentioned by Mbembe, which enable all kinds of hybridisation and reinvention, result from the process known as globalisation. And is the imperative behind 'self-stylisation' and self-performance not also an economic imperative?

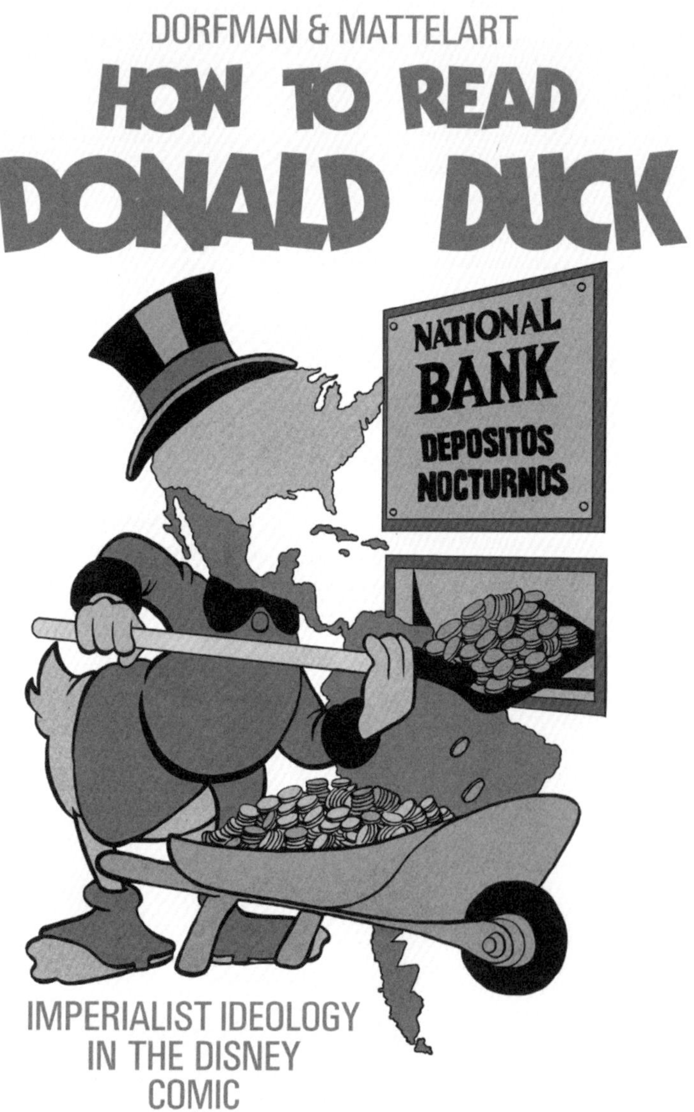

Front cover of Ariel Dorfman and Armand Mattelart's *How to Read Donald Duck: Imperialist Ideology in the Disney Comic*, first translated into English in 1975
Courtesy OR Books

Zones and Networks of Alter-Autonomy

The global order in its current (but rapidly disintegrating) form came into being between 1989 and 1991, when the collapse of the Warsaw Pact and the Soviet Union paved the way for a worldwide triumph of 'liberal democracy' and capitalism. It was in this context that the discourse on 'globalisation' burgeoned, fuelled by this expansion on the Western capitalist model, which coincided with cheaper (air) travel and the emergence of the internet. In the late 1990s, the antiglobalist or - as some argued it should be called - *alter*globalist movement, also known as the Global Justice Movement, emerged. With one of its slogans claiming 'another world is possible', alterglobalism aimed precisely at opening up other avenues of global collaboration. It marked the emergence of what one could call a global *autonomia* movement.

Often, texts on the subject tend to become inspirational homilies on Porto Alegre, on protests in Argentina or Occupy Wall Street, on biopower and transversal and instituent action, on the autonomist organisation of the *multitude*, against the sovereignty of Empire. In Michael Hardt and Antonio Negri's bestseller *Empire*, published in 2000 at the height of the movement, they took to theorising a multifaceted global multitude as the post-industrial proletariat:

> The proletariat is not what it used to be, but that does not mean that it has vanished. It means, rather, that we are faced once again with the analytical task of understanding the new composition of the proletariat as a class. [...]
>
> This is a *new proletariat* and not a *new industrial working class*. The distinction is fundamental. As we explained earlier, 'proletariat' is the general concept that defines all those whose labour is exploited by capital, the entire cooperating multitude.[32]

Though capitalist globalisation was triumphant in the 1990s, one should take the official rhetoric over the 'collapse of communism' with a pinch of salt. As early as the 1920s and 1930s, radical council communists argued that the Soviet Union was in fact a totalitarian form of state capitalism; later, renegade Trotskyists like C.L.R. James came to the same conclusion. Around the height of the Cold War, in 1960, James argued that what looked like an ideological contest between opposing economic and social systems - capitalism and communism - was actually a thoroughly capitalist battle for control of global market:

> There are many people who believe that Russia, because private property has been abolished, is not subjected to the fundamental movement of capitalism. They are quite wrong. Capitalism - I cannot say it too often - functions on the world market. Today the competition is not for the selling of goods. The competition is for total control of the world market. What does global mean? Global war! What are they fighting for? I hope there is no one here who believes they are fighting for democracy versus totalitarianism or vice versa. It is for total control of the world market, and it is not a question so much nowadays of the sale of goods. It is a question of the capacity to mobilise millions of men with great speed, to transport them with great rapidity and facility from one place to another; to be able to

produce armaments of all kinds and what is required by an army at the greatest possible speed. It is to produce ballistics. It is to produce satellites. It is to produce one of these things that go in forty minutes from one end of the world to the other – missiles. That is what the production of the modern country is geared to do, to keep people going, but essentially to produce these. You produce these during the 'cold' part of the war, and when you reach a certain stage and you begin to use them, that is the 'hot' part of the war.[33]

If competition on a global market was still cloaked in the garb of ideological conflict during the Cold War, after the collapse of the Warsaw Pact the rule of the 'free' market itself became the unchallenged ideology. This market is far from the natural and neutral structure for human commerce. It is in fact a construct that is shaped and maintained by national policies and supranational organisations such as the International Monetary Fund – who have tools to punish states that do not toe the line. While celebrating the market's capacity for innovation and efficiency, which ultimately would raise the standard of living and provide people with the goods and services they needed, neoliberal discourse turned a blind eye to the destruction wrought by processes of 'liberalisation' and to the different forms of colonisation involved – from invading countries to restructuring psyches and consumer behaviours.

Decolonisation after World War II was at times effected under US pressure; as the American government was well aware that the persistence of explicit, old-school colonies provided the Soviet Union with perfect ideological ammunition, more covert forms of neocolonial governance were quickly established. While the US pressed the Netherlands to accept the independence of Indonesia and, later, Indonesia's occupation of the remaining Dutch colony of Papua, in 1965–66 the CIA and the US State Department supported and helped organise anti-communist massacres that resulted in the deaths of at least 500,000 Indonesians, followed by the inauguration of a 'New Order' under President Suharto.[34] In Vietnam, US military support eventually escalated into a long war, with the US taking over France's role as colonial 'protector'. The Vietnam War turned into a fiasco for the US largely because politicised youth did not want to go and fight; subsequent US wars have relied on professional soldiers and mercenaries, with greatly diminished domestic opposition. It is crucial to remember that our 'globalised' world, including the art world, is traversed by neocolonial asymmetries and inequalities.

The philosopher Jean-Luc Nancy has argued that we need to oppose another concept to 'actually existing globalisation' in order to imagine and shape a true alter-globalism. In *The Creation of the World or Globalization* (2007), Nancy elaborates on the French term *mondialisation* as standing for a process that follows a different logic than that of market-driven, homogenising globalisation.

JEAN-LUC NANCY, *THE CREATION OF THE WORLD OR GLOBALIZATION*

Reprinted from *The Creation of the World or Globalization*, Albany: SUNY Press, 2007, pp.27-28. First published in 2002. Translated from the French by François Raffoul and David Pettigrew.

It is not without paradox that in many languages the French term *mondialisation* is quite difficult to translate, and that perhaps this difficulty makes it almost 'untranslatable' in the sense that the term has acquired in the recent *Vocabulaire européen des philosophies*. This difficulty lies in the fact that the English term *globalisation* has already established itself in the areas of the world that use English for contemporary information exchange (which is not necessarily symbolic exchange). There are therefore at least two terms (this being said without being able to take into account a considerable number of languages, which would introduce a supplementary perspective - which of course would be impossible) - two terms to designate the phenomenon that understands itself or seeks to be understood as a unification or as a common assumption of the totality of the parts of the world in a general network (if not a system) of communication, commercial exchange, juridical or political reference points (if not values), and finally of practices, forms and procedures of all kinds linked to many aspects of ordinary existence.

The French language has used the word *mondialisation* since the middle of the twentieth century - which seems to me slightly before the term *globalisation* appeared in English. The reasons for this neologism should be studied for their own sake. Whatever those reasons may be, the connotation of the term *mondialisation* gives it a more concrete tonality than that of *globalisation,* which designates, in French, a more abstract process leading to a more compact result: the 'global' evokes the notion of a totality as a whole, in an indistinct integrality. Thus, there has been in the English *globalisation* the idea of an integrated totality, appearing for example with the 'global village' of McLuhan, while *mondialisation* would rather evoke an expanding *process* throughout the expanse of the *world* of human beings, cultures and nations.

The usage of either term, or the search for an English translation that would keep the semantics of 'world' are not without a real theoretical interest: the word *mondialisation,* by keeping the horizon of a 'world' as a space of possible meaning for the whole of human relations (or as a space of possible significance) gives a different indication than that of an enclosure in the undifferentiated sphere of a unitotality. In reality, each of the terms carries with it an interpretation of the process, or a wager on its meaning and future. This also means that it is understandable that *mondialisation* preserves something untranslatable while *globalisation* has already translated everything in a global idiom.

One of contemporary art's premier 'global' events is the Venice Biennale, founded in 1895, during the heyday of European imperialism. Even now, the dominant pavilions are those of the former European empires - with the US close by. The artist Jonas Staal has argued that the map of the Venice Biennale is a 'more accurate' representation of the world than conventional world maps, showing the hierarchies much more clearly. For his smartphone app, *Ideological Guide to the Venice Biennale* (2013), Staal and his team provided critical readings of the various Biennale countries, their geopolitical and economic entanglements, and the actual presentations. For the French Pavilion,[35] which boasted a video installation by Anri Sala, Stephen Wright took up the theme of 'autonomy' within colonial empires, reminding us that to this day France has colonial outposts.

STEPHEN WRIGHT, 'THE AUTONOMY ARCHIPELAGO'

Reprinted from *Ideological Guide to the Venice Biennale*, available at http://venicebiennale2013. ideologicalguide.com/pavilion/france/ (last accessed on 19 September 2020).

For a middle power in spectacular decline, France comes off reasonably well amongst the united States of the Biennale: an Albanian-born, Berlin-based, artworld-respected artist, curated by an upper-level staffer of a big public institution, strikes near pitch-perfect balance. The parochial may shout a bit; art-marketeers will complain that Republican virtue continues to trump harder-edged market considerations, thus contributing to Paris's supposed eclipse from the dominant attention economy; but fielding this pair of middle weights seems both a smart and an elegant choice, inasmuch as it mirrors the paradoxes of autonomy – the watchword of France's geopolitical situation and of the artistic ideology it arguably incarnates better than any other nation.

Geopolitically, France has colonies in every time zone of the planet; the legitimacy for maintaining these 'overseas territories' within the colonial fold relies on the claim that they enjoy some degree of administrative 'autonomy' – a logic that requires a particularly elastic understanding of 'autonomy'. (Several years ago, a French president was chatting amiably with a foreign counterpart over a glass of champagne. 'I'm not sure what "autonomy" means in French', said the guest. 'I see you speak our language perfectly', replied the Frenchman.) The strategic redistribution of autonomy has become second nature to the elites of the Fifth Republic, because in their attention economy, the redistribution is all, the autonomy itself insignificant; the less traction autonomy is liable to gain in a given sector, the more it is to be encouraged. And the paradigmatic sector is that of art.

If Republican universalism and benevolence (along with the Eurozone that comes with it at no extra charge) can extend to clusters of islands in the South Pacific, the Caribbean, the shores of Newfoundland and that gigantic chunk of South America called Guyana, surely it can extend to any autonomous artist whatsoever, wherever he or she may be located, provided that location be squarely within the broadest framework of spectatorship. It is thus that autonomy opens not onto a horizon of emancipation but onto one of self-policing. For 'autonomous' art owes its fleeting moment of limelight in the attention economy to repressing a crippling double thought: that it must be art, just art, and that art is not enough.

Here we have the post- or neocolonial version of artistic autonomy as a heteronomously conditioned and 'strategically' allocated sphere of free play. Once again, artists – but now also curators – seem to play the role of both exceptional and exemplary subjects, hopping from one project to the next, from one residency to the next biennial, across a globalised world that is not only still marked by Cold War structures such as NATO, but also by survivals of the colonial era. Is there any *outside* to these dominant structures? The (unravelling) neoliberal global world order has been dominant and pervasive for decades, and has helped to shape even the exceptions to it. Such exceptions emerge in situations of crisis, in zones where the contradictions and conflicts produced by neoliberalism take on catastrophic proportions, and sometimes engender revolutionary projects – which in turn are often shaped by the *heteronomy* of globalisation.

In the 1960s and 1970s, certain postcolonial and anti-capitalist states held out the promise of organised resistance to capitalism to members of the Western intelligentsia. 'Third-Worldist' intellectuals and activists supported Cuba and former African colonies in their attempts at realising socialist societies. Cuba's Tricontinental initiative (which had its institutional home in the Organization of Solidarity of the Peoples of Asia, Africa and Latin America) garnered a lot of sympathy and support. No doubt the Western left's enthusiasm in part sprang from genuine belief in people's right to self-determination and resistance to late- or neocolonial exploitation. However, Third-World struggles were also instrumentalised to prove that while the Western working class had lost its revolutionary steam, oppressed peoples in Asia, Africa, the Middle East and Latin America were willing and able to continue the work of World Revolution. In his 1970 'Constituents of a Theory of the Media', Hans Magnus Enzensberger pinned his hopes on non-Western forms of media insurgency:

> The direct mobilising potentialities of the media become still more clear when they are consciously used for subversive ends. Their presence is a factor that immensely increases the demonstrative nature of any political act. The student movements in the USA, in Japan and in Western Europe soon recognised this and, to begin with, achieved considerable momentary successes with the aid of the media. These effects have worn off. Naïve trust in the magical power of reproduction cannot replace organisational work; only active and coherent groups can force the media to comply with the logic of their actions. That can be demonstrated from the example of the Tupamaros in Uruguay, whose revolutionary practice has implicit in it publicity for their actions. Thus the actors become authors. The abduction of the American Ambassador in Rio de Janeiro was planned with a view to its impact on the media. It was a television production. The Arab guerrillas proceed in the same way. The first to experiment with these techniques internationally were the Cubans. Fidel [Castro] appreciated the revolutionary potential of the media correctly from the first (Moncada 1953). Today illegal political action demands at one and the same time maximum security and maximum publicity.[36]

With its media wrested from capitalist ownership, Fidel Castro's Cuba seemed to embody the promise of a different (socialist) culture from Enzensberger's and many other 1960s leftists'. Yet over the years it became abundantly clear that Cuban media and cultural institutions were controlled not by 'the people' but by a party elite, much like in the Soviet Union. Tania Bruguera's piece *Tatlin's Whisper #6* (2009) was tailormade for the situation in Havana, at the opening of the Tenth Havana Biennial: here, in a theatrical setting evoking a famous image from the Cuban Revolution, people were given one minute of free speech. Bruguera created a situation in which Cubans were 'activated' and, from behind a microphone, allowed to 'talk back' to the regime. Even in the form of live performance, without any mass media transmission, this presented difficulties in the Cuban context. Yet the critical and media success of this work in the Western art world is not without problematic overtones. Mechanisms of control in networked capitalism tend to be rather more subtle and 'inclusive' than the crude mechanisms of exclusion and censorship in a country such as Cuba. What would an equivalent be in Western societies where complacent complicity with surveillance goes hand in hand with a patronising stance towards 'unfree' societies?[37] We are eager to cry 'censorship', and rightly so. But are 'free' societies really that free from censorship, and from self-censorship? What cannot, must not, be thought and shown?

If the Cuban revolution settled into a sub-Soviet dictatorship partly due to external pressure from the United States, a US-backed military coup brought the democratically elected Salvador Allende government in Chile to a bloody end in 1973. It was the Chilean model that the Marxist communication theorist Armand Mattelart actively supported, often in collaborations with Conceptual art impresario Seth Siegelaub, who ran the International Mass Media Research Center and the affiliated publishing house International General. Siegelaub published *How to Read Donald Duck: Imperialist Ideology in the Disney Comic*, the English-language edition of Mattelart and Ariel Dorfman's *Para leer al Pato Donald* (1971), a famously crude exercise in ideological critique, to be read in the context of the Chilean uprising against US economic and cultural colonialism.[38]

After the collapse of the Soviet empire, global capitalism continued to inspire local resistance and revolutionary movements in Latin America, such as the indigenous Zapatista Army of National Liberation (EZLN) in the south-east of Mexico, which began to manifest itself publicly on the very day in 1994 that the North Atlantic Free Trade Agreement (NAFTA) took effect; the Zapatistas rightly suspected that it would worsen the situation in Chiapas. In a society that still bears the marks of the Spanish version of settler colonialism, the Zapatistas draw on the will to resistance of the local indigenous (Maya) population.

For years the movement's main spokesperson was Subcomandante Marcos, who was highly articulate as well as photogenic – precisely because his face was always obscured by a balaclava. In the Zapatistas' struggle for autonomy in Chiapas, Marcos used literary and performative tactics of self-fashioning that negated his civil status as a 'natural person' in favour of artifice. Not of indigenous origin, unlike most EZNL members, Marcos's prominent role may not have been universally appreciated in the movement; in 2014, he changed his persona and name, becoming Subcomandante Galeano. In the following 1996 statement, the 'Sub' turned the tables on photographers working for the global news media. ·

SUBCOMANDANTE MARCOS, 'A ZAPATISTA POSITION PAPER ON PHOTOGRAPHY'

Available at http://www.nearbycafe.com/photo-criticism/members/archivetexts/phototheory/marcos/marcoszap.html (last accessed on 19 September 2020). First published in 1996. Translated from the Spanish by Monique J. Lemaitre.

Ladies and gentlemen:

Through this medium I point out that on the date of the first anniversary of the treason brought about against the EZLN and the will for a new peace of the Mexican people and world public opinion by the government of Ernesto Zedillo Ponce de León, there appeared in the Lacandon Jungle (better known as rebel territories against the bad government) two people: two named Francisco Mata and Eniac Martinez, males, to be more specific, who claim to be Mexican, and with the aggravating circumstances of being photographers (better known as cynical thieves), and they threatened the honourable public with their weapons (better known as photographic cameras), for which reason they were detained and handed over to the proper authorities.

They did not remain in anybody's custody aside from that of their own conscience (in a somewhat sorry state from what we can see), and they declared the following: that they come with the intention of taking pictures of Zapatista life in order to submit them to an Internet World event, and that they have no other aim than the telephoto photographers usually carry, that their intention is testimonial and artistic, that they did not receive any pay from the Zapatistas (as if we had any means to do so!) and that they did not pay the Zapatistas anything (which means that, aside from being photographers, they are stingy); that once their work in these dignified lands is over they plan to rush, rapid and swift, to their respective computers and to delight (that's what they think) the clients of Internet with their marvels (ha!).

Once the previous declaration had been taken down, the Sub (who surprisingly assumed the role of Local Private Ministry) declared guilty of the crime of image theft, with the aggravating circumstance of cynicism, since, says the Sub, the photographer is a thief who choses what he steals (which, at this stage of the crisis, is a luxury) and does not 'democratise' the image, that is to say, the photographer selects the pictures, a privilege which ought to be granted to the person being photographed. Once that said, the Sub condemned them to what is explained in detail below, but before that the Sub wants to talk about the images (better known as photographs) that these photographers (better known as the guilty parties) came to take and then …

As a Benjamin- or Enzensberger-style exercise in practical media critique in the budding internet era, the photographed subject becomes himself a producer:

Behind the ski mask, the Sub takes the camera and his revenge. During two years he has been on the other side of the lens, he has been the object and the target, the medium and the message. But today the Sub has decided to take his revenge and he has taken the lens from the other side, from the side of the history press photographers' take and, through them, the world who sees those pictures.

Now the Sub invites us to follow his pictures, to look from this side of the ski mask at what photographs don't say, at the trip they avoid, at the distance they mark.

The Sub's photographs try to build a bridge. A bridge that does not go from the 'reader' of the photographs or from the photographer to the place in which the Zapatistas sometimes live, sometimes die, and always struggle. The Sub proposes you another bridge, another trip, another 'reading' of the image. That is why the Sub has now picked up the camera from the angle which was forbidden to him, from the photographer's angle, from the spectator's angle.

The Sub takes a picture of the photographer taking pictures. The photographer discovers himself/herself being photographed and we can guess he is uncomfortable. Unsuccessfully he/she tries to recompose his posture and to look like a photographer taking photos. But no, he is and continues to be a spectator. The momentaneous fact of being photographed leads him to becoming an actor. And, as always, actors must assume a role, which is only an elegant way of avoiding to say that they must choose sides, choose a faction, take an option. In the mountains of the Mexican south-east there aren't many, and if we clear a bit the avalanche of fantastic declarations made by public officials of various kinds, we will see that there are only two options: war or peace. [...]

The photographed photographers haven't stopped feeling uncomfortable during the brief session of takes the Sub submitted them to. The great inquisitor that the camera's lens is was turned against its operators. Every time the diaphragm winks, the camera repeats the question that now travels through cyberspace and invades, as a modern virus, the memories of machines, men and women. The question that history always sets forth. The question which forces us to define ourselves and whose answer makes us human: On which side are you? The Sub leaves the camera in peace and takes back his rifle. He lights his pipe and bids farewell. The smoke which he leaves behind is already travelling through cyberspace proposing, asking, questioning…

The Zapatistas struggle against the Mexican state, having organised part of Chiapas into regions called Caracoles, which each contain several autonomous municipalities with self-organised infrastructures such as schools and clinics. Far from simply wanting to secede from Mexico in order to form a smaller state that has essentially the same juridical and organisational structure, the Zapatistas act on the belief that another world is possible. One might also say: another autonomy is possible, one neither predicated neither on the bourgeois-capitalist subject as the supposed bearer of an autonomous rationality, nor on a territorial sovereignty that is ultimately bestowed on the region in question by Empire. The project is about self-organisation from below, in local communities that may not always opt for the same organisational principles. Cookie-cutter universalism is rejected.

The Zapatista project has echoes in radical practices across the globe. The Russian collective Chto Delat, for instance, invokes Chiapas in the context of its endeavour to develop new, self-organised cultural spaces, beginning with Rosa's House of Culture in St Petersburg:

The political purpose of the new houses of culture is to raise, first and foremost, the issue of re-examining and reformulating the new class structure of society, in which we see the potential for the formation of singularities, i.e., new people, ready at a given historical moment to defend the values of an emancipatory politics and rethink the role of culture and aesthetics in processes of emancipation. This is happening in the Zapatista Caracoles in Chiapas, and it is happening in social centres around the world experimenting with principles of autonomy and protocols of openness. Autonomy is always naïve, as any micro-project is naïve in the big world of corporate capital, but only autonomy can launch a challenge and present new forms of production communities that disobey the logic of profit.[39]

The 'naïve' autonomy of which Chto Delat speaks may seem hopelessly optimistic. Is this a kind of 'prefigurative practice' that tries to create a future society here and now, even while current conditions must necessarily shape, limit and compromise the project? As Peter Osborne put it on the occasion of curator Chris Gilbert's resignation from the Berkeley Art Museum over his defence of Hugo Chavez's Venezuela, that 'there is no pure outside from the standpoint of which judgement on contradictory social processes can be pronounced. There are only passing opportunities in the deepening maze of contradictions.'[40] Those who are and choose to remain active in the international art world are of course profoundly entangled in deepening contradictions: they remain part of what they perceive to be the problem. Rather than attempt to ignore the problem, they can patiently engage with it time and again.

To boycott a museum – for instance, the Guggenheim apropos of its projected Abu Dhabi branch – is both to stress that this institution is not too important to antagonise and that it is too important to be let off the hook. One can make critical works of art for the gallery system, but why not (also) try to build alternative structures, such as Houses of Culture, that use the contradictions as working materials, that use crisis as an artistic medium. Why not contribute to the creation of zones of alterity that act as globalisation's immanent exceptions, as its dialectical counterpoints? These counterpoints are clearly not the end of anything, not the achievement of history in the here and now, but in however compromised – that is to say, actualised – a form, they are incursions of alternative futures into the present. In fact, if one considers that neoliberal globalisation is marked by a death drive, laying waste to the planet, such initiatives represent futurity as such.

In their statement, Chto Delat effortlessly shift from their Russian houses of culture to the organising Caracoles ('snails') of Chiapas; the difference in scale is striking. Chiapas and the Kurdish region of Rojava remain among the most prominent examples of large zones where embattled 'stateless' populations have realised forms of autonomous self-government; hence, these regions have galvanised attention and solidarity among those who may operate on a smaller scale, in contexts where no such full-on contestation of state power and of the forces of 'globalisation' seems possible.

In addition to mapping the world order as represented by the pavilions in Venice, Jonas Staal has worked with representatives of organisations that exist on the margins of the global structures of governance. His New World Summit (2012-16) and New World Academy (2013) mostly focussed on groups and movements considered terrorist or otherwise threatening to Empire, to global capitalism. As Dilar Dirik, an activist in the Kurdish Women's Movement and a PhD student at the University of Cambridge, explained in an interview with Staal in 2014, in contrast to some more specific organisations, such as Maoist political parties, the movement she takes part in traverses organisations such as the Kurdistan Workers' Party (PKK). Here, autonomy as 'living without approval' must necessarily become the rejection of frameworks that exist precisely in order to confer legitimacy and police the possible.

'LIVING WITHOUT APPROVAL: DILAR DIRIK
INTERVIEWED BY JONAS STAAL'

Reprinted from *New World Academy Reader #
5: Stateless Democracy*, Utrecht: BAK, basis voor
actuele kunst in collaboration with New World
Summit, 2015, pp.27-55. This edited version of an
interview that took place on 22 October 2014 at De
Balie in Amsterdam was revisited by Dilar Dirik
and Jonas Staal via email in February 2015.

Jonas Staal: You are an academic researcher but also an activist of the Kurdish Women's Movement. How exactly would you describe the nature of this movement, both geographically and organisationally?

Dilar Dirik: One could start off by deconstructing the words 'Kurdish', 'women' and 'movement'. Many people think that a national cause – a national liberation movement or nationalism – is incompatible with women's liberation. I agree, because nationalism has many patriarchal, feudal, primitive premises that in one way or another boil down to passing on the genes of the male bloodline and reproducing domination, to pass on from one generation to another what is perceived as a 'nation'. Add to that the extremely gendered assumptions that accompany nationalism, which affect family life, labour relations, the economy, knowledge, culture and education, and it becomes evident that it is a very masculinised concept. The Kurdish Women's Movement is named as such because of the multiple layers of oppression and structural violence that Kurdish women have experienced precisely because they *are* Kurdish and because they *are* women.

The Kurdish people have been separated historically over four different states: Turkey, Iraq, Syria and Iran. […]

Most, if not all, of the Kurdish parties in the four regions started with the aim of an independent Kurdish state. The idea was that we suffer this oppression precisely because we are stateless, and so if we – the 'largest people without a state' – have a state of our own, our people would no longer encounter such large-scale systemic violence. This kind of nationalism often emerges in colonial contexts. However, state nationalism is very different from anti-colonial movements that claim a national identity in order to assert their existence in the face of genocide. I am critical towards those who place Turkish, Iranian or Arab nationalisms on the same level as Kurdish nationalism: you cannot claim this without taking into consideration the radical unequal power relations that are at the foundations of this conflict. Yet this does not mean that nationalism is the solution or that a Kurdish state would pave the road toward genuine self-determination.

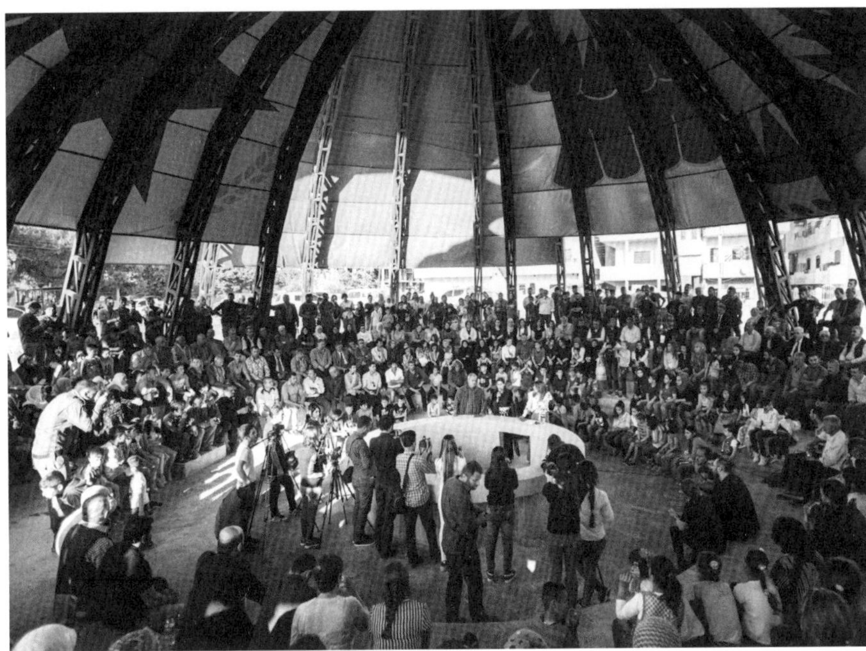

Event view, *New World Summit, Rojava*, organised by Jonas Staal, 2015–18
Courtesy the artist

See p.285 of this reader for more images

JS: This idea also contributed to the creation of the Marxist-Leninist Kurdistan Workers' Party (PKK), founded by Abdullah Öcalan in 1978, which led to the necessity of waging armed struggle against the Turkish government's repression of the Kurds. At a certain stage, the PKK's leadership changed its ideas concerning the goal of achieving an independent state.

DD: Indeed, the PKK started out with the aim of an independent nation-state as a reaction to state violence and systemic denial, assimilation and oppression. It emerged at a very conflict-ridden time in Turkey. In 1980, four years before the PKK began its armed struggle, a military coup d'état in Turkey had tried to wipe out the left and other oppositional groups. The PKK experienced many ups and downs, related to the guerrilla resistance against the Turkish army, the fall of the Soviet Union, the collapse of many leftist liberation movements and Öcalan's capture in Kenya on 15 February 1999, organised by the Turkish National Intelligence Organisation in collaboration with the United States' Central Intelligence Agency. It was in this context during the course of the late nineties that the PKK began to theoretically deconstruct the state, fuelled in part by the Kurdish Women's Movement, having come to the conclusion the state is inherently incompatible with democracy.

Statelessness exposes you to oppression, to denial, to genocide. In a nation-state-oriented system, recognition and the monopoly of power are reserved for the state and this offers some form of protection. But the point is that the suffering of the stateless results from the system being based on the nation-state paradigm. When you gain the monopoly on power, your problems are not instantly solved. Having a state does not mean that your society is liberated, that you will have a just society, or that it will be an ethical society.

The question is more systemic: Should we accept the premises of the statist system that causes these sufferings in the first place? Could we have a nation-state, a concept inherently based on capitalism and patriarchy, and still think of ourselves as liberated? In the Middle East, absolutely no state is truly independent. China, Russia, the US and European governments: they are the ones hierarchically controlling the international order.

This shift away from desiring a state was an acknowledgement that the state cannot actually represent one's interests, that the monopoly on power will always be in the hands of a few people who can do whatever they want with you, specifically because the state is implicated in several international agreements, including the North Atlantic Treaty Organization. That is why the PKK began to understand the importance of rejecting top-down approaches to power and governance. It concluded that there needed to be political structures that could serve the empowerment of the people, structures that would politicise them to such a degree that they internalise democracy. The work of the Kurdish Women's Movement was pivotal in that process. Patriarchy is much older than the nation-state, but nation-states have adopted its mechanisms. That is why the disassociation of democracy from the state is also a disassociation from patriarchy. [...]

In the nineties, with encouragement from Öcalan, women who experienced discrimination within their own ranks began to mobilise. Öcalan has always been supportive of women's liberation and has contributed significantly to the theoretical justifications around the autonomous organisation of women within the PKK. Because of this, however, he has also faced opposition. The 1990s saw the initiation of the Kurdish Women's Movement, but in the last ten years, the movement has gained much more strength. Contradictions such as class divisions have been tackled and new approaches towards women's liberation have been adopted in order to transform women's liberation from an elitist ideal to a grassroots cause.

In 2004 the PKK experienced a major backlash, with many people actually talking about the end of the organisation. This was at the same time when major international offensives against the PKK began. Furthermore, Öcalan's brother, Osman Öcalan, caused a major split in the movement by taking a feudal-nationalistic line. One of Osman Öcalan's slogans was 'We want to be able to marry too', because in the PKK, the cadres and the guerrillas are not allowed to marry or have sexual relationships due to their militancy.

Osman Öcalan's stance was perceived as an explicit attack on the women's movement. Many women broke away from the PKK, and some married men in the circles around Osman Öcalan. The morale of the women's movement suffered severely at this time because of the perception that Kurdish women should just behave like 'normal' wives. To be clear, the women's movement doesn't oppose marriage as such; the problem was the way that Osman Öcalan tried to undermine the women's movement by saying that their militancy, and thus their liberation, was not 'normal'.

Ever since, the women's movement has restructured itself to create new organisations. Now, its main body is the Women's Communities of Kurdistan (KJK). The aim is to form an umbrella organisation, rather than a single, decisive party. This could include the women's branch of a particular party, a women's cooperative, or a women's council in Europe, to name but a few possibilities.

Regardless of the forms such cooperating institutions might take, they are all part of one large movement. Today, due to this massive mobilisation, the whole world is talking about the Kurdish Women's Movement, not least because of its resilience against the Islamic State of Iraq and Syria (ISIS).

JS: You have described how the Kurdish Women's Movement and Abdullah Öcalan critiqued the state as being inherently anti-democratic, due to the patriarchal relations it embodies and its complicity in the structures of global capital. In Öcalan's prison writings, he refers to the political alternative as 'democratic confederalism', which is essentially a form of democracy without the state, and based instead on self-governance, communal structures and gender-equal political representation. How did the Kurdish movement respond when he articulated this radical proposal?

DD: Öcalan declared the ideal of democratic confederalism in 2005, while still in prison. As I said, at that time he had already rejected the strife for the Kurdish nation-state. For a movement comprising millions of people who anticipated an independent state, this concept of democratic confederalism was initially very difficult to grasp. It is difficult to reach the grass roots with the idea of a democracy without the state. In fact, many have accused Öcalan on abandoning the cause of 'independence', because they understand independence only within the framework of the state. It is very important to bear in mind the different realities and consciousness of people within the movement. In recent years, however, and through active practice, the notion of democratic confederalism has begun to resonate with many people.

The PKK and affiliated organisations managed to introduce the concept of democratic confederalism through council movements, autonomous organisations, communities and alternative schools in Turkey. In other words, models of self-organisation – central to the idea of democratic confederalism – were used to communicate that very same concept to the masses. Through active practice, they showed that an alternative to the state was in fact possible. Essentially, this boils down to teaching politics through practicing politics – to radically overcome the separation between theory and practice. [...]

The independent cantons of the autonomous region of Rojava, modelled after democratic confederalism, were announced at the same time that the Geneva II convention took place. So, basically, the response of the Rojava Revolution was: 'Well, if you don't invite us to Geneva II, to this major international conference, we announce our cantons; we claim our full independence with or without your approval.' This is the general stance of democratic confederalism, this is what it is all about: to work together and move forward no matter what is happening around you.

After this, jihadist attacks on Rojava only intensified. There were reports of jihadis being treated in Turkish hospitals. Had the world listened then, several massacres could have been avoided. Salih Muslim, the co-president of the main political party of Rojava, the Democratic Union Party (PYD), was denied visas four, five times to travel to the US to explain the threat of state-sponsored terrorism in the region. Sinem Mohammed, a prominent TEV-DEM representative, did not receive a visa to the United Kingdom, all because of outside political interests. On top of all of this, there are several economic and political embargoes on

Rojava. In 2014, even the Kurdish Regional Government of Iraq collaborated with Turkey in an attempt to marginalise the Rojava Revolution, because they wanted to be the dominant Kurdish force in the region. It is remarkable that the Rojava Revolution even happened and persisted in spite of these obstacles. Such obstacles actually account in part for why Rojava has been so successful, for had it been co-opted by a wider force, with very undemocratic interests, it might not have become a genuine revolution.

JS: That is to say that the revolutionary conditions that made it possible for the Rojava Revolution to develop were also partly due to the denial of the international order, which forced the cell-like structures of the Kurdish resistance to strengthen and become even more sophisticated?

DD: Exactly. It was a completely self-sustained effort – there was no support from anywhere. The revolution had to work in spite of this war and embargoes, so people had to come up with creative solutions. The People's Defence Units (YPG) and Women's Defence Units (YPJ), the self-organised armed forces of Rojava, even had to build their own tanks! The Syrian regime often used to say that certain products cannot grow in Rojava, but through experimentation, people learned that many vegetables actually grow very well in Rojava and have since created sustainable agricultural projects. This general self-reliance proved successful over the course of the revolution, especially as the fighting forces of Rojava handled their defence by themselves rather than relying on weapons or instructions from abroad.

Of course, it would have been great to have had support, but only from the right places – from leftist movements and parties, for example. Yet the fact that there was no outside support also nurtured the politicisation of the people, who learned to do everything on their own. But the costs and sacrifice were very high.

JS: In every revolution, however tragic, there seems to be the necessity for the creation of a situation in which there is collectively nothing left to lose: a total break with the structure that is oppressing you.

DD: What is unique about the Rojava Revolution is that it already had a solid ideological base. It was built on the ideas of democratic confederalism, of self-sustainability, self-governance, autonomy, true independence: not through the state, but in the sense of living without approval. This is in fact the legacy of the Kurdish movement philosophically affiliated with the PKK. It is something that the actors of this revolution will tell you themselves, but it is hard to accept for those who appropriate Rojava's resistance against ISIS for their own ends. Before Rojava, there were the autonomous councils created by the PKK in Turkey, for example, for which many people were imprisoned. The people of Rojava were not scared, because they knew the costs of their revolution, the costs of establishing something in spite of the oppressive dominant system and its attacks. That is why the resistance in Kobanê was so difficult for many people to grasp. That people would continue to resist right down to the last bullet, all for a different life – this philosophy and collective mobilisation cannot be treated in isolation from the military victories against ISIS. [...]

JS: At the end of the day, the geopolitical order seems more afraid of a democracy that is capable of organising itself outside of the state – critiquing and undermining that very order – than the idea of so-called terrorism.

DD: It is very interesting indeed to see how nobody wants to acknowledge the cantons, despite it now being very clear to everyone that the Kurds in Syria are the strongest opponents of ISIS. What would be a better way of supporting the resistance than acknowledging its administration? There is no challenging the system. Even the ideology with which women are battling ISIS is labelled as terrorist. To acknowledge Rojava would mean to confront NATO-member Turkey, to hold several Gulf countries accountable, to admit that Western foreign policy has failed, to expose the global arms trade. All that would cause a dramatic chaos.

JS: So, what you are saying is that when you acknowledge Rojava, you have to go through a similar process of confronting one's own internal oppressive structures, as those leading the Rojava Revolution have done themselves in order to arrive at the model of democratic confederalism.

DD: Why on earth would ISIS emerge to begin with? Why did states exploit the genuine desire for social change in Arab countries? Why did states promote new tyrants to take their place in these governments? Why did they support sectarianism? Why are so many young people in Europe joining ISIS? Why is the Rojava alternative, which looks like a potential perspective for the region, so marginalised? The answer lies in the fact that the global system is inherently flawed. That is why Rojava will continue to fight the system.

One could easily – all too easily – mock metropolitan artists and intellectuals who support rural and regional projects such as the Zapatistas' or the Kurds'. *Is this not a form of exoticising and primitivist feel-good politics? What relevance do these territorial struggles have to art-world practices and institutions, really?* To turn these rhetorical questions into an actual line of inquiry, the Invisible Committee's notion of territory – which operates on multiple scales – can be useful.

As the collective author of the much-discussed tracts *The Coming Insurrection* (2008) and *To Our Friends* (2014), the Invisible Committee has always been scornful of 'Negrist' rhetoric about a global multitude as a new revolutionary subject, a new proletariat. A central and striking feature of the Invisible Committee's writing is the call for the creation of 'zones of opacity'. Rather than having a pseudo-revolutionary multitude stage carnivalesque sit-ins in the capitals of Empire, the Invisible Committee advocates the active creation of opaque communes and zones in which the state cannot penetrate (a fight that has its obvious equivalents in cyberspace).

Today's territory is the product of many centuries of police operations. People have been pushed out of their fields, then their streets, then their neighbourhoods, and finally from the hallways of their buildings, in the demented hope of containing all life between the four sweating walls of privacy. The territorial question isn't the same for us as it is for the state. For us it's not about *possessing* territory. Rather, it's a matter of increasing the density of the communes, of circulation and of solidarities to the point that the territory becomes unreadable, opaque to all authority. We don't want to occupy the territory, we want to *be* the territory.

Every practice brings a territory into existence – a dealing territory, or a hunting territory; a territory of child's play, of lovers, of a riot; a territory of farmers, ornithologists or *flaneurs*. The rule is simple: the more territories there are superimposed on a given zone, the more circulation there is between them, the harder it will be for power to get a handle on them. Bistros, print shops, sports facilities, wastelands, second-hand book stalls, building rooftops, improvised street markets, kebab shops and garages can all easily be used for purposes other than their official ones if enough complicities come together in them. Local self-organisation superimposes its own geography over the state cartography, scrambling and blurring it: it produces its own secession.[41]

If the Invisible Committee foregrounds opacity, Chto Delat stresses publicness in their proposal for Rosa's House; its role as incubator of a counter-public.[42] It could seem curious that practices which share points of references such as Chiapas would give rise to such seemingly opposed positions, but publicness and secrecy have always been each other's doppelgängers. In its way, the Invisible Committee, too, attempts to create an alternative public – an alternative to what passes for the public sphere in the age of media conglomerates. The famous moment in 2010 when US right-wing commentator Glenn Beck frantically attacked *The Coming Insurrection* on Fox News was telling in this regard: in the service of Rupert Murdoch's corporate conspiracy, Beck used the Invisible Committee's insurrectionary language to whip up a reactionary frenzy in the service of the powers that be.

However, some of the radical autonomists who, to a greater or lesser extent, draw inspiration from the Invisible Committee may be said to feed the media precisely what they want: they become the perfect enemy, providing great excuses for clampdowns and for further turning to the right. After the riots at the G20 summit in Hamburg in July 2017, many German media outlets quoted *The Coming Insurrection* in their attempt to explain the violence of the so-called 'black block'. One journalist for a left-wing newspaper homed in on a live stream by the news channel N24: the right-hand side of the split screen showed a performance of Beethoven's Symphony No.9 with the various leaders in the audience, while the left side showed a simultaneous riot.[43] On the one hand, 'Ode to Joy' was used as social grease for a cabal of 'world leaders' including Donald Trump – a spectacular example of 'autonomous' high art's Babylonian captivity. On the other, the rioting autonomists produced an equally reductive and problematic counter-image of a different autonomy. The resulting montage at least put the image of harmony projected at the concert to a lie. That much is true, but at what cost and to what effect?

What remains is the imperative to realise autonomy within the city, both in the West and in the Global South, where the violence inflicted on communities is so much more stark than in the gentrification struggles of the West; 'in the outskirts of the world the system reveals its true face', as the Uruguayan writer Eduardo Galeano has put it.[44] The Mexico City–based art collective Cooperativa Cráter Invertido is profoundly indebted to autonomist and anarchist theory and practice as well as to the Zapatistas' self-organising in Chiapas. Mostly using the media of drawing, writing and (self-)publishing, Cráter Invertido has reflected extensively on urban and rural practice and the different territories they entail and generate, as well as on forging connections between different local and regional situations and struggles.

Released in the form of a self-published zine, 'The City is Sinking' – credited to 'H.K. revisited by pirate comrades' – was written by Cráter Invertido member Jazael Olguín Zapata. The text takes as its point of departure the fact that Mexico City is sinking due to the extraction of water from the ground on which it is built.

H.K. REVISITED BY PIRATE COMRADES, 'THE CITY IS SINKING'

Reprinted from *City-is/Ciudas-es/La ville-est*,
Mexico City: Cooperativa Cráter Invertido,
2016, pp.2, 3, 34–38. The text is here reprinted
unaltered, without editorial intervention or
standardisation.

Mexico City is sinking inside of its many linings and histories and (historical) violences. It is produced by the accumulation of diverse weights and psychosocial, political or economic forces that started boiling long ago in this enormous city (which foundations date back to 1325). It is a crushing force and a manifestation of something mundane and real: literally its buildings, plazas and streets are being sucked by its underground forces, swallowed by the swampy land. [...]

From the nucleus of catastrophe, life boils from within Monster City also known as Corpse City, Compost City: destiny lays over a mirror of civilization held by spilled blood and reckless behaviour. A Dried Lake and home of millions, Mexico City is deeply sinking into time and space with all of its inhabitants inside the irrational vortex of creative destruction that makes its daily routines happen.

Cities are simply not isolated from rural areas destinies, it's luck will always be interweaved. Within the urban-agro-industrial complex, symbiosis between rural and urban areas is vital for the reproduction of capitalism. It is in the rural areas, where food is mostly produced and where extractivism of minerals and energetic takes place, it is precisely where capitalism endures its resilience capacity. Looking for other ways of living beyond urban lifestyles, has nothing to do with the stimulation of new age dreams or 'new farmers' movement (mainly bourgeois idealizations of what 'living on the countryside' means), instead it means to deepen our critic for a better understanding of what the capitalist domination network means and how it is constituted, of how urban infrastructure is deeply linked to rural areas through specific spaces we may call intermediate such as highways, that are basically moving warehouses for commodities. We may continue to analyse our capacities to intervene, sabotage, blockade the dynamic transit of commodities and people in order to question the contextual problematic of capitalism transformed into space and its relationship with transit and communication, making visible that they are intermediate territories where capitalism-as-concrete-form flows. In these spaces disputed by velocity is were the vessels of capitalism reside, transit-spaces that are inseparable of hegemonic time dynamics. We may think of these spaces as ready to be framed as an embodiment of capitalism-as-a-crystallized-flux-form and consequently then possibly stopped-sabotaged-destroyed. Epistemological separations between city-rural areas, as most of the frontiers produced by human language, are artificial and therefore not absolute at all, we may actively defy them.

Referencing '[historical] communities in resistance, like indígenas communities in Mexico', who have 'confronted dispossession through specific forms, tools and practices', the text goes on to quickly sketch a genealogy 'from the sprout of the Autonomen in Europe in the seventies, to the Zapatista insurgency back in 1994' as moments in a history of 'constructing autonomy as a space of antagonist organisation against the state or corporate control'. It cites Berardi, then continues:

> The autonomous Italian movement of late seventies meant the proliferation of the communes, occupations, strikes, squats, but at the same time it produced the recombination of capitalism in its post/fordist era, continuing with the flexibilization of cognitive workers that brought the diffusion of class struggle and the individualization of the concept of autonomy into a series of supposedly alternative lifestyles mostly in urbanized areas. It translates into the present world, cruel and infamous, where even communes, squats, occupations, libertarian municipalities are not enough to subvert the destruction of the earth by neoliberal capitalism, especially, in contemporary megalopolis contexts where devastation of environment is daily practice.
>
> In order to generalize experiences that stand as concrete experiences of self-determination against neoliberal crisis, we are n the need to start deeply sharing alternatives that re reproducible and can be influenciable for the wide anti capitalist/anti statist/anti authoritarian struggles all over the urbanized world. This is how to start sharing profound alternatives must become real processes that influence ourselves and our communities to start taking individual and collective decisions that before we thought impossible, and to start facing directly all the contradictions that, for example, self-management process intrinsically produce. How may we leave behind work and start self-determined labor-process where we cooperate without competing, or how may we start working in collectivity for the maximum development of individuals in a communal ecosystem where our lives are not separated from the concepts we use to create our shared realities?
>
> In Mexico City, in the community-rooted areas, in the popular neighborhoods, in this specific and situated spaces is where certain communities inside the city find space to exist with dignity inside these Monster City that is devouring all signs of resistance. The experiences of autonomous urban organization defy daily structural violence building free spaces and self-organization outside the frame of the State and of capitalist management. The occupation of land and buildings, the generation of cooperative housing beyond the limits of legality, neighbourhoods blockade resistance against mega projects and urbanization are strategic tactics to breathe outside oppression and collectively care for ourselves, still through self-critique knowing about intrinsic limitations and reach of struggles that are focusing only in localities without envisioning coordination beyond specific territories in an internationalist perspective.

The elaboration of such an 'internationalist perspective' remains an urgent and difficult task. Possibly marked by some of the tenacious illusions that Povinelli seeks to dispel, a fragile and potentially ephemeral constellation (or coalition) has nonetheless emerged. Is another autonomy possible? Perhaps in tenacious survival and momentous events, in encounters and relationships, in determined and disenchanted practices that operate on the basis of enabling illusions – or ideals, as they were once called.

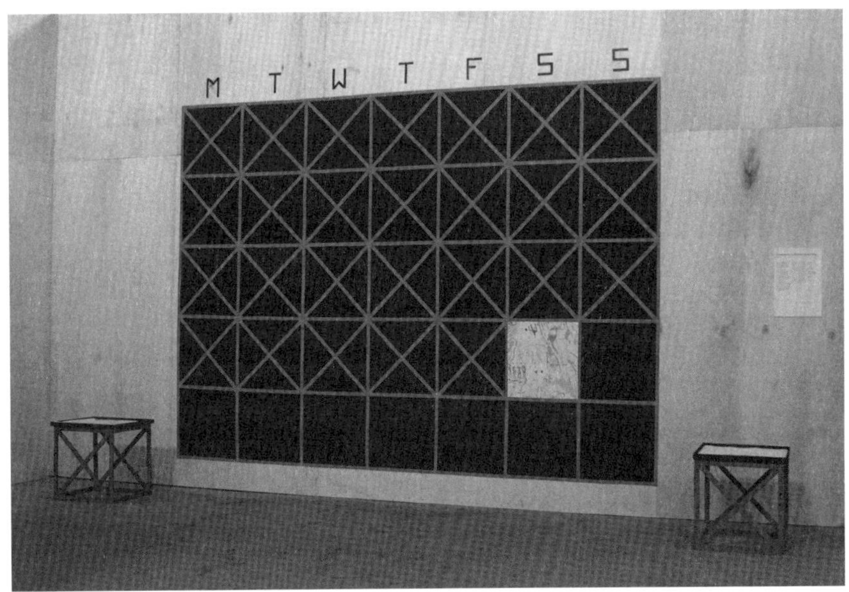

Installation views, Cooperativa Cráter Invertido, *Hoy (Today)*, Jakarta Biennale 2015

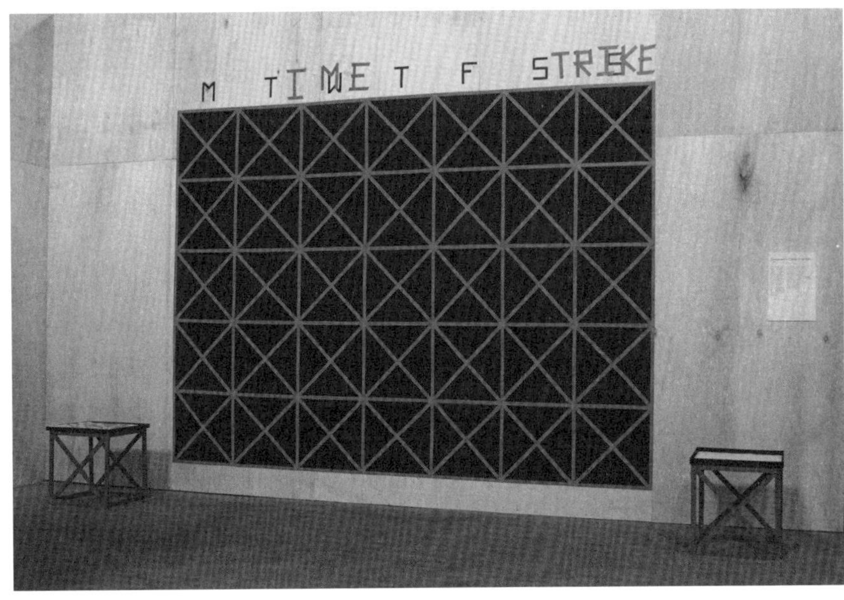

Notes

1   See, in particular, Gerald Horne, *The Counter-Revolution of 1776: Slave Resistance and the Origins of the United States of America*, New York: NYU Press, 2014.

2   Eyal Weizman, 'Are They Human?', in Nick Axel, Beatriz Colmina, Nikolaus Hirschn Anton Vidokle and Mark Wigley (ed.), *Superhumanity: Design of the Self*, New York and Minneapolis: e-flux architecture and University of Minnesota Press, available at http://www.e-flux.com/architecture/superhumanity/68645/are-they-human/ (last accessed on 19 September 2020).

3   Immanuel Kant, *Critique of the Power of Judgment* (1790; trans. Paul Guyer and Eric Matthews), Cambridge: Cambridge University Press, 2000, pp.90-91; select passages are reprinted in Part One of this reader, pp.34-35. Emphasis in original.

4   See Denise Ferreira da Silva, *Toward a Global Idea of Race*, Minneapolis: University of Minnesota Press, 2007.

5   Kerstin Stakemeier and Marina Vishmidt, *Reproducing Autonomy: Work, Money, Crisis and Contemporary Art*, London: Mute Publishing, 2016, p.58.

6   See David Lloyd, *Under Representation: The Racial Regime of Aesthetics*, New York: Fordham University Press, 2019. On the discipline of art history in particular, see Éric Michaud, *Les invasions barbares. Une généaologie de l'histoire de l'art*, Paris: Gallimard, 2015.

7   See Aimé Césaire, 'Discours prononcé par Aimé Césaire à Dakar le 6 avril 1966', *Gradhiva: Revue d'anthropologie et d'histoire des arts*, no.10, 2009, pp.208-15. On Césaire, Marx and Lukács, see Nick Nesbitt, *Caribbean Critique: Antillean Critical Theory from Toussaint to Glissant*, Liverpool: Liverpool University Press, 2013, p.309.

8   Fred Moten, *In the Break: The Aesthetics of the Black Radical Tradition*, Minneapolis: University of Minnesota Press, 2003, p.1.

9   G.W.F. Hegel, *Lectures on the Philosophy of Religion*, vol. 2, *Determinate Religion* (trans. R.F. Brown, P.C. Hodgson and J.M. Stewart, ed. P.C. Hodgson), Oxford: Oxford University Press, 2007, pp.546-47.

10   A good selection of Franz Boas's writings on indigenous American art can be found in *A Wealth of Thought: Franz Boas on Native American Art*, Seattle: University of Washington Press, 1995. Obviously, his 'good intentions' notwithstanding, Boas is still implicated in the colonisation of the Arctic and its consequences. The ship on which Boas arrived at Baffin Island for his 1883-84 collection was possibly responsible for bringing deadly diphtheria to the Inuit, as artists Rebecca Sakoun and Florian Göttke stress in their lecture and slide presentation *Collecting in the Collection* (2014).

11   Marius de Zayas, *How, When, and Why Modern Art Came to New York* (ed. Francis M. Nauman), Cambridge, MA: MIT Press, 1996, p.59.

12   Ariella Aïsha Azoulay, *Potential History: Unlearning* Imperialism, London and New York: Verso, 2019.

13   See Christian Kravagna, 'Toward a Postcolonial Art History of Contact', *Texte zur Kunst*, no.91, September 2013, pp.110-31.

14   See Part Four of this reader, pp.217-57.

15   See Sigmund Freud, 'Fetishism' (1927), *The Standard Edition of the Complete Psychological Works of Sigmund Freud*, vol. 21, *(1927-1931)* (trans. and ed. James Strachey in collaboration with Anna Freud), London: The Hogarth Press, 1961, pp.147-57.

16   C.L.R. James, *The Black Jacobins: Toussaint L'Ouverture and the San Domingo Revolution*, 2nd edition, revised, New York: Vintage Books, 1989,

17   Alexandre Kojève's lectures were edited and published after World War II by Raymond Queneau as *Introduction à la lecture de Hegel. Leçons sur la* Phénoménologie de l'Esprit *professées de 1933 à 1939 à l'École des Hautes Études* (Paris: Gallimard, 1947), and later translated by James H. Nichols, Jr as *Introduction to the Reading of Hegel: Lectures on the Phenomenology of Spirit* (Ithaca, NY: Cornell University Press, 1969).

18   More accurately (but uncommonly) known as the 'lordship-bondage' dialectic, or as the dialectic of 'desire' and 'recognition'. For the sake of consistency, and to preserve the language so central to Kojève's reading, the following discussion will retain 'master-slave' to indicate the relevant sections and transitions in the *Phenomenology of Spirit*.

19   G.W.F. Hegel, *Die Philosophie des Rechtes: Die Mitschriften Wannenmann (Heidelberg 1817-18) und Homeyer (1818-19)* (ed. Karl-Heinz Ilting); cited in Susan Buck-Morss, *Hegel, Haiti, and Universal History*, London: Verso, 2009, p.61.

20   *Ibid.*, p.115.

21   *Ibid.*, pp.15-16. Reproduced with minor amendments.

22   Homi K. Bhabha, 'Race, Time, and the Revision of Modernity', in Bill Ashcroft, Gareth Griffiths and Helen Tiffin (ed.), *The Post-Colonial Studies Reader*, 2nd edition, London: Routledge, 2006, pp.219-20, available at http://monumenttotransformation.org/atlas-of-transformation/html/r/revision-of-modernity/race-time-and-the-revision-of-modernity-homi-k-bhabha.html (last accessed 19 September 2020).

23   Anton de Kom, *Wij slaven van Suriname* (1934), Amsterdam: Contact, 2009, p.115. Translated from the Dutch by Juliette Huygen.

24   *Ibid.*, p.124.

25   Georges Bataille, *The Accursed Share*, vol.2-3, *The History of Eroticism and Sovereignty* (1953-54; trans. Robert Hurley), New York: Zone Books, 1991, pp.197-98. See also 'The Potlatch of Consumerism' in Part Two of this reader, pp.136-52.

26   *Ibid.*

27   Rachel O'Reilly and Danny Butt, 'Infrastructures of Autonomy on the Professional Frontier: "Art and the Boycott of/as Art"', *Journal of Aesthetics & Protest*, no.10, Autumn 2017, unpaginated, available at http://www.joaap.org/issue10/oriellybutt.htm (last accessed on 19 September 2020).

28   Jared Sexton, 'The *Vel* of Slavery: Tracking the Figure of the Unsovereign', *Critical Sociology*, 19 December 2014, pp.583-97.

29   See 'Autonomy of the Political' in Part Four of this reader, pp.226-37.

30   Gayatri Chakravorty Spivak, paraphrased in Lucy Steeds, '"Magiciens de la Terre" and the Development of Transnational Project-Based Curating', in L. Steeds (ed.), *Making Art Global (Part 2): 'Magiciens de la Terre' 1989*, London: Afterall Books, 2013, p.39.

31   Olu Oguibe, 'Art, Identity, Boundaries; The Rome Lecture', *Nka: Journal of Contemporary African Art*, no.3, Fall/Winter 1995, pp.28.

32   Michael Hardt and Antonio Negri, *Empire*, Cambridge, MA and London: Harvard University Press, 2000, pp.53, 402. See also Part Four of this reader, pp.217-57.

33   C.L.R. James, *Modern Politics* (1960), Detroit: bewick/ed, 1979, p.79.

34   This is the subject of Joshua Oppenheimer's film documentary *The Act of Killing* (2012).

35   In order to mark the fiftieth anniversary of the 1963 Élysée Treaty, the signing of which aimed to signal a period of reconciliation between the two states, France and Germany exchanged their respective pavilions during the 2013 Venice Biennale.

36   Hans Magnus Enzensberger, 'Constituents of a Theory of the Media', *New Left Review*, no.64, November-December 1970, pp.26-27; select passages are reprinted in Part Five of this reader, p.327.

37   In 2015, Bruguera was placed under house arrest for attempting to stage a new version of the piece on the Plaza of the Revolution in Havana. See Coco Fusco, 'The State of Detention: Performance, Politics, and the Cuban Public', *e-flux*, no.60, December 2014, available at https://www.e-flux.com/journal/60/61067/the-state-of-detention-performance-politics-and-the-cuban-public/ (last accessed on 19 September 2020).

38   Ariel Dorfman and Armand Mattelart, *How to Read Donald Duck: Imperialist Ideology in the Disney Comic*, New York: International General, 1975.

39   Chto Delat, introduction to *Chto Delat newspaper*, no.38 ('Houses of Culture yesterday, today and tomorrow'), p.2.

40   Peter Osborne, 'Living with Contradictions: The Resignation of Chris Gilbert and the Presentation of Politics in Recent Curatorial Practice', *Afterall*, issue 16, Autumn/Winter 2007, p.113.

41   Invisible Committee, *The Coming Insurrection* (2007), Los Angeles: Semiotext(e), 2009, pp.108-09.

42   Chto Delat, 'Rosa's House of Culture', available at https://chtodelat.org/category/c215-embodied-projects/ (last accessed on 19 September 2020).

43   Martin Kaul, 'Der Aufstand', *Die Tageszeitung*, 9 July 2017, http://www.taz.de/!5423733/ (last accessed on 19 September 2020).

44   Eduardo Galeano, *Days and Nights of Love and War* (1983; trans. Judith Brister), London: Pluto Press, 2000, p.170.

CODA:
HOMELESSNESS

Back in 1997, during the heyday of neoliberalisation, James Dale Davidson and Lord William Rees-Mogg penned a book titled *The Sovereign Individual*. The authors were the publishers of the 'Strategic Investment' newsletter, and their book is a hymn to a transnational or post-national über-class to come – 'the nation-state will be replaced by new forms of sovereignty, some of them unique in history, some more reminiscent of the city-states and medieval merchant republics of the premodern world'.[1] Referencing the rise of the internet and increases in bandwidth, the authors foresaw transnational communities whose 'participants will seek and obtain exemption from the anachronistic laws of nation-states'.[2] However, in an act of defiant anachronism, Davidson and Rees-Mogg also looked to the feudal Middle Ages and their complex geopolitical quilt of sovereignties as a possible role model. Presaging that individuals 'will achieve increasing autonomy over territorial nation-states through market mechanisms', they predicted the emergence of 'merchant republics of cyberspace'.[3]

Davidson and Rees-Mogg's treatise embodies the kind of Silicon Valley ideology that American venture capitalist Peter Thiel has taken to new heights. That Thiel is obsessed with attaining sovereignty vis-à-vis the nation-state, for instance via 'seasteading', has not, of course, prevented him from supporting Donald Trump's presidency, with its promise to restore national sovereignty, to 'make America great again'. Meanwhile, Rees-Mogg's son Jacob campaigned for Brexit while the company he co-owns, Somerset Capital Management, set up investment funds in Ireland.[4] This is the double promise of sovereignty: the one per cent get one kind, and everyone else gets national sovereignty – more particularly, the promise of a kind of national sovereignty in which many are classified as nonhumans, with classification wars that put the 'white working class' in a position of mastery over racialised Others.

While many are trying to construct territories and zones in which alternate forms of life and self-stylisation beyond survival on the job market are possible, the sovereign transnational über-class ideologised by Davidson and Rees-Mogg is redesigning territorial sovereignty to suit itself. Through its leading nation-states, global capitalism itself has created zones of exception, extraterritorial niches where regular (tax) laws do not apply; this, as it were, is the mirror image of the archipelago of autonomist pockets being created by contemporary social movements.

In an essay from 2015, Hito Steyerl calls attention to the proliferation of art storage and art transaction inside so-called 'freeports'. Freeport art is the perverse triumph of modernist ideals of autonomy: here, art as value is autonomous from even the most formalist of gazes. And of course, in theory almost any art can be freeport art – even 'critical' practices can, after all, become worthwhile investments. This only makes it all the more imperative to work against this reductivist realisation of 'the autonomy of art'.

HITO STEYERL, 'DUTY-FREE ART'

Reprinted from *e-flux journal*, no.63, March 2015,
available at http://www.e-flux.com/journal/duty-
free-art/ (last accessed on 19 September 2020).

Huge art storage spaces are being created worldwide in what could essentially be called a luxury no man's land, tax havens where artworks are shuffled around from one storage room to another once they get traded. This is also one of the prime spaces for contemporary art: an offshore or extraterritorial museum. In September 2014, Luxembourg opened its own freeport. The country is not alone in trying to replicate the success of the Geneva freeport: 'A freeport that opened at Changi Airport in Singapore in 2010 is already close to full. Monaco has one, too. A planned "freeport of culture" in Beijing would be the world's largest art-storage facility.'[1] A major player in setting up many of these facilities is the art handling company Natural Le Coultre, run by Swiss national Yves Bouvier. Freeport art storage facilities are secret museums.

Their spatial conditions are reflected in their designs. In contrast to the rather perfunctory Swiss facility, designers stepped up their game at the freeport art storage facility in Singapore:

> Designed by Swiss architects, Swiss engineers and Swiss security experts, the 270,000-square-foot facility is part bunker, part gallery. Unlike the freeport facilities in Switzerland, which are staid yet secure warehouses, the Singapore FreePort sought to combine security and style. The lobby, showrooms and furniture were designed by contemporary designers Ron Arad and Johanna Grawunder. A gigantic arcing sculpture by Mr Arad, titled *Cage sans Frontières* (Cage Without Borders), spans the entire lobby. Paintings that line the exposed concrete walls lend the facility the air of a gallery. Private rooms and vaults, barricaded by seven-ton doors, line the corridors. Near the lobby, private galleries give collectors a chance to view or show potential buyers their art under museum-quality spotlights. A planned second phase will double the size of the facility to 538,000 square feet. Collectors are picked up by FreePort staff at their plane and whisked by limousine, any time of day or night, to the facility. If the client is packing valuables, an armed escort will be provided.[2]

The title 'Cage Without Borders' has a double meaning. It not only means that the cage has no limits, but also that the prison is now everywhere, in an extra-statecraft art withdrawal facility that seeps through the cracks of national sovereignty and establishes its own logistic network. In this ubiquitous prison, rules still apply, though it might be difficult to specify exactly which ones, to whom or what they apply, and how they are implemented. Whatever they are, their grip seems to considerably loosen in inverse proportion to the value of the assets in question. But this construction is not only a device realised in one particular location in 3D space. It is also basically a stack of juridical, logistical, economic

---

[1]   'Freeports: Über-warehouses for the ultra-rich', *The Economist*, 23 November 2013.

[2]   Cris Prystay, 'Singapore Bling', *Wall Street Journal*, 21 May 2010.

and data-based operations, a pile of platforms mediating between clouds and users via state laws, communication protocols, corporate standards, etc., that interconnect not only via fibre-optic connections but aviation routes as well.[3]

Freeport art storage is to this 'stack' as the national museum traditionally was to the nation. It sits in between countries in pockets of superimposing sovereignties where national jurisdiction has either voluntarily retreated or been demolished. If biennials, art fairs, 3D renderings of gentrified real estate, starchitect museums decorating various regimes, etc., are the corporate surfaces of these areas, the secret museums are their dark web, their Silk Road into which things disappear, as into an abyss of withdrawal.[4]

Within the structures and operations of twenty-first-century statecraft, the counterpart to the freeport is the refugee camp. Another zone of exception in which certain laws have been suspended, the refugee camp is a negative freeport for non-citizens. As political, social and ecological catastrophes proliferate, the right in both Europe and the US have produced a perpetual panic over immigrants coming 'here' and 'taking our jobs' and 'abusing our welfare system'.

Chto Delat reflect on this in the video *Museum Songspiel: The Netherlands 20XX* (2011), in which the Van Abbemuseum is occupied by refugees – the institution becomes a refuge, the field of art erodes. Chto Delat's piece can be seen as a contemporary pendant of Hubert Robert's *Imaginary View of the Grande Galerie of the Louvre in Ruins* (1796), a painting that is one in a pair, with the other showing Robert's proposed redesign for the Grande Galerie. In the wake of the French Revolution, part of the Louvre building was just in the process of being transformed into a public gallery, and *Imaginary View of the Grande Galerie of the Louvre in Ruins* looks further into the future than its counterpart; the Grande Galerie, with its roof torn down and the sky laid bare, is now an ex-museum (though some relics, such as a version of the Apollo Belvedere, still serve as models for artists).[5] In Chto Delat's video, the museum becomes a ruin of its former self in a different sense: the white cube is still intact, but it becomes a refugee shelter nonetheless. Perhaps a sequel could show a freeport as a refugee camp.

---

[3]   'The Stack, the megastructure, can be understood as a confluence of interoperable standards-based complex material-information system of systems, organised according to a vertical section, topographic model of layers and protocols. The Stack is a standardised universal section. The Stack, as we encounter it and as I prototype it, is composed equally of social, human and "analog" layers (chthonic energy sources, gestures, affects, user-actants, interfaces, cities and streets, rooms and buildings, organic and inorganic envelopes) and informational, non-human computational and "digital" layers (multiplexed fibre optic cables, datacenters, databases, data standards and protocols, urban-scale networks, embedded systems, universal addressing tables). Its hard and soft systems intermingle and swap phase states, some becoming "harder" or "softer" according to occult conditions. [See Michel Serres, *La Guerre mondiale*, Paris: Le Pommier, 2008, p.115.] As a social cybernetics, The Stack that we know and design composes both equilibrium and emergence, one oscillating into the other in indecipherable and unaccountable rhythm, territorialising and deterritorialising the same component for diagonal purposes.' Benjamin Bratton, 'On the Nomos of the Cloud: The Stack, Deep Address, Integral Geography', lecture delivered at the Berlage Institute, Rotterdam, 28 November 2011, available at https://www.youtube.com/watch?v=XDRxNOJxXEE (last accessed on 19 September 2020).

[4]   An extremely intelligent remark from an audience member in Moscow added that this was to be seen as a huge benefit, as a lot of shoddy 'market art' would get safely quarantined without anyone having to see it. I sympathise very much with her point of view.

In Holland, the refugee collective We Are Here and its activist-academic-artistic supporters have insistently called attention to the situation of 'illegals', of rejected asylum seekers who are condemned to a perverse kind of autonomy, a life under precarious conditions. During Staal's *New World Academy*, members of We Are Here collaborated with art students on developing a plan for a cooperative building - possibly a converted office building sitting empty in the current economic climate - that would provide housing for the refugees, as well as for students and others, and include public functions like a restaurant. This would help to ensure that the project is not just about creating a stable home situation for this specific group of homeless people, important though that is, but also about maintaining visibility for a problem with which countless others struggle.

The extent to which such an endeavour would be concomitant with the legalisation and institutionalisation of the refugees was intensely debated. In a discussion, Tania Bruguera stated that this project clearly amounted to a form of institutionalisation, and that this should in fact be embraced. For 'illegals', it is particularly urgent that instituent practices need to find ways of using constituted, sovereign power. Bruguera emphasised that the restaurant, for instance, would have to be a 'real' restaurant, not some form of communal cooking dependent on donations, on charity. The problem with this, as Staal has stressed, is that such a construction is not feasible

Still from Hito Steyerl, *Liquidity Inc.*, 2014, colour video with sound and architectural environment. Courtesy the artist, Andrew Kreps Gallery, New York and Esther Schipper, Berlin

See p.286 of this reader for more images

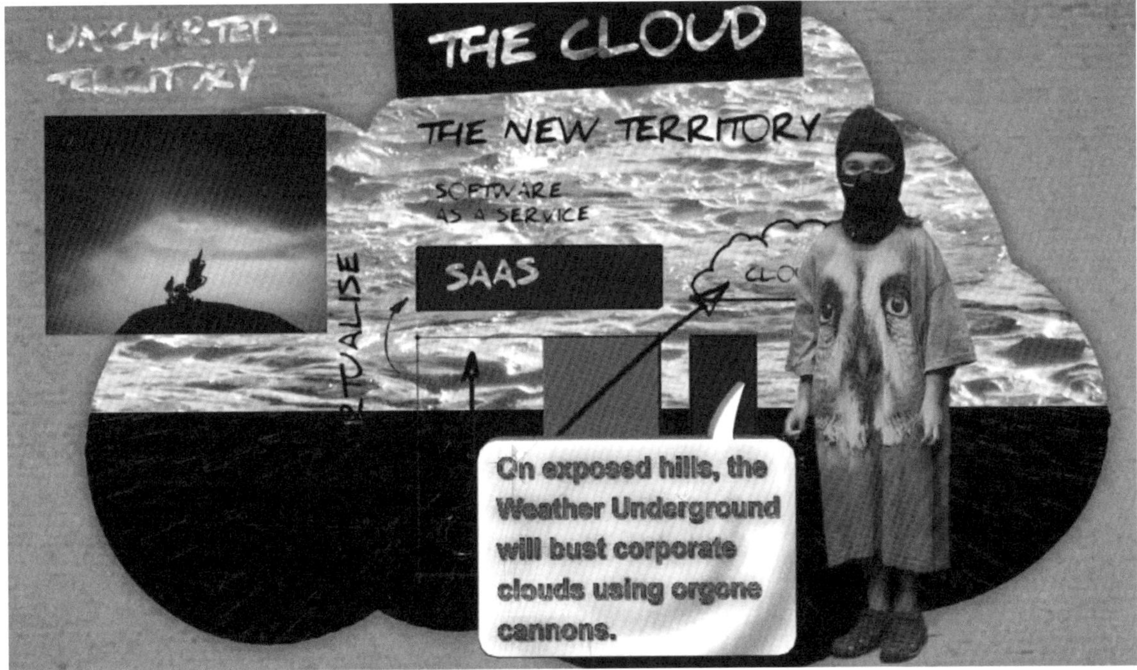

as long as the participants' status has not changed, for illegals cannot perform legal labour. However, in the context of artistic projects it may be possible to give them fees; this is a grey zone that has been explored and exploited. As the artist Hans van Houwelingen stated in the closing debate of the *New World Academy*'s We Are Here session, the problem is that the project-based economy stimulates artists to 'move on' once the show is over, but moving on is not so easy for many others.[6] Fissures, fractures, asymmetries: these are not to be wished away or glossed over; rather, they are materials for critical practice.

Following Friedrich Schiller, 'aesthetic education' always came with a suspicion towards art that remained pure art, mere art. Art needed to overcome its limitations and realise itself in life, socially: this is the programme that early German Romanticism bequeathed to the avant-garde. Art was not an ornament for the bourgeois home – though at various moments it was precisely the project of making art 'useful' by reintegrating art into the domestic that seemed to embody aesthetic promise. Being without a fixed abode, like those in We Are Here, automatically excludes one from the bourgeois life that is the home of 'art appreciation'. Neoliberal globalisation has exacerbated the 'transcendental homelessness' (to use a phrase coined by Georg Lukács) of the modern subject, and of aesthetic practice. In many cases it leads to literal homelessness and displacement. Anthropogenic climate change and the devastation and conflicts it generates will help to universalise the refugee condition. Where to go on an overheated and volatile planet?

Since global warming is the business model of today's reactionary populists, and since neofascists attack symptoms rather than address causes, it is no wonder that they both deny it and demonise refugees and other migrants. The transnational far right sees refugees as a dangerous, primitive (brown and/or Muslim) horde being welcomed by the cosmopolitan elite who produce and buy contemporary art, the elite intent on destroying and 'replacing' the white population. Neofascist and xenophobic narratives reject any sense of responsibility, complexity, complicity or dependency; the migrant Other becomes a subhuman entity threatening a freedom and prosperity 'we' have earned (at a cost we do not care to mention). Of course, it is perfectly true that contemporary art has been profoundly implicated in a process of neoliberal wealth redistribution that has affected certain white working-class and middle-class populations that now vote neofascist. One could argue that this means that contemporary art is precisely all too much at home in the world of 'globalisation', to the detriment of other worlds. In 2020, the machine of the global art world ground to a halt due to the COVID-19 pandemic, with national borders closing rapidly and air travel coming to a virtual standstill. Years before, Paul Chan had suggested that for art to be aesthetically operative, it cannot fully belong in the world of projects and productivism:

> This only brings to mind Groucho Marx, who once said: 'I don't care to belong to any club that will have me as a member.' If art is made to belong, it seems to me that it is the poorer for it. This is especially the case when art is made to belong to art itself. Echo reconciles. By forsaking the freedom realised in its own inner development, art affirms the illusionary reconciliation brought on by the state of belonging, when in truth it holds the greater potential of expressing, in a kind of non-judging judgement, just how unfree this belonging really is.
>
> Art is, and has been, many things. For art to become art now, it must feel perfectly at home, nowhere.[7]

Even as people were relegated to their homes in early 2020, practicing self-isolation, a 'new normal' was quickly established. Amidst an almost completely online attention economy, the imperative to produce or at least to self-represent and self-perform is as pronounced as ever. Those with 'nice' homes to work from are obviously in a privileged position compared to those in more precarious positions – such as the homeless or those seeking refuge. As usual, class and race (as well as age and gender) reveal themselves as 'pre-existing conditions' with potentially deadly consequences.

The self-isolation economy has proved an unexpected literalisation of an essential lesson of institutional critique: autonomy begins at home, with putting one's house in order. However, this house is a glass one, equipped with gizmos made in China with materials imported from Africa, and it is mortgaged to the hilt. In other words, starting with yourself means reflecting on your place within institutional structures, on the institutional structures in your own mind and their modus operandi. What starts as a critical engagement with a museum can quickly lead one to tussle with a multinational corporation, and self-organised spaces may discover that they have certain fundamentals in common with autonomous or sovereign zones in Chiapas or Kurdista, just as zones for non-approved forms of life are being created in defiance of the geopolitical order of global capitalism.

Immanent critique is likely to collapse into overidentification and pure affirmation if it no longer has any horizon beyond actually existing institutions, beyond actually existing globalisation; when its immanence is without moments of externalisation, its secularism is without moments of transcendence or transgression. Jean-Luc Nancy has characterised Christianity as the religion whose members try to be in the world, but not of the world.[8] Roland Boer has described Marxism in strikingly similar terms:

> [T]he tension within Marxism between being immersed in the world and yet not of it may be put in terms of a tension between secularism and anti-secularism. If we define the base sense of secularism as a system of thought and action, indeed a way of living that draws its terms purely from this age and this world, then Marxism is both thoroughly secular and anti-secular. [...] Marxism is engaged in a perpetual negotiation, a dialectic if you like, between rejecting and refusing the world of capitalism and struggling within it. Or, even more tightly, one works within the world in order to bring about its demise.[9]

We have come a long way since Schiller's *Aesthetic Education*. Or have we? We keep returning to certain questions, or the questions keep returning to us – on various scales, from the frustratingly modest to the impossibly grand. Throughout this reader we have emphasised that the aesthetic as a mode of perception, thought and practice is impure and a rejection of Enlightenment conceptions of the autonomy of reason, which is really an autocracy of reason. If genuine autonomy is the ability to choose one's dependencies, then clearly one's choices are often rather limited. This has been true for the majority of people for a long time, and in an age of environmental collapse and triumphant neofascism, even those who thought they had plenty of options may find themselves running out of them rather fast. This makes it all the more important to ask, time and again, whether there are really no alternatives to the politics and aesthetics of 'more of the same, only worse'.

Notes

1   James Dale Davidson and Lord William Rees-Mogg, *The Sovereign Individual: Mastering the Transition to the Information Age*, New York: Simon & Shuster/Touchstone, 1997, p.99.

2   *Ibid.*, p.30.

3   *Ibid.*, p.32.

4   See, for instance, Lizzy Buchan, 'Brexit: Jacob Rees-Mogg defends Ireland move by City firm he co-founded ahead of EU withdrawal', *The Independent* (UK), 14 June 2018, https://www.independent.co.uk/news/uk/politics/brexit-jacob-rees-mogg-scm-ireland-city-move-eu-withdrawal-dublin-a8398041.html (last accessed on 19 September 2020).

5   See *Hubert Robert 1733–1808. Un peintre visionnaire* (exh. cat.), Paris: Musée du Louvre and Somogy, 2016, pp.436–41.

6   Statement by Hans van Houwelingen at *New World Academy* public presentation, BAK, basis voor actuele kunst, Utrecht, 1 December 2013.

7   Paul Chan, 'What Art Is and Where It Belongs', *e-flux journal*, no.10, November 2009, http://www.e-flux.com/journal/10/61356/what-art-is-and-where-it-belongs/ (last accessed on 19 September 2020).

8   Jean-Luc Nancy, *Adoration: The Deconstruction of Christianity II* (2010; trans. John McKeane), New York: Fordham University Press, 2013, p.40.

9   Roland Boer, *Criticism of Religion: On Marxism and Theology, II*, Leiden: Brill, 2009, pp.29–30.

Acknowledgements

Thanks to Annie Fletcher, Juliette Huygen, Esmee Schoutens and Yen Noh